YOU CAN'T WIN A RACE WITH YOUR MOUTH

Howard A. Tullman

BLOG into**BOOK**

CONTENTS

ACKNOWLEDGMENTS

*O*ver the last 50 years, I've watched and worked with hundreds of entrepreneurs who have won many hard-fought and difficult battles to turn their dreams into reality and who have also lost as many contests as well. They would say that both the highs and the lows were important educational opportunities, but that the main life lesson was quite simple: the best of them took what they learned from both the ups and the downs and never gave up. In many cases, they ultimately did what older and more experienced professionals and other industry "experts" believed (and freely told them) was virtually impossible. Sometimes they accomplished this feat by not knowing any better; oft times by not listening to the naysayers or asking anyone's permission; and sometimes because they simply wouldn't or couldn't quit.

Through sheer force of will, a tremendous amount of hard work, and unrelenting perseverance, they eventually created an entirely new enterprise from an idea and they built something important – not only for themselves – but for many others as well. Some of their businesses changed the ways in which we go about our daily lives. Others made a more modest contribution, but the startup struggle just as surely changed those individual entrepreneurs' lives; the lives of the many people they touched and influenced; and especially the lives of those who worked alongside them in long-lasting and important ways.

And, although each of these businesses was unique, and the underlying trials, tribulations and circumstances were certainly different, there were common elements in the experiences of the entrepreneurs that I believe have a value for the rest of us far beyond the mere retelling of their specific stories. Extracting and sharing the primary principles, the recurring patterns, and the cautionary tales are the main reasons for this compilation. But why me you might ask?

I'm just as much an everyday entrepreneur as anyone you'll ever meet, but I've also spent more than 3 decades teaching about innovation, disruptive technologies, change management and entrepreneurship to thousands of students and business leaders across the world. In addition, I've built and transformed businesses over and over again which is an exceedingly rare circumstance since even the best of the entrepreneurial breed are lucky to have pulled off this most magical trick once or twice at most. And, in some of the most impressive cases, we'll never really know whether the ones who finally got it done were extremely smart or extremely lucky (or both) or maybe just in the right place at the right time.

As a result, I've come to realize in the process that the best people to document and explicate the lessons they learned aren't the ones who suffered the most and actually created and grew the businesses. They haven't been afforded the many chances and the time that I have had to synthesize the experiences into a coherent and consistent body of knowledge. In addition, not only are entrepreneurs not the most introspective of folks (even if they're willing to take the time to look back), but they suffer – particularly in the heat of battle – from selective memory, in-game amnesia, and an amazing capacity to get over (and forget about) the bumps, the mistakes, and the hard times and just get on with building their business. I believe that they're simply too close to the action to be an objective observer and it turns out that it's actually pretty hard to see the big picture if you're inside the frame.

So, to help my peers and those coming after along the path, I've spent the last 6 years writing a weekly column for INC. Magazine on anything and everything entrepreneurial and it's been an amazing and rewarding job. Any entrepreneur will tell you that bringing your idea into being and making it real is a lonesome, painful and often thankless task and one with no assurances or certainty of success. As a result, the slightest bit of support, even a little earnest encouragement, and especially impartial advice and a great mentor or two can make all the difference on those most difficult of days when you wonder – as we all do - whether it's worth it.

I hope this book will be my little contribution to your success as you travel down this road of well-worn hopes and dreams that we call entrepreneurship.

1 – TELL A SIMPLE STORY

Almost every day I meet and speak with young entrepreneurs trying to get their new businesses off the ground. I don't generally have a lot of time, but I always try to give anyone at least a few minutes to explain what they're trying to do and then I can decide very quickly whether it makes more sense to meet further with them. Frankly, what you can't basically say in ten minutes about your business or your idea really isn't worth saying. I don't think of these little chats as "pitches" (elevator or otherwise) – they're much more like speed dates where you're trying to decide very quickly whether what you're hearing makes sense; whether there's a real business or opportunity lurking there; and whether the person you're speaking to has the passion, enthusiasm and smarts to turn a good idea into a real business.

After 50 years of doing this, I can tell you that it's actually possible to make these initial decisions with a high degree of accuracy in a matter of minutes. Now I admit that I will definitely miss out on a few real opportunities and turn down or not pursue some very talented people, but, by and large – especially since we're all dealing with limited time and scarce resources – the system works and works pretty well.

And here's the main reason why – it's not that I'm so perceptive and smart; it's that way too many people make it too easy to turn them down because they're so unprepared to take their best shot in the moment when the opportunity is there and because they don't really understand how to make the most of that short window of time.

As we used to say in the music industry, it's really easy to tell when a song is bad, but only the public and the market will ultimately decide what sells. Note that I said "what sells", not necessarily what's good. The music business today is all about selling disks and downloads, not making great music. Always has been; always will be.

And it's the same story with describing new businesses. If you're all over the place; if you're trying to be all things to too many people; if your story is so complicated that it's hard to even follow; or if you've got a solution in search of a problem, it's going to be pretty easy to say "thanks, but no thanks". You've got one shot, one moment, and one opportunity to get right to the heart of the matter and the most crucial part of the entire process is to tell a simple story.

How simple? Your story should answer 3 simple questions about your company which, by the way, are the very same questions that will inform and guide your company for its entire existence. These answers are also every bit as significant for each and every employee as they are for any investors. So it's pretty important to get the answers right at the outset. The answers might change over time, but the fundamental questions never do.

Here they are:

Who are We?
Management and team members' <u>relevant</u> experience and credentials

Where are We Going?
Short and long term objectives and goals – abbreviated milestones – timeframe

Why?
What problem is being addressed and solved – time, money, productivity, status

Short, sweet and to the point. You've got to be a ruthless editor and there's no question that the hardest choices are about what to leave out, not what to include. You need to think of both detail and elaboration as forms of pollution. Cut to the quick. And stick to your story.

One of the nastiest things venture guys like to do to "newbies" is to ask them how big their businesses can be and how many opportunities and directions there are to grow the businesses. And when they charge off into the future and start building their castles in the sky; the VCs look at each other, roll their eyes, and say to themselves: "Boy, this guy's not focused at all."
It's an old but important trick from debate class – tell the story you need to tell, be relentless, stay on point, keep it short, and make the limited time that you have count. Everything else can come later.

Bottom line: tell a simple story.

It's almost impossible these days to avoid articles or conversations about disruptive innovation. And these discussions almost always start out asking why it is that large established corporations – even when they see the disruptors bearing down on their products, services or businesses – can't seem to react or at least to get out of the way before the new guys roll right over them. My answer is always the same: in these big, slow companies – "good enough simply isn't good enough" – and, as a result, they simply can't get anything started in time to make a difference. Whether it's analysis paralysis or too many cooks or postponing things until they're perfect or just the constant problem of resistance to changing things that worked for you in the past, it's a foolproof formula for failure. The solution in every company (big or small – old or new) is (a) to start with what you have; (b) to iterate like crazy; and (c) to fail fast.

It's absolutely clear that a good plan executed today beats a perfect plan that may never arrive. As Mark Zuckerberg from Facebook says: "Done is Better than Perfect". And it's equally obvious that nothing will ever be attempted if all possible objections must be overcome first. If these things were foolproof or easy, everyone could do them and would. One of these days turns out to be none of these days if you're not careful and on the case.

If you're going to try something new, you need to get the process started with the tools, people and resources that you have on hand and the crucial confidence that, as the project progresses, you will find and attract the right new people, the required resources, and the necessary tools. There's no perfect time to start anything – the best time is always now. And you can't rush it or wish these things into existence – it's like pushing a rope or nine women trying to have a baby in one month. Doesn't happen no matter how hard you try. But once you start trying and keep getting better every day, you discover that anything is possible.

Here's a great recent example. Aviary.com makes photo editing software – basically simple tools to help your pictures look better or different. When they started their business, the end users were the millions of consumers taking zillions of digital photos every day and, using a freemium model with ad revenue to follow, they put some pretty respectable early numbers on the board – say (at their peak) about 50,000 photos were being edited using their tools on an average day.

But they weren't growing fast enough in an increasingly crowded space and mobile was emerging around the same time as another game changing element in the marketplace. So they changed their model – just modestly – by targeting the large firms (think Walgreens for example) who were developing and digitizing photos for consumers and giving them the software tools for free to incorporate in their consumer service offerings. Turns out that there's an identifiable and addressable population of these kinds of firms so you can market to a couple of thousand targets rather than tens of millions of consumers and that's what they did.

Bottom line, they're now working with about 1500 firms. And what about the 50,000 photos a day that were being edited… well that number is now 5,000,000 photos a day. They got started; they watched the market and the opportunities develop; and they changed their approach and their offerings just in time to catch the mobile wave.

Iteration is the singly most important business process in the world today. The smartest way to develop and grow any business is incrementally – you start small and you scale rapidly. I call this idea "successive approximation" rather than "postponed perfection" and it applies to everything you want to do. You test the water and the depth of the pool with a toe or two, not by jumping in with both feet. And you try to never lose sight of your overriding plan; you just constantly adjust your strategies and tactics to suit the changes in conditions and circumstances. As Jeff Bezos from Amazon likes to say: "We are stubborn on vision, but we're flexible on details".

The iteration process starts with the belief that anything and everything can always get better. There are four simple steps:

(1) You Experiment
(2) You Measure
(3) You Analyze; and then
(4) You React and Modify

Once that's done, you start the entire cycle over again. The best businesses never stop the iterative process. As a result of the process, they may change directions, abandon a product line that isn't working or meeting expectations, or decide that an entire venture should be shut down. But they make these decisions rationally and quickly based on the facts – and above all, they learn to fail fast.

Being willing to "fail fast" by the way doesn't mean that you don't plan to succeed; it doesn't mean that you aren't confident in your idea and the likelihood of your success; and it certainly doesn't mean that you're going to give up without giving it your best shot. What it means is that you understand the concept of opportunity costs (knowing when your scarce time and resources are better spent elsewhere) and that you've learned the First Rule of Holes: When You're in a Hole; Stop Digging.

So don't wait for an invitation. Don't wait for a schedule. Don't wait for all the data you need. And most of all, don't wait until things are "just right" or perfect because you'll be too late every time. Start with what you have, get better every day, and keep moving forward. After a while, it gets to be a habit and a way of life.

The hyper-competitive world we now live in is full of fast followers. In our constantly-connected world of instantaneous information, every new business immediately spawns copy-cats, riffers, and discounters as well as cheap knock-offs and old-line traditional players trying to use their brands and their bigness to barge right into these new markets. Most of the low-end guys quickly learn to their dismay that no one wins the race to the bottom and that, in today's economy, even "free" isn't cheap enough in most cases because smart shoppers are increasingly jealous and careful with their time and their resources. Today's consumer rallying cry could well be "give me something of real value or give me a break and get out of my face".

Because the barriers to entry keep shrinking, it's just as easy for the next 5 guys to start a business like yours as it was for you. In fact, in many cases, when you invent and establish a new product, service, sector or approach, you actually make it easier for the guys running right behind you to succeed.

First of all, they ride on your coattails, your PR and your advertising in every possible way to explain their business. They're not pioneers breaking new ground; they're not inventing anything; they've just learned to say "we're just like X but cheaper or faster or closer", etc. Saying "we're just like Groupon but better" saves a shitload of time, money and marketing.

Second, they lean on your progress and success to establish their own credibility and to show their customers that the thing works and works well.

And third, they go to school on your errors and missteps so they save time and money by avoiding first- timer mistakes and by entering the product development and delivery cycle at a much more advanced and higher (as well as more stable) level than you did. The questions are so much easier when someone else has already worked out the right answers for you.

The fact is that while the barriers to real success are still just as high as ever, the barriers to effective competitive entry are almost non-existent. So what's a hard-working CEO supposed to do?

The simple answer is that you need to do it to yourself and do it to your business before your competitors do it to you. And the only way to stay in the game and pull this off is to keep raising the bar every chance you get. The world is divided into targets and gunslingers and, if you can't be a full-fledged gunslinger, then you'd better be a constantly moving target that's always a few steps ahead of the competition.

The test is "what's the best you can possibly be" and the answer is better (for the moment) than anyone else who's trying to do the same thing. And just because no one else has done something yet doesn't mean you shouldn't be aiming for it – you can't let other people's limitations hold you back. It's committing to a life of constant awareness (paranoia), continuous change and extreme flexibility as well as the willingness to eat and to abandon your "offspring" before they run out of steam. If you don't, you can be sure someone else will do it for you.

A good example of a great marketing company falling asleep at the switch is Nike. Simply stated, Nike owned the athlete for years. The coolest shoes, the coolest endorsements, the best technology and the coolest TV ads. When the Web came along, they put up a pretty robust website and made sure to show off their ads and their products and then – having fallen in love with their own videos – they just sat there resting on their laurels.

But the competitive race never waits for you. And, almost immediately, smart, fast competitors figured out that the real athletes weren't in it for the ads or the glory, they were in it for the blood, sweat and tears of the exercise and the sports. So a number of smart websites quickly emerged that served the real needs of the athletes – exercise programs, race training regimens, fitness tracking, socially connecting athletes with others who had like interests, athlete and team meet-ups, etc. – all aimed at providing real services and benefits to the athletes – not simply talking about it or trying to push products down their throats. But you can't win a race with your mouth.

And, in pretty short order, the real athletes (and plenty of weekend warriors as well) totally bailed on the Nike ad sites and moved over in the millions to these other service sites which were far more connected to their interests and far better uses of their scarce time. Nike blew it by not understanding that the expectations of customers are progressive – yesterday's novelties are today's old news. Nike failed to change their web offerings to meet the new needs and demands of their core customers and – as a result – opened the door for small, quick competitors to jump into the space with simple, straightforward tools and applications for runners and other athletes that permitted them to eat Nike's lunch.

Raising the bar means that you need to constantly outmode yourself and regularly cannibalize your products and services. It's not a linear or even an evolutionary process – it's utterly discontinuous and the fact is that what you're doing today may be meaningless tomorrow because the available technology takes a quantum leap and leaves your offerings in the dirt. The real test of Apple's relatively new CEO will be whether we see an iPhone 4S, iPhone 4X and an iPhone 4Z or we see a jump to the iPhone 5 that once again revolutionizes the marketplace.

The rate of change today is autocatalytic – each change creates the next change at a faster rate and leads to disruption and radical obsolescence – all driven by virality and almost perfect cross-market intelligence. If you want to stay in the game and run with the big dogs, keep raising the bar.

One last important thought – no one cares who made the first version of something – they only want to know who makes the best version.

There's a world of difference between failing and simply making mistakes. It's critical for entrepreneurs to understand and recognize the difference. I hear people talking about how proud they are that their last business or venture failed. They brag about what a wonderful learning experience it was. But it's all a crock and a waste of breath. Because you only fail when you give up and giving up is something that winners never do. Failing is failing however you paint it and, when you fail, it's game over. So, in my book, only cretins celebrate their failures.

Making mistakes, on the other hand, is absolutely par for the course and something we all do from time to time. It's a sign of a healthy, active and risk-taking business. The fact is that the only time normal people don't make mistakes is when they're asleep. Mistakes are a critical part of growing and expanding your company and, if you're not stubbing your toe from time to time, it means you're not moving fast enough and pushing forward. Skinned knees are part of the process. Rapid growth and constantly changing circumstances are inherently embarrassing – you need to get used to it. A thick skin helps a lot in a start-up because not everything in life is fair.

When I was first starting out several VCs told me that they never invest in businesses founded by lawyers because too many lawyers are more concerned about being "right" than they are about doing the things that are right for the business. They'd rather die than die of embarrassment. But the name of the game is to win, not to be right all the time. Being smart doesn't mean that you make all good decisions

– it means that you learn from your bad ones, don't repeat them, and make the best that you can out of them.

There are a few basic rules that will help you be just as successful in navigating the valleys you encounter along the way as you are in celebrating the peaks and high points of the journey.

Rule Number 1 – Make Cheap Mistakes (Fail Fast)

Not everything worth doing is worth doing well. You need to start small on new projects and be ready to scale swiftly or abandon ship as soon as the handwriting is on the wall. But be careful about the process –don't try to do things cheaply that you shouldn't do at all.

On the other hand, sometimes for a small, start-up company, being smart and cheap is the only way to meet the demands of your customers and to keep up with the competition. Even when the customer's demands are bullshit. Here's an example I had from the earliest days of Fed Ex.

We had a relatively new business called kiNexus which was providing thousands of college graduate job seekers' resumes on CDs to employers on a weekly basis so that they could sort and select interview candidates before they got to campus and often from several schools as well. Many of our actual customers were relatively low level HR people from big corporate employers and their jobs were mainly to schedule and support the "real" recruiters and, as you might imagine, they were insecure, demanding for no good reason and generally pains in the ass. Let's just say that they had issues.

In any case, around that time, anything in business that was time-sensitive and important was beginning to be sent overnight by Fed Ex and apparently the more Fed Ex packages you got, the more important you felt and appeared to the people sitting around you in your office. So one day in our little business, we started getting regular calls usually on a Thursday afternoon from a number of our customers insisting that they needed their CDs sent overnight Fed Ex (for about $40 a pop at that time) rather than by mail which was costing us 53 cents.

And we started doing it because we wanted to be responsive to our customers even though it was ridiculously expensive and totally unnecessary. And, because we were so conscientious, we'd regularly call the next day to make sure that the package was delivered on time. And guess what we found out? Half the time, the person wasn't on vacation for the next week or wasn't even going to be in the office that day. Most of the time, no one else could figure out what was so urgent about the delivery anyway. And generally, we felt like idiots. But the customer is always right – right?

So here's what we did. We made our own fake Fed Ex envelopes (see below) and we put 75 cents postage on them and sent them regular mail and never had a complaint after that from any of these guys. Ever.

Rule Number 2 – Don't Be Reluctant to Change Your Mind

Nothing in life is written in stone. If you're headed in the wrong direction or digging yourself deeper every day in a hole, the first order of business is to stop. Sticking to the original plan when the conditions on the ground have changed is foolish – you've got to be fast and flexible. To stick with a mistake is actually much worse than making it because delay only compounds and worsens the situation.

Rule Number 3 – Don't Dwell on the Past – Move On

It's always O.K. to admit that you've made a mistake. Make 'em. Admit 'em. Correct 'em. Forget 'em. A short memory and some in-game amnesia are critical. If you're worrying about the past, you've got a good chance of screwing up the future. You can't water yesterday's crops. So move on.

Rule Number 4 – Distinguish Mistakes from Systemic Problems

The best companies understand the very crucial distinction between mistakes (errors that happen once) and systemic problems (errors that happen over and over again) and they make it their business to track and aggregate these occurrences in order to eliminate the root causes of the problems. Mistakes will always happen, but the same mistakes shouldn't happen over and over again – those cases aren't mistakes, they're addressable problems that can be made to go away.

Rule Number 5 – Be a Big Boy or Girl

Don't try to hide a mistake or cover it up – admit it and get to fixing it. Show some remorse and make sure that people know you're taking it seriously. Let the appropriate people know it won't happen again. Don't waste your breath blaming others – you'll need it to say "I'm sorry". Take your medicine – don't sulk – just get back to work and get over it. And finally, don't ruin a good apology with a crappy excuse.

5 – YOUR BUSINESS PLAN CAN BE YOUR BEST FRIEND OR YOUR WORST ENEMY

In the near future young entrepreneurs probably won't even prepare formal business plans because they take too much time and they're generally out of date immediately upon delivery. That's just a measure of how fast things are changing in today's hyper-competitive global marketplace.

In fact, personally, I'd rather be sent a demo URL and/or a prototype (minimum viable product) than a 50 page business plan (which I'm not gonna read in any case) because showing me what you've done beats telling me what you're gonna do by a country mile. If you've got it, flaunt it. If not, come back when you do.

Given the ease of entry into most new markets, the growth of lean start-ups, and the relatively insignificant costs of most underlying technologies, the basic threshold for your product or service to be taken seriously by investors, vendor/partners or even prospective key employees has been raised significantly. Talk and type are cheap – show me something concrete that differentiates your business from the 40 other wanna-bes in the same space who also have good ideas.

But, by the way, the fact that a good solid business plan is less critical to the funding process and to the outside world in general these days doesn't mean that it's not a crucial document for you and your business. One of the great lines in Hollywood about screenplays goes like this: "the screenplay isn't always the movie that gets made, but it's what gets the movie made". So you probably still need to go thru the drill to get some early funding, but it's ultimately how you use your plan in your business and with your team that's really critical.

Your plan's value will depend entirely on how you develop and employ it – it can be a roadmap or a roadblock. At any moment in time, your business plan reflects your best informed guess at the future – it's an educated guess and not the gospel. And it's going to change a million times as you progress because that's what building a business is really all about – it's evolving and advancing a central idea through continually changing circumstances.

You should use a business plan as a tool and a starting point to recognize and measure changes (so that you can react to them and adjust your actions accordingly) and not as an operating manual to run your business. It's not a cookbook that you follow blindly as if it were set in stone. There's a lot to be said for consistency in some cases, but trying to stick to a plan that was written in the past assumes that you've learned nothing in the ensuing time or from the unforeseen events that you've encountered. In fact, in times of rapid change, your past experience may be your worst enemy.

One of the greatest business shifts in recent times was quite a surprise to the public when it was announced. In March, 2012, the Encyclopedia Britannica announced that, after 244 years (but only 11 years after the founding of Wikipedia), it was discontinuing the publication of its print edition. At its peak, 120,000 hard-cover sets of the books were sold each year. But, no one at EB was really complaining because, and here's the shocker and the surprise, the print editions at the time of the announcement accounted for LESS than 1% of their revenue. And instead of those 120,000 physical sets, about 500,000 households were now paying an annual fee for an online subscription which represented about 15% of EB's revenue. And the lion's share of their revenue came from the migration to and the ongoing sale of curriculum products (math, science, English, etc.) to customers around the world. They had quietly and quite efficiently responded to the entry of aggressive new competition and the advent of new low-cost delivery systems by changing their entire centuries-old business in less than a decade to a new, agile player in the information marketplace rather than the book market.

Too many businesses run into serious problems because they waste time trying to make the circumstances they find themselves in fit their plan instead of changing the plan to adapt to and respond to the new conditions around them. You can't become so reliant on the numbers and assumptions in your plan that you lose sight of the facts on the ground and in the marketplace. The fact is that the longer you benchmark or measure your progress to an irrelevant or outdated standard, the more time you waste and the more ground you give up to the competition.

A model or plan doesn't necessarily get you to the truth – eventually the "math" stalls out and something more human and personal takes over – this is what makes the final difference between success and failure – call it intuition or faith or just the unstoppable courage of your convictions – the fact is that great entrepreneurs are pioneers and they embrace change so early in the process that their decisions will never be totally justifiable by the numbers. It's the art of drawing sufficient conclusions from insufficient premises.

6 – HELP YOUR CUSTOMERS DO THEIR HOMEWORK

There are a lot of reasons why a prospect might make a first purchase from your company. Novelty, curiosity, lack of time to shop for or lack of knowledge about alternatives, pity or sympathy, effective PR and press, inexperience on their part, discounted initial pricing, great- looking marketing materials, fear of being left behind (the bandwagon effect) or shut out entirely (the scarcity argument), family or other connections or relationships, etc.

So, before you celebrate those early sales; drink the company Kool-Aid; or pat yourself too often on the back, take another careful look at the list. You'll notice that not a single cause or consideration really has anything to do with the quality of your product or service, the value of it to the user, or any of the other real-world measurements that matter in the long run. That's why first sales are easy compared to renewals where (for better or worse) you're dealing with an experienced customer and where nine times out of ten you're not even in the room (much less in the conversation) when the critical decisions are made about contract renewals or additional product purchases. It's this "second sale" (renewals or reorders) that secures the customer and cements the relationship for the long term.

And yet, way too many businesses take their customers for granted and then they're caught flat-footed and surprised when the customer quits or leaves. This is why – at all of my businesses – everyone understood for the day they started that renewals were just business, but that we took terminations personally. A termination was a slap in the face. Being "fired" by a customer was a kick in the teeth. And there was never anyone to blame except yourself because most terminations are entirely avoidable if you plan ahead and if you learn to do your customers' homework for them.

The first thing to keep in mind when you're trying to prevent customer attrition is that the guy who makes the renewal decision isn't usually the original buyer. He might consult with the first buyer, but, in general, he's a financial guy or an owner/check signer who's always looking to cut costs , reduce outlays, and to get rid of orphaned programs, services or subscriptions that no one uses any longer.

How does he know that no one is using some product or service? Here's the bad news – he doesn't have a clue and he doesn't really care. Because, in the absence of an advocate/champion within the business, the bean counter's rule is always to cut or cancel first and ask questions or apologize only after the screaming or complaining starts. And, since he guesses right so many times, he's pretty fearless. After all, it's not his ox that's getting gored, it's yours. And you don't even know the guy's name. He also knows that these days no one in the company really wants to be the person standing up and arguing for spending more money.

So how do you fight the invisible man who's about to cut off your oxygen and dump your product or service? Three little words: anticipation, preparation and ammunition.

<u>Anticipation</u> means knowing well in advance that a renewal is coming up and getting your licks in early and often. Any organization without a comprehensive renewal tracking and tickler system deserves to be run out of business and will be soon enough. One of the great innovations in this area was a system that American Hospital Supply developed to automatically restock the supply closets at the hospitals which were their customers. Their pitch was that this was just a handy way to make sure that no one was ever out of life-saving materials when they were needed, but the real beauty of the program was that it made it impossible for competitors to even get a foot in the door to sell their products since the supply closets were always full.

<u>Preparation</u> means taking the time to identify and recruit an internal champion – someone who works for the customer and whose job/life is made easier, smoother, or more profitable by using your product or service. Ideally, this person has the boss's ear or is the bean counter's buddy. He's your man in the back room who'll make your case when it's renewal time because it's also in his selfish interest to do that. But he can't do it alone or just using his wits and good looks. He's gonna need help.

<u>Ammunition</u> is the help he needs. It's the analysis, the backup, the homework that you do for him so that he's prepared and equipped to make your case and justify the renewal. Sometimes it's a spreadsheet; sometimes it's a couple of case studies; or a prop and sometimes it's a market/competitive analysis that shows how your product or service is helping to make/keep his business a market leader. These things take time and they don't happen by themselves, but they make all the difference in the world because metrics and measurements mean everything today and the guy with the black and white goods is the guy who gets the gold. Happy talk and generalities are no match for solid math showing dollar and cents results. And even the bean counters back off when you've got the facts and figures on your side.

One of the simplest and most effective props i ever made was for our customer satisfaction research business in the automotive industry. It turns out that, even though it seems obvious to all of us that treating your customers better will lead to happier customers and a more profitable business, in the car business, it's been hard for the manufacturers to directly connect improved CSI scores (customer satisfaction index) with increased profits because the most profitable dealers are often the highest volume dealers and in many cases their service departments and aftersales activities suck because they're primarily in the business of pushing as many cars out the door as they can.

So I needed a way to demonstrate to a bunch of car guys who were buying my research services (following up with customers to make sure they were happy campers, etc.) that the cost of the service were modest compared to the added profits they'd be making if they improved their CSI scores. I hired a professor or two and had them build me a formula that linked improved customer satisfaction to increased profits, but I knew that their fancy math wasn't going to get the job done. So I built a little sliding calculator that let the dealers see in black & white exactly how much in additional profits each incremental improvement in their CSI score would mean to them. All they had to do was slide the little card up and down and the profits were virtually in the bag. Here's the slider:

Was it accurate? I sure hope so. Did it work like a charm? You betcha. And why? Because we did their homework for them and gave it to them all wrapped up in a handy-dandy little "machine" to show their bosses and their bean counters.

And sometimes, that's all it takes to avoid those really ugly meetings and phone calls where the client quits. A little thought, a 50-cent prop that buys you thousands of dollars of business, and some basic salesmanship.

Anticipation, preparation and ammunition are the keys to owning your customers for a lifetime.

7 – MAKE ONLY THE RIGHT DEALS AT THE RIGHT TIME

Next to having great parents, choosing smart partners and making the right deals at the right times (and stages) in a company's development are the most important external variables in the success of new businesses. Because, in the hyper-competitive and global market we live in, no one has the team, the resources and the reach to succeed by themselves. In these complex times, well-constructed partnerships, carefully-structured joint ventures, and timely endorsements and other kinds of supportive commitments are critical components in helping a start-up build its brand, credibility, momentum and customer base.

But too many young companies these days are falling into the trap of thinking that constant deal making is preferable to actually doing the hard work and the daily blocking-and-tackling of building their businesses. Doing deals for the sake of the deals or because it's exciting and different or because you're bored is one of the biggest time sinks and wastes of resources imaginable. And worse, it can create the false impression of real progress and growth when, in fact, all that's really going on is an excited and hyperactive chain of eager start-ups servicing each other with VC funny money and/or by burning through their scarce growth capital to do so. It's a little bit of dot.com déjà vu and my sense is that it's especially rampant in the area of social media "consulting" firms.

A quick credibility test that helps sort this stuff out is to simply check out a company's customer list and, if the average age of most of the business's customers is roughly 3 to 6 months older than the age of the company itself (if that) or, if half the "customers" are incubator/accelerator suite mates or other companies directed and/or controlled by common parties and investors, then you're looking at this year's edition of "smoke and mirrors". Steer clear of these guys.

But don't stop looking or thinking about what kinds of deals and partners make sense for your business which mainly depends on where you're at and where you want to go.

And keep in mind that your own time is scarce, expensive and valuable – you can't chase every rabbit or dance at every dance – have a few clear objectives; know where your business presently is; and know where you're headed. These basic filters will help you identify the realistic prospects and the wastes of time. I've always used 3 buckets to describe any business and to help me answer these questions.

(A) Early - the business is emerging - deal objectives are:
    (i) Help to build and expand the customer base
    (ii) Prove the underlying technology

(B) Ongoing - the business is developing – deal objectives are:
    (i) Manage and deepen relationships to "own" your customers
    (ii) Control and expand your platform
    (iii) Promote and encourage product and service expansion

(C) Late - the business is maturing - deal objectives are:
    (i) Expand and integrate third-party offerings and services
    (ii) Win with scale
    (iii) Attack or eliminate competitors and potential new entrants

Having done more deals in more businesses than I can even count, I've got a few simple rules that have saved me tons of money, helped me dodge more than a few bullets, and added a few years to my life. Take 'em for what they're worth, but don't forget them.

(1) Never deal with the monkey when the organ grinder is in the room.
If the guy who can say "yes" and/or sign the check isn't part of the discussion, you're wasting your time. Too many little monkeys and paper pushers can say "no", but only the real decision makers can green light a deal.

(2) When you settle for less than you deserve, you get less than you settled for.
By and large, deals don't get better or sweeter over time. It's critical to make the complete deal BEFORE you sign the final documents. If you don't like something about the deal at the outset or you're uncomfortable with the people or the process, it's only going to get worse with the passage of time. Ugly babies rarely become movie stars.

(3) The easier the deal is to get done, the harder it will be to implement.
Keep in mind that most of the value of a deal is realized or lost during the post-signing implementation phase of the deal. And don't confuse silence or good manners with acceptance or agreement. It's better to bag the deal than to bury fundamental issues or differences and leave them to blow up later. Only the lawyers and their litigators benefit from leaving critical questions unanswered.

(4) Short term deals make much more sense for start-ups.

Long duration deals are very seductive and very dangerous – too easy to enter and very hard to escape. Always leave yourself an exit plan and an "out" clause even if it's expensive. It's better to be soaked at a later date than to be stuck in a bad deal for what can seem like a lifetime to a start-up.

(5) Don't chase a deal that takes too long to get done. Be prepared to walk away.

Necessity never makes for a good deal. It's like being at the bus station. There's always another bus (just like there's always another deal) coming down the road in any direction you're interested in heading. And don't kill the messenger if a deal doesn't get done - think of these as mini-R&D projects – you want your people to keep looking and keep bringing opportunities to you. Don't chop their heads off if a deal blows up – it may be the best result for all concerned.

(6) Do small deals on a regular and recurring basis – go for singles, not home runs.

Small, quick, additive/incremental deals that don't burn up critical management time or resources and that reach a "go" or "no go" point quickly are the way to proceed.

Endorsements are a great example of small but very effective deals which can make a huge difference to the prospects of a young company. Very few people truly appreciate the value of endorsements until they don't have them and their competition does. This is especially true in brand-centric markets.

When I was just starting my computer game development company and wanted to create some educational games as well as movie games, I decided early on that some crucial product differentiation was going to be essential. I went after the Where's Waldo name because I thought it crossed over between entertainment and education and that for children's education games – Waldo was a very meaningful icon for the parents who were the real buyers.

And, I even got to say that I actually did know where Waldo was.

As your company grows, the most important and hardest decisions that you will make will be about the people you hire and those you have to fire. There's a lot of talk these days about technology, but some things never change and the fact of the matter is that the ONE sustainable competitive advantage that any business can have for the long run is talented, committed and passionate people. Everything else erodes over time – especially technology which eventually in every case becomes accessible, cheaper and more broadly applicable by your competitors.

Many years ago I made this chart to track the price- novelty curve of technology which shows how the price of new technology diminishes over time and the other marketplace changes that accompany this process. (You'll get some idea of how old this chart is by noting that the software I used couldn't really even replicate a smooth curve.)

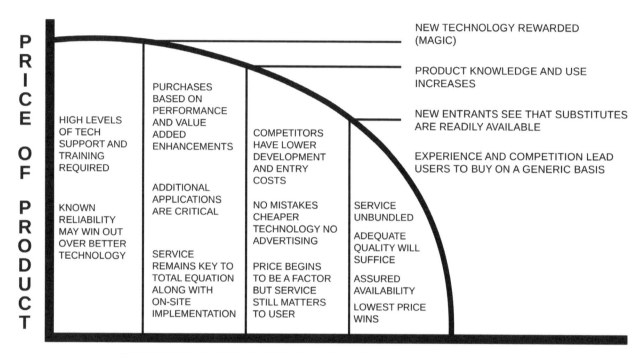

STAGES OF NOVELTY / DIFFERENTIATION

As you can see from the chart, while at the outset, new technology is almost indistinguishable from magic, by the time it becomes widely available and accepted, people basically take it for granted and price drives the discussion. As you can imagine, discussions about the lowest available price are never what we would call "happy talk".

But, good people, well-educated and motivated, just get better, stronger and more valuable all the time – especially if you watch their backs and stay out of their way. The real trick is to find 'em, hire 'em and keep 'em. Equally important is to move quickly to fire the people who aren't making it. Simple rule: Hire slow; fire fast.

(I'll deal with keeping your top performers and firing people who aren't in the next couple of posts, but suffice it to say that virtually NO ONE was ever fired too soon. Once you know that things aren't working out, you almost can't move too quickly to fix the situation. Every day you wait is one day too many and much too late.)

Let me start with a piece of bad news that comes from my friend Jay Goltz who says that CEOs are among the worst possible people to do their company's hiring. Why? Because, by and large, they're

(a) short on time and often distracted;

(b) great talkers and bad listeners because they're always selling themselves and their businesses rather than asking and learning about the interviewee; and

(c) too good-natured and trusting about people and not skeptical enough to ask the hard questions. So you may not be the best person in your organization to do this job even though there are few that are more important.

So consider yourself warned. Now, what can you do to at least give yourself a fighting chance of doing a good job? Here are a few ideas and rules that have helped me over the years:

(1) People lie about their resumes all the time.

I'm not saying this to get you down on mankind in general or anything like that. I'm just suggesting that it's perfectly reasonable to ask detailed questions about a resume and to take everything on it with a grain of salt or a tablespoon. I looked younger than my age for years (not sure when things caught up) and I once flew to France for a huge meeting with some folks over there involving millions of dollars. I got there – walked into the room – and was treated so shabbily by these folks (even taking into account that they were French assholes) that I was dumbfounded. I had lunch and went right back to the airport and returned home. I later learned that they saw me and having read my pretty extensive resume decided that I wasn't old enough to have done half the stuff written there and so I must have been lying to them. I wasn't, but it was a real lesson in managing information and expectations that I've never forgotten.

(2) Credentials are not the same as accomplishments.

Degrees are nice to have, but it's your deeds and the things you've actually gotten done that matter in the final analysis. And, there are plenty of "smart" people out there who aren't people smart. If you can't get along with the "natives" as part of an effective and collaborative team, your native intelligence doesn't mean squat.

(3) The best person you interview may not be the best person for the job in question.

Too many CEOs think that they should hire any great person who comes along and figure out a good job for them later. As important as it is to have super-talented people, trying to "warehouse" them (even when you're growing like crazy) is a losing strategy. Get a clear job description, understand the criteria for a successful candidate, and focus on filling that job.

(4) There are no easy jobs today.

Every candidate should have the basic required skills as a starting point. But the right prospects are the ones who have the ability to get the job done. Ability in any area is the successful combination of toughness (mental and physical), resourcefulness (flexibility and adaptability) and powerful concentration (focus and direction).

(5) Gray hair is a sign of age, not necessarily wisdom or relevant experience.

Young and (first-time) CEOs tend to get a point in the early growth of their businesses where they believe that they need to add some "grown-ups" to the management mix. There are usually a number of pretty standard excuses, explanations and reasons offered for these kinds of feelings, but ultimately the real driver is fear:

(a) fear of being alone and responsible;

(b) fear of being in way over your head; and

(c) fear of fucking things up. I can't make the fears go away, but I can tell you that 90 times out of 100 these types of lateral hires fail miserably and you will be the most miserable of all concerned because you did it to yourself and your company. There's not a simple or single explanation for the overwhelming failure rate, but generally the 4 main misses are:

(1) a quickly-emergent lack of energy (stamina) and enthusiasm;

(2) a totally absent connection to and comfort with the rest of the employees;

(3) an early tendency to criticize the way you run the business; and

(4) a focus and excessive interest in and emphasis on financial and compensation issues.

9 – MAKE ROOM FOR PEOPLE – PART 2

Once you've hired some terrific people, the next job is to hang on to them. Interestingly enough, that's getting harder, not easier, to do even in these tough economic times because (a) no one assumes any longer that they'll spend most of their career at the same place and (b) people these days don't commit to companies, they commit to other people and other people change and move on all the time. So how can you keep the stars (and the rest of the troops) happy, healthy and motivated?

First, nothing is more important than making room for people. All kinds of people – because talent comes in lots of different sizes, shapes and packages. We want the talent, but we aren't always willing to understand that it's a package deal. Some people like to work all night; some don't especially care to bath; some are insufferable and brilliant at the same time. You need to make room for these people and run interference for them if you want to build a great company. Too often, entrepreneurs try to find and hire people that look, act and talk like them and this never works beyond the first few employees. You need all kinds of people – even people just looking for a job – not a career and not looking to join your sacred crusade – just as long as they're willing to do their job and do it as well as they can. And honestly, your employees also don't have to love each other or go bowling every Thursday night. They just all need to show up and each do their jobs. Everything else is Kumbaya and gravy.

Second, you've got to talk straight to everyone, tell the truth, and do a couple of administrative things right away:

(1) define and nail down each new person's job and the reporting hierarchy;
(2) explain your expectations – tell people what you're trying to accomplish and what you're willing to sacrifice to accomplish it and make sure that they're signed up for the same trip; and
(3) establish the criteria to measure and evaluate success and confirm in writing that they are understood by everyone.

It's funny, but over the years, you learn that that the people from whom you really learned the real things of value (good or bad) were not the warm and fuzzy folks. They were sharp, hard-edged, driven people with a clear sense of purpose who were always asking more of you. And the real reason that those times were so instructive was that, in the midst of all of the blood, sweat and tears, and occasional screaming, you never doubted for a moment that they believed in you and believed that you were up to the task and could do whatever it took to get it done AND you knew that they would be there working and standing right beside you when you did.

It's great to shoot for the sky and have high expectations and to ask your people to work insane hours and move mountains as long as you never ask them to do anything that you wouldn't do yourself and as long as you're working side-by-side just as hard as they are. This whole area is a slippery slope. Keep in mind that getting the <u>most</u> work out of people isn't necessarily getting their <u>best</u> work. Ultimately, it's a quality, not simply a quantity game. Lots of people learn how to keep busy – the trick is to get things done and done right. Not all movement is progress.

Third, forget all this bullshit that every idea is a good one. Plenty of ideas just suck. Pretending that every idea is possible or worthy of consideration and discussion and trying to be politically correct and always constructive in your criticism is a formula for failure. It's nice to be liked; it's more important to be respected. And sympathy is a lot like junk food – it doesn't help anybody to lie to people or give them false encouragement or hope. Hurt feelings, bruised egos, skinned knees are all part of the growth process and critical to it.

Finally, your people are very important, but don't lose sight of the main chance. The name of the game is to create great products and services and to build a company that will last – it's really not about making people feel good about themselves and loved. Leave that to the clergy. Seeking consensus is about finding the middle ground, settling, and making people feel good about themselves and each other – it's a completely different objective than building your business and it has no place in the rough and tumble world of getting a new company off the ground. You can have higher aspirations, broader goals, and apple pie mission statements once you can pay the bills and afford those luxuries.

In much the same way, teamwork is certainly a wonderful thing, but in a start-up, it's mainly a means to getting the help you need to see your vision through to completion. Political correctness, consensus building and hyper-collaborative teamwork will only take you so far. You can't serve too many masters or chase too many rabbits at the same time or you'll end up with none. You're not a social welfare agency; you're not a church or a charity; and you're not your employees' shrink or family – you're a small, young business trying to grow into something important and that alone is a full-time job and then some.

The truth is that most of the world's great products and businesses – as well as most of the great inventions throughout history – were ultimately the result and expression of a single, uncompromising vision - albeit managed, massaged, and manipulated through a sea of change, confusion and compromise. That's your main job – define, defend and drive the vision. The reason that it's so important to always keep the vision front and center and so inextricably tied to your people is that great ideas can bring people, but ultimately it's something bigger – ideals – that keeps them together. We all want to be working for something that's bigger than ourselves.

In building your business, you have a small window and often a single chance, a passing moment and a fleeting opportunity to make something special and spectacular and to make a difference – if you have the courage of your convictions, the confidence in your abilities, and if you're willing to make and stick to the hard choices that will inevitably arise. The people choices are always the hardest.

There's no more challenging job in a young company than being the person who has to let people go. Everyone else gets to talk about what a tight-knit, stick together group the company is (just like a "family" of friends) and all that other touchy-feely stuff, but you're the one who has to deliver the bad news over and over again. And it's true whether you're the CEO or the head of sales or the HR manager – it doesn't really matter – it's a tough job for anyone. If you were unpopular in high school, you're already one step ahead of the game. It's not easy or always popular to be the boss, but then good leadership isn't a popularity contest. It's a given that you can't please any of the people all the time.

The truth is that your company's only as good as your worst employee and the best-run businesses are always looking to either retrain and upgrade or replace the lowest performing employees. Sometimes it's a breeze. We try to immediately fire any employee who doesn't try or doesn't care. These are cardinal sins in a start-up and there's no question that these people need to go – they're always the easiest decisions. And then the job gets harder and harder.

The next tier of troublesome employees is those who try hard, but just cannot do the job. You can be totally sincere and have the best of intentions, but still be incapable (or no longer capable) of doing the job that needs to get done. There are good people who are perfectly able to do a job poorly for a very long time before anyone has the time, interest, or guts to ask the hard questions about results rather than effort. These people need to go too, but you need to be as fair and firm with them as you can. And do them a real favor – tell them the truth.

Then there are the employees who are basically hard- working and dedicated, but who (for better or worse) can't fit into or model the corporate culture and behaviors. Every business that I've been involved with has ultimately been about hard work mixed in with a healthy dose of paranoia. We had lots of ways to reflect this ethic and plenty of signs all over the place. "Hard work conquers everything." "Effort can trump ability." "We may not outsmart them, but we'll outwork them every time." "Obstacles are those frightful little things you see when you take your eyes off the goal." "Just because you're paranoid doesn't mean that someone's not out to get you." And so on and so forth. And almost everyone we hired got the message and drank the Kool- Aid. Even the people who just wanted a "job" and not a career or to join a sacred crusade pretty much still worked their butts off.

But every so often, we'd hire someone who was just too healthy and well-adjusted to succeed among our tribe of crazies. We used to say that a relaxed man is not necessarily a better man. In one business, our internal motto was "let our sickness work for you". It turned out that it was important to let the other people see you sweat – not just the big deals – but the smallest details so they knew you cared. If you weren't just a little bit crazy about the work and the business, you were slightly suspect or worse.

I remember one special case where after we let someone go he wrote me a long letter and asked for a more complete explanation of why he didn't succeed with us. I decided to reply and ultimately what I ended up telling him is something that it's worth always keeping in mind when you sign up to be an entrepreneur. I wrote:

> *I'm sorry that complex issues like an individual's performance and work attitude get reduced to unfortunate shorthand phrases like "not hungry enough", "didn't want it", etc. in conversations with others who want to know "what happened?". We all know that work and relationships are far more complicated than a few pithy phrases. And we also know that, in their own mind, almost everyone wants to do a good job that they and others can be proud of. But here's the rub. Only a select few individuals are crazy enough (as we pretty much all are here) to subject themselves to the constant stress and heartache associated with starting and building new businesses. Our company is a very fast track run by a bunch of workaholic perfectionists. We all believe that that's what it takes to win against pretty fierce odds. And this is simply not the right place for everyone – especially people who want to have a family, outside interests and a normal life. I think it's very likely that you're simply too nice and too well-adjusted to work with the crazies around here and that's shame on us – not you. But it's the way things are. We wish you all the best.*

Ultimately, all of these situations come down to the basic choice – you can make one person miserable for a period of time when they lose their job, or you can end up with a crappy company where everyone's miserable because you don't have the guts to do the right things for the business. And once you start to carry people along who aren't performing, you take a tremendous <u>double hit</u> – you pay the price for the poor performer's activities, but that's nothing compared to the real harm. As soon as you fail to consistently fire non-performers, you start to lose your best people and that's what kills the company.

To do this right, you have to build a differentiated system from the start that provides different levels of rewards, acknowledgments and compensation for different people throughout the business. And you need to move quickly and regularly to identify and remove the bad apples before they spoil the whole place.

11 – YOU CAN'T ADD VALUE IF YOU DON'T HAVE VALUES

For new businesses, there are lots of things you just can't afford financially. Those things are typically (and painfully) pretty obvious. And I'm not just talking about fancy cars, frills, and bells and whistles. I'm talking about fairly basic, but sadly expensive, stuff. The good news, however, is that, as you grow your business, a lot of these kinds of problems will go away. I like to say that any problem that you can solve with a check isn't really a problem at all – it's just one of a million different choices you'll have to make as time goes on.

But there are a bunch of other things that start-ups also can't afford that have nothing to do with money. One of the most complicated and least talked about (in this feel-good, politically correct world we live in) is real values. You absolutely cannot afford to have the wrong values when you're building your business. In a word, you can't be pushing platitudes when you're trying to make payroll.

It makes me sick to read these retrospective (rewrite my life please) articles by people who've made it (sometimes thru hard work; sometimes thru luck; sometimes thru family ties or special connections; and sometimes for no apparent reason at all) talking about how important it was to their success that they had all these Mom & Pop, Apple Pie, and democratic (small "d") values as part of their businesses from the beginning. It's a complete crock. And what's worse is the fact that it can mislead other people into thinking that this is the way the real world works. But it's not.

As sad as it may sound and as bitter a pill as it may be to all the bleeding hearts and social scientists out there that have never run anything, the truth is that you need to adopt the values that are right for your business from time to time. As the joke *goes,* "These are my principles. If you don't like them, I have others.", but it's not really a joke. As a new company, you can't afford the luxury of having grown-up, fancy values when you are fighting for survival. And anyone who tells you otherwise just hasn't ever been there in the trenches looking right into the bottom or the wrong end of the barrel.

Now I'm not saying, of course, that you shouldn't have any concrete values, I'm just saying that the values that will make or break your business should and will change over time as your business and your team matures. This is actually a lot easier to show you than to try to describe. But first let me give you a few basics:

(1) Your core values need to be manageable and realistic for your business.
(2) Your core values need to be relevant to your business and your employees – not generic, but unique.
(3) Your core values need to be short and memorable – the shorter the better – ideally they'd all fit on the back of your business card.
(4) Your core values need to be as simple as possible, but no simpler.
(5) Your core values need to be repeated constantly and internalized by everyone in the company.

At TFA, my college, our five core values are clear to all. We believe in:

Unstinting Effort
Pride of Craft
Courage of Our Convictions
Loyalty
Excellence

Now, here are five core values from a large, mature corporation in our marketplace:

Fairness
Respect
Opportunity
Security
Inclusion

I hope the differences are obvious. Not one of these words conveys any energy or a bias for action. They're pretty much entirely devoid of emotional content. And even if I knew what some of these words were intended to mean in the way of behavioral guidance, they don't tell me jack about what makes the company stand up and stand out every day.

If you still don't get it, here's a visual aid:

Frankly, I couldn't build a fire under any group of employees with a stem-winder about inclusion or security if my life depended on it. In fact, in a start-up, attempts at too much inclusion are like ingesting a slow-acting poison that kills your response times, wastes enormous amounts of time and other resources, and almost always leads to mediocre results. I've said it before and I'll say it again – not every idea is a good idea – not every suggestion is worthy of extensive discussion - and democracy in meetings isn't really a virtue in and of itself. If I had the choice, I'd rather work for a tyrant any day than for a committee.

Again, there's nothing terribly wrong with these kinds of broad, vague values, they're just terribly wrong for a new, young business to try to live by or to live up to. And that's the real crux of the matter. You've got to make your core values real and you've got to make them matter or you're just wasting your breath. Company values don't break, they crumble slowly over time unless they are actively pursued and nurtured. It's a slippery slope and only you can stop the constant threat of erosion.

So, assuming you've got the right ones for your company's developmental stage and size, how do you protect and promote them? Three basic rules:

(1) Make your company values aggressive and demanding
(2) Make them inflexible and uncompromising
(3) Be totally intolerant of breaches

Once your values start to slide, it's almost impossible to recover. And believe me nothing is more central to your company's culture and your ultimate shot at success than getting this process right. You're the values cop.

And nothing is harder because it's NEVER easy to say what no one wants to hear and it's the easiest thing in the world to give someone a temporary pass or to overlook something in the moment when you should jump on it. But remember two important things: (a) past sins never vanish, they just wait; and (b) you can't talk yourself out of problems that you behave yourself into. You've got to insist on the proper behaviors and the proper attitudes and stick to your guns.

It's your job – it's not fun; it's not easy – if it was, we'd all be making $12,500 a year – and it's a constant process that requires continual vigilance.

To make your core values stick, you've got to be prepared to take it to people every day and insist that they get on the program or go somewhere else. Don't confuse someone's good manners with their willingness to change their behavior – you need to make sure that their commitments aren't just words - and that their apologies aren't just lip service. Any apology not accompanied by a change in behavior is an insult.

Today, because the barriers to entry into almost any business are so low and the costs are so modest, competitors can be in your business and in your face in an instant. And because much of the Web is still very much like the Wild West, prospects and customers have very little accurate information to go on in making their initial choices and evaluations of various products or services.

Website and service validation businesses represent an entirely new and interesting digital marketplace and Stella Service is one of the early leaders in the space trying to become the "Good Housekeeping" seal of approval for e- commerce and other sites. It's a fertile opportunity and you can bet that he'll have plenty of competition in no time at all.

But, because the need is a real one, everyone will eventually be much better served and become much smarter decision-makers by virtue of the immediate access they will have to timely and accurate comparative information concerning everything they are thinking about buying, selling, using, visiting or consuming. We're about to enter the Mocial world.

Mocial is just a mash-up of mobile and social, but what it stands for is a much more complex and important set of ideas and requirements. Mocial means providing:

(1) what we need;
(2) when we need it;
(3) wherever we are; and
(4) without asking.

Places and spaces will become intelligent and active and they will tell us relevant and particularized "stories" based on who we are, where we are and what we are doing as well as our prior contextual- sensitive activities and histories. Nudge commerce and next-generation suggestive selling systems will make a lot of the basic purchase decisions for us – especially in-store or online. Google Now is an early second-generation entrant into these kinds of services.

However, for the moment, as a result of inadequate and poorly distributed marketplace information, false claims and promises, bait and switch offers, and cheap prices are far too prevalent on the Web and unfortunately they're disproportionately effective for the moment. And even though price and value are two radically different things, it's often very difficult for your company to make your case in the few moments or seconds during which you typically have the buyer's attention.

Worse yet, in today's Costco-fied economy, besides price, uber-size seems to matter most to too many consumers. Measuring bigger is easy. Measuring better is much harder because it requires judgment and values. But it's not all that clear that most consumers care about long- term value especially given the highly-disposable nature and prompt obsolescence of so many of today's products and services.

As a result, you can find yourself trying to keep up with and compete against new entrants and other competitors who really have no skin in the game. Having nothing, they have nothing to lose – all they can do is mess up the market for you. And like finding a turd in the punch bowl, once the prices start to spiral down, things only get uglier and less appetizing. There's really no way back.

This is also why - for a real player - it's no fun at all to play poker for pennies. Playing for peanuts (or with people with nothing to lose) takes away the pain and pressure of making difficult choices and sacrifices. But even that's only half the story. The other reason that it's a waste of time to play for pretend stakes is that there is no real impact outside of the game if you lose. Ultimately nothing is more important to good decisionmaking than the ability to identify, appreciate and evaluate the costs and consequences of our actions. Not, of course, just at the poker table, but in all our business relationships and in our lives in general as well.

And please don't buy into this noise about there being room for everyone in the market and that more players just expand the overall market size. Your job is to kill the competition – if they're about to drown; throw them a nice large anvil to speed the process along. They want your family to starve and your kids to be homeless.

And even if these mopes were worthy competitors instead of low-ball artists, trying to compete on price or sheer quantity - especially for a start-up - is a very tough and risky choice and almost always a bad idea. This is why you don't wrestle with pigs – you'll both get dirty, but only the pig will enjoy it.

Not only are there no winners in the race to the lowest price, it actually turns out that, for many of us today, even "free" isn't cheap enough. This is because in many cases the costs of usage and adoption have a lot more to do with the calculated allocation of scarce personal time and precious resources rather than with just dollars and cents. In addition, there are always other and better dimensions to compete on if you're really doing your job.

So, as tough as it can sometimes be, the best plan is to ignore the guys in the cheap seats and concentrate on making sure that you're delivering a product or service that's worth the prices you're asking your customers to pay. In the end, that's all that really matters and that's what will win in the long run.

TULLMAN'S TRUISMS

FREE ISN'T CHEAP ENOUGH

Time has a nasty way of turning even your best assets into liabilities and even your happiest customers have a way of taking yesterday's "miracles" for granted (or worse – thinking that your products and services are old and tired) and looking elsewhere. They're always looking for the next new thing and the news media and the competition conspire regularly to stoke these desires for novelty and change.

If you're there to respond to these ever-expanding requirements and demands, you have a good chance of holding your own. But that's about it. On the other hand, if you want to grow your business, you need to anticipate these new consumer demands – not simply react to them – and you need a plan and a program to consistently get out ahead of your customers. Relationships that don't move forward and improve consistently deteriorate. One day, you turn around and the customer is gone. And by and large they don't give you any real warning; they don't generally complain; and they certainly don't ask your permission. They just disappear.

If you aren't aggressively watching your business and your customers and your competition, this situation won't be a problem for too long because you won't have any business to worry about. Suffice it to say, you can't sell anything sitting on your seat and you can't learn anything with actively and consistently listening to and for your customers. As you'll see, even when we try to listen, we often miss the main messages because we tend to listen primarily for what we want to hear – not what we need to hear.

Here's a quick example about doctors – some of the worst listeners in the world. One of my earliest businesses was Original Research II and our job was to measure customer satisfaction across many different industries. We were asked by a very large group of doctors to determine what considerations were most important to their patients and prospective patients. At the same time, we also polled all of the doctors in the practice to determine what they believed were the main drivers for patients. The results were fascinating and frightening.

Patients' Actual Priorities	Doctors' Presumed Drivers
Location	Specialty
Office Hours	Board Certifications
Free and Convenient Parking	Technical Skills
Insurance Coverage	Referrals - Word of Mouth
A Great Receptionist	Insurance Coverage

Needless to say, these results were the rudest of awakenings for the doctors. It was absolutely clear that a concerned and considerate staff was WAY more important than the most highly-trained surgeon on the team.

We did a similar project for bank officers and compared what they felt were important considerations for their customers to the customers' actual concerns and the primary causes for customer defections. There were a number of issues, but the overwhelming disconnect was that more than 67% of the customers felt that inattention was the worst possible sin and the largest problem – they could live with everything else – but when they came to believe that no one was paying attention to them, they stopped caring and left.

The bank officers, on the other hand, were largely consumed by mechanical and procedural considerations like price, interest rates, errors, credit decisions and paid only scant attention to the fundamental emotional consideration and customer desire of being appreciated and wanted. The only thing that we could say in their defense is that it was probably true that their primary interactions with the customers related to these process issues and that the customers probably felt uncomfortable expressing to anyone their personal feelings about how they believed the bank treated and regarded them. No one wants to be a number.

But here's the really sad part of this story. Failing to connect, cultivate and extend your relationships with your existing customers means that you are forfeiting the opportunity to harvest the easiest and most cost-effective additional profits available to any business. Spending time and money to find new customers (conquest marketing) is OK, but deepening your involvement with your current customers and increasing their average spend as well as locking them in for life (relationship marketing) is the brass ring.

14 – KNOCK ON OLD DOORS

Failing to connect and cultivate your existing customers means that you are missing the chance to grab some easy incremental profits. Deepening your involvement with your current customers and increasing their average spend as well as locking them in for life (relationship marketing) is the real key to building an increasingly valuable business.

I call this strategy "knocking on old doors" because these customers are already in the tent (which means there are no new acquisition costs) and you're already touching them (hopefully on a consistent basis) so now you simply have to up the ante and the incentives and you'll see some amazing results. And, by the way, upping the ante and improving your connections with these current customers doesn't have to cost you a dime more – it's usually just a matter of attention and focus.

Instead of spending money chasing new customers (conquest marketing) or trying to steal customers from the competition (often by competing on price – which is a bad thing to do any time), you should stick to your knitting and direct your energies and your efforts to the lowest-hanging fruit – the people you're already doing business with. Just do a better job of that and they will take care of the rest.

The other equally wasteful activity is to spend too much time fretting about why customers who do leave left. It hurts, of course, to lose any customers (especially when you're small), but when you do the math, you quickly discover that customer defections (unforced by errors) account for a few percentage points of total revenue - an amount that can quickly and exponentially be offset by redirecting the same funds and resources used in the "why'd they go" exercise to engaging more deeply and meaningfully with the next higher tier of remaining customers which is always a much larger and more valuable population. A small overall improvement in this pool of customers will mean a lot more economically than trying to chase a few people who've left.

And if that math doesn't convince you in and of itself, here's the closer from one consumer survey we did for our large banking customers. More than 55 percent of customer defections on an annual basis were caused by two uncontrollable and unavoidable events - death and job transfers or other geographic relocations. All the fretting in the world won't keep the family in town if father's new job or position is halfway across the country.

None of this is rocket science – it's just common sense. Happy, "cared-for" customers spend more. And "organic" customers (basically home-grown) spend LOTS

more than customers acquired through one-off marketing spends, promotions, and other incentives that may attract incremental customers, but don't create lasting connections to them. And sometimes customers leave you for reasons beyond your control. But what you may not realize is that the happy customers who stay with you also boost your business and your profits in a multitude of other ways. Here are some of the basic ways that your customers increase your profits when you "knock on old doors":

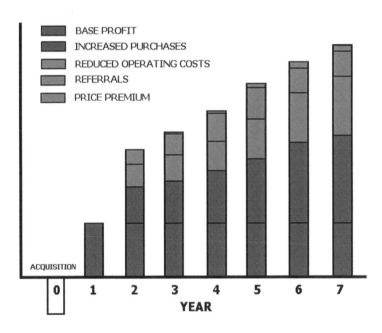

Yep, it's a fact. You can even charge your happiest customers <u>more</u> for certain types of status and premium offerings and they will stand in line to pay the tab. And they'll bring their friends, family and co-workers as well. So, the bottom line is that the care and feeding of your customers is even more important and valuable to your business than you imagined.

Constantly migrating your customers up the spending curve needs to be an on- going part of your marketing strategy even though it's technically "internal" marketing and, for that reason, it often gets overlooked or pushed aside. But if you want to "own" your customers for life, great service, careful listening and continual customer maintenance are crucial.

I t's more important to deepen your connection to your existing customers than to spend a lot of time and money trying to figure out why certain customers left. After all, while you might learn some things from the process, you can't really water yesterday's crops and, in any case, it feels a little too much to me like crying over spilt milk. Extract the necessary lessons, fix what can be fixed, and move forward.

But that's not to say that you shouldn't care about losing customers. Nothing is more important to your bottom line than preventing customer attrition and avoiding churn. I'm just saying that, once they're gone, they're pretty much gone so the real key is to hang on to them by "closing the back door". If you can't do this, and you're spending a fortune on the front end to pull in new customers while you're losing them out the back, your company's going nowhere fast. It's like kissing your sister or as Yogi Berra used to say about his road trips: "We're lost, but we're making good time." The truth is that, if you're losing customers as quickly as you adding them, you're not making or building anything – you're just treading water – and once you run out of money, they make you go home.

The name of the long and winning game is to "own" your customers for life and to anticipate, meet and, in fact, try to exceed their needs and their expectations throughout your relationship with them. The key word is "anticipate" and the biggest change in all businesses today is that we now have the tools and the data concerning virtually all of our customers that should permit us to totally manage our relationships with them if we invest the time and money to look at the available information and – most importantly – if we know what we are looking for.

Everything in life happens on a continuum (or a series of cycles) and your job is to monitor your customers' timelines and jump in at the appropriate junctures (long before the competition is even in the game) to make the next connection and the next sales.

This approach is equally true whether you <u>think</u> you are selling a product or a service. The smartest operators know that every business is really a service business today because the real nature of every business is that it's always about making the next sale, managing the next interaction or event, delivering an uninterrupted stream of service, etc. You never want the customer "to come up for air" because if he or she does re-enter the marketplace and starts shopping around, your job becomes a million times harder.

So the real task and the critical questions are always the same – how do I know when to act and how do I pre-empt/intercept the customer at exactly the right times in our relationship? The answer is actually easier than you would think because - even though the start and stop points on the cycle may vary by customer - at some definable and determinable point, every customer will move through the same cycle. You just have to understand and learn how to measure and manage the cycles.

Here's the most valuable chart you will ever see. Keep in mind that it not only applies to the customers in your business; it also applies to your current relationship or marriage and to every other significant connection you will ever have with other human beings. So use it early and often because it describes the critical cycle of consumption that governs our interaction with everything we love and value.

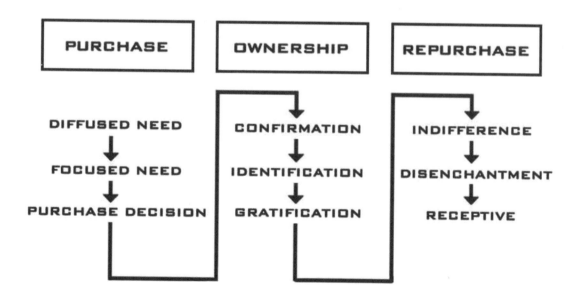

The "trick" as you might imagine is to consistently get your next "offer" in front of the customer somewhere right before DISENHANCEMENT so that you glide into RECEPTIVE as the only horse in town.

The chart below illustrates a more practical view of a consumption cycle that relates to the point in time (the "CROSSOVER POINT") when the remaining value of a consumer's car exceeds the amount of the loan balance which the consumer still owes on that car. From the standpoint of an automobile dealer, this is the ideal time to make a new offer to the consumer which basically amounts to a proposal to turn in his or her old car; get a brand-new car; and get a brand-new 48-60 month loan repayment book to go along with it.

Why is this a compelling offer for the customer? Because in virtually every case, the customer can be told that his monthly payments will remain the same EVEN THOUGH he or she will be driving a brand-new car. In addition, there's no car salesman to deal with; no time wasted negotiating; no anxiety about getting a fair deal or a fair trade-in; and, of course, from the dealer's standpoint, there's no competition.

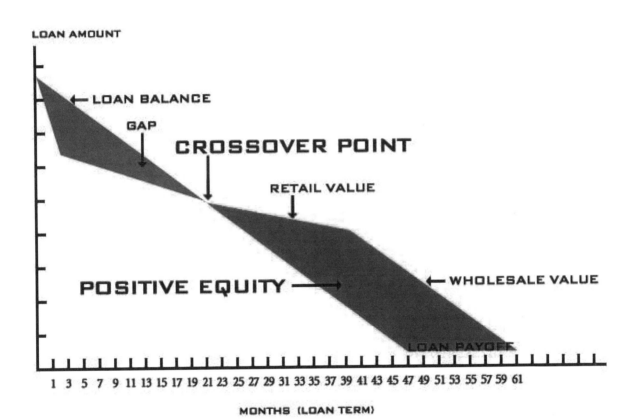

Now the cycles are going to vary dramatically depending on a variety of important considerations and they will vary from industry to industry as well. Some of the variables which will impact the types and durations of the cycles (but not the fundamental stages or phase within the cycle) include:

(1) how large and financially/emotionally important is the transaction;
(2) how often is a transaction likely to occur and what other connections/interactions with the customer will take place between transactions: and
(3) how easy is it for the customer to change vendors, services or products and how readily available are competitive offerings?

But, regardless of a given cycle's duration, there are similar cycles to be identified, tracked and managed in <u>every</u> business and properly managed, these cycles are the keys to closing the back door and keeping your customers for life.

I'm always surprised that even the smarter entrepreneurs, who understand how to segment their customers by "spend" and – within reason and usually discretely – treat them differently, fail to appreciate that simply approaching customers based on the dollars they contribute to your revenues is at best only taking into account a modest fraction of the whole story.

To really master the art and the science of customer retention, you've got to also understand where each customer is from time to time on the consumption cycle (as I described in the last post) and, equally importantly, you've got to determine what type of attachment the customer has to your business and the extent of the attachment that he or she has as well. And finally, you have to learn what viable alternatives and substitution capabilities the customer has and how compelling any available competitive offerings may be to each customer.

For the moment, I want to concentrate on the attachment issues because the conclusions you reach about these considerations will be the primary drivers of how you approach and treat each customer. Basically, you'll need to use different "strokes" (data, incentives and offers) for different folks if you want to succeed in holding on to the vast majority of your customer base. One size never fits all. And, the loyalty profiles of your customers will vary dramatically depending on the industry you're in and the specific kind of product or service that you are offering.

In the attachment universe, the first thing to determine is what type of connection is common within your industry and for your product or service. It's not as simple as you might think. And, if you do think this stuff is obvious or that you are already doing the right things simply because you "know" the answers to these kinds of questions (although you have to admit that you never really asked them or thought about them), then you're most likely in trouble already because anyone today who thinks that they have no "customer" issues or problems is just one step away from the cliff. The choice is always the same – innovate and improve your game or risk becoming irrelevant before you even realize it.

Step one is your industry/product. Soft drink and beer companies have it pretty easy. So do soaps, detergents, and deodorants. In fact, the most likely cause of a change in a beer drinker's preference is immediately following a divorce. Go figure that out. Probably not a lot of fond memories associated with your ex's brewski. But, in any case, in these industries you're looking at customers who have a clear emotional connection to the product and a reluctance to change or even try new products. They think they made a smart and conscious choice; they're sticking with it; and they're pretty good spenders as well. They're not going anywhere and you shouldn't allocate your scarce resources against this population because you always need to focus on changing the behavior of the "at-risk" customers – not necessarily stroking the ones who are already fat and happy. Call these guys the "HEART" group.

And, at the other end of the fun scale, in the life insurance business, you have an equally important group to ignore. This is another group that's going nowhere fast and maybe not until they die. I'd say that these people – by and large – apart from seeing the occasional FUD commercial on TV about your uninsured family ending up in the poorhouse and unable to bury you – don't even think about the product more than once a year; don't think there's any reason to change if and when they do; and aren't really even price-sensitive because who can figure out what any of this insurance stuff costs anyway. So, if the drinkers are emotional, these guys fall into the "just sit there" category. As long as you (or anyone else) don't disturb them, they're there for the duration. Same category includes your internet provider (notwithstanding a new bundle every day) and your credit card(s) company. It's just "too hard" to make a change that isn't precipitated by something. (By the way, this is not the same for car insurance decisions where there's so much ongoing and in-your-face advertising at all times that you're forced to consider apparent economic alternatives.) Call these folks the "BUTT" group.

The next and largest category (and the one you need to engage) can typically range very broadly across a lot of day-in and day-out necessity-driven products and services that we buy and consume almost every day – this can be our grocery shopping (but not personal hygiene items where we have an emotional connection as noted above); clothing for the kids; gas and maintenance for the car; etc. and here we're pretty engaged and VERY sensitive to and receptive to strokes. These are the folks who think a lot about their purchases (especially in these tough times) and they are regularly trying to evaluate, calculate and select the best deals. They are price/value/performance shoppers and they require a great deal of care and handling because of how quickly their loyalty and shopping habits can shift based on what you might regard as minor changes in price, packaging, bundling, etc. They need to be reassured and provided with continuing demonstrations that their choices and selections are the right ones. Call the guys the "BRAIN" group.

Take some time to figure out where you sit in this analysis and in the next chapter on closing the back door, I'll tell you what to do about keeping almost all of your customers on board for life.

When it comes to retaining your "BRAIN" oriented or analytical customers who represent the largest single portion of all of your customers in almost every circumstance, the process is straightforward and simple, but not easy to accomplish. You need to have a "conversation" with these people in order to address their concerns and provide them with the "strokes" necessary to convince them to stay.

But (a) you need to be very careful not to push or overstep their boundaries because they want to decide, not be convinced, in most cases; and (b) these kinds of "conversations" are almost always indirect and conducted passively rather than actively. It's not like sending someone a coupon in the mail or online or calling them up and telling them your dealership desperately needs used cars and how about trading in their car and getting a new one. And the job is much harder in industries where comparisons with alternatives are relatively easy and readily accessible and also where there aren't strong brand positions or attachments.

Keep in mind also that we're not talking here about unhappy customers (with or without a good reason) and we're not talking about customers whose changed conditions or circumstances have changed their requirements which in turn causes them to consider alternatives regardless of your efforts to anticipate and preempt such actions. Those cases require different approaches and typically aren't worth the incremental effort since the likelihood of a turn-around is small.

We're talking about generally smart, informed customers who try to act rationally and make the best and most cost-effective choices based on their view of the price/value equation which your products or services offer from time to time. And in most cases, they don't tell you if and/or when this process and the calculations are going on – they just do their thing. You've got to be your own best advocate and give them the tools, ammunition and ability to assess the situation and hopefully decide to stay.

Basically, there are 3 large buckets of benefits which you can manage and adjust to try to reach and convince these target customers. I call the buckets:

(1) Where's the Beef?

To borrow from Clay Christensen, the question here is how well does the product or service do its job? You need to determine how well you are doing relative to two metrics: the price/value equation (is it worth it?) and the cost of alternative solutions which may be readily available to your customers (where else can I find it?). Remember the old line that customers want ¼" holes, not ¼" drills. Whatever you can do to bolster and improve the customer's impressions in these two areas, you should do as quickly and as often as possible. The more benefits; the tighter connection; and the higher degree of "locking in" the customers and his or her peers to your service, the greater the likelihood that they will stay and not even consider switching.

(2) Where's the Heat?

The "heat" or, more accurately, the more friction that is built into your systems and processes, the more likely that there will be direct and negative customer reactions. Anything that takes too much time, requires repetition or seems to serve only your interests and not the customers' will be a problem going forward and a risk to your business. Remember that customers' buy for their reasons, not ours. Radio Shack has a pretty strong and flexible automatic return policy (even for cash purchases), but (for internal fraud prevention purposes), if you want a cash refund, they require that you supply them with your phone number. Turns out that for a lot of folks, this seems like gross overreaching and defeats the whole salutary basis of the general policy. The customer doesn't work for us.

Sometimes, businesses don't even really understand the "job" that the customer wants done and inadvertently make things harder or more expensive than necessary to meet the real requirements of both the customers and the businesses themselves. Customer loyalty punch cards are a well-intentioned retention device that (up until the advent of the new start-up Belly) was a literal pain-in-the-wallet (or purse) solution that was more often frustrating to customers instead of rewarding. How many half-punched cards can we jam in our wallet or forget to carry with us when we need them without bagging the whole bunch? Encouraging customers to consolidate their spending with you and return often is the holy grail, but only if the process is as painless as possible.

(3) Who's your Mama?

At the end of the day, everything in business and especially in successful selling is about relationships. The greater the connection and relationship that you can build with each and every one of these customers, the longer you'll keep them and the stronger they will be. Save me time or money or make me more productive and it's gonna take a very substantial and persuasive argument to make me walk away. And 9 times out of 10, price alone won't do it. The impression of "belonging"; being a special or top-tier customer; and/or receiving special perks and preferences are all methods that need to be continually expanded and built upon so that you constantly improve the connection to the customer.

No one sells a product anymore today – everything is a service in the sense that every sale should trigger a life-long customer maintenance program and strategy to maximize the long-term value of every customer and to help amortize their acquisition cost over the largest possible set of revenue streams and follow-on sales.

The best customers are those that "never come up for air" and then start to look elsewhere in the competitive marketplace because you've satisfied their past needs and their present requirements and you've anticipated their future desires.

TULLMAN'S TRUISMS

IT'S EASY TO MEASURE BIGGER - IT'S HARDER TO MEASURE BETTER

What kind of deal is a 90 Day Wonder. It's a transaction or an agreement where 90 days after you sign the papers, you wonder why you ever did the deal. And, <u>whichever</u> side of the table you're on – investor or entrepreneur - take it from me, you don't want to end up there – with a bucket full of regrets and egg all over your face. Even if Halloween's just around the corner.

There's a great old poker expression: "If you're in the game for 30 minutes and you don't know who the patsy is - you're the patsy." Needless to say, in any context, but especially when you're negotiating over money for a new business, nobody wants to be the patsy. And you can usually avoid it if you go into the negotiation process understanding even just a little about the needs of both parties; how those will change over time; and just how crazy most entrepreneurs get from time to time as their companies and their circumstances change and grow. Remember: as the Latin saying goes: "*finis origine pendet*" which means "the end depends on the beginning".

And keep in mind that I get to call entrepreneurs "crazy" because I "are" one. So please don't be offended. If you're a VC or other investor and I haven't previously offended you, it certainly isn't for any lack of effort on my part. I like to say that "asking an entrepreneur what he thinks about venture capitalists is like asking a dog how he feels about a fire hydrant". But I digress.

The fact is that, for many investors, each new deal and each new entrepreneur is a distinct set of experiences – so good, some not so much – and it's an ongoing education for both sides of the equation that can be very instructive and also very painful. Education is expensive, no matter how you get it.

So here are eight different things that it's really critical to understand and keep in mind as you start down the road of working with entrepreneurs. The first 4 are pre-deal; the next 3 are during the deal; and the last is when the business is most likely in the toilet. I've used bullet points throughout (with a couple of exceptions) to save time and space:

(1) Be Careful Not to Starve the Baby

Building new businesses may take less money today than it used to, but it still takes some basic amount of capital. In negotiating an initial deal, unfortunately both sides are perversely incented to starve the business. The entrepreneur wants to conserve his equity (you only give away your equity once) and to avoid early dilution at a low valuation. The investor wants to put as little capital at risk initially as possible although getting in early at a low valuation is an offset to this sentiment. The risk is that the business is undercapitalized from the outset and never has the resources necessary to get a serious start.

(2) Be Broader than the Boy Wonder

It's the investor, not the entrepreneur, who has to make sure that whatever deal is made adequately provides for the entire management team (key players) and for players to be named at a later date. For the entrepreneur, very often, the business is a mission and a sacred crusade and he or she would basically work for free. But this isn't usually the case for most of the other senior people - at least not to the same extent – especially if they were lateral and/or later additions rather than co-founders or early members of the team. Because entrepreneurs are so intensely committed themselves, they very often fail to appreciate the differing levels of commitment that exist among the rest of the members of their team and they almost always fail to adequately provide for the rest of their team when they are dealing with the investors. It's very rarely an issue of selfishness and usually it's just the fact that they're so focused that they're oblivious.

(3) Be Sure to Ask the Hard Questions and Don't Kid Yourself

Making an investment deal is very often a time-constrained process and, unlike a divorce proceeding where the lawyers on both sides are perfectly happy to bill their time and just wait until the parties calm down and get a little more rational before they try to get a deal done, in a typical business deal, everyone's in a hurry. And, because everyone wants to get to a deal, bad and ultimately unworkable agreements get made on a frighteningly frequent basis. Here are some of the things to watch out for:

Hard and time-consuming issues get papered over or buried to be resolved "later" by someone else (and sadly often through litigation) because no one wants to be the "bad" in someone else's day.

Otherwise smart and prudent people gloss over or entirely ignore their attorneys' advice on certain risks and with regard to undocumented or researched concerns (we regularly called our lawyers the Department of "NO") and focus only on the upside prospects of the deal.

In the interests of smooth sailing (and often with the excuse that "we have to live with these people after the deal is done"), even seasoned veterans will accept superficial assurances and smiles instead of concrete answers and go on to confuse good manners, pleasantries, and bad jokes with real agreement. The technical term we used for this phenomenon was "grin fucking" (where people are smiling through their teeth, but don't mean a thing they're saying) although there are a host of other equally descriptive and suggestive terms.

Too often, the negotiators push the problems forward and assume/delude themselves into believing that the fine details and rough edges will all be taken care of during the implementation phase of the transaction. All I can say about this is that – as a general rule in complex deals – (a) the easier the deal is to get done, the harder it will be to implement and (b) deals rarely, if ever, get better during implementation. Problems don't work themselves out or disappear – they fester and persist until someone takes responsibility for them and gets them resolved. Or, as the great playwright David Mamet once wrote: 'you can't polish a turd'.

Finally, instead of acknowledging and accepting that there are remaining open items and continuing uncertainties (that only time can resolve) and working together to construct metrics for determining the impact of possible outcomes as well as potential solutions to address changed economics, the parties engage in mutual fantasies and shake hands on deals which are full of holes and more porous than Swiss cheese.

TULLMAN'S TRUISMS

THE END DEPENDS ON THE BEGINNING

19 – AVOID 90 DAY WONDERS – PART 2

As I said in the last chapter, 90 Day Wonders are transactions or agreements where 90 days after you sign the papers, you wonder why you ever did the deal. And, <u>whichever</u> side of the table you're on – investor or entrepreneur - take it from me, you don't want to end up there.

You can usually avoid this situation if you go into the negotiation process understanding even just a little about the needs of both parties; how those will change over time; and just how crazy most entrepreneurs get from time to time as their companies and their circumstances change and grow.

The fact is that, for many investors, each new deal and each new entrepreneur is a distinct set of experiences – some good, some not so much – and it's an ongoing education for both sides of the equation that can be very instructive and also very painful. Education is expensive, no matter how you get it.

One of the problems, however, from the investor side, is that very often you've got young, relatively green guys representing the money and, because they don't have a great deal of maturity or experience, they tend to fall back on a standard set of approaches, formulae, repeated mantras (that they seem to think are infallible expressions of long-settled wisdom) and other inflexible (and often inapplicable) views of the deal that basically have worked for them (or – at least – that they got away with in the past. And, often for worse, they try to jam every deal into the same cookie-cutter mold and approach.

Part of this is simple inexperience and a larger part is butt-covering where they figure that they can always say – in their defense if the deal structure ends up sucking – that this was the way they were told to do it in the past. Just as they say that no young MBA ever lost his job at a VC firm by saying "no" to a deal; there's also no place in the partnership (or anywhere else) for a whole lot of innovation, clever new solutions or risk-taking. Shutting up and doing it like it's always been done is the tried and true course. Gag me.

In any case, in the last chapter, I covered three major pre-deal concerns that are critical for all investors to keep in mind as they start down the road working with entrepreneurs. The next 4 issues (which are covered below) relate to considerations growing out of the ongoing deal negotiations. And the last section covers some very common comments and a bunch of rationalizations that customarily start to be heard with great frequency when the business is most likely in the toilet or on its way there.

I include these last quotes of both investors and entrepreneurs because they function very well as early (but sadly not early enough in most cases) warning signs that the deal is in real trouble.

(1) Beware of Hurt Feelings and Hidden Agendas

Entrepreneurs are great rationalizers. Sometimes a modest delusion or a great rationalization is the only way you make it through the day when things are tough. As the old expression goes: if we knew how hard it was going to be and how long it was going to take; we would never have started on the journey in the first place. In start-ups, ignorance and lack of experience can sometimes be a competitive advantage – not knowing what you can or can't do opens up a far larger world of possibilities than settling for what's clearly doable and right in front of you.

In any case, in the context of negotiations, these traits play out in very specific and somewhat peculiar ways.

For example, to get a deal done, an entrepreneur will often accept (or really "settle for") terms and conditions that are unworkable and unrealistic just to get the deal done. He will sign up for the deal, but actually be crossing half his fingers and toes. Because entrepreneurs are eternal optimists (at least some of the time), they don't feel obliged to evaluate "either/ or" equations because they think (but don't necessarily say) that they can eventually have it all or at least recoup what they are giving up in the short term. When this doesn't happen, you have one very unhappy camper.

Investors need to be careful that they never accept a commitment in words rather than in spirit. This is the same situation that all employers have when an employee asks for a raise and is turned down. You have to be sure that the employee didn't "quit without leaving". Happy to take a paycheck and do a half-assed job while looking for the next opportunity.

Another example is that entrepreneurs hate to lose control of any situation. But the very give and take that makes for successful negotiations and deals is a back and forth process of concessions and give-ups which can be viewed constructively or bitterly by the entrepreneur. Too tough or aggressive negotiations (even when the entrepreneur "agrees") can build up resentments that accumulate and that will ultimately find expression in harmful ways as time passes and the business rolls out. It's ALWAYS better for the parties to feel that both sides have left something on the table.

Finally, entrepreneurs are quick to feel victimized and taken advantage of and they fear getting screwed in a deal much more than any concern they may have about the business failing. Anger and paranoia are major emotional drivers and part of the personality of EVERY successful entrepreneur. Investors want to make sure that the underlying anger that's always there isn't directed toward them. One of the saddest things about even successful entrepreneurs is that – in retrospect – even when the deal has gone well, they still feel "cheated" late in the game because they are convinced that they gave up too much at the start. I don't know what else to say about this except to point out that mental health has never be a prerequisite for entrepreneurial success.

(2) Back Off the Gas and Tap the Brakes

As the new business develops and expands, the interests of the investor and of the entrepreneur can easily diverge – especially if the deal has misaligned incentives which may be inherent in all deals rather than the fault of the parties. It's all about the relative perspectives of the parties.

Basically, the investor is always "on a clock" with at least one eye toward the door because his job is to ultimately harvest returns for his own funds or investors. More importantly, the investor knows that he will only have a small percentage of winners in his investment portfolio – some will be flat-out mistakes, some will be OK deals and some (maybe the worst outcome of all) will be the living dead – sideways deals that just hang on. So, when the investor sees a deal with real upside, he goes for the gas. He wants accelerated growth and he wants it sooner rather than later.

On the other hand, the seasoned entrepreneur certainly wants to expand his business, but he is usually focused on reaching profitability first and then growing from there. The main reason for this attitude is pretty obvious – the longer the business is losing money, the more likely the prospect that additional (dilutive) funding from the investor or others will be required. And, until the business is making a profit, other traditional and less costly means of financing growth simply aren't available. The second reason for the entrepreneur's attitude is that this is his business and he typically expects to be in it for a much longer time than the investor.

Bottom line - one is looking for a salable asset (near-term exit) and the other is looking for a self-sustaining and profitable business (long-term value).

(3) Business as Usual" Rarely is for the Entrepreneur

Every business encounters bumps in the road. They come with the territory and they are unavoidable. But, as inevitable problems arise, the older and more experienced investors react to the situations calmly and treat these things as "business as usual" problems to be dealt with rather than major catastrophes that are about to kill the company. In a real sense, "they've seen this movie before" and they've seen plenty of worse cases where some time, some planning and maybe a little luck got everyone through the storm in one piece. One of my favorite old-timers used to say that "things were hopeless, but not serious".

It's a completely different reality for the young entrepreneur who's going through the entire process often for the first time. To him or her, every problem is unique; they're all huge; and each one presents an existential threat to the business. While you might think this sounds a little extreme and over-wrought, it's completely real for the entrepreneur and it results in three material reactions which actually can have very serious consequences. In a sense, the business can get killed – not by the disease or problem – but by the reactions and the "cures".

In these cases, you can expect the following:

(1) The entrepreneur quickly concludes that the investors (because they aren't frantic) don't "care" or aren't interested in the business. This leads to ugly conversations and intemperate accusations which aren't helpful or constructive for anyone.

(2) The entrepreneur is irresistibly drawn to action – to doing something – pretty much anything – not because it's the right thing to do or a well-thought solution, but because the action itself is an antidote to the enormous anxiety that the entrepreneur is feeling. This leads to knee-jerk responses and wasteful actions which can usually be expected to do more harm than good. As Yogi Berra used to say, "We may be on the wrong road, but at least we're making good time."

(3) When you let everything become a crisis and be treated as an emergency, you lose control - not only of the agenda and of your scarce resources – but also of the ability to address and deal with the higher priority issues which are far more critical and which – if unattended to – can threaten the enterprise.

(4) Better an Unwanted Guest than a Broken Business

Sometimes, like it or not, the investor needs to be a bit of "a bull in the china shop" and barge in even if he's not welcome. Denial is a powerful tool for entrepreneurs, but it can also be a big problem. It's not a process where you can ignore the facts and try to make the circumstances fit the plan – all the parties have got to be willing and open to changing the plan. By and large, if you don't think your business has any problems or room for improvement, then you probably have a big problem. And, in any case, I'd rather see a pivot than an empty pot.

It's been my experience that entrepreneurs pretty much never want to or know when to ask for help – a smart investor needs to invite himself to the party. Asking for help is embarrassing to these guys and most of them would rather die than die of embarrassment. The fact is that, in many cases, the growth rate of a start-up is directly
proportional to the entrepreneur's tolerance for embarrassment. The thicker your skin – the further you'll go.

(5) You've Got to Bite the Bullet When Things Go Bad

Words that you want to watch out for.

Investor's Perspective:

This is Just One of Many Deals – I Need to Cut My Losses

I Can't Afford the Opportunity Costs of Spending More Time

Deals that Go Sideways are the Living Dead - Fail Fast and/or Pivot We've Got to Sell It to Somebody/Anybody

It's not Actually My Money Anyway – "Out of Sight/Out of Mind"

Entrepreneur's Perspective:

This is My Only Business – It's My Life and My Livelihood

We Need to Keep Fighting the Good Fight – We Never Give Up We're Just "this/close" to Turning the Corner

There's Always Another "Other" - Excuses or Explanations It's Just Money to You – It's a Crusade for Me

TULLMAN'S TRUISMS

DON'T CONFUSE GOOD MANNERS WITH AGREEMENT

20 – THE ONE WHO CARES THE MOST WINS

Remember when parents used to really care about their kids talking back to them or cursing? For a time, long after the weight and the sting went out of certain "swear" words and they were just words again in common use – albeit not universally, some kids (mostly younger brothers and sisters) still tried using them for effect and to rile up their folks, but it was pretty clear that no one actually cared that much. Sticks and stones, etc. Plus, and maybe most importantly, saying this kind of stuff and meaning it – even assuming that the kids knew what the words actually meant – were two dramatically different things. And their parents got that, refused to take the bait, and generally let a lot of "noise" just slide.

But their older brothers and sisters didn't waste any time in figuring out the most telling and effective new parental taunts to get under their folks' skins again and they deployed them so efficiently that even the grown-ups got with the program and adopted the new jargon almost overnight. And, somewhat amazingly, it was a single word that said it all for at least an entire generation.

And what was that word? It was "**whatever**" (shoulder shrug optional). In so many ways and so many circumstances and situations, "**whatever**" said it all and got the job done – smoothly and succinctly. And, what exactly does "**whatever**" really mean? It means "I don't care enough to care". So there!

It's one of those things that Aaron Sorkin only wishes that he could have added to the vernacular. For the moment, he'll have to settle for "ya think?" and a few other choice phrases that you can view <u>ad nausem</u> on the various YouTube *West Wing* or Sorkin compilations. And who's the very living embodiment of "**whatever**" every week on our TV screens? Of course, it's Dana Brody, the daughter from *Homeland*. If Carrie cares way too much about everything, Dana pretty much lets her Mom know every single episode that she doesn't much give a rat's ass about anything that her Mom cares about and she sure lets it show.

But why should any of this matter to you? We're pretty much in business after all – not entertainment, TV or the movies. But, as I've said before, no one sells a product any more – we're all in the service business now – where the key deliverable is the ability to create in the customer's mind the feeling of being sincerely cared for and cared about. Frankly, no one cares how much you know or how good you are at your job (except maybe if you're surgeons who apparently aren't required to have a personalities) - until they know how much you care <u>about them</u>. Caring costs a lot, but in the end, your people not caring is what kills businesses.

So the reason that the "**whatever**" phenomena should matter to you and your business is because the real message of "**whatever**" – which is an in-your-face, calculated, and painfully obvious indifference (however sincere or insincere it may be) - is a fact of life these days in too many places and, if you let it creep into your business and particularly into the attitudes of your people, you're screwed. Your customers will leave in droves. And they won't be back.

This is more critical than you think and something that gets overlooked too easily in the frenzy of rapid growth. I'm not talking about warm and fuzzy stuff – or Kumbaya crap – I'm talking about everyday execution of the fundamentals in your business. The truth is that, if as you grow, your people can easily get a little "tired" and think they have too much to do and that customers are a bother and too demanding and somewhat inconvenient, and when they start communicating that indifference to your customers, it's actually worse than you can imagine. It's like a slap in the face to the customers and they will pick up on it in a flash.

Why does it happen? First, it's not necessarily intentional and evil in many cases. Almost anything can get routine and repetitive and it's a short step from there to indifference. Second, passion isn't an infinite resource and it needs to be reinforced and replenished regularly. Third, today's younger employees are hard sells in a lot of ways. You need to keep in mind that at work they are generally more afraid of boredom than failure. And finally, anything that keeps growing and getting bigger always runs the risk of distancing your best people from the immediacy of the constant contact with your customers which is the very best feedback and reinforcement loop there is. Hearing the news – good and bad – from the horse's mouth is critical to keeping your people's heads in the game.

So, just like it's unsafe at night to speed so fast that you "overdrive your headlights" and can't see far enough ahead to safely stop in an emergency, a young company can outrun and outgrow its own energy and enthusiasm as it expands and burn out - not only lots of its loyal customers, but plenty of its best long-time employees as well. And when you do that, you find out that you've ended up with the <u>wrong</u> answer to the universal question: how big can we get before we get bad?

What can you do? You've got to spend the time and the resources to constantly reinforce the main message: that businesses exist because they have customers and taking care of your customers is ALWAYS Job Number One. Everything else can and should take a back seat to making sure that your customers know that you are looking out for them. And you've got to do it with a vengeance – with all your heart and all your energy. You don't get to fake it until you make it in today's super-savvy world. Second, the very best cure for employee boredom and indifference is challenge and curiosity. There is no cure for curiosity and your job is to make sure that your employees are always looking at new opportunities and new challenges. Finally, as always, focus. The smartest people I know care passionately about the few things in their life and in their business that really matter – the right things - and don't waste a minute or give a damn about the rest.

As you're trying to build your business and change the world, it's a good idea to remember that a different world can't be built by indifferent people.

Every business owner understands that, in addition to the many internal factors which can make or break a business, the cyclical state of the economy itself can also have a material impact on the success of your company. To a certain extent, it's like the weather - we can bitch about it all we want and blame those no-good politicians, but - in the end - we have only a limited ability to change these external market conditions. However, that doesn't mean that anyone should be sitting around feeling sorry for themselves and waiting for their life to get better.

I love the old Chinese saying: "Man stand for long time with mouth open before roast duck fly in". Good things in business don't happen by themselves (except perhaps in the movies) and, if you aren't making things happen and moving forward, you'll always be losing ground. So, in my world, we don't whine about politics, circumstances or greener grass. We believe that the people who succeed in today's hyper-competitive marketplace are the ones who get up and look for the right "circumstances" and, if they can't find them, they make them. Everyone thinks about changing the world, but no one thinks about changing themselves or their business. But, as I've said before, if you don't do it, someone will come right along who'll be very happy to do it for you or to you.

We've been treading water for too long and FUD (fear, uncertainty and doubt) has made us way too conservative. The big guys have been cutting back on their R & D budgets for years to protect pennies of earnings and thereby killing any prospects for new ideas and real innovation. And the little guys (like us) have been saving our shekels and not advertising or promoting our businesses. We need to start investing aggressively in the future (like we really mean it) or many of us won't have a future to worry about.

Now's the time to push our products and services and to demonstrate to everyone that we have the courage of our convictions. Not when the whole world finally wakes up and jumps back into the fray. I like to think of this running ahead of the pack as "getting ready to get lucky".

And, when you press your bets and bet on yourself and your future, you actually accomplish three other important objectives:

(A) You effectively set the pace for the rest of the market and you can become the market leader even if you're a tiny company;
(B) You reassure not only your customers, but your employees and your vendors as well; and
(C) You can grow your business at the expense of your competition without spending a lot of money since they've pretty much left the playing field to you.

Keep in mind this simple fact: increased market share is taken and grown NOT in good times, but in difficult times when everyone else is sitting on the sidelines and nursing their wounds. In good times, people want to advertise. In bad times, they have to advertise. If you don't, you die. The minute you hit the brakes, you start to slide down the sales slope.

Here's a case in point concerning Saturn.

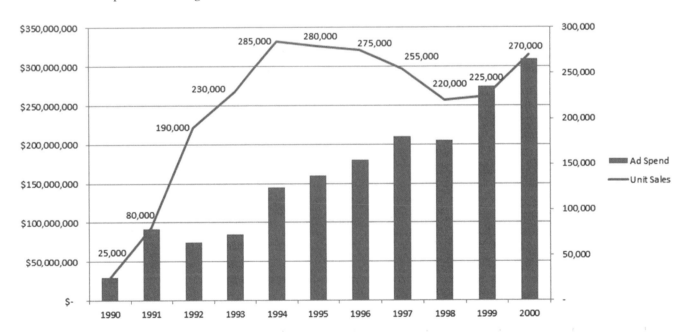

When sales dipped a tiny amount at the start of 1995, they started to cut their ad spending and that flattened 1995 and 1996 sales. Then they tried to get back into the game heading into
1997, but panicked when the sales didn't immediately recover and they cut back again on the ad spend. This killed not only 1997 results, but 1998 and 1999 sales as well even though they really accelerated their spend in mid-98. The bottom line (as the chart

clearly shows) is that trying to "save your way to success" (or even to improved bottom line results) is like trying to catch a knife. Most of the time, you just can't do it and it's very painful even when you do.

And here's a little survey of 600 U.S. companies whose revenues increased after the 1981-82 recession and what they did with their advertising during the recession.

Companies Increasing Advertising – VOLUME UP 275%
Companies <u>Decreasing</u> Advertising – VOLUME UP 19%

It couldn't be much clearer. Ya gotta spend real money to make money. Doing business without advertising is like winking at a girl in the dark – you know what you're doing, but no one else does. And please don't try to do a bunch of things cheaply that you shouldn't do at all.

Bottom line: get going. There are a number of things – large and small - that every business should do <u>right now</u> (especially if you believe that there's even a glimmer of light at the end of this long dark tunnel) to prepare for the better days to come. But there's one thing that is absolutely critical to understand - in good times to be sure, but even more so in tough times - you can't save your way to success.

TULLMAN'S TRUISMS

YOU CAN'T SAVE YOUR WAY TO SUCCESS

I said two years ago that - by 2020 - 90% of the U.S. population would have willingly agreed to provide at least some of their personal data to the MAW. I'm starting to think that my estimate was too conservative. The global pace of massive data acquisition is picking up steam and speed and it's definitely an auto-catalytic process - the faster the changes come at us, the sooner the next changes start to appear. So you need to get moving just to hang on.

There are many explanations for the acceleration, but the main and most important change seems to be that no one expected that all of the diverse behavior drivers (inducements, incentives, trade-offs, etc.) would converge on each of us so quickly, specifically, simultaneously and, frankly, pretty much inescapably. But that's where we're at - stuck in the middle of the M.A.W. - and getting in deeper every day.

The M.A.W. - in case you're wondering - is my shorthand for today's replacement for that tired old whipping boy - the evil military-industrial complex - which we were all told - dictated and controlled our lives. The M.A.W. is slightly more benign so far in that it doesn't so much control our lives every day as it engulfs and overwhelms us 24/7 with emotional and economic sticks and carrots which continually impact and influence our behavior.

The M.A.W. (the omnipresent collision of (M)edia, (A)dvertising, and (W)ork in every part of our lives) is the real environment in which we're all now living. And honestly we've all become willing participants (to varying degrees) in the program and relatively happy campers with the deals we're making and the results because no one wants to be left out or left behind. Springsteen said "we're livin' in the future and none of this has happened yet", but he was wrong. It's happening right now.

And, by the way, this is another party to which I hope you're not waiting for an invitation. You and your team need to get into the data marketplace with both feet before your business get priced out of the game by greedy middlemen happy to resell the data to you at a premium (DSPs and others) and before you get shut out of the market entirely by faster and deeper-pocketed competitors who will absorb all the available inventory.

Keep in mind that the key notion above is that "we agreed" to share and surrender this information. God only knows how much of our own information we have inadvertently or unwittingly parted with at this point in time. I'm simply talking about the extent to which each of us has made a deal - a conscious transaction - where we

have decided to trade and supply some of our personal data in exchange for some perceived value or benefit that we would be receiving in return. And by the way I don't mean "perceived value" in the pejorative sense as if these things weren't real and concrete. For sure, some incentives are virtual and slight at best (like digital badges and certain utterly inconsequential "achievements"), but many others have clear and direct financial and economic benefits.

What kinds of value or benefits are we talking about? The list grows daily. You trade your personal data because:

(a) We're all basically lazy and would rather do less work than more – Do It for Me is a lot easier than DIY;
(b) We hate wasting our time and re-entering the same info over and over in order to perform recurring activities of any kind;
(c) We become "invested" in an activity as a result of our prior effort and commitment and we just tend (due to inertia) to keep going with the flow;
(d) We've "connected" with others who are important to us in a shared context through the activity and it becomes convenient to continue and difficult to depart;
(e) We develop habitual behaviors and habits (online or otherwise) are just really difficult to break or abandon without a reason;
(f) We're actively "engaged" and "retained" by the smartest of the players so we stay; and/or
(g) We receive direct financial rewards for our participation.

When you add these up, we're talking about saving you time, making you more efficient or productive, connecting you with a community or group that's valuable to you; or that old stand-by – making you or saving you money. In many of the cases, it does basically come down to money. Almost everything does.

One of the neatest new deals has been created by a couple of the largest auto insurers in the U.S. If you let Allstate (thru its *Drivewise* program) or Progressive (thru the *Snapshot* offering) track your driving activities for a relatively short period of time, you can earn major discounts on your car insurance. It's a "win-win" for anyone who's a decent driver. I call this "swapping surveillance for savings". And we can expect to see more and more offers and opportunities like this.

It's pretty easy with tools like *FitBit* and other biomedical tracking devices to think that many of our daily activities will soon be available for researchers, marketers, economists, behaviorists, etc. to pay us for and acquire in order to study and sell.

And, by the way, it's definitely a two-way street. You can also pay up to be left alone. If you're sick of being swamped with ads on your Kindle, you can pay up and cut them off. At the end of the day, it's all just math and money.

But here's the bottom line. We're all involved in competitive markets today and it's really an arms race which will be won by the guys with the biggest guns, the best technology, and, above all, the most accurate and complete data.

Think of this as fair warning – your competitors are grabbing the goods and dropping big dollars for data and, if you don't want to be left in the dust, you need to get into the game as well.

23 – INNOVATION BEATS INVENTION HANDS DOWN

I'm always a little saddened when I see people (young and old) who are unhappy with their current job or position and who spend a lot of time sitting around waiting for the next big idea to occur to them or be dropped into their laps. They're about to invent the next Facebook - just as soon as the right inspiration strikes them - and those creative juices start flowing. And it's gonna be HUGE. Sometimes in these conversations, I find myself thinking of how thin the line really is between praying and whining and how easy it is to cross. Praying for something good to happen and whining because it hasn't yet – two sides of the same sad coin.

But that's not even the real problem. The main issue is that these people are thinking too large - not too small. They trying to invent some new killer product or service (which, in many cases, they would be unprepared and unqualified to develop and deliver) and they don't realize that there are important and substantial opportunities for important and lucrative changes and improvements sitting right there in front of them. Improvements in their current businesses - good, smart, simple and "small" ideas which could be winners for everyone involved and which they are already "experts" on. As Springsteen says: "From small things, Mama, big things one day come." The trick is always the same. Elegance and simplicity. How little of the current way we're doing things can we change to make a big difference?

I'm talking about the critical distinction between invention and innovation. These are two completely different and basically unrelated ideas. Innovation is quicker, easier and more profitable in almost every case than invention. Invention is about bringing new things into existence and hoping that the dogs will eat the dog food. Innovation is about applying existing and proven tools and technologies to traditional business processes in new ways in order to create new value. And by and large, no rocket science is required. You don't have to study Ruby on Rails or learn a new set of skills on the fly in order to succeed. Innovation is about "small ball" – a succession of base hits and quick scores rather than swinging for the fences and hoping for home runs. As Warren Buffett said a long time ago: "I don't like jumping over 7 foot hurdles, I like to find one foot bars that I can step over."

And the most amazing thing about this process is that, in many cases, it's not how different the new approach or solution might be, it's how much it's the same. How a simple shift or change can dramatically improve a product, service, or system and solve a problem or address a need that was sitting there for years and that, in retrospect, was painfully obvious. Of course, that's what the best entrepreneurs do – they identify and implement solutions where other people don't even see problems. Effective innovation is about seeing what everyone else may have seen and thinking what no one else has thought.

It's not as easy as that sounds (nothing ever is), but it's a lot easier than you might expect once you get the process started. And it is a process – a continual search for low-hanging fruit, easy targets and ways to apply tiny bits of existing and proven technology (or just better and more organized approaches) to inefficient, costly or unproductive procedures that have "always been done a certain way" in your business for no good reason or, even worse, for reasons that no one can still remember.

Let me give you a simple example. Insurance companies are desperate to know (as accurately as possible) how many miles you drive in the course of a year because that data has a direct correlation to the risks of your vehicle being involved in an accident and also to how much you should pay in insurance premiums. By and large, and even aside from fraud and sheer laziness, self-reported odometer information is woefully inaccurate. So the insurance companies continue to try to develop incentives and other ways to get their policyholders to give them this critical data in a timely and accurate fashion. New smart start-ups like Atlanta-based VEHCON (www.vehcon.com) are working with major insurers to develop mobile apps to help address these types of issues. But, to date – no such luck.

Now here's where innovation comes into the picture. Guess who else has accurate mileage information on just about every single insured vehicle on the road today and who already records, captures and stores that data. Car dealers. Car dealers record your mileage every single time you take your car in for service. They also capture the same data every time a used car is bought or sold. They are fully-automated; the data is sitting there to be electronically retrieved 24/7 from their management systems; about 85% of all the dealer management systems in the U.S. are supplied and serviced by one of two main vendors; and all these systems already connect in multiple ways to the web.

How easy would it be to build a retrieval system that polled (and paid) all these dealers on behalf of all the insurance companies and provided timely and current mileage on every car in America on a daily basis to the insurers? Pretty darn easy because EVERY single component of the new solution is tried, tested and already up and operating and the trick is simply shifting around a few of the parts of the equation to create a whole new service and thereby a large and profitable business.

It's just not that hard. And there are a million more opportunities just like this in every market, in every industry, and in every business just waiting to be discovered and capitalized on by smart entrepreneurs. It's not about strokes of genius – it's about steady, consistent, step-by-step improvement – that creates real long-term value.

Microsoft Excel is a curse. In its deceptive simplicity and ease of use, it has taught several generations of MBAs and entrepreneurs that creating the financial underpinnings for a serious business plan is basically just another form of word processing. It has insulated these aspiring business builders from the difficult and time- consuming - step-by-step - tasks of building a real case for a real business from the bottom up. Making a plan for the future without tying your analysis to the concrete experiences, results, and wisdom of the past is just a form of building castles in the sky.

As a result of the Excel explosion, we've seen the creation of thousands of mindless spreadsheets underlying hundreds of naïve business plans put forward by individuals who have relied on Excel to painlessly develop forecasts and predictions which haven't the slightest connection to any reality, but which look "marvelous" as Billy Crystal used to say. And then these folks (and their promoters, investors and enablers as well) seize upon these plans as if they were the Gospel expressed in rows, columns, and pivot tables and use them for support and borrowed credibility - rather than for analysis, guidance and hoped-for illumination – exactly the same way that a late night drunk relies on a lamppost. Welcome to the fantasy world of made-up metrics.

When you use a tool like Excel (that's fundamentally neutral) to generate hypothetical and hysterical numbers to make a theoretical case with no real foundation in fact or history and then you fall in love with the finished product, you're deeply into made-up metrics. Credible plans need to proceed from a serious grounding in prior, documented experience and results – they can extend those results into the future – I would call these "projections" and, while they are never certain, at least they are logical and well thought out. We used to call this process "precision guesswork", but at least we had a process and we knew where our numbers came from. "Predictions", on the other hand, are the results of those cases where people simply insert aggressive new growth numbers (without any clear justification, obvious cause, or decent explanation) and then use Excel to replicate, grow and run the numbers forward until they reach the sky.

When you get carried away with this approach, you tend to forget that building a real business is about producing results, not predicting results. It's actually easy to predict the future, it's just impossible to know when it will arrive. You can plan all the plans you wish, but you can't plan results – you have to do the hard work of making those happen – and that hard work starts with building a solid factual foundation for your numbers. Too many excellent Excel plans are just sterile exercises stuck somewhere between wishful thinking and delusion.

Another entire category of bogus business plans are crammed with so many fake facts and factoids and other accumulations of data that are only remotely relevant at best to the business being built. Grossed-up market size is always one of my favorites. "Our addressable market is everyone with two eyes in the world." Right. Fake facts are all the rage these days, but they don't help advance your cause. I think Seth Godin is a smart and thoughtful guy, but here's what he had to say in a recent blog post: "[Aside: More than a billion people on Earth have never purchased anything on sale at a store.]" Do you really think there's any factual basis for that statement? Why waste our time with this kind of stuff?

Even good facts are just facts – they're not props for arguments or support for conclusions – it's the conditions, trends, needs, and other market circumstances that you extract and extrapolate from the facts that help to explain, define and ultimately "sell" your business idea to investors, customers and partners. It's these larger drivers which you need to discover, document and master – and not cute anecdotes and fake facts – that will provide the real framework for the continual decisions you'll need to make as you move things forward.

Building a business in these tough times is about pushing your vision forward and adapting it where necessary through a sea of constantly changing facts and circumstances. But if you don't start with a fundamental idea – grounded in some reality – it's way too easy to get run around in circles or just lost in the shuffle. These are serious problems for young entrepreneurs because the triumph of the form of the materials over their real substance (slick spreadsheets) and misplaced reliance on irrelevant metrics (fake facts) can lead you to believe that you have your arms around your business when – in fact – you're swinging a big hammer, but you're trying to nail *Jello* to a tree.

I understand that nobody likes a quitter and that we all believe every captain should go down with his ship. These are among the few things in life today that everyone can agree on. But is this really a healthy attitude for the folks running a new business? Especially when they're spending other people's money at a ferocious clip? Sometimes you need to be smart enough to read the tea leaves and "quit when you're ahead" even if you're actually way behind and losing more ground every day. But how exactly do you ever know when enough is enough?

See - this is what's so tricky about clichés. We all grew up thinking that "quitting while you were ahead" meant grabbing your chips off the poker table and getting out of Dodge City (or Vegas as the case may be) with a pile of dough - even if your buddies tried to pull you back into the game and called you a sore winner for leaving <u>before</u> you started losing. Poker – as I'm sure you know – isn't really about making friends or being the most beloved guy at the table. It's about winning. Just like running a business.

And believe me, it's much tougher – personally and emotionally when the right time comes - to pull up stakes and shut down the business you've poured your heart and soul into than it is to piss off your poker pals over a few pesos. But it's part and parcel of the process - it comes with the job - and the final decision ultimately lands in your lap. So how can you figure out when the time is right?

There really isn't a simple answer or one solution for every situation, but there is a Rule that I have found to be useful in almost every case. I call it The Rule of 3 Ds and 3 Fs.

The 3 Ds are pretty simple. There are some things you've got to <u>DO</u>, to <u>DETERMINE</u> and to <u>DISCUSS</u>.

The main thing you've got to DO is to face the facts. If you can do this honestly, you'll be well on your way to the right conclusions about your particular situation. Because, while in good times denial is one of the greatest strengths of an entrepreneur, when things are moving in the wrong direction, you're simply can't afford to ignore them. And – at the end of the day – refusing to look at unpleasant facts and realities doesn't make them disappear or go away anyway. They don't vanish; they just wait and things in this life that don't get better only get worse.

People can have different opinions about the meaning of certain facts or circumstances and how to deal with them. It's funny that they'll call you persistent when you succeed and stubborn when you fail. But the facts always remain the same. They won't change by themselves and – once you do face them – you've got to have the courage and the wisdom to take the actions necessary to deal with them. In some

cases, that means that you need to close the doors. And sometimes, as the leader, you need to help your team and your employees reach these same conclusions. You've got to give your people permission to make the hard calls and the tough decisions.

The next thing is to DETERMINE your true feelings about the situation. If you focus on your feelings and think about these statements, you'll have addressed the second F.

(1) It's time to go when it's harder work to come to the office every day than any work you do once you get there.
(2) It's time to go when you find yourself spending more time talking to yourself at the office than to anyone else.
(3) It's time to go when you're constantly trying to do things cheaply that you shouldn't do at all because you can't afford to do them right.
(4) It's time to go when you feel under-appreciated, taken advantage of, and let down by everyone else in the place.
(5) It's time to go when you spend more time and energy at the office plotting your revenge than doing any meaningful or constructive work.

And let me just say on this score that, if you've actually ever run a business and you haven't experienced versions and degrees of all of these feelings, then you haven't really been an entrepreneur and you were most likely working for your folks.

The last task of the list is to DISCUSS your decision with your family and take their feelings into account. Family is the final F. Starting and running a business is just as tough – maybe tougher – on your family as it is on you. And because they aren't typically active in the business, it's even harder when things start to go south and they can't do much other than watch helplessly while you suffer. But here's the most important advice I can give you:

(a) there's always more work and other businesses, but you've only got one family;
(b) your family is a much more important extension and reflection of yourself than any work you do; and
(c) your work is just that – it's your work and NOT who you are. It doesn't make or define you – it serves you and when it stops being valuable and additive for you and your family, it's time to do something else.

For better or worse – and because life isn't remotely fair - when things are really rotten and we have no place else to turn, sadly - we don't turn <u>to</u> our families, we turn <u>on</u> them and we take a lot of the crap out on them for no good reason other than that they're there. This is some of the most real and devastating damage that a failing business can cause and it's the most critical reason to get out when the time is right and not to prolong the agony.

It's like staying on the *Atkins* diet way too long. You don't lose any more weight – you're just much more miserable to be around every day. Life's too short and you spend too much of it working not to find and do something that you love and can be enthusiastic about every day. It's never too soon to stop living someone else's dream and make your own dreams come true.

Enough sometimes really is enough.

TULLMAN'S TRUISMS

IT TAKES AWAY FROM YOUR SOUL WHEN YOU DO WHAT YOU DON'T BELIEVE IN

It turns out that the Three Musketeers had it half right. "All for one and one for all!" is a great strategy for assuring collaboration, teamwork and loyalty, but it can be a very dangerous approach in a start-up. This is because – notwithstanding the absolute best of intentions – it can lead to chaos in the kitchen with too many cooks and a whole lot of people trying to pitch in and "help out" who just end up being much more of a hindrance and a problem than if they simply minded their own business.

The fact is that, even if your business is short-handed and resource-constrained, you're not going to be well-served by people piling on to assist in areas where they don't have the skills, background or judgment to add value. Instead, they just get in the way or make things worse. Good intentions don't ever guarantee great results and, as the boss, you've got to politely tell these eager beavers to butt out. And you need to figure out a way to say "no thanks" without having them feel unappreciated, ignored or dismissed.

You don't want to crush their creativity or extinguish their enthusiasm, but you can't have your finance guys writing marketing copy (even in his alleged spare time) or your IT people trying to design your next product or service (unless perhaps you're in the IT business). And even then, if you are in the IT business, you still want your IT people taking care of their business and making sure that your servers and cloud connections don't blow up rather than suggesting new passionate, but sophisticated color schemes for your website.

Some skills are readily transferable and applicable across multiple disciplines, but too many people confuse energy, interest and even some skill with actual talent. I always loved it when I was making movies and people would dismiss a certain actor or actress and say that anyone could play that role. The truth is that the people up on the big screen are there for a reason – they have a certain electricity, attraction or whatever magic it is - and all the trying, practice, aspiration and desire won't ever help a million other wanna-bes duplicate their special presence. Stars are stars for a reason. They know that they can do one thing better than anyone else and the smartest ones do exactly that one thing and nothing else.

There's a reason that the people and companies that succeed in any line of business are those that focus their energy and resources and stick to their knitting. You need to be sure that both your company and your people have the same discipline. It's not even about what you actually say "yes" to and do, it's all about the many things that you have the guts to say "no" to and pass by even though they are terribly tempting.

This is all part of the process of what I'd call "getting real". It starts by admitting that democracy is not necessarily a virtue in all meetings; that not every idea is a good one or worth spending the group's time on; and that not everyone in the business is good at every part of the business or should be expected to be. And by the way, don't confuse bad ideas with bad intentions and don't forget that people can be terribly sincere and still have really stupid ideas.

It seems obvious, but I guarantee you that you'll find yourself stuck in these kinds of ultimately unproductive situations – especially as everyone in your company gets busier and busier – and the business continues to grow and expand. The basic nature of any start-up is a "let's get it done" attitude and, when things take longer than they should (with or without good reasons which may not be clear to everyone), there's a clear bias toward action – sometimes any action – and that's bad for everyone and really bad for the business because it encourages people who don't know what they're doing to roll up their sleeves and give themselves permission to try to do "something". Just because you can do something doesn't mean you should.

This is one of those cases where doing something really isn't necessarily better than doing nothing and waiting until the right people can get around to doing the thing that needs to get done and doing it the right way. It's hard for any entrepreneur to tell his people to hurry up and wait at the same time, but that's the right message. Stick to your knitting and mind your own part of the business.

It's downright dangerous for small companies (and especially start-ups) to deal with the corporate giants who dominate so many industries. They're the pachyderms; we're the plant life. And like elephants, they have great memories and recall how the world was; but no imaginations to see the world that will be. Still, because of the size of their markets; the fact that so many of them are dinosaurs who don't see the deluge about to drown them; and the fact that timely innovations and new technologies will ultimately turn their businesses around or put them in the ground, these are the places where the people who want to be real players need to be.

Entrepreneurs with great ideas and enormous energy (but limited time, resources and access) face a number of specific challenges in circumstances like these, but there are 5 things to keep in mind which can dramatically improve your odds of success.

(1) Right Church - Wrong Pew

It's easy to get lost or misdirected when you're wandering through the wastelands of these large companies. Too often people with new ideas get sent to (not to say "dumped on") the new media, innovation or digital guys and quickly forgotten. Typically the people who populate these departments are long on enthusiasm and short on cash and the ability to green light anything. It's critical to remember that big firms have many different pockets of serious money. If you spin your story correctly, you can often tap into community programs, marketing initiatives, charitable commitments or even diversity requirements – all of which are well-funded. Don't be shy about asking – sometimes success is simply putting a new cover on the same old book - or adding a novel twist to an old tale. But make sure before you start that you're in the right place.

(2) Right Pew – Wrong Seat

Even if you're in the right place with the right story, your proposal still needs to "fit" the customer's current interest and appetite. You need to make sure that what you're offering matters. This means that – when all is said and done – and you've busted your butt and hit it out of the park – and you've done it all with panache and a vengeance – you don't want to hear those two awful words from the client: "So what?" or something equally disappointing. You need to make sure that you understand the required size, scale and impact which will be needed to matter – to impress the client and his bosses – and to move the needle for them or you'll just have been wasting a lot of your time and energy. The problem is that even great results (high adoption percentages, significant engagement times, strong sharing and amplification, etc.) which are hugely significant and encouraging to the entrepreneur just don't matter if you're talking hundreds of active participants in your pilot and they're dealing with millions of card members or customers. I've seen major retailers do this over and over – they'll run almost any credible pilot project (especially one on your dime) for a new service or product, but they won't pull the trigger when the project is done because their metrics don't match yours.

And, if that wasn't bad enough, keep in mind that while start-ups run out of cash – big companies don't – and so they are more than happy to keep mediocre projects running for way too long – even though they may have mentally checked out some time ago.

(3) Right Seat – Wrong Guy

Another recurring risk in dealing with big businesses is that the guy sitting across from you can't say "yes". There are hundreds of people in these places who can say "no" – some of whom seem to have no other job than that – but you've got to get in front of the ones who can say "yes" and write the necessary check to put their money where their mouth is. As I have said before, you don't want to be dealing with the monkey when the organ grinder is in the room.

You've also got to be sure that you carefully explain how your proposal is incremental and additive to whatever it is that they are now doing and that it's not simply going to cannibalize their current sales or replace existing sales with less lucrative or valuable ones. We used to call these "kissing your sister" deals because they don't lead anywhere you'd want to be and you have a lot of motion and activity but no real progress or results.

(4) Right Guy – Wrong Time

I'm always amazed at how many entrepreneurs don't do their homework and understand the budget and buying cycles of their target customers and how these things are set in concrete and so tightly locked down that these people couldn't help you if their lives depended on it. I think this is because there really are no comparable restraints or barriers in the life of a start-up – everything is urgent, everything can be and needs to be done right now, and there's always no time like the present to do what needs to be done. But bad timing can be the quickest deal killer of all and – more to the point – if you show up at the wrong time, it's pretty obvious to the customer that you don't know much about their business, their calendars or their requirements. Don't make this amateur mistake.

There is one exception to this rule and that depends almost entirely on whether or not you have been lucky enough to develop a real connection and relationship with your buyer. If you have, then on occasion you will tumble into the Alice in

Wonderland scenario where the buyer lets you know that – instead of their budgeted funds being totally committed and/ or spent - they have excess funds which they need to spend before their budget year runs out to avoid having their budget cut for the following year. All I can say about these situations is – take the money and run.

(5) Right Time – Wrong Pitch

Sometimes the best way to get the order is not to try selling at all, but simply to focus on "helping" the customer understand the competitive dynamics of their marketplace. Fear is rampant in even the biggest companies and the greatest fear for many decision-makers is FOMO. The Fear Of Missing Out. Many market resources and opportunities are scarce or finite and letting these big guys know that there are other major players in the space who are about to shut them out is a very substantial and effective motivator.

One of my favorite old examples involves what I call cross-industry blocking alliances. These are cases where major players in different vertical market team up in a competitive game of musical chairs and the last company to find a chair (actually a partner) loses out big time and potentially for years thereafter. One of the great marketers of all times – American Express – was an early victim of this strategy and it cost the company millions of cardholders and billions of dollars. The story is very simple.

In the early days of frequent flyer programs, a very smart guy at American Airlines determined that miles could be used as an incentive not simply for flying, but for many other things (like car rentals and credit card purchases) as well. American quickly and quietly partnered with MasterCard. United in a flash (almost) partnered with VISA. And guess where that left American Express. Out in the cold without an airline partner which was credible and widely-available for business travelers. I suppose they could have partnered with Midway Airlines or with Greyhound and covered the bus market, but basically they were screwed for years. In the next several years, while AMEX topped out at about 9 million cardholders, VISA blew right by them and grew to almost 30 million cardholders in the same timeframe.

TULLMAN'S TRUISMS

ANYONE CAN SAY "NO"

An age-old question. If a tree falls in the forest, but there's no one there to hear it, does it make a sound? Who knows and who really cares? The better and more pressing question these days is: if the primary drivers for traffic to a website that you're paying money to advertise on are hacks, tricks and clever pet pix; what are the visitors who do show up (even assuming they are people and not tracking robots) really worth to you or anybody else?

I'd argue that they're not worth your time and certainly not worth any money you're paying for the very modest privilege of "entertaining" (in the loosest sense of the word) a bunch of morons with nothing better to do than to waste their time randomly clicking on just about anything. Instead of attracting people who might actually be interested in your products or services and also highly influential, you can end up spending money to attract mobs of easily-influenced people instead who probably couldn't explain how they go to the website if they were asked.

One of the things I always told restaurant owners about Groupon daily deals was that they were designed to attract "cheapies" to restaurants that were only looking for one-time deals instead of "foodies" who could become regular patrons and the true lifeblood of the business. And since I'm from Chicago and everyone's picking on Groupon these days, let me just say that we use it and that it makes sense for a lot of different kinds of businesses and situations IF you keep in mind 4 basic rules about when to do a daily-deals kind of deal:

1. The deal needs to drive new users and incremental revenue – not replace or cannibalize existing full margin revenues;
2. Your business can't be subject to capacity or size constraints which might result in the incremental traffic precluding access by and for existing customers and users;
3. The deal can't require you to spend or invest a great deal of upfront money with essentially sunk costs if the deal doesn't go; and
4. You can't put yourself in a position where taking on and delivering the deal gives you cash flow or other float problems.

But Groupon deals aside, there are still way too many companies "buying" into tonnage and volume (quantity rather than quality) and measuring their results by the wrong competitive metrics like "likes" and followers. As a result, the market continues to encourage young entrepreneurs to create (or basically make up) businesses which are all about buzz and bullshit rather than trying to build sustainable businesses which deliver real services and demonstrable results to clients and which have concrete economic rewards for those companies rather than cosmetic and superficial results that do nothing for any business's bottom line.

I keep seeing and hearing pitches and presentations predicated on prevarications, phony postings, and a pile of pictures that may be inexplicably popular, but have nothing really to do with anything and clearly nothing whatsoever to do with your products, services or business. As an example, I just sat through a highly- energized, but essentially empty, "presentation" about content and engagement which sadly, instead of being about ideas and approaches of substance, was all about scams and slick, but sleazy ploys to trick people into being traffic to sites for no good reason. A load of tactics and no real strategy or smarts. Or maybe they were really being just a little too smart for their own ultimate good. Because even if you're the biggest and fastest rat in the race, when the dust settles, you're still pretty much a rat.

29 – TWO WORDS EVERY INNOVATOR SHOULD KNOW

The most important rule of communication in business is a simple one. Say what you mean and mean what you say. Call it honesty, integrity or authenticity – the name doesn't matter, but the language you use and your willingness to honor and abide by your commitments makes all the difference in the world. A mixed or muddled message or a lack of support and follow-through can make everyone miserable and mean the difference between success and failure for your company.

Making and measuring meaningful metrics matters. Alliteration aside, there's no area where this kind of precision and diligence is more critical than in managing the process of business innovation. You need concrete criteria which are objectively determined, fairly applied, and precisely reported. And these need to be aggressively implemented and enforced without exception. If you get the message right at the get- go, you're golden and, if you screw it up and get started on the wrong path or with the wrong attitudes and approach, then you're gonna have a very rough ride and end up nowhere. Frankly, if you don't care where you're going, then any road will take you there.

One of the reasons we little guys win so often these days at least in the short run (and a central theme of the whole disruptive innovation theory) is that, as companies grow larger and more established, their value sets change and they no longer have the necessary flexibility and entrepreneurial attitudes that it takes to get things done.

The "grown-up" core values at a large corporation these days might look like these:

Grown-Up Values	Innovation Values
Fairness	Fierce Focus
Respect	Ready, Fire, Aim
Opportunity	Good Enough Is Good Enough
Security	Make Many Mistakes
Inclusion/Diversity	Fail Frequently

While the values that drive a successful culture of innovation are more like the ones in the second column. The truth is, as the Bible says (Matthew 6:24), that: "No one can serve two masters". Or, as I'm pretty sure Confucius must have said: "Man who chases too many rabbits catches none".

But aside from the values issue, the real key to successful and ongoing innovation is an understanding of the two concepts which really define the process: "mistakes" and "failures" and the critical differences between the two. Understanding and discussing these two ideas correctly in every conversation you have about innovation is crucial to the focus, clarity and momentum of the process.

If your culture makes your people afraid to talk about the likelihood of making mistakes, you're never going to succeed because, if we knew these things were all going to work out fine, they wouldn't be tests and experiments – they'd be sure things and, just like at the horse races, sure things are safe and comforting, but don't pay squat at the window when the race is done. So you need to make it O.K. to make mistakes just as long as they are quick and cheap and that you learn from them and – most importantly of all – be sure that they're original. It's important to make your own mistakes and not repeat someone else's.

The second important part of the "conversation" about mistakes is to appreciate and have a process in place that identifies and categorizes systemic "problems" and distinguishes them from "mistakes". It's a simple rule – a "mistake" which happens at your business over and over again isn't a "mistake" – and it's obviously not random - it's a "problem" that needs to be fixed. But only a tiny number of businesses appreciate this distinction and work to find the specific causes of and cures for the problems that cost them substantial amounts of time and energy and money over and over again for no good reason. Tracking these things down and eliminating them is just as central to improving your overall business processes as any new idea might be. Think of it this way – avoiding the potholes in the first place is a lot smarter and cheaper than getting a good deal from the guy towing your car to the garage to have your tire repaired.

Understanding how to talk about "failures" in the context of innovation is also simple to explain and understand, but hard to consistently implement. The good news is that bad examples are readily available and easy to find. People tend to approach failure in three ways – all of which are wrong:

(1) On the West Coast – especially in the venture capital community among people who are almost always investors (and not actual business operators), they "celebrate" failure and call it noble and a badge of honor. In addition to being simply BS, and, even if they were referring to the right concept of failure, to me the idea of a noble failure is an oxymoron. True failures truly suck – there's just no two ways about it.

(2) Then you have the folks who just refuse to accept the possibility and/or choose to ignore it which is merely stupid and short-sighted.

(3) And finally, you have way too many companies that expect and accept failure and all I can say about them is that companies that regularly expect and excuse failures don't ever try very hard to produce anything else.

And yet, while regularly dumping on all these folks, I talk about and embrace failure all the time. So where's the disconnect? It's all in the language you use.

First and foremost, a failure isn't the end. It may be the best you can possibly do under the circumstances. The real error is when you give up and stop trying. We never complain about failures – they're just approaches and solutions that didn't work at the time. In our world, failure is just another word for education. We try to give our people permission to fail, without an acceptance of failure because, while effort is great, ultimately it really is results that matter and move the needle.

Every entrepreneur knows about the "J" curve which predicts that things tend to get worse for a while before they get better and that's just part of the deal. So expect a bumpy road, but always keep moving the ball forward. Things will get better.

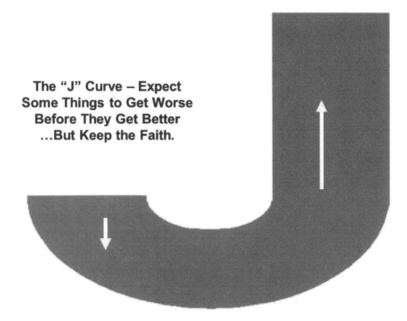

The "J" Curve – Expect
Some Things to Get Worse
Before They Get Better
…But Keep the Faith.

Our basic mantra is "fail, fail again, and fail better" – each time. And, at the same time, we are merciless about lack of effort or giving up too soon or too often.

The second and most critical part of the "failure" discussion is to focus on "failing fast". If you're in a hole, stop digging. If you're going sideways, bail out. You've got to remember that there's an opportunity cost to everything – whatever you're doing, you could always be doing something else and potentially more valuable to your business. So you've got to be downright greedy with your time which is your scarcest resource of all and very careful about how you spend it.

Saying "no" quickly and often helps immeasurably in this process. There's always too much to do and too many "opportunities" before you – saying "no" is your best strategic tool. And "failing fast and smart" is the methodology that makes this approach work.

I've learned that it really doesn't matter what you have to say or how well you say it if it turns out that nobody's listening. And this is just as true in your company as it is in the classroom or anywhere else. The days of the lecturing "sage on the stage" or the hectoring "lord of the lectern" are over – whether you're the boss who knows it all or anyone else. The one-way street called "I talk, you listen" has given way to a complex cloverleaf of conversation – everyone thinks they're experts; they've all got an opinion; and they expect to be heard and, more importantly, to be listened to rather than talked at.

Now I realize that - in certain groups and in certain parts of the country - the opposite of talking isn't actually listening, it's waiting to talk. But be that as it may, today, effective two-way communication is more essential than ever to reaching the most important goal – actual learning and true understanding – and making sure your audience gets, understands and appreciates your message. Because, at the end of the day, you can talk until you're blue in the face and you can explain things to people over and over again, but you can't understand for them. So, unless you're just talking to hear yourself speak, to be a successful communicator, you're going to have to make some changes in your game. Because, whether we're teachers or anyone else with a story to tell, we're all in a new kind of race and nobody's going to wait any longer for any of us to get with the program.

We're competing for scarce attention and sadly-muddled mindshare in a media- drenched, frenzied and frantic world where everyone's exposed to an ever-expanding mass of indiscriminate messages; where we're surrounded by a shallow and sleazy celebrity-driven culture that thrives on garbage, gossip and cheap thrills; and where – amidst the constant stream of stimulation – it's almost impossible to catch your breath or collect your thoughts. And, if you don't like what you're doing or hearing at the moment, just wait a bit and we'll give you something else.

There's a persistent fear out there that this new, ever younger audience is so over-stimulated, splintered, stressed-out and scattered that they can't really sit still for a second. It's as if they're all sitting on tacks – it's hard to concentrate in that position – especially if you never learned how to concentrate or focus in the first place. And we also encourage this constant motion and frenzy by pretending to believe in the myth of multi-tasking – or, as I call it, learning to do a bunch of things badly.

Too many people lead our kids to believe that they are somehow different and special and that they can do many important things simultaneously and do them all well. They can have their cake, the frosting, the whole nine yards, and eat it too.

Apparently, for anyone under 25 years old, the laws of life, gravity and physics have been suspended. But the truth is that, in trying to multi-task, you essentially learn to do a lot of things poorly and, worst of all, you eventually get completely comfortable with the illusion that you're doing something of importance or consequence. Instead of submerging yourself in anything substantive, you spend your time skimming over everything.

The most important thing that today's "multi-taskers" forget to do (and eventually lose the ability to do) is to focus, pay attention and "go deep". To be in the moment and to enjoy being there. To be there now. To give themselves wholly to an experience and let it transport them for just a short time to a different and hopefully better place and maybe, in the very process itself, to have it actually teach them a thing or two. And perhaps let them discover and learn something themselves (or about themselves) as they progress.

There is, however, some good news: the more things change (even today), the more the fundamental things remain the same. Good communication has always been about the substance of the "story" you've got to tell and it will always be that way – it's just the strategy and the delivery methods that have to be adjusted to accommodate a new kind of audience and the new and challenging environments that our new technologies are creating all around us. And it's important to remember that - as cool as our new toys and tools are - all the technology in the world still won't save a story that sucks. To make your story stick, you've got to make it shared and special. Or, as they say at Facebook, you need to make them care and you need to make them share.

Today, to break through the clutter and the noise and the massive distractions, and to engage, immerse and enthrall the new audiences, wherever they happen to reside, success isn't something that we will successfully be doing to them – the best and most successful practitioners of the new tools of effective communication will help the audiences learn and do things by and for themselves. Exploration rather than exposition will drive the future. Active involvement and engagement rather than partial and passive participation will be the hallmarks of successful new educational offerings wherever they take place in the office, in the field or in the classroom.

Creating compelling, immersive, interactive, experiential, collaborative, cross- disciplinary, and community- (or team-) based combinations of content and context is the only effective way forward. We need to build vehicles of all manner that will let us construct our own experiences and learning; that create the enticing environments where such adventures can take place; that proffer important questions, puzzles and challenges; and that ultimately give us the wheel, stand back, and let us make our own way through the vagaries and the mysteries of discovery which will define the new forms of communication and education.

lthough it shouldn't really come as a big surprise to anyone in sales, it turns out that selling someone something new and different is a lot harder to do than selling them more of the same or something that's just a little different and hopefully better. In fact, any salesman will tell you that the only thing harder to sell than something new is something people really don't want or need. That's when you know you're a real salesman. But, since most of us aren't super salesmen, we need to figure out other ways to overcome the simple fact that most people are just reluctant to try new things. Sometimes they're actually concerned or afraid, but mostly they're just inert – waiting for the world to happen to them – and not looking to try new things, spend extra money or take a chance on almost anything.

There are lots of reasons for this resistance, but the most basic reason is that we tend to like and to "go with" what we know. Tried and true solutions are safe, comfortable and relatively low risk. We're a conservative (not to say lazy) people and we're very happy to just get along and go along. This is probably a lot less true for entrepreneurs, but the sad fact of life is that the vast majority of the people buying whatever it is you're selling aren't gonna be entrepreneurs or risk-takers. And that's perfectly OK – it just means that you've got to learn to speak their language and put your selling proposition into a framework that they understand, appreciate and – most of all – are comfortable with. And it never hurts to make it your business to determine who the real buyers are and what the real drivers are for their decisions.

Let me give you a great example from my days of selling Xerox machines to law firms.

The first thing that you learn in dealing with law firms is that the senior partner who ultimately signs the checks rarely has anything to do with deciding the merits of the purchases he's paying for. He's too busy making money for the firm and it's not a good use of his time. This is also the case - 9 times out of 10 - with the owners of car dealerships. Generally, however, successful car dealers aren't spending their time making money for the firm; they're spending their money making time with hookers. But the idea's the same. And the minute something goes wrong, all these guys become screaming maniacs and want to fire the whole office. As a result, preserving the peace and quiet and not pissing off the boss becomes a consistent part of the purchase requirements.

The second thing you learn is that the other less senior partners in the law firm are a bunch of whinny, complaining assholes. I can say that because, for more than a decade, I was one. But here again, the real lesson is that life's too short to spend it listening to these bozos complain and, as a result, once again the decision set for law firm purchases has a lot to do with avoiding stress and strain and less and less to do with saving a few shekels. And, by the way, you wouldn't want to ask these nitpicking nutcases to participate in the purchase process under any circumstances if you ever wanted to get a decision made. Truthfully though they'd never let their fingerprints be found on any decision like this because it would theoretically keep them from second- guessing the actual decision-makers and from complaining about their conclusions.

So where does that leave us? With a simple rank order analysis of what you'd think the Xerox purchase decision set at a law firm consisted of and what the real criteria of the office manager (who's actually the buyer) turn out to be. In a survey of hundreds of professional office managers (including, but not exclusively, for law firms), the factors which consistently ranked highest had everything to do with keeping the machines up and operating successfully and almost nothing to do with costs. In order, they were:

1. RELIABILITY
2. COPY QUALITY
3. SERVICE
4. EASE OF USE
5. PRICE

And if you asked them honestly about their choices, they would initially offer you really nice clichés like: "when our copiers are working, our people are working", but the unspoken truth which eventually came out was always more like: "I want to keep my job" and "I don't want those assholes yelling at me." Saving money for the firm never entered into the equation.

The morale of the story is pretty simple. The most successful copier salesmen didn't pitch price, speed or performance – they focused on stability, security and the ever-golden "silence". They pointed their presentations directly at the pain points of the purchaser. And that won the day.

And the same approach and strategy works in almost any sales situation. You just need to remember 5 basic propositions:

1. Originality is overrated. Pioneers end up with arrows in their back - and not a whole lot more. Don't invent, innovate.
2. Novelty is a nuisance – it means expensive training; a new learning curve; and mistakes galore. Tried and true trumps all.
3. No one likes to cross the chasm – especially when they are first. Short, sure steps forward and a lot more of the same really sell.
4. Don't tell me how different your product or service is – tell me how easy and familiar and fail-safe it will be.
5. Analogies are better than apple pie. Show me anything I'm doing now and then tell me not how different things will be, but how much the same they will remain.

In the movie business, they call this process "high concept". You give me a snapshot that tells me all I need to know. Like using the latest slick and suave incarnation of Justin Timberlake to play the Frank Sinatra role in remakes of ANY classic Sinatra films. Says it all. I don't have to love the idea to understand exactly what you're telling me. Or having Tom Hanks play the Jimmy Stewart roles in anything except "It's a Wonderful Life". You get the picture.

Now think about what you're making and selling and figure out the same thing – what's the shortest pitch to get you on the path to a successful sale?

TULLMAN'S TRUISMS

IT'S NOT WHAT YOU LOOK AT THAT MATTERS, IT'S WHAT YOU SEE

Are we finally there? Should the last man out of tonight's late shift at the plant turn out the lights for good? Notwithstanding the success of "*Kinky Boots*" on Broadway, is the end of traditional manufacturing in sight? I'd say "yes" - albeit somewhat sadly. There are at least six different drivers for the demise. And they aren't the obvious ones that you'd imagine – I'm not talking about outlandish labor costs, ridiculous OSHA regulations, or protestors more concerned about pollution and plant life than production - although we can certainly thank the bozos in Washington for making many things in the world of manufacturing much worse over the last two decades. My thoughts are a little more basic.

Here are my 6 D's:

(1) Dirt

We lost the race for raw materials years ago as China and other more- foresighted countries scooped up vast quantities of all kinds of the mission-critical minerals, compounds and rare earths which are so essential to the production of the critical components of virtually everything cellular or digital in the world today. We don't have either the materials themselves or the right mindset any more. Maybe coal will stage a comeback. Here's hoping - not.

(2) Durability

In a world of instant gratification and rampant disposability - where the packaging we negligently discard costs considerably more than the products we consume - who really cares about manufacturing durable goods and long-lasting products when we'll be sick of the stuff anyway once it's no longer shiny ? Shiny never lasts. In addition, new 3D printing technologies will permit and encourage the development of even more low-cost, immediate and discardable kinds of products – all in the "use once and toss" family and none of which is good for our production facilities, our population, or our planet.

(3) Demand

Frankly, we'd rather not own anything these days. High maintenance costs, devastating depreciation of everything physical, rapid obsolescence driven by accelerating technologies, there's really no reason to buy anything for the long run. We're users and renters – not owners anymore. Zip cars are the "cars for people who don't want one" and that says a lot more about our lives today than merely about our transportation preferences.

(4) Desire

Life today just isn't about things because the best things in life aren't things. It's not really that the nature of things ever changes; the fact is that our desire for certain things morphs over time and our appetites change as well. There's no such thing as pride of ownership either – it's not politically correct – because we all know that people are more important than things and bragging about your property and your possessions just isn't cool any more. We're seeing more and more that bigger isn't necessarily better. And we're also becoming much less materialistic. In the "*Mad Men*" world of not too long ago, they would say that 4 things defined a man: his home; his car; his wife; and his shoes. Just think about how little this formulation has to do with the way we see our lives today and you'll appreciate the massive changes coming down the pike.

(5) Demographics

I wrote recently that kids don't care about cars, but the fact is that things are much worse for manufacturers than that. Apart from the prospect that today's kids may be the first generation that really isn't upwardly mobile relative to their parents, the fact is that - as soon as they reach the age where they would themselves determine and dictate durable goods purchases, they are finding that they don't have the dollars to do anything. Their folks stop buying them dolls, digital devices and indulging their every desire and they figure out pretty quickly thereafter that major purchases cost real money which they don't have and can't borrow. And instead of starting to save in order to eventually satisfy those deferred desires, they spend their time sucking down lattes from Starbucks. Everything today for Gen Yrs is about the experience and the adventure and the trip and not about things which are mainly a downer and a drag.

(6) Digital

Digital is dictating everything and it's worth a whole column itself. But one thing's for sure – the kids today (and basically anyone with a brain) realizes that good ideas - regardless of their size - last much longer and are worth a great deal more than anything you can make with your hands and that - in this world of increasing connectivity - ideas can spread across the universe in an instant. Even more importantly, in these times of increasingly scarce resources, ideas (and digital goods) have an amazing and unique property – unlike even the best physical objects. You can share an idea with someone else (and/ or everyone else) and then (unlike an apple or a Mac) – all of you have the shared idea – it's enhanced and expanded in its scope and its power - not diminished or lessened by sharing and broad distribution – and that's how we'll make our world will grow in the future – manufacturing new ideas – not new iPads.

33 – YOU ARE WHAT YOU ARE INTERESTED IN

When Facebook bought Karma (one of the leading gift sites) at the end of 2012, it was pretty clear that we were going to see a second iteration of Facebook Gifts - especially as the holiday shopping season started to heat up. Socially-informed commerce in various forms and shapes has been around for quite a while, but we're at another major inflection point now because of the impact of hyper-personalization and the far more precise and cost-effective targeting which is now available.

Keep in mind that it's a long-established principle that, if you give a consumer too many choices, they are far more likely to buy nothing than if you give them a limited and more relevant decision set. New young companies like Chicago-based Local Offer Network are jumping into this particular space as well with tools that deliver the "exactly right" offers to consumers visiting a site even the first time that the visitor appears. I call this "smart reach" and Facebook will be all over it – especially with Facebook Exchange.

Given the tools and resources that Facebook increasingly has at its disposal, they can now make the gift selection and giving process far more successful for the donor and also make the recipient far more likely to be happy with the gift. Remember that the excellence of a gift lies in its appropriateness, not simply in its value. And there are other important ancillary benefits as well. One of the reasons people get divorced is that they run out of gift ideas. Ergo – better gifts – less divorces.

So there's no question that this latest foray into "f-commerce" is going to be a big focus for the Facebook team along with a couple of other "interest graph-driven" initiatives like Facebook "Collections" which is their initial salvo in response to the explosive growth of Pinterest. If you want to get some idea of how interesting and accurate gift giving becomes when it's informed by detailed data about the interests and preferences and buying history of the friends and peers for whom you're trying to select a present, take a look at shopycat.com which is actually a product created by Wal- Mart Labs - but very cool nonetheless.

If you are more of a metrics person, here are some numbers to keep in mind – when a "friend" refers and/or recommends that someone they know take an action on the web – the impact (as compared to a simple ad solicitation) is major: recipients are 15% more likely to download something; 8% more likely to buy something; and – most importantly – when they do buy, the average order size is 22% larger. That's a lotta lift.

What's less obvious about the new gift-giving initiatives (the Lightbank/Groupon gang also invested in Boomerang in 2012 which is another gift site) is that, from Facebook's perspective, the dollars generated from gift purchases may be nowhere near as valuable in the long run to their enterprise as the purchase decision data which will be made available through these transactions as well as the implicit and explicit "connections" which each and every gift transaction will establish between their members. You can just imagine the opportunities for follow-on sales and service and the cross-marketing possibilities that each gift will create.

As I like to say, "personal data is the oil of the digital age" and Facebook increasingly owns the primary pump. And because birds of a feather flock together, other analytical tools will help correlate purchases with the buyer's presence in defined communities and other likely behavioral groups. Data, data and more data with virtually no acquisition cost and high degrees of precision and accuracy.

So the real "news" about Facebook Gifts is that we're continuing to see more and more indications of the next major seismic shift from the relatively simple social graph to the deeper interest graph. Because we (and Facebook in particular) have pretty much cracked the code on personal data and demographics (empowered in real-time by high-velocity computing), the next hurdle is pretty clear: "tell me what you're interested in and what you pay attention to and I will tell you who you are". And basically, if you're not where your targets and customers are and a relevant part of their world, you're nowhere. This is really where both Instagram, Aviary and Pinterest loom large.

As we see better and better tools to interpret and identify (and categorize) visual materials (photos and other images with videos to follow in the near future), we will see more and more emphasis on and influence of the players who are successfully aggregating these huge treasure troves of visual information. After all, a picture's worth about a million words these days if it's the right picture.

And speaking about the future and gifts reminds me that the future isn't a gift, it's an achievement that we work for and earn every day. Hard work is what makes our dreams come true.

But Facebook really is like a powerful steamroller and it rarely stops changing the rules of the game - and thereby - the world that we all live in today. The addition of Facebook Graph Search is really another major brick in the wall. But it's really a double-edged sword that will take some serious getting used to.

I've been worried for a while about the filter bubble and how narrow the search process was becoming as it increasingly morphed from a window on new worlds to a mirror reflecting back to us basically what we and our friends already know. Our peers are important, but how would you learn anything new if search was simply an endless loop?

I was also concerned about the death of serendipitous discovery which is the sheer joy we feel at a bookstore (remember those?) or a flea market (remember those?) when we come across something new and amazing and totally unexpected and it just makes our day. You didn't even know you were looking for something, but you loved it when you found it. And, of course, in search terms, you could never have constructed a query to find something you weren't seeking.

That's why I'm excited about Graph Search and why it will actually enable and enhance a lot of businesses (besides Facebook's) which could include yours once you understand some of the basics beneath the buzz.

First and foremost, GS is a return to the earliest days and, in fact, to the origin of Facebook. Think about it (even if you've only seen the movie) – it was about finding pictures of the hottest women on campus. And, clearly, it wasn't about women you knew (search); it was about women you wanted (desperately) to know (discovery).

GS takes the blinders and the filters off of the painstaking process of conscious search (does anyone really want to check out all of your friends' profiles one at a time?) and opens up a huge amount of additional social and personal and interest material that was always there, but which is now readily accessible. Broad content queries constrained by the limiters and filters of your friends is an elegant way to get right to the heart of the interest graph.

Two simple examples – how much better would a Groupon deal do if in 10 seconds I could ask Facebook which of my friends were already participating in the deal? Or have Ticketmaster's concert seating charts (enabled by Facebook integration) show me which of my friends already have tickets to the show and where they are sitting?

So, as you start to think about how to position your business and your product and service offerings in new ways to make them discoverable and sharable thru the new power of Graph Search, keep in mind the following three aspects of GS:

(1) Aggregation

GS does the heavy lifting for you and assembles the data and results of your friends' likes, preferences and interests across whatever cuts and selections you care to make and permits you to interactively build on your questions and broaden or narrow them on the fly. Single friends with MBAs who are living in San Francisco and working in the entertainment business? You got it in a flash.

(2) Filters

Instead of limiting your queries or your results in the background in ways that were never really clear, filters now take on a new ability to help you frame your selections, criteria and choices in ways that avoid overwhelming and unwieldy results and permit you to dictate limits of scope, time, location, images, etc. Friends who loved *Inglourious Basterds* and are actually up for going to see *Django* with me? Try that on Google.

(3) Engagement

For now, and this may change, assets like photos are "valued" and ranked and displayed in engagement order which – in Facebook terms – means that the more likes and comments a particular photo has, the more likely it will be to be surfaced. The reason I think that this criteria is in flux is that it's highly likely that the volume of activity around a photo may be exactly why it's the least likely photo that the person shown in the photo wants circulated.

We're headed into the next big burst of Facebook-enabled commerce (f- commerce) and increasingly millions of customers are going to be living within this Facebook economy and nowhere else. If you doubt that, just check out how many times the Facebook team during the launch events repeated the idea that "you never have to leave Facebook" to do anything that you want to do.

Each of these components of the new GS engine will change many of the ground rules for how (and whether) new and small businesses will be able to make themselves heard and get their messages out to their prospective customers in the clutter and the crowd. It's not going to be easier, but it will definitely be more interesting.

Here's one last word of advice. One of the great internal mantras of Facebook regarding the creation of all social web content is: what will make them care? and what will make them share? As you bring your products and services to market, keep these two questions top of mind.

34 – SLOW DOWN AND SAVE YOUR BUSINESS

Sometimes when I'm speaking to a young entrepreneur and talking about speed (or more accurately those times when I say that slowing down makes a lot more sense than hurrying down what will most likely turn out to be the wrong road), I get the sense that I could just as well be talking to (or yelling back at) the radio. It might make me feel a little better, but it doesn't really change much of anything.

I see that "glazed eye" look (which, of course, I'm completely familiar with from years of dealing with my kids) and I know that he or she is thinking just what I might have thought myself 30 or 40 years ago – when I'm sure I didn't listen any more closely to my own mentors. This guy is old – he doesn't want to charge up the hill because he's tired – he doesn't have the "start-up" spirit any more – it's ready, fire, aim – and balls to the walls. And I suppose that could be right in some instances, but not in my case. I'm always happy to charge up the next hill, but I like to know how many hills there are after that one and just who and what is waiting over the crest.

This is a much bigger issue than you would imagine for three reasons:

(1) Lots of young, eager and energetic young entrepreneurs literally get "hooked" on the adrenaline buzz and constant stimulation of living on the edge, doing something new and different every day, and even the whole idea of risking it all and they can't or won't take the time to slow down and catch their collective breath; to take stock of their situation; and to really think (for at least a little while) about what should come next for the business and the company. It's too easy today to confuse meetings for movement; mere motion for forward progress and smoke and mirrors for substance. Keep in mind that the critical mistakes made by businesses occur in good times rather than bad times and ultimately it's what you do wrong, not right, that has the greatest impact on your company and your success.

(2) The very culture of start-ups and the myth of killer customer service uber alles breeds a "can do" attitude that treats the everyday business as a constant emergency and a fire drill. Everything is here and now and very reactive. You have everyone running around fighting fires and no one minding the store. Basically you're being pushed by your problems rather than being driven by your dreams and it's a formula for failure and a great way to burn out your best people. A good test is to ask yourself whether you are working off your inbox (in which case you're reacting) or whether the business is working off your outbox (in which case you're leading).

(3) Managing and growing a business is all about carefully navigating and trying to hold your course through complex and constantly changing circumstances – finessing the details, but remaining firmly focused on the vision and the finish line. If you're totally consumed by the immediate, you aren't going to be asking the questions that will really determine the future course of your business because these aren't the kinds of questions that walk in your door and deposit themselves in your inbox. The really tough questions won't come to you – they will have to come from you. Your original business plan is a good guide and a useful reference, but only if you stop from time to time and use it to see where you thought you'd be, where you've been; and where you're headed. Otherwise you're flying blind and headed nowhere fast.

Going slow from time to time isn't about age or energy – it's about conserving your scarce resources and applying them smartly – it's about essential course corrections and changes – and, most importantly, it's about making sure that your team is with you and right there beside you and that you're continuing to bring them along and not running away from them.

And, by the way, the "speed trap" chat isn't the only somewhat difficult and painful conversation that I have on a regular basis with young owners and managers. The second least popular piece of advice that I offer is that "Not Everything Worth Doing is Worth Doing Well". Apparently this concept stinks of compromise, settling, and accepting necessary evils – all of which seem to violate some unwritten laws of entrepreneurship and the manner in which we are all obliged to conduct the sacred crusades which we call start-ups.

But, here's the deal – it's the truth and there're no two ways around it. The best leaders understand that you can't do everything at the same time, with the same energy and speed, and with all the resources at your disposal. This doesn't mean you're a sucker or a sell-out – it means – most of the time – that you're being smart and saving some dry powder for the next problem or opportunity. And it's equally foolish to try to do something on the cheap that you shouldn't do at all.

All too often I see people driving themselves crazy trying to accommodate foolish, unrealistic or insincere requests from investors, customers, vendors or even their own people and wasting their time and money in the process. And I know for a fact (which they won't often admit) that, in many cases, they're just going through the motions because they know it's stupid as well and that the end result won't actually matter to anyone. It's as hard to watch as someone trying to cut a roast beef with a screwdriver. When it's finally done, it's ugly and you've lost your appetite.

So give yourself a break – take some time – take stock – make some hard choices – and – believe me – your business will thank you.

So I'm standing at my neighborhood 7-11 and the two guys in front of me are staring at the brand-new *Belly* customer loyalty tablet which has been installed right there next to the box of beef jerky. The first guy asks the clerk what *Belly* is and, of course, the clerk has no idea. Now that's not a big surprise (considering the source) since the clerk can barely give you correct change, but it does tell you something about how critical it is as you're growing your business to make sure that your field training and implementation activities keep pace. Putting a pretty device on a deli counter isn't the same as getting the on-site implementation and integration job done. This stuff doesn't ever happen by itself. As it happens, and as Belly quickly shoots past 1 million users, in this particular case, it's no one's fault. The *Belly* program at 7-11 actually hasn't even formally launched yet. As usual, I'm in way too much of a hurry, but that's nothing new. As it happens, 7-11 along with *Belly* will be rolling out comprehensive field training to all of the participating stores before the launch date. But that's not really what I found so interesting about the discussion.

When the clerk struck out, out of the clear blue, the next guy in line chimed in and said he knew exactly what Belly was and he gave a short, but pretty accurate, explanation about how it was a "universal" (they only wish!) customer loyalty reward system that worked across multiple businesses so that you didn't need a bunch of different reward and frequent flyer cards – you could just use the Belly system. Pretty good I thought – clear and concise – although I was still mainly interested in paying for my drink and getting out of there. But his explanation also wasn't what I thought was really significant about their exchange.

What was really important was what happened next. The first guy who had asked the original question about Belly and now probably knew slightly more than he may have wanted to about what was going on turned to the second guy who had done such a nice unsolicited job of explaining and asked him the only question that really mattered at all. In fact, it was the exact right question. He asked him: "Do you use it?" and the guy said "Nope". And it was game over. Basically, I guess this tale fits into the "talk is cheap" or "actions speak louder than words" bucket, but I thought there was actually more to it than that. Because if your prospective customers know all about you and your business and they aren't using your service, you've got a lot more work to do.

Keep in mind that I think Belly is doing well – they're in 15 markets – dealing with major players like 7-11 – and already a great PR and marketing story. We see the Belly CEO, Logan LaHive, everywhere we look and – from an awareness standpoint – which is certainly step one in the process, both he and his launch team are doing a pretty impressive job of signing up users and getting their tablet devices into the market. They certainly have some viable competition like Five Stars or Spoton.com, but that comes with the territory, and interestingly enough Spoton has opted to date not to enter the Chicago market where Belly got its start.

One caveat that applies here (just as it does to Groupon) is that all of these guys have to be careful to make sure that the businesses they are targeting are the right kind of businesses for their service in terms of the profiles of each business's customers and especially the frequency with which each customer visits the business. While I realize that loyalty programs are specifically intended to increase customer connections and grow usage, etc., the fact still is that, if a customer typically visits a business twice a year, that business probably is not a prime target for Belly or any of the other players in the space.

So I'm not knocking or picking on Belly which I think is getting most things right when I say I'm concerned in general that, for many young and rapidly growing businesses, it's sometimes too easy to sit back and start believing your own press instead of continuing to press your bets and roll out your business. If you focus purely on awareness and the accompanying adulation, it's easy to lose sight of the much more critical measures of engagement, adoption, repeat use, and advocacy which are really the make-or-break determinants of the business. If you let the noise and the notoriety knock you off course, you can find pretty quickly that your connection to your "customers" can evaporate overnight.

And frankly, it's not really even enough that your users are using the service, they really need to be talking about it and promoting it if you want to ride the virality curve. They need to care enough to share and they need to do it quickly and to large numbers of their peers to really drive the growth you need. And, when I asked Logan from Belly about some of these related metrics, he said that they spend much more time on user engagement concerns than on PR and that they actually attract much more business through referrals than through self-promotion. If there are interested readers out there with their own opinions, I'd love to hear from you and so, I'm sure, would Belly.

We are increasingly living in times where the only thing faster than the adoption curve of new technologies and applications is the rate at which they are summarily abandoned by the same eager and early adopters. Before you push onwards and upwards and start shooting for the stars, you need to make sure that your product or service really matters to your users and that it makes a difference to them in terms of something they really value – time, money, productivity or status – are good criteria for starters.

If you aren't securing real attachment and engagement and if your attrition numbers are comparable to your acquisition numbers, you're a disaster waiting to happen.

I realize that each of us has our own version of the 3 biggest lies and I'm sure that everyone's list morphs over time depending on their own experiences and disappointments. I say disappointments because there are no happy outcomes from lies – even little white lies – so, by and large; I've concluded that honesty remains the best policy. It would be nice if the people who run our K-12 school systems (the management and the union "leaders") felt the same. But, regardless of whether they or anyone else responsible will ever admit it, there are certain real-world lies which persist – especially when they are repeated *ad nausem* by the highest politicians in the land - and these are so pernicious that it almost seems like our civic duty to call bullshit on them from time to time. As Thomas Jefferson said "a continual circulation of lies among those who are not much in the way of hearing them contradicted will in time pass for the truth."

Lie Number One, of course, is that everyone can afford to and should own their own home. I feel that this crock has pretty much imploded over the last few years although I sense a creeping rebirth of the same kind of delusionary thinking when I hear the President talking about how the JOBS legislation is such a triumph of democracy (small "d" for sure) since pretty soon every Tom, Dick and Harry will be able to buy and own cheap stocks and their "piece of the American Dream" through new and virtually unregulated crowd-funding vehicles which will let just about anybody with a "story" raise money from the masses.

Do I even need to add "whether this new class of "investors" can afford it or not" or "whether they have the slightest clue as to what they're investing in or the risks inherent in the investment"? Talk about learning nothing from the fake financial statements and phony real estate appraisals which let the crooked banks create huge numbers of bogus loans in order to lend just about anything to anyone. Imagine how closely anyone will be scrutinizing the net worths and required levels of sophistication of the tens of thousands of cab drivers and convenient store operators who will now become stock speculators on the side.

Lie Number Two – another favorite of the DC crowd is that every kid in American needs and is entitled to a 4-year college education whether they (and/or their parents) can afford it or not. And, frankly, whether they want it or not; are capable and likely to be successful in the pursuit or not; and/or whether they would be much better served and far more likely to ultimately find a job if they pursued a shorter, less costly, and better suited program to get some practical vocational training and to get on with their lives without mortgaging their future with student loan obligations.

Since I have an obvious dog in this particular fight, I won't say anything more on the subject.

It's the third big lie that's really killing our kids' futures and, not surprisingly, it has nothing to do with getting thru a college education- it's all about the diminished likelihood of getting to a college education. By the time many of these kids are of college age, the damage is already done and they're long gone from the system. And honestly, the ones who remain are basically no better served by the continued pretense that we're effectively teaching them much of anything useful or of value in today's globally competitive world. So what's the third big lie?

Lie Number Three is that in education, and specifically in the classroom, that "one size fits all". It's the job security lie that ignores how differently each of us learns and pretends that a single instructor standing in front of a classroom full of kids can effectively teach anything to all of them at the same time. It's true that the one thing this approach will convincingly teach each of those students is that we still think of schools as industrial-style factories turning out standardized automans with a premium on rote memorization and repetition rather than rigorous reasoning and problem solving. But it doesn't have to be that way.

All it takes is an honest acknowledgement that the current system sucks and that the solution is pretty simple. Not necessarily cheap; not universally available yet; and not easy to implement in the face of the fierce resistance to change which may be the only thing that many schools are still really good at – but a straightforward, not complicated, and readily accessible approach all the same. We've got the resources – the real question is whether we have the guts, the resolve and the strength to implement the necessary changes before we doom another generation of kids to lifetime under-employment, second-class citizenship or worse.

There's no magic here. It's pretty simple. You can call it differential or individualized learning or mass customization or a million other things. What matters is not the name, but the undisputed fact that we all learn at our own pace and often in dramatically different ways. The tools and technologies exist to build a knowledge- delivery system that fits and serves the students rather than trying to force every student to fit into an antiquated system that suits no one.

Imagine a class of students who are each is working with a device (could be a desktop, a game console, a tablet, a phone, etc.) that are all wirelessly networked and connected through the cloud to a dashboard for the "teacher" which shows each student's status, progress and level of success in real time. Instead of pretending that one size fits all or teaching to the lowest common denominator or having the smartest kids done with their work and bored in no time at all, the teacher (empowered by the simple dashboard tracking tools and adaptive learning programs) is able to track, react, and adjust the information being provided to each student as well as that student's learning experience continually as needed and on the fly. Some students will be right on time and on track; some will be looping through remedial exercises; others will be reviewing extracurricular materials or taking individualized pop quizzes or exams. The teacher can even share screens with individual students and provide hints, suggestions and other coaching without interrupting anyone else in the class or wasting anyone else's time.

Sadly today, our politicians mainly lie for a living and since they barely remember the lies they tell, you can rest assured that they have no recollection whatsoever of the promises they may have made. They can rant and rave all they want about everything that's wrong especially with for-profit education because it's easy pickings, but shouting a lie doesn't make it any truer.

If we're going to save our children's futures, it's going to be up to us to face the facts, tell the truth, make the necessary changes, add the crucial technologies that create leverage and scale without adding costs to budgets that are frightfully misallocated and hope it's not too late.

TULLMAN'S TRUISMS

WE NEED TO PRODUCE STUDENT WIZARDS, NOT STUDENT WIDGETS

I recently sent around a fairly direct (not to say harsh) memo to a number of our marketing folks which suggested that (a) being better prepared for certain meetings was a really good idea; and that (b) one great way to be better prepared was by making sure that they had seen and reviewed the videos and other materials which were going to be discussed in upcoming meetings before they got there – especially those specifically sent around by me.

Not only would this improve their participation and the value of their contributions to the meeting, but it would also avoid wasting my time and the time of many of the other attendees when we were forced to re-watch videos (which most of us had seen) so that we could all be on the same page during the meeting and have an intelligent and productive discussion. It seemed to me to be a fairly basic, straightforward and obvious request. Apparently, for at least some of the people, I wasn't being sensitive enough to how awfully busy they are and how hard it is for them to keep up with things. I guess that expecting people to do their jobs and telling them when you don't think they are has fallen out of fashion and is bad for morale. Shame on me.

But it got me thinking about motivation and about how too many of us have the whole motivation and incentive thing ass-backwards. In the same way that too many people still think that education is about filling empty vessels (our kid's heads) with facts and figures rather than about igniting a passion for learning in them and creating environments that engage and excite them, way too many folks think that motivation is something that we do to other people. That it's the boss's job to be the team cheerleader and keep the troops pumped up. Basically, that this motivation business is an external process and a management tool which has to be learned and religiously applied to keep the wheels of the train from falling off.

But I think that's completely wrong. Real motivation comes entirely from within. People who pump themselves up stay pumped and succeed because passion and commitment and a true appreciation of why you're doing something and how it ultimately benefits you (and your family, etc.) are things that doesn't wear off or wear out and not some slogans, some incentives or some stupid party tricks that you read in some Dale Carnegie book. The simple truth is that there's no way to excite or motivate or inspire people that isn't grounded in their own perceived self-interest. And that's perfectly fine and the way it should be. No one's really against anyone else in business – they're just mainly interested in themselves and looking out for Number One.

So, if you're a leader and you want to effectively influence others, the process is actually pretty simple: you've got to talk about what they want (their future) and you've got to show them how to get it (the path) and then get out of their way and let nature take its course. They will take the information and – if they're engaged and excited about their prospects, their projects and their futures – they will create far more compelling and comprehensive reasons and justifications for working their butts off than you ever could because each of them knows exactly what's really important to them and you'd have to be a mind reader to even try to guess.

So forget about thinking that motivating your team is something you do to them and focus instead on doing things for them which removes obstacles, adds resources, clarifies directions and goals, and reduces friction so that they can see clearly what's ahead of them, how to get there and what's in it for them. The smart ones will be highly and authentically motivated all by themselves and the others will soon be working somewhere else.

TULLMAN'S TRUISMS

YOU CAN EXPLAIN THINGS TO PEOPLE, BUT YOU CAN'T UNDERSTAND FOR THEM

38 – WHAT I LEARNED FROM MY WAITRESS

I believe in life-long learning. I also believe that you can learn something of value from almost anyone. Everyone's an example - sometimes a good example - sometimes not - but always instructive. The key is to extract the wisdom from the wood chips and apply the lessons to your own work and/or life. It's easier said than done. For years, I've had a favorite waitress at my neighborhood deli named Brenda. I hate to wait for anything, but I'm happy to wait for a seat in her section because I think she actually improves my digestion. And she always shows me something. This week I learned three important things. It's always somewhat remarkable because very few people actually get tips <u>from</u> their waitress. So pay attention.

(1) Repeat After Me

I noticed that she has her own way of taking orders. She repeats everything that I say right back to me – word for word. And there's a curious comfort in that which is very reassuring. How many times have you had some smart-ass waiter stand there while you're reciting your very complicated choices and requirements and not write anything down or repeat a single thing? Did you really feel confident that your food was going to fill the bill or were you just a little anxious that maybe Wally the Waiter didn't really have the world's greatest memory and that your potatoes were coming with peppers whether you liked it or not? Not exactly the warm and fuzzy feeling that makes for return visits.

But the most important part of her process actually wasn't that she always got my order right. Her mimicry sent me a specific and powerful message. Not only was I being listened to; I was being heard. And I was being heard by someone who actually cared about me and about getting my order right. That emotional impression - that recurring result - the ineffable feeling of being "important" and cared for - is the absolute heart of great customer service. Getting the order right is basic execution. Getting the listening part of the process correct – basically adding communication to the conversation - was even more important. It's that old cliché – I don't really care how much you know until I know how much you care.

Way too often today we're distracted when we're supposed to be listening. We're texting or typing. We're multi-tasking or (not so discretely) checking our monitors for new email. And we're sending a very clear message to the person(s) talking to us. It says "I might seem to be listening, but you're not really being heard because my mind and my attention are obviously elsewhere" or it could be saying "I'm actually anywhere, but here in the moment and you don't really matter." Frankly, nothing could be worse for your people, your customers or your business.

If your customers don't think you're concerned about them or listening to them, they won't be customers for long. And it's even worse internally. If your people bring you problems or concerns and you seem too busy to listen or to be bothered, it won't take them too long to conclude that you don't care. They'll stop coming to you and, far more critically, they'll stop caring themselves. It's when your people stop bringing you their problems that you know you have a real problem.

So, if you're going to have a meeting - make it as short as possible - make sure it's necessary and not window dressing or make-work - and make sure it matters (so you aren't meeting for the sake of meeting). And then, if you're gonna do it - do it right. Be there 100%. Pay attention. Listen carefully. Take notes. Give them some feedback and a reaction. Make sure your people know they're being heard.

(2) Do What You Can Do

My waitress doesn't own her restaurant and therefore she doesn't get to set the prices on the menu or the size of the portions. She doesn't determine the daily specials and she can't guarantee that they've got my favorite fruit on any given morning. Sometimes there are things simply beyond her control – like a new cook or busboy who just can't get things right. And shame on her for forgetting the surcharge for sharing. And - heaven forbid - she better not ignore the "no substitutions" rule which apparently is the Eleventh Commandment of the Bible of the restaurant business. So, given the many things that can get in the way of her delivering the kind of service and experience which makes a difference to her customers, she has developed her own simple strategy. She does what she can.

That may sound simplistic and somewhat random, but it's not that at all. This isn't some arbitrary process. It isn't a case of flouting the fat cats or trying to get away with something. The fact is that it's good for business to take care of your "friends" - the regulars - the special customers who represent the recurring foundation of the business. And that's exactly what she does and here's how she does it.

You say you don't want the green beans that come with your meat loaf. But the rules say "No Substitutes". Well, she doesn't substitute anything – she just piles on extra potatoes and lets you know it's a double portion. Not so good for the waist line, but great for making sure you know you're special. She can't change the rules, but she works her magic with the ladle. She works with what she has control over and she does what she can and it shows and – believe me - it matters. This is her own individual solution. When you incorporate this kind of flexibility and empowerment into your entire organization, you become Nordstrom's – the epitome of empowered employees and a great place to shop.

The trick that can make a difference in your own business is to figure out how to encourage initiative and how to give all of your people permission to make things special for your customers in their own personal way.

(3) Don't Worry, Be Happy

If our jobs were fun every day, I think they'd eventually change the name and stop calling it "work". But at the end of the day, every job turns out to be a direct reflection of the amount of time, effort, commitment and passion you put into it. There are really no boring jobs; just people who are bored with their jobs because they lack the energy, attitude and imagination to make something great out of every day. The best bosses I know make it their business to find the pumped-up people in their places and make sure that their excitement, enthusiasm and energy is shared and communicated throughout the organization.

What I love about Brenda the waitress is that she absolutely refuses to let anyone be the "bad" in her day. On her worst day, she's a smile waiting to happen and you just can't knock her off her stride because she makes it her business to make your day in some little way. Her enthusiasm is absolutely authentic and completely contagious. There's no question that it's possible to take the joy out of any job. But you couldn't get her down if your life depended on it. This isn't just about being Peppy Pearl every day – it turns out to be communicating a different and far more important message.

It's about attitude and respect. It says that her job may not be rocket science or Earth-shatteringly important – but she takes great pride in how she does it and she puts herself entirely into the process. She expects you to appreciate that and to respect her effort and commitment to doing the best job of her job that she can do every day. And, unless you're completely unconscious, you do.

TULLMAN'S TRUISMS

THE HARDEST THING TO DO IS TO LISTEN

We've been told practically since birth that a lot of the success we hope for in business (and in life) will come from being a good listener and from being <u>really</u> good at following directions. Consistency is another highly regarded and very traditional virtue along with learning from our experiences. But what if - in a world driven and dominated by technology that is changing much faster than ever before and picking up more speed every day – all of this conventional wisdom was basically wrong?

What if past experience wasn't your best friend, but your worst enemy because it was no longer predictive of virtually anything and, worse yet, because it was actually an impediment to the kinds of disruptive change and innovation that we need today to remain competitive and ultimately to lead the global pack? Letting go of what has worked for you in the past isn't ever easy, but it's ever more critical that these kinds of questions be a significant part of the decision set.

What if being consistent wasn't the smart thing to do (that is – to keep doing things the way you had always done them), but was actually fairly stupid in that it meant that - in the months and years that had intervened since you initially made a plan and started executing it – you hadn't learned anything that required changes, updates, pivots or even dropping whole lines of unproductive or unprofitable business? As Emerson said, "a foolish consistency is the hobgoblin of little minds." And frankly, who really needs more hobgoblins – whatever they are?

I'm especially concerned these days about a different kind of directions (in the compass sense of the word (North or South – to or from) rather than meaning "instructions") and how important it is going to be for all of us to understand and appreciate the ways in which the flows of critical information, assets and resources have reversed their directions/polarities over the last few years so that we can quickly adapt our businesses and our operations to address the new and very different requirements that these changes dictate. And to understand the necessary changes, we're going to need some very smart people and some strong compasses (rather than historical road maps which aren't worth much these days) to help us find our way.

What's the absolutely simplest example? The obvious fact that ubiquitous connectivity, information sharing and universal access have turned every form of publication, broadcast and communication (formerly one-way or one-to-many) into a bi- directional or multi-directional conversation (at least two-way or more). The "I talk, you listen" model of anything (media, sales and marketing, education and training, and even governance) is totally toast. Everyone's an "expert"; every opinion (based on facts or factoids) registers and counts; and sadly, in many cases, the biggest blowhard beats the brightest bulb. Sheer tonnage today trumps tact and very often the truth. This situation can't last, but it's what we've got to deal with today. The goal is to find the new business opportunities and advantages hidden in the piles of gossip and garbage.

And what does the omnipresent cloud and the massive amounts of content of all kinds which now reside there tell us about the changed directions? It tells us that we're entering a world of PULL where we'll pull (and extract) information and intelligence from the cloud as and when needed and where we're in control of the information equation rather than PUSH (and swallow) where we're simply passive consumers of whatever crap is forced down the pipelines and feed to us. There's just too much noise, too much information, and too many complex and overwhelming decisions coming at us for anyone to effectively process the data and make wise choices.

But that's exactly the kind of information overload that makes for great opportunities for those companies which can help us choose, niche, filter, process and decide what makes sense for each of us. Companies that can help us find just what we're looking for (and no more) will set the standards for search in the future because "knowing" is going to be an insurmountable task for anyone whereas "knowing where to look" to find the answers will be the new name of the game. Chicago-based SimpleRelevance (www.simplerelevance.com) is a start-up developing and providing cost-effective analytical tools for the "rest of us" to make smart choices and sense out of masses of available (but not necessarily readily accessible) data in a cost-effective manner.

The truth is that – in virtually every commercial exchange – the information equation has been reversed because of the improved access (for better or worse) which buyers have to group intelligence, shared opinion and pricing data which were formerly held and controlled solely by sellers and the playing field for negotiations has been altered in the consumers' favor forever. And this isn't simply a matter of getting a better price on some product or selecting a smarter service provider for your lawn care.

It's clear that no industry or profession is immune to these directional shifts. Medicine offers two great examples. First, in the old days, we picked a doctor (usually through family connections or other word of mouth) and then – if necessary – the doctor told us which hospital he or she was connected with and that's where we went for our surgery or other procedures. There was no choice, no shopping around, no arguing – just "doctor's orders". In the near future, that order will be completely reversed for the vast majority of patients in America. We will pick or be assigned a health services organization and that company will specify and dictate our hospital, our doctor, and even to a very large extent our course of treatment or non-treatment. Accountants and clerks we've never met will decide whether we "need" (and their companies will pay for) certain tests and medication rather than our doctors.

And if these changes didn't make our doctors feel somewhat diminished (to say the least), just think about how drug advertising has changed the game and turned them into glorified waiters and order takers. In the grand old days, if we were sick and saw our doctor, he prescribed any necessary medications. In fact, that ability – to write scripts - was the defining legal characteristic of being a doctor. Today, thanks to TV and the web, we go into the doctor's office and tell him that we need the "purple pill" or a Z- pack and we won't take "no" for an answer because we saw it on TV and now we're the experts. Talk about TMI. And, as a result, the doctors spend their days arguing with us about ads we've seen on the tube rather than telling us what we need (or very often) or don't need for our problems. And if we don't like their answer or their reluctance to give us what we think we need, increasingly, we can go to see a nurse practitioner or clerk at our neighborhood drug store and get our fix right there.

As the information around us expands and implodes at the same time, and we are all swamped in the unceasing flow of data and TMI, we're looking at another major inflection point (or - as Yogi Berra would say – another fork in the road) and, while it's not very clear what lies on the path ahead, it's obvious that if we don't make some hard choices and just stand still, we'll be run over. Where you head is less important today than the fact that you keep moving and head somewhere. When you get to the fork in the road, take it.

There's an old adage about successful entrepreneurs which states that, if they knew how long and hard the start-up process was going to be, they wouldn't have set out on the journey in the first place. I think this may be true for a small fraction of entrepreneurs – mainly older career-changers who bail before they begin – but that it doesn't apply to the majority of the target group because (a) they're gluttons for punishment; (b) they basically wouldn't believe you even if you swore on two stacks of bibles; and – in any case – (c) they wouldn't listen to you (even if they thought you might be right) because their passion typically overwhelms their perspective as well as whatever objectivity they might still have. Bottom line – time, blood, sweat and tears - and a lot of hard work don't scare anyone who's really trying to make something important happen.

But what really kills any good entrepreneur is the fear of getting the short end of the stick in a negotiation and/or the feeling of being taken advantage of. These concerns are serious parts of every entrepreneur's mental make-up (when and whether they admit it is a different story) and they can lead to serious issues and problems down the line for all concerned. As often as not, they end up being the hardest problems to deal with when a business is about to be sold – the entrepreneur's somewhat naïve and long- standing expectations rarely match the realities of the situation. There's a simple reason for this recurring outcome and it starts very early in the investor/entrepreneur relationship. Very frankly, most young entrepreneurs don't spend anywhere near enough time doing the fundamental math that is crucial to answer the ultimate and very simple question – what am I going to end up with in my pocket when this deal is done? This isn't about being greedy or focusing too much on yourself – it's about setting reasonable metrics for success and aligning – to the greatest extent possible – the respective interests of the parties. If you spend some time early in the process addressing these kinds of issues, you can save yourself a lot of stress and some ugly surprises way down the line.

I've been working with several small teams of young guys with big plans and big ideas and a pretty clear and realistic view of what it's going to take to succeed. They're all fully prepared to climb any mountain, scale any wall, and honestly do whatever it takes to succeed from an effort and commitment standpoint. But they have only the vaguest idea of how to even think 3 to 5 years ahead and to try to calculate and understand the economics that will obtain at that time and which will really determine the value of their interests in the business. They need help in a hurry. But there's some good news. It's just not that complicated.

The very best negotiators go into battle (and these really are battles) with a range of expected outcomes. They may not always achieve the highest and best results, but at least they understand the various possibilities and they can prepare - mentally and emotionally- for them. Young entrepreneurs are so focused on the short run - get the money and get the business started - that they never sit down and really do the math. They don't spend the time to extend and envision the likely financial outcomes (given the required phases of funding and the time frames involved) and, as a result, they cut and/or accept deals way too often that doom them to end up at the end of the road with a bunch of nothing. They work their butts off; they get the funding they need; and they create jobs and a great company, but when they turn around and finally focus on their own finances, they discover that while they definitely bet the ranch, they personally ended up with a lot of other people's gratitude and a pocket full of rocks. That's not how the world is supposed to work, but that's the hard truth in too many cases.

And here's another little piece of bullshit that needs to be put to bed. No one else is gonna do it for you. When it comes to bucks, you gotta look out for your own bacon. No boards of directors will do it for you. Your buddies have their own agendas and their family's mouths to feed. And you'd be surprised at how little time these days supposedly astute investors (who've typically never run anything) spend worrying about the management's compensation and incentives of the people running their portfolio companies. When everyone in the world wants to be an entrepreneur, you could almost forgive these guys (although I never would) for being arrogant enough to think that even the best founders and CEOs are just cogs in the big wheel of business - readily replaced, grateful to be in the game, and a dime a dozen. And while their facts aren't necessarily wrong, their philosophy in this regard is short-sighted and stupid and just results in a lot of angry and unhappy people.

So, as someone sitting across the table from a team of smart, seasoned scumbags (sorry - did I really say that?), how do you - the relative novice - try to develop a strategy, a rationale, and an attitude (at least as important to the process) to carry you successfully through the multiple series of negotiations that you'll be part of as you build (and fund) your business. You need to build a roadmap in reverse. It's not that hard, but it's absolutely essential to securing the right results for you. It may not always work, but if it's rational and realistic, it's at least a working framework and a hook to hang your hat on. Keep in mind that in reality no one knows anything for sure about this process. There are no "one size fits all" rules. There's no gospel or black letter law - every deal is different, every deal is personal, and every deal depends on the parties and their relative degrees of preparation, passion, and patience. In the land of the blind, the guy with the reverse roadmap wins.

So what exactly is a reverse roadmap? Think of it as a rigorous exercise in developing a realistic analysis, a set of often reduced expectations, and a target set of rational (ideally achievable) results. And the rule of thumb for doing this couldn't be simpler - if you know where you want to end up and you've developed several reasonable routes to get there, you're just that much more likely to avoid detours, distractions, and nasty dilution and to reach your goal. On the other hand, if you're so head-down and focused on funding the day-to-day and fighting the fires and you don't take time to focus at least a little on your future (even though I know there's no hurry 'cause you're gonna live forever), you're not going to be that happy when the dust finally settles and you discover, from a financial perspective, that the whole painful struggle looks in retrospect like you spent your precious time kissing your sister instead of stepping out with Shakira or jet setting with J Lo. But it doesn't have to end up that way.

Now keep in mind that I'm not talking about your business plan. I know that you've got a business plan. And I'm sure you've also got a pile of financial projections for your operations in every size and shape. I'm talking about a fiscal projection for your future pocketbook. A tiny little cheat sheet that keeps you on track which you can keep in your wallet, paste on your forehead, or write down on the back of your business card (if you still use one). The numbers may change over time and need to be updated to reflect new facts and circumstances, but this little tool will help keep you focused when it matters on the ultimate goal line. And because you have a "plan", every conversation you have on the subject is clearer and convincing because we all know the guys on the other side are just winging it - or worse - making it up as they go.

What you need to succeed is just a piece of paper with a few columns (3) and a few rows (4 for each round of expected financing) on it. It might help to have 2 or 3 basic business metrics on the page as well, but it's not critical because this exercise is all about funding. Here is the entire matrix:

	Year One	**Year Two**	**Year Three**
BUSINESS METRICS			
REVENUES			
HEADCOUNT			
CURRENT ROUND			
FINANCIAL INVSRS			
STRATEGIC INVSRS			
POST-$ VAL			
MGMT STAKE (%)			
MGMT VALUE ($)			
NEXT ROUND (DATE)			
FOLLOW-ON INVSRS			
NEW INVSRS			
POST-$ VAL			
MGMT STAKE (%)			
MGMT VALUE ($)			
THIRD ROUND (DATE)			
FOLLOW-ON INVSRS			
NEW INVSTRS			
POST-$ VAL			
MGMT STAKE (%)			
MGMT VALUE ($)			

Don't have all the answers at your fingertips? Not to worry – no one else does either. But start the exercise and slowly you'll develop some level of comfort with the process and put up some real numbers on the board. Some may be wishful thinking – but the way I see it is that wishful thinking beats not thinking about and planning for these things by a mile. Remember, in basketball, it's "nothin' but net", but in business, it's ultimately all about "net worth". You can't let your passion warp your long-term perspective because you don't get that many great bites at the apple and you need to make each one count especially when you're riding a winner. Winning takes some getting used to and a lot of hard work, but it's the name of the game.

I'm convinced that not only does every rose (think: customer, not garden) have its full complement of thorns, but that – in the case of start-ups - it seems to be the case that the prettier and larger the rose, the stickier and more challenging its thorns can be. And if there's one situation that's among the most difficult, it's the case of the 800-pound gorilla buyer who's an early and crucial customer (often representing a make-or-break deal for the whole business) and whose demands and requirements would drive a saint insane. If you're starting a business and you haven't seen this particular movie yet, trust me, it's just a matter of time.

Even though we all say that - in the final analysis – what start-ups need more than anything else is paying customers (and presumably the more and the bigger the better), the fact is that one or two big customers don't make a business and, worse yet, they can actually reduce your chances of success in the long run. It's critical to remember that too much dependence on one big customer can: (a) divert your attention from the real prize which is to diversify your business (and your risks) among a broad spectrum of customers of all sizes and shapes; (b) drive you nuts with customization and one-off development and configuration requests which can actually consume precious and scarce resources and end up making your base product offerings not viable or salable to the larger population of "regular" customers; and (c) put substantial and unwarranted downward pressure on your pricing which will reduce the critical early operating margins that are essential to any start-up's survival. You need healthy margins as early in your business as possible to give you some cushion and breathing room and to offset the mistakes and problems that you're sure to encounter.

How you negotiate with and respond to these "big dogs" can impact your fledgling business for years to come and, more specifically, the outcomes of these kinds of negotiations can be critical to: (a) your ability to fully and fairly price your products and services going forward ('cause you ain't gonna make it up on volume); (b) your ability to grow and expand your business according to your priorities and best interests; and (c) most importantly of all, your ability to attract and secure additional strategic and sizable customers who will often be direct competitors of these initial customers.

This is a page I've ripped right out of the book of "be careful what you wish for" and plenty of people will be happy to tell you that big early buyers can be too much of a good thing for a young company in many different ways (staffing and scaling issues, financing and cash flow questions, quality delivery and control problems, etc.), but they don't go on to tell you what to do about it. And there actually are some good reasons for their reluctance to "talk turkey" apart from the fact that many of them are just "consultants" who are basically a bunch of blowhards talking a good game, but disappearing when it's time to actually roll up your sleeves and do something.

One real reason why a lot of the conversation and writing around these crucial issues are so painfully broad and general rather than specific and useful is because there are too many variables and diverse concerns for any one approach or set of answers to cover even the majority of the most typical cases. I understand this "one size doesn't fit all" situation as well as anyone and so my basic plan here is to give you some ideas and strategies for handling just one of the most important and recurring demands that large initial customers can make. It's one that I've found over and over again is likely to raise its ugly head sooner or later in almost every instance regardless of the industry, product/service offerings or other circumstances.

It's the demand for exclusivity and it's a killer. But it's a bullet you can dodge if you're prepared in advance with a series of reasonable explanations as to why it's actually not in that customer's best interests to insist on exclusivity. If you do this well enough, it may actually sound like a favor that you're doing for them rather than a product of the fear for your fleeting future that it's actually designed to mask. And keep in mind that this needs to be an ongoing topic of discussion and reinforced regularly with the customer because when you're dealing with these guys, the negotiations often just begin after the contracts are signed rather than coming to a happy conclusion with the stroke of a pen.

Since efficient and timely access to accurate and extensive information (especially personal and intent data about your customers and prospects) is going to be the major competitive weapon of the future in most competitive marketplaces, and since so many of my own businesses have been in these areas, my suggestions tend to reflect specific arguments that have consistently worked for me in the past in industries as diverse as automotive, insurance, hospitality and technology.

I assure you that these haven't exactly worked overnight and not without some interim concessions and "necessary evils" thrown in, but, in the long run, they will get the job done. Most of your customers will also put a major premium and considerable value and importance on the quality of the information and data that you are employing and providing and their perspective in this regard forms the foundation for several of the more compelling arguments.

So you might say: "I can't work exclusively with you because:

(A) it's important to both of us that the information, research, evaluations, prices, data, analysis, etc. (hereafter the "material") that we are relying upon for you and supplying to you be INDEPENDENT of your organization; and/or

(B) it's important to both of us that the "material" be OBJECTIVE and NEUTRAL and that the outcomes and results derived from the "material" are fair and unbiased in every respect; and/or

(C) it's important to both of us particularly as against third-parties (consumers, regulators, governments, etc.) that we quickly develop an INDUSTRY STANDARD which is agreed-to and accepted by all of the parties in the marketplace and which our company aspires to become; and/or

(D) it's important to both of us that we have enough customers and scale to permit us to make the necessary research and development INVESTMENTS which we could not undertake or afford on behalf of a single client or customer – regardless of its size; and/or

(E) it's important to both of us that we grow quickly enough and have a broad enough customer base that we can actually provide REDUCED COSTS of our products and services (but not artificially depressed prices) because we are able to realize the economies of scale and amortize our capital expenditures over the broadest customer base possible; and/or

(F) it's important to both of us in order to service your requirements on a national basis that we have other customers whose presence in certain parts of the country is larger than yours and whose commitments will justify GEOGRAPHIC EXPANSION into areas where your business alone would be insufficient to support our roll-out or operations.

Keep in mind that there's no simple formula for success or failure in these things. These approaches will help – some better than others – and some may not apply at all. Don't try to use every argument all at once – negotiations can often be wars of attrition and you want to always save a new argument or two for next time so that there will be a next time. But, if you work through each of them and try to determine for your own business (and on your own terms and in your own words) how similar ideas might help support your position, it's safe to say that you'll get a much better outcome than going in blind. If you know the pieces going in, you're much more likely to walk out with at least part of the pie.

Sometimes, by the way, it's clear that you just have to take what you can get now and hope that you can get what you want (and will ultimately need) down the road. If you wait too long or push too hard, you may find that you will just miss the whole deal. So try these arguments and see how well they work for you, but be careful not to be such a hard-ass that you end up throwing out the baby with the bathwater.

TULLMAN'S TRUISMS

YOU DON'T KNOW WHAT YOU CAN GET AWAY WITH UNTIL YOU TRY

I spent some time recently with a very talented and thoughtful team of young entrepreneurs from Pathful (www.pathful. com) who were developing some new analytical tools to help non-technical website owners determine which parts of their websites were effective for them (driving engagement, conversion and ultimately sales) and which other parts either weren't as successful or, worse yet, were actually damaging to their business because they aggravated, frustrated or confused visitors and ultimately turned them off.

This is a bigger problem and a much bigger deal today for business owners than you might imagine (and, most likely, it's a problem for you as well) because – while everyone tells us (regardless of our size or type of business) that we need a website – no one (including the companies who build and host the websites) ever tells us (the site owners) with any precision or detail whether the website is really "working" for us and/or whether it's worth the time and investment which we've made (and continue to make) in it. Try it yourself. If you call up your website developer, provider or host today and ask how your site is doing, at best, you'll get some "up-time" data and maybe some traffic information, but nothing that really deals with the real metrics and ROI of the website.

As I learned more about this new business, one very appealing aspect of their SAAS-based service was how highly automated the back-end processing and reporting systems were going to be and how – as a result – they could cost-effectively offer some basic versions of their products, services and reports at prices which would be reasonably affordable and which would appeal to early-stage businesses (as well as many Mom & Pop businesses) all of which they clearly understood wouldn't and couldn't afford or justify the costs of licensing and implementing some of the higher-end and much more expensive analytics packages which have been in the market for a while. Another of the best aspects of their new offerings was how quick and "easy" they said it would for a business to deploy their software and start getting valuable feedback. They simply had to "add a couple of lines of Java script" to their site and they were ready to roll. Just like implementing some of Google's basic tools.

And that's where I started to get worried that they were about to become victims of their own narrow environment and technical expertise. Because when you're sitting in a start-up incubator or a shared tech workspace killing it with your team and you're all surrounded by dozens (or even hundreds) of other smart, young techies who eat Java script for breakfast, it's a lot like living in an echo chamber lined with mirrors.

Everyone hears what they want and perhaps even what they need to hear in order to keep going, but - by and large - they simply have very little idea of how life actually works outside their bubble in the real (very pedestrian and non-technical) world. Especially if one of your prime market target sectors are young and small businesses. Telling a small business owner that all he needs to do is to "add a little code" to his website is a lot like handing him a pen knife and telling him that it's cheaper and easier to just do his own root canal. And he doesn't even need to make an appointment.

And there's a second, equally problematic, aspect of this type of situation which I call the "curse of creeping functionality". It's driven by talent and enthusiasm and the best of intentions, but it can really hurt a start-up by resulting in product offerings that are too complex and ambitious and way too over-engineered and technical for the larger market. They may suit and please the earliest adopters, but they're gonna freak out the crowd. The fact is that the "boys in the back room" just want to keep on building great code and adding more and more to the company's products, but here's the nasty news: new products and services have to satisfy the immediate needs of prospective customers and current users and not the egos or desires of the company's managers and engineers.

For so many companies today that are tech-based, this is a really difficult growth phase to navigate and it can easily lead to hurt feelings, abrupt departures of key employees and plenty of other problems including a lot of passive-aggressive behavior and foot-dragging from the geeks. But if you're the CEO and you're building the right kind of business, then you've also got to be the customers' and users' advocate; rein in the troops; and make sure that your products meet the market's needs and not the other way around.

Existing users are incrementalists – they are generally at least willing to try system enhancements and updates as long as these are not disruptive of their ongoing activities. New prospects, on the other hand, are always looking for an easy on-ramp and a simple way to start. They don't want to read a book, take a training course, or spend a week getting up to speed – they just want to get started. For the vast majority of customers, too many bells and whistles (products that "can do whatever you want") are not attractive enticements or incentives; they're perceived headaches and anticipated heartburn in the making. Prospects and new customers don't want tools that can do "anything" – that's not a meaningful or useful concept for them – in fact, it's most often off-putting and too vague to help convince them of anything. Basically, they want solutions to serious, finite and obvious needs that they have to solve pressing problems which are important to them. Now I will admit that they may not even know that they have some of these problems until they're "sold" on the need for a solution, but I can also promise you that they want a solution in a box and not a set of D.I.Y. instructions telling them how to build the scaffolding and infrastructure that they'll need to solve their problems.

Now, don't get me wrong. For many companies with the right staff and support, adding a powerful, effective and inexpensive tool like this to their website would be a no-brainer and a very smart thing to do. I understand that not everything can be natural, easy, user-friendly and taste like chocolate. But for the millions of little guys all over the country who really need and could benefit from this kind of objective, third- party review of the value and effectiveness of their sites, identifying the problem for them, but then offering them only a partial solution which they can't take advantage of or implement themselves is a waste of everyone's time and effort.

And yet, if you step back and really look at what the customer's problem is that you are trying to solve (what's the "job" that needs to get done) rather than getting locked into a perspective of focusing on all the great things your new service and software can do and create, it's actually pretty easy to figure out a better answer and a much better offering. In this particular case, the problem is very clear: if the customer is paralyzed or afraid or incapable of adding the couple of lines of simple code to his website, you've got to figure out how to add it remotely (or through a channel partner like BrightTag www.brighttag.com) for him. Once it's there, everything else is easy. I'm thinking something along the lines of a next-generation, no-brainer InstallShield kind of download that the customer just emails to the host of his site although an interesting question is whether those gatekeepers are gonna be happy to help or pains in the ass to get around.

Basically, you've got to solve the WHOLE problem for these little guys and, once you figure out how to do that, you discover that there's a huge, readily scalable market sitting right in front of you. And as long as you entirely solve at least part of the problem, it's not critical at the outset that your solution does everything, addresses all the issues, provides every form of report, etc. That can all come later – but only if you can get a foot or two in the door and get started. This is really what disruptive innovation is all about – start small, listen aggressively, iterate and then scale.

And the best part of this approach is that, once you can eliminate the major barrier to acceptance (the Java script addition to the website in this case) and get yourself onboard, you discover that the bar for substantial success is embarrassingly low. Sometimes simple is more than sufficient for a large segment of the market. Good enough in this case can be more than good enough. You can make this low-end, high- volume, automated version of your product or service easier, simpler, and less robust, etc. because these companies aren't power users or sophisticated buyers; they're customers who would be grateful for any help in this area. And the more hand- holding, explaining, and straightforward analysis that you can do for them, even at the most basic level, the more appreciative and satisfied they will be.

TULLMAN'S TRUISMS

YOUR DOG DOESN'T NEED EMAIL

I'm pleased to report that, even though we're still a few light years away from flying jetpacks and cars that drive themselves, we have officially entered the age of mass customization. Thanks to a couple of powerful new tools and technologies, businesses – large and small – can employ a game-changing approach which enables them to turn a long-time marketing fantasy into an everyday operating reality. It turns out that - in this age of (a) hyper-personalization, (b) readily-available and inexpensive access to interest and intent data, and (c) high-velocity computing – you <u>can</u> actually be all things to all people. And, more importantly, you can tell <u>each</u> and every one of them individually exactly <u>what they want to hear</u> – no more, no less and right to the point. Marketing, media and politics will never be the same.

But it's the businesses - especially smaller companies and start-ups who can't afford the brute force and big money approach which their larger competitors employ (with admittedly mediocre results since dollar bills will never equal brain cells) which should most quickly see what is happening and figure out how to turn these changes into opportunities to (a) reduce their operating costs; (b) maintain or even shrink their headcount without diminishing their ongoing and critical interaction with their customers; and (c) provide faster, more relevant and highly personal products and services to their customers. And – as a result of their stealth, speed and precision (provided they move quickly) – they will be the big winners for the next couple of years until the big, fat corporate players catch on and try to catch up.

But, as with all good things, in order to intelligently and cost-effectively employ mass customization in your business, there are some basic concepts that you'll need to understand (I call these Tullman's "Tenets") and also a few "tricks of the trade" which will help you determine (a) if this is the right strategy for your business and then, if it makes sense to adopt this approach; (b) how to best adapt the fundamental philosophy and the generic process to your customers' specific and requirements and needs.

Tullman's Tenets

(1) There are Only Nine Stories in the Naked City

We all like to think that we are different from everyone else and unique in many special ways. This might be true in some philosophical sense, but to marketers and statisticians, we're pretty much all the same within some very narrow and easily determinable ranges. This is actually nothing new – more than 90 years ago, in 1921, a guy named Georges Polti demonstrated that in the entire history of drama and story- telling throughout all of time, every single tale could fit within one or several of the 36 dramatic categories that he established. When you hear them say that there's nothing new under the sun, this is what they're talking about and yet – in our daily lives – we don't really appreciate how common and recurring certain themes and ideas are.

This lack of common understanding is one of the main tenets of mass customization because it means that – in virtually any situation or evaluation or analysis or sale – there are only a finite (and actually relatively few) things that are right or wrong with anything. The vast majority of behaviors, scores, actions, approaches, etc. all fall within a very limited range of standard deviations and this means that we can immediately shrink what would to an outsider appear to be the insurmountable or massively time-consuming and costly tasks related to responding to; evaluating; selling or otherwise messaging millions of people into a completely manageable and fairly trivial set of responses which apply to and can be persuasively and convincingly communicated to 99% of all the individuals within any targeted population.

And here's the best part – for the few special cases, the unique or crazy people, the frauds and thieves, etc. – you can absolutely forget them. They don't matter and that's the charm of the immutable laws of large numbers. This is how actuaries stay in business. Only idiots and academics worry about the tiny groups at the extreme fringes of any population. Let them be distracted and get all wrapped up in their hair- splitting undies; the name of the game is the greatest good and impact for the greatest number of people. Scale is what sells and what matters and mass customization permits even small players to address and interact with massively scalable audiences.

With tools like these, I guarantee that you can sell shoes to a snake. And when it's done right – the outputs (the messages you're sending) end up being halfway between a fortune cookie and a horoscope. Basically we all want to believe these things because they mostly "fit" and frankly we don't have an alternative or a better option. And, it's always nice to think that you're appreciated and being singled out for personal attention. Hah!

(2) A Few Things are Important, Most are Not

We don't have multi-processing computers built into our heads (yet) and, as a result, we're still pretty much constrained by the limitations of our brains and the fact that basically we can effectively juggle maybe a few balls (or ideas) at once, but frankly not that many. We know in fact that the more choices that people have in a shopping context; the less likely they are to choose anything. If you chase too many rabbits, you're most likely to end up with none and therein lays another important part of the mass customization strategy. The clearer the vision – the fewer the choices – the quicker the decision. Systems that reduce the noise and chatter and simplify the selections and choices for the consumer win.

This is why we still rely on brands – they are mental shorthand for a set of attributes and features that we desire and they save us the time and the brain damage of evaluating and making a new set of choices. Tell me a few important things quickly and convincingly and you're miles ahead of the competition. In fact, the power of a good story and the value of a great brand are exactly the same – they help us put complex facts into a proper context – and by delivering their message with energy, passion and emotion – they make it easy for us to follow along. Simple stories – well told - build powerful long-term connections. And the truth is, by giving us the facts and the "evidence" to support our often foregone conclusions; they address another fundamental human condition. We are far better persuaded by reasons and justifications that we "feel" (rightly or wrongly) that we have reached and discovered on our own than by anything offered in support of the same conclusions by third parties. This is why advertising today needs to attempt to be informational and additive rather than simply persuasive.

(3) More Data is Not the Same as Better Information

Let's face it – we're drowning in data. Big data. Fast data. Global data. But sadly, it's not making us any smarter because having more data isn't the same as having better decision-making information. So, in addition to fewer overall inputs, we need smarter and simpler outputs that we can readily absorb and efficiently act upon. Here again, mass customization can help convert a pile of facts (call it "knowledge if you like – I'd call it "noise") into simple wisdom (recommendations, advice and solutions) and relatively painlessly get us all much further up the learning curve.

But keep in mind that this approach is far from obvious because only a small number of people actually understand the elegance and power of simplicity. The vast majority of us think that something simple must be cheap or insufficient or incomplete. The truth is that excessive elaboration (too much of anything technical) is actually a form of mental pollution. It doesn't clarify our thought processes – it muddies and mucks them up. We need a better and quicker solution.

You can call it "precision guesswork" if you like. We don't really know anything for sure today – we make educated and calculated bets based on what we believe (or what we are convinced of) and what we believe is informed by and based on our experiences, but those experiences can be easily aggregated, simplified and shared primarily because they are so frightfully typical and common. And this sharing is what a mass customization strategy enables – quick, scalable, simple solutions (hopefully smart as well) for the largest audiences possible.

I call this "the consultant in a can" system. We're swamped; we're stumped; we need help and here's the bottom line – something sufficient this Saturday beats the heck out of something super next September. Give me a story and a strategy and keep me moving forward. I need a cure for what ails me most right now – I'm not really interested in your crusade for perfection (or the greatest software never sold) – I want a product or a service that does a few important things for me really well and I want it right now – perfect can wait for another day.

(4) There's an Art to Being Wrong with Confidence – It's called Logic

The final basic element of mass customization is to have the courage of your own convictions. If you don't believe it and believe in it, you're never gonna be successful in selling it to anyone else. Your solution is better than any of the alternatives and provides real immediate value to the users – regardless of how many of them there are and/or how many of them receive only slight variations of the same advice. Don't be embarrassed – don't apologize – just go sell it and see how well you do. You'll be very pleasantly surprised. And if you need a handy attitudinal reminder while you're out there in the field, use one of my favorite mottos: "Sometimes wrong; never in doubt."

For quite a while now, I have been talking about social media and how all businesses need to incorporate a social media strategy into their day-to-day operations. I always added a couple of words of caution to my presentation with one of the main recommendations being that each company needed to "start small and scale" its efforts as its management determined (through relentless trial, error and measurement) what actions were really working (driving engagement, conversion and sales – not keeping the CEO's 22-year old son-in-law/company intern busy for the summer) and which were not. This measured and iterative approach still makes a lot of sense to me when you're talking about adopting new additive tools and technologies for your company. But it's not a life philosophy that makes sense for every business or every entrepreneur who wants to start a business.

Unfortunately, for a lot of entrepreneurs, the phrase "start small and scale" has taken on a life of its own and it's become a business mantra that can lead them astray or – worse yet – create unrealistic and/or inappropriate expectations and pressures on people who just (for a variety of their own good reasons) want to start a new business and create new jobs and opportunities, but who don't necessarily plan - this week at least - on changing the world. Not everything or every business has to be gigantic. Not everything has to happen at light speed. There's actually more to life than just increasing its speed. And, not every product has to cure cancer, taste like chocolate and cost a dollar. Hence, my new suggestion for some of you: it's perfectly O.K. to "start small and snail".

We all have to take a moment to understand that it's completely acceptable for some people (regardless of their skills and talents) to want to do something with their lives that is smaller, simpler and, at least in some ways, less taxing on them and their families and that – even if they only add a few new jobs to the economy and make a few folks happier, healthier, better-trained or educated, etc. – that this is totally cool and their choices don't make them bad or lazy people or disappointments to their parents or to those of us who are so presumptuous that we would have picked a different path for them. We should all stick to picking our own paths – it's tough enough and actually that's my real point.

There are a lot of different ways for someone to be an entrepreneur and as you start down the path, I think that it is very important for you to take the time to decide where you (and the company you want to build) will fit on the spectrum. For your convenience and consideration, I've divided the universe into a few different categories to get you started on the analysis and I've included a few short thoughts and formulations that should help flesh out the categories. Take your time and be brutally honest with yourself (and maybe even consult any other interested parties – family members, significant others, prospective business partners, etc.) – proper alignment now will save much angst and agony later in the process for all concerned.

In addition, you'll find that, once you have made up your mind and picked a path, it's a lot easier to explain your strategy to other people and to avoid that gnawing and nagging feeling that maybe your plans aren't grand or special enough. It's often harder to tell your friends and employees that changes are necessary than to deal with your clients and competitors. Remember you're in this for you (and yours) and not to please other people or have them live vicariously through you. If you look to others for fulfillment, you will never truly be fulfilled. All of this stuff looks easy to the people who don't have to live through it every day and make it happen.

So here's how I see it:

(1) **Happy Camper – Like My Life – Enough is Enough – Work for Myself**
It's Not What You Do, But How You Do It.
To Be Happy, Set Yourself a Goal that Commands Your Thoughts, Liberates Your Energy and Inspires Your Hopes.
If Your Happiness Depends on Money, You Will Never Be Happy with Yourself.

(2) **Trade Offs – Concerned about Work/Life Balance – Family Matters**
Making a Life Consists of More than Making a Living.

(3) **Measured Growth – Careful about What You Grow into – Size Matters**
I Want to See How Big We Can Get Before We Get Bad.

(4) **Run Away Train – Didn't Plan It – Trying to Hang On – Get Some Help**
Speed is Useful Only if You're Running in the Right Direction. All Movement is not Progress and All Change isn't for the Better. You Can't Control the Winds, but You Can Adjust the Sails.

(5) **Speed Demon – Disrupting Existing Markets– Leading the Way Forward**
If Your Team Looks like a Bunch of Ferrets Pumped Up with Double Espressos, You Need to Take a Break.
There's a Point in the Process When the Thrill of the Speed Overcomes the Fear of Failure, but It's not a Happy Point.
It's the Reason that There are Rarely Skid Marks When Start-ups Fail…They Hit the Wall Head First and Full On.

(6) Ruler of the Universe – Changing the World – Nothing Else Matters
People Who Change the World Have an Original and Obsessive Vision. It's More Likely to be Based in their Dreams and Aspirations than in their Experiences, but It's Just as Real.
Too Much is Not Enough for Rulers of the Universe.

It's your choice and it's pretty much within your control as long as you think about it. If you don't control your destiny, you can bet someone else will. Even if it's a long, hard road, it helps to have a vision of where you'd like to be; how you'd like to live; and an idea of how you'll get there. Otherwise, you'll soon learn the wisdom of that old cliché: life is what happens to us while we're making other plans.

TULLMAN'S TRUISMS

DON'T THINK YOU'RE WORKING FOR SOMEONE ELSE

Just about everything today is a double-edged sword. As much as we want passion from our people and a relentless commitment to the "cause", some moderation can be just as meaningful in many cases. We want a single-minded dedication to success, but surging mindlessly ahead can cause just as many serious setbacks as substantial scores over time. Speed doesn't help if you don't know where you're going. In fact, almost anything you do to excess comes back (in pretty short order) to bite you in the butt.

I see this all the time with young companies where the desire to be rapid and responsive makes everything into an emergency (however appropriate that may be) and - too many times – the rush of the urgent (and often immaterial) displaces the attention that needs to be paid to the really important things that will ultimately make a difference for the business. Not every situation needs to be turned into a crisis and not every customer issue or demand is critical and time-sensitive.

As often as not, giving a little time and a little more thought to a measured and smart response to a given situation pays larger dividends in the long run (for you and the customer) than taking a knee-jerk swat at the problem and hoping for the best. So, in certain circumstances, you can actually be too responsive, too reactive, too eager, and too quick for your own good.

But, in all my years of thinking about these things, I never really thought you could be "too" focused. I've said and believed for years that an obsessive focus on a few critical parts of your business was probably the most important discipline that you needed to master in order to succeed. Turns out I was wrong and you can be "too" anything if you're not careful.

My thought always was to be constantly mobilizing "all the wood behind a single arrowhead" so that you could maximize the force and impact of your activities. This is how you avoided being "a mile wide and an inch deep" in your business and essentially diluting your results (or doing a crappy job) on a lot of different things.

Many years ago, the Japanese figured this out in a process that they called the "hard drill" where they knew that they couldn't take on multiple industries because they were too time and resource constrained so they would identify a single industry (think about how they took over the copier business) and then deeply and directly attack that marketplace rather than wasting their efforts on several industries and not making a dent anywhere.

But, these days, there are new critical considerations – principally due to the prospect of aggressive and rapid disruptive innovation which now threatens every market. Because of the low cost of competing and the ease of market entry; because of the speed of change and its discontinuous rather than evolutionary nature; and because businesses are facing both traditional and non-traditional global competitors, the strategy of bearing down and looking straight ahead turns out to risk putting you and your business at a competitive information disadvantage because you literally may not see the competition and the problems coming.

Not only are many of the most serious threats likely to arise from way down the food chain; others are just as likely to jump into your market from adjacent and seemingly tangential sectors where various technical, legal or geographical barriers previously precluded such actions. In the old days, the typical process of competitive responses was a five step progression:

1. Ignore
2. Ridicule
3. Attack
4. Copy
5. Steal

But, if you aren't on the lookout and don't see these guys coming, they're likely to roll right over you before you know what happened. We may have a new Man of Steel these days, but our domestic steel industry was completely destroyed by quick, cheap foreign steel producers who started at the very bottom of the market creating things that no one else even wanted to make and then quickly moved up from that base to take over the entire business.

The bottom line: you've got to pay attention not only to the business you have and the competition that you can see, but also – and maybe even more critically – you've got to keep a sharp eye out for the guys lurking just over the hill who are getting ready to eat your lunch if you're not on the ball. As the saying goes, just because you're paranoid doesn't mean that someone isn't out to get you.

I see way too many young entrepreneurs spending way too much time and energy worrying about their furniture, fixtures and equipment (FF&E in the trade) way too early in the growth and development of their fledgling businesses. This isn't the way to grow anything that lasts. I like to say: "Let's rob the train before we spend our time splitting up the loot."

In the same way that your company needs to have a changing set of core values as you grow, you need to focus on things at the outset that are a lot more significant than color schemes and coffee tables. There's a right time for everything and – while it's true that people need a decent place to come to work – it's a lot more important to give them some very good and compelling reasons to come to work than to worry about what the place looks like when they get there. Offices are a necessary part of the deal, but they're not sufficient to get the business built if you aren't far more focused on your people and your culture. It's the messaging, not the materials that matter.

Alignment ultimately trumps architecture and design. The reason the Aeron chair is so well-known from the dot.com days and such a cliché today isn't because it was a beautiful and well-built chair; it's because these $1200-plus chairs were the complete embodiment of the wretched excess and stupid spending that characterized the self-absorption and arrogance of that time. Build your palace after you're profitable.

In the meantime, there are some things to keep in mind when you are trying to figure out how to have the environment you're putting together support and reinforce the culture and the values that you want to embed in your business from the beginning. This isn't easy to do with scarce resources and limited time, but it's possible if you do what you can and don't overdo it. And please, if you remember just one thing above all, don't try to do something cheaply that you shouldn't do at all. If your budget is brutal, do a few things well and forget the rest. In the long run, quality and smart choices matter most.

In the last ten years or so, with my design partner, Barbara Pollack, we've built out over 300,000 square feet of space for various businesses; made as many mistakes as you can make in the process; and learned a lot about what not to do as well. Here are a few of the most important take-aways.

(1) The Ten Second Test – First Impressions Matter

It's a *Head & Shoulders* world – we rarely get a chance to make a second impression so you need to make sure that the first impression people have of your business is at least favorable - and ideally - fabulous. At Flashpoint, the elevators you ride to get up to our main space are tired, slow and tiny. I always tell guests (as we're riding up) that they shouldn't be concerned because the 70 year-old elevators are the oldest technology they're going to see at our college. Once they hit the main lobby upstairs, they're immediate blown away by the technology, the art and the wide open spaces in front of them. It's a visceral reaction and it's effective 99% of the time. Bankers and accountants are the rare exception - they immediately wonder how much all this amazing stuff cost – and they have no imagination to boot.

(2) The Ultimate Audience(s)

While it's clear that you're building your workplace primarily for your employees, it's critical to remind yourself and your people that virtually every visitor to the space is a crucial part of your audience for one reason or another. And I really do mean almost "every" one.

I'm not talking simply about clients, customers, vendors, media, parents, students, business partners, regulators and other employers, I talking about everyone who comes to visit. We once saved a deal and closed on the last day of the month because our FedEx guy returned (basically on his own) to make a second re-delivery at our offices.

When we asked him why he would go out of his way at the end of his day to do that, he said he knew how seriously our receptionist took her job; he knew how important what we were waiting for was to us; and he wanted to do his part because he loved coming to our offices. He said it was one of the few places he visited where you could feel the energy and enthusiasm when you got off the elevator and you could just tell that everyone just cared. Culture is contagious and it starts at the front door.

(3) The Main Message – 3 Key Themes

As you start to think about the environment, the impressions, and the culture that you're trying to create in your space, you need to appreciate that you're going to have to make some tough choices and pick a fairly narrow and focused message which you want to communicate clearly and consistently throughout the entire facility. You can't make everyone happy and you can't be all things to all people so you need to decide on what's most important to you and to the business and take your best shot. The worst possible strategy is always the straddle. Trying to address too many constituencies or too serve too many masters ends up with a messy, muddled and misplaced message. Go with what makes you proud and what you feel is the way to put your best foot forward. At least you'll know that one person is happy with the result.

The theme of your message will depend on the nature of your business and the phase of its development as well as a number of other factors. There are obviously many different themes, but 3 of them are commonly used in instances of start-ups or turnarounds where – if you do it right – you have a decent shot at starting with a relatively clean slate and inventing or re-inventing the vision as you go. The big 3 are these:

(a) Functionality – Transformation and Change
(b) Authenticity – All about Work and Accountability
(c) Aspiration – Creative Expression, Execution and Craft

Each of our last 3 projects presented a different challenge.

(a) *Kendall College* was a 75-year old failing college in desperate need of a turnaround and a transformation. Everything about the rebuilding of Kendall had to do with creating a flawless and technically advanced platform for the faculty of chefs to teach their culinary magic to successive generations of passionate students in a unique learning environment. Everything in the brand-new facility spoke to precision, professionalism and minute attention to detail and those messages formed the heart of the reborn culture of performance and excellence.

(b) *Experiencia*'s two "worlds" – Exchange City (a collection of operating business in a 20,000 square foot "city") and Earthworks (4 distinct "natural" environments filled with real animals) – were practical work and learning environments for inner-city 4th and 5th graders, but they couldn't succeed as plastic or pretend places or as Disney-like fantasies. They needed to be grounded and serious places where the visiting students would achieve new levels of authentic responsibility, performance accountability, and team-based, peer- driven learning that they had never experienced before. Watching the students rise to the occasion and seize the new opportunities before them was an unforgettable daily experience.

(c) And finally, *Tribeca Flashpoint Academy*'s message to a population of under-appreciated and under-served students – surrounded and encouraged by their true peers for the first time in their lives – and challenged by the newest facilities, technologies and industry tools available – was very clear. The sky alone was the limit and everything was within their grasp if they made the commitment, had the passion, and did the work. It was all about craft, execution and aspirations – not to say dreams – and it became a special home for creative expression, collaborative and immersive learning, and the next generation of digital leaders for our country.

And when all the dust settles and all the paint dries and you finally get a chance to catch your breath and see what you've built - what you'll realize at the end of the journey is that it's in the building process itself – with all the messy twists and turns, upsets and mistakes – and all the pains and joys – all the highs and lows – that your team ultimately comes together and the fundamental foundation of your culture is formed.

It turns out that what you built is nowhere near as important as how you and your team went about the process of getting it built. Cultures are funny that way. You can try to explain it to people, but you can't understand it for them – they've got to live it to make it real.

47 – HOW TO TALK YOURSELF OUT OF A JOB

It's time to bring back *The Peter Principle*. Not the BBC TV series, but the idea that meritocracies work to eventually promote people beyond the level of their actual abilities. And this time, it's not as a management concept about premature or inappropriate promotion – it's as a warning to everyone under 30 who are not grateful for the jobs they have and who want more – especially too much more too soon. If ever there was a time to be really careful about what you wish for, it would be right now.

So what's *The Peter Principle* anyway? Of course you can *Google* it, but *Wikipedia* is much faster and easier. The simplest phrasing is that "employees tend to rise to their level of incompetence." It was initially a humorous formulation until people started to see how accurate a description it turned out to be. But no one really talks about it anymore today although it's far more prevalent than ever in our government; our military; and especially in our schools.

And, if you're young and not careful, it's a quick way to lose your job. In fact, I just had to sit through a very painful and embarrassing meeting where a perfectly decent and talented young man was unsuccessfully asking for his old job back. But his old job had been filled. And basically, because he had vocally and aggressively sought the new job that he really wasn't right for; he had essentially "hoisted himself on his own petard". This one you'll want to definitely *Google* which will take you straight to *Wikipedia*.

Young people today seem to understand only half of the phrase "up or out", but it's a fact of life. I encourage everyone to aspire to greater things and to take their best shot – but only (a) when they are prepared; (b) when they understand what they're asking for; and (c) when they're prepared to live with the consequences of things not working out.

So don't be in such a hurry that you leap before you look. Before you jump for that new job; you just might want to honestly answer these questions for yourself.

(1) Make Sure You Understand What the *Whole* New Job Entails

If you just focus on the perks and the apparent rewards of a job, you often miss the whole package and especially the baggage that comes with the benefits. Especially in sales, there's a whole lot of ugly lifting that goes with getting the job done. I had a client once who won some hugely profitable government contracts and it seemed like a piece of cake. Then I spent a week on the road with him going from one Army base to another entertaining procurement people in cheap, smoky bars for hours on end and dealing with a stream of insufferable self-important assholes and I decided that life was way too short for that shit and you couldn't pay me enough to put up with it for a second. He knew it too, but it was a choice he had made and it came with the job.

(2) Make Sure You Can Do the Job

Hope and wishful thinking aren't good tools for advancement. I suppose that in our dreams we all think that we can do anything, but in the real world our "can do's" have to keep up with our "want to's" or we end up in deep doo doo. This is where honest assessment (and maybe even asking some other people whose opinion and judgment you respect) comes into play. The very last thing you want to do is to test the depth of the pool with both feet – it's a great way to end up all wet - even assuming that you don't drown. As they say in the South: "if wishes were Porsches, poor boys would drive".

(3) Make Sure You Really Want the Job

The grass is almost always greener. It's like guys watching TV – they know what's on – but they <u>want</u> to know what <u>else</u> is on. Travel and time out of the office sounds great until you miss the first few family occasions, a few school recitals, and spend a few too many rancid nights in the *Red Roof Inn*. Other jobs are so stressful and so 24/7 that the sacrifices they entail (family, friends, etc.) simply aren't worth it in the long run. There's always more work – you've only got one family.

In addition, some jobs look easy from the outside and some may actually just be easy. But you'll find that the hardest work is actually to do nothing or next to nothing. And here's the truth – real happiness doesn't come from doing easy work or just phoning it in. It comes from doing hard work really well. If you don't put the effort into something, you never really know and appreciate what it's worth. And remember that your work and how you feel about it has a lot to do with your sense of self – if you'd rather be doing anything but your work; find something else to do.

(4) Make Sure It's a Real Job that Matters

Sometimes, the easiest way to get someone to shut up and get them out of your hair is to say "yes". You want to be sure that you're not ending up with a make-work job and some lip service that your boss created just to stop the constant chatter. You need to make sure what you're doing matters. Otherwise, you might as well be Dolly Parton's feet. It's great to throw yourself into things and work hard at something, but you want to work hard at something that's worth doing.

In addition, in today's economy, you've got to look at each job through two distinct lenses. Does it have meaning? Does it have value? If no one values or cares about the results of your efforts, it may be meaningful to you, but does it really matter to the business or your bosses? If not, it won't be around for long. In the book and newspaper business, and a world of user-generated crap, I think that real editors must ask themselves these kinds of questions every day and I bet that they don't like the answers.

(5) Make Sure You Know Who You'll Be Working With

Some people you may get stuck working with (above or below you) can turn the best job in the world into a miserable experience. I'd rather work with tree stumps than some of the people I've had to deal with over the years. I think that some people are only alive today because it's against the law to kill them. Try not to end up working with or for them. And while you're at it – try not to work for someone who has more problems than you do.

(6) Make Sure that Management is Committed

It's not easy to look a gift horse in the mouth – especially one that you begged for, but you need to make sure before you sign up that management and the company will provide what you need to succeed: funding and other resources; authority to get things done; enough time and runway; and, most importantly, some agreed-upon metrics for what will constitute success. Without the proper tools, time, and a measurable set of objectives and goals; you'll be chasing your tail in no time.

(7) Make Sure that You not Getting Just Enough Rope to Hang Yourself

I don't want to be too cynical, but here's another fact of life: it's a lot harder to have to flat out fire someone (especially someone you'd like to keep, but can't afford) than it is to let them work themselves out of a "new" job that just doesn't end up working out. Believe me, it happens more than you'd imagine.

So, here's the bottom line: do your homework <u>before</u> you open your mouth and ask for that new position. It will save you a lot of heartache and maybe your current job as well. Sometimes not getting what you think you desperately want is the best break of all.

TULLMAN'S TRUISMS

YOU CAN'T TALK YOUR WAY OUT OF PROBLEMS YOU BEHAVE YOURSELF INTO

Iwrote recently in these posts that originality is overrated and that it's a lot easier, less costly and more productive to be an innovator (making the wheel spin faster and with less friction) than an inventor (trying to come up with the next great wheel). And I certainly still believe that. But, it's even smarter to find someone's else's great idea (which has already demonstrated some traction and success) and to quickly put your personal twist and stamp on it and make it your own. In today's competitive world of fast followers, constant iterative improvements, and repeated riffs on every product and service, no one thinks of this approach as "stealing" anymore. It's a just another form – like imitation - of financial flattery. And today, the smartest players have built entire businesses and strategies around systematizing and streamlining this routine of rapid rip-offs in order to make sure that their competitive entries will win the race.

The guys at *Rocket Internet* in Germany would probably say that they invented this approach and they have certainly been at it for many years with great success. They've sold "clone" companies to *eBay*, *Groupon*, *eHarmony*, etc. But, when you look carefully at their strategy, you can immediately see that they've focused almost entirely on one vector – geography – as the dimension along which they will launch their competitive businesses. If someone has a great U.S.-based business (like *Groupon*, for example, in the old days), these guys will build and launch a *Groupon*-clone in their marketplace as quickly as possible and hope that, in addition to being a local success because it's already a proven approach - if they grow it fast enough - then one day *Groupon* will come along and buy their business instead of launching a belated competitive entry into the space. And, of course, this is exactly what has happened for them several times already.

But, when you "slide to the side" and decide to attack adjacent and related market opportunities, it turns out that geography is only one of many possibilities and each of the possible variables presents open-ended chances to build additional highly-successful and cost-effective versions of the core product or service. I have found, however, that very few businesses of any size or maturity (but especially young businesses) do anything more than a cursory and sporadic examination of these kinds of prospects because they have no procedures in place to make these reviews happen on a regular basis and no tools to help them organize and structure their analysis.

The truth is that the whole thing is a lot easier and more straightforward than you would think, but you do have to commit to doing it and you have to make sure that the entire management team buys into the process. That said, every single business will have expansion adjacencies along 5 basic vectors including geography. The first part of the program is to understand the vectors and how they apply to your business in particular.

The 5 vectors in the simplest form are as follows:

WHO?
Types and Composition of Customers and Other Purchasers
Second and Third Tier Direct and Derivative Types of Users
Demographic Aggregations and Other Differentiated Groups
Un-Served or Under-Served Populations

WHAT?
Product or Service Additions or Extensions
Product Mixes, Packages or Bundles, Pricing & Discount Variances
New Applications and Uses – Different Degrees of Utilization
New Forms of Access and Slicing/Dicing of Offerings
New Data Products and Solutions Generated by Core Activities

WHERE?
Anywhere – Geographical
Everywhere – Global and Ubiquitous
Mobile – Remote – Free of Place or Other Restrictions

HOW?
Changes in Organization
Changes in Delivery or Service Processes – Degrees of Interaction
Networks and Collaborative Contributions and Consumption
Changes in Available and Employed Technologies
Changes in Partners, Vendors, Agents, Distributors

WHEN?

Any Time
All the Time
Real Time
Persistent – Without Asking – Location-Based or Triggered

I'm sure that within these generic buckets there are many additions, variations and other increments as well, but these five are a good start to kick off the investigation for any company.

Keep in mind that it's far more important to get the process started and to then build in additional detail and complexity rather than waiting until some "perfect" and all-inclusive framework has been developed by too many participants (or a committee or two) over too long a period of time during which interval nothing gets accomplished.

The second part of the program is to determine whether and which of the identified opportunities are "ripe" in terms of your timing, your available resources, the competing or conflicting internal opportunities, the external competitive considerations, and the relative value/potential contribution and risks of each choice.

These considerations can also be readily organized into a basic time and action decision matrix.

WIN BIG (RIGHT ACTION, RIGHT TIME)	**MISSED OPPORTUNITY** (RIGHT ACTION, WRONG TIME)
WASTED EFFORT (WRONG ACTION, RIGHT TIME)	**LOSE BIG** (WRONG ACTION, WRONG TIME)

TIME

After these broad cuts are made, you can then weigh the relative impact of the other considerations listed above in reaching your final decisions.

TULLMAN'S TRUISMS

INNOVATORS SEE WHAT EVERYONE ELSE HAS SEEN, AND THINK WHAT NOBODY ELSE HAS THOUGHT

49 – WIKI-WORK: FREE TO BE WHERE I WANT

I'm convinced that if, by virtue of someone's magic wand, we instantly had freely-transferable (and truly portable) and reasonably-priced insurance coverage for everyone (regardless of prior conditions and other similar insurance company scams and dodges) who was presently gainfully employed in the United States, we would instantly see two amazing occurrences:

(1) a GIGANTIC movement to new jobs, new start-up businesses and other new and exciting opportunities by millions of employees who are presently trapped in horrible, useless and unproductive jobs because they (and their families) are prisoners and/or hostages of their existing insurance coverage and their prior medical histories; and

(2) an equally ENORMOUS boost in overall growth and productivity as well as in our nation's GNP as the talents, energies and skills of these insurance "slaves" were suddenly freed up and applied to valuable, innovative and exciting new ventures of every size and shape.

There's a great deal of conversation these days about why productivity increases and technology advancements are no longer resulting in improved median income levels for huge segments of the population and why only a precious few people and businesses keep getting richer and richer as a result of these drivers. It turns out that for many years and until very recently even the best economists were misled by the purely coincidental parallel movements of productivity improvements, job growth and increases in median income. It turns out that there's no necessary connection and that productivity or technology improvements don't have to necessarily help or financially benefit the vast majority of us. Life still isn't fair or – as that great old William Gibson saying goes – you might say "the future is already here – it's just not very evenly distributed".

Another huge time sink is the constant conversations about skills gaps and the need to retrain zillions of workers to equip them for 21st century jobs. I don't feel that these concerns are misplaced; it's just that - when entrepreneurs look at issues like these rather than bureaucrats and politicians – we focus on the lowest hanging fruit and the solutions that can give us immediate results and the most bang for our bucks. The real name of the game is to overcome the horrible resource displacement that's a product of our stupid politicians and our restrictive and anti-competitive laws and policies and of the antiquated ideas about insurance coverage, education, etc. that prevent the kinds of real changes and simple solutions that could make quick and comprehensive contributions to our overall economy and to the economic well-being of millions.

I've said my piece about insurance, but consider that the entire world can access educational videos now anywhere and anytime except in one place – in our school classrooms – where state restrictions driven by teacher union lobbyists prevent even smart and forward-looking teachers – from using these "free" resources in their classrooms to provide their students with the "best of breed" kinds of instruction that are now available. As hard as this is to believe, in states like Illinois, "virtual" instruction has to be delivered by an Illinois state-certified instructor. Interstate commerce – forget about it. Globalization – don't bring that stuff in my house. And as to the morons who are our political representatives – all I can say is that: "if horses could vote, there would never have been cars".

The truth is that we've got plenty of talent, plenty of skills and plenty of people in this country right now – but huge numbers of workers are in the wrong places doing the wrong jobs – and all because we haven't figured out two crucial things: how to increase their mobility so they can move to better positions and better paying jobs (portable insurance for a starter) and, in the case of the millions of place-bound and otherwise location-challenged workers - how to bring the jobs to them which I call for ease of reference Wiki-Work (web-distributed, massive scale, collaborative work executed in bits and pieces) to effectively recapture millions of man hours of lost time and productive effort.

The models and examples are there. The solutions are fairly obvious and not costly. There are entrepreneurs just waiting in the wings all over the world to jump on these problems. The question is when and whether we have the will and the courage to make the changes that will make a better world for generations to come.

I like to think that the best entrepreneurs are masters of cutting to the chase. They're very focused, of course, but more importantly they're especially efficient because they don't really have any other choice. Scarce resources, limited time, and a regularly shrinking bank account do a whole lot for your concentration. And the non-stop streams of decisions (large and small) which they face every day are roughly like living in a batting cage with a machine firing fastball pitches at your head every 15 seconds. It means they've got to be 'on purpose" and "on point" all the time. Patience isn't exactly a virtue in this kind of frantic fast-forward environment and tolerance – especially of time-wasting doofuses – is a very rare commodity.

In addition, because entrepreneurs live in a world where they need to be constantly calculating opportunity costs, the smartest ones are always asking themselves the same two questions:

(1) Is what I'm doing right now moving us forward toward the goal; and
(2) Is what I'm doing right now the highest and best use of my time and talents?

Frankly, if you're not asking yourselves these same questions at least a couple of times a day, then your people and your business are running your life and making your choices for you instead of the other way around which is how it should be. You always want to run the business based on your outbox and not your inbox.

It's absolutely true that (starting with Steve Jobs) some of the sharpest and most effective CEOs I have known over the last 30 years might seem like arrogant, asocial and abrupt assholes to most people (and that's when they're in a good mood), but, in their hearts (or what's left of them), they're just aggressively optimizing their time and their opportunities on a continual basis and constantly assigning new priorities to things in real time. They aren't being rude or dismissive; they're just attentive to things that they regard at that moment as more important. They're doing what they think is right – right at that moment – no more, no less and no promises as to what the next moment will bring. That's just how it works.

To say that they don't suffer fools lightly is a gross understatement. The truth is that they regard most people as something between a nuisance and a necessary evil. But the fact is that we need leaders like this to make important things happen and they can't all be charming social butterflies even if they had the time which, of course, they don't. As the old saying goes: "money doesn't come from singing. It comes from work."

So it usually falls to other people in the organization to help the fiercely focused founders and CEOs figure out how to deal with the people who are simply doofuses, masters of make-work, and/or wizards of window-dressing and who, for better or worse (and mainly for worse), are not only necessary evils; they're generally part of the whole package that comes with your decision to accept third-party financing whether it's high-end angel investors, private equity groups or traditional venture investors.

If you take their money, you get to take all the crap that comes right along with it and you're supposed to smile at that prospect. Thank you, sir. May I have another? But, smiling or shrugging (just don't get caught sulking), every entrepreneur needs to figure out how to deal with these people because they're here to stay. It's not easy (it's a little like putting out a fire in your hair with a hammer), but it does help to understand who you're dealing with and how you can help. Frankly, anything that you can do as a senior team member to help your fiercely focused CEO manage this process and also to run interference for the rest of the folks on the team couldn't be more valuable.

First, and foremost, remember who you're going to actually be dealing with from day-to-day.

I guess there's a version of the old "bait and switch" routine in every business – the car guys may be the masters, but the VCs and PE guys aren't very far behind in the BS business. You start out talking to a guy who could buy a small country and end up working with people who can't approve a pepperoni pizza for a party without checking with personnel. It's a rude awakening and disappointing for sure – but it's just another part of the business that you need to get used to. The trick is to get the rules of engagement straight at the outset and to not let the turkeys get you down.

Second, you need to remember that these folks basically have never begun or run anything.

By and large, you'll learn that they are consumed with matters and minutia of form over substance. They worry much more about font sizes and folders than about the actual facts and figures of the business. It's all about presentations and the "process" rather than real prospects and progress. None of these guys wants to give their Emperor(s) the bad news. I call this the doctrine of "no new news is ever good news". Their absolute worst nightmare is to EVER be the bearer of changes, surprises or any bad news. They know only too well what happens to the messenger.

Third, generally the players that you're unlucky enough to get stuck with really don't have day jobs.

As far as I can tell, their main occupation (other than making work for you) is to somehow justify their own positions. They can turn the simple scheduling of meetings (the more the merrier) into major undertakings and marathons of telephone and email tag. And they think the meetings themselves are the end game and that counting meetings counts – rather than what gets done in the meetings. And it gets worse. Everything they touch has to be over-analyzed; repeatedly chewed over; and ultimately cleared with everyone including the dog in the lobby. It's a painful, time-wasting process.

Finally, I really wasn't kidding about the pizza. These people have absolutely no ultimate authority to do or approve anything (other than hiring outside consultants on your dime) without running back and clearing it with a multitude of higher-ups. The only way that you can ever lose your job at one of these investment firms is by saying "yes" to something. No one ever lost their job by saying "no" and that's not going to change in our lifetimes. So it's pretty much a waste of your time and your breath to ask these guys for anything since they can't write the check in any event. You don't want to be dealing with the monkey when the organ grinder is in the room.

So, what can you do to keep things moving forward for the business in spite of these people?

(1) You can't completely ignore them, but you can take your time in responding and this will actually save you time and effort in the long run because – as often as not – they'll never follow up and pursue many of their demands.

(2) You can do whatever you can to contain and limit their involvement (and thereby protect at least some of your team's time) by insisting on being the funnel for all their interactions with and inquiries to the team.

(3) As a test, you can initially respond to certain requests simply and quickly and then determine whether anyone is actually reading, reviewing and/or acting upon any of the submitted materials. Much of the time you'll never hear another word on the subject because it's likely that no one will even be looking at the stuff requested.

(4) But, sadly, here's the one thing you can't do: you actually can't try to go around these mini-gatekeepers in order to try to get to the real decision makers because – just like in any classic John le Carre espionage novel – it turns out that everyone on their side (top to bottom) is a part of the program and needs to preserve the fiction that their plans, processes and procedures actually make sense and work. No one, including the Emperor, wants to ever hear otherwise.

TULLMAN'S TRUISMS

THEY HAVE TO PAY YOU, BUT THEY DON'T HAVE TO THANK YOU

I've always been partial to Thumper's Dad's advice about communication. In case you don't recall it from the *Bambi* movie, his Dad said: "If you can't say something nice, don't say nothin' at all" - at least as Thumper recalled it. And, as it happens, this is pretty good advice for small talking animals, but it's a really bad way to run your company. You can't build a successful business based on a culture that values quiet, courtesy and consensus over honest conversations, constructive criticism and confrontations where necessary. Politely keeping the peace can't ever trump telling the truth. The best operators know two things for certain: (1) the truth only hurts when you don't tell it and (2) the truth only hurts when it should. I realize that sometimes it's very hard to tell the truth, but it's just as hard to hide it and a whole lot less productive.

White lies and other pleasantries are worthless – they're a lot like eating junk food – you get a temporary lift, but no nourishment; the problem persists; the emptiness returns; and nothing gets done in the meantime. And when you encourage people to lie even a little, you learn quickly that people who will lie for you will eventually lie to you. Better a few bruises and battered egos than a bankrupt business based on bullshitting each other. And honestly, it's just so much easier for everyone because when you always tell the truth, you never have to waste time and energy trying to remember your lies.

Frankly, an aggressive culture where people stand their ground and argue their cases makes for much better ultimate decisions as long as people are arguing for the right reasons. The right reasons are to get to the truth and the best results for the business and not because people need to be right and won't shut up until they grind everyone down and wear everyone else out. Make your point; say your piece; and sit your butt down. Don't argue with the truth.

You want your people to fearlessly face the facts. As one of the great old Hollywood moguls used to say: "I want my people to tell me the truth even if it costs them their jobs". But seriously, unpleasant facts don't fade away when you ignore them – they fester – and refusing to look at them won't change the situation or improve things until you do something about them. Facts may change, but the truth never does. And waiting only makes things worse. It's a funny thing about the truth – the truth doesn't have a time of its own. There's never a better or best time to tell someone the truth – the time for truth is always <u>now</u>.

I think all of the foregoing comes down to a few simple "rules" which you need to share (somewhat obsessively) with all of your people (not just newbies in orientations) on a regular and recurring basis. My suggested and very basic rules are as follows:

(1) Tell the Truth

No shades, no strokes, no "smoothing" the news or softening the blows – give it to me simple and straight. Figures don't lie, but they often don't tell the whole story. Make sure that the metrics don't get in the way of a clear message. As they say, everyone is entitled to their own opinion, but the facts are the facts – you don't get to pick and choose them.

(2) Tell It Timely

Nothing ugly really improves over time. Don't wait to bring me bad news. The sooner and shorter the better. I need a brief, not as book. Nothing elaborate – just accurate information delivered on time and in time.

(3) Tell Everyone

Don't assume that everyone else (or anyone else) necessarily knows what you know. Spread the word. In addition to the general virtues of transparency and making sure that eventually the message does get thru to the right people; going wide makes it more likely that meaningful and actionable information will also get to people who need whether you even realize that or not.

(4) Tell It 'til Someone Listens

I don't think that, in most businesses, you can <u>ever</u> over-communicate relevant and time-sensitive data. But you will often encounter people who fall into two problem piles: (a) people who don't want to say what nobody wants to hear; and (b) people who don't want to hear what needs to and has to be said and spread throughout the organization. These folks are master manipulators and they typically follow the standard three-step routine in dealing with "inconvenient", but sadly true facts: (i) first they aggressively ridicule; (ii) then they violently resist; and finally (iii) they get with the program – claim that they knew it all along – and treat things as obvious and self-evident. You need to keep spreading the word until you're sure that you've done as much as you can reasonably do to let the folks in charge know what you know. If they don't listen after that, so be it. It's frustrating and depressing, but in many businesses, it's a fact of life. As Bruce Springsteen says: "When the truth is spoken and it makes no difference – something in your heart goes cold". After a while, if it's clear that you're wasting your breath, find a better place to be.

(5) Tell It All the Time

And finally, truth-telling is not a sometime thing. As with everything else that matters in your business, it's an everyday, all day part of creating and maintaining an environment where the organization learns and grows and where things continue to improve through a constant iterative process. You can't make innovation through iteration work if you don't have a constant and accurate flow of data telling you what's working and what's not and where you're going wrong.

SOON IS NEVER AS GOOD AS NOW

In today's frantic, fast-forward environment of accelerated discovery of everything combined with the pressures of the constant quest for the newest "new' and for exponential excitement and stimulation on steroids, it's hard to know what a start-up should try to hang on to and make its own. We're in a time where the rate of abandonment is ten times faster than the rate of adoption for new mobile applications across every material age cohort. We're all great grazers these days, but we're harder and harder to corral for the duration. It seems clear that nothing is "the future" for very long these days and the cycle time between blips as well as the mean time between surprises (good and bad) keeps shrinking. In the world of 6 to 15 second videos, Andy Warhol's old 15 minutes of fame seems like an eternity and a tired remnant from another time.

Where everyone's trying to make the biggest splash, it's way too easy to lose sight of what really matters in building value for your business. You can easily lose the substance if you're spending all your time chasing shadows and shout-outs. You've got to set a steady course and a strong pace, but you can't get ahead of yourself – you want to move without undue haste, but without rest or interruption as well. I know that today – probably more than ever - immediate user engagement is certainly a critical component for a successful business because it's a race and no one is going to wait for you, but the truth is that, even in the near term and certainly in the long run, simply novelty, notoriety or even having the biggest, boldest launch in the history of man won't get the most critical job done. The trick is to live a lot longer than your launch. Even the best launches (think of Steve Jobs and *Apple* of old) are like forest fires or tornadoes – there's a lot of light, heat, sucking and blowing at the beginning and at the end, if you're not careful, you'll lose your business and/or your house.

There's no doubt that customer engagement is essential, but sustainable user/customer retention (which doesn't need to be maintained constantly maintained by one-off efforts and/or repeated, massive and costly marketing salvos) is the whole ball game. Increasing retention isn't easy, but it's a lot easier to achieve when you understand the basic behavior drivers involved and then build your own program to support and optimize these types of connections and incentives for your users to return and remain.

The best and most successful players in this area are masters of what I call "manufactured addiction". It's the art of making sure that your users will love you <u>even more</u> tomorrow than they did yesterday. And all it takes to succeed is a basic understanding of human nature and a plan that capitalizes on some of our most basic emotions.

Here's the short list of the fundamental ideas and the emotional "drivers" that your engagement and retention plan should incorporate:

(1) We are basically lazy at heart. We'd rather have simple and stupid things done for us than do them ourselves. Especially boring and repetitive things. We'll happily exchange our loyalty for improvements in our productivity, savings of time and effort, or other actual dollar benefits. Everything today is a "deal" – we engage in constant calculations of the personal and typically immediate value of various proposed transactions – and – as often as not - we make these repeated determinations automatically and almost unconsciously.

(2) We hate to waste our time and we especially hate redundancy. It's like watching paint dry except that paint only has to dry once. How many times have you found yourself in situations where you are asked to supply (in one way or another) the same information again and again. I think that (other than making well people physically ill) requiring millions of us to repeatedly complete ridiculously redundant documents may be the most horrible injury that hospitals have regularly heaped upon the human race. Socially-engineered tools and underlying systems (like the omnipresent *Facebook Connect* button) which avoid the constant need for new site users to re-supply the same data over and over again and which have the additional bi-lateral benefit of saving programming costs and other work for the owners and operators of literally more than 10 million independent websites and services to date are extremely powerful connectors and hugely successful retention devices.

(3) We don't know when to quit. Once we have mentally "invested" our time and energy into any enterprise or activity, we are much less likely to abandon it. We believe for no good reason that even trivial actions over time have a cumulative value (although we couldn't quantify it or explain what it might be) and that as a result of our steadfastness and continuity, we're sure to get lucky and be rewarded someday. In addition, we seem to always believe that our switching costs are much higher and more onerous than they actually are – especially in today's highly-portable and mobile world of the cloud. We're just suckers for the daunting power of the *status quo;* we are resistant to all unnecessary changes; and – as a result - we are virtually incapable of bestirring ourselves and choosing any less-than-overwhelmingly-compelling alternative to doing almost anything. And even the most useless, trivial and fleeting rewards (ranks, powers, badges, scores, etc.) make the choice to leave just that much harder.

(4) We don't want to disappoint our friends. The more "connected" we believe we are in any context to numbers of others (especially our friends, neighborhoods, families and peers), the less likely we are to cease an activity and the longer we will remain – even when the activity or venture has largely ceased to hold any personal interest for us or provide any real value to us. Misery loves company and we often underestimate the power of peer and other social pressures even among grown-ups. It's the contagious power of the crowd. And, for ourselves, there is a palpable (and demonstrably solipsistic) sense that

- in "leaving" even the most useless environment, website or other fruitless activity – we are abandoning our "friends" and depriving them in some sense of the benefit of our continued presence. As if they really knew or cared.

(5) We all do much more from habit than from rational and conscious choice. The repeated use of and reliance upon any product or service tends to take on the attributes and associated behaviors of a habit and habits for humans are very hard to break and die hard. When habits are reinforced by peer pressure, collective action and other group dynamics, the "locked in" nature of the commitment becomes even more difficult to dislodge. We don't appreciate how "sneaky" and powerful habits can be because they begin as weak tendencies (which we think of as intentional preferences) and their power isn't readily apparent to us until they become so strong and controlling that we discover they are actually embedded and compulsive behaviors which are very hard to break. Make your product or service easy to use, readily accessible and friction-free and you'll own me.

(6) We all want to be leaders, not losers, and everyone today keeps score. This is why cab drivers who couldn't necessarily count to 10 can quote you precise opening night movie box office grosses for their favorite films. We're competitive – especially with our friends – and (at least on both coasts) in many cases, it's even more important that our friends lose (place lower on any list you choose) than it is that we win. It's a little like the two guys running away from a hungry bear. You don't have to beat the bear – you just have to outrun the other guy. This means that, while leader boards have a certain definite appeal, peer-to-peer comparisons are far more compelling because – while you may not know the leaders – you always know want to know where you stand relative to your friends. I call this the "peer-spective" approach because although everything is relative, only things that are relevant to us as individuals will really compel or change our behavior. We're all status conscious and it turns out – pretty consistently – that while even money and other financial considerations will max out, there's no clear limit on the power of meaningful status-flavored achievements and rankings to drive increased and extended performance in both business and social contexts.

(7) We live in a "what have you done for me lately?" world. Just like Walmart and Costco religiously change their end-caps and in-store displays every week so that customers are always seeing something new, any site that doesn't feed the new, fresh content beast is doomed. Return visitors come with a set of progressively higher expectations – not only that the site will "know" them and simplify their progress – but that they will be offered new and extraordinary experiences and challenges or opportunities on each visit. Yesterday's miracle is today's table stakes and the ante is always being upped. There are two solutions to this problem. One is to hire more people and constantly obsess about the need to create clever new content. This is almost as bad as doing nothing and much more expensive. The second, and far smarter way to go, is to free-ride on obvious and available content that is being generated regularly and consistently by other providers. I'm not talking about stealing and I'm not talking about just copying super-popular content from elsewhere. I'm talking about simply setting down with a national events calendar and building a full year of piggy-backing your content currency strategy off of the constant and recurring flow of events, activities, anniversaries, holidays, films, etc. that beat a path to your door (as well as everyone else's) all year long. This seems so obvious that you would think it would form the foundation of virtually every site's programming and yet almost no one (except GOOGLE which does a new header every day) takes the few hours of creative thinking and organization that would make sure that they had a fresh, new, almost automatic stream of content ideas which the entire rest of the entertainment, news and media world were engaged in promoting for them. How much easier and cheaper could it be?

(8) And finally, we all want to drive the train. In their personal relations and leisure time, many young and active social media users want to have as much impact and control as possible to make up for the frustration, helplessness and impotence they often feel at work. This sets up an interesting problem for many websites. If everything is too easy to accomplish, secure or achieve, the users lose interest; they aren't being challenged in any respect; and they don't value the results of their efforts. They want an active role in the process – they want to be the accelerating gas pedal which will drive the experience rather than the speedometer which only measures and displays the results. They want to see how their efforts and actions make a concrete difference in their status and/or their results. I suppose there are some people who would accept a fundamentally passive experience, but they aren't really the attractive and active users you looking for. As Yogi Berra used to say: "you can observe a lot by just watchin' ", but this isn't baseball. We want the people who make things happen – not the ones who watch what happened – or worse yet - the ones who wonder what happened. When your users are part of figuring something out and accomplishing even interim goals, they're going to be much more committed to the enterprise and to its success. The best and most compelling sites convert initial involvement into active engagement and then engagement into return and retention – all as a part of one seamless process. And, equally importantly, the most enticing sites are fast. Whether we realize it or not, every time we visit a site, in one way or another, we're expecting and hoping to learn something and the key to effective learning is the immediacy and accuracy of the feedback. We're not checking the calendar here – we're watching our watches because the cycle time for everything these days is in minutes, not months. Everything is in the moment and if you want me to come back, you've got to deliver the goods every time I visit.

Some people are just made to be entrepreneurs. It's genetic and they couldn't be anything but. Many of these guys knew early on that they couldn't ever work for someone else. They were just horrible employees. Others became entrepreneurs because they were influenced and pushed down the path by their circumstances, fate, and good (or bad) fortune. It also helps to have started a few businesses when you were very young. And it's definitely formative to have been fired – especially more than once – from a job you actually cared about. Finally, your family dynamics matter more and in more different ways than you think. Sometimes that's a good thing – others – not so much.

At the moment, I'm beginning to wonder whether, in addition to cheap technology and generally lower barriers to entry, a good part of the latest massive stream of new start-ups spreading all across the country isn't being generated at least in part by the last grand gestures of hundreds of helicopter parents (mostly Moms) in every city who still can't quite cut the post-college cord and who want to give their little boys and girls one last boost along the road to bountiful.

And so they provide comfort and continuing financial support for Junior's latest venture – regardless of the merits – and this spawns businesses that have no business being in business and a host of other problems – not the least of which is that the money that could be helping to build the right kinds of new businesses gets pissed away on feel-good fantasies funded by misplaced and misguided generosity – not to say – clueless charity.

I get that part of this situation is an age-old dilemma – whether parents should spend their time preparing their kids for the path and then set them off on their way or continue (for way too long) trying to prepare the path for their kids – and – very often – ending up just getting in the way. Too much support and ongoing financial participation (especially from friends and family) is always at best a mixed blessing for a new business. And that's really the much more important question at the heart of this whole thing – the latest frenetic burst of market madness – start-ups starting up with no rhyme or reason – based on ideas that are a dime a dozen – which employ lots of otherwise lost kids in made-up jobs – all of whom would be much better served getting any real job with an ongoing business where they might actually get their lives started and learn something.

Here's a hint. If your "job" has you and your friends living in someone else's fantasy funded by their friends and family (for as long as the money lasts), there's simply no good that can come of it. And you'll all eventually learn that – even in smart start-ups - money actually disappears much faster than it can be raised and secured and that - unless you can build a sustainable cash-neutral business that no longer requires regular dollar infusions from relatives or investors, you're just prolonging the business's inevitable demise.

Having too much or too easy funding doesn't usually help the growth process – it dulls the entrepreneur's edge – it hides the reality of what makes a business real (mainly paying customers and modest profits) – and it seems to me that it makes these kinds of businesses much less likely to succeed. If it ultimately doesn't matter to the powers that be (or the family) whether the business makes it or not because Mommy will always make sure her kids have a safety net, a soft landing and a place to stay, and everyone in the company knows that, the real question is whether this kind of non-critical consideration is likely to do the young business much more harm than good.

There's no question that most experienced entrepreneurs would tell you that being "comfortable" and secure in your shoes is a curse worse than almost any other when you're getting started. Working without a safety net is part of the process. You need to be a little scared, plenty hungry, and always wondering about making payroll and other ends meet. In addition, there are major personal and psychological issues in terms of the folks who are in the boat with the fortunate entrepreneur (and who have made their own sacrifices and commitments) when they realize that there aren't enough life vests and rafts to make sure that everyone has a happy ending. And finally, if you've always got one foot in and one foot out of the boat (and safe on shore), it's not the kind of true commitment that's going to inspire anyone.

Now before I start getting cards and letters from folks complaining that I'm picking on Moms, let me tell you exactly what the vast majority of successful entrepreneurs will say when you ask about their families and their relationship with their folks. First, they'd tell you that their parents were very often self-employed. Second, they'd tell you that they were the oldest or the only child. And finally, they'd say their Moms were spigots of unconditional love and that their relationship with their Dads wasn't comfortable or competitive (or even non-existent) – they'd say it was "strained" – whatever that means - and that's why the cash flow in these cases of (often covert) assistance comes overwhelmingly from Mom. Dads may help in other ways, but this kind of money comes from Mom.

So your Mom clearly does matter to your business, and surely parental support can be a plus in some cases, but that might not be good news if her "contributions" are actually holding the business back.

I like to be supportive of almost any implementations of new, exciting technologies – even when I think that some are definitely "solutions in search of a problem" or the latest and greatest examples of "software that only the designer's mother could love", but there are limits and sometimes you see something so sad; so ill-conceived; and so poorly executed that you have to speak out just to avoid all of us toiling in these fields from being tarred and feathered with the same brush or beaten over the head with the stupid stick.

I'm very excited about the prospects of augmented reality across many different fields including education, entertainment, marketing, etc., but the recent *Haagen-Dazs* lid top "Concerto Timer" AR demo – available free in the Apple iTunes store [https://itunes.apple.com/us/app/haagen-dazs-concerto-timer/id670015815?mt=8] is so awful that it's likely to set the entire AR field back a century or two.

The premise is that you take the ice cream container out of the freezer and then you use your phone to download an app and then stand somewhere nearby and watch an AR-generated music video that appears on top of the ice cream container lid for the two minutes that *Haagen-Dazs* thinks you should wait for the ice cream to reach the ideal temperature for consumption.

The only thing that's remotely smart about the whole thing is the hook to a charitable donation for honey bee research and preservation for each of the first 15,000 downloads, but frankly, I'd pay the 5 bucks directly to the charity myself just to have the time back that I wasted on the demo and a promise that I'd never have to try to watch the thing again.

Where should I start?

(1) **Who exactly is the audience and how old are they likely to be?**
If anyone is experimenting with new, cool AR apps, it's tech-savvy kids and young adults – not grown-ups.

(2) **Who thinks that kids today are listening to classical Bach violin pieces?**
Bach Inventions No. 14 for violin and cello? Really? Have these guys spent too much time in the freezer?

(3) **Who waits 2 minutes for anything today – especially ice cream?**
We live in an IG world – Instant Gratification. Waiting for your wine to breath might make sense after you unscrew the lid. My ice cream melts in my mouth.

(4) **Who is going to stand anywhere for 2 minutes (like an idiot) holding your phone precisely focused on a pint of ice cream while it "tempers"?**
I thought it was painful to watch paint dry. But this is much worse and you only have to watch paint dry once. Here, because the video isn't persistent, it disappears the second you move your phone away from the lid so you have to stand like a mime (while your arm cramps up) to watch something you wouldn't choose to watch on a bet.

(5) **Who can even see the image clearly or hear the music being played?**
Using *Kinect* to capture the image of the performer rather than playing a clean, simple video (if you absolutely had to) was unnecessary and foolish overkill – like using a sledgehammer to kill a fly – and resulted in bad sound, poor video quality, and overall a completely disappointing experience. What were they thinking?

There are already plenty of intelligent uses of Augmented Reality technologies and some very smart applications that are finally getting traction and which even make good business sense because they supplement and add to the user experience instead of wasting our time. This clearly isn't one of them.

We have always been told (in a quotation wrongly attributed to Ralph Waldo Emerson) that, in terms of innovation, if we built a better mousetrap, the world would beat a path to our door. As it happens, the mousetrap (as we know it today) was invented a few years after Emerson died, but this hasn't prevented the issuance over the last hundred years of thousands of patents for new mousetrap designs along with additional thousands of failed mousetrap applications.

But what's the smartest strategy for a business when the guy or girl next door has already built a better mousetrap? Within reason and the bounds of legality, you'd think that the best plan would be to copy his or her solution and incorporate it into your own processes as soon as possible. Instead, over and over again, whether it's because of our own egos; some unstoppable craving for originality; the "not invented here" syndrome; or just expensive stupidity, we insist on re-inventing even the best wheels.

Now, I'm sure there are instances when pure ignorance is a reasonable defense – if you don't know there's a better way, it's hard to criticize you for not adopting it. I'm also certain that the vast majority of even the most conscientious website managers and marketing gurus don't know that there are new tools being brought to market every day which can help you quickly discover how your business is performing in a competitive context and how your website (or, as I used to call it, "your front door") stacks up against the competitor down the street or across the country. I'll tell you about one of the newest and coolest analytical tools (*Pathful*) in just a moment.

If you're not making it quick and easy for your site visitors and prospects to find quick answers, simple solutions, and a short path to success, you're making your life a lot tougher than it needs to be. And if you can readily determine that your competitors are doing a better job than you are in this area, then the solution is simple. Copy their best approaches and practices and make them your own. Frankly, this is nothing to be ashamed of – it's happened since the beginning of time. This is the reason that there used to be gas stations on 3 or 4 corners of the same intersections or why there are "car dealer" rows and auto parks where competitors sit right next to each other. A good location is a good location. The fact that the other guy may have gotten to that corner first doesn't mean squat unless you're too proud or foolish to park your business there as well.

So what does this mean in the simplest terms for your website? Well, *Pathful* is a new young Chicago-based company that's built some basic tools which can quickly <u>and objectively</u> tell you how effectively your website is doing its job. How well it works – how quickly it gets your customer to and through the point of purchase - because, as they say at *Google*, data beats opinions.

So this isn't a question of how pretty or cool the site is. There's no data point for "cool". And who really cares how much Bob likes it – even if Bob's the boss. His opinion is just that – an expression of one man's preferences and prejudices – not a way to set a smart strategy or build a great business. I'm all for educated guesses and your intuition is sometimes a big help in moving from a "so what?" solution to something spectacular. But start with the facts as your foundation. And that's what *Pathful* can help you do – answer the two most critical questions as to how you're doing and how you stack up against the competition in terms of the operational effectiveness of your site. Getting your customers to their goal so that they give up their gold.

Pathful's analysis addresses and answers a lot of questions and concerns, but the two that always jump out at me (and which are clearly interdependent) are the following: (1) Speed – how quickly can I get to the answers I need? – and (2) Clarity – how clear and free of distractions and detours is the path to success? Here's a simple case in point where 5 different organizations websites (A, B, C, D & E) were tested head-to-head on the Speed spectrum and graphed against Satisfaction. No surprise here – we don't like to wait – we want our answers and we want them now. And the longer we have to wait, the less positive our experience. And, if that wasn't bad enough, keep in mind that this analysis relates ONLY to the people who toughed it out and got to the finish line – not to the large numbers of people who bagged it at various points along the way because it just wasn't worth their time or continued effort or they ran out of patience.

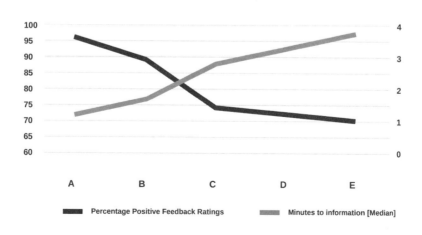

COMPARISON OF "SATISFACTION" TO TIME TO GOAL FOR 5 SITES

The second equally significant component was Clarity and the analysis there was equally instructive. I'm only going to show you the best path and the worst path of the 5 (the displays are a little unwieldy), but you'll get the point. The squares are the right steps and the circles are detours and distractions. These paths proceed from the top of the charts down and – even though each of these two sites had basically 4 steps to get to the finish line – you can clearly see how easy it was for people to lose their way on the worst site – and how often that happened.

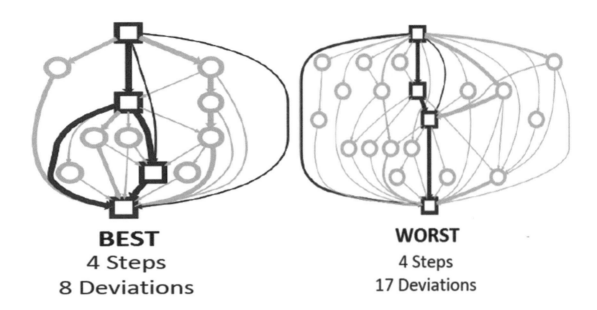

COMPARISON OF TWO SITES' PATHS TO GOAL

This really isn't rocket science. Think of these charts as potential roadmaps for your business, get in touch with *Pathful* or some other source of comparable and objective data, and get busy.

One of the hardest things to learn in successful selling is to leave well enough alone. The trick – once you actually do make a sale – is to shut up and leave. Don't keep talking; don't overstay your welcome; don't get greedy; and don't try to gild the lily. Get the goods and get out. But there are two basic tools in sales that are even harder to master – especially for young entrepreneurs.

First, you've got to learn how to directly ask for the order. But even more importantly, you've got to adopt the discipline; develop the thick skin; and practice the persistence that it takes to ask for the order every time you get the chance. Without embarrassment. Without hesitation. Without apologies. And without blaming it on someone else as in "my boss makes me do this." What exactly does this mean? It means actually remembering to ask for the sale every time the opportunity presents itself; making sure that you do it with a vengeance; and creating as many opportunities to do so as you can. Every time you try - you get better. Practice actually does make a difference. You want to always be closing the sale.

If you're apologetic or reluctant or only half-convinced yourself that the customer needs to act and act now to sign the dotted line, or if you're sitting back in the weeds waiting for people to call you, then you might just as well save your breath and shut your doors. You can't sell anything sitting on your ass. And – as with most things in life - saying certainly doesn't make it so - only doing makes a difference that matters. Knowing what you should do or talking it to death, on the one hand, and actually executing on the plan – quickly, confidently, and consistently - are too often worlds apart. Success really starts when you just start doing the heavy lifting of getting the job done.

As I look around these days, I see more and more instances where the people who should be focused on closing deals are spending their time and energy making excuses for their clients and customers and justifying their inaction and lack of concrete results. The economy sucks – so what? Someone is still selling things – just not your folks. The recovery is really slow. Big deal. People still need someone's products and services. It oughta be yours. "Understanding" your clients' issues and problems is a very nice theoretical approach (actually I think it mostly sounds better in the literature than it works in real life), and when it gets in the way of making a sale, it becomes a much bigger problem for your business and one that you need to promptly address and solve.

Salesmen who emphasize customer empathy and offer a collection of "good" excuses for missing sales aren't really doing much of anything for your bottom line. It may help them feel better about themselves and their poor performance, but it won't get you across the goal line. Nothing happens without salespeople who want to sell your product. My best-ever sales manager had a simple (and admittedly crass) analysis which has always stuck with me. His view of the sales world all came down to a single idea: "somebody's gotta sell this shit". Feeling sorry for your customers doesn't really get anything done. You've got to nip this attitude in the bud and get your people back out there on the street selling. If they're not in the game, you can bet that someone else will be taking up the slack and making the sales. I hear these sad stories about missed chances & lousy excuses from companies every day.

One of the worst excuses of all is being told by the customer that the timing just isn't or wasn't right. You'll learn soon enough that it's always too early until it's too late. And nothing's a worse feeling than dropping the ball with a customer who keeps putting you off and off and then - when you finally do get around to calling again, they tell you that you're too late because they went with someone else. The longer I'm in business the more I realize that there's never a perfect time for the customer to buy because most of them would just as soon not buy if they don't have to - so it's the salesmen's job to control the clients' calendars; to always be in their faces; and to be there whenever the customers are ready to buy. It's all about "at-bats" and always asking for the order. Lots of important things are lost for lack of asking.

And here's an interesting fact. As brash, impolite and aggressive as most entrepreneurs appear, the fact is that they're no better (or more capable) than anyone else when it comes to this crucial skill. I don't think society in general has gotten a lot more gracious and polite lately (in fact I'd say it was exactly the opposite), but for some reason, young people today are reluctant to push and/or to appear to be pushy. Some otherwise tough and smart entrepreneurs I know would rather die than die of embarrassment. They don't think it's cool to let people see you sweat. They don't understand that it's a good thing – not a bad one – to show everyone exactly how much you want something and what you're willing to do to get it. Sometimes I even think that – in their hearts and heads - they themselves doubt their products and services and this also makes it hard for them to throw themselves into the game full-force with body and soul. That tired old joke about sales has more than a kernel of truth. They used to say that the main difference between a car salesman and a computer salesman was that the car salesman knew he was lying. Maybe a little self-doubt also comes with every new digital business and maybe that's not a bad thing.

But, as I've talked to a bunch of these guys and girls, the real issue turns out to be simpler and – by the way – easier to resolve. Entrepreneurs aren't used to being told "no" and they don't like it. So they avoid it by not putting themselves on the firing line often enough and it slows down their businesses and their growth. It also sets a lousy example for the rest of the sales team. But I've got a simple mantra that can save the day.

All you need to do is train everyone in your business (including yourself) to repeat this phrase a couple of times a day – especially in the selling season – and it'll be much more helpful than all your pep talks, sticks and stones, sugary sweets and other threats and incentives combined. What's the phrase that I use to keep bouncing back up and taking the next step and the next shot and asking for the sale every day?

I say to myself and my team: "it's only a "no" for now". And, you know what, almost every "no" is exactly that – it's a "no" until it's a "yes" and it'll only be a "yes" if you keep asking.

TULLMAN'S TRUISMS

SOON IS NEVER AS GOOD AS NOW

57 – DO MARGINAL MENTORS REALLY MATTER?

I'm fairly certain that there's an overabundance of highly-verbal and successful people who are flattered to be asked and more than willing and even excited about the prospect of giving sporadic advice to young entrepreneurs. I say "sporadic" because - even in the best and most structured and organized incubators, accelerators and other start-up and tune-up support facilities - the mentoring process has a lot of hit and miss qualities. People drop by for an hour or two – rarely actually up-to-speed on the business in question or the critical issues on the table – and then they listen briefly to the entrepreneurs, nod sagely, take their best shot at some quick suggestions and advice and then leave. And sadly, the next guy dropping in to meet with that same team might have identical or completely opposite advice.

It's no doubt a learning experience for the entrepreneurs, but I'm not really sure what they're learning or gaining from the process. I believe that when you take the time to give someone advice (and you take their time as well), you're obligated to do what you can (in terms of preparation, connections, referrals, etc.) to make sure that it's not just lip service or a bunch of empty clichés.

Some of these "advisors" are one-hit wonders themselves and it's not really that clear whether their particular success was mainly due to a good idea, good partners, good timing or simple good luck – not that there's anything wrong with any of these elements – and I'd rather be blessed in any business with all of the above if I had a choice. But you have to wonder – as you're listening to their war stories – exactly how much transferable wisdom they've gained from the experience and, more specifically, how much they've extracted and generalized from their situation which will be of use and value to your own business.

Giving advice is a form of high-minded, self-congratulatory nostalgia for these folks in many respects and, in addition, it's frightfully easy in these situations to tell someone else what to do because nothing is impossible for the person who doesn't have to do it himself. What's more, a lot of these people will tell you to take a hard line on something and stand up on principle until push comes to shove and then they're long gone. I like to say that a principle really isn't a principle until it costs you something.

Another aspect of the process that's somewhat problematic is the matter of money. Money doesn't care who makes it and having a lot of money – as we all know from experience – doesn't really make you wise or make you a class act. And I realize that rich entrepreneurs sometimes complain that when you have money, people tend to doubt your talent. But in many cases that's exactly the fact. And, for me, it's really hard to pay a lot of attention to the advice of someone with no skin in the game. I like people who put their money where their mouth is. My favorite trader (I realize that's somewhat of an oxymoron) likes to say that "until you have a position, all you have is an opinion" and I agree.

Any entrepreneur's time is precious and constrained – if you're going to spend it listening to anyone for any substantial amount of time, make sure (as best you can) that they know what they're talking about and that the conversations are worth your time.

Here are a couple of thoughts to help you through the process.

(1) As Simon and Garfunkel said so well in *The Boxer:* "…a man hears what he wants to hear/and disregards the rest". Listen carefully, weigh everything with a grain of salt, and try to determine why the person would (or should) know what they're talking about. Then take the best and leave the rest.

(2) If the person is also a prospective investor in your business (and one that you think you'd like to have and could live with), remember that listening to advice very often accomplishes far more than actually heeding it. Be patient, nod your head a lot, agree with their observations, and then go on and do what you think is best for the business. Frankly, I think in crazy times like these, lying probably gets more businesses started than money.

(3) Try to remember that personality and rapport are not substitutes for credibility and knowledge. They make for pleasant conversations, but just because someone's a really good guy only rarely also means that he knows what he's talking about. These are people you'd happily buy a drink for, but never lend any money.

And finally, keep in mind the strange paradox that there are people who can give you extremely useful and valuable information and direction, but who can't get out of their own way in their own businesses and who would be the first to admit that they really don't do a good job of taking their own advice. Don't follow their example, but listen to their suggestions.

Sometimes, while you are waiting for that amazing *Instagram* moment when your ship comes in and the entire world beats a rapid path to your door, you've got to remember to take care of business. And I mean that literally. Too many entrepreneurs today are so focused on the big, broad score (going viral worldwide overnight and other similarly-extravagant visions) that they lose sight of the many opportunities right in front of them to make deals that can help to pay the bills and keep their business in business.

I've decided that we need a new shorthand term for this particular flawed fantasy of massive virality and – for simplicity's sake – I'm just calling it CCC. (I have my own personal reasons for this choice.) Think of it as "collaborative crowd consumption". This isn't about crowd-sourcing or crowd-funding as much as it's about simple crowd-sharing. We all know what B-to-B businesses look like and B-to-C companies aren't that tough to understand either. But understanding C-to-C-to-C isn't as easy.

Getting a handle on how to analyze and evaluate; encourage and accelerate; and ultimately measure the prospects of success for a company setting out to trigger the mysterious process whereby millions of energized consumers suddenly take up your cause as their own; start aggressively promoting and re-distributing your products for free; and become engaged advocates of the entire experience (and of your business) is a much more complex and difficult problem. I'm not sure that there's any easy or clear answer (and, in any case, even the best of these outcomes takes some time), so I'm just suggesting that, in the meantime while you're waiting, it's smart to keep busy taking care of the business that you can secure and manage.

I realize that a lot of small deals aren't as exciting as world viral domination or even highly visible big wins (and I also realize that chasing too many rabbits can be painfully distracting), but big deals (and instances of really rapid and extensive consumer adoption) present all kinds of issues of their own. They take a lot of time and resources to get done; they're generally a lot less profitable since you lack negotiating leverage as a young company dealing with big guys and since you're accelerating ("investing") in the growth curve well ahead of any expected or anticipated significant revenue streams; and they spread you and your team far and wide. In addition, it's always risky to put so many of your eggs in any one basket in the early stages of your development.

The old dot.com idea of getting big fast probably still makes sense if your only goal is building a business to get bought by somebody bigger. But even if that's your idea, there's no guarantee that you'll get there and – with scarce resources and constrained capital – going solely for the gold may be actually betting the whole business on getting the big break.

I think that a smarter strategy is to allocate at least a little time and some sales or biz development talent to deploying your product in the B-to-B market which will often be practically standing there knocking on your door and asking to be serviced and sold. If you're concerned about your hot new offering leaking out before your grand world-wide launch, you can "white-label" it, strip it down or price it up (as against the eventual consumer deliverable), or impose other time, location or distribution limits on the B-to-B versions.

What you don't want to do is turn your nose up or your back on business that will pay the bills and bridge the gap to the hoped-for mass adoption. Even in our new instant information world where everyone knows everything in an instant, this is a pretty modest exposure risk and a pretty prudent approach. And it can be quite profitable to boot because the marketing costs can be minimal and, in a real sense, you're basically taking orders and filling requests rather than trying to drum up demand and manufacture a mass movement.

So while you're pushing that big boulder up the hill, getting ready to glide down the other side, and waiting for the avalanche of accolades and adoption to appear, don't forget to take a little time to investigate these additional avenues of opportunity:

(1) **Limited Players.**
Are there one-off cases, applications, promotional uses, or other ways that you can provide your product or service exclusively to a limited number of partners, brands, vendors, verticals, or in pilot programs which will give the participants a new marketing boost, a competitive edge, a novel solution, or a gee-whiz gizmo which will set them apart in their markets from their competition and for which they will happily pay a fair amount of money as a marketing project cost or as a promotional expense in a bulk payment or fee-based transaction rather than on a per-user (consumer) basis?

(2) **Alternative Markets.**
Are there commercial or industrial uses for your product or service which don't risk large-scale exposure to consumers and which can be priced on a service provider or system solution basis rather than by the bite or even initially free as may have to be the case for ordinary consumers? Keep in mind that these types of deals can often be predicated on higher and more powerful and complex uses of your offerings because of the differences in the skill levels and training of the targeted user populations which may enable them to be more quickly trained and/or – with a little good luck – you may even find that there are groups of users already familiar with and capable of adopting your new tools and technology and readily applying them to existing problems in their businesses. They've just been waiting for a solution to come along.

(3) Different Geographies.

Are there self-contained or relatively closed markets where you can launch versions and variations of the product or service for evaluation and fine-tuning purposes without letting the entire cat out of the bag? As much as we hear about global this-and-that and about constant connectivity and ubiquitous market information, the fact is that you can do a great deal of testing and limited market trials effectively under the radar by simply selecting the right geographies. There are many towns throughout the country untouched to date by the democratization of data. The trick is to get in, run your trials, and get out as quickly and quietly as possible. Remember that media attention at this point doesn't matter and mainly doesn't help. This approach won't really help you test product virality, but it's fine for determining utilization patterns and basic product viability.

All in all, the bottom line is pretty simple. You always need a Plan B while you're waiting to be wonderful. A plan that keeps things moving and makes you some money in the interim is a pretty nice straddle and you'll also learn - in retrospect and almost every case and business – that the biggest money turns out to be in the smallest sales

TULLMAN'S TRUISMS

DON'T TRY TO GET TO HEAVEN IN ONE NIGHT

I think most of the end-of-season Demo Days are officially over now - at least for a while. It's hard to be sure as the number of accelerators, incubators, and shared office facilities continues to race toward almost 200 different entities - just in the U.S. - and everyone else also wants in. Seems like someone's got something going somewhere every time you turn around. Still, having sat through half a dozen "days" in several cities in the last couple of months and watched more than 50 different pitches, I have a few suggestions for the teams and the teachers/mentors/coaches while we've got a bit of a breather.

I realize that it's easy to carp or complain from the cheap seats (and overall each year the players and the pitches are getting better and more mature), but since I've been there myself literally hundreds of times, I feel entitled to offer my impressions. You can take 'em or leave 'em, just don't ignore 'em until you've read 'em.

(1) One Size STILL Doesn't Fit All.

Too many of the pitches were just too long. Early enthusiasm and energy turned into fatal fatigue when it felt like the last few minutes were just filler. Not every company or business needs ten minutes to tell a compelling tale. Say your piece - keep the emotional level high - and then sit down. Elaboration after a point is just mental pollution. Here's an old rule that has served me well over the years - "Just Because You Can Doesn't Mean You Should".

Sometimes I swear that it felt like even the guy (or girl) on the stage was just going through the motions. A separate, but related, issue is the risk of leaving your "A" game in the rehearsal room - too many rehearsals; too many coaches; and too many sleepless nights. Adrenaline will only take you so far and some of the presenters just seemed pooped to me.

(2) Templates are Tiresome.

Your story and your style need to be front and center and everyone's story is different. The type of pitch (high energy, deep detail, quick quips, pretty pix, etc.) should depend completely on the specific message you're trying to send and the type of typical investor that you're targeting. Go with what makes sense for your story, not some set of boilerplate presentation slides where each team just fills in the blanks. Different strokes make sense for different folks.

Maybe your team is terrific and should be a major part of the pitch (after all investors mainly vote on the jockeys and not the horses), but the tenth time the audience sees the infamous smiling team slide, it's just tiresome and too much. Put the bios in a booklet or just bag the whole thing if your team isn't demonstrably a compelling competitive differentiator. You'll have plenty of time to introduce the team down the round.

And maybe it's just me, but I'm also pretty sick of meeting "Bob", the prototypical user or target customer, who has all the problems your product or service is going to solve. It's a painful and tired trope and it needs to be dumped from every demo as soon as possible.

(3) Don't Let Your Dress Be A Distraction.

I think that - as a general rule - wearing your team's t-shirt may be the safest bet of all. Dressing up or down or too distinctly is risky. The last thing you want to happen as you walk on to the stage is to have anyone looking at you rather than listening to you. Crazy clothes, hiked-up heels, bushy beards, etc. all subtract substance, attention and focus from your story. It's just the way people are and it's not gonna change any time soon. Make your statement some other time and place.

I realize that there are plenty of smart and savvy people who choose to dress or wear their hair in a certain style, but in this narrow context, I think that a fashion faux pas can start you off with a crowd that wonders if you're serious and why would you want to start with that extra monkey on your back? This is a steep enough slope as it is – starting out in a rut of your own making – makes no sense. First impressions REALLY matter when you've only got a few minutes to make your points and your best case. And you don't get a second chance to make that first impression either – there are no "do-overs" on Demo Day.

I feel the same way about humor. Jokes are really hard to set up and pull off and they're risky. You just don't want to take the chance that your gag or stunt will fall flat and the crowd will start feeling sorry for you rather than swayed by you. They might still buy you a beer during the break, but they'll be a lot less likely to bet their bucks on your business if they think you're a clown. And a bad one at that.

(4) Case Studies Generally Suck

Talking about your own results – user acquisition, revenue growth, major contracts, new strategic partners, etc. moves your story forward and makes a lot of sense. But trying to explain (as the clock keeps ticking) the details of a case study – even one with impressive results – is just a waste of too much precious time and – by and large – always a bad bet. You've got to set up the case; introduce the client and their problem; explain the context and the actions; and show the success – and all the while the audience is hearing the client's name (not yours) and you're talking about the client's business (not yours) and it's just too easy for everyone to get lost in the weeds. And frankly, they're not that interested in a one-off anything.

The depth of the discussion required to make a sensible explanation simply isn't worth the distraction. Just claim the results – "We saved these guys millions." – and move on. Details to follow. You can make the point that the product works without putting the audience to sleep.

(5) Funders are Fierce Followers

I was amazed at how many companies said that they had raised X or Y dollars toward their goal, but didn't take the opportunity to say who their investors were. If your backers are willing, it's worth the time to tell us who are they. Brand name investors betting on your business sends a very clear and concise message to the rest of the crowd that they should get on board. The bigger and faster the bandwagon, the better the fund-raising results.

You should never forget that investors don't fear losing their money anywhere near as much as they fear being the only investor who does. Nobody today really wants to go it alone if they don't have to and, if things go bad, at least they'll have company in their misery.

TULLMAN'S TRUISMS

THERE'S ALWAYS ENOUGH TIME TO DO THINGS THE RIGHT WAY

If you think that it's hard to get a new business off the ground, you should really try shutting down a start-up or two in order to appreciate what serious stress means. If there's a lonelier and more depressing spot for a young entrepreneur to be in, I can't really imagine what it would be. Especially because there's rarely anyone – inside or outside of the business – and even at home - that you can talk to honestly about the prospect of closing your company down. Even your banker and your attorney will start to turn a little green around the gills and get that slightly vacant look in their eyes when the prospect is raised that they might not get paid or repaid. You'll find that their advice and answers slow down somewhat (it's like English is their second language and they have to translate stuff in their heads first before they speak it to you) and – all of a sudden - everything feels somewhat tentative. I realize that this kind of situation always sucks, but it's a fact of life and in the next year or two - as more and more start-ups run out of gas and out of runway because they can't raise their next round of financing – it's going to become a front-and-center concern for everyone who's active in any capacity in the early-stage investment space.

So get ready and, when it happens to you – directly or indirectly – wherever you happen to be in the food chain, don't start thinking that people are against you (or generally out to get you - although you could be pardoned for occasionally thinking that when things look especially dark), just try to remember that it's simply the fact that they're much more interested in looking out for themselves and their interests first and foremost than they are in going out on a limb to save your bacon. As they like to say, it's not personal; it's just business. But, of course, it's your life and your business that's on the line.

And it's you – and often you alone – who has to sit up at night and worry about when to pull the plug. By the way, after setting out to change the world and seeing that it's not happening, it takes just as much strength and courage to plug the plug as it did to set out on the journey in the first place. It's pretty easy to sign up new employees and talent when the till is full; it's a lot more challenging when you're inviting people to come on board what may be your version of the *Titanic*. And it's pretty easy to pump up the troops and send them out on critical sales calls when you know you've got the cash to cover their credit card charges. Not so much when they might be unknowingly bankrolling the business and when you know that that's the last thing they can afford to do if they'll be out of a job entirely in a couple of months. Things can get pretty darn ugly fast when you hit that slippery slope. And the sense of isolation and abandonment that you feel is only made more extreme by several other considerations which we rarely think about in the rush and excitement of the initial creative process as we're building the business.

Nobody Tells Ya Nothin'

For one thing, which I'm trying to partially address right here, while there's a vast amount of reading and writing that's readily available concerning every aspect of launching a business, there's almost nothing you can turn to for help when your business is headed south. People are fond of saying that, if you want to be there at the landing, you've got to be there from the launch. But the truth is that you're largely on your own when things go wrong because no one wants to be there (much less talk about it or plan for it) when the business is about to crash and burn. Plan B's are generally OK. Plan F is nothing anyone wants to hear anything about until it's way too late in most cases to make a difference. It's a lot like the overwhelming lack of interest we see in writing a will or buying a cemetery plot when you're 25.

In addition, many investors and even close advisors who might be able to give you some help and guidance (although usually not more cash) are way too quick to jump ship when your deal gets in trouble and the funding starts to run out. Experienced entrepreneurs (who have been to this movie before) will tell you that this is just another part of the process and that being left in the lurch comes with the territory. But even knowing that this is commonplace doesn't provide much comfort when it's your place that's in the creditors' cross-hairs. When people start to lose their confidence in you, they are driven much more by their fears than by their hopes

The Pendulum Swings Both Ways

Opportunity costs (just like pendulums) cut both ways. At the outset and when you're a star, everybody takes your calls and wants to be your best buddy. As I like to say: "they'll love ya when you're leading and leave ya when you're losing". Everyone quickly seems to have better things to do than to sink additional time and effort into a deal that's moving sideways or backwards. VCs call these companies "the living dead" and can't wait to move on to the next big thing. The attitude today – more and more in light of the massive number of opportunities – is this: "anything that isn't a clear and obvious winner is a loser". I don't think we're gonna change human nature any time soon, but especially for first-timers, it's important for you to know what you can expect from these folks (not much) in hard times. When things get really rough, your partners, managers and best employees will – by and large – give you a better shake than outsiders, but they too have families, obligations and futures that they need to be attentive to and responsible for – and, in another sad, but true fact of life, it's the most qualified who quickly learn that they have other options and alternatives and they're more likely to leave than the rest of the team. But don't worry apart parting with hard-to-find, terrifically talented people. Here's a little secret – save your business first, then restock your larder. Great talent is attracted far more by the opportunity to solve important problems and by demonstrable unmet demand for the business's products and services than by peanuts, perks and promises.

Tune the Team for Tough Times

Talking about the team, there's an old football rule that, if you want to win consistently, you play your best 11 (the most effective and cohesive team) and not your 11 best (the best individual performers). When you're in trouble and picking the people to keep, this is a CRITICAL concern and often a very tough call. You may have to fire your second best salesman to be able to afford to keep the guy who keeps the servers humming. And as much as it feels like you're throwing away a part of your future upside; when you're in survival mode, you need to first make sure that you'll have the funds to have a future at all. Figure out the functions that really permit the stripped-down business to still function and have a shot at success and go with the people that can make that happen. Among other things, you'll very likely find that it's some of your younger and newer employees rather than the older and more experienced ones who are best suited to this type of a struggle.

Kidding Yourself is Not a Competitive Advantage in a Crisis

One of the reasons young entrepreneurs succeed is that they don't know what they're unable to do. In addition, they refuse to allow their actions to be constrained by the limitations of others. As a result, because they didn't know something "couldn't be done", and there were no rules against doing it, they often end up accomplishing things even though they had never been done before. Their ignorance and abundant confidence in this context is a competitive advantage. They think that they can solve every problem with the application of unbounded enthusiasm and great energy. But the world of counselors, creditors, and courts combined with the constraints of a cash crunch isn't a place of unplowed new ground. There are hard and fast and painful rules and procedures that constitute this environment and they're expressly designed to limit flexibility, restrict movement, and slow everything down. Entrepreneurs sell dreams which they often quite honestly believe. But just because something is exciting and has the ring of truth about it doesn't mean that it matches the realities of the situation and the facts on the ground. Saying doesn't make things so and all the confidence in the world won't make up for a lack of cash. As Charlie Brown used to say: "How can we lose when we're so sincere?"

Entrepreneurs are Super Superstitious

Forget your WPO & YPO forums; strategy seminars and trade shows; your PPMs and IPO plans; and all those other "helpful" resources for a while. These kinds of activities are wastes of precious time that you can't afford and they also won't help a bit. But not for the reasons you might imagine. They won't help because the fear of failure is highly contagious and exhibitions of honesty and vulnerability in most cases don't encourage other entrepreneurs to share; they tend to drive them to shut down and disappear. Even guys you've been close business associates with for years and years aren't gonna be there to help you over these hurdles. The sooner you realize this; the more time you'll save and the less disappointed you'll be in your buddies. No one else is really gonna help bail you out or supply the silver bullet – it's all on you.

So what can you do to at least start to prepare yourself mentally (sooner rather than later) for the prospect that your turn in the dunk tank may be right around the corner?

Here're four crucial rules to keep in mind:

(1) **Don't Wait 'til It's Too Late**
As I suggested above, very few people who haven't been through this process multiple times have any idea of how soon you have to acknowledge your problems and start moving to fix them if you're going to have a fighting chance of saving the ship. You think for example that you can always quickly let people go and stop the burn, but you don't take into account issues like accrued vacation pay, severance, continued insurance benefits, expense reimbursements, etc. and every one of these things keeps the money meter running long after the people may have departed. In addition, there's the opposite side of the coin as well – every day that you move closer to running out of cash – but keep operating the business, you're adding creditors and obligations that you're going to need to resolve in some fashion. A scary example (and just one of many) is the issue of unpaid employment taxes, deposits, etc. which can quickly become personal liabilities for management and directors. Trust me; you don't want to go there.

(2) **Don't Slice the Salami Slowly**
If you have to eat a bunch of ugly frogs, it's a good plan to eat the biggest one first. If you're going to try to save the business, the necessary cuts have to be quick and deep and over as soon as possible so the survivors can get back to work and stop worrying that they are the next to go. Trying to save a couple of people or a marginal job or two is the worst thing you can do. It's never easy or pretty, but doing it piecemeal and over and over again is an early death sentence. People do better

absorbing one big shock and getting over the loss than they do dealing with the uncertainty of a series of continued small and ineffective cuts.

(3) Start Looking for a Salvage Sale

It may be that you've got a great team or a great idea or a cool new approach or something else going for you. The problem is that to win today, you need <u>all</u> of the above plus a bunch of time and cash. And you've got to know how to run an entire business which might not really be what you're great at and – without a bankroll – no one's interested in waiting around while you learn on the job. However, there are lots of companies looking to acquire whole talented teams; to fold in technologies or tools that they haven't yet built for themselves; or even to start an entire division doing what you hoped to do as a stand-alone business. But you've got to start looking as soon as you start to see the handwriting on the wall. Frankly, even a fire sale – especially one that provides going-forward jobs for the folks who hung in there with you – is a LOT better outcome than extending your struggle for a few months and then crashing directly into the concrete wall.

(4) Shoot for a Soft Landing

If you're never planning to pass by this way again, feel free to just smash into the wall, bail out and shut the place down, and leave waves of unhappy folks in your wake. But, what goes around does come around and most young entrepreneurs are very likely (especially these days) to want to get back up on the horse and try it again. The ONLY way you will have the slightest chance of doing this is if you preserve your integrity and credibility by trying to do everything in your power to shoot for a soft landing where you leave as few people holding an empty bag as possible. This goes for vendors, partners, employees, customers, creditors and Uncle Sam as well to be sure. Remember that at these times, you riding a very emotional see-saw and constantly teetering between support and blame from everyone around you.

There may not be enough money to make anyone happy or whole, but careful cash management, full disclosure, good timing, and self-sacrifices will go a long way toward at least generating some understanding. Remember that (unlike friends and families) professional investors (and most decent angels) have seen these scenarios many times and know what the possible outcomes are. Shame on them if they didn't make their commitments with their eyes wide open.

But they'll still be checking to see whether you handled a tough situation like a professional. One amazing way to surprise them is to think about an early shutdown and a partial return of their unspent capital. Here's the bottom line: if you can't see a clear path and a way to win; there's very little reason to waste your time and energy (and your investors' money) on trying to lose more slowly. It's never the hills on the road forward that matter; it's how you handle the ruts that tells the real story for the future.

Bottom line: failing to plan for a possible failure shouldn't be confused with people who are planning to fail (a lack of confidence or commitment) and just going through the motions. It's a much worse failing – it's failing to honor the faith and belief that people had in you. There's always more money – your reputation and credibility are much harder to preserve and restore once they're gone.

The promise of the cloud can be very seductive and the adoption in every industry of cloud-based solutions provided - by and large - by new, young companies offering all manner of software as a service (SaaS) solutions continues to accelerate. The prospects of reduced capital expenditures and smaller IT staffs as well as ubiquitous access and perpetual uptime are very compelling for any business.

And while I realize that there are a few big, long-established players (like Salesforce.com) in the SaaS space; if you look carefully, most of the major and more substantial players have concentrated on infrastructure plays while most of the new, interesting, and potentially highly disruptive software solutions are being offered by young players who have elected to ride on that newly available infrastructure which is inexpensive to access (though not to build) and to assemble their products and service offerings on top of these industrial-strength platforms which are being provided by Amazon, Microsoft and others.

But those new young entrants present three serious and essentially structural risks to businesses looking to move to the cloud which every CEO needs to appreciate and evaluate before making such a move. The truth is that not every "cloud" has a silver lining and – as the head of a growing company – before you bet your entire business and begin to migrate mission-critical services and offerings to the cloud - you need to be sure (a) that you really understand who you're signing up with; (b) that you appreciate what you're signing up for and what you're <u>not</u> getting; and (c) that you have an accurate picture of the risks that you are taking and how they compare to the <u>potential</u> benefits of a move. The devil is always in the details and, in many cases, the devil you know and have worked with for years (with all the warts and all the complaints) may still be a better bet for your business than a crapshoot on a company that's still getting its shit together.

Only after you get solid and complete answers to a few, very critical and important questions should you think about moving forward. These aren't easy things to determine or simple inquiries to make, but you won't get a second chance if you move prematurely or if you pick the wrong vendor/partner. You could end up entirely out of business. So take the time and commit the resources to do the necessary due diligence and to look hard before you leap. They're called "clouds" for a reason – they're not remotely transparent – they're totally opaque.

Here are some brief thoughts on the three most critical concerns and one final suggestion:

Who Are These Guys and Are Their Interests Aligned with Mine?

When you're first starting out and trying to build a new business, there's a tremendous emphasis and tons of pressure on management to keep increasing revenues. Make the sale and move on to the next. But, for the customers, the rubber really meets the road when it's implementation time and that's when the SaaS sales guys tend to be long gone. And, because installations, training, configurations and the entire process of customization for individual users don't drive "new" revenues, the senior management and top sales guys at too many of these SaaS start-ups have little or no interest in these "down and dirty", but crucial parts of the migration process. I think that this is totally because they are focused solely on the top line and compensated accordingly.

But, even if you want to give them the benefit of the doubt, and you say that – because they've never done it before – they don't understand that software development is basically a business of brief moments of creation embedded in a lifetime of maintenance; it still doesn't make life any better or smoother for their customers. Essentially the basic SaaS *modus operandi* is to sell the stuff in and then leave the rest of the work to third party consultants and integrators or to the customer. Bottom line – they're into sales, not service or support, and you can easily end up – under the best of circumstances - with a partial solution and a load of headaches.

What Am I Getting and What Do I Only "Think" I'm Getting?

Not only is the SaaS solution sometimes half-delivered; it's also often half a loaf when you look under the hood. In some ways, it's a competitive advantage to be young enough not to know any better and not to know what you can't do. Entrepreneurs regularly bite off too much and promise far more than they can deliver. Business as usual – buyer beware – no harm, no foul. But other times, especially with first-generation software programs, the initial set of buyers are involuntarily turned into the last beta testers and – believe me – that doesn't make for happy campers. In this context, I like to say that SaaS software changes and upgrades aren't released; they escape from the engineers. Newbies seize on the "lean" methodology jargon as an excuse to launch all kinds of undercooked and half-assed products, but we're all pretty tired of hearing that flaws are actually features, and not bugs. And, in addition, it turns out that, by "lean", they don't even mean simply-designed initial MVPs; they mean that they plan to learn what works and what doesn't by leaning on the users and letting them live through all the hiccups and mistakes.

Young entrepreneurs rarely understand the difference between a software program and a software product. Developing a robust and stable software product (with programs incorporated into it) which will hopefully be used by hundreds or thousands of customers in a wide variety of ways and contexts takes at least TEN times longer and far more effort than developing a basic software program or solution for a private user. This where all that nasty, time-consuming, and highly-detailed work called implementation, configuration and customization comes in which – by the way – rarely scales.

Are the Savings, Flexibility and New Functionality Worth the Risks to My Business?

Drivers of electric cars suffer from "range" anxiety. They worry about whether their current charge will last long enough to get home or to the next charging station. Thoughtful and attentive SaaS users should suffer constantly from "change" anxiety for two reasons. First, another portion of the half-a-loaf problem is that, as a SaaS customer (whether you realize it or not), you only get effective control over your part of the total package. This makes for the serious likelihood of some very nasty surprises whenever the main operating system in the cloud is changed, updated or otherwise revised – with or without ample notice to you and rarely with testing sufficient to confirm that the new versions will work with your install. Think of the overall installation as having two parts (theirs and yours) and ANY time that the two parts get out of sync, you're basically screwed.

Ultimately, I feel that the real problem is a structural one – the vendors are worried about enhancing and improving their main set of offerings and solutions and you're praying (because you've spent a small fortune configuring and customizing your end of their system so that it works with and for your business) that whatever changes they make won't damage or disrupt your operations. I hope that you don't think for a minute that there are ANY SaaS vendors out there who test their new updates and revisions against every customer's installation and usage BEFORE they release the new versions. That would be far too difficult and time-consuming as well as impossibly costly to staff and support.

And it gets worse. No small start-up can realistically afford (whether they admit it to you or not) to build and be running a completely separate development environment alongside their production systems. That's just not the way the world or the money works in the start-up universe. And, as a result, they release their changes into the production environment and – as noted above – they do their testing on you and your business in real time. This is the fundamental risk of a cloud-based solution. One size and one version or system will never work for any serious number of customers and frankly the attitude in the SaaS world isn't to make the system work for the customers. Once these businesses have any real traction and installed bases, their attitude is that you need to decide whether their system will work for you and – if it doesn't – they respectfully suggest that you change your business processes until it does.

One Last Thing to Think About

And remember one final thing – in addition to determining whether the vendor's sales people are telling you the truth and whether the references they provide are legitimate and satisfied users (or just fellow victims looking for company) - you have to weigh and consider the agendas and the motivations of the people inside your company as well. In every case I have seen (or suffered through myself), there are well-intentioned and sincere people on both sides of the decision with decent reasons to support their arguments and then there is usually another collection of people who are scared to make any decision that they might be blamed for; afraid to rock the boat or change things; committed to prior solutions that they endorsed or recommended; protecting their own job, people, turf or fiefdoms; and/or just too lazy to want to do the work that it takes to do one of these migrations well. They are rarely incented to give you the straight scoop.

Information (along with hard questions and sharp edges) has a way of getting smoothed out and softened as it wends its way upward in your organization on its way to your desk. That's just another fact of life – regardless of how big or little your headcount is. Just be sure you have all the facts before you make your move.

I f you're a smart and strategic entrepreneur running a start-up today, you should be spending part of your time trying to pare your business down so that you can focus your people and resources on doing just those things that you're terrific at (or going to be terrific at) and – at the same time – trying to shed everything that doesn't really add value to the process. If something you're spending time and money on isn't building an advantage for you and helping your business to create one or more sustainable competitive edges, you should be doing something else. Think of it as outsourcing *uber alles* – you need to bag everything you can't do a lot better than a million other people because just doing things as well as the next guy won't cut it anymore. Average is over.

In the not so old days, people used to look critically at businesses that were somewhat "virtual" and often accuse them of being composed mainly of "smoke and mirrors" – politely suggesting that these enterprises were really scams because there wasn't an obvious "there" there. Essentially, there weren't enough concrete, computers and other serious capital expenditures to give prospective investors or customers comfort that the business was secure, solid and real. Today, most of those same folks would call you "stupid" if you were buying and building your own servers; handling your own HR and accounting; and fundamentally failing to farm out every other function that you didn't need to staff and run yourself because it was core to your company and central to your strategy.

But selecting the right vendor/partner for the various services you are seeking to outsource isn't as easy as you might imagine because everybody lies. Everyone tells you what you want to hear and virtually everyone will basically say that they can do anything that you need done. So, I've developed a pretty straightforward checklist and I've found that – even if you don't always get the straight scoop and a full answer – by the time you've worked your way through these questions, you'll have a gut feeling as to whether this is someone that you want to be in business with and frankly that's about the best that you can do in a case like this. You won't be an entrepreneur if you didn't go with your gut more often than not anyway, but here at least you'll have a framework to help make sure that you cover the basic bases and that you don't go off half-cocked just to get the process over so you can get back to your more important business. Actually, getting these selections right is VERY important business and critically important to your business as well. So don't sell it short and don't try to rush it – it's worth the taking the time to do it right the first time so that you don't end off in a few weeks or months doing it all over again.

I call these things the 5 A's although in this age of everything inflation, you'll see that there're more like a dozen A's in the mix. Some are more objective criteria than others and those you can get some help answering by the standard methods. As an example, it actually does make sense to do some customer and reference checks before you sign on the dotted line. Others are impressions and feelings that you should try to elicit in the course of your conversations. And speaking of conversations, get yourself in front of the people who run the business – not the salesmen who sell business for them. It's those guys that you want to be looking at – eyeball to eyeball – when you're trying to decide if they'll go the extra mile and really look after your interests and your business when things get bumpy – as they always do at some point. If the right people are willing to show up and make the right kinds of commitments and assurances, and if you believe them, then you've done about the best job that you can.

So here's my short list of A's.

(A1) Ability and (Actual) Accomplishments

This one is pretty easy and referenceable. You need to make sure that they've actually done (and done well) the particular work you're asking them to do. Law firms, as an example, are notorious for saying they can do anything, but you really don't want anybody "learning" how to do something on your dime. You want the people who have done it before - not the ones who watched - or the ones who think they can do it. This is stuff you can (and definitely should) check out with their existing clients and customers. And while you're at it make sure they have the resources and the capacity to take your additional business on and to handle it from the "get-go" - not grow into it and try to add people to support it over time.

(A2) Anal and Accountable

This one's about personalities and whether they're a "fit" for you and the way you do business. Find a place that takes things personally and you're most likely to find some folks who are just as anal and driven as you are about how things should be done. By the way, these people may sometimes drive you crazy – but in a good way. Just expect some strongly expressed opinions and you'll do fine. There's always a right way to do things - you've just got to find folks who care about doing things that way and who are willing to commit the time, people and other resources necessary to do the job that way each and every time. This is the culture you want in your own company and it's essential that the people and firms helping to support you share the same work ethic and "take no prisoners" attitude. Otherwise, you set up a second class of service and your people start wasting their own time and energy pointing fingers and complaining about the work that the outsourcers aren't getting done on time and on the money.

(A3) Aggressive and Assertive

In building your external team, you want people who are leaders in their own markets – people leaning forward and into the game, not coasting or resting on their laurels. These people don't come cheap, but they're worth the investment. You will never save your way to any success worth securing – spend the money and do things right the first time. These people also tend to be fast and aggressive and they will challenge you to move quickly yourself as well. And - God forbid - they agree with everything you suggest or propose. There are only two scenarios in the real world where this kind of obsequies agreement and compliance occurs: (a) when two people consistently agree on everything, one of them is excess baggage at best and should be gone; and (b) when two people agree on everything, it turns out that one of them isn't engaged or listening and that's as bad for your business as the guy who bends over at every opportunity. Good people ask hard, direct questions and won't be pushed aside or put off. If you do that too often, they'll just pick up and leave.

(A4) Adaptable and Ambidextrous

We live in a world where's there's no "business as usual" left anywhere and you need to be sure that the partners you're picking are committed to changing with the times and changing all the time because the stark choices today are: change or die. Some deaths will be abrupt and some will be painfully slow, but you can be sure that people trying to pitch yesterday's solutions and ways of doing business to growing companies trying to address tomorrow's problems and the new challenges that arise every day are basically the walking dead and doomed. In addition to just the volume of sheer change that needs to be addressed, there's a related concern which is equally crucial. Vendors who still believe that one size of anything fits everything or that one approach or solution automatically scales and applies to most of their customers aren't people you want to be in business with because that's another sure formula for failure. Everything today needs to be customized and hyper-personalized to suit the precise and very exacting needs of each customer. Your suppliers need to be flexible enough to go in multiple directions at the same time (offering competing, conflicting and contradictory solutions to different parties) and to understand that – with today's rates of change – that what worked well for you yesterday might just be a major problem for you today and tomorrow for sure. It won't be easy for them to track and manage all these variables (and they would much prefer not to have to try), but if they don't learn to adapt their products and services along multiple and alternative vectors, they won't be of much help to you and they won't be around themselves much longer.

(A5) Always Additive

I don't like people who come to play – I like people who play to win. There's always a better, cheaper, faster or more efficient way to do things and I'm sorry to say that you personally aren't going to have the time, the bandwidth or even the ability to figure everything out yourself so you need to surround yourself with teams of people who are domain experts (in each of their areas) and count on them to contribute new ideas, approaches and solutions that will move your business forward. People who are there just to save you a dollar (or to make themselves a dollar) aren't going to be the ones to make a major difference for you. People who can add to the equation and keep raising the bar are force multipliers and you need to get them on-board and then get out of their way. Remember that customer expectations across the board are progressive – if you're not pushing the ball forward, you're losing ground to someone.

And, by the way, since every business is always "selling" themselves (and their products and services) to someone, you might take a few minutes to ask yourself how well your partners, vendors, customers, suppliers, and employees would say that your own company satisfies the 5 A's in dealing with them. Looking in the mirror isn't always a narcissistic exercise – sometimes it's a harsh and necessary evil – and a very effective way to see the most accurate reflection of how the outside world sees your business.

TULLMAN'S TRUISMS

BE SMART ENOUGH TO KNOW WHEN YOU SHOULDN'T TRUST YOURSELF

Having just heard the Winklevii twins try to "explain" to a very skeptical Dealbook audience the rationale for their Bitcoin investment and what an exciting new form of currency it has become (nothing less than "Gold 2.0" so they say), I still had trouble figuring out exactly how Bitcoins were likely to change the financial instruments and payments world as we know it. But maybe that's just me.

Bitcoins are definitely a fast, fluid, flexible and "free" solution for effecting money transfers and those attributes are certainly among the most compelling components of any new and demonstrably disruptive technology. But considering the Ozian aspects of its mysterious founder, the apocryphal stories of its formation, and the vagaries of its current administration as well as the utter lack of transparency regarding many of the mechanical functions which allegedly make it work so smoothly, it's just hard to have a great deal of confidence in the whole thing.

So, for my two cents (no pun intended), as far as new "currencies" go, I'd rather bet on the best/worst tendencies and reliably consistent behaviors of ordinary people. One thing I know for sure is that we all revere status and that we all love to keep score and - most of all – that we love to compete with each other and especially with our friends and family. In fact, in many cases, just winning isn't really enough, it's just as important to know that your friends lost.

So I'm staking my claim on "status" in all its forms and flavors as the next great "currency" and, more importantly, as the most cost-effective and accessible influencer of changes in consumer behavior which is available to smart businesses of every size. Traditional forms of advertising are antiquated and virtually invisible – broad-scale, brute force marketing clearly costs too much and returns too little – but status abides. And now is the time for you to learn how to incorporate these new behavior drivers into your relationships with your customers and prospects.

The fact is that we always knew that status mattered. But it's only with the comprehensive hyper-personalization of the web (thanks principally to *Facebook*) that these days we actually have to be whom we are because the days of Internet anonymity are long gone. And, as a result, it's become possible for any business to:

(1) confer upon and award status to others (particularly its customers);
(2) to reliably create, measure and track status, achievements, accomplishments, etc. on a massive scale; and
(3) to broadly distribute and publish the results in real time to audiences – large and small – that matter to each and every one of us.

Lists of all kinds, leader boards, badges, rankings, etc. are some of the most obvious incarnations of the status tracking/ measurement syndrome that's accelerating and being supercharged by social media. And these trends aren't limited to consumer forums – they're impacting and sweeping through the business environment as well. One of the earliest manifestations of this kind of behavior was aggregating "friends", "likes" and "followers" before we all came to appreciate that having too many friends wasn't exactly a good thing. At the same time, these early aggregations were generally enabled by a set of activities that consumers could directly manage and partially influence – if you spent the time, you could up your game and change your position. But today, that's much less true especially when you compare the old systems to today's tools like *Klout* and *Kred* which are primarily beyond the control of individuals.

I realize that *Kred* has certain self-reporting activities ("uploadable moments") that give its participants some sway over their individual rankings and ratings, but essentially these new measurement systems profess to be aggressively independent and objective even while they entice and encourage us to engage in activities which they claim to be influential in their calculation and evaluation processes.

And, by the millions these days, people are taking the bait and changing their behavior in the (most likely vain) hope that their actions will improve their stature and standings within these artificial (and largely irrelevant) hierarchies. I say "largely" irrelevant because – the fact pretty much is – that without a fairly robust and demonstrable *Klout* score these days – you can essentially forget about even getting an interview with a top tier advertising agency, PR firm or social media team.

But what does all this have to do with you and your business? Simply this. If you want to keep your customers and, in fact, deepen and extend your connection and relationship with them, you need to understand how these new notions of shared notoriety and the concept of manufactured addictions (where we repeatedly engage in activities for no real economic benefit or actual purpose other than improving our rankings or status on some utterly arbitrary listing or leader board) can be used by you to build better and more beneficial bridges to your customers which will increase their commitment and loyalty to your products and services.

There are basically 3 simple elements to the status equation which almost any business can create and implement (at little or no cost) and – in each instance – your job is to create the levels, tiers and plateaus (almost exactly as if you were building a typical computer game for your customers to play) which will help you generate the kind of quasi-competitive environment that triggers and spurs on this kind of compulsive/obsessive behavior and builds Power Users. Power Users who quickly become – not simply your most lucrative customers – but – even more importantly – your strongest, most authentic, and most aggressive advocates and promoters.

Here's a basic outline of what you need to think about and construct in the context of your business:

(1) Provide Increased Recognition for your Power Users

You need to develop a simple system to provide, document and publish the increased status and recognition which you are affording your most important customers. There are several companies already in this space who provide various programs with levels, award schemes, badges, etc. that can be easily adapted to your requirements. Just make sure that you take the time to personalize the offerings so that they don't just seem like the latest and greatest canned incentive program that some consultant sold you.

(2) Provide Expanded Access for the Power Users

As every restaurant, night club, airline and sports team learned long ago, there's always a "best" seat in the house and there are people who will do whatever it takes and stop at nothing to be granted access to those rarefied levels and locations. In the purest business context, this can range from special service lines, extended hours or credit considerations, concierges, accelerated processing or transport programs, etc. Here again, the incremental resources required to deliver these kinds of programs are trivial compared to the long term lifetime value of retaining these high-end and often hyper-active customers.

(3) Promote "Ownership" by letting Power Users Actually Influence the Business (or at least let them "think" that they are)

To a very real extent, the smartest companies today are designing programs and incentives which basically "hire" their own customers to work for them and encourage them to do significant amounts of work in the name of influence and ownership. Insurance companies are increasingly creating more self-service options for their customers and positioning these things as conveniences and tine-savers for their customers rather than cost savers for the companies which, of course, they are as well. Obviously, Wikipedia's 70,000 "editors" believe (and rightly so) that they are influencing the end product on a daily basis. And they will continue to do so without any thought of compensation so long as their efforts are acknowledged and so long as they don't feel that anyone is making a buck off of their hard work and good will. Users groups have been around for quite some time, but the difference is the immediacy with which, and the concrete ways in which, the influence of Power Users is implemented by these companies in virtually real time.

Frankly, this whole approach is just today's rife of the old Tom Sawyer fence painting scam. As Tom said to Ben: "Does a boy get a chance to whitewash a fence every day?" And a bit later, Ben asked Tom: "Say, Tom, let me whitewash a little." And the rest, as they say, is literature. Some things never change.

TULLMAN'S TRUISMS

SILENT GRATITUDE ISN'T MUCH USE TO ANYONE

In today's hyper-competitive marketplace, the most sought-after and desirable employees are the ones whose bags are always packed – not because they are disloyal or disinterested – but because they recognize that "up or out" is the way of the world today.

If you're not ready, willing and able to step forward and seize the next best opportunity – within or outside of your own company – then you'll discover pretty quickly that the people making the decisions and the key personnel selections will start to look right past you when the best opportunities are on the table.

They need people who will jump at the chance to move across the country, take on new and uncertain challenges without the slightest qualms, and – most of all – who understand that there are no guarantees of comfort, security or success these days – just the guarantee that anyone standing still (or "just" doing their job) will be blown away by the people who are doing a whole lot more and who make their interest, aptitude and attitude known.

The world today is divided into targets and gunslingers. Hot shots and has-beens (regardless of your age). Everyone is in someone else's sights and plenty of people are gunning for your position. That's why it's a good idea to keep your boots by the side of your bed – just like the firemen do.

And it's also important to remember that it's not so much a case of taking you for granted (although there are certainly elements of that) or any dissatisfaction with your current performance – it's much more about attitude and the feeling on management's part that you're not likely to be the person to take the business to the next level – regardless of the level that you're at and regardless of how important the particular assignment is.

If it's not abundantly clear that you want it (whatever the "it" happens to be) a lot more than the next twelve guys and that you're prepared to make the commitment and the sacrifices necessary to see things through and get the new job done and done well and on time and on budget, then it's very easy today for the company to find someone else who's a better bet.

So what can you do to increase your favorable odds and your visibility without overstepping the bounds of propriety or pissing off your peers? Here are a few things you can do now to get ready to be great.

(1) Sharpen Your Sights and Step Up Your Skills

It helps a whole lot to know specifically what you're shooting for. Chasing too many rabbits usually results in ending up empty handed. Set a goal, make a plan, and go for it. And while you're waiting for good things to happen, make sure you're constantly honing and updating your skill sets, adding new tools and technologies to your war chest, and learning all the while from anyone and everyone willing to share with you. Good listeners are in terribly short supply and you'd be amazed at how much valuable information people will part with if they know you're interested and that they're appreciated. Soak it all up – lifetime learners are superb sponges – and that's a good thing.

(2) Streamline Your Story and Skinny Down Your Price Tag

It's actually quite possible to be too much of a good thing in the job market and to be perceived as over-qualified for a new position that you'd absolutely kill for. It's nice to be subtle and to stay above the fray, but that's not what people are looking for today. They want people who want it and want it bad and who aren't afraid or ashamed to admit it. Those who never ask rarely, if ever, get what they want. Most of the things in life that just drop into your lap don't really belong there, aren't really worth that much, and generally result in a mess of one kind or another.

Don't try to be so delicate or oblique that your message and your interest get lost in the process. You want to be sure that, when the time and circumstances are right, you're in the game and on the short list and that you make your interest, appetite and aptitude for the new position known to all concerned. Don't ever assume that anyone besides you knows what's best or just right for you and shame on you if you don't tell them.

And, if you're not careful, you can also easily price yourself out of a new opportunity before you even get a chance to have a conversation with the people doing the search. You never really want to negotiate against yourself, but it's very important to make sure that the folks around you (and above you) know that money isn't the thing that matters the most to you.

Money is just the way that people without talent try to keep score. Doing important work; doing it exceptionally well; and getting the right, timely results is what ultimately counts and where the real satisfaction in your work will be found. Making it critical that you get a bump in your current compensation into the prime consideration in your ongoing search for your next career move is a major mistake that is most likely to lead to a very rocky road going forward. Prove yourself first – it always pays off in the long run.

(3) Scrap Your Sidekicks (Entourage) and Bag Your Baggage

Package deals may work great for travel agents and casinos, but they don't help in the hiring process. In fact, they're a drag and a major hindrance. People who try to bring too much baggage with them don't get a shot at the brass ring. You need to worry about yourself – first and foremost – and then, once you've made it over the hurdles and beyond the barricades, you can always reach back for your buddies. But, in the beginning, the old, time-tested rule still applies: he travels fastest and furthest who travels alone. It may be a lonely journey at first, but at least it's not crowded.

And try also to lose as many of the other typical kinds of impediments as possible if you really want to make a successful move. As sad as this is to say, the fact is that the more integrated into and tightly bound you are to your community and your surroundings and your outside activities, the less likely you are to make it onto many a short list. There's nothing wrong with this (from a social and family standpoint it's probably a very good thing), but you should understand that there's an embedded choice that it represents unless you actively signal and communicate otherwise which will have serious career consequences.

We're in a global race these days and you've got to be willing to get up and go where the action is whenever you're asked. And - make no mistake – you will rarely be asked twice because there's a long line right behind you of folks ready, willing and able to step right over you and into those new, bigger shoes if you hesitate in the least. They might be younger, unmarried, childless, and not house or condo bound, etc. and they are raring to go.

So, while it may be a conscious decision and the right choice for you and your family, just be aware that family and community ties are just that – "ties" that can restrict and limit your chances to move onward and upward – whether anyone ever admits that to you or not.

TULLMAN'S TRUISMS

TALENT & HARD WORK ARE NO SUBSTITUTE FOR SELF-CONFIDENCE

I think an end is in sight. That giant sucking sound which accompanied the annual flood of all the smartest quants, developers and systems engineers being swept up and into the giant banks, hedge funds, VC/PE firms and other financial institutions (never to be seen again) may finally be quieting down.

More and more talented programmers and engineers are bailing out – looking for better, not necessarily bigger – and leaving the "friendly confines" and the comfort of their current positions to look for new opportunities. And "confines" they really were. Turns out that, once you actually got into that tantalizing temple of men and money, you'd quickly discover that at the end of the day – however much money you were making and however well-appointed your digs were – you were still a troll in the tunnel. And it wasn't anyone's idea of the Tunnel of Love.

And, of course, the most ironic aspect of the situation is that the new attitudes and behaviors which are driving these alternative occupational choices are more apparent and more consistently present these days in many an employment calculation even though the long economic drought is finally beginning to abate. Big bonuses are back and sadly it's still way too much "business as usual" on Wall Street. You'd think nothing ever blew up and, of course, since no one with any true culpability was ever punished, it's like the whole deal happened to some other guys and we all just read about it in the papers. And, for sure, since this is a culture that never learns its lessons, you can expect a whole lot more of the same down the line.

So it's a lot more "show me the door" than "show me the money" these days. And really, for the good guys, the job was never about the money anyway – it was always about the work and not about the perks. It had much more to do with the idea of and the freedom to tackle the really challenging problems which were fundamentally changing the way in which the world's financial markets worked.

And it's not like we've solved all those issues; it's just that today is all about tweaks and tweaking (just like twerking) is nothing to write home about or brag about to your hacking buddies. It's the difference between inventing the Model T, on the one hand, and worrying about how long the fins and tail lights should be on this year's model, on the other.

So the smartest guys aren't locked-in, laser-focused, heads down and grinding out new code any more. The truth is that they're realizing that they're not chained to their desks and they're heads up and heading for the door in droves. So, if the shoe fits you, you need to start thinking about the same things if you don't want to be left behind in the new digital Gold Rush. Get going, get out there while the getting is good, and make sure you get yours.

Now I know that this is an easier thing to say than it is to do for many people and that most developers and engineers are surprisingly conservative whether they'd admit it or not. Structure and stability is a goal in their code and a major virtue in their lives as well. And that's why I'm going to share a little secret with all of you which should make the process a lot simpler, safer and more comfortable.

Here's the secret: You Can Always Go Back. (Better)

Now what exactly does that mean? It's really simple. If you're not an asshole when you leave (and you don't leave anyone in the lurch), they'll always take you back in a heartbeat if things don't work out better for you out there in the "real" world.

And just why would they do that? Because on the round trip, you'll be a better trained, more experienced, and especially more up-to-date candidate for the position. The fact is that everyone gets stale and everyone gets a little lazy. So if you've been in a job for years and you're working with the same code base and working on variations and tweaks of the same problem set, you're just not likely to also be the one guy in a thousand who spends his weekends making sure that he's current on everything new that happening. And you're also not likely to be the guy who wakes up one morning with a ridiculous and counter-intuitive approach to handling some problem that's been staring your whole team in the face for months or years. Radical change and disruptive innovation come from the outside of organizations, not from the people in charge or the one's maintaining the status quo.

So, instead of being a scarlet letter or something to be ashamed of (as if you were disloyal and abandoned ship), the fact that you joined a start-up trying to change the world or spent a year or two learning a new set of mobile tools or some crazy new e-commerce platform isn't a bad thing – it's actually a career-booster, even at your old place of employment. I've seen it happen a million times already – if you're good and newly- gung ho to jump back in, only someone who's a complete management moron would hold a grunge and bar the door back in. If they're smart, they'll ask you if you've stumbled across 3 more guys who also want to join up and also have new skills, new strengths, and a new outlook on how to approach the key issues. As long as they're not bitter and happy to have you back; you're actually in a better position and a better hire than anyone else they could find because you know the ropes and the mess of legacy spaghetti that they call their code.

So what are you waiting for? There's a big wide world out there waiting for you to rattle a few cages and make some critical, game-changing changes. And you can do it. And, worst case, you can always come back. Better.

I'm always surprised how often even very sharp entrepreneurs don't understand the importance of always making sure (through repeated and consistent communication with their team) that, even as their people are chasing new sales opportunities and falling in love with the newest and coolest marketing tools and tricks, they aren't losing their focus on the basic blocking, tackling and execution that help to consistently pay the bills. Essentially this entails nothing more than taking really good care of your existing customers. This may seem a bit old school and even a little boring, but it's a tried and true way to build an increasingly valuable enterprise.

I have always called this basic business strategy "knocking on old doors" which means working harder to deepen your connection to and your involvement with your current customers and thereby to increase their average spend ("share of wallet") as well as to lock them in for the long haul. It's critical for new businesses to always remember that customer churn is the ultimate enemy of increased profitability. In the frenzy of a hot start-up, it may appear that customers are easy to come by because the adoption rate of anything shiny and new these days is remarkably high. But the abandonment rate is 10 times higher than that and if you're not quickly connecting with and retaining these new customers, they'll be gone and you'll be running on a treadmill and going nowhere fast.

Your existing customers (the newest and the oldest) are already in your system and you're already regularly interacting with them (hopefully effectively) so - rather than spending scarce money chasing new customers or trying to steal customers from the competition - you just need to do a better and more expansive job of servicing the guys you've already got and the cumulative results – particularly year over year - will knock your socks off.

It's pretty much a given that happy and "cared-for" customers will simply end up spending more with your company over time. And "organic" customers (basically home-grown) regularly spend LOTS more with better margins than customers acquired through one-off marketing spends, promotions, and other incentives that may attract incremental customers, but don't create lasting connections to them. Think of the pain and suffering caused to thousands of small restaurants by Groupon 1.0 which drew tons of "cheapies", but few returning "foodies".

Happy customers also boost your business and your profits in other ways. They not only buy more (and at better prices); they are also easier and less costly to service; and they're a great and active source of referrals. Especially in the new age of tech-enabled social media, constant connectivity and collaborative commerce, this is the "new" news.

An active, well-run program that drives, encourages and rewards ongoing and authentic customer recommendations and referrals (and incents them to take ownership of the relationship) will generate 5 to 10 times the bottom-line results in terms of actual revenues as any of the other traditional tools including trade shows, print media, and even direct, in-person sales calls. And the results are far more obvious and measurable as well.

You can pretty much forget entirely about trade shows – they're toast. Expensive, inefficient and unfocused: they burn out your people; generate a bunch of worthless leads from lookers, not decision makers; and divert your attention from the things that matter most. If the real decision-makers are even "in the house" at these things these days; you can be sure that they aren't walking the floor and looking for you.

Similarly, in most businesses today, the people still using printed media are so far behind the curve that they might just as well take the money they're spending on creating and delivering print solutions and burn it. In fact, I think – especially in older traditional markets like car sales – that more print/newspaper advertising is driven today by inertia and superstition than by smarts or strategy. You hear older dealers (usually in businesses not run by professional managers) say: "It's how we've always done it – why should we stop now?" Scary, but true.

And frankly, even ignoring the growing presence, utility and efficiency of net-based meetings and demos and video conferencing services, the math today for most products and services simply no longer makes sense or justifies having your sales people on the road trying to sell new customers face-to-face. Wining and dining might be great for your sales people, but from the perspective of busy management personnel in well-run businesses, it went out with the 3 martini lunch quite a long time ago. Good managers want decision-making data about proposed solutions presented as quickly and clearly as possible and they want it now – not in two weeks when the salesman can stop by.

And, if you asked them, your existing customers would also tell you that they're perfectly happy with regular phone updates and new product suggestions or even timely email communications if they are properly managed and valuable rather than just random and unfocused promotional materials. This is known as "the ATM phenomenon". Is there anyone left in the world who would rather deal with a bored and borderline teller rather than a rapid-fire ATM machine for virtually any banking transaction? By and large, if you take a careful look, you'll find that your customers feel pretty much the same about their interactions with you and your sales force. Especially if you have a strong CRM program in place which is primarily focused on capturing the lifetime value of each customer.

But strong, long-term customer connections don't happen by themselves. You need to continually and aggressively work on new ways to keep your customers engaged and invested in the success of your business (as well, of course, as in the success of their own businesses). This process is pretty well understood, although rarely consistently executed.

But the less well-known and clearly under-appreciated tool for customer retention that's even more important because of its competitive deterrence as well as its retention benefits is the need to do everything in your power to increase your customers' switching costs. This is what I call the process of "making moats" which not only keeps your customers in the stable, but also makes it much harder for the competition to reach them and induce them to move. Effective "moats" can come in many forms, sizes and shapes and only you will be able to quickly determine which are the easiest and most cost-effective for you and which make the most sense for your customers.

Keep in mind that I'm not talking here about things like long-term contracts with overlapping expiration dates or similar "legal" constraints which keep folks in the fold. I'm talking about arrangements, value-added tools and data, and other barriers to switching or leaving which arise as a result of things you build and deliver in the ordinary course of your business operations which actually improve the customers' experience and also – as an added benefit – make it much harder for some other competitor or vendor to steal them away.

As I said, the examples are too numerous to list, but there are three industry characteristics which will help you discover and develop the moats which will matter the most in your business.

(1) Complexity

The more that you can do to streamline and simplify essential, but complicated processes for your customers and increase their productivity by saving them time and avoiding redundancy; the "stickier" your connection with them will become. Sometimes these may be complexities built into your own systems, but more likely these are aspects of doing business within a given industry or system where you can accumulate and share – exclusively with your customers – procedures, documents, regulations, and other resources that are necessary to the business, but not necessarily readily-accessible or even known to occasional users. Pre-populated forms; access to associated information like applicable state taxes; drop-down lists and boxes with regularly used choices and selections; embedded estimators and calculators, etc. are all valuable add-ons and the more detailed and industry/user-specific your incorporated add-ons (think of these as "power tools") can be made; the more valuable they will become to your customers and the harder they will be for competitors to replicate.

(2) Compliance

Many industries are more highly regulated than most people can imagine and it takes years of painful and costly experience (often through trial and error) to develop the internal resources and personnel who are sufficiently skilled at navigating these regulatory environments to permit a given company to successfully compete with other established players. But, in many cases, these companies come to rely very heavily on their vendor/partners because a substantial amount of the industry wisdom and compliance knowledge is actually in the hands of the vendors rather than the companies themselves. This is primarily because the vendors are regularly interacting with the state and federal regulators on behalf of multiple clients and parties whereas a typical company's involvement will be much more infrequent and sporadic. The more that you (as a vendor/partner) can add additional functionality and the products of your broader experience to your offerings (turning your "products" into more valuable "services" and consulting), the more locked-in, the customers become.

(3) Consistency

As strange as it may seem from the outside, in many cases, it is often the third-party vendor/partners of large corporations who are the ONLY parties who actually have the data and the ability to advise and assure these large, unintegrated organizations that their various departments, divisions and affiliates are operating in a consistent fashion across the business and in a manner consistent with the company's own rules, regulations and policies. To a certain extent, this is another value-added service where you have the opportunity to provide quasi-managerial functions for your clients who simply don't have the internal capacity or organization (or sometimes the necessary information systems) sufficient to handle these tasks themselves. They really can't tell the left hand what the right hand is doing and they operate at their peril (especially in highly-regulated industries) because of this. As a result and as you begin to gather and archive more and more information about their business's functions and organization, you become an increasingly unique and valuable asset and basically irreplaceable. In an era with increasing management and employee turnover and diminishing institutional memory at all levels, being the keeper of the company's operational history and one of the few places they can turn to assure compliance and consistency throughout their company is a powerful lever for your business and a major deterrent to your competition.

Bottom line: if you want to hang on to your customers for the long run (which is really the name of the game for successful businesses) and go beyond the basic CRM programs that are table stakes these days; you need to erect exit barriers (moats) which raise your customers' switching costs; provide substantial disincentives to migration; and help to exclude competitors. Focusing on their needs to reduce complexity, increase compliance and assure consistency throughout their businesses is the key to keeping them.

In picking prospective partners or deciding which potential investors make the most sense for your business (assuming that you have the luxury of making such a choice), nothing matters more in the short run (and in the long run) than the proper alignment of the interests of the parties to the deal. Today, there's plenty of fast money to go around; lots of people it would be easy to live and work with; and plenty of players who, on paper, would make great partners. But if your dreams are different from theirs and your ultimate desires diverge, it's just a matter of time before the venture's wheels get wobbly and the vehicle runs off the road. And what's really amazing to me is how quickly the disconnects in these deals can appear and how obvious in retrospect the differences which drove the parties apart seem to any objective viewer from the outside.

I suppose though that, if the people on both sides of a deal want it to happen so badly, they're more than willing to ignore those ugly little facts and warning signs that don't fit conveniently into the big picture. Their hearts are probably in the right place, but their heads are stuck somewhere dark and entirely different. In this business, you've got to always remember that no deal is <u>much</u> better than a bad deal and that there's always another deal right around the corner.

And it's also crucial to appreciate that sometimes a deal can be critically important to one side (maybe even a life or death opportunity for a start-up) and, for the people on the other side, who are big, fat and happy, "corporate", and secure in their jobs; it's just another transaction – maybe even just a "take it or leave it" experiment – and basically nothing more than another day at the office rather than a make-or-break shot for a new business. And truthfully, whatever your business is, you don't want to be on the wrong side of this equation.

And we aren't talking about just amateurs here; these are some of the smartest guys in the room and in the media and entertainment businesses who are making these kinds of fundamental miscalculations. And this isn't a one-off case or an incidental "miss" where it's only a bad mistake or two – we're talking about quite a few. In fact, in the most recent YouTube example, there were hundreds of businesses and thousands of people and hundreds of millions of dollars involved and they still totally missed the boat. They went from being industry heroes ("content is king") to being non-entities and essentially homeless in less than a year. All because they had the wrong ducks in the wrong rows and no alignment.

So, when you see dozens and dozens of content deals all implode in a relatively short period of time, it's worth taking a closer look at what went so terribly wrong so quickly. After all, these weren't fake Wall Street junk securities or made-up collateralized mortgages – these were mostly deals that seemed pretty solid, but nonetheless went swiftly up in smoke. Not every one of them failed – but basically for its $300 plus million, YouTube ended up with a bag or two of beans and a couple of very expensive lessons.

Having been in the content creation business myself many times, I predicted the minute I heard the first announcement about these deals that the vast majority would fail because I thought that none of the "celebrity" or athlete creators appreciated how challenging it was going to be to try to create a constant stream of fresh and credible content for a 24/7 channel and how hard it is to keep up with the ravenous and constantly-changing demands of today's short attention span audiences.

My sense was that they thought they'd take YouTube's money (after all, who wouldn't take a million bucks with no real strings attached?) and then dump a bunch of pre-existing video material and other stuff they had stored or left over somewhere in the can into the new streaming services. Basically this looked to me like another generation of people trying to create just the latest pile of digital shovel ware – reusing old tired stuff - and trying to cram it into new delivery vehicles.

And while crappy content was undoubtedly a contributing factor to the failure and I was right about the results; I was basically wrong about the primary reasons that explain why this massive venture failed. The three main reasons things blew up were all about the alignment (or lack thereof) of the parties. It's hard to get to a happy ending when you start out headed in different directions. Same bed; separate dreams. And that's what happened here.

In July, 2012, YouTube announced that it was going to immediately spend $100 million to fund the development of 100 different web-based channels whose content would be developed and delivered by a diverse collection of producers, celebrities, entertainers, athletes, etc. – the vast majority of whom had never done anything like this before. This "Original Channels" initiative (eventually supported by another $200 million in YouTube marketing funds) was largely abandoned in less than a year and officially wiped off the map (shades of Stalin) a couple of months later at which point even a Google search couldn't find the original landing pages for the project.

So what went wrong? There were basically three critical miscalculations:

(1) The parties' understandings of the scope of their respective commitments and of the duration of those commitments were misaligned.

As obvious as it seems in retrospect, building and maintaining a media channel is an ongoing and constant process which not only never really ends, but which also requires continuous incremental investment – not simply for marketing – but for new production costs as well.

To the extent that the "producers" of these new channels thought in any detail about this situation, they were applying the traditional "network" model where a first season's "pilot" production is funded by the network and, if the show is successful, the producer looks to the network for additional funding to produce additional shows. Some of their confusion is completely understandable because both YouTube and others (like Netflix more recently) are completely comfortable calling themselves content networks even though it's not really clear (certainly in YouTube's case) that they understand what that means.

And, notwithstanding all the talk about next-gen networks, YouTube's perspective on the whole matter was completely different from that of the talent. They were applying the seed capital model and assumed that they would provide each channel with funds sufficient to launch and then it would be the responsibility of each channel's producers to obtain follow-on funding to the extent that the channel was gaining traction and initially successful.

In addition, as noted above, while this was serious business for the producers, it was pretty clearly just an experiment on YouTube's part and, in a fashion entirely consistent with their particular engineering mindset and analytical methodology, as soon as the data demonstrate that a venture's not viable, they turn off the spigot and move on to the next project.

What's the moral of this part of the story? You should never confuse a gift horse with a guarantee. And the "real" networks are not much different – they love ya to death until the day they don't and then they're gone.

(2) The "product" offerings and the prospective YouTube audiences for them were misunderstood and misaligned.

Not too long ago, and unrelated to the YouTube channel initiative, I had the chance to work with 4 of the leading and most popular "performers" on YouTube to produce some marketing videos for a new music-based video game. Each of these individuals/groups had spent several years developing a growing and loyal subscriber base for the karaoke music videos that they were creating (basically in their bedrooms) on a regular basis and they had hundreds of thousands of followers.

These 'performers" weren't well-known or media celebrities in any traditional sense, but they were pioneers in the emerging area of "camming" and they were all beginning to make an actual living doing their thing. They were creating personal and authentic connections with growable niche audiences and the "connections" they were building had as much and actually more to do with their personalities and patter than it did with the actual music they were making which was – after all – just their karaoke versions of pop songs.

What was very clear was that their audiences and followers (and, in fact, almost all of the steady YouTube video consumers) had absolutely no recurring interest in celebrity performers, traditional media stars or entertainers and jocks. Sure, they might drop in to watch one version of the new JT or JZ video on the day it was released, but essentially, if they were going to commit to anything on a continuing basis, it wasn't going to be some plastic performer that they knew was simply doing it for the money. They were looking for "real" people generating content that was not too far from material which they believed (rightly or wrongly) that they could produce themselves if they had the time, resources and inclination. Polished material, professional production values, synthesized sounds, etc. were all just a little too slick for their tastes.

So when YouTube launched the channel initiative with far more emphasis on the "hype" than the "heart" and somewhat cynically selected a bunch of performer/producers that they believed had significant niche followings which would follow them indiscriminately anywhere, the YouTube users basically weren't interested. Ultimately, the only channels that made it were the guys that had pre-existing channels and some decent traction before the new initiative ever launched.

What did they miss here? The real attraction, connection and engagement mechanism was not the songs or the sounds; it was the apparent accessibility of the talent and the shared social aspects of the group self-organizing around these performers as a connected community that was the underlying reason why large volumes of YouTube users were adopting and following each of them.

Sustainable YouTube success is predicated on <u>nobodies</u> developing significant <u>niche</u> audiences of true fans with shared ideas, values and perspectives and a strong sense of belonging to a community of their own making rather than fleeting and totally fickle followers of mass-market, made-for-the-media celebrities who have no authentic or actionable connection to anyone.

The lesson here is really about listening. There are plenty of ways and lots of tools to effectively listen to your customers and users today and to develop offerings consistent with their interests and appetites. Trying to create and launch new products and services in a vacuum and then trying to force-feed these with celebrity hook-ups and heavy marketing dollars on users who are already drowning in better choices is the worst kind of arrogance and stupidity.

(3) The timing and the scale of the channel development initiative and the fundamental adoption culture of the YouTube audiences were misaligned.

You would think that one thing which the guys from Google/YouTube would be aware of was the adoption/abandonment behavior of the active users on their sites. Another thing would be the law of averages and the unlikelihood that, out of 100 newly-created anythings, any more than a very few would ever be viable channels or worth watching. And a third thing would be that even the most committed and dedicated user/viewer has a finite amount of time to consume media and the average user couldn't possibly be expected to sample more than a few new channels in any reasonably short period of time. But notwithstanding all of these factors, these guys just went right ahead and basically launched everything at one time.

Consistent growth and sustained engagement on YouTube is absolutely a function of user acceptance and the passage of time. Audiences build slowly over many months and only if the content being offered maintains a high level of consistent quality. While it is true that certain individual videos (for reasons that no one can explain) go viral and, in a relatively short time, can have millions of views, this has nothing to do with the idea that users would subscribe to or otherwise return regularly to a video channel to see updates and newly-added content without considerable marketing, substantial and highly-favorable word of mouth, aggressive sharing, etc.

But, instead of adopting some type of measured roll-out where small curated groups of additional channels (perhaps related in terms of subject matter) were added on a regular basis over several months, the YouTube channels initiative tried to blow out all of the new content (basically a "spray and pray" approach) and that's why essentially more than 90% of the channels failed to find any sizeable and sustainable audience.

What's the lesson here? Apart from the utter lack of awareness and respect for the way their own users operated and slowly accepted new material, and the sheer presumption that they either knew or could dictate what their users would like to see, they basically spent almost a year trying to push a rope. That is, trying to convince an over-served and essentially disinterested universe of viewers to change their basic consumption patterns overnight and to seek out and at least sample multiple instances of untested and unproven content.

There's only one explanation for why anyone would buy into this entire venture. It's the same classic observation made by William Goldman about Hollywood as far as what movies will sell and succeed. His conclusion was simplicity itself. He concluded that "nobody knows anything".

TULLMAN'S TRUISMS

IT'S NOT WHAT YOU'RE SELLING, IT'S WHAT THEY'RE BUYING

I want to thank the ADL for this tremendous honor and especially the ADL staff for all of their hard work in pulling this amazing dinner together so smoothly and professionally. I want to thank Governor Quinn, Mayor Emanuel and President Preckwinkle for joining us tonight and for their kind and generous comments.

I also want to thank our clergy for their inspiring participation in tonight's event. And finally thank all of you – especially my wife, daughters, and granddaughters – all my girls – and my extended family as well and my broader family of so many people who have honored me with their presence here tonight and with whom I've been privileged to work for over 50 years in so many different, exciting and challenging businesses.

I'm flattered and grateful that you are here for me and appreciative as well of your support for this most-deserving and important organization. I'm sure they could have found many more-deserving recipients, but I'm very happy they chose me and very proud to be here at this particular and tremendously exciting time in my life and in all of our lives. We're on the cusp on changes of an impact and magnitude unlike any we've experienced in my lifetime and it's going to be quite a ride.

They say that timing is everything and, as you probably know, I've just retired after 6 long, but extremely gratifying, years of building Tribeca Flashpoint Academy into the country's leading digital media arts college and , far more importantly, of training and enabling many hundreds of talented graduates to be effective and compelling storytellers. And it's the power and the accompanying responsibilities of storytelling that are the ties that bind my comments tonight to the mission and the ongoing efforts of the ADL.

Storytelling is the way we teach and the way we learn. The stories we tell others help us to share our knowledge, experience and wisdom. The stories we tell ourselves give us faith, courage, inspiration and the strength to bear on against seemingly insurmountable odds and obstacles. But the stories we tell our children and those they create and tell themselves are the most crucial of all because these stories can heighten a child's horizons and broader their perspectives or, in the next instant, they can crush their creativity and condemn them to a bleak and soulless future.

Stories play a crucial role in all of our lives and they aren't neutral. Stories are lessons embedded in language (whether written, spoken or seen – or all of the above) and they can bring us together or they can tear us apart. Sadly, in today's socially-fueled and fired media and technology frenzy, we've done a great job of enabling and empowering enhanced expression – where our stories (for better or worse) spread instantly around the world, but we've done a lousy job (especially with anyone under 30) of explaining the ethical and moral responsibilities that come with the expanded power to persuade and the weight and impact which the stories we now tell can have on other lives.

In a recent song, Same Love, Macklemore talks about how readily we call each other hurtful names "behind the keys of a message board" and about the harm and the pain that these rote and thoughtless actions can cause. It's just too easy, too insular, and far too separated from any concrete consequences today for people to launch hateful and deceitful speech and spiteful slanders with a few keystrokes on their computer or phone. We're not going to completely stop this behavior any time soon or maybe ever, but there's help available from the ADL in the form of education and encouragement (of the amazing kinds that you're heard and seen tonight) and in the form of reporting, refereeing and record-keeping that helps us all better appreciate the scope and magnitude of these problems and the new stresses and strains that they are increasingly putting on the social fabric of our society.

Too many young people (present company excepted) in our frightfully permissive and over-parented society learn early on that they can do no wrong – that they're all entitled and exceptional – top of the heap and talented beyond measure – and that even the worst actions are ultimately free of consequences or accountability. But it's just not true and, frankly, it's organizations like ADL that can help us tell the next several generations what's right and what's wrong. And if ADL wasn't there to help explain, educate and enforce the right values and behaviors, I'm not really sure who would step into that particularly unwelcoming void.

Before I close, I want to say something about my newest job as the incoming CEO of 1871. I couldn't be more excited about the opportunity especially because I have always viewed my career (as varied as it may seem from the outside) as a very coherent continuum where I have tried to move from strength to strength and – at the same time – to bring along with me all the experiences of the past (good and bad) and many of the key people who've made the prior successes possible. I've talked a lot about stories tonight and I see the job at 1871 as a chance to turn hundreds of stories into start-ups and to turn hundreds of ideas into invoices. It's all about making realistic dreams come true and about the dedication, hard work and sacrifice that it takes to make that happen. In many ways, it's similar to the way we helped the students here tonight stand before us and make their dreams become realities as well.

So I'm proud to be here tonight to support the important and ongoing work of the ADL; I'm totally blown away by the students' stories that we saw and heard tonight (it does give me hope); I thank all of you for being here; and I promised to get everyone out of here and home by 9 o'clock. Especially me. So good night and God bless.

I have to laugh and just shake my head when people tell me that they are working on the digital strategy for their business or reluctantly ask me to help them figure out what they should be doing about social media as if it's a new form of head lice or psoriasis or something equally disgusting, contagious and unavoidable. It's a little like saying that you've decided you're going to spend a little time each day breathing – even though you're pretty busy with a bunch of other commitments – because it seems like the smart thing to do.

Digital technologies and social media channels and the new degrees and depth of "connection" that they enable are so mission-critical these days and so pervade every aspect of what we need to be doing in our lives and companies – as every business in the world migrates rapidly from analog anything to digital everything – that the incorporation of these powerful tools and technologies isn't an option or a choice, they are inevitable additions to your arsenal and, frankly, the sooner the better. I see the two alternative paths as very binary – you can engage or you can be extinct. Change and grow or die – pretty stark choices. You can face the facts or you can be like that lonesome old fax machine sitting in the corner just dreading the day when it will finally be unplugged and trashed.

This is a major topic which is well-suited for a series of columns, but, for the moment, I just want to give you a short list of the 5 major dimensions of enablement which digital is bringing to the game. If you ask yourself what you are doing or about to do in your business to take advantage of these new resources, tools, technologies, channels and perspectives which are now available basically because of the digital datafication of everything, you'll get a head start on your peers and competitors. It's not an easy process or a short path, but it's already well underway and you need to get with the program or get left behind. It's always the same story: you can make the dust or you can eat someone else's dust.

One crucial aspect of this ongoing and highly-disruptive transformation which the mass media really doesn't seem to appreciate is that the most critical attribute of the Internet is NOT its immediacy or its low cost; it is the heightened direct access to identified individuals, the ability to accurately measure and react to their ongoing engagement in real time, and the media spend direction and accountability that it enables.

Here are the 5 vital vectors:

(1) Superior Customer Targeting and Offer Optimization

I've talked before about hyper-personalization (customer demographics) which morphed quickly into determining and tracking interests and attitudes (customer preferences and desires) and now we're moving forward again to anticipatory actions which let us drive and leverage future customer behaviors. This is a page right out of the canon of Steve Jobs who basically said that consumers don't know what they want until we create it and show it to them. Or as Henry Ford might have said about consumer demand for the Model T: If I had asked people at the time what they wanted, they would have said they needed faster horses, not automobiles.

(2) New Levels of Analytics & Insights Based on Speed & Scale

Size is nice, but in today's world, speed is what kills. It's not the big guys who are moving the needle today; it's the fast and responsive guys. Everything we're doing today in marketing is time-compressed and the rate of required change continues to accelerate. You'll never see smart marketers buying 12 week campaigns any longer and then sitting back and hoping things work out well. We have tools to see how things are trending in our campaigns on a minute-to-minute basis and today that's the standard for reacting to those behaviors as well. We're not talking about an A/B testing world any more. We're talking about A to Z systems that can launch 20 alternative offers to a small (and inexpensive, but representative) segment of a target list; collect and collate the responses in real time (minutes rather than months); prioritize the winning pitches and kill off the losers and then launch the winners against the larger lists and continue this iterative process all day long. No one said it was gonna be easy – just essential. And the ante just keeps getting upped.

If you haven't seen and started to use GOOGLE Product Listing Ads (PLAs), you're late. But what's most important is to understand – not how much more appealing a GOOGLE search response is which features multiple responsive product images and pricing from local merchants – you need to appreciate how much more work this represents for each local merchant. Every product has to be imaged, catalogued, loaded and priced (realistically, the pricing almost needs to be dynamic for your particular offerings to remain competitive) and the whole thing needs to be actively managed and updated constantly. It's a whole every day job just to stay in the game and increasingly it's going to have to be machine-driven and informed – much like programmed stock trading. But who's going to create and supply these kinds of tools for SMBs to permit them to remain competitive in these new, high-speed marketplaces? I see this whole area as just another amazing set of opportunities for entrepreneurs. But even if you're not building the new tools for the rest of us, you'd better be doing something in your business to respond.

(3) Ability to Change Consumer Behaviors in Real Time

If you're always reacting (regardless of how quickly) to the behavior of the consumers you're trying to reach, in today's world of high-velocity computing, you'll always be behind the curve and behind your competition because the game is now to get ahead of the consumer and to "know before they go" so that you can be there when they arrive. Sites like www.chango.com offer these kinds of tools for smart marketers with response and reaction times in the area of 10 milliseconds – faster than a webpage can load. As you can imagine, if I'm taking search results (what you found) and I'm trying to launch offers to you in response to those searches, I'm going to <u>always</u> lose out to the competitors whose tools and technologies enable them to determine what I'm looking for and present me with those choices rather than waiting for me to ask or find the answers on my own. It's a world moving from diagnostics (historical analysis) to prognostics (anticipation and prediction) and you need to get your business on the bus or you'll be left behind.

(4) Two-Way Channels for Ongoing Consumer Conversations

The ability to have ongoing, long-term, unmediated and bi-directional conversations with our customers on a massive scale provides us with the tools and channels we need to increase the lifetime value of each customer (LCV). Nothing is more directly connected to profitability than growing your share of each of your customers' spend and improving your retention of those customers. You now have the ability to determine - not simply whether your customers are seeing or hearing your messages, but whether they are listening to them and responding to them in meaningful ways. We've moved from a broadcast world (call it "spray and pray") to improved and more targeted unilateral communications and now we're moving forward again to two-way talks and credible conversations.

(5) Concrete and Readily Available Metrics – CAC, CSI, CRM

Data is the Oil of the Digital Age. If you don't already understand how critical access to and the constant measurement of the data which drives your business has become to your survival (not simply your success), there's not much I can add to the discussion. As Louis Armstrong used to say: "If you have to ask what jazz is, you'll never know".

TULLMAN'S TRUISMS

HAVING TOO MUCH EXPERIENCE KEEPS YOU FROM BEING ABLE TO QUICKLY ADAPT

Having been in sales for most of my adult life (and frankly what entrepreneur isn't always "selling" something), I try to never be rude to even the most clueless or incompetent salesman because I know what a tough and thankless job sales can be. But recently I stopped taking one guy's calls and began just hanging up when he started directly calling my cell phone. (I've also been ducking my barber's calls, but that's a different story.)

All I can say is that I'm very grateful for Caller I.D. these days because – although most of the time I'm strong enough not to hate, this guy was treading on the thinnest of ice. And why? Because he simply wore out his welcome and – with me at least – once you've burned that particular bridge, there's really no way back. Life's just too short to deal with ignoranuses. And, in case that's a new word for you – it's people who are both ignorant and assholes.

But the saddest part of the story is that I went out of my way to give him all kinds of fair warnings. You can't push a rope no matter how hard you try and I fundamentally wasn't interested in what he was selling at the time. Unfortunately, he was just in too much of a hurry to hear me – even assuming (which might be a stretch) that he was interested. The truth is that it's a very thin line between persistence and pestilence, but it's pretty bright and obvious if you're paying attention and listening to what your prospect or customer is saying. This shouldn't be that hard a concept to master.

The fact is that all long-term success in selling always comes from two things – even in this crazy, time-constrained and chronically impatient world in which we are living – building relationships and being patient. And, by the way, I can't believe that I'm saying this – the world's most impatient guy and a long time sufferer of hurry sickness, but it's actually true. Trying to press a sale on an unwilling buyer at the wrong time is a waste of effort and energy. Patience always achieves more in the long run than force and, as I always say, even the strongest "No" is just a "No" for now. But not if you burn down the place and wreck your relationship in the process.

In sales, you're always dealing with people's perceptions which can shift in an instant – they're erratic and discontinuous – so, for a long time, you're it and the next moment, you're out - if you're not careful to thread the needle between obnoxious and irresistible.

I've got a few ideas and suggestions to share with you to help you think about ways to keep the conversation moving forward without crossing the customer's comfort line and throwing out the baby with the bathwater.

(1) Small Serial Successes

Great sales people will tell you that winning is almost never about hitting home runs or bowling someone over in a first meeting with your bravado and BS. It's about solid and consistent base hits – an unbroken series of successful gestures and increments - that lead over time to a relationship based on trust and then a sale. There are times when it's more important to walk away and wait for the real deal than it is to grab a quick sale (whatever your sales manager might think) which may or may not make ultimate sense for the customer. You have to learn to communicate a sense of urgency without seeming to be in a hurry. If you can't move things forward, it's a good time to move on and wait for a better moment.

(2) Someone is Always Selling

As they always say about stocks, they're not bought, they're sold. Selling is about momentum and – at any moment in a conversation – someone is selling – it just might not be you. If you find yourself leaning back on your heels and suddenly on the defensive, you've lost control of the conversation and, most likely, you've just met a master salesman who happens to be your prospective customer at the moment. You always want to be selling from strength and not seeking sympathy or someone's pity. It's OK to agree with your customers and even to empathize with them and all of their problems – as long as you don't end up (with the tables turned) agreeing with their very good reasons for not buying your product or service. And one more thought on this topic – as soon as you start talking about price – you're on the slippery slope and headed in the wrong direction. It's better at that point to pick up your marbles and pack your bags and come back when you're got a better story to sell.

(3) Sell Something Else

When you're selling something that nobody really needs, you'd better actually be selling something else. This is why perfumes are sold by smell, sex and status rather than dollars and cents. And why alarm systems are sold by images of burglars and broken glass – by smoke, security and safety concerns – and almost never on price.

(4) Manufacture "Maybes" and Reasons to Return

In sales, closure is as bad as cancer. A million "maybes" are better than having the door definitely shut in your face. So it's important to always have a plan to prolong the conversation; to have something (however modest) that the customer can say "Yes" to; and to always have a reason to return. Good selling is telling – explaining without a hidden agenda – adding to the customer's knowledge base – and being an impartial source of this type of "education" – and even of juicy industry gossip – is a way to make sure you're welcome to return.

Effective competition has always been multi-dimensional. One-trick ponies and businesses that were strong in a single area (product, technology, sales or marketing, etc.) but short in others rarely succeeded in the long run. By and large, there wasn't enough time to fix their shortcomings before the fast followers not only caught up, but quickly provided solutions which were quicker, cheaper, easier to implement or just better designed and more responsive to the real needs of the market.

The first movers and pioneers often identified and defined the problem, developed early approaches and simple solutions, and made all the early mistakes that are always part of the process and they basically set the table. And then, in too many cases to even count, an army of imitators rolled right over them and ate their lunch. One rule will never change – in the end, consumers don't ever care who was first, they only care whose product, service or solution is best when they're buying.

And today, I think it's an even tougher game because some of the fundamental terms of successful competition – especially for start-ups – have changed and the winners (as always) will be the companies that catch on quickly and respond to the new conditions. Sometimes that means moving forward and sometimes that means getting back to basics. These days, we're in a world where there's plenty of capital, there're more than enough customers, and there's even a growing talent pool in many industries and areas.

The competition today is not for capital or resources – it's for the consumer's attention and – for better or worse – you're competing for that attention – not simply with your direct and indirect competitors – you're competing with EVERYTHING that gets in the way of or in front of your message. Don't believe me? Check out your phone (which we do on average 150 times a day) and just scan your messages and news feeds. Family, friends, photos, phonies, ads, alerts, offers – it's unending and filters aren't much help so far. In fact, the initial GOOGLE filters are worse than no help – they actually make more work while you try to find buried messages and important information that some machine or moron at GOOGLE decided weren't worth your time.

It's just a fact of life that the channels to the consumer (and to all of us as well) are congested, confused, clogged, and increasingly costly and it's just way too easy for your message to get lost or drowned in the deluge. Media today is everything that gets in the way of communication. And there's only one thing that could make the situation worse. Spending money that you don't have and can't afford to waste on pushing out a confused or muddled message.

So we're back to that very basic idea that - in communicating with your customers and prospects - getting your message right is even more important than getting your message through. And here's the deal – one is the number. One message, one voice, one spokesman – end of story.

If you're the entrepreneur, I'm hereby giving you permission to tell everyone else to suck on it. It's your show, it's your story, and it's your game to win or lose. And – in the end – it's not about a rampant outbreak of the Egola virus (and don't let anyone else tell you otherwise), it's about effectiveness.

(1) It's Never Everybody's Turn

I realize that a company consists of many people and that many of them are making important contributions to the growth and development of the business. But I just don't care about them or their hurt feelings when they don't get their turn on TV or in the spotlight. Find other ways to recognize and reward their contributions. Democracy isn't a virtue in effective messaging – consistency, image, clarity and communication are all that matter. Let the whiners be the co-captains of the company bowling team.

(2) It's Not Really About You

It's always possible that you aren't the best spokesman for your business or that you're not comfortable in the role. If that's the case, just find the best person you can for the job. I'm assuming that you're smart enough to know your own limitations and desires. (Of course, if you can't successfully sell yourself and your idea, you might just as well forget about being an entrepreneur anyway – although I do realize that the selling doesn't necessarily have to be done on TV or in the spotlight.)

The real point is that – if you do sign up to do this job – it's not an ego thing – it's because it's hard enough to get a clear and concise message out there into the world and the more you can simplify the process - streamline the ideas and the images – and structure the conversations, the more successful you will be. You could teach other people over time to do this, but it's a waste of time in the early stages of the business to even try. Just do it yourself – it's faster and far more impactful.

And keep in mind that delegating your messaging to anyone else – especially outsiders and consultants – is a total disaster. The media may not know much – but they do know the real thing when they see it. And messengers and middle-men just don't work anymore. Like it or not, entrepreneurs today are mini-rock stars and that's who they folks want to see and hear from.

(3) It Really Does Work – Especially for MSM

The media doesn't know anything other than what you tell them. They're lazy and time-constrained. The easier and faster you can make it for them – think one-stop shopping – the happier and more responsive they will be and the more often they will be back. They need "go-to" guys and girls – experts and advocates - not inarticulate amateurs or losers who can't clip on a lav. They don't want a dissertation or a skull session – they want a sound bite. And they're just as grateful to get your message – quickly and easily – as you are to share it with them. Remember that it's not about education – it's about entertainment and selling suds and soup. You're just filler between the ads so they don't all run together. So make your message your ad – short, sweet and smooth.

And that's the drill. Just do it – over and over again – every opportunity you have – obsessively and repetitively. Repeated messages are remembered messages. Stay on message – people take a long time to listen. Don't apologize – don't share the spotlight – don't play nicely with others. Just get out there and get the job done. Even the wanna-be web stars in your company will eventually thank you.

TULLMAN'S TRUISMS

GREAT LEADERS ARE GREAT SIMPLIFIERS

Every entrepreneur I know talks about being a first mover. Very few of them actually think deeply enough about what this really means. And, unless you actually understand what it means to be a <u>smart</u> first mover and you carefully analyze how to fully take advantage of the competitive opportunity, you might just as well be talking about the winter and all your conversation will have about as much impact on your business as whining does about the weather.

The conversation really needs to start with all the very good reasons NOT to be a pioneer. Pioneers aren't automatically entitled to anything except maybe some arrows in their backs. If you don't have an ongoing strategy and a specific plan to seize upon the opening that you've created by being ahead of the pack as well as the ability to keep moving forward and raising the bar, all you've done is set the table for someone else to roll right over you and eat your lunch.

It's tough to be first. Here are a few of the key reasons why:

(a) You've got to learn about the new marketplace and the new customers – exploration and discovery is expensive, uncertain and time-consuming.

(b) Once you know your story and your pitch, you've got to explain it to your team and to your prospective customers – education is also very expensive especially with new and disruptive products and services

(c) You really don't know what the demand for the new offerings will be, but you have to invest and build the team and the delivery capacity in advance (at least for the initially expected responses) and not everything in life can be a variable cost or bought on the fly from AWS.

(d) You can expect that the buyers' needs and demands will quickly change over time and you'll have to be ready to adapt and respond quickly to these changes before fast followers can "one-up" your product or service and steal your customers. Customer expectations are progressive.

(e) In establishing the market and defining the new product or service offerings, you have to commit to certain investments and parameters – 24/7 availability might be a good example – and then – unlike your competitors – you discover that you're saddled with these early commitments while other players aren't and – even worse – when the customers really can't tell or don't care about the differences in the offerings.

(f) It's quick and easy for competitors to imitate your product or service and sadly it's also much cheaper. You can expect almost immediate price competition and pressure on your margins.

(g) Too many things today on the Internet are just a click or two away and customers can jump quickly and easily to alternatives. There are very few powerful impediments to these kinds of shifts and some of the traditional barriers (like brand) are no longer significant advantages.

On the whole, not such a pretty picture. And it doesn't get any better or easier because if you really want to capitalize on your early advantage, there are more than a dozen considerations and calculations that you need to take into account and which will ultimately determine how smart and successful a first mover you will be. You need to design your approach, your marketing, and even your timing to try to optimize each of these dimensions of the problem for your benefit. As you will see, some of these things cut both ways and you'll need to make some difficult choices (and some rapid changes) as you move through the process.

Here's a summary list of the things you need to be thinking about if you want to win.

(1) Hide the Ball from the Competition (Lack of Information)

As you are rapidly coming up the learning curve about the new business, you have to do as much as you can to avoid educating your competitors and to keep them from quickly (and more cheaply) imitating your product or service. Let them make their own mistakes and not learn the shortest paths and the best answers from watching your stumbles.

But this gets tricky because you've got to weigh a bunch of constantly competing considerations. First of all, your customers need product information and other assurances that you're for real. Second, your investors and lenders (as well as future financiers like VCs who couldn't keep a secret if their life depended on it) need details, progress and performance reports, and even competitive information. And finally, you need to think about all the standard issues like PR, marketing and promotion concerns because you've got to get the word out about your product or service in the broader market.

And the Web, if anything, has made these concerns even worse. Instead of a quiet and confidential test or launch, the minute you put up a functioning website, the whole world can basically see it; copy it; reverse engineer it; and claim that they can do it better and frankly, the general population of consumers out there can't really tell the difference.

(2) Competitive Ju-Jitsu (Delayed Response)

Disruptive early entrants often succeed because their larger, in-market competitors may be unwilling to immediately cannibalize their existing businesses and/or may be constrained by legal or regulatory considerations (think AirBnb or Uber) or by other reasons such as concerns for near term financial results. In addition, it often just takes large organizations a frighteningly long time to recognize, evaluate and formulate a competitive response to new threats and entrants particularly when these new players enter at the low end of the market.

(3) The More the Merrier (Economies of Scale)

This is pretty obvious. As your production increases and your facilities and resources can be more fully and efficiently utilized, your costs come down. More importantly, in a market with limited overall demand, the next few potential players can't find enough customers to scale up to a size where they can compete effectively with you.

(4) I'm not Necessarily Smarter, I've Just Been Doing It Longer (Producer Learning Curve)

In addition to cost savings, the longer you are producing and servicing customers, the more efficient and experienced you become -especially with respect to their specific needs and requirements – and the more knowledge you gain which is not readily available to competitors or new entrants. Compliance issues, regulatory requirements, security and confidentiality considerations all create new and highly effective barriers.

(5) Inertia is a Wonderful Thing (Buyer Switching Costs)

When users find it costly or time-consuming to switch - even to a better product – the guy who got there first wins. High switching costs are usually associated with cases where (a) the products are expensive and long-life (durable goods); (b) where the buyer needs to make large co-investments; (c) where it's expensive and time-consuming to seek out and evaluate alternatives; and (d) where the buyers have to invest a great deal in training costs.

(6) Take My Word for It (Reputation)

Today, there are many products and services that the consumer really can't accurately evaluate until they've been bought and used. So buyers adopt and rely upon shorthand references such as your brand equity and the length of time you've been around and then equate these with quality and stability. First in good; but best is better.

(7) The Gang's All Here (User Multiplier Effect)

First movers get to ride the product adoption ramp and take advantage of the fact that certain products dramatically Increase in value and utility as the number of adopters grows. This is basically Metcalfe's Law of the compounding value of networks. Products of this kind also create tremendous market pressure for standardization which moves the market toward a de facto standard.

It probably wasn't much fun to be the only guy on the block with a fax machine and no one to fax to. As a result, a particular product or service can quickly become the market's means of coordination. No one wants to be left holding a Zune.

And not too long along, the VHS video tape format killed the Sony Betamax because, when Sony refused to share or license its technology, 4 or 5 other manufacturers all adopted the alternative VHS standard and it won the hearts and minds (and dollars) of the consumers.

(8) Smart Buyers Buy Blue (Buyer Evaluation Costs)

As new buyers are confronted by competing offers and have significant costs, time constraints and other difficulties in evaluating them, they try to Free-Ride on the presumed analyses of the larger and better informed players in the market who have already signed up with the market leader. As they used to say: "No one ever lost their job buying IBM."

(9) It's So Crowded No One Goes There Any More (Advertising and Channel Crowding)

Early entrants have less crowded and competitive venues and spaces as well as more alternatives for advertising and distribution channels. As the market becomes more congested and the competition for the consumer's attention grows, everyone's messages get dimmer and it becomes far more costly to create and build customer awareness and/or to secure shelf space. Late entrants typically chase smaller niche opportunities or have to buy access and distribution thru third parties.

(10) It's Lonely at the Top, but at least It's Not Crowded (Pre-Empting a Product Position)

First movers have the chance to choose the most attractive (typically high-end) positioning in a market which then creates future opportunities to expand and diversify the product lines at lower costs and with less competitive resistance. Premium pricing which early adopters are willing to pay as well as aggressive and influential word of mouth creates self-fulfilling buzz and increased demand.

(11) Not Everyone Gets a Great Date for the Prom (Channel and Partner Selection)

There are demonstrably better channels, representatives and distribution partners in every market. Once these are paired off and spoken for, late entrants settle for the remnants and their products suffer by comparison. More importantly, in some cases, there are only a limited number of acceptable and appropriate strategic partners in a market and, once they are committed to a competitor, there's very little chance of finding alternative and viable partnerships.

(12) Musical Chairs (First Call on Scarce Assets)

First movers get the opportunity to control and lock up scarce facilities, end caps, websites, locations, suppliers, and other resources including key personnel. Slotting fees and other costs emerge later. Typically, early on, these scarce assets are available at lower relative costs as well because the sellers/leasers don't initially identify or appreciate the levels of future demand and the scarcity of their offerings.

(13) Do It My Way (Opportunity to Define Standards)

The chance to define, control and continually advance the product or service standards in the market and to keep raising the bar for the competition is invaluable. Frankly, the federal and state governments, by and large, no longer have the personnel, skills or resources to regulate these matters in many industries and, as a result, the smartest and fastest operators are seizing the initiative. Standards Drive Scale.

(14) Leave It to Larry (Institutional Barriers)

This is another area where governmental shortcomings have created a void. As the number of applicants, entrants and competitive offerings in a market grows, the time, ability and interest of various institutional parties, regulators, suppliers and other gatekeepers to deal with, support and accommodate all of the potential players rapidly diminishes. Pressure mounts on new entrants to obtain connections and other access through existing players at much higher, brokered prices. Charges and costs emerge for validation and vetting actions, hook-ups, access to scarce personnel and services or unique data feeds which dramatically raises the operating costs for late entrants.

(15) Save Something for A Rainy Day (Early Profit Margins)

You're gonna make mistakes and have plenty of false starts. But first movers can command the higher margins associated with new, novel and often scarce products (for a period of time) and this lets you build up some cash reserves for the future price battles to come and, in some cases, you can even do some early price cutting to discourage other entrants.

TULLMAN'S TRUISMS

IT'S NOT WHO'S FIRST; IT'S WHO'S BEST

I don't mind people who are easily or regularly confused. At least they're thinking and, frankly, confusion is a higher state of knowledge than ignorance. And, most of the time, I don't even mind blissful ignorance. A great deal of the early enthusiasm in building a business comes from a combination of ignorance, bad information and wilful self-delusion and - as often as not – it helps you get over a bunch of those early humps.

And the even better news is that, with some time and some education, ignorance is basically curable. That's why, having spent the last decade or so building and rebuilding colleges, I've always liked the old expression: "if you think education is expensive, try ignorance". Although I wouldn't say that the most important education for an entrepreneur is ever found in the classroom – it's always found in the streets and in the trial-and-error process. Really effective education, for better or worse, takes you slowly from cocky ignorance to miserable uncertainty because real knowledge is essentially discovering and acknowledging the extent of your ignorance (notwithstanding whatever crazy conjugations Donald Rumsfeld may have come up with) and then moving forward to fill those gaps.

Ignorance really is a big part of the start-up game and, in some cases, it's almost a competitive advantage not to understand or appreciate just how tough, costly and long the process of building something new and important can really be. I always say that, if we entrepreneurs knew how hard the journey was going to be, we might not have started down the path in the first place. And, ultimately, the truth is that ignorance won't necessarily kill you or your business; it's just guaranteed to make you sweat a lot. So I'm OK with some ignorance. But what I really can't stand is ignorance combined with arrogance and I see way too much of this around me these days. And there's nothing more frightening than arrogant ignorance in action.

I'm sure that you've experienced these things as well and there are many forms of the problem, but I want to focus on a single instance which, and this may just be my painful past experiences talking, I think has everything to do with your age. Those of us of a certain grand old age were raised with a lot of rules and one of the most fundamental rules of all was that you asked permission before (not after) you did something.

Now I know all about it supposedly being so much better in our crazy and aggressive start-up culture to just rush straight ahead and try to get a jump on things and then beg for forgiveness afterwards (instead of asking for permission) – and believe me, I've been there and done that a bunch of times. But there was a pretty critical distinction - I might have often rushed ahead without permission, but I leaped without as much information as I could possibly gather before I moved an inch.

And, here's the bottom line: the way you get the information that you need is very, very simple. You don't guess, <u>you ask</u>. As hard as it is to believe, this seems like a foreign concept to an amazing number of young entrepreneurs that we deal with every day. If you ask the right people for the required information and/or direction, the odds of your going off half-cocked and being dead wrong are virtually zero. So why wouldn't anyone with a brain take a minute, catch their breath and ask before they acted?

I think that the problem is arrogance. They're too smart for their own good and too lazy at the same time. This is the triumph of hubris over homework. "I don't have to ask – I'll just jump and, if I mess things up, so be it. Someone else can clean up my mess". And when the mistakes do happen and you ask them why they didn't spend the marginal few minutes to get the goods and get things done right (the first time), they hide behind these silly platitudes from B school. I call this ignorance acting in the name of initiative. They'll say things like: "I thought you wanted me to think for myself" or "I was just taking the initiative" when the truth really is that they were being arrogant and assumptive and, worst of all, too lazy and/or too proud to do the preparation and ask for the assistance that they needed to do the right thing.

I don't see this going away any time soon, but it's important as a leader and a manager (especially in a young company where communication is so critical) to make it;

(1) more than O.K. for anyone to ask questions (not stupid or embarrassing) and to make it
(2) very, very clear that everyone needs to be sure that they have all the information available before they act and that
(3) they understand that there's no upside in guessing what anyone wants or expects or assuming that they know what the right actions are through some process of divine inspiration.

It couldn't be easier. Don't guess, ask.

74 - WHAT'S UP WITH DOCS?

As a former (or maybe I should say "reformed") lawyer, I understand all of the financial and other pressures on the legal profession these days and I sympathize with the guys who are just trying to make a living. But I'm also aware that, at the very same time we're trying to make it simple, faster and easier for startups to raise money (thru the JOBS Act among other initiatives), the lion's share of the lawyers working with new, early-stage businesses and entrepreneurs are still basically pretending that they need to redraft and reinvent the wheel every time they create a set of totally boilerplate, Seed or Series A investment documents and, worse yet, they're charging way too much for their services. I realize that it's getting harder (with more and more attorneys graduating every year) to find challenging and lucrative work, but that's no excuse for making work where it's not required.

And that's not even the end of the problem. Because many investment communities in a number of major cities and states are just beginning to fully embrace and encourage more centralized and concentrated efforts (as well as physical locations modeled after our 1871 start-up facility in Chicago) which are intended to channel, support and promote the growth and dramatic innovations inherent in entrepreneurial businesses, these areas lack the institutional knowledge, professional networks, and standard business practices (for better or for worse) which are one of the few charms and virtues of doing business with venture firms on either coast.

As a result, even after your new business has spent a small fortune (certainly in your eyes) on a set of basic corporate and investment documents, you now discover that you have the privilege of paying for an even more costly (and less beneficial or valuable) process where the competing lawyers on multiple sides of even the simplest investment seek (almost always at your total expense) to justify their own fees and their existences by engaging in stupid, irrelevant and time-consuming (and, oh yes, fee-generating) nit-picking and fly-specking of the same old documents that people (and businesses in exactly the same circumstances as yours) have successfully used without changing a single word or provision for many, many years. It's wasteful; it's offensive and presumptuous; and now is the time to put an end to it.

The truth is, as far as Seed round and even Series A investment documents go, there's just nothing new under the sun and the sooner we all agree (city by city, state by state, or whatever) to a standard, universal and stipulated set of basic documents which can be made available to all parties at a realistic (and modest) cost, the sooner we'll stop ripping off young, eager entrepreneurs and their backers and investors and let everyone get down to the real business of building their businesses. It's actually amazingly effective for an entrepreneur (regardless of the amount of leverage he has or lacks in a negotiation) to simply say to his counsel and to the other side that these are the documents that everyone he knows are using and that he's not prepared to start doctoring them up for anyone's benefit. And the really good news is that it's the truth and it's readily and immediately verifiable. What could be smarter, easier or more efficient? And why aren't we doing it nationwide?

So here are five simple steps for you to get the process started on the right foot regardless of where you're located and without respect to how many deals you've done before.

(1) Make Sure Your Lawyer Knows His Stuff

Every lawyer says he or she can do anything. They teach you to say that in law school because it's a good practice for getting hired. The truth is that doing deals is a specialized area and some attorneys in town and some firms focus on the work and do it better, faster and more regularly than many others. Even more importantly, they know all the other attorneys who also do deals for a living and they know the shortcuts, code words, standard provisions and restrictions, etc. because they all do it every day. And some of them can even help you get your funding by introducing you to their clients. Go with a pro – not Joe who will try to learn the ropes on your time and on your dime.

(2) Ask Him (or Her) to Use the Standard Documents and Ask for a Flat Fee

Ask for the standard package of documents and for a fixed fee. Make it clear that your feelings won't be hurt if the actual forms and paperwork are done by an associate and not by the Big Guy himself which is what's going to happen in any event anyway. This saves everybody a lot of time and cuts down on the phone tag where you call the partner (who doesn't know anything about the status); he calls the associate (they both bill you for the call); and then generally a secretary calls you back with an update. Just send Sally the secretary some sweets and have her keep you in the loop.

(3) Read the Documents Yourself Until You Really Understand Them

You don't have to be a lawyer to understand the elements of a basic deal and shame on you if you're stupid enough to need to pay your lawyer to read these documents to you or for you. It's your business and your livelihood that's on the line – so spend the time and get smart at least once on the document package - because (God willing) you'll be seeing the same documents every time you do a new deal in the future. You don't have to be Perry Mason or Einstein to figure these things out and, frankly, if your lawyer isn't using a set of documents written in pretty plain English which just about anyone can understand (give or take a few special phrases which won't ever matter to you anyway), then he's not doing his job.

135

(4) Tell the Guys on the Other Side Exactly What You're Doing

Tell the investors exactly what you're doing and don't be ashamed of the fact that you're being smart and cheap at the same time. If they have any brains, they cut the same kind of package deal and reduced fee arrangements with the attorneys on their side a long time ago. And if they're smart investors, they understand that it's actually - at least in part - their money that you're spending on those legal fees rather than on marketing, product development or sales.

(5) Exchange and Sign the Papers – Get Your Money – Get Back to Business

Don't be a pig on valuation. Take whatever they're giving. Take the money and run before they change their minds. Get back to building your business. Thank me later.

TULLMAN'S TRUISMS

EXPERTS OFTEN POSSESS MORE DATA THAN JUDGEMENT

75 – BE A ROLE PLAYER OR ROLL YOUR OWN?

There's a lot of conversation these days about being an entrepreneur and starting your own business and it's very reminiscent of the early dotcom days when everyone thought they'd spend a few dollars, quickly build a website, and just wait for the bucks to start rolling in. Everyone knows how well that worked out for the lion's share of the companies, but many young people today haven't taken the inescapable lessons of those frothy times to heart. They think that starting a business is like learning to swim the hard way – you jump (or a helpful parent or older sibling tosses you) into the deep end of the pool - and everyone (except maybe your older brother) hopes you quickly figure things out and that you don't drown. To put this vignette into the proper perspective, the end of this particular fantasy would be that you'd swim a couple of lengths and then emerge as a slightly better swimmer than Michael Phelps.

In addition, there's another strain of embarrassing arrogance floating around the West Coast where the "Y" guys maintain that they can identify a good, young and talented team of guys with a mediocre idea and then, by magic and the massive application of money, their "expertise", and their network connections, invent a new and better business for the team to build. This is, by and large, utter BS and the few pivots and successful examples that have worked out shouldn't mislead the vast majority of us into thinking that this approach makes the slightest sense. Your idea may change over time and, in many cases, it will have to, but at least it's your idea. If you're plowing someone else's field or chasing another man's dream, at the end of the day, you're just a hired hand. So stick with making your own best ideas real – this startup stuff is just too hard to be doing for someone else. And I get that everyone's dream these days is to be working for themselves building an exciting new business. That's where we'd all like to end up, but that's not where the journey starts.

I spoke recently to a young man who said that he had decided that he really wants to work for a technology startup. I, myself, would like to grow at least 10 inches and play center for the Celtics. I'd say we have about the same long-term prospects because just wanting doesn't make anything so. It's good to have desire, but the details don't take care of themselves. Passion needs to be melded with preparation and planning. A goal without a concrete plan to get there is just a daydream or a delusion. Your plan doesn't have to be the world's greatest anything. It doesn't have to be complete; it doesn't have to be perfect; and it's going to change a million times along the way, but it's a place to start. As we used to say in the movie business, "the screenplay isn't the movie that finally gets made, but it's what gets the movie made."

And, as many times as I have said that an entrepreneur's ignorance can be a competitive advantage in some respects, the truth is that you don't get into this crazy game simply by knocking on a business's front door and asking nicely. If wishes were fishes, every boy would be driving a Porsche. But hope alone is not a strategy for success.

And that's why, when I was asked the question about whether it's better at the outset to be a founder or to work for a startup and learn the ropes, it wasn't even a close question. The odds of achieving some ultimate happiness and financial success are at least 1000% better if you take the time to learn your craft and develop a valuable set of skills in some area that interests you and where you've got some aptitude. After that, the sky really is the only limit.

So plan to be a great employee and to grow into an important role player <u>first</u> and build your future path and your next plan from there instead of from nowhere. Just one note of caution – try to work for someone who can actually teach you something of actual value – not a person who's been doing things the same way forever or someone who's 15 minutes older than you and learning the job as he or she goes. Also it's a really good idea to try to work for someone who has fewer emotional and mental problems than you have.

So that's job number one – get started, start learning, and go from there. Then, and only then, can you start thinking about your next step. Just like Cinderella, if you want to get a great job at a great company, you've got to bring something to the Ball. You'll need the skills you developed in the jobs you've had before (not anything you learned in school) along with a killer work ethic as well as unbelievable persistence. With that kind of package, you're actually worth hiring.

I'm afraid that we're developing another generation gap and this one isn't merely cosmetic (can't stand those tattoos!) or aurally aesthetic (can't stand that music!) or even extreme economic (why "own" anything). It's far more important than any of these fairly superficial differences and preferences – albeit I recognize that they are crushingly important to the hosts of TMZ and Access Hollywood.

And it's far more pressing and critical than the angst and quasi-parental concerns these weird choices engender in us grown-ups. I can deal with all the questionable choices that many young people are making today because I'm relatively sure that we all made similar (or much worse, but probably less long-lasting) choices in our youth and yet, amazingly enough, we're still here, standing tall, and giving them advice and the "benefit" of our wisdom – such as it is.

But I'm not talking about something that's a preference or an option that we can take or leave – I'm talking about a problem that threatens to undermine something so fundamental and basic to the conduct of business (and especially to early-stage angel investing) that almost everyone (other than those in the film or music business) has always taken it for gospel and for granted. They say every day in the film business, "I'll love you 'til I don't" so get used to it. But that kind of fleeting attachment or commitment and the complete absence of sincerity that's "just business" in those worlds isn't the way we hope and expect that the rest of the sane (and square) business world conducts itself.

That's why I'm getting increasingly concerned about this very basic idea. I recently heard Alan Matthew (a long-time successful options and commodities trader) express it forcefully in about 15 different ways throughout a recent talk he gave to several hundred entrepreneurs at 1871. He said that, in every deal he does, and in every transaction: "My word is my bond." And it's just that simple – especially in the trading pits in Chicago – where the entire ecosystem depends on trust and the ability for everyone to rely on the commitments and honesty of the other players. But the problem is that - even as essential a part as this attitude is to how we do business in Chicago - I don't think we're doing a good job of communicating this very critical concept to today's young entrepreneurs. Too many of them live in a different conceptual world – one driven by situational ethics. And it sucks.

Telling people half the story or what they want to hear instead of what they need to hear isn't a funding solution – it's an invitation to a later slaughter. And it's usually the entrepreneur and the management team who will ultimately get killed. So it makes sense to share ALL of the news all the time – if for no other reason than to just save yourself all the grief coming down the line. The truth never hurts unless it ought to and sometimes it's a powerful wake-up call for all concerned. There's never a really good or special time to decide to tell the truth – the time is all the time.

But, if you haven't been there (to make the right choice regardless of how hard or discouraging it may be or how it may impact your financing or prospects) and there's no one more experienced around to guide you because you're running full-speed ahead and you're also making it up as you go, it's far too easy to take a quick slide down that slippery ethical slope. And once you lose someone's confidence, once they come to believe that you don't share and abide by their fundamental values, you will never get their trust and support entirely back.

And, honestly, because a whole generation of kids have been told (at least since second grade) that they're amazing, exceptional and completely unique, it's just a short step for them to conclude that the ordinary rules don't apply to them and that morals are just for little people and that they're way above that somewhat mundane conformity and far too smart for it as well. An old friend of mine used to say – by way of excusing virtually anything disgusting that he managed to do - that exceptional people deserve special concessions. I'm afraid his disease may be spreading.

As I often kiddingly say when I'm talking about building your company's culture and instilling critical values in your people and your business processes: "These are my principles. If you don't like them, I have others." But that's always intended as a joke because – in the real world – we don't get to pick and choose when to honor our promises and commitments. We say what we'll do and then we do what we said we'd do. It couldn't be more straightforward – you don't get to be truthful some of the time or sometime later or when it's a better or more convenient time. The truth doesn't vary based on circumstances.

And frankly, I'm not even sure that, in some cases, this is purely an issue of intentional dishonesty or immorality. I think it's just as much a lack of experience and education combined with way too much enthusiasm. Entrepreneurs can talk themselves into anything (I call this the "that hooker really liked me" condition) and, once they do, they want to sell it to the world. But whenever you find that you're having to shade the truth or forget some ugly facts in order to convince yourself or talk your team or some investor into something that you're not even sure you yourself buy off on, you're probably not doing yourself or anyone else a favor. It's almost inevitably a bad deal which you should back away from as quickly as possible.

And, while it's great to be highly motivated, it's not even a little cool if no one trusts your motives. It takes a time and hard work to build any kind of relationship, but just an instant and a suspicion (a long way from proof) to destroy it. And I know just how hard it is to say things that no one wants to hear, but that's part of the leader's job – it's not delegable and it's not optional.

It takes a great deal of experience and a whole bunch of broken dreams and busted relationships to appreciate that to be trusted is a much greater compliment than to be loved. Entrepreneurs – without a doubt – need and want (first and foremost) to be loved. It's part of the sickness which drives us. But, at the end of the day, trust is the only thing that you can really take to the bank.

I was recently part of an all-male ARA panel discussion (moderated by Sandee Kastrul from i.c. stars) and held at 1871 in front of another 250 women to discuss The Male Perspective on Women in Technology. I thought that it was a very enlightening session for all of us and - after the necessary disclaimers about why any woman would ever care what any men thought about this subject - and why there weren't any women on the panel - we got down to a mostly serious discussion (with a few laughs about men who cry) talking about what could be done to help improve the current – pretty depressing – percentages of women in the technology sector. Bob Miano, CEO of Harvey Nash, said in his comments that the numbers have remained flat and pretty constant for the last several years according to their annual surveys.

The panel discussion was prefaced by a short keynote talk by Brenna Berman, the CIO for the City of Chicago, and she noted (essentially on the issue of who cares what the guys think) that some of her most valuable mentors over the years had been men who had assisted and supported her progress throughout her career so she certainly believed that their thoughts and concerns were, in fact, pretty relevant. I felt she handled this touchy question very well and that her opening comment was a helpful and instructive observation which cleared the modestly tense air a bit before our discussion started.

Of course, not everything was roses after that. In the blogs following the event, she was quoted (I'm assuming accurately) as saying that she thought, on occasion, that the male panelists were giving answers that didn't fit the questions and that it would have been interesting to see (at the same time and in the same context) how women panelists might have answered those precise questions. For my part, I thought that - across the board – the male panelists gave straight and honest answers to the best of their abilities and avoided any kind of politically correct crap, but, of course, this is what makes horse races. And, as someone else noted, we were a group of guys who fundamentally believed that we were on the right side of this issue anyway and so I doubt that we were necessarily full-fledged members of the target population whose mindsets needed to be changed or expanded. I said in my opening comments that I've been gender-blind in my hiring decisions and team compositions for more than 40 years and that I was plenty proud of the fact that every business I've built had women as part of the senior management from the beginning.

In any event, I came away with a couple of thoughts and pieces of advice that I would share especially with all the young women in my various ventures who are just getting started in the business world or in the world of building their own businesses. These were mainly drawn from the comments of the other panelists although I will take credit for eventually providing a pretty good answer to the main "curve ball" question of the night even though I ducked it when it was first asked by saying that I had promised my team in writing that I wouldn't answer that particular inquiry.

(1) Wallflowers Aren't Really Welcome

Roger Liew, the CTO of Orbitz, made a very important point which – in my writings – I've usually short-handed by saying either that "feasibility will compromise you soon enough" or "don't let other people's fears or limitations hold you back". There are always plenty of people willing to tell you why you can't do something and it's very important that you yourself not be one of them. Roger had his own very interesting experiences about assigning women on his team certain high-visibility and important projects and then having to convince them (not to say "beg them") to step up and take on the job. His point was that no guy would ever say he wasn't up to the task (whatever the task was) and neither should any woman especially because they should know that their boss or manager wouldn't have asked them to take the job if he or she had any doubts in their ability to get it done and done well. You need to know that in any business everyone "wings it" from time to time and the key to success is simply that some people do it much more confidently than others. So don't be afraid to step forward when you next have the chance and don't ever sell yourself short. You'll always miss 100% of the shots you don't take.

(2) Leave the Baggage in the Lobby

Matt Hancock, Executive Director of the Chicago Tech Academy High School, said that, if he had only one piece of advice for young women entering the tech world, it would be to forget all the "expert" advice and all the "Dos and Don'ts" about how to act in the workforce and just leap right in and go with the flow. He called this "dropping all the baggage" and showing up as you are. If you let your contributions and actions speak for you and use the skills that you uniquely possess, you can make a real impact and a difference. I'd say it slightly differently, but the point is the same: all the good advice, pre-game coaching and helpful hints in the world won't ultimately make you a better you. Everyone's an expert who doesn't have to do these things themselves. Only you can make these things happen for yourself and it helps a lot to be sure that you don't get in your own way while you are doing just that.

(3) Being Passionate Isn't a Bad Thing

The closing question of the night was the closest thing to a curve ball and dealt with a very touchy area. The question was: "How do you suggest coming across confident without being perceived as a "Bitch" or overly aggressive?" I'm sure that there are a number of good hints or suggestions in the literature on this subject, but I thought that the right approach wasn't to try to outline rules of behavior or language suggestions which would have just amounted to piling on more of Matt's "baggage" (see above). The truth is and the best answer (for me at least) is that you need to change the conversation and the lens that you're looking through.

Aggression is so weighted and ugly a word that I can't think of any context in which we would truly value it (except maybe in pro sports where we reward violent actions by morons already being driven mad by steroids) and so we need to put that particular word aside and have a smarter and more productive discussion. Talking about a fierce passion to succeed, on the other hand; or about an uncompromising commitment to a cause or a business; and/or discussing a "take no prisoners" attitude are all positions and postures that we heartily endorse and, in fact, hope to emulate in our own behavior. Passion is just the flip (and far more attractive) side of aggression and that's how we should answer the question. The ones who want it the most and care the most are the ones who make things happen.

Passion is what moves mountains and makes the world move forward. Passion and unflinching optimism are force multipliers. There's never enough to go around because these qualities are always in short supply. So, the bottom line is self-evident. It's short-sighted and stupid to discourage anyone's (males or females) energy and enthusiasm and it's long past time that we got over the rhetoric and the pointless characterizations and started focusing our efforts and energies on who can best help us make a difference in the marketplace and create real results.

TULLMAN'S TRUISMS

THE ONE WHO CARES THE MOST WINS

Two weeks ago was the 25th anniversary of the World Wide Web. Even for those of us who were there at the very beginning, it's hard to remember a time before the Internet. But the sad truth is that the Web, as we once knew it, is disappearing right before our eyes. Does anyone type "www" as part of an URL anymore? Does anyone type a URL anymore or really want to type anything? I think not.

We'd rather swipe a screen or press a button on our phone or, better yet, just tell our phone what it is that we need. In fact, whether we like to admit it or not, we'd actually much prefer for our devices to "know" what we need before we ask based on our preferences, interests, location, prior behaviors and profiles. Then, without having to ask, we'd just have the answers handy and readily available when, where and whenever we need them. I call this modality "MOCIAL" – the merger of mobile and social – which is driven and enabled by constant connectivity, high-velocity computing, and by the massive stores of data about all of us which are now accessible to virtually anyone at little or no cost. These new capabilities and tools set standards of speed and performance as well as expectations of immediacy and accuracy that even the very best websites can't hope to compete with. And the competitive bar just keeps rising. The truth is that we're all suckers for speed and simplicity – save me time and make me more productive and I'm yours.

Today's reality is that websites are pretty much yesterday's news and the vast majority (to the extent that they haven't already been practically abandoned by their owners) are destined very shortly to be orphaned or consigned to the virtual dustbin. They're slow on a good day and too often plagued by latency issues; they're fundamentally static rather than interactive; far too many still aren't built or optimized for mobile use; and even the most conscientious webmasters can't really keep the data on these sites current because everything is changing way too fast. High velocity computing can rapidly supply the framework and the appropriate context for delivery, but that's not the same as effectively generating authentic and engaging content as opposed to rote and routine responses. And very frankly, adding a couple of widgets, a sidecar Twitter feed, or a few other flashy bells and whistles doesn't contribute anything much to the utility equation or to the perceived value of a visit. Too often searching the web these days is an exhausting and unproductive waste of time unless you know precisely what you're looking for.

And things aren't ever going to get better because all the positive movement and all the vectors are pointing in the wrong direction for anyone to even imagine a day when websites will once again matter. Mobile online use has convincingly overtaken the desktop and the usage gap is growing every quarter across all cohorts and age groups. In addition, and most strikingly, over 80% of the current mobile online use is now channeled opaquely through applications rather than overtly and transparently through browsers. This migration to mobile applications (and the closed-off connection conduits that they create) have created what I call the "App Gap" for Google because you can't measure and you certainly can't monetize what you can't see.

And the rapidly widening social gap is even more problematic for Google. The vast volume of meaningful traffic, the influential action and engaged activity, and ALL of the buzz and energy are focused today on social actions and sharing and not on search or research. Search is a sporadic, need-based and linear process. When it's done in the moment, it's done. Social is an emotional, expansive and ongoing sharing experience which is not only contagious, but exponential in that it grows and builds on itself. As a rule of thumb, and at least until you get burned or reach a certain age, the more you share, the more you're inclined to share in the future because you become increasingly psychologically invested in the process. Information may want to be free, but it turns out (no surprise here) that we want to be with our friends. There are a number of complex and powerful drivers behind these group and cohort-based behavioral changes, but one thing is abundantly clear – none of this is good news for Google.

As the novelty of "search" has worn off and the pure excitement of spontaneous exploration has dissipated, search has changed from a joy to just a job. It's an incidental and reflexive part of our day and nothing more. The more efficient and informed that search became; the less interesting and serendipitous it was. It was the triumph of the dispassionate engineers – all about dispatch and discipline (speed and results) with all the drama and passion of discovery being drained away. In a sense, Google did its job too well.

Today search is a heavily-manipulated mirror (reflecting back and confirming what we already know) rather than a window on new worlds. Among other critical differences from the much more intriguing Facebook interest graph approach is that in order to launch a Google search, you pretty much have to know where you're headed and you need create at least a modestly informed description of what you're looking for. The search box doesn't fill itself. It's not an adventure; it's a task. It's not a place we want to go these days; it's a place where we have to go when we need to accomplish some narrow and specific inquiry. The web today is about work, not wonder. And it's lonely out there as well because search is a solitary enterprise and we're all social animals.

The App Gap is just Google's latest problem as it struggles to continue to matter in a marketplace where the playing field has changed radically while Google's core offerings really haven't. Google needs to find a way into these new activity spaces, but many of its belated and reactive responses (and even its new and somewhat novel offerings) have fallen way short of the mark. Google was great when the web was about links, pages and anonymity. But when Facebook made it personal and the smart phone made it social and mobile, Google simply lost its way. You can't engineer emotions and you can't arbitrarily construct connections and engagement with others.

Shopping and social are where it's at today and, in those sectors, Google's become an also-ran. Maybe not quite as much of a yawn as Yahoo, but nothing to write home about for sure. Far more people search every day for products on Amazon than on Google even though its new Product Listing Ads (PLAs) are arguably better suited to mobile search than Amazon's offerings. The problem is no one knows they're there because no one sees them. And why is that? Because search isn't sexy or exciting any more. If there's one thing worse than being a chore or a commodity, it's being a tool or a utility. And the situation in the social sphere is even worse. Google+ has plenty of what I would characterize as "manufactured" members, but they're generally ghosts and they're not engaged with the service and – worst of all - they're simply not sharing. G+ has about 2% of the social sharing activity today while Facebook has over 50%, Twitter is at about 24% and LinkedIn and Pinterest account for another 19%.

If you don't have a substantial seat at the table, it's hard to have anything meaningful to say about the game or to the players. Without a window into Facebook's world; some perspective on Pinterest; or any idea of what's happening on Instagram, Twitter or WhatsApp, it feels like Google's on the outside looking in and you have to wonder how much longer Google's advertising model will make sense to the major media and advertising buyers. If you're not where your advertisers' targets are spending their time and money, at the end of the day, you're nowhere.

Google

For better or for worse, in today's autocatalytic technology-driven world, where every change accelerates the speed and frequency of the changes to follow, gamers (of all ages) are the virtual canaries in the coal mine. The disruptive innovations and the market transformations which the gamers' behaviors consistently predict are felt and rapidly found across every industry sector and, in general, across the board. As gamers go, eventually (and increasingly quickly), so goes the rest of the world.

It was the gamers' rapid abandonment of expensive, bulky and static gaming consoles (PlayStation and Xbox) in favor of light, portable, and mobile devices which not only built companies like Zynga into almost overnight market leaders, but, much more significantly, presaged the world's online migration from the desktop to the mobile world. Mobile today is everything and everywhere and our smartphones are the direct descendants of yesterday's handheld gaming devices.

And there's still much more to be learned from the actions and choices being made by gamers every day which will change the ways in which more and more businesses price their products and services and the manner in which they interact with their prospects and customers. We're looking at the end of fixed pricing for anything and entering an ala carte/all the time world. Bulk packaging, bundled products, and even bargain pricing are all breaking down in favor of a single consumer demand driven by a desire for freedom of choice and flexibility – I want "everything by the bite" – whatever I want, whenever I want it, and wherever I am. And it's the gamers who have shown us exactly how these demands will soon find their way into every business.

It's helpful to start by looking at which approaches didn't work over time in the gaming space and why they didn't.

First and foremost, subscriptions and long-term commitments haven't achieved anywhere near the scale and player penetrations that were anticipated. The fundamental reasons are fairly clear – commitments of any kind and continuing obligations are out. Any online game company will tell you that the most active participants won't commit to spend a dollar in advance, but will spend ten dollars – a dime at a time – all day long.

Second, fixed pricing, downloadable paid games and pay-per-play models have also failed. The only companies making real money today (over a million dollars a day in virtual sales) are the companies deploying freemium games where players are charged for upgrades, increased weaponry, powers or skills, or other virtual goods.

So what are the lessons for the rest of us? Three basic propositions underlie the gamers' decision-making process and these ideas are already on their way to your market and your products and services if they're not already there.

First is Investment

The best and smartest games let the users set the effective price of each session or game each time they play. Some days it's a little bit and some days it's a bundle. The point is that the customer is in control. Your pricing strategy needs to incorporate and evidence the same kind of flexibility.

Second is Commitment

The best and smartest games let the users decide how much or little they want to spend each time they play. Some days it's a lot of time or money (each being a material kind of a commitment) and some days it's just a lark to kill some time. If you do things right, you can be all things to all people all of the time. But your products and services need to be accessible across a broad spectrum of pricing and consumer choices and not a simple set of fixed offerings.

Third is Valuation

The best and smartest games let the users decide on exactly how much the experience is worth to them each time they choose to play or continue to play. All the market research and pricing guidance in the world doesn't compare to just letting the customer determine the value of the experience. If your products or services provide real benefit and value to the users, you will discover over time (and over the lifetime of a continued customer relationship) that your best customers will actually pay up for the right experiences rather than try to be bargain basement buyers.

And focusing on the value of the experience is doubly significant because today no one under the age of 30 really cares about possession or frankly about owning anything. Everything is about utility and experience. Social and sharing. Ownership (buying "stuff") is a burden today – not simply because so much of the readily- disposable technology we see and use every day is outmoded and obsolete in roughly the time it takes us to master the things in the first place – but because, in addition, we would just as soon not assume the obligations and the commitments that come as part of the package.

Bottom line: I know that one size, one model, one strategy will never work for everyone – but one thing is true beyond question and that is that your best buyers will tell you that everything is better by the bite.

I'm planning to go postal if I hear one more person pontificating about "pivoting". I know it's the biggest business buzzword of the last couple of years (I guess "disruptive" will just need to suck it up and settle for second place), but we don't have to beat the concept to death. It's not like it's a genius new idea or something.

I do get it. I've said it myself in many different ways for way too many years. Sometimes – especially in a startup - you need to change directions and sometimes – especially when things are going sideways – you just have to stop dead in your tracks (no matter how far down the wrong road you may have travelled) and start again. This is the First Rule of Holes: If You Find Yourself in One, Stop Digging. You shouldn't ever lose sight of your vision; but it's more than O.K. to alter your course – in fact, it's essential in today's rapidly-changing world to constantly react to changes in your circumstances and to the competitive environment that you find yourself in from time to time.

But here's the thing: (and let me say right up front that I never really liked Algebra or Geometry that much) – I think a Pivot can't be more than a sharp 90 degrees. It's an adjustment – a course correction – and only rarely a complete abandonment. And I think that beyond a Pivot (or maybe 2 Pivots at the most), you don't have a process or a plan, you've got a problem. And that's what I think of as a Twirl. If you're just spinning around in circles and grabbing at straws ("twirling" instead of pivoting), you're wasting your time (and, most likely, someone else's money), and you need to give it a rest. This kind of frenzy might be the right way to roll at a weekend hackathon or in a brain-storming contest or competition, but it's no way to build a business. If you keep changing your UI, redesigning or repositioning the product or service before it's even out the door, morphing the mission and the mantra, etc. – you're missing the boat.

So sit down, catch your breath, and take stock of where you're at, what you're really trying to accomplish, and whether you're even moving in the right direction. It's easy to get caught up in mindless activity. In fact, it's actually a pretty effective (albeit very temporary) cure for the anxiety and fear that every entrepreneur lives with. But it's not a solution or a strategy for success.

There is one small bright spot. It's not really your fault. It's the fault of these lean startup zealots who have misled a whole generation of young technologists. They've got the horse behind the cart and it's really tough to make any headway that way. This MVP (minimum viable product) bullshit needs to stop. It's actually <u>not</u> alright to have your first customers be your last beta testers. Because in this world of rapid reaction and instant abandonment, you don't get a second chance to make a first impression and – as a young business with limited resources - you don't have the time or the resources to hang in there until you get it right. In the first instance, it's about research and analysis rather than reacting to external stimuli and revising your story, your pitch, your product or your approach every few weeks. Getting it right at the beginning these days is the whole ballgame. The way you start the journey ultimately determines where you end up.

The truth is that you've got to find a need and a problem to solve before you rush ahead and start building the solution. This isn't fun and it's hard to excite your engineers and your buddies about taking care of business before you starting building your bundle or your software stack, but it's what you've got to do. This is slow, nasty work where you have to go out into the real world and do your homework. You need to find and ask prospective customers and users what their pain points are, what problems they need solved, and – most importantly of all – what and whether they are prepared to pay for a solution. Then you can build a product or a service. We need to be talking about MVA – Minimum Viable Audience (aka "real customers") and then you can use the MVP methodology to iteratively build increasingly responsive offerings for your users.

I say fuck this "Field of Dreams" nonsense. The customers aren't coming. They won't find their way to your door because, not only don't (and won't) they even know you exist, they could care less about you and your dreams unless you've got something real, timely, and cost-effective that addresses a pressing and irresistible need that they have and one which they admit to and acknowledge having. Something they can't find a reason or an excuse to say "No" to. That's a real product. Not a fantasy.

Right now, we've got thousands of business builders who have been told that it's all about the technology when the truth is that it's all about the targets – the real needs of real customers. This isn't something that you fix in the shop – it's something you solve first in the field. Stop pivoting, quit twirling, grab your hat, get out of the office and hit the road, ask the right people the right questions, and you just might find your way to a business worth building.

81 – DON'T BUILD YOUR BIZ ON A PINNACLE

It used to be a sign of disrespect and condemnation to say that someone had their head in the clouds. They were foolish dreamers or cock-eyed optimists - certainly not the kind of down-to-earth folks firmly grounded in reality that anyone with any brains would want to bet on and/or invest in. Thoreau wrote about people building castles in the air (which he said was where they should be), but then he cautioned that the next steps needed to be putting solid foundations under them.

Right now, you can't go anywhere without hearing or seeing another pitch for SaaS and enduring multiple arguments for putting your products and services in the cloud. I wrote about SaaS not too long ago myself although my view – then as now – was a pretty contrary one. (See: Why SaaS is More Dangerous than It Looks. http://www.inc.com/howard-tullman/why-saas-is-more-dangerous-than-it-looks.html). As it happens, being in the cloud today is supposed to be way cool. Everyone will tell you that it's definitely the place for your business to be. But I'd say "maybe". Because I think it depends entirely on what kind of business you're planning to build and whether you've built the right foundation for moving forward.

This is because sometimes - especially in the world of technology - you learn that the more things seem to change, the more they stay the same and you eventually realize that they're no different than they've always been. I don't want to rain on anyone's parade, but the cloud's no more a panacea and the answer to all things than any of the other wondrous tools and technologies that came before it. The cloud can kick-start you or kill you if you're not careful. And sadly, if your head's stuck up there in the haze and you think the cloud's gonna solve everything for you and your business, you're likely to be just as mistaken and wrong-headed today as you would have been years ago which was – by the way - long before we all discovered the supposedly silver linings inside all those newly-accessible and suddenly transparent clouds.

If your business plan and model are appropriate, the cloud could be a big help, but if your model makes no sense, nothing including the cloud will make much of a difference. Because when you really look closely, you discover that the cloud's not magic or another Oz – it's just a virtual place in cyberspace - an environment to operate in - and for your startup to be successful anywhere - in the ether or down on Earth - you've still got to build a business that's well-grounded and smart. There's no question that the cloud's cheap and easy in many ways, but there are plenty of things that you just shouldn't ever do for your business and trying to do them cheaply is much worse than not doing them at all. So it pays to do your homework before you head into the ozone. And, in particular, that's why, when you're thinking about the cloud and your business model, it's so important to pay attention to exactly what you're trying to build.

Pinnacles are a Problem

Pinnacles are generally very tall and relatively thin. They're a very precarious foundation for a business because they don't provide a broad base of user engagement or commitment or support and they really limit your ability to connect to your customers and, more importantly, to react to and/or cushion the impact of adverse developments. The cloud encourages us to chase the world and boil the ocean from Day One because those opportunities are theoretically there for the taking. But, if you fall for the long thin line (essentially the polar opposite of the long tail), you find that you're stretched way out (a mile high and an inch wide) and that a relatively modest upset, piece of bad news, or other disturbance can really knock your whole enterprise off course because your real connection to so many of your remote and very distant customers is so tenuous. To build a smart business, you never want to be spread too widely or have too thin a connection to your users and this is how I see a number of businesses today.

You want to be focused, but not single-threaded – you want to be straight, but not narrow – and you always want to have a couple of ways out of the tight spots. And it's pretty easy to drink your own Kool-Aid if you're not careful. For example, if you're disrupting and revolutionizing an industry where the standards of response time and performance were historically measured in days or weeks, you don't have to introduce your new solution and your initial metrics in terms of minutes or hours of turn-around time. Give yourself a break and some breathing room. It's always easier to improve than to walk the customers back from some insane, unscalable and hyper- costly benchmark that you simply made up.

This is an area where too much information – being too data-driven – can actually limit your opportunities and your upside while increasing your vulnerability because you can fall in love with the measurements and lose sight of the critical relationships and your real business objectives. Take measuring turn-around or response times (as noted above) or tracking geographic penetration as examples.

Measurement is a relativist thing and when we are constantly measuring our results against purely pre-defined goals and objectives, it's too easy to develop a case of tunnel vision. As the data tell us that we are drawing ever nearer to the goal ("our uptime is great and our response time is terrific") and we convince ourselves that we're getting better and better ("we have customers in 50 countries"), we lose sight of the fact that (a) these may be easy things to measure, but they aren't necessarily the important things to focus on or optimize for the long run; (b) too much of a good thing probably isn't a good thing if it's too soon to manage it; and (c) there may be much larger and broader opportunities over the horizon and outside of our immediate zones of interest and – while we're feeling so good about our near-term progress – someone else is out there getting ready to steal the main prize out from under us.

Because the cloud can so readily and inexpensively connect us to many or just a few users everywhere and because it enables degrees of unimaginable and constant connectivity, it is very seductive and it's very easy to run down these rabbit holes and lose your way. You can quickly end up over-extended, undermanned and unable to meet the commitments you've made to your users and customers. It's pretty lonely and uncomfortable sitting on top of that pinnacle wondering what went wrong. But at least it's not crowded.

TULLMAN'S TRUISMS

IT'S TOUGH TO SEE THE BIG PICTURE WHEN YOU'RE INSIDE THE FRAME

Last week I had the privilege of sitting on a panel with two extremely successful serial entrepreneurs (Sam Yagan – founder of *OkCupid* and now CEO of *Match.com* and Chuck Templeton – founder of *Open Table* and now MD of the ImpactEngine accelerator at 1871) which was moderated by my good friend, Rob Wolcott, who runs the Kellogg Innovation Network (KIN). The title of the panel was slightly longer than the typical length of my blog posts (so I don't want to repeat it here) and no good entrepreneur stays on point anyway - so let's just say that it was an evening of quips and networking tips from a bunch of very smart and experienced people. I learned and laughed a lot (and caught a few things that were new ideas to me as well) and I thought I'd share a couple of the highlights.

(1) Walk the Walk and Wear the T-Shirt

I'm usually the most under-dressed guy at grown-up events like this, but Sam Yagan was wearing a *Match.com* t-shirt under his jacket so, from a sartorial splendor standpoint, it was pretty much a draw. The more important point was what Sam said about why he was wearing the shirt and what wearing the shirt says about Sam. He said that, as the CEO, he's always selling and promoting the business and that it's a critical part of that process that everyone he meets knows that he's all-in, fully-committed, and sincerely does believe that Match.com will change your life for the better and, if you've got the time, he'll tell you how and why.

My friend Slava Rubin who co-founded *Indiegogo* (and is now the CEO) always wears a company t-shirt when he travels. He's plenty proud of the business he's built too and it shows the minute you meet him and you'll miss your plane for sure if he gets started talking about the company and the latest and greatest crowd funding successes that they've helped to make happen. He says, of course, that his shirt's a comfy way to roll, but the real reason is that he knows he's going to pass a bunch of people on the trip and it's the cheapest form of subliminal advertising he's come up with so far which also saves him a bundle on marketing.

It's all about authenticity, believing in your business and yourself and walking the walk. Leaders lead by example or they don't really lead at all. The day you're not comfortable in your role, in the business, or in the company t-shirt, is the day you should find another place to be. If you're not excited about what you're doing and proud of the place you doing it, do something else. This stuff (building new businesses and changing the world) is just too hard and life's too short to go to work every day without a spring in your step and a smile on your face. Not everything will ever be fun and easy, but as long as it matters and you're making a difference, there's no better place to be.

(2) You Never Know Who's Going to Bring You Your Future

Rob Wolcott likes to say that at KIN he tries to never leave serendipity to chance, but Chuck Templeton told the audience two different ways that – in the early days of his business - he manufactured and mined his own serendipity. One was a process and one was an attitude and they both helped him build his earliest networks of supporters and sponsors and also – crucially – helped him fill in the gaps in his knowledge and experience by reaching out to others for help.

The process was pretty simple. He'd read every issue of what - for a few minutes back then - was more or less the hot tech industry magazine (**The Industry Standard**) – which he described as an early version of **WIRED** (although the fact is that **WIRED** was started about 5 years before it) and when he read about people doing things that seemed interesting and relevant to his business, he would reach out to them and ask them for a few minutes of their time to answer his questions. Not only did he learn a lot about stuff, but he said that he also learned a lot about how many people were so generous with their time and how they would actually take the time to help a total stranger. The moral of the story was pretty simple – it never hurts to ask – and it can often turn into a real opportunity and it's always an education.

The attitude was also pretty straightforward. He said that you should always keep an open mind when you meet people and that you should never underestimate them because you really just never know who's going to turn out to have the keys to the kingdom. Or as I like to say: you never know who's going to bring you your future. Every encounter, every meeting, every conversation is a chance to learn and also to build and extend your network. Everyone's an example – some to emulate and some to avoid like the plague – but you'll never know which ones are which if you don't invest the time to explore the possibilities and have the right attitude while you're at it.

I've been talking for several years now about how important it is to appreciate that – in today's complicated, ADD-addled, and increasingly cluttered and noisy world – it's become mission-critical in trying to sell anyone anything that marketers understand the new imperative that how, when and where you reach your prospects (and your existing customers) is at least as important as the content of the message you are attempting to deliver.

It's absolutely clear today that the context in which your message is transmitted and received by the target is MORE important to its successful communication and reception than the construction, creativity and even the contents of the message. I call this idea "Smart Reach". Smart Reach is all about the need to deliver engaging, demonstrably relevant, content to your target at exactly the right time(s) and place(s).

And here's an initial hint – in the game today, it's not just about "different strokes for different folks"; it's about fashioning radically and consistently different messages to be directed at the same folks depending entirely on the times and places and contexts in which you're attempting to reach them. And it's also about understanding and appreciating that to do this right; you need an entirely new formula: you should be spending no more than 25-30% of your time and energy of creating new content. The rest of your resources should be focused on planning, channel selection, distribution strategies and real-time measurements of the results so that you can course correct and better shape your campaign as it rolls out.

It doesn't really matter these days whether your content (or offers, incentives, etc.) is the coolest unless it reaches the right audiences. And, because content (standing alone) isn't laser-sighted or heat-seeking; it's gonna need serious help. Just like the fat old chicken sitting on top of the fence post, it's not gonna get there all by itself and it's not gonna get the job done without planning, positioning and an aggressive and focused push from you to help break through the channel clutter and reach the customer.

A staggering number of folks who you'd think were otherwise fairly intelligent don't seem to realize that their literal competitors (the sales folks and businesses who are out there selling directly competitive offerings and competing every day for market share in the same sectors and industries) are only a relatively small part of the problem.

You don't get to compete for the sale until you win the race and the constant competition for the consumer's attention.

And in competing for the customer's attention today, which - right along with our time in general - is the scarcest resource we have, the list of distractors, obstructions, barriers and filters just continues to grow larger and longer every day. You're up against family, friends, breaking news, sports, music, medical issues, travel, charities, every kind of media, and even sleep-deprivation. And believe it's hard to sell new shoes to someone taking a snooze or a noon-time nap.

And that's why no one can afford to get these things "almost" right. Today, as always, "almost" only counts in horseshoes and love – not in the marketplace. And almost everything is easier to get into than to get out of – so it's critical to get off on the right foot with the right focus. There's too much money involved, the stakes are far too high, and the consequences if you misfire or waste your ammunition with poorly- timed or poorly-placed salvos are dire. They don't beat you – they just send you home and give the prize to someone else. And I recognize that there's no simple solution or crystal ball to tell you in every case or in any case what the exact right approach should be and that will be a determination that you'll have to make on the fly and over and over again. I certainly don't know and the thing that's for sure is that one size or one approach will never fit every case.

But let me give you just a new idea and a couple of questions to think about as you're analyzing your own programs which I hope will give you a new perspective on the problem. It's a very simple and time-tested idea. You want to be there when the customer wants to buy what you're selling. Because that's the only time that matters and it's a short window that opens and shuts in a snap.

But because you can't really read their minds (yet), you need to settle for the next best thing – smart reach. Think about (a) where you want to engage your targets and (b) what they will be doing when you do and (c) why that's the best possible time for you to make your pitch to them and then figure out how to get your message in front of them – at that time, in that place, and in the context of what they're doing. Reach me at the right time and I'm all yours. Reach me at the wrong time; interfere with or interrupt something that I'm doing which I regard as more important at the moment; get in the way of my friends or family or even my work and you've just wasted my precious time and your scarce and now wasted money.

Context is king.

It's great to be living and working in Chicago. We're west of all the fear and frenzy that make New York so nutty and east of all the fame seekers and fruitcakes that make the Valley so frothy and volatile. In Chicago, we build businesses, not bubbles, and - in our city - bootstrapping is seen as a virtue to be proud of, not as a vice of the petite bourgeoisie.

So it was a welcome note of normalcy to hear Jon Medved (the founder and CEO of OurCrowd – the hottest equity crowding funding operation in the world – coming all the way from Israel to tell the assembled entrepreneurs (during his presentation at 1871) that "flat is the new up". Loosely translated, he meant that there's no shame in taking in additional capital and bolstering your war chest when the opportunity presents itself and when the investors are ready and willing regardless of whether you're also able to secure some immediate step-up in the putative value of your early- stage business.

It's important to always remember, as Jon also reminded the audience, that the only truly fatal mistake for a startup to make is to run out of cash. When you do that, they send you to the showers. Everything else in the life of your business is fixable. As I used to say, anything that you can fix with a check isn't a problem; it's just another choice. But when you run out of cash, they pretty much run you out of town.

Now you might say that Jon's a VC (and he is, but I think - in his heart - he's really more of an entrepreneur) and that it's in his interest to keep the valuations of the follow-on rounds of startup financing flat rather than constantly and automatically ticking up – especially those deals in which his fund has invested. And that would also be true. But that's not really the main idea or the overall message that I took away from his comment. I thought that there were some pretty valuable thoughts embedded in that simple descriptive phrase.

And I think that now's as good a time as any – maybe the best of times – to take a moment to reflect on where things stand and where we're headed in today's pretty bullish (at least for new businesses) investment environment. Because it's easy for bullish times to lead to bad behavior.

Let's start with a simple statement and a word of caution: the worst mistakes in business are made in good times, not in bad times. It's a remarkable fact of life that a small (and shrinking) bank account does a great deal to focus your attention on the things that are mission-critical and existential. You stop taking limos to the airport pretty quickly when you're starting to worry about next week's lunch money. I've been right there several times and, while it's good for your waistline, it's a lousy way to live.

But when funds are theoretically much easier to come by (at least in the current opinion of so many of the pundits and pontificators in the tech world) and the funds are being offered in ever-increasing amounts, it's a very attractive time to grab the gold and it's also pretty easy to lose your way and lose sight of the main and more important goals for your business. That's why an emphasis on the mainly artificial bogie of <u>interim</u> valuations (the math) is woefully misplaced when what only really matters is getting the investment (the money).

Until you sell your business or take it public and take a bunch of chips off the table, interim valuations are just so much chatter and cheap talk. Not worth the time to talk about and temporary fantasies at best. It's a lot like wetting your pants in a dark suit – it gives you a nice warm feeling for a moment; no one else really notices or cares; and you end up stinking up the place.

So when the opportunity presents itself to boost your bankroll; strike while the iron is hot and remember these three basic rules of early-stage fundraising.

(1) Getting money is just like eating appetizers. You do it when they are being served. Don't be reticent or late to the buffet.
(2) Don't be a hog on valuation. There are a million other deals competing for those same funds – many are just as attractive as yours and some will be much better- priced than yours. Pigs get fat; hogs get slaughtered. Just like on Wall Street. Easy money is what everyone <u>else</u> raises – getting yours will always be hard until it's done and in the bank.
(3) Take more money than you need because you <u>will</u> need it – maybe for good reasons (radical growth or expansion) or for bad reasons (disappointing or delayed results) – but need it you will.

And ultimately, if you can't entirely resist being a bit of a hog on valuation; at least be the practical one just like in the storybooks. Take all the money you can get; say "thank you" (and not another word); and run like the wind.

I wrote recently about my concern that too many young entrepreneurs had what I called "situational ethics" and that they believed that it was "nice" to tell the truth (or the whole truth) when it was quick or convenient, but that it certainly wasn't essential – especially when it got in the way of getting something else done. A little inaccuracy can save a ton of explanation – if you don't care about your reputation or your customers.

Sadly, too many of these characters don't really care about anything but themselves. Certainly they have no time or truck for things as vague as honesty and some kind of basic business morality. It's like they were raised in a values vacuum. These are my values, but if you don't like them or they don't suit, I've got others as well. Something to fit every occasion.

Then – when the truth gets out and they've got to explain to millions of ripped- off and disappointed users - they go for cheap excuses and try to paper over the problem with legalese and after-the-fact improvements to their boilerplate policies and written disclosures. Worse yet, I see too many cases where there's an even more upsetting and gratuitous attitude toward their customers (who, after all, are millions and millions of young kids with their own "whatever" attitudes) – they not only take them for granted; they take them for idiots who just really don't care about these things or wilful co-conspirators who are just as likely to forget and forgive a little "mistake" here or there in the service of the greater good – making a lot of money and sticking it to the man. After all, what your parents can't see or share, they can't bust your chops about what you're not supposed to be doing once they do. Snapchat and sexting _uber_ _alles_.

And now, we have the two Snapchat co-creators who have stepped up to be the poster boys for flagrant fiction followed – once they've been caught red-handed in their lies – by slick and superficial attempts to say they're sorry. Saying you're sorry doesn't mean a thing unless you mean it and it isn't worth a thing if what you're sorry about is getting caught – not screwing up in the first place.

Their mediocre and self-serving mea culpa blog post is a complete crock. "We were so busy building" that we didn't pay "enough" attention to the very things that were the core principles and the basic value proposition of our product – privacy and ephemerality. It turns out that the government has determined that

(1) the "snaps" don't necessarily disappear in a few seconds;
(2) that Snapchat's claims and promises about privacy were lies;
(3) that the alert notification system was also flawed and by- passable; and
(4) that private location and other data were being collected even though Snapchat expressly said that this was not happening.

The fact that they've settled their "dispute" with the FTC's division of privacy and identity protection where they were accused of deceiving their users and multiple misrepresentations to consumers about how things actually worked and with whom they've now agreed to hire an independent expert watchdog for the next 20 years doesn't mean squat and certainly doesn't give me any confidence that anyone has learned anything useful from this episode. I'm just hoping against hope that the tens of millions of people who have been duped decide that maybe there's another product or service that does the same job (maybe even a better job) and that it's a smarter tool and place to do the stupid things that they want to do.

But all of this noise isn't really the lesson for smart entrepreneurs who are trying to create real businesses and real value for themselves, their users and their investors. The point is much simpler – it's just too easy today to build something that looks good and seems to solve a problem or create a solution on the surface – this is the triumph of form over substance – but, if you're in such a big hurry to get something out there in the market and you don't take the time and invest the hard work and the necessary resources to build the infrastructure necessary to really deliver on your promises into your product or services at the beginning, then ultimately you haven't built anything real or lasting. Your solution won't scale. Your design won't survive real due diligence. Your prospective acquirers will be happy to take the concept, but not the code or the crew. And you'll find out that you built a toy – not a technology and wasted a lot of time in the process.

The biggest shame in the Snapchat story is not that they were unethical egotists; it's that they were bad engineers.

I wrote recently about "smart reach" and the need to understand that how, when and where you reach your prospects (and your existing customers) is as important as the content of the messages you are hoping to deliver. People who are socializing aren't likely to be in shopping mode; people who are chatting aren't generally consuming; and people digitally scrapbooking aren't really looking for new medications – whether they may need them or not.

These days the context (where they are and what they're doing) often trumps the content (what you're saying or selling) unless your messages get both active engagement from the consumer and are accurately aligned in terms of your target's time, interest and attention. Blindly launching your campaigns into indiscriminate channels (regardless of their aggregate volumes) like *Facebook* where the active users' likely behaviors aren't coincident with the actions you seeking from them is just too sloppy and too costly an approach for virtually any business today. These channels are readily accessible; they may even relatively easy to use and to measure (at least in terms of tonnage but not real reach); and they may not actually appear to cost that much (ignoring the obvious opportunity costs). But there's very little economic benefit in wasting your scarce bullets on bad marketing regardless of the CPMs or per-piece cost. And, frankly, these days the crowd in general is crap. You need to focus on the folks who matter – not the masses – and make your message real for them.

These mega-channels are simply the wrong places to be looking for new business or anything else unless you have thoughtfully crafted and precisely targeted your messages. It's exactly like spending the night looking for your lost keys under the nearest street lamp. Not because that's where you think you lost them, but because the light is so much better there. Lazy marketers use these big fat channels because everyone else is doing the same thing. It's like a drunk uses that same street lamp – for support (and comfort) rather than illumination.

To succeed today, you need real visibility into relevant behaviors and a strategy/plan to move yourself away from the crowd and to do your own thing. If you want to beat the Babe (or the big guys in any business), change the game. That's why, while understanding context is certainly an important consideration to keep in mind and one that you need to take into account when developing your marketing plans, it's only one dimension of the new data and metrics-driven approaches to digital marketing that are changing the game and increasingly distancing the winners from the also-rans.

To really understand what's going on (especially in terms of the ongoing social conversations which, for better or for worse, are impacting your business every day (whether you realize it or not), you need to focus on

(1) the multiple dimensions of these social conversations; and
(2) who's having them; and
(3) who's listening to them in order to spend your time, energy and resources wisely and, more importantly, to be sure that you are targeting and successfully reaching the right audiences.

Today, the fact is that no one with a brain wants to reach millions of easily influenced nobodies – regardless of how many fractured flicks they watch every day or even how many "allegedly" fervent (and generally faithless) followers they may have. Even faithful followers only matter to a marketer if the reason they're following an influencer is directly connected to the messages they're trying to extend and expand. Asking a Justin Bieber fan about Bach is a lot like asking Mrs. Lincoln how she enjoyed the play.

The only goal that really matters today is to get your messages in front of highly influential people (think digital multipliers and megaphones) who are tightly connected to significant (and fairly sizeable) niches of active and desirable individuals whose actions and attitudes they can directly influence (amplification) and whose behaviors as consumers, voters, or other cohort members you are looking to change and direct into actual results – not wishful thinking.

To do this successfully, you need to look at the whole story and at all four of its sides. Even more to the point, the big guys in the social listening spaces (*Radian 6*, *Buzz Metrics*, etc.) are all myopically focused on just one part of the equation (**WHAT** is being said and the apparent sentiment associated with it) and – as a result – if you hurry, you can jump ahead of them and deliver some valuable and truly-differentiated products and services to a marketplace that is ready, willing and able to buy anything that makes economic sense and that makes common sense out of the tsunami of meaningless data that they're swimming in right now.

As noted above, equally as critical to effective social listening and deliberate message delivery is a determination of **WHERE** the conversations are taking place (context) and information about **WHEN** the conversations are taking place (time). But it's the 4th dimension – the **WHO** is speaking and what are his or her relationships and connections to the ultimate target audiences as well as his or her ability to amplify and extend the messaging thru expressions that sway and influence (power to direct or drive behavior) the targets that is the vast unmined terrain and opportunity zone.

Klout.com and *Kred.com* are the pioneers in the individual influence measuring space, but at best these are mechanical attempts to count frequency, volume and potentially the extent of one's connectivity without a great deal of time or thought being devoted to the true weight, value and influence of the sum of these connections. These are brute force approximations and solutions that are barely workable and of little real value beyond generating some industry bragging rights and hype. This, of course, didn't keep *Lithium Technologies* from buying *Klout* recently for $200 million. I wish them lots of luck in figuring out exactly what they got and what to do with it.

But bigger and better versions of these types of tools are desperately needed because the stakes are high and so – as a result – are the opportunities for new disruptive entrants into this space. It's clear that today even the best language parsing engines and related algorithms are no match for the old family connectivity trees built out of bright colored Post-its tacked to the wall or the white boards that we see every night on the tube in the police procedural shows like *Law and Order*. You can't tell the players without a program and a scorecard and the best computers can still only do our bidding (and massive data assembly), but not our thinking (yet). The companies which build the products and services that help us identify, reach and influence the people who matter (the highly influential and deeply connected prime movers) and who – in turn – can move the markets and the marketplace will be the next generation of big winners.

We don't care about the wisdom of the crowd; we only care about the wisdom of the people we care about.

TULLMAN'S TRUISMS

EGGS HAVE NO BUSINESS DANCING WITH STONES

Today, for a startup, especially in the tech space, money just doesn't matter anymore. There's more money available today – even for mediocre stories and half-baked ideas - than anyone knows what to do with. And there doesn't appear to be any end in sight with more and more investors than ever before all frantically chasing the shiny new things and the few deals that they hope are really exceptional. As always, it's still a great big crapshoot in any event because (just like we say in the music business), it's easy to tell when someone's got a bad idea, but it's a lot harder to figure out the one-in-a-million deal that's gonna break through. So if you've got something special to sell and people are beating a path to your door, now's the time to let them in.

And there's another game-changing aspect of the money game which is equally important. In addition to having fairly painless, reasonably-priced and readily-available access to a great deal of cash, virtually every startup today actually needs millions of dollars less to get their businesses up and operating. In fact, they can even get themselves far enough along the way to hit a few major milestones on what we used to call "chump change". It's not like the good old days when capital was a central concern (and critical to your business's credibility and success) and you needed to raise a real war chest because – at least back then - you couldn't launch your company on sweat, smoke and mirrors with a few servers rented from AWS. But today, for better or for worse, you can pretty much get the ball rolling with some relatively modest funding and then you just have to start praying hard for both traction and momentum. However, it's still important to keep in mind that just because the barriers to entry are much lower; it doesn't mean that it's any easier to succeed. In fact, if you don't have all the tools you need; it's actually much harder to break through the noise, clutter and competition to get yourself and your business noticed.

So, if money isn't the be-all and end-all gating factor these days, what really does make the major difference in a startup's likelihood of success? I'd say that it all comes down to how you handle your talent. You can teach someone all about technology, but you can't teach talent. Talented and highly motivated people have always been and will always be the only, long-term, sustainable competitive advantage for a business and managing this particular resource is something that you need to do from the very first day of your business. In addition, we are starting to better understand that talent management is an ongoing, maybe every day, kind of job and not some kind of lay-away plan where once a year you try to make all the folks happy with raises or bonuses or options (or at least less unhappy) and then you generally try to forget about these things for the rest of the time or until something blows up in your face. We see this particular phenomena and the hyped-up emphasis on talent acquisition and accommodation in Major League Baseball right now where the balance of power (and compensation) has shifted dramatically from the on-field and dugout managers of the clubs who used to run the show to the corporate GMs who are the guys responsible for tracking down, tempting and securing the talent.

Now I realize that there are already plenty of treatises, textbooks (remember those?) and thoughtful articles out there about the need for (and the clever ways of) attracting, nurturing and retaining talent, but these things are generally written by people sitting on the sidelines like corporate managers, business school professors and HR professionals. Frankly, it takes a lot more talent, strength and energy to start, grow or change a company than it does to run one. And, as I like to say about picking surgeons if I'm having an operation: I want the guy who's done a hundred operations; not the guy who's watched a thousand. My life, and the world of startups in general, are not about "say", they're all about "do". So, I want to get down to brass tacks and into the trenches and talk about three critical things to keep in mind when you're dealing with the people who will make or break your business.

(1) Exceptional Talent is a Package Deal

A very important part of your job is to make room for people. Talent comes in strange and wonderful packages and – while we're happy to have the upsides – we are all too often not willing to understand that there are going to be trade-offs that come with the deal. You don't get to pick and choose and you've got to make sure that there's a place for everyone (including many who don't speak, act or look like you) in your business whether or not they believe that bathing is optional or prefer working all night long to showing up before the bell rings in the morning. Productivity is what you're looking for, not punctuality.

(2) Your Business is as Bad as Your Worst Employee

While it's still true that the best and most talented software engineers' contributions are a multiple of those made by the next group of smart programmers or designers; it turns out that there's a more important overall consideration. It turns out that the damage done by even a modestly underperforming employee is far more negative to the overall company efforts than the added benefit of those people punching above their weight. And tolerating mediocre performers is not only a horrible example for the rest of your folks; it's a contagious disease that can sink your ship. This means that another part of your job – not the easiest and certainly not the most popular – is to promptly and regularly get rid of the losers. And this means even the people who are trying the hardest. It's a sad thing to see people who have just enough talent to try, but not enough to succeed. Nonetheless, for your business to move forward, they need to move out and you have to be the agent of those changes. Waiting never helps in these cases. These situations don't fix themselves and I have found over the last 50 years that I have never fired someone too soon. Think about it and get busy.

(3)   Even Your Superstars Need Support

I used to say that talent and hard work are no match for self-confidence, but over the years, I have discovered that every one of us has serious moments of self-doubt and crises of confidence. With extremely talented people, it's a special problem in their maturation and development. In their early years – whether it's in business or in baseball – the superstars can mainly get by on their sheer talent alone at least until the going gets really tough and the competition starts to even out the score. Then, at some point, they fail – in a project or in a pitch – it's inevitable and that's where you need to be standing by to help. Because it's only after you have failed – only once your raw skills and talent have let you down – that you realize that the really great talents are those people who combine their talents with thought and preparation – those who can add the power of discipline to their talent are the ones we come to call geniuses down the line. But this is a precarious juncture for these people who've never before known a rainy day or caught a bad break and, without some support – whether they ask for it or not – there's a risk that they can fall apart and never get their risk-taking confidence and their mojo back. If you've had it your own way for too long, you can come to believe (or at least convince yourself) that even luck is a talent. But it's not. At these times, if you want to hang on to these precious people, you need to be there to help.

TULLMAN'S TRUISMS

HIRE PEOPLE WHO FIND THEIR SATISFACTION IN ACHIEVEMENT

Not exactly sure what "oblivion" means? Well, take a minute and look it up. And, in a way, that's precisely my point. Some of you will already know what it means; some of you will think you know (Goethe called this frightening phenomena: "ignorance in action", but it's actually a case of ignorance begetting inaction); some of you will take the time to look it up and be the better for it; some of you just won't care (shame on you); and most of you will say (hopefully to yourselves) that you just don't have the time.

But, of course, you do. Here's a tip about time: if you really want to do something, you'll find the time and a way to do it. If you don't, you'll find an excuse. The fact is that - even in our frantic and time-constrained world – we have all the time that we need (or we can make the time) for the things that we are actually interested in. And if you're not interested in life-long learning and in constantly trying to make yourself smarter and better-informed, you're not gonna be of much value to anyone (including yourself) and you certainly won't be able to compete effectively in the new knowledge economy. And this isn't just an attitude that you'll need; it needs to be a prominent part of your company's culture as well unless you also want your company to be an afterthought or yesterday's news.

Today, one of the greatest obstacles to progress isn't ignorance; it's the illusion of knowledge which – as often as not – is bound up in our arrogance and our reluctance to admit that we may not know it all. Real knowledge today is as much about knowing the extent of your ignorance (what you don't know) as it is about what you actually do know. Now don't get me wrong. I'm not trying to do some rhetorical Rumsfeld rap here – I'm just sayin'. And, unlike Rummy, I think there's good news on the horizon and a pretty simple solution to the problem.

Ignorance fortunately is curable; stupidity sadly is forever. We can't save most folks from their own stupidity or laziness, but I'm hopeful that we can help you get everyone in your business focused on getting better and smarter all the time with a simple turn of a phrase. Because even if ignorance doesn't kill you; it's certainly gonna make you sweat a lot more than you need to. So here's a simple suggestion on how to change the conversation and the culture in a few words.

The next time anyone anywhere says "I don't know", tell them that that phrase no longer means "they lack knowledge"; it just means that they're lazy because they didn't take the time to find out. DON'T KNOW = DIDN'T LOOK. Because the answers to just about anything we need to know today are out there; we just need to go find them. And to paraphrase Yoda: it's not about "trying" half-heartedly to find the information; it's about doing it with a vengeance. And, to remain competitive in today's economy, your team needs to know where to look and how to find the right answers fast. Because you can be sure that someone else is right behind you looking over your shoulder for the same advantage.

Sometimes it's a really short journey. It's not even about automatically searching the web. In many cases, you just need to do a better job of knowing what's going on in your own shop. I call this the "If P & G only knew what P & G knows" syndrome and it's applicable to every business – large and small. The answers, my friends, aren't always in the stars; sometimes they're in ourselves. In other cases, even a simple web search will provide more relevant and actionable information than you can imagine and more real value as well. It's not always that easy – so tenacity and perseverance matter as well – but the rewards for persistence are clear.

But your people have to have the intention, the inclination, and your permission to look – a bias toward investigation and learning – and not the self-satisfied and smug attitude that they already know everything worth knowing. Education isn't cheap; but ignorance is beyond costly. I recommend getting a t-shirt for the ones who just refuse to get with the program (while they're packing their bags) which says: "I DON'T KNOW AND I'M TOO LAZY TO GO FIND OUT". Not knowing is a sin; not caring about not knowing is grounds for termination.

The fact is that, except for your lawn sprinkling system, I'm afraid that there's nothing left in our world that can operate on the "set it and forget it" principle which made life so easy for so many people in the past. The vast amount of data; the prospect of constant feedback and trend information; and the ability to change the behavior of our customers in real time are all raising the need to be (a) on the case, (b) in the know, (c) all the time. Not knowing isn't even a bad excuse anymore; it's a death sentence for your business.

One of the most interesting parts of my job at 1871 is listening to our member companies. For most entrepreneurs, effective and patient listening is a fairly foreign concept. They think that the opposite of talking isn't listening; it's waiting to talk. Partially this is because they think that they have to always be selling and they're always trying to fill any dead air and suck all the oxygen out of the room. But sometimes, you just need to catch your breath and let the other guy have his say. As it happens, bits of actual wisdom are the rewards you often get for listening when you would have preferred to speak.

These days, I think that listening is a rare and highly undervalued skill. It's an area in which every one of us could use some improvement and developing good listening skills can make a world of difference for your business and in your leadership. Listening carefully is the highest form of courtesy and professionalism. As my Mother used to say: "this is why God gave us two ears and only one mouth." If I had only listened back then, there's no telling where I'd be today.

So every day I get to hear as much and as many of the trials and tribulations of the hundreds of entrepreneurs who work here at startup central as I can stand. I try to be patient and objective as long as they have taken the time:

(1) to do their homework and get prepared;
(2) to organize their thoughts and their questions; and
(3) to specifically identify the areas where they think I can help or at least advise them. Folks who just drop by to shoot the breeze quickly find themselves shooting it somewhere else with someone else.

If they're not prepared and if they have that little respect for my time; it's hard to imagine that they would really care about my thoughts and opinions or that I should waste my relatively scarce time sharing my reactions with them. I think this is a very fair expectation on both sides of the discussion – whether you're the "oldie" or the "newbie" in any conversation; you need to bring it or don't bother coming.

And, of course in the course of the conversations, generally when I'm asked, and often whether or not I'm asked, I'm not especially shy (and rarely polite) about giving them my impressions and the alleged benefit of my years of experience which may occasionally keep them from making the same mistakes that I made in similar circumstances. Sometimes, I discover that they're trying to create solutions before they've spent enough time listening to their customers' problems which is a lot like working in the dark. Other times I find that just the act of having someone seriously listening to them (who doesn't have an attitude, an interest or an agenda) does wonders for their mental health and their anxiety levels. But that's not to say that I think that these skull sessions should be warm and fuzzy chats.

I like to save the "strokes" for their co-workers, friends and families. Honestly, I'd rather be fair and frank than spend my time beating around the bush and worrying more about their feelings than their future. My process is aggressive and unapologetic – I'm trying to make them and their businesses better – that's all there is to it. It's never about me. But it does have a lot to do with argument and challenge – pressing and pushing them to think about the tough issues and the non-obvious answers - rather than supplying their standard responses. I want to make sure that they have the courage of their convictions and the willingness to stick by their guns. We often describe this posture as "sometimes wrong, but never in doubt."

That's because you need a thick skin to succeed in this crazy startup business and the internal and external calluses which will ultimately come to protect you are developed and grow strong in the crucible of confrontation (and hard questions) and not in courteous conversations steeped in superficial compliments. Some babies are just ugly – and some ideas just suck. It always helps to tell it like it is and the truth only hurts when it should.

Having said all that, I'd still certainly rather have them not just listen to my advice, but take it as well. I do vehemently believe that great serial entrepreneurs are masters in pattern recognition and – in the startup space – there are very, very few problems and very little else that represent truly new issues or – as the courts say – cases of first impression. In 95% of the situations, for better or worse, these are "movies" that I've seen before. Everyone I know and those I speak to about this who have made it their life's work to consistently light up new businesses will tell you that – while you're always gonna make new mistakes – the real key to succeeding more often than you fail is to avoid making the same mistakes over and over again.

I can't speak for the many guys who've been successful once in this business of new businesses – I'm sure that even they aren't sure whether they were terribly smart or terrifically lucky or, most likely, a bunch of both. It's never really that clear whether their particular success was mainly due to a good idea, good partners, good timing or simple good luck – not that there's anything wrong with any of these elements. I like to say: "Just because you've done it once doesn't make you Jesus."

And I've written before about marginal mentors and on the subject of how little having made or accumulated a lot of money has to do with having the mental horsepower and the chops to help someone drag his business out of a ditch. Money doesn't really care who makes it and having a lot of money – as we all know from experience – clearly doesn't make you wise.

But for those of us who have lived through the very prolonged and painful process of successfully birthing businesses over and over again, it all comes down to listening and paying attention. And to one more important thing: the winners are those who learn to listen patiently without losing either their self-confidence or their temper.

I sit through lots of meetings these days wondering how so many smart people can be so oblivious to some of the web's harshest realities. They work so hard and they're so creative in most parts of their business and yet they consistently overlook the singly most obvious shortcoming in their plans for global domination. These aren't mediocre mopes or deluded dreamers – they're great technologists, really sharp systems engineers, dynamite designers and even prominent professors. But, far too often, as they pitch their products, services and amazing ideas, what always comes through to me is the sad fact that they just don't get it.

What's the horrendous hiccup? Ya gotta get it out there before it's gonna do you any good. I call it Digital DARE which stands for Distribution, Adoption, Retention and Engagement. If you can't get your mobile application on my phone (distribution) and convince me to initially try it (adoption) and to then keep it on my phone (retention) and finally to use it on a recurring and fairly frequent basis (engagement), you've got nothing to talk about. And each of these steps in the success path presents different challenges and hurdles.

I see this same syndrome with all the new frenzy around content marketing. There's a fierce focus on content creation coupled with "Field of Dreams" fantasies about the ease of digital distribution. The hard truth is that if you're not spending almost as much time thinking about (a) how your message will reach its intended targets (and how you will know [measure] that it has) as you are on (b) developing the message itself, you're just kidding yourself.

In the old days, when we were still talking about desktop computers (before the world moved to mobile), we used to say that "if it ain't on the screen; it don't mean a thing". The point back then was that ideas and talk were cheap whereas execution and delivery were much more difficult. Fascinating features and functions didn't cut it if they weren't in the code base. And all the wonder and wishful thinking in the world wasn't going to get the product shipped and launched. Then, once you shipped your product, the bar was quickly raised again and, at that point, distribution and penetration were the whole ballgame. Yes, that was way back then, but it's just as true and as critical to your success today.

And while the screens we're dealing with may be smaller and much more mobile, the job is still exactly the same. Distribution and adoption are all that matters in the first instance and the competition is tougher than it has ever been because, while there are billions of phones in the aggregate out there in the world, each and every individual user gets to choose what occupies the prime positions on his or her own device. It's just like the real estate business – location and placement are everything. As I've said now for several years - the scarcest piece of real estate in the world is the front screen of the smartphone.

And if you think the adoption curve on cool new technologies is quick; wait until you see how fast these fickle fanatics abandon the latest and greatest anything in favor of the next bright shiny thing coming down the road. Especially anything that's a novelty rather than a necessity. Not only is nothing the future forever; the fact is that it's hard to hang on to a prime position even from week to week without some powerful staying power. The basic rule is: "out of sight, out of mind". Getting there is plenty hard; staying there is harder still. If you're depending on me looking for it; you better be sure that I love it or I'm not gonna make the effort.

So, if you want to be taken seriously (however amazing your application may be), you've got to address the critical concerns which will be front and center in every investor's mind. And while there are no simple solutions, it helps to spend some time thinking about the different ways that you can get over the hurdles and who can help you in the process. Because especially today, these things take tough teams and strategic partners. They never happen by themselves because no one has the time, talent or money to bring it home all alone.

Think along these three dimensions:

(1) Utility – Make It Multi-Purpose

The more functionality that your application provides; the more value it creates for the end user and the more likely it is to succeed. In addition, engagement and retention are frequency games – the more reasons I have to use something; the more instances in which it saves me time or money; the more likely I will be to retain it and keep it close at hand. But don't make it bulky. Feature creep and too many functions is a sure formula for failure. Interestingly enough, excess complexity is exactly why *Facebook* is now slicing and dicing the FB mother lode into a series of single purpose mini-apps. But it's a doomed effort because the sheer number of the individual mini-apps will assure the eventual abandonment of many of them simply because the vast majority of consistent users (MAUs) will pick a couple of core favorites and forget the rest. I realize that it's a straddle, but the winners will be the ones who strike the right balance.

(2) Ubiquity – Make It Multi-Channel

The more channels and locations through which the end users can encounter and obtain your application; the more likely it is to find its way onto their devices. This is all about distribution partnerships and about engineering as many different "win-win" formulations with channel partners as you can manage to put in place. You want to be everywhere the user looks and the "go to" solution for whatever problem or need you're addressing. If you do this right, you're going to spread your application's availability horizontally across the universe of uses in multiple channels and this will provide you another significant advantage against individual vertical channel solution providers who simply won't be able to match the volume and scale that a single multi-channel horizontal solution can achieve.

(3) Universality – Make It Multi-Cultural

You've got to go global from the get-go. Sure the U.S. is a huge market, but it has never been easier or less expensive to make sure that your solution is available and works around the world. I hear stories every day about the power of the web and especially the cloud and how users – acting entirely on their own - are adopting new products or services world-wide without their makers spending any material marketing dollars or trying to put a bunch of feet on the street. Make it easy to go big and broad. Just like the most successful global movies are short on explication and long on explosions; you want your application to be a vehicle that basically doesn't care or even know about the identity, language or other attributes of the content processed through it. This is precisely why photos work so well in so many contexts and sharing applications. What you see is exactly what you get – no more, no less, and no one cares.

TULLMAN'S TRUISMS

TO GET WHAT YOU WANT, YOU HAVE TO DESERVE WHAT YOU WANT

While I'm sure that philosophers for many years to come (if they're still around) will continue to wrestle with the question of whether a tree falling in the forest makes a sound if there's no one there to hear it; today's pressing dilemmas are more social and digital in nature. Whether we like it or not, while that tree may still be all alone in the forest, we're almost never actually alone these days and the advent of constant connectivity and two-way datafication is changing the ways in which we behave in surprising and unexpected ways.

We're connected to our friends and family, our co-workers and employers, a multitude of info-grabbing apps, and frankly a whole host of other folks, businesses, and agencies that we hardly know or know much about. And because our "phones" – actually I'd call them digital trackers that happen to make phone calls – are transmitting our thoughts, actions, locations and activities – actively and passively – knowingly and not – all day long, the communication and surveillance loop is persistent, omnipresent and unending.

It's like we have a digital Jiminy Cricket strapped to our waists instead of sitting on our shoulder – but the end result is virtually the same. Your tracker may not be offering moral support (or judgments), but it's tracking your movements all the same and sharing those with the world. And, as we all know from Professor Heisenberg's uncertainty principle, we behave differently when we know we're being watched (and/or measured) and this is why we like to say that "what gets measured is what gets done".

Now, if all this surveillance and digital peer pressure results in more exercise or other positive activities and actions, I suppose that's a good thing. But there is definitely such a thing as too much of a good thing and I'm thinking we're getting pretty close to the tipping point. And you may think that you're immune from these kinds of influences (and for the moment that may be true), but it's only a matter of time (and which poison you pick) because, in the end, they're gonna get us all and most of us will come along willingly.

As our technologies become more and more mobile and miniaturized (and – at least for now – wholly dependent on the life of our batteries), it appears that the power of constant connectivity may be at least as enslaving and annoying as it is theoretically empowering. And, just as an aside, is it too damn much to ask the phone manufacturers to have a phone whose battery lasts at least through a reasonably long business day? I love the new kinetic battery guys (like MyPowr.me), but do we really need to be carrying yet another device with us just to have enough juice to make it home at night?

In any case, I'm not just talking here about dedicated/obsessive users of any stripe: email junkies, crackberry addicts, selfie sickies, or even Google glassholes – I'm talking about anyone wearing a Fitbit, Jawbone, heart-monitoring watch or any other gizmo that charts and communicates athletic, calorie-burning or other aspects of your activity. The fact is that these powerful little guys strapped to our waists can be constructive coaxers or demanding dictators. We're seeing new (non-chemical) kinds of addictions – manufactured right before our eyes – in fact manufactured by us for us - which are built on datafication systems driven in large part by peer and partner pressure. These programs are beginning to change our behaviors at scale. And it's equally clear that there are psychological changes which are accompanying the introduction and adoption of these kinds of systems.

If you don't believe that this is a problem here and now, just see how you react when you discover midday that you forgot to sufficiently charge your device and it's no longer measuring your activity. We've all already experienced the angst associated with our mobile phones dying, but this is even worse. And, if you really want to go "cold turkey", just see how hard it is to put your device on the bed stand one morning and try to "leave home without it". I don't think you can do it.

Why is this so important for all of us and especially for the next several generations? It's not because I really care whether you're a few steps ahead or behind me in tonight's rankings or that your place on the leader board is far above mine. These are just the measurements and outcomes of the disease. The disease is that our technology now connects us and lets us work as long and hard as we want. All the time if we like.

The seductive power of constant and ubiquitous connectivity is that we don't want to turn it off. We don't want to drop out or disconnect. But if each of us doesn't start to think about limits and boundaries and rules, there won't be any end to anyone's day or anything meaningful left in our lives outside of work. The Fitbit anxiety is just the "canary in the coalmine" and an early symptom of the bigger problem. And the bottom line for each and every one of us in the most personal terms is very simple.

There's always more work, but you've only got one family and one time to go around this crazy life. So I'd say that now's the time to start thinking about how to balance all of the things that are really important in making a life (and not just in making a living) and try to get some sense of balance and proportion back in your life before it's too late.

92 – YOU DON'T GET A SECOND CHANCE TO MAKE A FIRST IMPRESSION

I call this the *Head & Shoulders* rule: most of the times in business you don't get a second chance to make a first impression and yet that simple fact of life is by no means as obvious and well-understood a phenomenon as it should be. Since we're talking here about "real life" and there are no second acts, rehearsals or do-overs; it's critical to make sure that the first impression people have of you and your business is at least favorable - and ideally - fabulous.

We're designed by nature to make lightning fast decisions (it's all an outgrowth of our earliest "fight or flee" instincts which were developed for self-preservation and to keep the animals we encountered from eating us) and we make these kinds of snap judgments hundreds of times a day without even thinking twice about them or the process. It's a visceral operation – mainly subconscious - and it's far more accurate (in 99% of the cases) than many people and especially behavioral "experts" like to admit. Turns out you can judge a book by its cover. Just not in the ways we used to think about these things.

In the old days, if you wore crappy old clothes to go out and look for a new car (which might or might not have happened to have been clean), the car salesmen would size you up in a flash and basically either ignore you completely or hand you over to the newest and youngest guy on the floor. Today, if you wear those same old duds to go car shopping, after, of course, you've checked everything out first on the Internet, the salesmen can't take the chance that you might be a major "in the money" code monkey or a mobile mega-millionaire and so they have to try to treat everyone who walks into the dealership in the same fashion.

But while this approach might be good rules of the road for the car sales biz and you can get away with dressing like a slob while you're shopping; it's a different story in any social or business context where the decisions you make in terms of your dress, your appearance, or any other aspect of how you elect to present yourself to the world) can influence – for better or worse – other people's impressions of you, your values and your ability to make smart and appropriate choices. People don't know how smart you are when they first meet you; but they can tell in a flash – based in some cases on nothing more than your appearance – that you've made some woefully bad choices sometime in the past. And it's a very short hop from there to "I don't care" or worse.

So we're still judging books and people by their covers – we're just drawing different kinds of conclusions from the data – less about economic circumstances or purchasing power and more about attitude, competence and overall good judgment. This is not to say that you're not always free to ignore other people's impressions and reactions and make your own choices; it's just to remind you that these are, in fact, conscious or unconscious choices that you're making and that all the choices we make come with consequences. And as you get older, you learn that who you are and what kind of life you get to live is largely the sum of all the choices – good or bad – that you've made along the way.

I recently wrote about one part of this problem in connection with the question of what to wear when you go on stage for your Demo Day pitch. I thought that your team's t-shirt was probably the safest bet of all, but mainly I was trying to suggest that you stay within the basic guidelines and avoid overdoing it in any direction – you don't want the way you're dressed to become a distraction. And the last thing you want to happen as you walk on to the stage is to have anyone looking <u>at</u> you rather than listening <u>to</u> you.

Crazy clothes, hiked-up heels, and bushy beards all subtract substance, attention and focus from your story. I realize that there are plenty of smart and savvy people who choose to dress or wear their hair in a certain style, but in this narrow context, I think that a fashion *faux pas* can start you off with a crowd that wonders if you're serious. Why would you want to start with that extra monkey on your back? This is a steep enough slope as it is – starting out in a rut of your own making – makes no sense. You should "make your statement" some other time and place.

And there's another monkey that it also makes sense to avoid if you can. Good people (that is to say most consumers) are somewhat patient, largely understanding, and – most importantly – inclined to give almost anyone the benefit of the doubt. But when you present yourself in a fashion that feels more like desperation than design or style; and you put it out there with an "I dare you to say something" attitude; you forfeit the benefit of the doubt.

Now the stakes are changed and you've got to do everything you're doing <u>really</u> well because you've essentially given up the standard margin for error. If you're gonna be right up in my face; you better not slip up because it's a very slippery slope and a very long road back. Make the slightest mistake and the person standing opposite you changes in an instant from "Get Along John" to "Judgmental Joe". People go from neutral to negative in these situations in seconds. We've all been there and done this ourselves.

So if you're gonna have tats all over your body or nose rings in your nostrils; just understand that you're walking a tightrope of your own making. On any given day, you can make it across with no problems, but you've made the job a lot harder and more perilous than it needs to be. And don't think that it's easy to fix the situation or repair the damage with a smile and a few sweet words. You can't talk your way out of problems that you behave yourself into.

There are degrees of everything – very few things in our world today are absolute. The amount of regular attention we pay to various matters and things; the extent of our patience for our loved ones, peers and others; and the wide range and intensity of the up-and-down feelings we experience at home and at work every day are all highly variable and emotionally-charged elements of our lives. If variety is the spice of life; it's equally an unsettling, challenging and countervailing offset to the security and stability that we all also relish.

At the same time, some things are for sure. You can't be all things to all people; you can't dance every dance; and throughout your life, you've got to make some hard choices, lots of sacrifices, more than a few compromises, and then you've got to live with them through thick or thin for a very long time. The truth is that you can't really hedge your bets when it's your life and the really important parts of it on the line. We become the sum of our choices over time and those choices determine the kind of person we end up being and how the world sees and values us.

What we become isn't a necessary result of fate or destiny. It's certainly not foretold or pre-ordained in any sense just as there are no guarantees when you start a business. And I don't believe that it's beyond our control and our ability to bend and shape the outcomes to match our desires if we consciously, actively and continually apply ourselves to the task. Throughout our lives, we remain a work in progress. Iteration isn't just a business process; it's a strategy for a life well-lived as well. And the good things that we all hope for don't happen by themselves; you've got to pay attention and make them happen.

One of the most critical choices you'll need to make when you start out in your career is exactly what kind of person you want to be. I think it's somewhat back in fashion these days to be a workaholic. For some of us, it never went out of style. Almost everyone today wants to be an entrepreneur; build a business; and be a big honking overnight success. But that's only part of the story. Just as we say at 1871 that ultimately it's not about making money, it's about making a difference; it's also about more than making a living – it's about making a life. And the "you" you become is a big part of the life you build outside the office right alongside your business.

It's really important - in the frenzy of the work and the world - that you don't lose your sense of purpose, perspective and proportion and risk losing yourself in the process. Your business and your work will always be what you do. These things are not who you are. And it's critical right from the start that you not confuse or conflate the two. This isn't as easy to manage as you may think. Today too many of us worship our work; we work at our play (fitness uber alles); and we play at what little worship we make a part of our lives. Where're the soul and the value in that? And – assuming that we want to – how exactly do we get ourselves back on top of things before they veer entirely out of control?

To handle the constant barrage of useful information, occasional insights and useless chatter as well as the increasing assault on all of our senses and, in fact, just to get successfully through the day; we need a new plan. You can drown in many ways today - in data, in documents, in deliberations and in endless discussions. So, the fact is that we each need to develop new skills (for managing both the data and the people in our lives) which probably most resemble the triage process in any emergency room. It's all about radical and rapid choices – as always – but there are many different kinds of choices in the mix.

At work, we tend automatically to focus on the fiercest fires and the highest flames. We let a great deal of how we spend our days and how our attention is directed be driven by the newest crisis rather than remaining in some kind of control and attending to the critical things that really matter. Attention is a slippery substance (a lot like mercury); easily and quickly redirected and readily dissipated. If no one is paying attention to the right things and the things that count, people just stop caring. Once you stop paying attention to the people in your business that are important and they stop caring about you and your business; they'll go someplace else to find someone else who does pay attention and who does care. It's just a matter of time. But that's mainly the business side of the equation.

As the number of physical, mental and emotional inputs we absorb each day continues to increase; our attention spans are shrinking and it's easy to fall back on systems and formulae and – before you know it – just by force of habit and circumstance, we're applying the same approaches and mental checklists that work so well at the firm or in the factory to our friends and families. This is where things can go very wrong very quickly. Because some of the people decisions we're confronted with every day aren't mathematical or subject to standard rules and procedures – they're choices about others, about feelings, and about our relationships. These concerns are fundamentally different, non-mechanical, and far more complex and they defy easy explanation. People aren't products, positions or policies – they're our co-workers, friends, and family. There's no fixed formula for getting these things right.

But it's just as much our job and equally incumbent upon us to decide all day long what's truly important in these inter-personal instances - both in the moment and in the long run – and to spend the time and direct the required attention to making sense of these situations with the same passion and energy that we apply to our business problems and concerns. It's a given that there's never enough time in the day (and that's never going to change); there's never enough of any one of us to go around (cloning may help this someday); and it's way too easy to find an excuse rather than finding the time to deal with these issues.

But here's the bottom line: your family (when you have one) will be a much more important extension of yourself than any work you do. There's always more work - you only have one family. And, believe me; good friends are also few and far between. Friends are the family that you get to choose – they're hard to find; even harder to leave; and impossible to forget. So as you make 'em; make a plan to hang on to them. They're as important an investment over time as anything else.

Take a little time now to decide how you'd like things to turn out when you look back in 50 years at your accomplishments, your family, and what you've built. It's all right there before you; it's all possible at the moment; and ultimately it's all about what you're going to make of it.

TULLMAN'S TRUISMS

THERE'S ALWAYS MORE WORK, BUT YOU ONLY HAVE ONE FAMILY

I t's not just Country Music that we rely on to say the simple things that need sayin'. And the Blues don't have any monopoly on tellin' it like it is (or how it ain't) or the way it should be. The fact is that, over the years, many songs from other genres have also told some basic stories which then resonated with millions of listeners and turned those "hits" into timeless classics. The format was inexpensive and the songs were "popular"; but that said nothing about the depth and reality of the feelings they successfully evoked. Even big boys do occasionally cry - as does everyone else. Music moves us all to extremes.

Sometimes, but only rarely, the elements that drove the widespread appreciation of these special tunes were the song's memorable hook; a special intro (like Keith's on *Satisfaction*); or a guitar solo (think Carlos Santana) that seemed permanently stuck in our minds. Most of the time, however, it was the immediate and intimate connection that we had with the lyrics which sealed the deal. They seemed to be speaking directly to us and "killing us softly" with a sensation of unexpected emotion. They surprised and touched us because they spoke to and about the very things that were important in our own lives. The truth is that music and music alone has both the power <u>and</u> our permission to enter our lives every day and excite and move us in these magical ways. As Sara Bareilles says in *Brave*: music can turn a phrase into a weapon or a drug.

But putting all the "love" (including love of country) and all the "loss" songs aside, what strikes me is that the singly most successful and consistent message in the largest number of classic songs (which are as powerful and telling today as they were on the day they were written and first performed) is one that's just as significant in our business lives as it is in our personal affairs. It's about the importance of being there.

Think about it.

What have you got "when you're down and troubled and you need a helping hand"? Of course, you've got a friend.

And who will "take your part when darkness comes and pain is all around"? Simon and Garfunkel - for sure.

And for all those times "in our lives when we all have pain - we all have sorrow"? We know we can lean on … Bill Withers.

Everyone needs someone in their lives that they can count on – someone to call when there's no one else to call. And, these days, with radical change and ongoing disruption being a constant part of every business, the most valuable people in any company are the ones you can count on in a crisis or a crunch – the "go-to" guys and girls. The people who are there in a pinch and who you just naturally tend to run <u>to</u> – not <u>from</u> – when the feces hit the fan.

This isn't part of anyone's job description. And it's not something you can create on the fly or on the spot. It's a visceral feeling that you just get about the people who've got it. But here's the good news. It's something you can build over time (like any other part of your reputation) and it's something that you can work on and work at every day that you're at work and – over time – if you're truly committed and your efforts are sincere and authentic; you can make it happen.

And, just in case it's not obvious, there's no better investment you could possibly make in your career or your future than being the <u>first</u> stop when someone's looking for help and not the <u>last</u> resort.

So what does it take to get it done?

(1) Stay Up (Perspiration)

Be the early bird at the office. Effort and energy trump talent all day long. And it never hurts to be the night owl too. Not the guy who's the last to leave the office TGIF party, but the person who puts in the extra time to make sure that things are done right the first time. Turns out that the buddies you buy beers for aren't very often the ones you'd bet your business on. And, as often as not, while you're bellying up to the bar (or buying someone a breakfast burrito the next morning); the real winners are back at the ranch taking care of business.

(2) Step Up (Passion)

Make sure that everyone knows you're interested and available. That you're excited about the business and the opportunities and that you really want to be a part of the program. Ya gotta want it and it's gotta show. You need to put it out there and understand that all anyone can do is say "no" – they won't eat you. And – if you keep asking – I guarantee you that it'll only be a "no for now" and it'll be full speed ahead soon enough. You won't get your shot if you don't take every opportunity to try and you'll miss 100% of the shots you don't take. Anyone who tells you it's not cool to be out front and eager these days will soon be changing the bottles on the water cooler while you're being welcomed into the club.

(3) Study Up (Preparation)

Even in the world of great entrepreneurial BS-ers, it actually does help to know what you're talking about. "Wingin' it" is good for sports bars and on Thanksgiving, but it's not a strategy for success in business. As I said recently, saying you don't know something these days isn't a commentary on your lack of knowledge – it's a confession of laziness and lack of interest – because the information is out there today; it's mostly a matter of looking. And if you cared; you'd care enough to get the answers before the questions were asked. The kind of knowledge, research and situational awareness that matter don't grow on trees or happen automatically or without help. You've got to put in the time, do the looking, and ask for assistance (when you don't have or can't find all the answers) in order to be ready when someone asks you for a hand.

(4) Stand Up (Principles)

You can't create value if you don't have a set of real values of your own that consistently guide and inform the way you behave. Charismatic leaders can attract a lot of followers, but the attraction is to themselves rather than to something greater and more important. Cause leaders bring the multitudes along with them in support of doing things that matter and make a difference not simply to a single business, but in terms of a broader and more general good. It's important for the people you work with (and for) to understand that – while we don't expect anyone, but a monk to be utterly selfless – you believe that the best plans and the best businesses are focused on creating situations where everyone can be benefitted and where it's a win-win-win all around. Not easy to engineer or to pull off, but very important in the end.

(5) Stick to It (Perseverance)

Execution is everything. Keeping at it – getting knocked down and picking yourself up again – making it clear that you won't settle for less or take "no" for an answer – these are all behaviors and traits that give off a certain vibration that the big dogs in the business will quickly sense and pick right up on because (a) it's absolutely a part of their own DNA and (b) it's also a big part of what got them to where they are. Winners have a Spidey-sense about other winners and, while their ears don't exactly perk up like a dog's; you can't miss the shift in their interest and attention when they encounter another of their own species. Wanting to win is fine – wanting to do the work that it takes to win and to keep at it until you do win is what makes the difference in the end.

That's all it takes. You can make it happen and there's no time like the present to get started. It's a lifelong iterative journey and the good news is that it gets better all the time.

If there's a goal or an endpoint to the process, it's very simple. When the chips are down and the fat's in the fire, you want to be the one who people can count on.

TULLMAN'S TRUISMS

BE THE ONE THEY CAN COUNT ON

People casually talk about "the cloud" as a platform, but it's not. It's just an alternative method of data conveyance. Most simply stated, it's a part of the pipe that gets you to and from whatever platform (think resource repository) you're looking for where you can access, connect to, interact with, and/or extract whatever you need. The cloud has solved the classic distribution dilemma which has dogged millions of young businesses since the beginning of time. How do I get my product or service offering out there to the masses? Solving that riddle is far more possible today through multiple channels – especially the app stores – than ever before.

In the old days, the name of the game used to be all about location. But in today's hyper-mobile world of constant connectivity, location is essentially immaterial (work itself is also no longer place-based) and effective distribution is all that matters. The cloud (basically for free to the end user) makes access ubiquitous and response time close to instantaneous. This is compelling and tremendously helpful (as well as cost-effective), but the real value and the ultimate power still resides with the parties who control the contents and the underlying delivery platform itself – not in the pipes. We see tiny, but very clear examples of the relative power of the players every time some cable company tries to extort additional carriage fees from content providers. All these games eventually end up in the same way – the guys with the goods get the gold – and the pipe guys are sent packing and back to the woodshed.

But when I talk about platforms, I'm not talking about the basic technology platforms (iOS6, Jelly Bean or Windows 8) that run our devices; I'm talking about the data, content and transaction platforms (or you might think of them as bi-lateral networks) which are sitting on top of these enabling technologies and which connect us with the data we desire, cool content of every kind, necessary products and services or simply other people.

And by the way, if you're wondering why there are only 3 mobile platforms (actually 2 ½ to be honest); that will tell you something important in itself about the power of platforms. Platforms are central to the "winner-take-all" realities of the world of technology and they help to create the inevitable concentration in these markets where one or two winners outdistance the field and then enjoy disproportionate and substantial profits for as long a time as their dominance persists. And these windfall and excess profits – if aggressively deployed – can further accelerate the ability of the leaders to pull away from the pack in many different ways. Excess cash can be applied to securing priority positions and placements in critical channels, crowding the channels themselves and closing out available ad inventory or other exposure available for competitors, predatory pricing, etc.

The fact is that, in markets fundamentally driven and dominated by (a) two or three central platforms, (b) mission-critical technologies, (c) ubiquitous operating systems; (d) enabling networks; or (e) products with very little, possibly zero, marginal production and distribution costs; over some reasonably short period of time, there will consistently emerge a clear and obvious winner, a strong number two and then a bunch of midgets and also-rans. There's just not enough volume or oxygen in these intensely competitive markets to support a half dozen winners. All of the structural considerations inherent in the ways we (as customers and consumers) elect to narrow and concentrate our choices rather than broadening the scope of our inquiries and our horizons also help to reinforce and precisely dictate the result we see over and over again in these case. Whether it's time constraints, an interest in efficiency, pure ignorance, sheer laziness or just basic human nature, we all tend to pick (and stick with) our familiar favorites.

There are a number of other contributing factors to this recurring outcome which are less personal – demonstrated economies of scale, market-dictated centralization and standardization requirements, and, of course, the power of Metcalfe's Law which first described and defined the exponential growth characteristics of networks and how that growth rapidly increased the network's power, resilience and value. The more power and connections a business had to and with its users, the more powerful and profitable it would become.

Metcalfe's law with certain subsequent refinements and embellishments stated that the value of any network (originally consisting of connected and bilaterally communicating inanimate devices, but these days counting nodes of any kind including people and/or users) was proportional to the square of the number of connections. If anything, in today's world of constant connectivity where every one of us is tethered to one or more devices at all times, the predictive power and nearly universal application of Metcalfe is even more relevant.

So your mission is pretty clear. If you want to find the prime position for your business to capture value from whatever back-and-forth activity is going on in your industry; you're going to want to identify the convergence points within the market – through which virtually all of the traffic and commerce needs to pass – and that's where your business needs to be. If you can locate the hub (not the spokes) and get yourself on the gatekeeper gravy train; you will learn very quickly just how powerful a position this can be. Being paid even a little something every time anything moves over a network adds up to a whole lot of everything in pretty short order.

And here's the deal: you don't have to be some Colossus astride the harbor to pull this off. Smart little guys can often construct effective horizontal platforms more quickly and economically than the big vertical (and siloed) players who dominate many (mainly oligopolistic) markets. You just need to understand the basic building blocks and the dynamics of what makes a particular platform prevail. And you need to plan to be a platform from Day One. Believe me, it's not something you stumble into.

So what do you need to know and be thinking about in terms of creating a persistent and winning platform as you try to build and properly position your own business?

(1) Do Something for the Market that the Major Players Can't Do Collectively or for Themselves

There are any number of industries where the major players are prevented by law or regulations from collaborative or cooperative efforts (very often these laws specifically target pricing issues) which are almost automatically regarded by the authorities and regulators not as helpful, but as predatory, exclusionary and anti-competitive. This makes it very difficult to structure and organize some market solutions that might ultimately be very beneficial and cost-effective for the consumer and which – at least arguably - ought to be of equal interest and concern to the same regulators. At the same time, these situations create great opportunities and openings for little guys to come out of nowhere and create sustainable new solutions.

So, in the case of the book publishers and Apple (albeit at Amazon's urging), the government attorneys have sued, fined and/or settled with almost all of the players for "conspiring to fix book prices". But, in the streaming music space, (where the music moguls seem to have finally learned a few lessons from the Napster debacle), we have Spotify and Shazam and others providing new services to consumers. And guess what? By creating industry-wide platforms for music delivery, these aggressive little startup companies not only blew the big guys away, but – even better yet – invited them in as investors. At last count, Spotify investors included: Sony BMG at 5.8 percent, Universal Music at 4.8 percent, Warner Music at 3.8 percent and EMI at 1. 9 percent. Also Merlin holds a small stake. The story is pretty much the same with Shazam where Sony, Universal (Vivendi) and Warner (Access Industries) each invested the exact same amount of $3 million. Could the message they are sending be any clearer? A very convenient and "legal" way for the very same guys who couldn't do it themselves to do it together thru smart startups building next-gen platforms.

(2) Create Criteria or Objective Benchmarks that Become the De Facto Industry Standards

A second path to becoming an industry platform deals with a different issue that again is common in many industries and presents new opportunities in all of them. In markets dominated by a few majors, a common problem in organizing and improving the efficiency of the market and creating better visibility (and "apples-to-apples" price comparison capability) for consumer is the lack of common and consistent nomenclature and the fact that each of the players has adopted and is psychologically "stuck" with their own numbering, identifying and classifying systems for their products even though the products offered by multiple players are functionally and often physically identical.

There are a lot of reasons for this – companies that believe that their branding and reputation will permit them to charge the consumer more for a product that is basically a commodity come to mind as the type of player which will resist market standardization. But they are basically losers (or will shortly be) in the new world of transparency where even the laziest consumer willing to do the minimal amount of research can access almost perfect pricing data in a flash. Another reason for the resistance to change and improved market organization and efficiency is simply company pride of authorship and the "not invented here" syndrome. This is "how we do it" and we always will do it this way – flash – until the market tells them otherwise by moving quickly away from them. And a final complication is simple overkill. Many companies for reasons ranging from tradition to the requirements of antiquated legacy accounting and control systems have way too much information associated with every product in their inventory and accounting systems. This does nothing good for anyone and, in fact, creates additional impediments to the company's speed, competitive responses to changed market conditions, etc.

Not surprisingly, the solutions which are changing markets like these are again being created by startups who are unhampered by all the historical and traditional concerns (as well as the ego issues) that make it hard to innovate and improve the old ways of doing things in the big businesses that dominate these industries.

And, in addition to being free of the constraints of the past, these startups bring a fresh approach which can best be described by three critical words: "Good Enough Is". They aren't trying to write the Magna Carta for product classification or the Geneva Convention (worthless as that may be in its own right) for generating inventory lists; they are just interested in building a simple new solution that spans horizontally across the many market players and focuses only on the common and critical components and characteristics that matter to the market when specifications and purchase decisions are being made. Nothing needs to be perfect – nothing needs to be the "be-all and the end-all" – the solution that gets you started just needs to work and be good enough to get the job done. Things can and will always get better, but they won't ever happen if you don't get something started in the first place.

Need a simple example? Think about eBay way back when. No real product specifications. No serial numbers and other details. Not even photos in many cases at the beginning. But it became a powerful trading platform in very short order because it was a sufficient system to get the required job done. While customer expectations are definitely progressive over time; they're pretty primitive and modest at the outset of a new experience.

(3) Offer the End Users/Customers Independent and Consistent Evaluation Documentation

A third type of platform is one which creates a resource for buyers and sellers to access accurate, independent, and consistent documentation about the location, availability and costs of various products (often used or refurbished) which is not often available from the sellers or manufacturers of new equipment. In theory, the best type of platform for this particular need would be an active marketplace, but because it is often difficult and time-consuming to assemble a critical mass of buyers and sellers at the outset and sufficient transaction volume as well – the marketplace is a nice and desirable tool for generating the pricing and supply/demand data about various products – but it's not necessarily the only solution in the short term.

Better and more accurate information is always preferable, but in some cases, any information that helps the parties make smart and more informed choices is better than nothing. When I started CCC Information Services in 1980, the goal was exactly this – to provide in digital formats better, more accurate, and more timely information about used car prices for insurance adjusters and ultimately for consumers to use in settling insurance loss claims. 35 years later, the same basic platform that I built back then is still in use and CCC is still the industry leader in the insurance vehicle valuation space.

What's so great about working with innovative startups every day at 1871 is that I get to see new and exciting game-changing examples of businesses addressing some of the same issues I dealt with decades before, but applying them to new markets and opportunities. One case in point is MarkITx (an early 1871 company) which is building a platform to permit Fortune 1000 companies to efficiently value and then buy or sell the billions of dollars of used IT equipment that they have to update and dispose of every year.

Right now, in 90% of the cases, my impression is that the only important consideration for these companies is getting rid of the old stuff (someway, somehow) in order to quickly make room for the new stuff. The fact that they regard it as "junk" and that they have foolishly written the equipment down far too quickly on their books results in them leaving tens of millions of dollars on the floor of the shipping dock while some junk dealer drags the old stuff away.

A system like the one MarkITx is already putting in place for major firms with enormous dated equipment inventories that simply and accurately not only shows them the actual residual value of the pieces that they were about to pitch, but then also painlessly enables them to sell those items for cash on the barrel head has been a long time coming. But it's here now. And, just as you would expect, once you've got your shop set up on this kind of an automated system with a disposal schedule, etc. and you can just look forward to the "found money" rolling back into your coffers on a regular basis, you don't even think about doing something else or going elsewhere.

(4) Invest Your Resources in Infrastructure Individual Market Players Couldn't Justify or Afford to Create for Themselves

Another of the opportunity spaces for platforms are in markets not dominated by a few big guys, but consisting instead of a million little guys – none of whom are in a position to make the commitment or the capital investments (as well as absorbing the people costs) of funding the costs involved in launching, marketing and operating a central organizing platform for their industry or marketplace. As I said above, platforms don't happen accidentally and getting the word out about a centralized and ubiquitous utility platform is very tough and very expensive.

I'm somewhat surprised that even sophisticated business journalists often don't really get what's going on in these spaces. One writer whose opinions I generally respect commented on Uber and said he wasn't even sure that Uber was a technology company. He acknowledged that they used smartphones, but so, he said, did every other business these days including taxi companies. Frankly, he just didn't understand that it wasn't about the phone you used, it was all about the classic Ghostbusters question. Who ya gonna call? That's the name of the platform game. Sure everyone in the city could just call some random cab company on their phone from wherever they happened to be and hope for the best, but that's not a solution that anyone with any smarts thinks is a winner.

To solve this riddle, you've got to be top of mind with the consumer; have immediately responsive city-wide coverage; have a critical mass of participating drivers – 24/7; build a system to instantly connect them all thru a single distributed platform; and then have lots of cash and staying power and hope for the best. Anyone who thinks this isn't a technology business won't know a Tesla from a Model T.

So, at the end of the day, one thing is absolutely clear. It will be the companies driving and controlling the centralized and coordinated connections we need through the hubs, the networks, and the other emergent channels which will be the ones which can extract market-driven premiums from the communications, transactions and commerce moving through them. These gatekeepers (many of them startups who built the critical platforms) will keep a very fair share of the gold. Nothing primes a platform.

One of the recurring conversations I have with startup teams at 1871 is about their "bad" board members. I discount a fair amount of this talk because I have been on both sides of this particular table many times and I understand that most first-time entrepreneurs would be "pleased as punch" if their investors just sent over a bag of money, dropped by once a year for a nice meal, and waited patiently for the day they could help ring the bell at NASDAQ or just start clipping their coupons. More seasoned entrepreneurs understand that a strong, engaged, experienced and additive board is every bit as critical to the business's long-term success as any other part of the company's management team.

Nonetheless, I think this is an important issue as well as one which, for a lot of obvious reasons, is very hard for the entrepreneurs themselves to raise and discuss with the men and women on their boards. It also turns out that these issues are very hard conversations for the board members to have among themselves as well - even when they very clearly recognize the problems that may exist with certain directors.

The truth is that in many cases these days, you don't really get to pick and choose your fellow board members. So these concerns are just as much issues for the board members as they are for the entrepreneurs. The last thing that a new business needs is a situation where you have a bunch of micro-boards where certain board members communicate with other members of the board on sensitive issues, but not with all the members of the board. That leads to very mixed messages for the entrepreneur and a lot of hurt feelings – often, I have found, to be the result of mis-directed or inadvertently forwarded emails.

Also, more and more these days, you have very diverse boards (from an experience standpoint) and, in many cases, this situation puts very seasoned investors at the table with a bunch of angels (or industry-savvy "strategic" directors) who may have initially put their money in the deal (or their company's money in the deal), but who have very little to add as advisors going forward either because: (a) as angels, they lack any significant and useful business or investing experience; or (b) because as strategics, they often have no real "skin in the game" and tend to be reluctant to commit to much of anything in the way of hard decisions. I don't think you have to love your other board members (or even like them a great deal), but as a foundation for an effective board, you do need to have at least some basic respect for their opinions and expertise.

In other instances, the interests and agendas of the board members can radically diverge early on and make for some very stressful and difficult sessions where it's not always clear who is acting in the company's best interests and who is looking out for their own interests and agenda. I see this type of problem arise regularly in cases where the entrepreneur quickly falls out of love with certain investors either because: (a) they're too critical and over-involved at the outset (these kinds of businesses don't all happen to get built overnight) or (b) because the entrepreneur feels (often rightly so) that there were unkept promises and undelivered connections, relationships, introductions, customers, etc. which turned what looked like a promising connection into a bad arrangement from the entrepreneur's perspective. Sadly, in the constant frenzy of early stage fundraising, entrepreneurs make a lot of bad choices out of necessity and most often fail (with respect to board members) to heed that very important hiring advice about hiring slow and firing fast. Needless to say, it's very, very hard to ask someone to get off your board a few months after they've joined.

All of these considerations can be made better or worse by the behavior of the parties. I think we all know what the entrepreneurs can learn to do better, but I thought I would share a few of my observations regarding directors and also describe some of the behaviors and attitudes that seem to be at the center of these kinds of unfortunate situations. If the shoe fits, you know the rest.

Some successful entrepreneurs (even one-time wonders) can be great angel investors. Their decision speed; bias for action; appreciation of the ambiguities and uncertainties inherent in creating a brand-new business; and their commitment to seeing things continue to change for the better are all important advantages and reasons to have them as investors. But as board members, it can quickly become a very different story. Many of the very same skills, talents and attitudes that are benefits on the battlefield can be brutal in the board room. Among other things, they often suffer from "founderitis" – roughly described as "my way or the highway" and that just won't cut it at all in someone else's board room.

Great listening skills are an important part of being a board member and not something that entrepreneurs generally have in their bag of tricks at the outset. And I'm not sure that compromises, concessions and building consensus are even a part of the entrepreneurial DNA. So, as the CEO, you want to be careful before you invite too many bulls into your very fragile and young china shop. And as an entrepreneur acting as a director, it's a good idea to try to check your ego at the door.

Here are a few other tips from the trenches that I hope you'll also keep in mind.

(1) Family.
We aren't yours. Just because your wife and kids don't listen to you at home doesn't mean you get to take it out on the guys you invested in. You're not our Dad and you're not Mr. Rogers. So spare us the homilies and the heart-to-hearts.

(2) Flyovers.
Showing up is table stakes. Being prepared and focused is what we are looking for in a good board member. If your attention span is roughly akin to a Mexican jumping bean; try taking some Adderall and come back when you're calm. As far as drive-by mentors go; we say tell them to keep on drivin'.

(3) Fables and Fantasies.
Just because it happened to you doesn't make it interesting or important to us or to the business. And just because things turned out well doesn't necessarily mean you had anything to do with it. Impress us with data; not dicta. Data always beat opinions.

(4) Forget the Format.
The value and timeliness of the information is what matters; not the volume and weight of the board book. We'd rather have the right facts on a roll of toilet paper than a perfectly-bound book of boilerplate slides and a bunch of bullshit. Directors who are more concerned with form than substance tend to be the same guys who are more concerned with punctuality than productivity.

(5) Focus on the Forest; Forget the Trees.
It might seem like the directors' job is to get into the weeds, but it's not. Their job is to set the broad strategic directions for the business and to hire and fire the CEO. The directors don't need to be minding everybody in the business's business; that's the CEO's and his team's job – not theirs. It's counter-productive, annoying and a great waste of time to try to end run the chain of command. It's there for a reason that smart directors understand and respect.

TULLMAN'S TRUISMS

GRAY HAIR IS A SIGN OF AGE, NOT WISDOM

Where is it written that a 26 year-old is entitled to a 6-figure salary? The rampant grade inflation at our colleges and universities where everyone's apparently an "A" student and where grading on a curve is just for old-fashioned curmudgeons like me is nothing compared to the ego and compensation inflation that's also going on all around us. Salaries always spike when there's tons of easy money chasing deals, but today it seems like the finances of too many startups are entirely out of whack with both reality and with their own wherewithal.

We used to believe that the cash and other compensation which you earned were reasonably correlated to the contributions that you made to the business. "Made" in the past tense – not those you were hoping or expected to make in the future. But today, recent graduates and new employees (especially in tech businesses) want to be paid on the come and - in addition to being unbecoming and overreaching – these expectations are choking a lot of young businesses because it would appear that almost no one in management knows how to say "No" anymore. In fact, I'm not sure that any of these young CEOs really want to say "No" (and here's another change from the past) because the salaries being paid to the people working for them are a pretty good justification for the amount of their own compensation as well. So no one really has the guts or the motivation to slay the Golden Goose until it's too late.

I'm afraid that, if we don't take some time to review the situation and maybe re-set some of the benchmarks, we're going to see a lot more businesses abruptly hitting the wall when the cash runs out before there's any real traction for the business and before the results start to show. You can shift your strategy and pivot like crazy if you've got the funds to stay in the game, but when you run out of cash, they send you to the showers and then straight home with your tail between your legs.

What's interesting to me is that this problem is pretty much restricted to the new young tech companies rather than the established Silicon Valley technology businesses that have been in the game for many years. In part, this situation is probably because a great deal of what used to consume a significant part of early-stage funds (capital expenditures, connectivity costs, etc.) are really no longer major components of getting a new business off the ground. So there's more theoretically "free" cash to spend on disproportionate comp packages for the management and key technical employees.

In fact, the big tech guys not only understood the salary and comp problems; they appear to have adopted an entire – basically illegal - plan to deal with it. That hasn't worked out too well for them at the moment, but you can't blame them for trying. At least they were a lot smarter than the legal profession which basically blew itself up (and killed a number of major firms) by engaging in an insane annual competition to see which firms could pay the largest starting salaries to their newest associates. Year after year for no good reason they would pay newbies tens of thousands of dollars more than their existing employees and brag about it to boot. I'm sure that the stupidity of this competitive process wasn't lost on the senior management at Apple, Google, etc. An interesting aside is that one of the only companies not accused of participating in this comp-fixing scheme was Facebook which was also run by the youngest guy on the block.

In any event, and however they came to the realization that some collusion was in their aggregate best interests, we're all reading these days about the latest class action lawsuits asserting that certain executives at the biggest tech firms on the West Coast got together and agreed not to poach talent from each other by starting bidding wars for engineers and other workers with specialized technical skills. They allegedly had an aggressive and quite overt enforcement policy among the major firms and an ongoing and active involvement from the most senior managers in the whole process. Most recently, the judge rejected a major settlement offer by the leading firms (about $325 million) saying that she thought it wasn't enough money for the damage done to the hundreds or thousands of employees who got screwed.

I'm not sure how the litigation will turn out for the parties (I know the lawyers will make a bundle), but I'm certain that I can understand some of the underlying motivations (not, of course, the morality or legality) of most of these guys. It's hard enough to get great talent and almost impossible in the hyper-competitive and completely immoral world of the Valley to hang on to your best people because everyone is basically chasing the same players and most of those players are chasing the next "big bucks" offer. Frankly, I'm surprised that it's taken this long for this whole story to leak out.

And I would have expected nothing less because company loyalty doesn't matter much out West and job longevity is pretty much a joke. We may have fewer superstars in Chicago right now (that's changing as we speak), but, while the culture and the people here are just as competitive, we also value commitment and keeping your promises. Our best employees basically stick around. They're here and in it for the long haul – not for the easy exits – and not for the next best offer.

But that doesn't mean that there isn't a big issue around compensation in Chicago and every other tech-oriented big city these days that's causing a lot of headaches and heartaches for young entrepreneurs who are trying to build their businesses with limited capital.

I understand that in every market there's an ongoing competition for talent, but there's also a lot of talented engineers and others walking around these days wondering exactly what to do with themselves. There are a lot fewer sure things than you'd imagine; not everyone's got a game-changing idea or a world-beating business; and there's not all that much appeal (or upside) to becoming employee 98,001 at Apple.

And whether you want to acknowledge it or not, it's not a free or perfect market for talent anywhere because a great many of us are constrained by other considerations – family demands, education requirements, location and the risks of picking up and moving across the country, etc. – and these concerns also all factor into the choices that we can make.

So I think that right now it's almost as hard (however talented you may be) to find a great opportunity (and the one that's right for you) as it is for businesses to find all the talent they need. And I'd suggest that this is a healthy kind of equilibrium that serves us all in the long run and that should encourage all of us to try to keep our personnel costs somewhat in check.

As I imagine Jesse James used to say: it's always a better idea to rob the train first and then split up the loot. Or as Kanye says: *"I got a problem with spending before I get it. We all self-conscious. I'm just the first to admit it."*

TULLMAN'S TRUISMS

BLOOM WHERE YOU ARE PLANTED

One of the great TV ads of all time featured a crotchety old Chicago woman (Clara Peller) whose plaintive 3-word inquiry ("Where's the Beef?") became a national catch phrase and a huge advertising home run in terms of brand awareness and sales for Wendy's restaurant chain. Every comedian, late-night television host, news commentator and politician seized on the expression and couldn't use it enough.

For at least an entire year after the commercial first aired, it became a very succinct way to challenge the substance of almost anything or anyone – even politicians like Gary Hart. It was a socially-acceptable form of 80's shorthand and a speedy substitute for those who formerly referenced the ancient (1837) and time-honored Hans Christian Andersen tale of the child who noted that *The Emperor's New Clothes* were notably absent.

And – amazingly enough – this lightning-fast phrase craze swept the country in 1984 – long before social media made it possible for the most trivial comment by a second-rate celebrity to become a worldwide "triumph" or "travesty" overnight. But today, among too many young startups, the latest and greatest craze – with roughly the same caloric count and value - is "lean" everything.

I find myself thinking fondly of Clara's pronouncement whenever I have to sit through another bogus business review session where someone with the bare bones of an idea is trying to convince a group of otherwise intelligent investors that there's a real business opportunity buried beneath all the bullshit and that (a) all of the shortcomings of the story being spun and (b) all the gaps in the gospel aren't actually problems at all. They're not bugs, oversights or misses; they're the intentional result of trying to be "lean" and trying to launch "something" (not to say "anything") to get the ball rolling.

I'm not sure when it got to be OK to try to do the least work possible in developing anything that you were seriously trying to do well, but maybe I missed a memo or two. And, as a result, when I hear these pitches and have people telling me that it's the minimum viable product, not the meat of the matter, that actually counts; I remember that Clara knew better and that this entire lean startup movement not only misleads and misdirects people into building mediocre products and potential services, it's also much more of a curse that ails us than any kind of a new cure.

We're encouraging an entire new generation of young entrepreneurs to rush things out to prospective customers; to throw a bunch of stuff against the wall; and to see what sticks. In the old days, people thought this might be a good way to test to see if the spaghetti was <u>al dente</u>, but it actually wasn't. Pasta that sticks to the wall is most likely overcooked and too gummy to taste good.

Like so many other things in life, there's no simple shortcut or quick way to do these things right. It takes time and craft and patience to build things that will matter and last. "Quick and dirty and out the door" sucks as a strategy for successful startups. Maybe you can never be too thin or too rich, but a startup can clearly be too "lean". The ultimate goal isn't to build skinny startups – it's to build smart ones.

I understand that it would be naïve to delay your launch until you thought you had every single detail exactly right and that, by waiting, you'd ended up building the completely perfect product or service. We know that, over and over again, even the experts can completely overlook glaring interface flaws or other obvious omissions that the simplest novice user will see right off the bat. And it's equally arrogant to assume that you can't learn a single thing from the marketplace or your users. But that's just a different problem.

As I see it, there's a basic flaw in the common understanding of the "lean startup" concept and then there are 3 main problems with the way most young entrepreneurs are trying to adopt and implement the methodology.

The Basic Flaw

Even the best MVP ("Minimum Viable Product") won't succeed without an MVA. An MVA is a Minimum Viable Audience (that's my simple shorthand for a bunch of potential buyers). Long before you start creating your product, crafting your code, and designing your UI; you need to find out if anyone gives a damn about your idea and your proposed solution. This isn't easy work. You have to actually get off your butt and get out into the field and find and talk to actual people – not your co-founders or your folks – about what you're hoping to do.

You have to find actual problems that are generating real pain for a large number of people. You have to determine whether those people recognize the problem, appreciate the pain, are willing to admit that they have the problem, and are willing to pay for a solution. Then you might have a fighting chance to define and build a viable solution.

And you have to also recognize that: (a) there's an infinite demand for the unavailable (anyone can say they'll buy something that you don't have for sale); and (b) the easiest way for a buyer to get you to leave them alone is to say "Yes" and "Come see me when your product is ready" and then show you the door.

The 3 Key Problems

(1) They Won't Care

If you haven't done your homework first and identified the right pain points and the right target customers, you might as well take a hike because no one wants the cure for no known disease; no one is going to invest in solutions in search of problems; and you'll end up building and wasting a lot of time on the greatest software never sold. The way you start the process determines where you end up and these businesses are hard enough even for the people who do all the proper research, preparation and planning. A goal without a plan is just a daydream on someone else's dime.

(2) They Won't Suffer

The idea that you can dump some partially-baked solution on your first prospects and that they will help you figure things out is another pipe dream. Trying to make your first users into your last beta testers is a stupid waste of everyone's time today because smart users want simple solutions that work right out of the box, not more problems. And it doesn't really matter what the problems are – implementation, training, support, stability, or security – they're all just more noise and aggravation that busy people don't need. We are very quick to try and even adopt things that work for us, but we're even quicker (by a multiple) to dump the stuff that doesn't. And while there is an obvious trade-off between the degree of the customer's pain and the customer's otherwise heightened expectations, in the end, no solution that simply swaps one set of problems for another is going to get out of the gate.

(3) They Won't Wait

As the Heads & Shoulders people always say, you don't get a second chance today to make a first impression. Customers won't (and don't) wait for you to figure things out and – for sure – if your first attempt falls flat, you can bet that they won't let you come back. We hear too often about products that aren't released, but simply escape and others that aren't ready, but run out of time and race into the market. It's ridiculously easy to burn your bridges and impossibly hard to rebuild them when there are fast followers and copycats galore standing in your wake and watching your mistakes. Customers don't want stories or excuses; they want workable solutions.

The Right Way

There is a right way to do this and it's pretty simple. Do your homework and find an important unmet market need. Recruit the right early users who are invested (by virtue of their own desires) in your success. Build your MVP to their specifications and with their input and buy-in. And then prepare to enter the perpetual iteration loop.

Launch, Measure, Modify, Re-Launch and Repeat the Process ad nauseam.

Successful solutions today are all the same – moments of mad creativity followed by months of maddening maintenance. Continually raising the bar and improving your offerings is the only way to stay in the game.

I get that everyone wants to be the boss. But the truth is that very few people have the necessary set of emotional, technical and intellectual talents, skills and tools that it takes to succeed over time in building a new business. This is even more of an issue when you're trying to finance and grow a startup in the critical period when it begins to gain some traction and starts to scale. Sure, you can try to hurry out there and hire some grown-ups to help, but if you've got the wrong person in the driver's seat, you're never going to get the business to the next level. And sometimes, you're the only one who honestly knows that you're the wrong guy or girl for the job.

The list of what it takes to succeed is a long one and I've written about these various attributes before and how challenging it is to have to balance so many competing considerations at the same time. You've got to walk that thin line between pushing the envelope and being somewhat patient so that you don't get too far out over your skis and crash. You've got to be demanding and also delicate – getting the most out of your people isn't the same as getting the best from them. Making room for people is all about different strokes for many different folks. You've got to have a thick skin to ward off all the naysayers and know-it-alls so you can keep going and an open mind so that you can not only hear, but also listen to and learn from, well-meaning and smart people when they tell you what you're doing wrong and how things will need to change in order for the business to grow.

And all the while, you've got to keep your head up high and not let anyone see you sweat or worry. Leadership is an ongoing performance art and you're never offstage. It's an all-consuming constant juggling act and it never slows down or gets easier. And because there are always so many different things going on, it's very easy to get spread a mile wide and an inch deep – to keep jumping from one crisis to another without taking a breath - and it's very hard to find the time to do what it is that you do best which isn't everything for anyone. But no one's gonna go out of their way to tell you that or to tell you to take it easy. It's all pedal to the metal and balls to the wall. They've all got their own agendas and going slow isn't anyone's idea of how to get ahead today.

And that's the really bad news – spending the lion's share of your time trying to be all things to all people, running around like crazy, and trying to do a little bit of everything that needs to get done may not be your highest and best use or the way that you can make the greatest contribution to the ultimate success of the business. But it isn't ever easy to admit to yourself or anyone else that you may not be up to the job you're in. And it's even harder to share the truth with the other people who also need to hear it. It's never easy to say what nobody wants to hear. And it's especially difficult and more than a little scary for any entrepreneur to acknowledge that maybe they're not the best person for the top job.

The *Peter Principle* is still alive and well – it's just slightly different and more complicated when the person who's the problem is also the founder or co-founder of the business rather than someone pushed or promoted into a position that's over his or her head. I'd call this problem the *Founder's Fallacy*. The idea that every talented engineer or coder comes equipped with the skills it takes (or even the deep-down interest or desire) to lead the business or that he or she will automatically grow those abilities as time passes is a foolish fantasy.

And oftentimes it's actually the entrepreneur who figures these things out first. But knowing what should be done, admitting it to yourself and getting it done are very different things. But, when corrective action is required, if you don't initiate the process and try to guide it; you can expect one of two outcomes: (a) the business will start to go sideways, stall out, and eventually fail; or (b) the investors will finally work up their courage (and overcome their own fears and reluctance) and they will come for your head. It's much, much better to get ahead of the wave than to get pulled under and washed out.

There isn't one approach or formula that fits every case, but there are three basic ground rules that govern this process and you need to work through them and see where you and your business stand.

(1) Be Honest with Yourself

We each have our own strengths and weaknesses. We need to play to them and not ignore them. But, even more importantly, each of us has things that we love to do and other things that we abhor and do poorly. The trick is to find the highest position possible where you still love doing what you're getting paid to do. Nothing is all fun and games (that's why they call it "work"), but the more time you can spend doing what you want to do, enjoy doing, and are really good at doing; the better the results for the business.

You need to ask yourself honestly if you're really enjoying coming to work every day or if you're increasingly frustrated because a million inconsequential things keep getting in the way of you getting the things done that you – and probably you alone – need to get done. If you're honest about it, you'll start thinking about getting someone else in there pronto so you can get back to taking care of the real business.

I'm watching this scenario play out in at least three young businesses right now. And every case is remarkably similar – you've got a guy who's great at analysis and data acquisition trying to deal with the banks and accounts payable – you've got a fabulous salesman trying to supervise day-to-day operations while he's standing on one foot at the airport waiting for his next flight to see a big new prospect – and you've got a guy who loves machines and hates people worrying about HR matters. It turns out – he's slowly learning - that even the smartest machines demand a lot less of you than people do. It's not a good thing that he hates people, but – for sure – dealing with people is not something he's good at.

The bottom line is that they need to quickly get real and make a better plan and they need to do it before their businesses fall apart or they get tossed out.

(2) Be Honest with Your Backers

Your Board and your investors won't pretend to be even slightly happy to hear that you want to hire your own replacement even though they may well be secretly relieved that they didn't have to force the issue. After all, this is really one of the only two things – overall strategy being the other - that they should be concerned with even though they generally spend way too much time in your shorts and in the weeds of the business.

But even if they're expecting it (or fervently hoping for it), this is still a complicated conversation that you need to handle exactly right. Any leadership transition is challenging even when the ship is steady and it's even more risky and perilous when the company is in the midst of a growth spurt. So expect everyone to be somewhat on edge including, of course, you.

To start out on the right foot, you're gonna have to get over your own feelings of failure and inadequacy which can quickly poison the discussion if you're not careful. You brought the idea to life; you got the ball rolling and now it's time to hand the reins over to someone else so that you can return to doing what you do best.

Be careful here that you don't get angry at the investors (or the world in general) for not appreciating you enough, not giving you the unlimited time and funds you needed to realize your dream, and/or not having your back and being disloyal to you (after all the sacrifices you've made for them) when the chips were down. I'm sure these sentiments are already familiar to you and that I'm not telling you anything new. But you have to put this stuff behind you. You need these guys on your side as much going forward as you did getting to this point.

You also have to deal with two additional emotional concerns and you need to convince the Board and the investors that you can successfully handle these feelings as well.

The first is the loss of control. Entrepreneurs are all about authority and control. So it's understandably very hard to let your baby go – even a little bit – and everyone who's been through the process knows how quickly problems can arise if there's not a clean and complete handoff. You can't have two CEOs and you can't set up a situation where your key people – for whatever reasons – start to shop for the answers/decisions that they're looking for from whichever one of you seems the likeliest to agree.

The second is the fear of being forgotten. Entrepreneurs very quickly get used to the spotlight, the strokes and the applause and it's hard to walk away. They don't want to be forgotten or no longer regarded as essential to the company's success. Sometimes this can turn into a serious problem where the prior boss acts in ways that sabotage the business. You would think that everyone involved was working in the same direction for the company's success, but human beings are a little more complicated than that. It's just a little satisfying to know that the guy stepping in to fill your big shoes isn't finding things quite as easy to pull off or as straightforward as they looked when you were running the show. The Germans may have invented the idea of *schadenfreude*, but it's alive and well in every C suite in this country as well.

The bottom line here is that you have to be out front and very clear with the Board and the investors that you're 100% on board with the transition plan and willing to do whatever it takes to make it work. One of the leader's most important jobs is to create the next generation of leaders.

(3) Be Honest with Your Buddies

The people who are going to be the most concerned and anxious about your decision are going to be the ones you are closest to and most dependent on. They're gonna feel abandoned, disappointed and more than a little angry that you're leaving them in the lurch - even if you're not. Sometimes the hardest part of being the boss and making the tough calls isn't fighting off your competitors; it's having to deal with the hurt feelings of your friends. But those feelings can't keep you from doing the right things for the business.

Startups are a lot like circuses and political campaigns. Intensely high-energy and high stakes exercises carried on in incredibly compressed timeframes. While the circus is set up and all over town; it's all bright lights, excitement and superstars. Once they strike the tents and move on down the road; it's an empty arena, some broken dreams and sawdust all around. Once a startup reaches a certain size and level of maturity, some of the early dreams and hopes (or delusions) also die and some of the people who got you there can't take you any further.

Political campaigns are even worse. You drive yourself and your team crazy trying to beat the other guys and then – when you win – the difficulties really begin because now you've got to make a series of impossible people choices and position selections and everyone in the running is someone who's been there from the start and helped you make it all happen. There are no simple answers and all the decisions are hard. But it's just another part of a job that no one ever said was gonna be easy.

The bottom line here – amid all the tears and hard feelings that will most assuredly be part of the process - is to be honest and to set out the circumstances and your choices as simply as possible. And then to remember that you can explain things to people, but you can't understand those things for them.

Today, we have a much better and clearer view of where technology will take us over the next few years and how it will continue to significantly alter our lives. The primary focus – per my own personal crystal ball – will be on "efficacy" – products, services, systems, software and things that help us get other things done – more quickly and more economically. The overwhelming emphasis will be on saving us time, saving us money and making us more productive – these are the metrics that make for businesses that will consistently make their builders money as long as they continue to deliver the goods. Moonshots (literal or figurative) don't really matter in the Midwest – concrete results do.

I realize that simply shutting down the spam-spewing email systems of the world would make us all more effective, but I don't see that happening. I also don't expect to see many bionic anythings and I think we'll also have to wait quite a while for social robots and other intelligent household helpers. In fact, I wouldn't expect any dramatic advances or new "miracles" any time soon because the upcoming changes will most likely be both much more mundane and also tremendously more beneficial in ways that really matter to us. The next several generations of high-tech advances won't be about inventing new things - they will be about making the everyday objects we deal with in our day-to-day lives smarter, more responsive, and more helpful to us.

These developments will be driven by two (now fairly obvious) considerations: (1) every one of us is constantly connected to the Internet cloud by increasingly intelligent devices which will all compute; and (2) our basic expectations (which are forever growing and expanding) are that we will use these connected devices to provide us with what we need, when we need it, wherever we are, and without asking. This is the new world which we will come to call the Internet of Everything.

We'll make smarter choices every day about a wide variety of things based on vast quantities of better information which will be available all of the time in the palm of our hands. And many of the basic decisions which are required will be made quickly and automatically for us by high-velocity computers living somewhere in the cloud based on the unimaginable quantities of data being generated by every action we take, every move that we make, every venue we enter, and the trails of digital exhaust that we will leave behind wherever we go.

So what exactly are the kinds of things that we can reasonably expect to see today or in the near future? Things that will seem super cool tomorrow and which, by next year, we'll all take completely for granted.

Here are 3 categories of intelligent device-driven interactions that will become everyday parts of our lives.

(1) Who Are You Lookin' At?
The new Samsung phones turn off their screens when we aren't looking at them. New photo apps won't snap a picture if we're not smiling. Others won't take the shot until we signal them by making a fist. Our slabs and tabs are looking at us just as intently as we continue to study them.

(2) Who Are You Talkin' To?
New cloud-connected pill bottles will remind us to take our medications and just how much of each prescription we should be taking. New haptic utensils and clothes will vibrate to remind us to slow down when we're eating too fast and speed up when we're walking too slowly.

(3) What Are You Waitin' For?
Our phones (which we call mobile "trackers" that just happen to make calls) will alert merchants as we enter their stores to send us immediate, totally-personalized offers, specials and coupons on the way into the store when they're useful instead of wasting paper and trees printing long receipts that never even make it out of the grocery bags once we leave.

There are many more examples and these are just brief glimpses of the future. Exciting, challenging, and constantly changing. Buckle up.

101 – PERSISTENT "PROBLEMS" ARE GREAT FOR GROWING BUSINESSES

Woody Allen once said: "If it weren't for problems, the work day would be over by 10am." But, being Woody, he thought that having a day full of exciting (and sometimes frightening) problems was a bad thing. I think it's a sign of great management and a growing business. Woody's ideal world of slow, steady and predictable everything – with Tuesday nights forever spent playing the clarinet at Bemelmans Bar – is dying a little more every day. Nostalgia is not an engine of growth – it's a nasty nightmare composed of equal parts of apathy and avoidance. Maybe this is why Woody's movies keep getting set further and further in the past which he clearly pines for.

And while the truth is that the view out of the rearview mirror is always clearer and less buggy than the straight-ahead scene rushing up at you outside the windshield (as you're flying down the highway); those businesses which are spending their time looking fondly backwards and celebrating their prior glories and the status quo are sure to run off the road or into a wall even sooner than they expect. Clinging to the sterile past is a real problem. Embracing messy, but inevitable change is the only real solution.

Our world today isn't neat and tidy or even well-organized any more – it's a big complicated, uncertain and confusing place – just like a startup. Encountering, analyzing and addressing new problems – day-in and day-out - are crucial components of the ongoing developmental process of your business. This is an iterative process and a continual practice which hopefully never ends because we know that, in building a great business, there's never a finish line.

And we also know there are no guarantees and that little or nothing is certain in a brand-new business. A business that's expanding and bursting at the seams will never perform exactly as expected or predicted (or as written in some "ancient" business plan that you wrote 90 days ago) or, for that matter, like any other past business you've ever been involved with. Even the best businesses will have bumps and slides, rough edges and difficult patches, pleasant and other surprises, and a whole bunch of unexpected and unintended consequences. You can call all these things "problems"; I'd call them opportunities in the making.

The trick (there's always a trick) is to create a business which offers you a steady stream of the right kinds of problems. A strong leader treats problems as normal, not special or unique. Good problems energize us – bad problems drain us dry. Good problems are about too much or too many – bad problems are usually about too few or too little. Too many orders, too much demand, and too many new opportunities – we should all have these difficulties because growth solves a lot of problems. But no one wants to hear about too many defects and returns, too little production capacity, too many overdue receivables, etc. Ultimately, good problems are almost always about the future – bad problems are generally about making up for or cleaning up after the past.

In addition, as a bonus, having a boatload of big, brain-busting and bewildering bogies that your teams are constantly chasing has another important benefit. It's the surest way to attract the best, brightest and most talented people around. Because, in today's hyper-competitive recruiting world, it's no longer about snacks, scooters or snap chatting; the game-changing people – the ones who will matter the most to your company's future – are looking to work at the companies doing important, challenging and meaningful work which is directed toward solving major concerns and addressing serious cross-industry issues.

So, although it may take some time, you need to get used to the idea that your business isn't unique and that you'll always have a set of pending problems (as will every other business) and the only differences between you and everyone else will be in the severity and the volume of the problems at any given time. Don't let it get you down – and don't take it personally. Instead, just get busy identifying the problems, categorizing them and knocking them off as quickly and smoothly as you can.

To help you get started, here are a few things that you should keep in mind.

(1) There's never only one right answer to a problem.

We're used to thinking that, if we apply ourselves and just keep at it, eventually we will find the one and only best solution to whatever the problem is. I always believed that, if I worked just a little harder, a little longer, a little more creatively, I would eventually figure it out. And when that magic moment arrived, everything would be perfect. What I discovered over time is that while there's always an apparent solution which is neat and simple and even inexpensive, it's almost always wrong. The trick is to avoid settling for a makeshift or partial solution which only hides or defers the real problem and to keep looking for a better answer. You never want to try to do something cheaply or quickly that you shouldn't do at all.

(2) There are some problems that you will never solve.

Some very difficult problems never get solved, they just get older. And in many cases, this is because these aren't problems – they're facts of business or life that you simply have to learn to live with. In these cases, you don't want to waste your time and energy – you need to understand that your best course of action isn't going to be to fix the problem; it's going to be determining how to cope with the problem and the fact that it's not going anywhere any time soon.

(3) There's no way to create a solution without listening to the problem.

We live in such a hurry up world these days that I often see teams of highly eager and energetic engineers swarming a problem and coming up with solutions that are created in a vacuum. Trying to find an answer without spending the time and effort needed to carefully listen to the problem is just like working in the dark. As often as not, this approach generates solutions in search of problems and not real results.

(4) The facts (and the problems) won't disappear just because you ignore them.

Deferring a discussion and/or a confrontation doesn't avoid an eventual problem; it just makes it much more likely that the next time around, it will be a full-blown crisis. If you refuse to face the facts honestly and openly; they won't evaporate – they'll accumulate. If you leave a small problem alone long enough, it becomes a big problem and one that is much more difficult to solve. Very often even good managers don't understand that any problem which you can solve by writing a check isn't a problem; it's just an expense. You don't have the time or the bandwidth to be penny-wise and pound foolish. Pay the man the money and move on.

(5) There's a pony somewhere in almost every pile.

Much of the success that you and your company will have in handling problems will ultimately depend on your own attitude and how you approach each new issue or concern. Problems can be looked at as constant burdens or as potential bonanzas and all of the members of your team will take their lead from your behavior. Great companies have interesting and exciting problems that are likely to blossom into new and expansive opportunities. Great leaders can make even ordinary problems into people magnets which attract and draw the most talented employees into the process and engage them in the challenges surrounding the solutions. It's all in how you define and articulate things.

At the end of the day, this problem business is pretty simple. You're not alone – everyone has them. You can't ignore them. You can't solve them all. You can't solve them by yourself. And most of all – you can't let your business be pushed by your problems. You want it to be driven by your dreams.

Way back when, in April of 2013, Scott Case and I participated in a rapid pitch program called Enrich Your Pitch at the INC. GROWCO conference in New Orleans. The competition featured all veteran-owned and operated businesses as the presenting companies. It was an impressive group and I was especially taken with an eager guy named Joseph Kopser who was pitching his relatively new business, Ridescout. At the time, I didn't realize quite how new it was.

Joe didn't win the grand prize, but he says that the press and the exposure from the event were worth their weight in gold from investors and helped him keep afloat and raise crucial funds at a very precarious time. He also told me - much more recently - that - at the time of his GROWCO pitch - he barely had a beta version of his idea and he was having an impossible time hanging on to users. In any event, we hit it off in the Big Easy and have been in regular touch ever since.

Now flash forward about a year or so, and Joe picks a luncheon at 1871 in Chicago as the place to launch Ridescout in the Midwest. The business literally exploded after that event into another 66 cities in a matter of weeks. It was a spectacular rollout and Joe has been running around the country ever since with 69 total active markets and several hundred ride providers. I thought I knew exactly what his game plan was – in fact – I wrote about the basic components of the strategy in two recent INC. columns about the power of platforms which are described below, but I still wanted to hear it from the horse's mouth.

Luckily for us, Joe still finds time to swing by his 1871 Chicago office on a regular basis and, most recently, in addition to promoting Ridescout, he's become a vocal and very active supporter of a new initiative that we have launched at 1871 called The Bunker which is an incubator and support program for veteran-owned businesses with a particular focus on technology. The Bunker is led by Todd Connor who is a Navy man and it launched formally a few weeks ago as part of the 1871 2.0 expansion program. We were honored to host the event which was attended by over 300 interested supporters, members, investors and vets as well as by U.S. Senator Dick Durbin, the senior senator from Illinois. And, of course, Joe was there at the Bunker launch as well because giving back and helping out is also a big part of who he is and what he wants to do with his life.

And then – just a couple of weeks later – came the big announcement that Daimler, one of the world's largest car manufacturer, had acquired Ridescout and entered the ride-sharing business. Quite another impressive step up for a startup that was scrambling to survive a little more than a year ago, but that's how it happens if you're in the right place with the right team and the right idea at the right time. And, of course, it never happens by accident.

So I sat down recently with Joe to ask him exactly what the secrets were to that drove the rapid national expansion and brought about all the good things that followed. And, in a word, he said that he basically built a "platform" which, of course, was music to my ears and exactly what I had assumed. And it's amazing how closely his description on the critical building blocks mirrored my recent INC. pieces.

What the Power of the Platform Means for Your Company covered parts 1 and 2 of the strategy: (a) do what the big guys can't do for themselves or won't do by working together; and (b) create de facto industry standards that organize otherwise unstructured data and markets.

Joe figured out early on that each of the alternative transportation providers was operating in a silo and the last thing that any of them cared about or was focused on was cooperating on sharing route and cost data - even if such a combination was clearly desired and highly valuable and beneficial for the end user. Basically, Ridescout built the bridge between these islands and created a comprehensive platform that served the consumer's needs.

Even more importantly, Joe understood that each vendor had their own language, terminology, interfaces, etc. and that the absolutely last thing any consumer needed were more individual apps on their phones which didn't talk to each other and which couldn't even be effectively compared with one another without investing an inordinate amount of time and energy.

The need for a one-stop shopping experience and an integrated solution was clear, but no one was really in a position to get the job done. Needless to say, the first mover would have a major shot at organizing the entire space, setting the industry standards, and becoming the market leader. Ridescout rode to the rescue.

The Primacy of the Platform dealt with the third major consideration: invest your energy and resources in building infrastructure that the individual players in a given market can't afford to do by themselves.

So the need was clear and there was a major opportunity, but Joe also needed to assemble the technical team that could get the job done quickly and in a fashion that was immediately scalable. He needed to build a platform and an overall solution that accomplished 4 things:

1.   It was absolutely critical to figure out how to translate, aggregate and normalize the data which needed to be "grabbed" from sites, suppliers and vendors from all over the country into a consistent set of formats. Building the ingest tools and the translation programs were major time and dollar investments.

2.   It was equally important to build a single interface for all sharing by vertical – in other words – all bike shares needed to ultimately look the same thru Ridescout regardless of the city you were in – and the same was true for all car shares, transit and rides for hire. No one else was stepping up to fund the development of a single standard and one which also needed to somehow account for the outliers in certain areas whose particular approaches needed to be melded into the overall system.

3. The system and the backend had to be scalable and robust enough on Day One to accommodate the flood of data (and hopefully users) as well as demand from newly interested participating vendor and partners – once they woke up – on a national basis and the process needed to be as automated as possible.
4. The overall solution set needed to be extensible and always backwardly compatible because the only way to make sure that Ridesout maintained its leadership position was to constantly be raising the bar by adding features and functionality that responded to the input, suggestions, complaints and increasing demands and expectations of all the participants including the various governmental bodies in each geographic location. As it happened, the fact that Ridescout took a very conciliatory and collaborative approach to the city managers and regulatory bodies as they moved from market to market turned out to create a very substantial barrier for other potential new entrants.

Ultimately, time will tell, but Joe's off on an exciting and exploding ride and nothing beats a well thought-out and a well-built platform as long as you keep raising the bar.

TULLMAN'S TRUISMS

THE TRUTH ONLY HURTS WHEN IT OUGHT TO

Where should I start?

Best Buy is bombing out. They should think about changing the name to Better Buy as in "better buy somewhere else that's gonna be around for the next few years" just in case you need them. It's morphed into a bunch of mini-showrooms for the mobile phone and computer companies and a hands-on demo facility for Amazon shoppers who want to handle the goods before they order online. The increasingly random product mix and the way they change their in-store locations so often make it almost impossible to find anything. It's like a torture maze designed by Conan the Floor Planner. Basically, they're spread a mile wide and an inch deep trying to be all things to all people and to have a little bit of everything for everyone and it's an impossible mission.

The concept of the long tail works – but only in the virtual world - for a simple reason. The web permits <u>infinite inventory</u> which no one in the real world has the cash, the resources or the shelf space to replicate in terms of its breadth or depth of available alternatives and choices. This is one of the main things that killed Blockbuster. Back in the day, we used to call them "Boxbuster" because they stacked tons of empty VHS boxes all over the store to make you think that they actually had something in stock that you wanted to rent (like a hot new hit film) once you asked for it. But when you did ask, nada.

Sears/Kmart (remember Sears?) is also sinking like a stone and they just cut Lands' End adrift for no greater or more apparent reason than they gave when they bought it in the first place. It was a desperate attempt to move upmarket and it went nowhere. Saying doesn't make anything so – you've actually got to change your actions in order to change your culture and to change the public's perception of your position in the market. This stuff doesn't happen overnight even if you're actually committed to making it happen which is somewhat of an open question in Sears's case. Similar attempts to reinvigorate and modernize their sub-brands like Kenmore and Craftsman have also been stillborn. Sears is a proud and historic brand, but it's probably just history these days. Some things are beyond redemption or salvation. Shopping at Sears is a chore and today no one's looking for more work.

And Radio Shack – the original store for geeks, model makers and operators of all sizes and shapes - is a wreck in the midst of the greatest boom in demand for technology and gadgets in history. If anyone had a chance to naturally migrate their business from hobbyists and Trash 80s to the big time in computing devices, it was these guys and they basically got rolled over by everyone else. In addition, with the whole world moving from analog to digital, they completely missed the movement from physical "kits" to digital everything. The Maker movement was their last best shot and they never even stepped up to the plate on that one. At this point, someone just needs to tell these guys to lie down because they are badly burnt toast.

Sears is in no better shape than Radio Shack. Nothing's worked since the Kmart deal. Kmart buying Sears was like taking poison to get even with your enemies and expecting them to die. It's another case of identity loss. Walmart (480B) owns the low price position. You could make an argument that Target (73B) owns the middle-class style and fashion spot although probably not for long – way too many new players moving into that space – and there is no more fickle class of consumers than their targets. And Sears plus Kmart (36B) owns nothing. They have no direction, no passion and no soul. Everything they do these days is short-sighted – it's like wetting your pants in a dark suit. It gives you a warm feeling for a little while, but no one else notices.

How did it happen? First and foremost, they all got caught to varying degrees in the muddle in the middle. Or maybe in the middle of the muddle. Today to compete effectively you just can't be beige or average and their stores and their offerings were basically "so what" in every possible category. If you don't stand for something in the consumer's mind and carve out a demonstrable and defensible niche, you're nothing. You can't save yourself with advertising, promotions, coupons and circulars – these days any kind of "brute force" spray and pray advertising (regardless of the channel) is just the unavoidable cost of being boring. And the proof of the pudding is that there are still companies getting it right. Interestingly enough, they are also still way too reliant on the old-fashioned techniques, but their in-store chops are second to none.

Maybe the best example today is Costco which has clearly figured a bunch of this stuff out. And considering that they started 20 years after Walmart which is the 800 pound retail gorilla, it's impressive that they are doing more sales today (109B) than Target and Sears combined. What exactly do they know that the others don't and why is it important to your business as well?

(1) Family Fun

They've made it fun for the whole family (even Dads) to go shopping again. They've made it an adventure (instead of a chore) to hit the store and see what's new. They get that we're deep into the Entertainment Economy where every environment needs to be immersive, informative and engaging. And they have figured out that the main reason that all the stats suggest that the lion's share of typical consumption decisions are controlled by Moms is because the Dads aren't there most of the time when the shopping takes place. Once you add Dad back into the equation, the average spends of trips where two parents are present (rather than just Mom) increases by more than 40%.

(2) Here Today, Gone Tomorrow

The guys who run Costco are also masters of FOMO – Fear of Missing Out. Every other big box store tells you that they have unlimited quantities of everything to convince you that they will never run out of what you're looking for. Costco convinces you every week that it's your very last chance to grab that item or you'll never see it again. Why else would you buy your Xmas decorations in the middle of October? It's because you sincerely believe that, if you don't, you'll be totally screwed, your family will gleefully remind you of what you missed out on for months thereafter, and you'll be the only one on your block who didn't grab the goods while the gettin' was good.

(3) Run and Gun

They also understand that we all live in a world where IG (Instant Gratification) is the name of the game. I want what I want and I want it now. And they don't leave these things to chance or to even the smartest computers. They know that, while you're waiting in the checkout line, you've got next to nothing to do and that's when their super-salesmen descend with their scanning guns to check out the contents of your cart and let you know how much you will be saving – right then and there – if you switch up to a higher level of membership. In fact, if your order is big enough, you might even come close to covering the annual bump in the membership cost while you're just standing there and – for sure – if you're a regular volume shopper, you'll be miles ahead of the game in just a few weeks. It's easy, it's true, and it's right there – right now.

The moral of the story is pretty clear and simple. The expectations of consumers and customers are progressive – to hold their attention and their affection, you've got to keep making every new visit an adventure and an experience. If you don't, they won't be your customers for long.

TULLMAN'S TRUISMS

THERE'S NO SUBSTITUTE IN LIFE FOR PAYING ATTENTION

I have consistently said (for longer than I care to remember) that, at least for me, there's a really simple test to evaluate the viability of an idea for a new B-to-B business. Does the proposed product or service save the end user time; does it save the customer or client money; or does it increase their productivity? If so, let's talk further. If not, take your plan and take a hike.

Now I understand that there are ideas for businesses that are intended to address other social objectives and that you can't measure those kinds of endeavors solely by their financial bottom line, but that's not what I'm talking about here. And frankly, those types of businesses are not representative of the vast majority of the proposals that I see every day. So, while there are clear exceptions to every set of rules, I'm sticking with my 3 simple questions until someone shows me a better approach.

And, of course, the ultimate dream is to find a business that does all of the above. It's not really as hard as it sounds especially today when new technologies are ripping through every old line traditional industry and turning things upside down. I see businesses every day that are disrupting the old ways of doing business simply by taking steps, obstacles and costs out of the old way that things have been done forever and dragging those businesses into the new world.

And what is so interesting to me is that the lion's share of the opportunities and new solutions (medical technologies are an exception) don't necessarily involve newly invented or untested technologies – they are nothing more than cases of smart people applying proven and industrial strength technologies to eliminate waste and inefficiencies and improve outcomes. This is the critical difference between invention and innovation. Innovation is smarter, faster, less expensive and less risky than trying to invent the next big thing from whole cloth. Good technology is necessary for great products and services, but it's not sufficient in itself to get the job done.

The new and inexpensive technologies which are now available pretty much everywhere are certainly enablers of the digital revolution (as is the rise of mobility and constant connectivity) and these tools make the process improvements and new solutions feasible and cost-effective, but it remains true that the real drivers of disruptive change are always the same: entrepreneurs (who probably didn't know what "couldn't" be done) and who look at things that everyone else has seen for years, but think something new and different and then go on to build something that changes the whole ball game.

Amazingly enough, once you have the cutting insight that changes everyone's perspective of whatever problem you're trying to solve, you discover that the "app" or the new technology is a conduit that is helpful in the process, but it's generally not the central reason for the appeal and attractiveness of the new approach. A good example is *Snapsheet* which is using mobile technologies (phones and cameras) to change the way that insurance adjusters do their work. Consumers simply use the *Snapsheet* app to take a series of photos of the damage to their car and upload it to *Snapsheet* where a room full of experienced adjusters immediately evaluates the damage and determines how the loss should be handled. Losses can be settled in hours rather than days or weeks. And that's just the beginning.

Snapsheet is one of those rare companies that are delivering a beneficial solution to auto insurance companies across all 3 of my test vectors. Time, money and productivity.

(1) Save Me Time

Claimants get settlements in hours. They don't have to waste time sitting around their house waiting for an adjuster to show up. The adjuster doesn't waste his time (and half a day) driving all over the city to look at a fender bender. In addition, using readily-available data, adjusters can instantly determine based on the age and mileage of the damaged vehicle whether any repair is appropriate or whether they should just "total" the car and write a check on the spot.

(2) Save Me Money

Insurers save boatloads of money avoiding the costs of providing rental cars for their insureds. Transportation and fuels costs shrink dramatically. Faster settlements have less unhappy parties and significantly fewer supplementary payments.

(3) Increase My Productivity

Adjusters can process far more claims every day because they aren't wasting travel time and gas on useless trips. In addition, they're sitting in a room surrounded by other expert adjusters instead of being The Lone Ranger standing out in some cornfield or driveway trying to write an estimate. Faster, better, more accurate and fully documented transactions mean happier insureds and employees as well.

But the thing that is so striking is that the major benefits from using *Snapsheet* don't really arise from the "app" or the underlying technology – any mobile device that can capture and send images could get the job done – the real value arises from smart (and now obvious) improvements in the efficiency of the adjusting process. This is why the best businesses don't lead with their technology – they lead with solution selling addressed to known and obvious problems.

Along time ago a very wise old man said: no one cares how much you know until they know how much you care. The ability to consistently demonstrate this type of paramount "personal" and emotional concern to others (about whatever the current issue or matter under discussion may be) is an essential ingredient in the make-up of any successful politician (or husband). We absolutely prefer sweet, "sincere" and somewhat stupid leaders (like Uncle Joe) to serene and severe smarty pants (like President O) who we know in our hearts don't care a fig for us common folk and, basically, would just as soon not dirty their hands dealing with our pedestrian problems. You just can't let those minor day-to-day disappointments get in the way of your grandiose thoughts and big dreams. And if you don't ever deliver on the dreams, well who's really counting anyway – let's just move right along to the next fundraiser.

And, when we (as consumers, customers or an entire country) feel like this, we proceed to act accordingly - by withholding our approval, our support and, most importantly, our commitment. President Obama's functional failings (too many to count) and basic inexperience and incompetence are nothing compared to his complete inability to manage the drama, emotion and theatre of the Presidency in a way that not only instills some (admittedly fast fading) modicum of confidence in his operating abilities, but - much more materially - convinces us that his Spock-ish heart is occasionally in the right place and in our corner. Where's that master of empathy - Doc "Bones" from the Enterprise - anyway when we desperately need him in the dawning age of Ebola?

We don't hear too much these days about anyone being the smartest guy in the room anymore (as if he ever was when either Clinton was within the same zip code), but we do believe that our President's trapped in a womb of his own making surrounded by the same unskilled and useless advisors that he's had around him from Day One plus some guy whose main job is apparently to keep the basketballs inflated at all times. Forget the nuclear football that we used to worry about having close at hand at all times; now it's all about tee times and clean, white Titleists.

You might regard this all as both old news and cheap politics, but managing these types of emotionally-charged interactions and exchanges (where – as often as not – the customers don't tell you the real problem or their actual feelings until: (1) it's too late; (2) the connection with them is irreparably broken; and (3) they're long gone - is also a critical component of how you and your business need to carefully approach the new world of "social" everything where everything's a two-way conversation and everyone gets a vote whether we like it or not.

Today, the context is somewhat different, but the fundamental idea of demonstrating your interest and concern to your intended targets hasn't changed much. The basic objective is to figure out how to make me care and then how to make me share. I'm happy to spread and even amplify your message (as long as it relates to and resonates with me and is delivered at the right time, place and context) by sharing it with my friends and throughout my network as long as I actually believe that the message, the concern, and the process are all authentic. So how do you go about getting it right? And who exactly knows what they're talking about since the majority of the people talking about this stuff have: (a) been doing it for about all of 5 minutes and (b) couldn't find their asses with both hands even if you gave them a hint and a head start.

Sadly, right now, there are about a million people full of suggestions, systems, tools, tips and tricks of the trade for making this whole social thing happen for you – social media consultants are definitely part of a growth industry where there don't appear to be any required credentials although being the biggest blowhard on your block is a definite benefit and being a diva in your own mind doesn't hurt at all either. It also helps to be in your early 20s just as it does in Hollywood where a bunch of equally ill-equipped and uninformed folks are running businesses while they keep looking over their shoulders hoping that no one will figure out that they have no idea what they're doing either.

And then there's also a growing number of morons and scam artists who think that you can "fake it 'til you make it" in this social media business. I'd say they're having roughly the same degree of success as the guys who thought that the makers of Preparation H should also make a lip balm while they were at it. I wrote about these bozos a while ago in these pages. (*The Trouble with Social Media*. http://www.inc.com/howard-tullman-the-trouble-with-social-media.html). Sadly things have only gotten worse with pseudo experts on "virality" being all the rage today. There's a reason that the blind leading the blind don't end up getting anywhere.

I'm not sure that anyone has all the answers for your business (or that the best answers won't change again by next week), but there are three basic ideas that it's important to keep in mind as you develop your own social media plans.

(1) Less Messaging is More Effective (A Little Goes a Long Way)

Just because you can doesn't mean that you should do certain things. High on that list is inundating your intended targets with tons of repetitive email, interruptive and inconsequential texts, run-of-the-mill offers, mixed and confusing messages, etc. – all of which are doubly destructive. First, by burying your important communications in a pile of non-stop crap, you lose any prospect of commanding the attention of your targets and you also run the risk that your channel may be shut down entirely either by the end-user or by the email guardians in the sky. As the poets used to say, if I had more time, I would have been briefer. Second, by bundling the important material with the mundane and mediocre mass, you cheapen the entire set of messages and make it easier to dismiss your whole effort. There's a reason that people hate bulk mail and it's not just its weight and crappy production values. If you're respectful of my time and interests (and at least semi-polite while you're at it), I'll be happy to help you get the word out.

(2) Give Me Ammo, not Ads (I'll Be Fine)

Information-sharing is a contact sport and it's also a highly competitive one. People – especially those who regard themselves as major influencers in any area – don't just want to know what's going on, they want to be the first to know. But they're not looking for the run-of-the-mill chatter that *Access Hollywood* or *Tech Week* had last week, they want the straight goods and they want the good stuff that will position them as knowledgeable and in the thick of things. Factoids and fluff aren't going to move anyone's needle – you need to develop real facts and substantive information that will stick and stand up to scrutiny and then you need to get it out to your advocates and net promoters as soon as possible - before it all becomes yesterday's news. The bulk of active social sharing now takes place in a matter of hours – the same day - not some days thereafter – and if you miss the first wave, your message will just get lost in the froth that follows.

(3) You Can't Push a Rope (You Won't Have to)

Save your breath and save your money. If you have the right message and a great story, you don't have to sell anyone on selling it for you. The people you want to reach (for their influence and their ability to build your story) – the major influencers in any space - are like the scorpion who rode across the river on the croc's back and then stung him anyway. When the croc asked why (after the scorpion had insisted that he would never do any such thing), the scorpion replied – "it's my nature – it's what I do." Here's the dirty little secret – you don't have to chase or push these folks – just like the scorpion, they also can't help themselves. They have to share and they have to push these stories out there or they fear that they'll no longer be relevant themselves. So don't sweat the distribution part of the program until you've built a rock-solid and valuable story and then let it fly. Sometimes the best push you can provide is to take a step back and watch things happen from the sidelines. Never let 'em see you sweat.

TULLMAN'S TRUISMS

PERPETUAL OPTIMISM IS A FORCE MULTIPLIER

106 – OPTIMIZING, NOT MAXIMIZING, YOUR TEAM'S OUTPUT MATTERS MOST

Today, and every day from now on, the tools and technologies that permit us (and others) to observe and document more and more detailed information about everything that we (as well as all those around us) do, see, pay and say are continuing to exponentially increase their power, scope and accuracy. Data is the oil of the digital age and we are generating unfathomable amounts. Not only are we swimming in it; we're leaving a trail of digital exhaust everywhere we go to be captured, analyzed and output in real time and in ways that will increasingly permit third parties to anticipate and attempt to influence and change our behaviors. This flood of facts creates amazingly attractive opportunities and chilling challenges at the same time.

I'm not really concerned about big data and big government and the NSA; my interests are much closer to home and all about how we are using all this new information to most effectively manage and grow our businesses. I've said (practically forever) that keeping score matters and that, in most businesses, what gets measured (acknowledged and rewarded) is what gets done. I haven't changed my belief in this regard so much as I have come to believe that we are putting too much emphasis strictly on the numbers. Numbers don't lie, but they never tell the whole story. They can only take you so far before they top out and you need something more qualitative and experiential to get to the right conclusions.

Peter Drucker's dictum that: "if you can't measure it, you can't manage it" has created a whole generation of analysts and others who are often so focused on perfecting their business's processes that they lose sight of the business's purposes. I hear managers all the time talking about the need to get more work out of their people when they should be trying to get the best work out of them. Optimizing, <u>not</u> maximizing, the team's output is what matters most to the ultimate success of the business. Working smarter and more impactfully - not necessarily longer or harder - is how you ultimately move your business away from and ahead of the competition.

So I think that we have to be exceedingly careful these days that we don't let the ease of access and use and the ubiquity of massive amounts of quantitative performance data cause us to over-emphasize the math and measurements in our businesses (and in our lives) and thereby lose sight of the far more important qualitative attributes of what's going on and the meaning and value (rather than just the metrics) of our various activities. Not everything is easy to measure or quantify, but that doesn't make these things less important; it just makes our job as managers tougher. Human nature (being what it is) means we tend to gravitate toward the easy and the concrete rather than the harder and often vaguer vectors involving attitudes and behaviors. But when you get so comfortable with and wrapped up in the measurement process that it becomes a goal and an end in itself, you discover pretty quickly that it loses its effectiveness. In today's frenzied work world, it's easy to confuse movement with progress – but not all motion is forward – and lots of activities that run up the numbers aren't remotely productive. Measuring more is easy; measuring better is tough.

And when you let the numbers basically drive the train, you also give up two important advantages that are critical to your success. First, the goal isn't to be the thermometer; it's to be the thermostat. It's not about measuring the heat; it's about generating and controlling the heat. You don't want the analytics to lead you; they're a useful benchmark and a guide for course corrections, but it's on you to set the direction and move the business forward. Second, when you get so focused on specific and concrete financial results (sales targets, growth rates, etc.) and you direct all your team's energies toward getting as close to achieving those numbers as possible; you actually limit your ultimate upside because you lose the ability to think and see beyond those immediate goals. This means that when a game-changing opportunity, a quantum shift in your sales prospects, or an out-of-the-box new direction appears; your team may be so heads-down and in the weeds pushing those budget numbers that someone else will come along and grab the new brass ring.

I think that there's some middle ground here and some ideas that can help you balance the temptation to take the easy way out with the need to deal with all the facts – even the fuzzy ones – in order to get the full picture. Here are three important perspectives to keep in mind:

(1) Elaboration is a Form of Pollution

Tell your team to keep it simple. No one gets paid by the page or the pound and shorter is almost always better. I've found that when people expand and extend their plans, proposals and presentations, there's a high degree of likelihood that they're concerned about the value of their pitch so they try to bury it in a boatload of facts and figures, charts and citations, and everything else that just hides the hard truth. It's better for everyone for your people to put things right out there – front and center – and take their medicine if that's what's called for. If you torture the numbers long enough, they'll say whatever you like, but that's not any way to get to the truth or the right result.

(2) Not Everything is Worth Doing Well

Tell your team that everyone's always on the clock. There's an opportunity cost associated with everything we do and choosing what not to do and how extensively to do the things you need to do are critical in any startup which has scarce resources and even less time. One size or one approach never fits all of the possible cases. Some things just don't warrant the full court press and it's important to make sure that everyone knows that that's O.K. with you. Other things shouldn't be done at all and you should <u>never</u> try to do things cheaply that just aren't worth doing. It's never easy to turn people down or say "No" to marginal choices, but it's part of the job and comes with the territory.

(3) No One's Ever Measured How Much the Heart Can Hold
Ultimately, the value of the critical connections your people make every day with your clients and customers can only be roughly approximated by even the best math. But it's those daily personal and emotional interactions with your empowered employees that build the crucial engagement as well as the lifetime value of those buyers for your business. You need to give your team permission to do what's best for the customer in the moment that the opportunity arises. If they need to consult a rule book or have a calculator handy to do the math, they'll lose the value of the moment every time. The best businesses don't worry about the number or sheer volume of moments – they work to make each moment matter.

TULLMAN'S TRUISMS

NOT EVERYTHING WORTH DOING IS WORTH DOING WELL

It's National Magic Week. I've been a "professional" magician since I was about 9 years old and I firmly believe that nothing in my training or background (except my mother's raising me to have a level of ridiculous confidence which was utterly disproportionate to my actual looks and abilities) has had a greater impact on my success as an entrepreneur than practicing magic for my peers and their parents. Every prospective entrepreneur should have to learn to perform and "sell" a dozen tricks to an unruly crowd. The lessons learned are good for a lifetime.

Frankly, the kids in the birthday party audience were always easy to control and to fool…the parents (especially those paying me to perform) not so much. They always insisted on seeing how the tricks were done and, as everyone knows, a good magician never tells. Managing the adults and telling them "No" was a learning experience that was at least as valuable as learning how to deal from the bottom of the deck or to pull a sickly little rabbit from a hat.

And the truth is that - as much as people ask you for the explanation or to "tell them the truth" - they actually all prefer the magic of the illusion to knowing how the effect was accomplished. They just don't realize it until it's too late. Because once we know how the trick was done, it loses all its power to amaze, inspire and confound us. No one really wants to see how the sausage was made.

If this is starting to sound a little like an entrepreneur's daily journey; it's not a coincidence. Selling yourself and your team and your investors on your dream every day is itself a magical act. Starting a new business is a triumph of imagination over intelligence and passion over experience. Because – as I always say – if any of us knew how long and hard the actual process was going to be, we probably would never have started down the path in the first place.

Startups have a great deal in common with magic.

First, they involve masterful storytelling. When you look closely at a magician's performance, you realize that the power and the passion is in the dramatic way that the trick is explained and the story is told. The effect (the action) is just a technical process which is more about engineering than emotion. Capturing and conveying that excitement and enthusiasm is what the best entrepreneurs do every day.

Second, they involve the willful suspension of disbelief – at least for a while. We don't believe for a minute that the woman is going to be chopped in half, but we go along with the gag and the guillotine and our hearts race all the same as the blade descends. Setting off to change an industry, invent a new way of doing things, save thousands of lives, etc. isn't something that happens every day, but these things will never happen if we don't believe that they can and try to turn those dreams into realities. Feasibility will compromise us all in the end, but we have to believe in our dreams – however impossible they may seem – and never let the turkeys get us down.

And finally, we are blessed to be living in an age of amazing new technologies available to millions of people across the world. The truth is that any sufficiently advanced technology is basically indistinguishable from magic anyway. If we continue to create and capture the multitude of opportunities out there today to combine our vibrant imaginations with our powerful new technologies, we can all be magicians in our own right. If you can dream it, you can do it. Because, as they say at Disney, the magic's the magic within you.

TULLMAN'S TRUISMS

NOT KNOWING THE RULES OF THE GAME CAN BE AN ADVANTAGE

I wrote a few months ago about the importance of keeping your eyes open for opportunities to grow and expand your business outside of your core markets and expertise by looking into "adjacent" areas which would afford you the chance to extend your product and service offerings into new geographies and across other dimensions and vectors without substantial new investments or even significant changes in the basic elements of your programs. See http://www.inc.com/howard-tullman/five-reasons-your-market-is-bigger-than-you-think.html.

I called this basic concept "sliding to the side" which meant attacking readily-accessible and proximate markets along new lines which might include identifying and targeting who the new customers were, what the required and desired offerings might be, and/or where, when and how your products and services were going to be delivered in order to meet the needs of the customers and clients in these new markets. This was an idea based on looking outside of your traditional market and sector definitions and then moving in directions that might well be outside of your comfort zone, but which offered rich rewards if you were successful and only modest financial penalties (and probably some wasted time) if things didn't ultimately work out. That was an *inside/out* approach to growing your business.

Equally valuable and again - something that's right before your eyes (if you're looking) – is the idea of lateral learning which is an *outside/in* approach to improving how you are doing things. Basically, instead of working to extend your areas of impact and influence beyond the virtual four walls of your business, here the new idea is that you explore, examine, evaluate and incorporate the best approaches and ideas you can find outside of your own shop and you pull them all into your operations as quickly and seamlessly as possible. You're never going to have all the great ideas yourself or develop all the best solutions internally, so feel free to copy or steal the best of breed answers from anyone and any place you can. Just don't copy their mistakes. Keep in mind that while education is something that is allegedly done to you; learning is something you're responsible for doing for yourself.

I call this concept "lateral learning" and here's the secret: you will absolutely learn as much or more from the people working around you (both in your company and outside) about how to step up your game and improve your prospects as you will from any mentor, teacher, class, book or lecture. When it works well, you discover that you're looking at things you've always thought you've known and understood, but in new and exciting ways. Think of this process as stepped-up and hyper-intelligent osmosis – where you consciously increase the focus and the energy devoted to checking out what and how others are doing things – some even better in the moment than you are – so that you can ultimately get to the point where you look around and no one's kicking your butt or doing your business better than you. Get started today and see what happens. There's no limit to what you can learn if you're not afraid to ask or too embarrassed or shy to inquire. But learning doesn't happen by itself – it's got to be part of an ongoing program and commitment to continually iterating and raising the bar.

And the fact is that you can try this strategy any place and in a variety of ways. But there is no better place to take advantage of learning laterally (from your peers, neighbors, role models and even competitors) than installing yourself in an active and constantly growing startup incubator (like our best-of-breed 1871 facility in Chicago) where there are literally hundreds of businesses in a single massive space and thousands of people working every day to create, develop and grow them every day. When most people talk about why young entrepreneurs should try to get into an incubator (or accelerator), they often focus on some of the obvious emotional components ("it's lonely trying to do this stuff on your own"; "there's a lot of energy and encouragement available in these places; etc.), but it's the serendipitous learning and the amazing synergies and happy accidents that happen every day in these environments that are the things that will really make a difference for you and your company.

And, equally important, the very best incubators aren't glorified coffee shops and co-working real estate plays; they are exceptional places that are purpose-built and run and managed every day to create a constant flood of educational opportunities, critical thoughts, game-changing ideas, new approaches and technologies which change and expand every day because new people are constantly moving in, moving up and/or moving out of the place. They may be growing or about to be going, but the one thing that's for sure is that they are spending every day just like you facing the same kinds of challenges, coming up with new and novel solutions, and suffering all the ups and downs of the startup process that we know and love so well. And you can learn more from them – their bumps and bruises – triumphs, trials and terrors - than from just about any other source.

You might argue that colleges and universities are equally fertile environments for this kind of energy and excitement, information exchanges and aggressive testing of new ideas, and rapid change, but you'd be dead wrong. Sadly, our bulk of our higher education system is about the repeated regurgitation of conventional wisdom and the creation of self-congratulatory dissertations which purport to validate "new" versions of old and tired news. While validation is really important in parking lots, it has very little to do with change, exploration or discovery. And concepts like commercialization, monetization and moving concepts from the labs (and sterile papers and articles) out into the real and very messy world where they can make a difference in people's lives are equally foreign ideas.

In addition, our universities lack just about everything that really matters to the process of disruptive business innovation and new company creation: (a) there's no existential requirement to get some customers and sell something because the professors will always have their jobs and their tenure; (b) there's no sense of urgency to make payroll because they always get a paycheck and there's always another quarter or semester around the corner with a fresh crop of anxious students; and frankly, and most unfortunately, (c) there's absolutely no reward structure in place at any of these places for the slightest risk-taking or for even thinking about making real changes in the way things have always been done. And if the sad combination of those things didn't suck all the juice, mojo and enthusiasm out of these places, it's also downright uncool at college for the "adults" to be passionate and excited about anything outside their academic ivory towers or to be seen as promoting or marketing just about anything. So it's just not happening at So What U.

On the other hand, in an incubator, if you're open to it, you learn by looking, listening and doing every day. This is because you get to free ride on three important trends that are driving rapid and radical change at light speed throughout the tech economy and even in more basic industries as well. Keep an eye out for these 3 drivers:

(1) Solution Migration

What's good for the goose is often just as good and helpful for the gander (except, I suppose, right around Thanksgiving time) and so we are seeing more and more instances where a quick and effective technology solution (or even one that took years and millions to develop and perfect) in one industry (like precision drug dosing cartridges) is ported and rapidly migrates to other industries (like self-service food and beverage providers) overnight and with just as much success and impact. Smart players in almost every major industry (except the U.S. government) have figured this out and are aggressively pursuing these kinds of parallel research and investigation programs. And they're also stepping up to invest in and buy more and more startups as M & A is rapidly becoming the new R & D.

(2) Cross-Industry Pollination

An entirely separate, but equally extensive area for lateral learning is more about behavioral benchmarks and expectations rather than technologies. Seeing what works socially in adjacent businesses; seeing what it's reasonable to ask of and expect from consumers these days and what the *quid pro quo* needs to be; understanding the new dimensions of self-service and constant connectivity; etc. are all inquiries and directions of investigation that are crucial components of how you bring your business to the new digital marketplaces. Just because we haven't previously expected customers to be responsive to certain changes in the way we do business or we have never before asked people to behave in certain new ways doesn't mean that these aren't very significant directions (and potentially opportunities for enormous savings) for your company. The trick here is to let someone else do the first round of experimenting and seeing what and whether anything blows up in their faces before you make your moves. Clearly, as a recent example, the Netflix debacle with Qwikster where they tried for two weeks to split their business into two distinct pieces and almost immediately lost hundreds of thousands of customers and millions of dollars kept a whole lot of other companies from jumping off a similar cliff with their pricing plans. It's always better to let the other guys make the first mover mistakes and then to be a smarter fast follower.

(3) Inexpensive Adaptation

It's not critical or essential that your version of a copied or borrowed solution be gold-plated or crazy expensive at the outset. Try it first with duct tape and chewing gum and see what happens before you bet the farm. You'll learn a lot, maybe you'll lose a little, but you'll never know what can work for you if you don't try. Just don't put both feet into the pond until you know how deep the water is.

Each of these approaches offers value and opportunities for your company as long as you spend the time to think about what they can bring to your business. Keep in mind that the power and value of a change isn't necessarily related to its size. Sometimes the most valuable and important aspect of these things isn't about how much you have to change to make a difference, but exactly how little a change needs to be to make a big impact.

Recently, I've been involved in a series of negotiations and discussions with a number of young entrepreneurs in and around 1871 (and elsewhere throughout the country) about a variety of topics regarding their businesses. Some of these conversations have been about the nature, usage and pricing of their products, services and content; some have related to the strength of their existing and emerging competition and the need for additional strategic partnerships; and many have been discussions about cash (or the impending lack thereof) and the pressing need for new rounds of financing.

On the last topic - new money - it seems clear to me that way too many of these guys (and girls) are getting miles ahead of themselves (and the actual results and progress of their businesses) and feverishly talking about raising big chunks of venture capital at very healthy and stepped-up valuations when they should be thinking about grabbing more angel money, generating some real revenue from actual customers, and figuring out how to get their businesses to break-even before their bankroll disappears. They're just in too much of a hurry to get everything done; they're losing sight of the need to make real connections with investors before you try to hit them over the head with your proposals; and they're trying to have it all in a heartbeat which almost never happens. Part of this is just that even the best fundraising process still inevitably takes some time - just like pregnancy. Sadly, nine women still can't have a baby in one month and you can't push a rope or an investor beyond reason and expect any real results.

To make things worse, I keep hearing about more and more expensive and time-wasting pilgrimages to the West Coast where these same people are meeting and pitching a dozen or more different VC firms and basically getting their heads and their porkpie hipster hats handed to them at every meeting because they're wasting everyone's time and - even in the Valley - they expect a little more than just pipe dreams and wild ass projections that grow to the sky. As they used to say about the Internet, and now they say about investment dollars, "the money's there all right; it's just not evenly distributed."

The fact is that there is plenty of capital everywhere these days (no need to drag yourself across the country in either direction), but there's no more money available for half-cooked concepts or half-baked businesses than there ever was. Your story and your numbers (and your valuation which is presumably based on them) still all need to make sense or you're just kidding yourself. Passion and extreme self-confidence can fill in some of the more glaring gaps, but there aren't too many smart investors around who've suddenly been hit with the stupid stick. I understand as well as anyone the pressure to make payroll, but you've got to be a little prudent about the process.

So, as you might imagine, these aren't easy chats to have with fired-up (and also very nervous) entrepreneurs and a bunch of these conversations have gotten pretty heated and intense. All of that's fine with me and pretty much business as usual and, frankly, it's even to be expected. I'm all for pushing the envelope, aggressive selling and persistence, but it helps some time to leaven the lectures and the "lessons" with at least a little patience and some perspective. In addition, a little listening to what people are consistently telling you doesn't hurt either. And just because someone else you heard about pulled a miracle off in record time with even less results than you have and found some whale of an investor almost overnight doesn't mean jack for your prospects.

But what I am really concerned about is that I'm seeing rampant examples of another epidemic of "egola" where the entrepreneurs are just so far out there with their demands and their expectations that they're becoming their own worst enemies. They're as bad as the Tea Party bozos and just as tone deaf and incapable of compromise or thinking about alternative paths, taking less money for the moment, cutting their burn rate so their runway extends, etc. And, not surprisingly, when your "asks" are off the charts and astronomical compared to other folk's (especially prospective investors') views of the real picture, it makes it ultra easy to say a quick "no" and send you on your way. And this is exactly what is happening right now to companies which are full of good ideas and good people, but too full of themselves to understand and keep in mind the three most basic rules of negotiating good deals.

The first is the ancient business prophecy and truism that: what comes around goes around. Hopefully, if you're good and smart; this won't be your last rodeo or the last time you'll be in front of these very same investors (all of whom talk to each other regularly about the deals they're seeing) and it's really important for you to play the long game - pushing too hard and burning your bridges when you get turned down or over-reacting in any way is simply stupid. And coming to see these guys too early with too little is also a reflection on your judgment and your credibility that it will be hard to walk back and rebuild if you take your shot too soon and you're not prepared for the hard questions with concrete facts and good answers.

The second hoary axiom is that the best deals are those where everyone leaves a little bit on the table. I call this a "nibble for next time" and it lets everyone feel like a winner who got some of the things (but not everything) that were important to them. Everyone also feels a little pain, but they can go back to their boss or their team with a few scalps on their belts to show how well they did. And, most importantly, they feel that the other players were reasonable and that there are opportunities down the line to talk and deal again. That little nibble you left is a modest investment in the deal next time.

The third rule is that - at the end of the day - in every business people care much more about how their deal was negotiated and completed than they do about every little detail or talking point or even the final outcome. If your attitude going in is mature and healthy, you've got a good shot at getting a solid deal that makes sense for all concerned. But if it's all about winning and "your way or the highway" and it's not even enough that you get your way unless the other guys give in or give up; your deal's in trouble from the get-go.

This is because not only is implementing any deal at least as challenging and tough as getting the deal done and documented in the first place; successful implementation and integration will be a hundred times harder if the guys sitting across the table from you can't stand the sight of your face because you were a pig or an asshole during the negotiations. You can't burn down the village and then expect to be welcome at the native's weekly pig roast unless you're the pig on the spit. No one needs that kind of welcome - it's a lot like inviting a turkey to be your guest at Thanksgiving dinner.

So the lesson is that sticking to your guns and asking for all that you're entitled to is fine, but there's always a hard-to-read line past which you'll have gone too far. The only thing likely to bring you back is the good will (and a little slack and forgiveness) that you've accumulated throughout the process and the fact that you acted like a mensch from the beginning.

TULLMAN'S TRUISMS

IN THE END, PEOPLE CARE MORE ABOUT THE DEAL PROCESS THAN THE DEAL POINTS

Self-service business solutions are all the rage these days and that's good news in many cases. These kinds of programs can save us all a great deal of time if they're implemented properly and, frankly, in some cases – like ATMs – there's little question left today that we actually prefer the machine solutions to dealing with bored and indifferent tellers. But when self-service is poorly done, in big box stores for example, it can feel like you're wandering in the desert for days without ever seeing a helpful human being. And, as often as not, when you finally do come across a living, breathing person, it's generally not their department or they have no clue as to how to help you.

It's always struck me as very sad that so many of these large organizations with hundreds or thousands of front-line, customer-facing employees don't seem to understand that it's not simply about the rote training of their people; it's about building and reinforcing their team's self-esteem. If you can make their jobs "important" (whatever they are) and make them feel good about what they are doing every day (however seemingly mundane it may be), the people will get their jobs done and done well regardless of how many hours of lectures and useless training they have had to endure. Pride is just as contagious as Ebola and it shows.

And when big companies push the acceptance envelope too quickly or too aggressively, even in apparently modest ways where they are basically trying to save a few bucks, they can end up shooting themselves in both feet. A recent example from one of the nation's biggest banks is very instructive. To save money, they stopped sending deposit envelopes which had previously been printed with the return postage pre-paid. I guess they figured that, if their customers were mailing in a deposit, they could afford a stamp. Not the worst thing in the world, but chintzy nonetheless.

But I stopped by one of the bank's many branches a few weeks ago when I had used up my last envelope and asked for a few of those new "pay your own postage" mail deposit envelopes for future deposits. Amazingly, they told me that the branches aren't being given any envelopes to give out to customers for mail deposits. And, if you can believe this, when I asked them what the current address was for the mail deposits, they had to spend 5 minutes looking it up and they wrote it on a piece of scratch paper for me. I guess now you need to provide your own envelopes and your own postage. Seems like the beginning of the end of mail deposits or maybe they just don't care about the customers' needs any more. In any case, I'm not banking there anymore. Would you?

But I'm not really that concerned about crappy traditional self-service which I would call abuses and poor uses of the "Help Yourself" model. I'm more interested in where we're heading with the new technology-based approaches that shift a lot of the burden of interaction, authentication and other effort to the consumer. These programs might better be described as the new "Help Me Help You" model. And here too, as with most of these things, success or sucking is in the details and in the execution because - when it comes to service, everything matters.

It's also critical to understand the ever-changing boundaries of the typical consumer's acceptance of these increasingly intelligent (and somewhat invasive) automated interactions which are being driven by the adoption of new in-store technologies. These solutions are predicated on our increased mobility and connectivity and also depend and incorporate the staggering amounts of real-time data which our devices can now provide to interested and activated merchants.

Here are just five examples of what you can expect to see in the retail area alone:

(1) In-store displays that send texts and/or talk to you as you pass by them;
(2) Systems that track what you've purchased and suggest what you may have forgotten;
(3) Dressing rooms that read RFID tags on your selections and suggest alternative choices;
(4) Phone apps that make cosmetic recommendations based on analyzing your selfie; and
(5) Systems that project digitized versions of clothing or other products onto your body

Ask yourself just how creeped out you would be as each of these systems becomes more and more personal and personalized. And yet, realistically, as long as these exchanges are designed to provide real value on both sides of the deal – saving us time or money or helping us make better and smarter choices, I think that we've just seen the beginning of this trend and we will see expanding variations of it in every business very soon – including yours.

I wrote recently that it was important in trying to keep your own business on the leading edge of what was happening with emerging new technologies and other potentially disruptive changes for you to invest the time and make the effort to keep an eye on both the players and leaders in your own industry and also the smart and aggressive companies in adjacent spaces and market sectors where innovations that are transferable and readily-applicable to your own company's offerings and ways of doing business may be taking place. I called this process "lateral learning". (See:http://www.inc.com/howard-tullman/when-to-steal-from-other-founders.html)

I noted there that - as often as not - the observations that really paid off were those about companies which were testing for and continuing to politely push the acceptable limits of consumer behaviors and which were basically asking exactly what it was fair or reasonable these days to expect consumers (and especially your regular customers) to do as their part in the day-to-day transactions that make up our businesses. These companies are doing all of us a great service because, frankly, if these questions were not being asked and the responses acted upon; we'd still be doing a whole bunch of things in the old-fashioned and inefficient ways that worked for us in the past. Change doesn't happen on its own and someone needs to keep raising the bar and asking "why not" a lot.

But, if you want your own business to succeed, you really can't leave all the heavy lifting to the other guys and keep riding on their coat tails. The problem with the "After You Alphonse" strategy (playing it slow and safe and letting the other guys go first) is that, by the time you finally wake up and smell the coffee, they're over the next hill and miles ahead of you. And, the fact is that you're the ones who are supposed to know your markets, your customers and even your competition the best and so you're really the most likely candidates to figure out where things are headed in your industry, how to apply these new tools to your business, and just how far to go before you've gone too far.

TULLMAN'S TRUISMS

IF CHANGE WERE EASY, IT WOULD HAPPEN BY ITSELF

111 – IF WE ONLY SEE WHAT WE'RE LOOKING FOR, WE NEED TO LOOK A LOT FURTHER AND WIDER

The Internet has transformed our lives in so many ways that it's almost impossible to keep track of all of the momentous changes. Things that we tend (unfortunately in some cases) to take for granted today would have been thought of as works of magic or astonishing miracles just a decade ago. And no one expects the rate or volume of these changes to slow down any time soon. If anything, the rate of change will continue to accelerate because the growth of our technological capabilities and of our knowledge base is now increasing exponentially in almost every area. It took 13 years to sequence just one percent of the human genome and then just one year thereafter to complete the remaining 99% of the entire DNA process.

So part of our jobs – in addition to adopting, exploiting and incorporating these massive changes into our businesses – is to try to make sense of their broader implications and the impact that they will continue to have on our society as a whole. If everything wants to be free, we still have to figure out what that really means for you and me. And even more importantly what it means for the world we're building and leaving behind for those who will follow us. If you can't develop systems that spread and share the amazing benefits and bounties of these technologies to much broader portions of the total population, then the digital revolution will have failed to realize the greatest part of its potential and our own enterprises and adventures will fall far short of the heights that they could have achieved if we had successfully captured the benefits of including all of the human resources which are now efficiently and economically accessible to us in the overall equation. And so it's incumbent upon all of us to make the extra effort and to reach beyond the easy and the obvious solutions if we're really going to differentiate our businesses and set ourselves apart from the pack.

If I had to choose the most important difference today in the way that we go about our lives and our businesses, it would be the way that technology (and the mobility and connectivity that it has enabled for all of us) has so radically changed the concept of "place" and the old-fashioned idea that any human endeavor today is location-bound or limited to a single geography or place. We can live virtually anywhere these days and we can work productively from just about everywhere. And we can attract, recruit and employ people with remarkable skills for our companies from all across the world (and also from our own backyards) and, if we don't, you can be sure that our competition will figure out how to use this abundance of talent for their own benefit.

We, as a country, are very early into this process and, frankly, way too much of the emphasis to date has been on outsourcing and cost savings instead of "insourcing" where we pull these new resources into our businesses and take advantage of their capabilities and brains instead of trying to just save a few bucks on their hourly rates. No one ever saves their way to success. Your own plan for the future needs to be wide enough to build on this world-wide opportunity and also narrow enough to understand that the answers for you could just as readily be next door as in Nairobi. Because stay-at-home Moms, college kids, and people who are smart and willing, but still physically bound to a specific area can all add enormous value to your business. It's nice to think globally, but you might find your future just as easily at the corner grocery store.

If I had to pick the second most important difference today in the ways that we could (and should) be conducting our businesses and a change, as well, that offers just as many benefits and unexploited opportunities as the newly global and expanded nature of our talent pools, it would be that we need to use the new digital tools and extended connectivity to unlock another vast resource by reaching out to capture the still-vital skills and knowledge of our older citizens – many of whom are technically "retired" or otherwise unwillingly sidelined, but quite far from desiring to be inactive or ceasing to make a continuing and productive contribution to our economy. The fact is that - in our hearts - we never really grow old. We only grow old when our dreams are replaced by regrets. My sense is that growing old is simply something that busy people don't have time for – whatever their chronological age may be.

Just as gray hair is a sign of age, but not necessarily wisdom; it's equally true that it's also in no way reflective of the ongoing value, skill sets, and capabilities (or capacity to work effectively) of millions of our "senior" citizens. And not to simply work – but to work smart. As the classic expression goes: "the young people know the rules; the older folks know the exceptions." The burden is on us to extend and expand our ideas around where critical work can take place and by whom it can be profitably performed to homes, senior living facilities, remote locations and even retirement and university communities. There's a reason we like to hire young carpenters, but old physicians. In the next few years, we can convert the old guard into the vanguard of a new push for increasing the utility and productivity of millions of our older, but not old, citizens.

The thought that simple age or a mere lack of digital facility is a disqualification for people with decades of accumulated technical and institutional knowledge, great judgment, and extensive business experience is just another foolish example of wretched excess that we could perhaps afford when we had surplus talent and resources to burn, but which today is a painful oversight that deprives our economy of important incremental sources of skill and intellectual horsepower which are essential as we continue to lose ground in the new global battlefields.

Happy days are a mixed blessing for startups. Growing rapidly is definitely energizing and exhilarating. And it can be plenty enervating as well so you need to try to pick your best shots and also to conserve some of your energy and resources for the inevitable bumps along the way. It's pretty easy these days to grow your top line in double digits every month – especially when you're starting from scratch - but that's only one metric of many that will matter if you're trying to build a real and sustainable business. Maintaining a conscious and thoughtful balance between all of the vectors of your business's growth is tough, but it's essential to your ultimate success. Overemphasizing any one of the objectives or the directions in which you're moving forward runs the serious risk of tilting the whole enterprise into an unrecoverable tailspin. Getting big quick is nowhere near as critical as getting good consistently at what you're doing and learning to do it well over and over again. And racing like crazy to be everywhere as soon as possible killed millions of startups in the dot.com era and hasn't been demonstrated to have worked that well for much of anyone this time around either.

And it's also easy in these days of quick and easy money chasing deals to get carried away doing the fundraising fandango and running around the country looking for new investors and new money instead of minding the store. That's a good way to end up going nowhere fast. There are lots of people with their own agendas happy to blow smoke up your behind and tell you that you can walk on water (and everything thing else that you want to hear) and also how they can help get you there for a piece or a fee or a few shares. And you can also kid yourself all day long and claim that all the road trips, all the pitches and all the demo days, conferences and speeches are great for brand-building and marketing, but somebody near to you who's paying attention (and whose counsel you respect) probably needs to tell you to give it a rest and get back to paying attention to the basics of the business that got you this far so far.

I understand that sometimes all the motion and all the activity is just one way to try to suppress the anxiety that's also part of the startup process and I get that sometimes, truth be told, even while everyone else is hooting and hollering; it can feel to you like you've got a tiger by the tail and that you're barely hanging on for dear life. One moment may be jubilation and the next sheer terror and very often it's only you (and a precious few others in the company) who may know just how close to the edge things are really running. That technology that looks so slick from the outside has more gaps and holes - with only duct tape and chewing gum solutions holding it together - than anything MacGyver ever dreamed of. You can find yourself moving daily between sadness and euphoria, but, at least on most days, you don't have the time to be bored although I don't think that's much consolation. And those are the good days.

Even more importantly, apart from the everyday emotional drain of the run-up roller coaster ride, and the funding frenzies and flavor-of-the-week fashion shows, the kind of radical ramping of revenues which the new digital economy enables (mainly because the barriers to inexpensive customer acquisition and product distribution are virtually non-existent) can disguise and/or conceal a host of operational, accounting and control problems which are guaranteed to come back and bite you and your business in the ass at some future (and usually worst possible) time. And the future may not turn out to be that far off because – if you take your eyes off the ball and get carried away – you may find that you don't have that much of a future to look forward to.

The truth is that far more critical mistakes are made by entrepreneurs in good times than in bad times and many more promising companies lose their way and are killed by distraction, indigestion, and the inability to focus and/or handle hyper-growth than end up starving because they ran out of cash and slammed into a wall. I'm seeing way too many young companies chasing expansion and new markets before they have a firm and consistent grasp of how to successfully and repeatedly execute and deliver their core business services in their initial marketplace. There's a reason that the smartest entrepreneurs nail it first and then scale it.

If you want to quickly determine whether your own ship is more than a little out-of-control and whether you're a bit too far out over your own skis, ask yourself these few questions and try to answer honestly. By and large, the NSA notwithstanding, no one else is generally listening when you talk to yourself. But, of course, this only helps if you're not only talking, but listening as well.

(1) You've Got No Middle Management
The business was easy when you did everything yourself and made sure it was done right. Now you find yourself looking around for someone to pick up that job and do it with the same passion and attention to detail as you did, but there's no such animal in the place. No one's as careful or as crazy as you and it shows because balls start getting dropped all over the place. It's not necessarily that they don't care; it's just that they don't know any better and they certainly don't care as much.

(2) You've Got No Idea of the Money in the Bank
If you had to guess how much cash was in the bank or whether the important bills were getting reviewed promptly and paid on time – especially those submitted by the folks who were there for you when you needed a break – and you were honest, you'd admit that you just don't know and – worse yet – you just hope that someone else does. But guess what? The guy in accounting just wants to process the weekly checks – he's not checking half the things that fly over his desk – and the people in purchasing don't have the time or the inclination to look for the best deal or the smartest deal – they've got a budget and they're gonna spend it – one way or the other. It's not "their" money anyway.

(3) You Forgot What a Customer Looks Like

When's the last time you were meeting with some of your oldest and best customers instead of bankers, brokers, journalists and other entrepreneurs? Not only don't you see many of these important customers; you never take the time to stroke them any more either. And they do notice the difference – they just might not mention it to you, but they do. Not to worry, however, because this is a self-liquidating problem. Customers' expectations are progressive and, if you're not improving and building a better connection and relationship with them on an ongoing basis, you won't have to worry about them for too much longer. They'll be gone.

TULLMAN'S TRUISMS

YOU CAN HAVE IT ALL, BUT YOU CAN'T HAVE IT ALL AT THE SAME TIME

113 – DON'T HIRE THE WRONG PERSON EVEN FOR A GOOD REASON

It's the holiday season and everyone wants to lend someone else a helping hand. But let me just say, without seeming too Grinch-like, that, while I heartily agree with the idea and the sentiment, it's important to remember that – even in the working world – charity begins at home. It's sweet to be Santa, but not if your business suffers as a result.

There's an old (and somewhat naïve) adage about friends and finance. When you're considering making a loan to a friend, you should give a lot of thought to which you'd <u>most</u> prefer not to lose: the money or the friend. The reason that the adage is naïve is that, in the vast majority of cases, you can almost certainly count on damaging the friendship and/or losing the friend entirely – <u>even</u> if you get the money paid back.

There's something about being in debt to a friend that's awkward and humbling and just never bodes well for the long-term life of the relationship. So it's much smarter (albeit not often easy) to be a good enough friend to give your buddy a straight and simple "no" rather than starting down the slippery slope of becoming a lender. Better a friendly refusal than an unwilling promise.

I got to thinking about this when one of our startup CEOs asked me an interesting question recently about hiring. He had heard me talking about the "*Hotel California*" syndrome here at 1871 – that's the idea that no one ever really leaves our place even if their particular business idea doesn't work out. As *The Eagles'* song says: "you can check out any time you like, but you can never leave". Instead, at 1871, the smartest of the guys whose businesses have gone sideways or who've run out of cash before they found their footing or their market niche have an interesting reaction.

They don't sulk. They don't make excuses. They don't expect the world to owe them a living. Instead, they get busy. They start looking around; they do their research and homework, and then they try to attach themselves to a better and hopefully more viable idea at another member company with more traction and momentum. It's very Darwinian, it's productive, and it works all day long.

I think that this is one of 1871's greatest accomplishments – to have built an organic community that's so additive and supportive of everyone here that it's almost as if there's a safety net that assures a soft landing and a new start for the serious and committed folks who want to stay in the game, get right back up in the saddle, and get rolling again.

Now, of course, there are two sides to this process and honestly the job's a lot harder for those on the helping and hiring side than it is for the guys (and girls) looking for their next gig. And that difficulty, in fact, was exactly the subject matter of the question which I was asked.

It went something like this: How do I figure out if it makes sense for me (and for my company) to hire someone whose business just blew up? Especially if it's someone I feel like I know pretty well; who I think is smart and committed; and someone who's been working 3 desks away from me for the last year – head down – 24/7 – balls to the wall? In fact, I have to admit, that there were plenty of weeks when – just watching from the sidelines - I felt like a slacker compared to this guy. So really, what more about him (or her) do I need to know and what are the right questions that I need to ask in order to find out whether this is a smart hire?

I'd say that there are five basic questions that you need to ask the person and to get clear and convincing answers to before you move forward. And, by the way, don't expect this to be an easy or comfortable conversation. It should be hard and it should be honest because it's important to get this right at the outset or you'll regret it for a long time later.

So here are my five questions:

(1) Are You Done with Your Dream?

It's not ever easy for an entrepreneur to give up on his dream, but it's essential for you to make sure that you're not paying someone to work for you whose head really isn't into the game and who's spending the bulk of his time and emotion trying to figure out how to resuscitate his old business and get the show back on the road. There's no lie detector test for this kind of thing – you've just got to look each other in the eye and decide whether there's a real commitment to leave the past behind so that you can count on getting the full attention and energy that are required directed toward the success of <u>your</u> business

(2) Are You Down with My Dream?

It's easy to fall in love when you need a job. That's not enough of a commitment to make things work in the start-up world because it's never just a job. It's signing up to give the dream everything you've got and you really have to care about the vision, about making a difference (not just a paycheck), and your heart needs to be in the game just as fully as your head. This is an essential part of the down-and-dirty conversation that needs to take place and the best candidates will tell you upfront what they like about your idea and your program and what they think could be changed or could be better. But they can't be signing on with the idea that - once they're in the clubhouse - they'll have a chance to start rearranging the furniture and changing things. They need to buy into your dream and then help make it better – not try to turn it into their dream. And they need to sign on 100% on Day One. If they have serious reservations, they need to work someplace else.

(3) Are You Already Ready to Re-Up?

A dying dream is a debilitating thing and sometimes we don't even realize at the outset just how hard a hit we took or the extent of the damage done. It takes a while for the reality to sink in and for all the conversations to take place where a hundred random people ask you how your business is doing and you have to break the news to them. Every one of those "chats" is just more salt in the wound that you were hoping was getting better every day. I get that it's great to get over the past and pick yourself up off the floor and move forward, but you also need to catch your breath and make sure you're settled before you start off on the next adventure. Catching someone too soon on the rebound isn't any better an idea in your business affairs than it is in your love life. Make sure the new guy is really ready to start and knows what he's signing up for.

(4) Are You Sure You Can Be Second Chair?

There's only one seat at the top and one captain of the ship and you need to make sure that everyone understands the pecking order from the get-go. And, just to be clear, this isn't just something to get straight between you and the new hire – it's important that it's clear to the whole team so that everyone knows what to expect and how to proceed. It's easy to fall into a trap here and start talking (while you're still in the "selling" mode of convincing the guy to come on board) about being "partners" in the journey and working closely together. And, while that's a good ultimate goal, it's a bad way to start the new relationship off. You're the boss in your business. He or she <u>used to be</u> the boss in their prior businesses. The new relationship needs to be clearly understood from Day One.

(5) Are You in It for the Long Run?

You don't want to waste your time and money training and integrating the new guy into your business if he simply regards it as a stop-over on his way to his next start-up. You're not a way station to anywhere and – while there are no guarantees that anything will last forever or that everyone will ever work out perfectly, you can't afford to have someone coming into the business who already has one foot out the door. Make sure they're there for the duration or don't do the deal.

I feel a little like Smokey the Bear talking about an ounce of prevention and going through these things which should be fairly obvious to all of us, but which, in fact, too often get lost or overlooked when we're in a hurry to get a good new guy on the team. All I can say is that it's a lot better to avoid the potholes entirely than it is to get a great deal on the towing service that comes to bail you out of the hole.

TULLMAN'S TRUISMS

DON'T EXPECT PEOPLE TO LISTEN TO YOUR ADVICE AND IGNORE YOUR EXAMPLE

As the year draws to a close, and we all get a little break from our day-to-day activities (and from the regular crises and fire drills that accompany them), it's a good chance to find some time to catch your breath and spend a few hours just thinking – and not doing anything else, but thinking – about the year ahead and where you want to take your business. I'm not talking about some foolish New Year's resolutions (like Zuck's optimistic, but stillborn, daily "thank you" plan) or your desire to definitely get in great shape this coming year or to be a much better person in 2015. I'm talking about thinking strategically about how you can make the next 12 months a lot more valuable and productive for your company.

This isn't about some make-work exercise, crystal ball predictions, or chart drawing contests – it's much more basic than that. It's not about making roadmaps – it's about your mindset. It's about you and you alone taking a moment to take stock of things and to ask yourself some very basic questions. There's plenty of time for group activities and facilitated/moderated conversations (whatever you might think those are worth) and/or sharing your wisdom with the team. But, first and foremost, you've got to make sure that you've got your own head on straight and fully back in the game.

None of us does enough of this simple exercise these days (we've all got plenty of explanations and excuses for why this is) and, as a result, too many businesses lose sight of the main chance, the critical things they need to be doing, and the most important questions they should be asking. Questions like: why did I get into this business in the first place? Am I doing any good and/or making any difference that matters? Does anyone outside of my friends, family, investors and employees care about what we're trying doing?

And while you're at it, I wouldn't waste much time reflecting on the past 12 months since:

(a) there's nothing left that you can practically do about them;

(b) you oughta already know what you did right and wrong since you lived through it and hopefully learned a lot from the experience; and

(c) fretting over mistakes and missed opportunities doesn't really move anything forward. You want to build your future on strength and resolve and not on regrets and "shoulda, woulda, couldas".

But those are not even the main reasons why it's not effective to spend a lot of time looking backwards. Looking in the rear mirror is distracting and a great way to run off the road if you're not careful or to smack into something big and ugly that would have been a piece of cake to easily avoid if you had been paying a little attention to the outside world and, even more importantly, to what your customers are doing and saying about their own pressing needs and their current desires. Customer expectations are progressive. If you're not on top of them, you'll be at the bottom of their list of choices soon enough.

And the most important reason that you don't want to get all wrapped up in reliving and analyzing the past is that it's almost always an invitation to largely look inward. To spend your time navel gazing, making excuses, and bemoaning the bad breaks. It's mainly about you and your issues. And that's not where you need to be focusing your energy, your research, or your efforts as you try to get the business set for the New Year.

You need to get out and find out what's going on now outside the four walls of your business because that's where your future will be found and fixed or frittered away. We can surely learn from the past and we react every day to the present, but we can leverage and change the future. But that kind of change won't happen by itself. You've got to be asking the right people the right questions. And, right now, that's your most pressing job as a leader.

And here's a flash: you will never get straighter or more useful answers to your questions than the ones you get directly from your customers. The truth – with all its wonders and warts – comes from the consumers and the users of your products and services. They don't have any other agendas (apart from always wanting a lot more for a lot less) and they're the real reason you got into this startup mess in the first place so pleasing them and addressing their notions, ideas, and needs seems like the obvious thing to do. But it doesn't happen if you don't do it.

And here's some more breaking news: you might just discover (when you take the time to think, to look, and to ask) that there's a bigger and better opportunity right under your nose which you've been practically tripping over for months or years without ever noticing. One of our 1871 startups (We Deliver) thought they were in the delivery business for small merchants until they discovered that what those many businesses really needed was a mobile ordering app for their products and services which they couldn't afford to build for themselves. Even more importantly, when you roll up hundreds of those businesses into a one-stop, mobile ordering app that consumers quickly learn about from all the individual merchants – you basically create a destination platform (with critical mass) that also makes life a lot easier and more efficient for thousands of shoppers who can now aggregate and bundle their purchases from multiple sellers into a single transaction. And, by the way, all those additional products don't end up delivering themselves so the new platform approach also drove the basic business to new heights as well.

If you want to take the plunge, here are a few of the main questions to ask yourself. It's a pretty simple process, but, as you'll see, the results can be game-changing.

(1) What's the problem you initially set out to solve?

(2) Are you trying to solve the same problem today or doing something different?

(3) Is the problem still important to your customers and worth paying you to solve?

(4) Are there cheaper, quicker or easier solutions to the problems offered by others?

(5) Are there new, more important or different problems to be solved?

You'll notice that all these questions – in the first instance - address the customers' problem(s) and not your products or solutions. This isn't just a question of semantics. If you don't understand the pressing problems of your customers, you have no chance at all of building a successful product or service to solve them. You can keep building the greatest software never sold or the cure for no known disease, but you won't be building a business that will be here at the end of next year.

TULLMAN'S TRUISMS

WE'RE USING A LENS SHAPED BY THE PAST TO VIEW THE FUTURE

These days, for better or worse, professed experts in every conceivable area of business are a dime a dozen and, in most cases, I'd say that they (and their alleged expertise and invaluable advice) are worth just about that much. And, in all events, they are clearly worth considerably less than you'd spend on a good cup of coffee. And just like spoiled cream can kill a great cup of java; out-of-date ideas from people who the developments in new technologies have clearly passed by should be date-stamped with the understanding that their time has come and gone and that they're no longer worth listening to – politely or otherwise.

It seems that everyone claims to be an expert on something today and they're shameless and more than happy to sell you (and everyone you know) their various services for a tidy sum. Some of these people are one-hit wonders trying to re-invent themselves and it's not clear whether their prior "success" was mainly due to a good idea, good partners, good timing or simple good luck. So you have to wonder – as you're listening to their war stories – exactly how much transferable wisdom they've gained from their own experiences and how much of that knowledge will be of use and value to your own business.

And, just like cigarettes, I think a lot of these characters ought to come with a large warning label (maybe something like "take this advice with as many large grains of salt as possible") because – in addition to wasting your time and money – these people can be clearly be harmful to your business. And their misdirected guidance can take years off your life - just like a pack-a-day smoking habit. In today's high-velocity and hyper-competitive markets; speed kills (in a good way) if it's you that's moving down the road. But if you're heading in the wrong direction because you listened to the wrong advice; you could find yourself way behind the curve and trying to play catch-up with your competition.

Now, I'm sure there are always valuable things to be learned from others and that - within their own experience base and their given areas of expertise – there really are experts who can add value to your strategy and your business if their input is timely and current. But it's not easy to separate the wheat from the chaff or to figure out who can really give you a helping hand and your money's worth. Your time is a scarce and precious resource and it's always constrained. If you're going to spend it listening to anyone for any substantial amount of time, make sure (as best you can) that they know what they're talking about and that the conversations are worth it.

I think that there are a few guidelines and ideas to keep in mind when you find yourself having to evaluate situations like this.

(1) Process Experts Have a Longer Shelf Life than Domain Experts

A domain expert knows a lot about what to do in a specific area or situation and in a defined space or industry. That knowledge is the stuff that spoils quickly over time if it's not refreshed and renewed – especially with regard to new technologies. It's critical to be a life-long and continual learner. A process expert knows how to repeatedly do things effectively in whatever situation or industry you happen to be in. Successful serial entrepreneurs call this skill "pattern recognition" and it means simply that many situations present problems that aren't materially different (regardless of the specifics) from those that seasoned operators have seen and solved hundreds of times before. Guys who know the proper approaches and have mastered the change management process never go out of date.

(2) An Expert's Knowledge Can Exceed His Experience But Only Rarely

There's a lot of delusional mythology around the extensibility of skills and expertise. Much of this BS is promulgated by the people trying to sell you their services even when it's an obvious stretch and a complete leap of faith to believe that they can really add value based on their actual backgrounds and experience. Even the most successful players need to know and – more importantly – admit the limits of their skill sets. You only need to recall Michael Jordan's abortive career as a professional baseball player to see what I'm sayin'. Lawyers (as a race) are also great at never saying "No" to doing anything regardless of their actual qualifications. They're always ready to take the fee and the assignment and then you have the privilege (and the risks) of paying for their OTJ learning curve and education. Not a smart choice – ever. You need to find the right person with the right experience and tools in the right industry (your industry) and not try to make do or accept someone saying that what they did elsewhere is easy to apply to your situation.

(3) Knowledge is Subject to the Law of Diminishing Returns in Most Cases

In addition to simply going stale or out of date, whatever accumulation of knowledge and expertise you may have and apply to your situation, you should understand that it can only take you so far. It's true that we are always learning, but that doesn't mean that we are necessarily getting smarter in the process. After a certain point, the facts and figures and past wisdom run out of steam and this is when the best entrepreneurs really earn their stripes and their keep. It's at the point when you need to use your best judgment; your intuition; and a little prayer (which never hurts) to get you over the last hurdle and through the woods to the finish line that you learn whether you've got what it takes to succeed. No one else can do it for you. No one else can make those last calls and choices. It's all up to you because – in the final analysis – and in the critical moments of decision – no one knows your business better than you.

(4) Hire the Expert Who Can Get You There, not the One Who Says He's Been There Before

In business, just as in your sex life, especially as you get older, it's important to remember that past results are no guarantee of future performance. A track record is an important and very valuable part of the evaluation process for any expert, but you're not headed backwards and your job is to make sure that the people you are planning to work with have the desire, the energy and the skills to help you move your business forward.

TULLMAN'S TRUISMS

DON'T ASK DIRECTIONS FROM SOMEONE WHO HASN'T BEEN THERE

The New York Times recently ran a piece on how the traditional and lengthy MBA programs were under growing pressure because – in addition to questions about the actual economic value of such costly offerings - their emphasis on corporate finance and strategy was increasingly being seen as irrelevant to the skill sets required in today's competitive marketplace where success is largely driven by speed, constant iteration, and the rapid abandonment of bad ideas. See N.Y. Times article here: http://www.nytimes.com/2014/12/26/business/mba-programs-start-to-follow-silicon-valley-into-the-data-age.html?ref=technology&_r=0 .

As hard as it may be to believe, it's possible that, in the next few years, the stigma attached to the MBA may even increase. If that happens, I'd say it was no big deal or any great loss because it's been years in coming; it's well-deserved; and it all began when the top schools became more concerned (if not obsessed) with inflating their annual rankings in a single magazine (*U.S. News & World Report*) than with the rigor and relevance of their courses. In cultures where punctuality is more valued than productivity; where there are no rewards for risk takers; and where maintaining the peace is more important than making progress – what else would you expect?

But what really bothered me in the article was the description of the ongoing, frantic, and utterly expected and lemming-like responses of the business schools to the problem. The author said that they were going to "follow Silicon Valley into the Data Age" by adopting the best practices they saw in the outside world and adding courses in stats, data science and A/B testing. Focusing on A/B testing – as if it's the new tool in town - when the rest of the world (powered by high-velocity, real-time computing and a flood of data drawn instantly from the marketplace) is simultaneously testing and evaluating variables ranging from A to Z is like trying to get the very best price you can on a great new VCR. Or building a new buggy whip.

It's so backward and embarrassing that it's almost hard to believe. The only thing more frightening than this kind of technical ignorance in action is the idea that some of our best and brightest students at these schools are being subjected to out-of-date and hidebound academics making bad, group-think decisions which are very much akin to the tech-blind leading the oblivious.

Trying to create market-responsive and timely training solutions without really understanding what massive changes are going on in the marketplace and what new decision-making tools and other resources have been created by the rapid expansion and deployment of new, low-cost and ubiquitous technologies; the growth of market and transactional transparency and measurement; and the impact of constant connectivity to the consumer – whenever and wherever – is like working in the dark or in the Dark Ages. It's not that MBA students aren't being trained in the use of data to make better informed decisions – it's that they are being trained by faculty members who are so far behind the times that they don't even know what kind of data now exists or the power of that data to be applied in new ways to predict and change behaviors in real time.

Matters of education around data and technology which are this important to our country's economy are probably too important to be left to educators. The right solutions and our future progress are going to be dictated and changed by active disruptors with unique and original ideas that are far more likely to be based in their visions (and even their dreams) than in their own practical experience or prior education. The changes required are discontinuous leaps forward and not linear extensions of legacy systems and programs. In many ways, it's as if the world is finally waking up to the fact that our existing educational institutions just don't have the tools or the chops to get the job done any more. These schools are selling their students what they have to sell and not what it takes today to succeed.

And just to be clear, so also are you in your own business. We all get stuck in these ruts after a while in any business and – as we start out the New Year – we can all learn how to pull ourselves out of the mud if we look closely at the 3 basic reasons that cause the problem. Because remember, if you only do what you've always done; you'll only get what you've always got - or a lot less – because nothing is standing still today and – if you're not getting better – you losing ground.

As I see it, there are basically three reasons why we (and so many of our institutions) so often end up in such a sorry place where we're going sideways at best and – more likely – slipping backwards.

First, we need to understand and acknowledge that the way we have conventionally done things to date is neither inevitable nor the only or best way to accomplish the results we are seeking. In addition, the results we are getting from our efforts today aren't the ultimate results or the maximum amounts we can achieve – they're just what we can do now. These aren't limits dictated by the inherent conditions or the available resources – they are limits determined by our present lack of vision as to what is possible and will be possible as our tools and technologies continue to improve. If we accept the current state as our limits, we limit our ability to grow beyond them. If we only see what we are looking for and we accept that as a boundary, we'll be left behind by those whose vision exceeds their grasp and who are hell-bent on continuing to grow until that is no longer the case.

Second, when we talk about the future, we need to develop a new language and vocabulary because – at the moment – our ability to share and explain our dreams and visions is bound up and limited by the words and phrases we have at hand. In the context of the business schools, when you are completely surrounded and consumed by the day-to-day operations and the commonplace, there's very little prospect that you can successfully look outside of yourself and your surroundings to see what's really going on. It's like trying to explain the ocean to a fish who's lived in that environment all its life. What you've always taken for granted, you lose the ability to change. Large educational institutions are completely reliant on predictability and linearity – they need the trains to run on time – and they hate surprises. But in the real world surprises and the joy of discovery mean everything and they are the very stuff of change. And this is why it's so sad to see discussions about moving from A to B when the real opportunities are to think about moving from A to infinity and beyond.

Third, we need to steal yet another important idea from nature. Goalless planning and progress. In nature, evolution doesn't proceed toward some known, defined or even arbitrary goal. The movement is not <u>toward</u> anything; it is movement away from constraints. Everything in nature wants to be free and unlimited. The goal is never to grow to a certain place or size – it's to never stop growing in every possible direction. And nature offers neither rewards for growth nor punishments – there are only consequences.

As we look to the future, we also need to adopt the same type of methodology for goalless planning – we need to keep moving forward and measuring our progress – but without accepting the idea that there is <u>only</u> a defined and known goal in mind. This is too minor and petty a vision to permit us to leap forward. The very nature of the future is one of moving targets and new challenges and we can only hope to be prepared for the opportunities that those present if we are looking forward and upward rather than working with our heads down and grinding out some steady progress toward a goal that was out-of-date the day it was established. Fluid goals and objectives are messy and hard to measure and they are difficult to incorporate into institutional compensation and reward schemes, but the fact that they are challenging and complicated only means that the businesses and the institutions that first master these new approaches and systems and build upon them will be the ones that lead all of us forward.

So our businesses and our schools need to change and change quickly. But not without first understanding that there are major systemic barriers to effective change which need to be addressed and changed as well before real progress and improvement can occur. Otherwise, the very nature of the inquiries and the initiatives adopted will be uninformed by the right analysis and information and pedestrian at best. They will be just about as effective as the drunk looking for his keys under the street lamp – not because he thinks he lost them there – but because the light's better.

TULLMAN'S TRUISMS

DON'T ALLOW OTHERS LIMITATIONS TO DEFINE YOU

It's the beginning of 2015 - a new budget year for many businesses - and - for a whole bunch of us - this means the start of another painful year of trying to live with a bunch of made-up numbers which – in all likelihood – aren't really even of our own making. They're driven by all kinds of external considerations including, but not limited to, the requirements of management; the needs and demands of investors; and, frankly, by the apparently universal belief that every new year's numbers need to be bigger and better than the prior year because – contrary to the scientific evidence – in the start-up fantasy world - apparently trees still can grow to the sky.

So you can look forward to twelve more months of trying to make someone else's dreams (or delusions) come true. Sorry to be bursting your bubble so soon in the season, but now's the time when it's still possible to have some honest conversations with the appropriate parties and to make some simple adjustments and changes in your projections and budgets that will make everyone's life a lot easier and more rational and – most likely – will also make for better ultimate results and happier folks as well.

Now I understand the need for ongoing growth (although some companies these days would do a lot better to slow down their growth efforts until they could convincingly demonstrate to someone that there was a profitable bottom line and eventually some brighter light at the end of the tunnel) and I also appreciate how the whole annual planning "process" works as well as anyone. So my problem isn't with the basic procedures; it's with some of their most central and sorely misguided underlying assumptions.

We go about the budgeting process in the same way each season and we never seem to learn – even with the demonstrable results staring us right in the face year after year – that: (a) not every aspect of any business can be defined, measured and documented in the same way (one financial or analytical approach – for sure – doesn't fit all) and (b) not everything in a business can be predicted or calculated in advance with mathematical precision because – try as we might to prevent it – sometimes the world and the people in it just have other plans. But we soldier on and everyone plays the same game of making forecasts (with an occasional wink on the side) and the numbers get generated and rolled out and that's when the real problems start. Because even though we all know that these are "best guesses" at best; too many people on the outside take them for gospel. They seem to have forgotten that saying alone doesn't make anything so.

Sure you had "input" and you told everyone that there were a lot of uncertainties again this year and the bean counters listened very attentively (and even sympathetically for a while) to your suggestions and advice, but ultimately when the rubber hit the road and - whether you liked it or not, they needed some concrete numbers from you to plug into their big old spreadsheets so they could crank out the upcoming year's budget documents, it turned out that they weren't leaving your office without them or willing to take "I don't know" for an answer. So you held your nose, bit your tongue, and did your best at making a few wild-ass final guesses to fill in those nasty gaps in the numbers. And then you went about the rest of your day hoping that the numbers wouldn't eventually come back to bite you. But you didn't feel good about it. And that's the rub. It's hard in your heart to sign up for a story which you yourself don't believe and it's even harder to execute. Even your most fervent prayers won't help because you can't pray a lie.

So, is there a better way? Can we fix even a small part of the problem and save ourselves a lot of pain in the process? I think so. I say – especially where we are dealing with matters that are demonstrably beyond anyone's ability to predict or control – that we just admit to that simple fact and adopt a new strategy which I call the "fence it and forget it" approach. It's clean, straightforward, ridiculously easy to administer and – as a bonus – it leads to results which are likely to be far closer to the eventual truth which makes it much easier for everyone to get a good night's sleep because they're not worrying about things they can't really do anything about.

And, while you will have to decide for yourself which are the best situations in which to apply it, I can guarantee that, once you get the hang of it, you'll never look back regardless of what kind of business you're in. Let me give you two radically different cases as examples from each end of the spectrum. The first is a church which runs a soup kitchen and tries every year to keep up with the growing and unpredictable demands of its clients and the second is a sales business where expensively wining and dining the buyers is still the way the game is played.

Case One – The Churches

Yep, even a church needs to have a budget and watch its expenses. But when it's crunch time and it's freezing cold outside; no one gets turned away or goes hungry at the soup kitchen - regardless of the budget or the best laid plans. That's just not the way the world works. And so, year after year, the end is always the same. It's sorta shame on the operators because it ended up costing more than they had planned to feed all the folks who showed up. Of course, everyone knows that no one knows how many folks you're gonna have to feed until the year's over. But nonetheless, the board blames you for spending too much to do too good a job of doing your job.

Case Two – The Clubs

No one ever said it was easy to manage your sales team's T & E expense line or to make sure that every meal really mattered and helped to make a sale. Or to determine (whatever the post-trip Salesforce notes may have said) that every trip needed to be taken to close a deal or to keep a customer close. And believe me, you can drive yourself and your team crazy sweating the small stuff like this. And that's really the point – it's small potatoes in the grand scheme of things and you can't let it get under your skin. Worrying about whether $50,000 over the course of a year is going to be pissed away on drinks and dinners when you're trying to make your company's first $15 million year in top line revenues a reality is a waste of your time which – well-spent - is worth a lot more than the measly $50k.

So what's the solution in both cases? You're worried about the sales guys taking too many trips? Take your best guess at what the number and costs should be – add 5% to be safe – and tell them that that's all they get for the year and it's on them to make it work. Same deal for the pantry – try your best to estimate the volumes and the costs – set the best budget amounts you can and add a small cushion and then you're done. That's the number and now it's mainly in God's hands.

What have you done? You put the problem in a box – you fenced it in – and then you were able to forget about it and focus on the much more important things that really matter. It's simply (1) constraining the problem and then (2) being content to live with the consequences and then, most importantly, (3) forgetting about it. We've got to all learn to live with some conscious and intentional ambiguity in our businesses if we want to make them better in the long run. We just can't sweat all the small stuff.

Now I know that this idea – conscious ambiguity and cost indifference – will make all my most anal and controlling friends (and every accountant in the city) anxious, but we've just got to admit it. We don't know everything and never will – we can't find out everything even after the fact – we can't predict everything (and wouldn't that be boring anyway?) – and we can't control everything. So what. Get over it and pay attention to the important stuff and to the places where you can make a real difference.

Here's What You Do

(1) You pick some categories and you determine a budget number for each – your very best guess. You put the numbers out there for the team.
(2) You make it clear that these are serious numbers (but not written in stone) and that you expect everyone on the team to live with these numbers and try to make them real, but you don't kid yourself or them about it or obsess about it every day.
(3) You let the chips fall where they may throughout the year and you spend your days doing what really matters.
(4) Next year, you can take a look back and see whether the numbers need adjusting. It never hurts to be a better estimator as you learn.
(5) You congratulate yourself on how much less stressful your day seems now that you not concerned with policing all these petty matters or worried about a few bucks one way or the other – cause that's all these things will ever mean to your bottom line.

Here's Why You Do it

(1) You do it to put an end – once and for all – to all the false precision and made-up metrics that used to creep into your budgets and destroy whatever real credibility and integrity they may have had. Once everyone knows that no one knows for sure – that it's always our best honest guesses, it's a lot easier for people to put their heads down and go for the gold because everyone's in the same boat pulling in the same direction.
(2) You do it to give your team the clear message that you have confidence in them and that you trust them to make the right choices and decisions in the field and in the moment that no rule book and no budget will ever be able to address in advance. Because it's a real plan and a real budget, everyone can buy into it and take ownership and responsibility for the numbers – not lay them off as someone else's concern – and "owners" at any level in your business are exactly the folks you want minding the stores and pinching the pennies whenever they can.
(3) You do it because you've got much bigger fish to fry. No one likes to waste money – whoever's money it is – and so when you see that kind of behavior going on in your business – it's not about the money – it's a message to you and the rest of management that those folks don't feel good about the business and that's the real problem that you've got to fix. You won't see it or be able to recognize and fix it if you wandering thru the weeds worried about nickels and dimes.

I've seen the future and it's a flywheel. Not a physical flywheel, but a system that – for all intents and purposes – is actually its more expansive and digital equivalent. A system that replaces the momentum which a flywheel creates and gathers as it spins and accelerates with the expansive digital power which we have come to call the "network effect". Actually, my favorite flywheel these days isn't a physical or digital object at all – it's a relatively new, second-generation (or maybe a third generation) ad tech startup business based in New York which is called *Simple Reach* (www.simplereach.com) and which has built tools and a measurement/content distribution platform that permits publishers and brands to make much more effective and intelligent use of all of the branded and sponsored content they are creating to help them burnish their brands and better connect at a higher level with their customers.

The network effect (which was first formulated by George Gilder and is now generally known as Metcalfe's Law) is basically a description of the expanding value of a communications network as it adds additional nodes or links. The rate of growth in the intrinsic value of the network is not linear, but exponential and multiplies ever faster as the network expands. What *Simple Reach* has done is create an enterprise model where its customers themselves (as well as interested third parties who may be prospective customers) increasingly help build *SR*'s business and grow its user and customer base (without any direct compensation) mainly because it serves their own selfish and competitive interests to do so. There's no more authentic and convincing promoter and marketer for your business than a satisfied customer who makes it his or her business to invite more people to the party. That's the flywheel in action.

Why do they do this?

First because it dramatically increases the value of the *SR* tools and services for each of them in their own businesses. You can never go wrong counting on smart business people to act in their own self-interest. From the brand's standpoint, each new publisher added to the *SR* reporting network increases the brand's ability to more fully measure – in a unified and standardized manner – the value and impact of its spending on a given campaign. From the publisher's standpoint, each new brand added to the program (by the publisher or independently by *SR*) which then has the ability to extend its ongoing and new campaigns and its marketing spend to that publisher's channels creates more revenue opportunities and more of a one-stop solution set for the publisher.

And second, because the publishers (and frankly the agencies as well) really have no choice but to adopt such a system because their own customers are starting to demand that they use the *SR*methodology and provide them with the results which they can then readily fold into their own analysis. Sometimes a given brand will have learned about the *Simple Reach* service from a different use case with a different publisher (or obviously from *SR* itself – although they do very little sales or marketing right now – relying mainly on word-of-mouth and cross-referrals) and then – in discussions with other publishers, the brand will expect and often specify this type of data and reporting and make it clear that – if such support is not available – it will be pleased to take its business elsewhere. Frankly, no publisher today can afford to be without these kinds of offerings which are really the newest and most powerful windows to the digital world.

And finally, because, if the middle men (publishers or agencies) don't provide these services to their customers (the brands), the customers will go right around them directly to *Simple Reach* and sign up for the services. And, as it happens, that's already beginning to happen as the ultimate brand customers start to understand that they need these tools for all their marketing channels and not simply for the initial channel (or agency or publisher) which may have brought the *SR* service to their attention. Frankly, the brands already see themselves more and more as content publishers anyway and so it's a simple step (no pun intended) to contract directly for these kinds of resources – especially when – as noted above - they provide constantly more efficient one-stop shopping and integrated surveillance and tracking dashboards.

This is the kind of growth engine that you want to hang your hat on and then hold on tight for the rapid ride. And it's the kind that's very hard to come by and, as often as not, may end up flying off the track and throwing everyone for a loss. But if you find the right engine in the right marketplace and environment and your guy is the first player there, then the extent of the potential upside is hard to imagine.

It's not simply that (a) pervasive and truly additive platforms – once in place – are almost impossible to dislodge and (b) that increasingly technology spaces are becoming more and more "winner take all" plays; it's that the momentum and the earning potential accelerates at such an overwhelmingly rapid pace that even the biggest players can't respond quickly enough to the new competitive threat or use their size and resources effectively to offset the early advantages of the growing cash cushion of the first mover.

Especially in the case of a new business, that cash cushion provides several layers of comfort and security. First, management can focus on the business, not on what often – in new growing businesses - feels like perpetual fundraising. Second, early mistakes are less likely to threaten the business's existence since the business can pivot if necessary without payroll becoming a problem. Third, the customers are comforted by the bankroll and much less concerned about betting their business on the newest kid in town. Fourth, the company can afford to support simultaneous pilots and trials for far more customers than most startups. And finally, there's very little pressure on the pricing of the business's services since the company doesn't have to engage in price cutting in order to win new accounts.

But there's an even more powerful factor at work in cases like this and it's the "lock-in" investment (not in terms of dollars, but in terms of tangible business benefits) which creates powerful barriers and overwhelming switching costs even for those clients and customers which are willing to consider any kind of shift or movement. Both of these considerations are not matters of dollars and sense; they are concerns that anyone attempting to switch and losing even a moment's time or presence in these fiercely competitive marketplaces would be irreparably damaged and disadvantaged to such an extent that any such considerations would never be worth the risk.

As a result, flywheel businesses enjoy another interesting benefit – the customers seek out and readily agree to multi-year contracts - which is somewhat counter-intuitive when you are dealing with new, young companies until you realize just how quickly these kinds of new data services become mission-critical to the customers and just how addictive and additive they can be. The customers (who ordinarily would be reluctant to make longer-term commitments to a startup) quickly start to attempt to sign multi-year agreements for two reasons: (1) they become concerned about the startup's overall capacity to meet the growing demand for its offerings and they want to be sure that their own needs will continue to be met; and (b) as they incorporate the new company's products and services into their own businesses, they want to be sure that the company sticks around and stays in business.

As long as the startup retains the ability over time to continue to raise its prices and otherwise adapt and improve its products and services, this is nothing but great news for the new business because it creates unexpected levels of stability, predictable future revenue streams, and assurances that the company's future is sufficiently secure that it can make appropriate growth plans and also attract first-class talent to what would otherwise appear to be a far riskier opportunity.

So what does all this say about the future of content marketing (which continues to grow like crazy as the big brand advertisers try to create viable and continuing substantive/emotional connections with their customers) and what do you need to be thinking about for your business as you try to determine how to most profitably spend your digital marketing resources?

First, it's important to understand that we are moving into the second generation of the digital marketing revolution. If the first generation was the brute force ability to get your material (content) and your associated messages out and in front of the digital consumer (on every device), the second generation is all about tracking and measuring the efficacy and amplification of those efforts and getting better at getting it out there all the time. It's no longer about tonnage – it's all about transparency and touching the right targets at the right time in order to deliver the appropriate information and incentives to them.

Second, especially in the media/publishing marketplace, accountability is now the be-all and the end-all. No one takes your word for anything these days – no matter how much wine you pour down them - it's a "show me or see ya" world and the winners are the ones with the documentation and the ammunition to make their cases. If you can't convincingly connect spend to traffic to engagement (and organic sharing) and ultimately to conversions and concrete results, you really can't compete for much longer in this space.

We know most of these initiatives won't work, but we need to know which are working and which aren't as soon as possible so we can tactically adjust the aggregate dollar spend in order to optimize our dollars and our results. The old idea that you would simply "set it and forget it"; spend ratably the same amounts across various campaign channels; and sit back and wait for the results might have been the only way to go in the old days before we had real time responses and metrics, but it's a lazy and stupid strategy today.

And even discussing the best post-campaign documentation feels a lot like too little and too late because it's fundamentally about after-the-fact analysis and not utilizing ongoing actionable insights. The best players are focused on prognosis (prediction and real-time adjustment) rather than diagnosis which is basically all about looking backwards to see what worked. You want to be able to shift the sands under the consumers' feet and up the ante when you see where it makes sense to increase the spending behind already successful sharing in order to press your bet, amplify the impact, and increase the return on your initial investment in the development, creation and delivery of that content.

And so, in this newest media world, the real winners will be the ones who can not only help their clients track and measure effectiveness in real-time, but whose tools permit them to immediately take the next and most critical actions to accelerate and double down on what is working before these fleeting opportunities pass them by. It's an old venture capital rule of thumb – you feed your winners and you starve your losers. And that's where the guys at *Simple Reach* really come into their own as their rapid growth and multi-line expansion are showing. As I always say, you want to be there when the customer wants to buy and *Simple Reach* helps its clients track and get the right messages in front of the right customers in order to reach them at the right moment – when they are receptive and ready to buy.

It's that simple (no pun intended), but it's not easy and these guys are simply crushing it.

I've said for many years that ultimately technology is not a long-term sustainable competitive advantage because – as the cost of any new technology continues to plummet (which it eventually does in every case) – it becomes a commodity that is readily affordable and available to anyone in the marketplace. So what is it that sets the best businesses apart – regardless of their size – or any momentary advantages which their latest technologies may provide? It's their people – dedicated, passionate, committed and hard-working - that ultimately will make the difference between success and so-what. Finding, attracting, hiring, retaining and fairly compensating the best and brightest folks you can locate is the only way to assure your future.

And that's true in part because it's almost never the technology itself that makes the critical difference anyway – it's the smart application by the members of your team of these technologies to solve important and substantial business problems that will set your company apart from the rest. In many cases, the technologies and the problems have been around for a long time; what was missing in the past was the clear and new vision, the inspirational spark, and the guts and initiative to make a change.

And - while there are certainly cases where the invention of new technologies opens doors and possibilities which we never before even contemplated – as often as not – most of the new, game-changing applications aren't instances of any special rocket science (the technologies are typically already built, stable and even industrial-strength as well as readily scalable); they're simply cases of having talented people who see things differently (than everyone else has in the past) applying what are often very simple and basic technologies in ways that accelerate, improve and enhance traditional processes and solutions in order to save time or money (or both) and increase their customers' productivity.

Easy to explain; hard to execute. And it always starts with people. But it's not simply about super smart people. It's about having the people with the right mindset and attitude. People who want to stick around and do the heavy lifting that it takes to make a difference and build a real business. Things that don't happen in a flash or overnight. The truth is that an ounce of loyalty these days is worth a pound of cleverness because, in the tech space these days, we have a highly mobile workforce with fewer geographic ties than ever before, less practical constraints, commitments and obligations (other than student debt), and a much higher propensity to jump from job to job – often for the cash and the perks – but just as often it would seem for the sheer cumulating of diverse work experiences. So, especially for new, young companies, the singly most crucial component of the entire HR equation is retention. That's why it's so great to build a business in Chicago where people better understand and appreciate the meaning and value of a long-term commitment as opposed to the Valley where everything seems to be about quick scores and compensation. Frankly, if your employees are always looking for their next job, a new title, and a bump in their comp; they're not taking care of your business in the way they should.

But, here again, too many companies make the mistake of thinking that increasing retention is a product of something that you can actively do "to" people. This is the same fallacious reasoning that leads old time college professors to think that the measure of their success is what and how they teach when, in fact, it's what their students learn that really matters. Today, no one commits to a company anymore – they commit to other talented people whom they want to work with; they commit to solving challenging and substantial problems; and – in the best places – they commit to ideas that are bigger and more important than themselves.

These are fundamentally internal and often emotional (not necessarily rational) considerations – not something that's driven by décor, desserts, drinks or dogma – and not something that the company can manufacture or manipulate. You need to have people in your business who are loyal beyond reason because building a new business is just that tough – everyday tough – in every way. And real results aren't ever the product of rules and regulations and orders- they're the product of commitment and – even more importantly – of perseverance. So if your workers have one foot out the door and their eyes on some other prize, you're not building the foundation that you'll need for the future.

It's a funny thing – when you're first starting your business – when it's just an idea; it's all about story and contagious enthusiasm. But as you start building your business; it's all about the long haul – perseverance, perspiration and execution. To win over time takes character – to bear up when things are going south or sideways – takes grit and heart. And it takes a firm and full commitment – not a drive-by or toe in the water approach – and not just in words or cheap talk – but in an all-in spirit. It's like an eggs and bacon breakfast. The chicken makes a contribution; the pig makes a commitment.

So ultimately, it comes down to this. You can set the stage; you can create the surroundings; and you can certainly say all the right things, but you can't make the ultimate commitment for anyone but yourself. And there are very few tools to help you in this process – there are no spreadsheets or budget line items or litmus tests for these kinds of strengths and choices. Although when you've been at it for a while, it's easier than you would think to figure out who's not a keeper. So what is it that you can do to tip the scales in your favor? In the end, all you can really do – as Bruce Springsteen would say - is to try to make an honest stand. Tell your people what you're trying to accomplish and why. Tell them what you're willing to sacrifice in order to accomplish that goal and what you expect of them as well. Tell them the truth and the costs of getting there – whatever those costs may be. And hang on dearly to the ones who step forward and sign up.

I spoke recently about the impact of technology, connectivity and social media on the real estate business at a series of events sponsored by various brokerage companies and industry associations involved in the commercial (non-residential) real estate marketplace. These were very interesting forums because – while there's obviously a great deal of interest and concern among the key players and a real thirst for knowledge – I also came away with the feeling that the actual appetite for change was tempered in many instances by the idea that change was a good thing as long as the change was something that happened to somebody else.

A consistent inquiry in all of the Q & A sessions that followed my comments was how I expected the new technologies to alter the traditional and highly-personalized ways in which this type of business had been conducted for decades. You may think that the real estate business is all about "location, location, and location," but - in the final analysis - it's actually about continued confidence in the people you rely upon and longtime trusted relationships. And the one thing that we know for certain these days about trust and relationships is that the rise of social media and the constant presence of cell phones has been brutally difficult on both. It's really hard to hide in plain sight.

In my responses, I spoke about a variety of developing trends and oncoming changes including the need for a new type of employee – a digital native if you will - with the requisite attitudes and skill sets to be able to successfully function in an industry which was in the process of rapidly moving from a relationship-based world of intentional opacity to a bright, new and deeply democratized world of improved information, high degrees of visibility and data-driven decision-making.

I went on to say that this wasn't a thing about the age of the new players – it was about their willingness to adopt the emerging technologies and the newly-available tools and it didn't really matter whether the "newbies" were book smart or street smart as long as they understood how they would need to operate in the new digital world dictated by the twin agents of ubiquitous mobility and pervasive connectivity where every participant in any transaction had ready access to timely and relevant data.

But – in the overall flood of interesting and occasionally fearful questions – there was a single question – asked without the slightest hesitation or apparent discomfort – which really stood out from all of the rest. The truth is that what this long-time broker asked me was much more of an amazing admission by him rather than a question for me which is why I found it to be so interesting. I think it's also why so many others in the audience – brokers, builders, owners, lessors and lawyers – squirmed just a little bit and found the conversation to be somewhat uncomfortably close to home.

His question was short: My entire livelihood depends on the inefficiencies in the real estate market and ill-informed clients. How does my future look?

My first reaction was to think back to the early days of the computer business. We used to say that the primary difference between a used car salesman and a computer salesman was that at least the car dealer knew he was lying to you. Here was a broker saying that his success basically depended on the relative ignorance and lack of market knowledge of his clients.

Then I thought of that economist clown (and MIT professor) who was quoted as saying that the Affordable Care Act was purposely drafted by the Obama team with intentionally confusing language that was carefully designed to take advantage of "the stupidity of the American voter." Another arrogant academic moron who obviously feels far superior to the mere mortals who pay his salary. You really have to wonder how exactly these people live with themselves? But I digress.

In any case, I told the broker who asked that question that he was screwed. I didn't add: "as well you should be," but that wasn't really lost on anyone in the crowd. And please understand that this isn't especially about integrity in many cases. I think it's just a human condition in too many people who think that - as long as "good enough" is sufficient - they don't have to invest the time, energy and hard work that it takes to do the best possible job for their clients. They're willing to settle for doing just the kind of job that gets them through the day - especially because they believe that the clients don't know any better. But, from today on, the game's really changing because the clients will know a lot better and insist on a lot more. And that's what's so exciting (and so scary and threatening) to so many.

In the brave new world, asymmetrical information-based relationships will be a thing of the past and a fair assumption will be that everyone who cares will know anything that matters and that they should. Two words say it all: transparency and efficacy. The smart players today (buyers, sellers, clients and consumers) want to know as much as they can about every aspect of the conversations/ transactions that impact them and they're going to increasingly insist on direct and immediate access to all of the relevant data. And then, when the data dust settles, they're going to make their choices, selections and decisions based on real metrics, real visibility and real bottom line results.

The players who prevail going forward won't be masters of the shell games, bait and switches, and other tricks of the trade that used to be the way things were done – they'll be the ones who are upfront, out front and leading the charge to the future where the best economic deals for the clients will prevail and where the chips will fall where they should – not because of ignorance and a lack of good information, but because of diligence, dedication and a lot of hard work.

"There is nothing more frightful than ignorance in action."

(Goethe)

I was thinking about these poseurs who call themselves "opinion journalists" and what an oxymoron that is and, more importantly, how these halfwits must make the skins of the sadly shrinking population of real journalists crawl.

I realize that it's a source of very cheap labor (and these publishers are certainly getting what they're paying for), but I still have this old-fashioned view that even stupid and Iil-formed opinions ought to be based on some semblance of real inquiry and some modest factual basis rather than random rants written to order and based on factoids and fiction.

Sure I understand that it's quicker and easier just to make these "opinions" up (forget being there or doing any of the real research) and to claim to be relying on someone else's reporting - especially when you're trying to juggle a few too many commitments all at the same time.

And I also get that there's nothing easier in this media-crazed world than to find someone willing to say whatever you need said for whatever reasons and in support of whatever agenda they may have. But that's no better than just talking to yourself and certainly no more helpful or instructive. In fact, having these people just stand in front of a mirror and talk to themselves might be the least damaging and most narcissistically satisfying thing that they can do.

All of this wouldn't matter except that - as we continue to dilute and degrade what passes for journalism - it becomes harder and harder with a straight face to tell our kids that thoughtful, intelligent and civilized public discourse and the aggressive discussion of competing ideas and viewpoints is one of the most important foundations of our democracy.

We want our kids to learn to think and reason – not to rant – like the naysayers trying to sell newspapers (though thankfully not for much longer) or the bozos on cable or in Congress. Children and young adults today are facing an unprecedented flood of indiscriminate information (and a bunch of crappy, one- sided opinions as well) and they need to learn how to filter the flow, evaluate the relative strengths and weaknesses of the various positions, and ultimately decide what they believe.

This isn't rocket science, but it is a scientific process and it's one that is just beginning to be taught in some of our schools and it's gonna rock the very foundations of our educational system because it's about teaching our kids how to think and think for themselves rather than memorizing a bunch of conventional wisdom spewed by a "sage on the stage" which may or may not have any real value for them in the future.

As I have watched some of our EDtech companies at 1871 (especially *ThinkCERCA*) roll these new programs out to schools, it has been a joy and a wonder to see how quickly the students adopt the new approach and move from passively sitting back as the old wisdom washes over and right past them to leaning into this new world where they actively take control and responsibility for constructing arguments and building the foundations for their own education. Tell me - I might listen. Show me - I might learn. But let me do it myself and I own it for life.

Watching the kids using *ThinkCERCA*'s tools to build their arguments step by step starting with their <u>Claim</u> – then gathering the <u>Evidence</u> for it – then explaining their <u>Reasoning</u> for it – next addressing the <u>Counter Arguments</u> – and doing it all in <u>Language</u> appropriate to their audiences is an amazing experience. You can just feel the difference – they're taking responsibility and control and ownership – and it shows in their posture, in their faces, and in the results. This is exciting stuff and the sad sacks that call themselves journalists could learn a lot from these kids who actually know whereof they speak.

Tom Kartsotis and his brother Kosta built *Fossil* (FOSL) from scratch starting in 1984 (when Tom dropped out of college and was scalping football tickets in Texas) and turning into a global lifestyle brand and a public company with 14,000 employees which - 30 years later - sells $3.2 billion worth of bags, watches and clothing a year and has a market cap of more than $5 billion.

Tom retired as the Chairman of *Fossil* in 2010 and these days Kosta runs the *Fossil Group* while Tom (through his private equity firm – Bedrock Manufacturing) has turned his primary attention to a new challenge – *Shinola* (www.shinola.com) - an analog watch manufacturing and marketing start-up in a profoundly digital world. With 7 retail stores, close to 400 employees making great wages, and an exploding online demand as well for its products which now include multiple lines of watches, high-end bicycles and other accessories, the company is well-positioned to help Detroit and to create the next big lifestyle brand. And, amazingly enough, it's really just getting started.

The Kartsotis brothers are pretty private guys and rarely – if ever – talk to the press or any other media. They understand the power and importance of getting their brand and their "story" out there, but they prefer to do it guerilla-style and face-to-face rather than through the traditional channels. So Tom and some other key members of his team (including *Shinola* President Jacques Panis) agreed recently to sit down with me and a couple of dozen of our 1871 entrepreneurs in our Chicago startup incubator to give us the inside scoop on *Shinola*.

Tom shared some of the lessons they've already learned (as the company nears its third year of existence) in building a "new" manufacturing business in an era of high-tech and digital everything; he talked about the size of the opportunities they see ahead of them and the openings and market gaps that they are targeting; and he answered a bunch of questions from the founders of some of our own most exciting startups. There were plenty of concrete take-aways that were relevant to every entrepreneur in the room and I've summarized a few of the most important ones below.

I Wish I Could Say That We Had A Plan

Sometimes you just have to believe, get the process started and have confidence that - with a lot of effort and persistence - you will get there – even when you're not exactly sure where there is. It helps a lot to have a vision and a dream and a compelling story. Shinola is about pride and craft, making things that matter and last, and honoring our past as well as the future. It's a no-nonsense notion combined with a lot of nostalgia and it's the real deal. No one believed the *Shinola* team when they explained what they intended to do (to start a watch factory in a 100-year old office building in Detroit) and Tom thinks that there are still some folks out there shaking their heads, but now they're wearing *Shinola* watches and riding their *Runwell* bikes. He also noted that there will surely be bumps in the road and false starts which you'll simply have to manage through. He said that they've had plenty of hiccups, but they just kept their heads down and plowed ahead. Nobody ever said building a new business was easy. He pointed out that their idea for a Tall Men's store in Tokyo didn't work out real well – but he was just kidding.

If We Take Care Of Our People, They'll Take Care Of Our Customers And Our Business

Shinola pays its people well; provides amazing medical benefits; and even pays them above-market wages while training them right in their own factory. Everyone spends time in the company's retail stores because listening to the customers is the best feedback you'll ever get. But – far more importantly – *Shinola* believes and shows everyone that anyone can succeed if they're willing to work hard and put in the time and effort that is required. The company celebrates their successes and some of the most important team members – who started with *Shinola* as guards, janitors, delivery people, etc. – are now in charge of critical parts of the operations and continuing to grow and learn more every day. Success breeds success and believing that your people are your most important asset and that they can always be better is the only way to keep raising the bar.

We Start With The Best Product We Can Find (Or Imagine) And Then Make The Numbers Work

If you aim for the stars and being the best you can be, you very often get there. If you ask people why not and why something can't be done a new way; you'd be surprised how often you get the answers and the results you looking for. The Shinola team brought in the best Swiss watch builders in the world to train their people. They built a first-class factory that's as clean as a surgery suite. And they guaranteed their products for life. These aren't small hurdles or tentative commitments – these guys are all-in, but they also understand that they've got to make the numbers work for the long term so that the businesses can scale. It's reverse engineering on steroids and a fierce attention to every production detail and source of materials and it's opening up new opportunities for the company and its many U.S.-based supply partners. *Shinola* believes that - penny for penny and pound for pound, their people can learn to build better products at competitive costs with far higher quality in Detroit than are now being manufactured anywhere else in the world.

If Your High Prices Are Propped Up By Huge Marketing Spends, You're Ripe For Disruption.

The traditional high-end luxury watch industry has benefitted from enormous mark-ups and margins which are largely dependent on the manufacturers' very substantial brand advertising and marketing spends. *Shinola* saw an open space in the market and an opportunity to offer a high quality product at price points which were still very profitable and yet only a fraction of the pricing which the traditional brands were maintaining through their massive ad campaigns. The *Shinola* team believed that you can make a great product and a great living (and even give back to your community) without being greedy and taking advantage of the consumer. These days the *Shinola* watches are the entry point into the higher-end, luxury watch sector of the business even while they are also seen by consumers as solid, workman-like, precision products suitable for everyone.

It's not easy to be all things to all people, but it appears that everyone knows and loves *Shinola*.

SHINOLA

Have a pretty simple test for determining whether whatever you're doing has the makings of a real "business" or whether it's just an expensive hobby or a lark or a solution in search of a problem. If you can't quickly show me how you're saving me time, saving me money or increasing my productivity; I'm going to be showing you the door. Not because I'm rude, but because I'm more interested in invoices than wild ideas and new theories and the first step in the long road to getting paid is identifying real pain points and creating practical solutions for them that someone's willing to pay you to provide.

Now I understand that this is more of a modest Midwestern approach than you might find in El Lay and that things are a lot less buttoned down on the Left Coast, but I'm good with that because I'm not looking for the next billion dollar baby. There are way too many easier ways to go and a lot more low-hanging fruit and opportunities where the odds of building viable businesses and succeeding over and over again (instead of just once in a lifetime) are just a lot higher. Business plans that demonstrate great returns for investors on exits of $100 million or thereabouts rather than moonshot stories about billions to be made on some crazy bet on bionic baby foods are a lot more palatable to me.

But, when you're starting out, you soon discover that there's almost always another hurdle right behind the one you just vaulted over (it's a lot like mountain climbing in that respect - always another peak) and that – however experienced you may be - things never get that much easier. Once you've identified the problem and are on your way to solving it for your target customers; you've got to make sure that you're in the "need to have" and not the "nice to have" category or you'll be wasting a lot of time and money chasing the wrong rabbits. As often as not, the biggest hurdle isn't even coming up with an elegant and cost-effective solution; it's getting people to accept the prospect of change and to adopt your answer to the problem. Sometimes even serious savings won't overcome the comfort and security that comes from staying with the same old solution.

And, beyond that, I've also been finding lately that even the mission-critical business ideas that make it through my first set of filters have to address another (typically 800 pound) elephant in the room and that is the question of whether they're building something that's going to become a free-standing and independent business or whether they're developing a great function, feature or add-on which is going to be swallowed up, ripped off, or rolled over by one of the big guys in their space in the near future. Here's the truth: all the bells and whistles in the world won't save a partial solution. It's not that it's a bad thing; it's just not enough to get the entire job done or to be defensible over time. You need to ask yourself the hard questions about your position and your plan now so that you can get busy and figure out how to position yourself and your business on the strategic roadmap of the big guys without ending up as road kill.

And, in case you were wondering, this isn't a new problem or question. And some of the players to watch out for are the same big guys from 10 or 20 years ago – *Microsoft*, *Oracle*, *ComScore*, *AT&T*, etc. – basically it's whichever companies are the long-entrenched stakeholders and "powers-who-be" in your space – not because they're great innovators or disruptors, but because: (a) they're increasingly well-informed about who's doing what very well out there (damn those demo days); and (b) they're fairly fast followers with great gobs of money; and (c) they have the people, resources and patience to hang around and keep buying and trying until they eventually get things right in the long run.

The only good news about the big guys is that there is another group of them (think *AOL* and *Yahoo* for starters) who are so lost, so behind the curve, and so desperate to deliver something for their shareholders that they are constantly running around and throwing money at the shiniest new things in a panic and – if you can stand the short term pain and the forced smiles (until you take your money and leave to start your next business) – and if you're not a zealot or a greed head about sticking with this particular startup (because there's always another good idea right around the corner), you should think about taking a bunch of their money to build your own war chest before they wake up and smell the coffee and they're replaced by the next savior CEO.

On the other hand, if you're interested in staying the course, there are a few things to keep in mind in building your business (while you still keep one eye looking over your shoulder to see who's chasing you and running right up your tail) which will help increase your odds. Here are five ways to work it out so things will hopefully end well.

Be a Black Box as Much as Possible

Due diligence can be a double-edged sword and you have to be very careful about over-educating your potential acquirers who are also your most likely competitors. This is a very slippery area and it reminds me every time about the disappointment and disillusionment we all feel when we learn how a magic trick was done. We never say: "Wow, what a wonder that they were able to fool us so completely". We always say: "Aw, that's so easy anyone could do it." It's surprisingly close to the same situation when you pull back the curtain too soon and let the seekers see your secrets. The most typical reaction (baseless though it may be) is for these folks to conclude that - with the right amount of time and money - they could readily rip off your ideas and do it themselves. The good news is that they are generally full of crap about that, but the bad news is that it often kills the deal before they learn that very few things are as easy to do as they are to talk about.

Be So Good that They Can't Ignore You

The bar today in big companies for implementing even modest innovations is pretty low. By and large, these guys are moved by external demands far more often than any internal movements for change. They're still stuck in the mode of trying to save their way to success and they think it's all about heads rather than about what's inside those heads. They typically react (slowly at best) to three outside drivers: (a) their competition brings a new offering to market and they need a quick competitive response; (b) their customers see and begin to adopt new processes and solutions and the customers demand that their products and services conform to the new ways of doing business; or (c) they see a new tool, product or service in the market offered by a new player that bears directly on their own offerings and they quickly determine that this is a game-changer which they need to own (rather than try to build themselves) because they simply lack the internal capacity to do otherwise. If you've built something that good, there's no better place to be.

Be So Cheap that They Can't Bear to Build It Themselves

I'm not a big fan of the whole lean thing or even MVPs unless they've been previously market-validated, but there is a clear virtue in representing an initial solution which a company can quickly buy and bring to market – even if it's not comprehensive, industrial strength or the whole enchilada on Day One – because you're being compared to the substantial internal costs and additional headcount (which - in every case - will be a multiple of what you've spent or hired) which any acquirer would have to incur in order to replicate your product or service even if they are already essentially in your space or business. They know it's a painful process today to add people to any business and they also know that the only thing worse than making a headcount request is to try to tell their internal development team leaders that they have to add a new project with a reasonably high priority to their already lengthy lists and then having to sit back and listen to the even longer list of whys that isn't ever gonna happen.

By and large, the big companies today are so bound up in trying to address enterprise concerns and fix legacy issues that they have very little time for new projects and products. This is why buying (as long as the entrepreneur isn't a pig on valuation) is so much better for them in many cases than trying to build something that will never make it to the top of anyone's list of priorities. Just one head's up though if you're the guys being bought. Keep your bags packed because once you're inside the place, you'll quickly find that you'll have no more ability to command additional resources than the guys who were there in the first place and – worse yet – they may try to use your team and whatever resources you do have to solve their other problems instead of building your business.

Be So Fast and Agile that They Can't Keep Up

Elephants (and big businesses) have long memories and remember the way the world was, but - because they're totally consumed in the process of keeping themselves fed every day and keeping the trains running on time – they have little interest or ability to look or think ahead - and virtually no appetite for changing the status quo. Today, however, speed and agility are everything and their sheer size is often an albatross that these companies have to drag forward as well as an impediment to course corrections and competitive responses. The one virtue of startups that these big companies do seem to value and appreciate above all (and one that makes acquisitions so attractive rather than internal R&D efforts) is the freedom we have to embrace rapid change; the ability to adapt and pivot; the absence of a huge installed base and the demands of backwards compatibility that weigh so many innovative efforts down; and – perhaps most of all – the ability to get going – to move quickly – to understand that things may never be perfect at the start, but that we'll never get started at all if we wait until they are.

Be So Spread Out that You Can't Be Easily Swatted

I don't really believe that any startup should get so far out over their skis and ahead of themselves that they're "a mile wide and an inch deep" because there are huge execution risks in terms of support and maintaining effective connections to your customers, but there are exceptions to any rule and – in the case of presenting your business to the big guys – because they bring their old attitudes and ways of doing business to the bargaining table with them – it can be a big deal to look a lot bigger and broader than your business really is. This is because they – by and large – still think of geographic expansion as a costly "bricks and mortar" kind of roll- out process and they just don't get the cloud and the fact that there are very modest dollar costs to distributing almost anything digital today to everywhere in the world. So to them the fact that you're 5 minutes old and already in 50 countries seems like a substantial and valuable accomplishment (which they do know would cost them a bundle in their own organization to duplicate) whereas, to your IT guys, it's just a fact of digital life and a huge pain in the ass to support and maintain.

I love the constant frenzy of activity at 1871's front door. With more than a thousand people a day regularly passing through that portal, things are always poppin' as our new Governor would say. So it's a cool and very energizing sight for all of our visitors and for all of the other "civilians" who stop by for a press conference or to join a special guest who's visiting or who come simply to attend a class, lecture or luncheon.

And it's great to see that our hundreds of generous professional mentors who drop in for scheduled office hours or workshops with the member companies also love the buzz and the contagious enthusiasm of so many entrepreneurs of all ages who are actively engaged in inventing the future. I'm sure they're all hoping that some of that special start-up sauce will rub off on them.

But for our full-time members who regard 1871 as their day-to- day (and plenty of nights as well) place of business, it's increasingly a somewhat different story and reaction. After the buzz wears off a bit, they're much more concerned with taking care of business and it turns out that that's not as easy to do as you might think in the middle of an entrepreneurial petting zoo.

So we're cutting way back on the "show and tell" at 1871 and we've restricted the scope, duration, size and volume of the constant tours in order to respect our members' desire to reduce the traffic and the distractions which are the somewhat inevitable result of being one of the most popular places to visit on the planet. Failure is often an orphan, but successes have plenty of parents and others happy to share in the reflected glory and the associated bragging rights so 1871 can sometimes feel like a non-stop circus.

But all of this is pretty straightforward and manageable and probably doesn't have much to do (you might think) with the issues in your own business. However, as we've listened to our own "customers," we've begun to discover in their conversations and, more importantly, in their own actions and behaviors that there's a bigger issue at work here (no pun intended) and it's applicable to millions of businesses which have moved – over the last ten years or so – with the encouragement of architects and designers looking for the next new thing and also at the urging of social scientists seeking equality and democratization around every corner - to building floor plans and office configurations that are increasingly free-form, socially-structured and wide open in large parts of their operations. What we've discovered in our own inquiries and conversations with our members is simple. Open is over. The theory that wide- open spaces would do a world of good for improved multi-level communication, dramatically increase serendipity, and promote the sharing of just about everything - not to mention having the additional appeal of reducing the costs of constructing tons of private offices – turns out to be just the latest triumph of form over function and the continual search for novelty and differentiation. What we're finding is that a workplace where you can't get any serious work done isn't a workplace – it's a bad joke. Call me a curmudgeon, but I don't really want to hear every morning – immediately upon their staggered arrivals – a report for the "group" from each of my co-workers about their nightly clubbing, consumption and conquests – even if I cared. But, as often as not, I don't have a choice.

Anyone with the slightest powers of observation can see that it's a fool's game to try to have a private conversation or conduct any serious business when you're sitting in a place that sounds like a supermarket on Saturday morning or Chuck E. Cheese at Christmas. Headphones may help, but they're their own source of fiddling and distraction and they put an end to any pretense that there's gonna be more communication between seatmates when the whole world is individually wrapped up in their own little audio wonderlands.

The fact is that we're watching more and more pilgrimages where our people pick up their work and their laptops and wander –wasting precious time - because they're looking for a respite from the roar and a place where they can hunker down and get something done. These sad sojourns for solace and silent spaces are actually pretty clear statements (people voting with their feet) that we need to rethink the latest spatial strategies and – at a minimum –start thinking in all our offices and businesses about segmenting and segregating spaces (think "no cellphone" zones) where we effectively will be heading back to the future. There's something frightening productive about a little peace and privacy that we've seemingly lost sight of.

And we should also put to rest this utter canard that our younger team members have some mystical multi-tasking power that permits them to shut out all the noise and other distractions and yet still lets them benefit from the joys of sharing and constant community. Multi-tasking is a fiction foisted upon folks who just don't know any better. It's doing a mediocre job at a multitude of things rather than doing a deep and productive (and focused) dive into something that you actually need to get done and done well.

It may be that part of the multi-tasking confusion comes from the fact that the newer people have never known any other way of operating and that they are less insistent on the levels of productivity and results that we have always expected and have even taken for granted. But if that's the case, it's on us to fix it before things get worse and we start settling too often for getting something done when the goal should be getting what needs to get done done – when it needs to get done –and as well as it can be done – all the time.

We can't blame all of these concerns on our spaces or any other simplistic explanation, but removing and repairing what we can address and change is a good start. I appreciate that there are probably appropriate common areas where it still makes sense to encourage interaction and random activity – intersections and interchanges where potentially additive and informative encounters are encouraged – and even places (within places) where you can move to temporarily and thereby opt into the congestion, conversation and community if you wish.

But no business today can afford to be Times Square everywhere all the time. Open is over.

If you haven't been in a *Best Buy* store lately, you'll be surprised to find that – almost on a weekly basis – the Blue Ray/DVD department just seems to be shrinking right before your eyes.

My guess is that - among all the big retailers - it's now a flat-out race to the bottom (and to the mid-aisle disk dumping bins) between the BD/DVD guys and the CD department heads whose in-store footprints are also approaching Lilliputian dimensions (not just at BBY, but in every other consumer electronics retailer as well) although the space share shift in the audio department seems to be slightly offset (or disguised) by the huge growth and substantial variety of new offerings in the headphones department. Thank God for *Beats*.

I think that *Best Buy*'s management is basically giving it up – waving the white flag - and just conceding that they're fighting a losing battle on too many fronts to continue the war. But they may be missing the boat because they're playing 100% defense (cost-cutting) instead of trying to get ahead of the curve and repositioning themselves to serve the <u>new</u> needs of their customers before their few remaining customers abandon them entirely. This isn't anything new in the category of Business Management 101 – the demands of customers are always changing and you either change with (or ideally ahead of) them or your customers go somewhere else. What has changed is the speed of the changes going on and how quickly you need to anticipate and then react to those changes in behaviors, attitudes and demands.

Here's what we know for sure today. Companies that have effective online <u>and</u> offline channels consistently and significantly outperform their competitors who are still using only a single channel – typically bricks and mortar. It's all about the interplay between the channels and about the mix of offerings in each and, most importantly, it's about the need to continually innovate and add new functionality, products, services and solutions to <u>both</u> channels rather than starving one and trying to double down on the other. Honestly, I think that the big box retailers bought into the inevitability arguments which were constantly being promoted by Amazon's press and PR blitzkrieg a little too soon and much too completely. As a result, now that the boat has pretty much sailed, I think we'll see that 2015 will be known hereafter as the year in consumer retail when the "tale of the long tail" really came true, but only because the major retailers helped stage their own funerals instead of fighting back.

And, as convincing as the long tail arguments seemed to be on the surface, it's turning out that the infinite inventory and instant availability attributes of the long tail were only part of the causes of the retailers' ongoing difficulties. These superficial factors masked - to a certain extent - another major contributing behavior. The hidden problem was that these freaked-out retailers are killing themselves slowly. They were trying to catch a knife and each concession that they made to reduce their in-store inventory exposure and their overall physical merchandise offerings turned out to make the overall situation even worse because – from the standpoint of even the most willing consumer – this process quickly became a self-fulfilling prophecy.

No one wants to waste a trip to the store once they're convinced that what they want won't be there anyway. This is the old *Blockbuster* paradox coming back to life – *Blockbuster* always had loads of empty display boxes for all the popular films and plenty of old product, but none of that week's hottest hits in stock. In other words, they had everything you didn't want and nothing you needed. And, what is also very clear today is that, while we're not watching any fewer movies or TV shows or listening to any less music (or – in fairness to my good friend Don Katz – consuming less "audible" content including music), we are increasingly accessing and absorbing whatever the desired content may be in virtually every manner except sitting in one place and "playing" a physical object on a fixed and immobile device.

So the critical underlying issue isn't decreased demand. I think that it has a lot more to do with portability. The rise of mobile computing and the ubiquity of constant connectivity has definitely put extra pressure on the old delivery systems and technologies and the big box retailers haven't done any more to address this transition than the booksellers. In a world where everything wants to be streamed, *Best Buy* needs to think of their stores as digital gas stations and provide fast, cheap and exclusive fill-ups on new music for their customers on the spot – in the store and online, too. The music is the real message, not the medium of delivery. We don't need shiny disks to share our sounds any more. *Best Buy* should stick to selling fans and fridges which won't be going digital any time soon. Phones and headphones will probably sustain them for a while because these objects (of both necessity and desire) remain highly personal, tactile and touchy-feely tokens in our lives. If you don't believe me, ask yourself how totally reluctant you are to ever hand your phone to someone else. You'll show them stuff on it all day, but sharing it with someone else is another story.

Right now, we're in the age of IG (Instant Gratification) and the immutable law of IWWIWWIWI. (I Want What I Want When I Want It). Every industry (even relatively new and fairly digital ones) will be changed significantly as we continue to move from the analog world to a world of digital everything. And new major businesses will be built in the cracks and the gaps created every time the big guys fall asleep at the switch.

Take gift cards, for example, and consider the very rapid rise of *Raise* (<u>www.raise.com</u>) which runs an online, mobile-enabled, exchange that sells partially used gift cards to consumers at a discount. And they don't just sell you the cards while you're sitting on the couch at home; they sell you the exact gift card that you need at a discount while you're standing in the checkout line at the store. Exactly what you need; precisely when you need it; and instantly. They sell you a *Target* gift card at a discount to the face amount of the card while you are standing in line getting ready to pay for your purchases at *Target*. Can you stand it? Can you even believe it? Well it's true. Right in the store. Right on the spot. And there's much, much more to come.

Your job is to anticipate how these kinds of game-changing shifts will impact your business because your business may be next in line. There are no simple answers, but there are a few things to watch for and to try to get in front of instead of waiting until it's too late and then spending a lot of costly and painful time playing catch-up.

(1) You need to constantly monitor and dynamically adjust the dollar allocations of your commitments to each of the channels you are using to reach your customers in as close to real time as possible. And the more channels you effectively employ, the higher your likelihood of ultimate success – especially because the vast majority of digital distribution channels are relatively ridiculously inexpensive to use.

(2) You need to monitor the ongoing migration of the traditional products and services in your sector or industry as they move from the analog and physical world into the new digital economy. Some will survive the transition; some will morph into new offerings; and some will cease to exist, but managing the life cycles of all of them will be crucial to your success.

(3) You need to watch for the emergence of new delivery channels and systems for both your own products and services and, more importantly, for the sale and delivery of competitive or substitute goods which may be better priced, more readily accessible, easier to use; or more easily incorporated into the ways in which your customers are now conducting their own businesses.

(4) You need to watch for new consumer behaviors which are probably the most difficult to anticipate and also the most rapidly disruptive because of the speed and ease with which massive numbers of consumers can migrate to new solutions with virtually no switching costs or training requirements.

The bottom line never really changes. The customer has a constantly increasing array of choices, a limited attention span, and a relatively fixed amount to spend on whatever you're selling. The winners in the competition for those dollars will be the players who are most attentive to the customer's changing desires and most immediately responsive to their demands.

In the end, notwithstanding the appeal and power of the long tail, it's not a game of vast volume, it's always about the ultimate connection you build to your customers and the concrete value which you deliver for them.

TULLMAN'S TRUISMS

YOU DON'T WANT TO BE AT THE AIRPORT WHEN YOUR SHIP COMES IN

Please stop streaming stuff that sucks. No one cares. No one's watching. And, just because you can do it doesn't mean you should. And, as hard as it is to imagine, just because it happened to you doesn't make it interesting to us. You're constantly cluttering up the channels with your crap. And it seems like the spread of cheap video tools and technology isn't helping the situation – it's actually making it worse because now every clown with a camera can be a digital media publisher. Technology used without talent is less than a tool – it's a tragedy.

And even new innovations like *Hyperlapse* compression video which can speed up and smooth out the video viewing (without the shakes and constant jumping around) can't fix the presentation problem because when we're watching speakers (as opposed to road trips), there's no way to accelerate the accompanying (and obviously necessary) audio without sounding like Mickey Mouse. Media (or technology) that gets in the way of communication is less than useless.

UGC used to mean User Generated Content which contained – at least occasionally – some useful, meaningful and authentic material. Now, as far as the glut of webcasts which are indiscriminately spewing out massive amounts of video (and, frankly, podcasts aren't typically much better), it pretty much means Unwatchable Gratuitous Claptrap.

But it doesn't have to be that way if the makers would only take a few minutes (that's all anyone has anyway) to put themselves in the viewer's shoes. If we need help sleeping or want to be bored to death, there's always C-SPAN. And, as trite as it seems, we really do prefer quality over quantity - especially when you're asking us to commit our scarce time and – even more importantly – our attention to your offerings. It's not a volume game; it's not supposed to be a Friskies buffet; it's all about choice and value.

So next time you're getting ready to stream a talk or a panel or any other event, do us all a big favor and do these four critical things:

(1) Get a producer/director

A stream is NOT a show. Get a real producer/director (not a camera man or worse yet a tripod) who actually knows that not everything that everyone does or says during a program is worth capturing for posterity and who also knows the difference and can make intelligent choices. Get a second camera and a switcher and also (if there are slides or other presentation materials) get clean, legible digital copies of those materials as well. Incorporate the audience into the shoot. Make the visuals interesting and not static and use the zoom so we don't feel throughout the show that we got some of the worst seats in the house.

(2) Get an editor

The real value of these kinds of video-captured events isn't the few people who watch for a few minutes simultaneously online. They will generally get bored or go blind fairly quickly and bail out. If there's any lasting and archival value, it's in what use you make of the content after the fact. And to create intelligent, informative and useful content that someone will be willing to watch, you need an editor who knows the material, understands the goals, and can turn out the kind of product that you and your organization can be proud of. Vary the camera angles, intercut the slides, add some audience reactions, etc. It's not hard – it just takes some time and some thought. And it's a real talent also – not just something that people learn how to do. As Liz Taylor's 7th husband said: "I know what to do, but the challenge is to make it interesting."

(3) Give us the good stuff

Let the editor do his or her job. Cherry picking has gotten a bad name somehow, but we don't care to watch introductions that we can read, administrative announcements for the room (and we don't have to silence our cell phones), sponsor acknowledgments, or coming events calendars. Do you see where I'm going with this? Cut the crap and give us the beef – the good stuff – the 10% of the conversations that matters and from which we can learn something new. Content ultimately is cheap; wisdom is invaluable and worth watching.

(4) Give us a break

15 minutes of anything today is a lifetime. We're starting to see 7 second commercials for a reason. So decide early on what the outside time limit of your piece is going to be and then hold your editor to delivering the best material he can within those constraints. The best people will tell you that constraints encourage more creativity rather than the opposite as you might think. Think highlights and high value rather than heavy lifting. And respect the target audience's time above all.

When the dust settles, you want to be sending out something that people will want to see. Don't let your media get in the way of your message.

In the "been there, done that" category of mistakes that you should only make once, I would award a place of high honor to the idea that startups should spend their scarce capital and limited resources trying to "earn" their way into the hearts and wallets of big customers by selling strategy as a door opener. By "strategy," I mean various attempts, presentations, mock-ups, etc. designed to show these big guys the disruptive and scary future and how your company can help them successfully navigate through the coming tough times for their businesses. Here's a flash – these attempts at show and tell (which are really just some smart guys showing off) almost never end well for the little guys – that's you – and, worse yet, it deflects your best people and a lot of your focus in the wrong direction.

I realize that there's an ego component to this stuff and also some bragging rights about who you're pitching and getting in front of. But egos aside, the bottom line is whether anyone is going to be writing you a check any time soon. The method doesn't work, the metrics are always muddled at best, and, for sure, the math is a killer because you rarely get paid anything for the privilege of spending your time chasing these guys. To be successful, you need to develop, design and incorporate your strategies and your solutions into your offerings rather than trying to use them as come-ons and commercials for how well you'll eventually do for the customers.

And, of course, the biggest and saddest joke in this formulation is the word "selling" because - in 99 cases out of 100 - startups aren't selling anything – they're really giving away their time, knowledge and insights for free. Some folks think of this approach as "bread on the water," but I'd say this isn't a loss leader or an intelligent marketing cost; for a startup, I'd say it's much more likely to be a business buster. You end up spending your precious time educating a bunch of folks who often turn out to be indifferent ingrates at the end of the process and politely tell you that (a) they've decided to do it themselves (which we all know that they can't do - even if they steal your ideas); (b) that they're gonna do it elsewhere; or – in many cases because of fear, inertia, or ignorance - that (c) they're not going to do it at all. And only you and your team are that much worse for the wear.

And – if that wasn't bad enough – you'll also learn quickly from your investors (after a couple of these expensive adventures go nowhere) that they thought they were buying into a product or service business and not a consulting firm. They don't want explorers and educators; they want executors. They don't want you strategizing; they want you selling. Fully engaged in turning your ideas into invoices. They're gonna tell you that they'd rather see a month of consistent singles and doubles than wait 3 months hoping for a home run which may never come. As a scrambling startup, you just can't afford that kind of investment.

So forget it. But just in case you can't resist the temptation or the bogus blandishments about how bright you are (think: "that hooker really liked me" in cases of self-delusion like this), here are a few things to keep in mind to help you avoid a total wipeout.

(1) Don't Get Pushed Around

The biggest bullies in big companies are the boys with the least actual power. They can say "No" all day long, but they can't say "Yes" and they know it. They couldn't greenlight a project if their life depended on it - unless it happened to cost a lot less than a latte. So they spend their time taking their frustrations out on you and tormenting young entrepreneurs who don't know any better with big empty promises of good things to come down the line. And – in the meantime – they're only asking for the sun, moon and stars – all for free – because that's pretty much all they've got to spend.

Here's the straight dope: you don't have to give away or prove anything to these guys because they don't matter. Find the folks who can actually sign a check and get in front of them. They're a lot easier to deal with and they can make a real deal happen. They're also a lot nicer too because they don't have a big chip on their shoulders. And they know that - if you want something of real value – you have to pay for it. If you pay peanuts, you get monkeys.

(2) Get Profitable First

Too many complimentary pitches and big bunches of brainstorming freebies will mean too little inbound cash flow and that means trouble for any startup. You need to have an aggressive containment strategy (a limited number of ongoing anythings and that's it) and you need to be sure that your sales team isn't taking the easy way out by selling air and getting paid nothing for it. It's not a "win" when all the commitments and all the costs are on your side of the table. The real focus of management needs to be on making sure that you are identifying and signing up paying customers. The size of the individual deals is nowhere near as critical as the cash.

Another important bonus is that these deals don't take as long to launch or as long to complete as many of the bigger ones might.

The truth is that you simply can't afford to pass up the small fish while you're waiting for the whales. See http://www. inc. com/howard-tullman/why-small-wins-beat-big-ones.html. Big companies are one of the last refuges of the slow "No" and there's just about nothing worse for a startup than that. A fast rejection (it only hurts for a bit) is always better than being stroked and strung out by a guy who gets paid to have meetings rather than to make decisions and progress. Once you're making even a little money, you can consider whether to roll the dice on some bigger proposals. Don't be a hurry.

(3) Get A Pilot Project

Don't leave the conversation once you're in the room without something. A trial, a test, a pilot, a prototype, etc. These are all good ways to get the ball rolling, but not for nothing. And equally important you must make sure that there's a clear and express agreement on just what you're committing to do and what exactly will constitute success and the steps to follow afterwards. If the metrics and measurements aren't properly aligned and apparent, you're as likely as not to get to the end of the project and have nothing to show for it because you didn't get the right rules established at the outset.

And don't think that any agreement is better than no agreement because a bad beginning agreement can set the wrong tone for the whole relationship. And don't think that only newbies make these kinds of mistakes. *YouTube* and plenty of celebrities make $300 million worth of these mistakes just a little while ago. See http:// www.inc.com/howard-tullman/ three-lessons-from-youtubes- programming-disaster.html . So get something, but make sure you know what you're getting yourself into.

(4) Get Paid

If you don't ask, you don't get. You know what your stuff is worth (or you should) and you shouldn't be embarrassed to say that you stopped giving it away for free a while ago. We have all heard the stories about what great reference clients some of these companies will make for your business and these tales are basically BS because everyone in the industry who matters knows that the very same guys make a habit of never paying new companies anything for the chance to test their products or services. They never pick up the check and, after a little while, they start to lose respect for the companies that keep working for free. Just like the patsy in the poker game; if you don't know who it is after 30 minutes of playing (or too many free trials), it's you.

(5) Get Partners Who Are Already in the Door

There are a lot of big companies scared to death these days of everything digital and under tremendous pressure from their own customers and clients to figure things out in a hurry. This kind of demand would be encouraging overall except that these companies simply aren't built for speed in anything and that's where the opportunities are being created for clever young companies with the chops and the technology to get these kinds of jobs done quickly, relatively cheaply and - most importantly - quietly. Think of the big guys as today's Trojan Horses. They're already inside the walls – they have the relationships that would take you years to build with the biggest brands and players around – and they are hurting for help. They can make good partners and you can make them look good as long as you're careful to make sure that your IP and financial interests are protected and that they aren't selling you the same bill of goods about future fortunes that their clients will try to do.

TULLMAN'S TRUISMS

STRATEGY IS WHAT YOU DON'T DO

I was part of a recent Oxford-style debate in Chicago where the proposition under consideration was that "Entrepreneurs are born, not trained." It was the classic nature versus nurture type of heated argument between two pairs of seasoned senior executives and serial entrepreneurs. And truth be told, I think that each of the advocates in the debate (except maybe my debate partner, Amy Wilkinson) could have easily argued in favor of or against either side of the proposition. Amy herself was pretty hardcore on our side of the argument (we were the "built" team) and she had some pretty strong ammunition as well based on her most recent research in the field.

In fact, the entire contest was especially informed and influenced by Amy's participation since she (after 5 years of serious investigation interviewing dozens of hugely-successful company founders) had just published a new book on entrepreneurs called *The Creator's Code*. I'd say it's a must read for anyone who wants to understand what it takes to survive and succeed in the startup world. I don't want to try to summarize it because I couldn't do it justice and because the many concrete examples in the book which are drawn from one-on-one conversations with all of these people are invaluable additions to the book's own concrete conclusions. But – as noted below – while you definitely need the big names and boffo stories to move the books off the shelves, the real value of her years of diligent research and analysis is how the findings can help all of us everyday entrepreneurs be better at accomplishing what we're trying to do.

Amy's book identifies and describes a cluster of distinct abilities that will sound very familiar to any serious entrepreneur, but it also makes the more interesting assertion that real break-through success depends on the presence, not of some of these talents and capabilities, but of ALL of them at the same time and in the same person. Her research shows that every one of the six essential skills which she had identified were present in each and every one of the male and female entrepreneurs in her study.

The underlying study basically focused on the founders of companies which had reached $100 million or more in revenues over a 5 year period. Rapidly growing and highly impactful companies. Every one of the founders she spent time with is a household name today to millions of people, but not a single one of them would call themselves an overnight success. Nor would they say (even though the premise of the book is their skill sets) that they achieved their successes alone. And, in fact, one of the six essential skills is the ability to network and draw talent and resources to your ideas. These narratives are all about striving, persistence, passion and even patience which is something we rarely talk about in this context, but it's invaluable to understand that you should never confuse a clear view of where you're headed with the time or distance that it will take to get there or how difficult the journey will be.

Amy's research also demonstrated that the more times a given individual exercised these abilities and the more businesses he or she created over time, the better they got each time at the process and the higher the likelihood that they would again be massively successful. Practice and application make increasingly perfect. Perhaps the prime poster boy (and serial entrepreneur) in the book is Elon Musk for obvious reasons – although, as she noted –nothing was sure or obvious (except his raw intelligence) when he started and – in fact – Elon faced the abyss multiple times in several of his most successful ventures, but he never stopped believing. By his own admission, he taught himself a great deal about a number of different industries and, throughout his journey, he learned immense amounts from each and every bump in the road. The bottom line of Amy's research and the most compelling conclusion was that all of these critical tools and techniques can be _learned_, honed, and improved upon throughout anyone's career and over successive instances of starting new businesses.

Note that I use the term "learned" rather than "taught" because so many of the individuals in Amy's study were not classically advantaged or trained in the areas of their ultimate triumphs. In fact, they were almost all more scrappy and "street smart" than brilliant or "book smart" in the areas that really mattered to their eventual businesses. This distinction – of course – became a major bone of contention in the debate itself. Our view was that becoming an effective entrepreneur and a business success was about experience, iteration, and learned craft (as well as a full measure of good fortune) rather than some genetically-determined destiny that inescapably assured you of eventual success. At the outset of the debate, the audience was informally polled and they agreed substantially (60-40) with our side of the argument. The trick was not to lose them over the course of the discussion.

Our opponents immediately attempted to pigeonhole us in the academic world and repeatedly stressed that their view of the "training" under discussion was the type that could only take place in the narrowest confines of colleges, universities and graduate programs. We countered that they were attempting to make a distinction which made no real difference in the real world. Where and how you gained and developed the skills didn't matter a bit – the point was that none of these talents appears fully-realized and ready to roll at birth or at the outset of anyone's careers.

As you might expect, there was a lot of loose talk about crazy people, college dropouts, about people happy to take insane risks, about fatal optimists, and about the absolute cream of the crop – those few super entrepreneurs whose names we all know and revere. But, when the dust settled, the thing that struck me at the end of the contest was that we are actually doing so many aspiring entrepreneurs a real disservice by focusing on the very few Michael Jordans and the Lang Langs of business (who may be amazing or may just be the luckiest people alive at the right time and right place) rather than on the thousands of equally successful (if considerably smaller) entrepreneurs who are working just as hard every day to build their businesses and who can really learn and demonstrably benefit the most from the important lessons which Amy's book has to share.

Uber is a great story, but the real growth and expansion of new businesses and the creation of new jobs will come from the hundreds of businesses that apply the new lessons of the sharing economy and "*Uberize*" their own businesses and industries.

Similarly, there will be *Airbnb*-ish solutions brought forward in many market sectors. All of these successes will be driven by individuals who master and intelligently apply all of the essential skills which Amy sets out in her book to their own enterprises and not by the ones who think that the key to success is to emulate Travis or Zuck by rocking a hoodie and then sitting by the roadside waiting for the lightning to strike. Hope is not a strategy for success. Hard work, perseverance and iteration are.

Finally, in the interests of full disclosure, I have to confess that by the discussion's end – due in no small part – to the underhanded and reprehensible behavior of our opponents (and some pithy comments about the height of NBA players and other flagrant grandstanding), the audience was somewhat swayed in favor of our opponent's position and the gap in opinion was narrowed although we ultimately prevailed in a purely mathematical sense. Small solace.

TULLMAN'S TRUISMS

THE PERSONALITY THAT MAKES A GREAT ENTREPRENEUR HAS NO REGULATOR OR SHUTOFF VALVE

Many years ago I saw a great cartoon that completely encapsulated the leap of faith that is a crucial part of every entrepreneur's dream. The drawing showed a guy standing under a series of thought bubbles reflecting the development of his great new business idea – each one stepping sequentially from its creation thru its development and on to its commercialization – and right smack in the middle of the chain was a modest little bubble which read "miracle happens here". For me, that simple illustration said everything there was to say about how critical faith and perseverance are to the success of a startup. And how sometimes - to get from here to there – it's not about seeing; it's about believing. You have to believe it first; concretely envision it next; and then, ultimately, you can convince others to see it as well.

But, in addition to that initial take-away, what I have retained all these years later is a completely different thought about that critical link in the process which has helped me to understand and formulate inexpensive, practical and rapid solutions in many cases for small and large businesses which can help to move things forward without asking anyone to bet the farm. This isn't a new concept in some respects – we've all heard the idea of "try it before you buy it" for years. And I used to remind my MBA students that you never wanted to test the depth of a puddle by jumping in with both feet. Making cheap mistakes and getting over them is an art form.

But this simple concept continues to be a major challenge for large businesses who want to introduce new ideas and innovations to their businesses, but who are also are trying to deal with the need to deploy enterprise-wide solutions and manage the spaghetti code of decades-old legacy systems. They long for the speed, flexibility and low costs of the startup world, but they're stuck in an environment where the passage of time and the prior investment of millions of dollars makes it harder and harder to change or abandon the constraints of business as usual. They need an approach which will let them investigate and iterate before they invest and integrate the new solutions into their core operating code. And they need a buffer to be sure that – while they're trying and testing the new tools – they aren't infecting or disrupting the ongoing business. This is actually easier to accomplish than it sounds, but – by and large – it's got to be done in partnership with outsiders who can take a fresh look at the situation and create solutions which – very frankly – the people who got you to the breaking point are the least likely to come up with. The people who built and created the problems aren't going to be the ones who fix them.

My solution – which I call "sneakernet" - isn't ground-breaking or revolutionary – it's just the absolute heart and soul of how startups think about these things – and it's also something that these big businesses just can't seem to independently arrive at as an efficient approach to solving their problems. They need our help to get over that first hurdle of "good enough" where you're just doing something – quick and dirty – with duct tape galore – in order to get the ball rolling and to get things going. It won't be pretty – it certainly won't be perfect – but if you wait until it is, you'll never even get started.

As with everything, we start with a definition. It turns out that - in the real world - properly defining the problem gets you more than halfway to the solution. And, as often as not, the solution that you need to get the ball rolling is something that's painfully obvious and sitting right in front of you. Very often, it's not a step or two forward; it's a look backwards at how things used to work and how they were done before all those ponderous and sclerotic systems and expensive computers got in the way.

So what exactly is a sneakernet?

It's a solution that doesn't try to solve 100% of the problem on Day One or create a comprehensive and complete, stem-to-stern, process that will cost too much and take too long and which will - most likely - never see the light of day.

It's an approach that says: if I was starting from scratch and just had to get the thing from here to there, how would I do it? And we all know that you wouldn't try to do it (while you still weren't even sure that it would work) by trying to directly connect it to your main operating systems – even if you could.

It's a back-to-basics perspective that recognizes that sometimes shoe leather and sneakers are better system connectors than 6 months of re-engineering, thousands of wasted man hours, and unending attempts to get two separate systems to talk effectively to each other.

When we couldn't solve things the hard way, we took a much shorter and simpler path and just walked the data from one system over to the next. And even when we had to re-enter critical information and notwithstanding the redundancies, the truth is that we got the job and the tests done and we actually saved time, money and a lot of sleepless and sweaty nights.

If you can't breach the four walls of an enterprise or legacy system and get your job done directly, the next best attack is to step back and do things the old-fashioned way for a while – especially when you're just trying something new.

For example, if you can't readily or inexpensively integrate a new mobile ordering system with your old payment system (and you know you absolutely can't), then do it the easy way. Capture the orders quickly and easily from the new mobile system (thereby making your customers a lot happier), print them out, and then quickly walk them over and re-enter them into the payment system which will take it from there. That's a classic sneakernet approach.

It won't scale, but who really cares? For the moment, you're just trying to see if the dogs like the new dog food. It doesn't need to be industrial strength – it just needs to get the job done – and no one really needs to know what's or who's behind the curtain. It's really not important how or who moves the critical information; it's just critical that the information move.

It's smart because you limit your investment and your dedicated resources while you are still able to effectively test the consumer's interest and appetite in the new approach.

It's <u>secure</u> because there are none of the data issues that a real-time connection might entail and which would give your IT people ulcers for sure.

It's <u>swift</u> because it is supplementary and additive to everything you are now doing and can be immediately implemented without any material changes or integration into your current operations. To those ancient and immovable legacy systems, it looks exactly like the "same old, same old" but you're actually appending new solutions to the system.

It's a sneaky sneakernet.

TULLMAN'S TRUISMS

EAT THE ELEPHANT ONE BITE AT A TIME

If you thought it was difficult to start a new business in the education space, you'd be right for sure. But it's even harder to do something in the adult education space and that's very unfortunate because we - as a country - are in dire need of more companies providing cost-effective and results-oriented retraining and up-skilling programs especially to adult learners whether they be career changers, new job seekers, or just folks whose continued employment and value to their companies is in question because their own skills haven't kept up with the growing technical and digital requirements of their jobs.

Having large numbers of people in any of these three particular populations sitting on the sidelines looking for new opportunities without having the requisite training for the new positions which are available and currently going unfilled represents major losses to our economy - not merely because these individuals aren't working - but also because they represent a wealth of accumulated institutional knowledge that will be lost if we can't figure out how to connect and enable them with the new technologies and move them and their aggregated wisdom forward and into the digital economy. So creating better and more effective systems of adult education and re-skilling are critical, but they're hard and especially hard for startups mainly for one overwhelming reason.

I call it the "curse of cohorts" and it's a bitch. School teachers and even college professors by and large have it easy in the cohort department. As I used to tell my faculty, sadly we keep getting older while the students every year are the same age and, of course, that's precisely the point. Our traditional education system does the selection, segmentation and other sorting for us so basically the majority of students in any class are roughly the same in terms of demographics, prior experience and education, and - maybe most importantly - expectations and aspirations. Classes are for all intents and purposes cohorts by definition and can be addressed and dealt with from a curricular perspective in a single and consistent fashion.

I don't mean that their individual needs are the same or that they will be learning in the same way or that they should even be taught in the same manner because differentiated learning is the future of all education. And don't get me started on how stupid the "one size fits all" model of teaching is. But at least in a given group within a given class, there will be some prerequisites and some fundamental external and known alignments. And we also know for sure that their common and overriding objective is to complete the class and graduate.

Unfortunately when you get to adult education, it's a vastly different ballgame. It's almost impossible to figure out who will respond to your ads (in whatever channels you launch them) and realistically what each and every one of the prospects will be expecting to get in the class and to get out of the class. I used to joke that, if you announced a class on Excel, you'd have respondents looking for a new headache cure; rank beginners who'd never used a spreadsheet; and masters looking for new strategies to crank up their pivot tables, etc. A course on Ruby on Rails would unearth model railroaders and aspiring gemologists among others searching for the keys to the kingdom.

And those are just the types of disconnects that arise regularly over subject matter and course materials and coverage. When you add to that unwieldy mess, the additional and considerable confusion over outcomes, next steps, and what the extent of the actual preparation is expected to be, it's amazing that anyone can manage this process at all. Some of the students expect that 12 weeks of coding instruction will turn them into entrepreneurs; others plan to immediately jump into a mid-level, high-paying programming job at a major corporation, and still others think that - with enough passion and energy - you can actually wish a real business into existence. Turning even the best ideas into invoices takes a lot more than that. In fact, the matchmaking function itself may be the absolutely hardest part of building a sustainable and profitable adult education business.

Frankly, if I had the time, I'd quickly build a national registry of the course offerings from all the different providers in every city that would be the "go-to", one-stop place to find exactly what you were looking for. It would have its own tipping-point mechanism built right in so that each specific class would launch and go forward only after the minimum required number of appropriate and interested people had actually signed up for it. Hard to believe that it doesn't already exist, and yet, it doesn't. But, alas, that's for another day.

Right now, if you're intent on trying to help in this space, I've got plenty of scars, lots of experience, and some specific tips for you.

(1) Find A Channel (Outbound)

Trying to reach your cohort of ready, willing and able students (who are also qualified) among an unbelievably diverse population of potential adult learners who are hopefully interested in precisely your particular offering in a specific location and at fixed times and dates is an expensive and ridiculously expensive proposition and one which (if you were to tell the truth) has continual customer acquisition costs far in excess of what you can realistically charge a given student for your course offering. You're not gonna make it up in the volume either. Because unlike a college or university, too many adult courses are one-off deals where there isn't even a way to claim that you can amortize your acquisition costs over multiple sessions or courses which will eventually be taken by each person once you've incurred the cost to track them down and attract them to your program. This is much harder than finding a needle in a haystack – it's more like continually sticking yourself with the needle and hoping that eventually you'll get used to the pain.

So you need an outbound, cost-effective communication channel to reach your targets. You want to ride on someone else's back and rely on their bucks to help you get the job done. This is a lot easier than you think because fashioning win-

win partnerships these days are all the rage. In particular, membership organizations a (think AAA or AARP) are all under growing pressure to demonstrate the value they provide to their members in order to retain them when so many of the things they traditionally offered to their groups are now available elsewhere and often at no cost. So find yourself a free ride – associations, membership organizations, alumni groups, etc. and choose the ones most closely aligned to your offerings and see what happens.

(2) Find A Feeder (Inbound)

A staggering number of traditional schools (high schools, colleges and universities) aren't giving their graduates the concrete and practical skills that these students need to secure one of the massive number of good-paying and challenging jobs which are being created in the digital economy every day. We need more vocational training at every level of the education chain and this is the precise niche that high-end, technical adult education programs can fill if we regard them as "finishing" schools and education extenders and enhancers rather than as places for grown-ups to occasionally pursue their hobbies, dreams and passions.

The traditional schools aren't going to get around to changing their programs any time soon (the community colleges are actually beating them to the punch), but their students (and graduates) are starting to get the picture and they make great targets for these kinds of programs even before they're officially done with school. It's easier than you would imagine to get the word out about what you're doing on college campuses and much, much less expensive than other channels. Keep in mind that the students still do listen to certain of their professors and they have considerable sway. You never know how valuable a testimonial or an endorsement can be in helping to convince your prospects to sign up with you until you run into a situation where you're the one without someone else in your corner helping to vouch for and "sell" your product or service. Having two Profs pitching your programs is worth a lot more than piles of pamphlets at the student union or persistent emails and other promotions.

(3) Find A Food Chain (Upward Bound)

More and more, the singly most discouraging words that I hear from the "graduates" of so many of these short-term courses is that – now that they have made the investment, spent the time, and learned whatever, they really don't know where to go or what to do next – either because the actual training they've received is only part of the story (some, but not all, of the skills or tools that they need to really move forward in their job search, etc.) or because there's no placement support or service from the training provider to help them take the next critical steps.

Now I realize that – as good as your intentions may be - you can't do everything for people and you can't push or pull people forward all by yourself. All you can do is to show them a possible future and a defined path to get there. You can tell them everything that is necessary and just what it takes to succeed, but you can't understand these things for them. Ultimately, it's on them. But it's up to you to show them that there is a path for them and that it's real and manageable if they're willing to make the effort. It's simply not enough for you to mentally draw some invisible line and take the position that your responsibility stops there.

I realize that it's one whole and pretty difficult task to just do a great job at the education part of the process and that most of the people offering these courses aren't even equipped (and they certainly don't have the necessary time and/ or resources) to run a placement service when – very frankly – they're constantly scrapping to fill their own next bunch of classes. So – if you can't do it yourself, it's critically important to make yourself a place in one or more food chains and become a feeder to the groups and organizations who need the very people that you're training – even if the training isn't one hundred percent of their requirements – because they're not only the logical employers, they're also willing and able and equipped to fill in the missing gaps with their own on-boarding processes. It's another win-win situation. You inexpensively source qualified and interested people for them – they fill the bill and finish the process further down the line for you.

I started writing computer code when I was in high school in a special program at the Illinois Institute of Technology. This was in the early 60's and long before there was such a thing as a personal computer. I continued coding through my college years where I distinctly remember carrying rubber band wrapped decks of punch cards to the Vogelback Computing Center at NU every night and praying that there'd be some decent output the next morning when I returned to pick up my job. In the early 90's, I designed and developed computer games for multiple platforms. So I'm a geek to the gills and no one believes any more than I do that computer literacy is an absolutely essential skill for student in this country if they want to have even a fighting chance of succeeding in the digital economy.

But, having said that, I think that there's a material difference between computer literacy (which I think of as awareness and curiosity) and simple computer coding (which I think of as learning some specific skills and processes). Parents today (along with older job seekers and career changers – who are also prospective students) have to be careful to make sure that they don't go crazy with coding. Learning to code is a desirable skill to be sure, but it's just that. It won't make your kid a better person. It's not a solution to all that ills civilization and it's certainly not the right path or course for everyone – at least not until their expectations and aspirations are properly aligned with a realistic view of what they can expect at the other end of the process. And for adult "students", they too need to appreciate that it's not a cure-all; it's not a business in and of itself; it's not a shortcut to building an earthshaking application; and it's not even a certain path to a dream job. It's a great beginning and a solid foundation to build on.

Of course, if you don't care where you end up, then any path will get you there. Taking a coding class is as good a way as any to spend some money and kill a few weeks or months and - for high school kids - it's a great addition to their future college applications. But if you're going to make the investment of the necessary time and money, you should also give some thought to where you're headed and why. And, if you're trying to move your own work life forward, upskill your capabilities, or give an edge and some valuable education to your kid, then it's really important that you understand what anyone can and should realistically expect when they set out to learn to code. There are terrific reasons for almost anyone to take the plunge – they're just not the ones you might typically expect.

Coding is a tool – it's like a ladder which will get you to a higher place – but what's the point if there's nothing for you on the top shelf when you get there? You can't exercise your skills in the abstract or in a vacuum. You need to apply these new skills to important problems which people will pay real money for you to solve. Otherwise, the truth is that basically – after all that time and money - you'll be all dressed up with nowhere to go.

And, given the rapid rate of change in the tools and platforms that we are using every day, it's also important to understand that the specific technical skills that you learn in even the best programs at the best schools will go rapidly out of date or out of fashion. But that's completely OK (and to be expected) because the real value of learning to code isn't in the mastery of the tools; it's in the development and the internalization of the rigor, the analysis, and the critical thought processes that are the crucial foundational skills of all great programmers. The true value of these programs is in the learned processes and not in the typically trivial outputs. I'm almost certain that the world doesn't need another scheduling service or sharing site. But we need all the critical thinkers and change agents that we can create.

And, frankly, these should be the skills that smart parents want to equip their kids with - as early as possible - because they are life-changing – not mainly because of the implications for heightened college admission or employment prospects – but because (just like debate class or chess club) they provide your offspring with a methodology to approach and attempt to resolve whatever challenges and problems they will be facing in the future. They won't be put off or paralyzed by these prospects – they'll have learned to take them on and vigorously attack them. To find the critical path through or around the problem. I call this "approach behavior" – it's leaning into the wind and moving forward rather than standing still or turning away from difficult situations. And it's a powerful life skill for anyone.

And there are a few other invaluable skills and ideas as well (the ABCs) which coding teaches and these are the real outputs that matter in the long run. There are others for sure, but here are my most important ABCs:

(A) Approximation

Successive approximation is better than postponed perfection. Done (for the moment) is always better than perfect sometime down the line because the world isn't waiting for you. You learn early on in creating code that it's a constant series of small steps (with a ton of failed attempts included) which slowly get you to the end result. Each accomplishment is itself only the next level in the process. There are no shortcuts and doing things right takes time and patience. All of the great ideas are cumulative – they incorporate disparate components and elements which eventually combine to deliver a solution which is broader and more effective than anything that came before. But nothing ever happens if you don't get started.

(B) Better and Better

Code can almost always be faster, cleaner and more efficient. You want to copy everything that came before except your mistakes and make it even better. Raising the bar, constantly iterating, and building upon your successes is the reason that there's never a finish line in these businesses. It's also because every business today is engaged in an arm's race with tons of other people (copycats, fast followers, etc.) who are running right behind you and going to school on your code and your solutions so they can build quicker and cheaper ones. If you don't constantly improve on (and even cannibalize) your own products and services, you can be sure that someone else immediately will.

(C) Curiosity and Confidence

The best competitors today are those who are constantly learning and re-learning everything about their businesses. This requires an openness to change and an immense curiosity which continues to ask how things can be improved and why things are still being done in certain ways. Entrepreneurs see the same things that everyone else has seen, but think about them in new ways, and they are willing to explore new alternatives. Coders share this same type of unrestricted perspective. They rarely ask why; they always ask why not. One of the most satisfying parts of the entire development process is when you get the rush of excitement as you come to understand something you've known all along, but in a new and different way. Daily epiphanies; adrenaline bursts; and the alchemy of creating something from scratch are some of the greatest joys of the job.

TULLMAN'S TRUISMS

WE'RE MORTGAGING OUR KID'S FUTURES BY SADDLING THEM WITH YESTERDAY'S SKILLS

Too much of our planning for growth these days is predicated on incremental improvements, brand extensions, product re-sizing, territorial expansions and the like. These are attempts to capture market share available in readily-apparent adjacencies rather than through undertaking new journeys and adventures and they're generally safe and sound bets for big companies. One problem with this approach is that these are paths and choices that are demonstrably evolutionary rather than revolutionary – they're great add-ons, but rarely will they generate needle-moving numbers. Sure bets guarantee small margins. The standard "no one ever got fired" process is all about taking carefully-qualified steps forward instead of making quantum leaps.

But it's becoming increasingly clear that this heads-down, "grind it out" approach (which might have been entirely prudent and reasonable in less flush or chaotic times) keeps many of us from seeing and seizing certain kinds of disruptive and game-changing opportunities which are being enabled today primarily by the rapid spread and availability of new low-cost technologies and by the dual explosion of ubiquitous mobility and connectivity. If we are principally focused on getting as close as possible to achieving our currently defined goals and objectives (and our operating numbers for the quarter or the year), it's just not very likely that we're going to look beyond those targets and over the horizon in order to see the less obvious and more extraordinary areas of possible change.

The truth is that we just don't have to do things in the same calculated and mechanical ways that we always have in the past and we especially don't have to construct the kinds of capital-intensive, costly and time-consuming foundations (including, but not limited to, every kind of bricks and mortar solution that is out there today) which were required and essential supports in the past, but which today simply constrain us and slow us down. This isn't simply that old familiar conversation to the effect that "we didn't need better buggy whips or faster horses, we needed cars"; it's an even broader commentary than that. We don't need the horses, we don't need the stables, and, frankly, any day now, we may not need the drivers themselves.

What we need is new inspiration and new approaches that are disruptive and discontinuous – not linear extensions – but true experiments with admittedly unknown outcomes and results, but which also represent the prospect of exponential potential gains. And the very good news today is that these types of new solutions can be implemented in less costly ways than ever before so that the real risks and downsides of continued experimentation can be constrained and largely mitigated.

It's also encouraging to see that these innovative approaches aren't limited to new businesses, but are being incorporated in the strategies of plenty of large and old line companies as well. Admittedly, in some cases, they are acting belatedly and defensively rather than leading the charge, but at least they are moving in the right direction. But whatever the age and size of your business, you need to be thinking about the steps you should be taking to distance and differentiate your products and services from both the competition you can see today and the much more threatening and extensive competition still to come. And, even more importantly, you need to ask yourself what – if anything – is the sustainable competitive advantage that you are hoping to create for your business so that it can compete in the future on anything other than price which is always a race to the bottom for any business.

No one can tell you the specific steps you will need to take to make these jumps, but here are two interesting and instructive cases which are worth continuing to watch in order to see how they might be applicable to your own situation. One is a done deal and one is an open question.

(1) The Book Biz is About Anything But Books

Please don't call anyone in the book biz a "publisher" these days just because – if you twist their arms – they might sell you a book. The "P" word is definitely out and the new industry buzzwords are all about adaptive learning and learning management systems, etc. Why is this seemingly semantic change so interesting? Because – for all intents and purposes – it reflects the decisions made by all of the biggest book publishers in the land to just throw in the towel and pretty much leapfrog right over the digital book business without even trying to explore those kinds of content offerings. It would appear that they're leaving the field wide open for Amazon and Apple, but maybe they know something that isn't obvious to the rest of us. There may not be any there there any longer.

If you ask them why they didn't aggressively pursue the protected digital distribution of their content, it turns out that their decisions weren't really based on the usual considerations which continue to plague the music and film industries – theft by pirates, cheap low-quality duplication, peer-to-peer sharing, etc. It turns out that they concluded that the intrinsic value of the content itself which they had to offer was being slowly ground down to nothing by:

(a) the actions of the content creators themselves (rather than the actions of others as was the case in music and movies);

(b) highly-efficient used book marketers;

(c) the advent of MOOCs; and

(d) free webcasting of lectures and classes by universities and professors all over the world - so they just decided to jump right over the challenging and unprofitable distribution game and move to building proprietary and protectable learning systems which they could market and sell to their same customers and which would assist in teaching whatever the content might be and, more importantly, measuring the results of those efforts.

(2) A New Lease on Life for Libraries?

Libraries aren't much better off than books these days and cities and schools of every size and shape are trying to figure out what the library of the future will look like and – very frankly – what real functions it will provide which justify its continued existence and provide some kind of differentiation from so many other public and private spaces. There are about 120,000 libraries in the U.S. these days and the vast majority (pretty close to 100,000) are in schools and universities. And you can be sure that in almost every instance, there are other users, groups, departments and facility management professionals who are coveting those large (and largely empty) spaces in their institutions for a million other uses. The one thing that we know for sure is that relying on "tradition" in order to support the old ways of doing things won't do the trick much longer. Tradition these days is just a delusion of permanence and - most often – it's just an easy excuse for those who don't want to change.

So the challenge that I would leave you with is to think creatively and disruptively about what will we do with our libraries now that books are increasingly a thing of the past? Should they simply be community spaces? Safe harbors for kids after school? Coaching and supplementary education places? Or just rows and rows of recycled desktops for accessing digital everything. Right now, this is a very open question. You should regard it - not as a closed book - but as a very large volume full of empty pages.

TULLMAN'S TRUISMS

WHEN YOU GO UP TO THE BELL, RING IT, OR DON'T GO UP TO IT

Paul Simon and Art Garfunkel had it right and they actually didn't even know it. I think that today they'd still probably be embarrassed if someone called them "computer geeks" or said that they had perfectly articulated the newest and smartest solution we've seen in some time for the legacy and enterprise-wide computer system problems that continue to plague many of the country's largest businesses. But the fact is that they said it all in a song.

The correct solutions today (and the enormous set of opportunities they create for smart young businesses) for a great deal of the legacy leftovers, remnant and orphaned protocols, and general "spaghetti code" confusion that continues to impede important process improvements, speed and efficiency enhancements, and any amount of material innovation in these big businesses are actually pretty simple. Some of these things are sitting there in plain sight, but they're overlooked by the guys who've been staring at the same stale whiteboards for years and retreading the same tired paths. Rehashing the same old stew isn't going to help anyone get ahead.

The simple answer - as the boys used to sing in the 70's – is all about building a "bridge over troubled water". It's not about trying to implement the latest desperate attempt (in a long, sad series of stop-gap measures and bulked-up bandages) which simply adds complexity to the current code base and postpones the necessary progress to the ultimate solution. You can't save your way to these kinds of radical solutions and you can't do it on the cheap either. But you won't get anywhere at all if you don't have a new and clear vision of where you're headed.

Here's the hard truth: the guys that got them there and built the problems that these companies are living with today aren't gonna get them to the next level of solutions. They're committed to their code with their embedded approaches and they're stuck trying to drag those ancient albatrosses forward into the future. It's a heavy load; it's the wrong strategy; and it's doomed to be more of the same under the best of circumstances. There's only one way you're headed if you're looking through the rear view mirror and that's backwards.

Frankly, to solve these kinds of problems, these companies need to get help and a fresh set of uninvested eyes from the outside and they need a strategy that builds a new, streamlined and simply sufficient solution right over the top of the problems (a "bridge") rather than another massive rewriting project that takes forever, costs a fortune, moves the same deck chairs around, and basically repaints the flagpole. Even the best Band-Aid is no bargain in the long run.

And what is very interesting is that these aren't cases where the new kids on the block are going to be suggesting new things to be doing or even new ways to do them – they're creating bypasses, express lanes and other new streamlined and fast channels to get the work done. They know the inputs; they know the desired outputs and results; and they're free to determine the least costly and most efficient ways to connect them. It's as easy as that once you get over the old news.

It all comes down to a simple realization, but it's one that's very difficult for the folks whose history is closely tied to what's been built in the past to admit. They need to acknowledge that their hard work and voluminous body of code can be readily and easily replicated and, in fact, efficiently superseded by simpler and more straightforward solutions. Today it's not about the size of the effort and the lines of code created; it's about speed and throughput and – as often as not – the simpler and more elegant the code, the faster the results generated and the happier the end users.

The trick for the old guys is not to take this stuff personally. No one said that life was fair or that anything lasted forever. And the trick for good managers is to acknowledge that the rules of the game have changed and – while it's not exactly fair – it's something that needs to be recognized and lived with.

The best approach (and it's still not an easy one) is to recognize and appreciate that the guys who built the ships that got us to this point were the explorers and the trailblazers and the real inventors in many cases, but their path was long and hard and costly and full of false starts, wrong paths, broken code, etc. along with plenty of do-overs. But they still got there and that's a true accomplishment and something to be respected.

Unfortunately now for them, whether it's fair or not, the new guys with the new eyes get the easy job – they already know where the goal line is and they know what works and what the users need and now they have a much easier job – they simply need to build a bridge that spans the old code and connects the past with the future as quickly and inexpensively as possible. And that's all about execution rather than exploration and that's what it's going to take to finally break out of the restrictions and legacies of the past in order to build the paths to the future.

The way forward isn't through the morass; it's over the top.

It turns out – in a perfect world – that much of what every kid would ideally learn in school is, in part, a working familiarity with the same attitudes, approaches and outlooks which we try to have our aspiring 1871 entrepreneurs internalize as a lasting part of their overall experience with us.

Today, there's no question that we learn a great deal through indirect lateral learning (see http://www.inc.com/howard-tullman/when-to-steal-from-other-founders.html) which comes principally from our observations of the trials and tribulations (and the successes and failures) of the others around us who are engaged in similar or parallel activities. Not only does misery love company; the fact is that the cheapest and least painful education available today is making sure that you don't repeat someone else's mistakes while you're building your business. In addition, peer-to-peer communications are a constant and growing part of our lives and thus we also learn every day directly from each other and from others across the globe.

When you combine these new knowledge sources with the many independent media and content channels which are now readily and continually available to all of us, it's increasingly clear that most of us are learning as much or more from the digital universe as we have to date or will hereafter learn from any traditional and/or formal education programs.

And, although the debate continues to rage as to which startup skills can be taught, it's very clear that a great deal can be learned by new business builders who immerse themselves in the critical and creative entrepreneurial mass which an incubator like 1871 provides – especially when all of the other component parts of the startup ecosystem are also present in the same physical location – including hundreds of other new entrepreneurs, universities, VCs, experienced serial entrepreneurs and committed mentors, angel investors, city and state representatives, substantial educational resources and programming, alumni businesses, etc.

But we need to figure out exactly how to make sure that the policies and programs in our schools are designed and organized in ways which help our kids learn these same entrepreneurial life skills as early and as fully as possible. It's not about filling their heads with ancient philosophies and rote facts; it's about filling their hearts with a passion for learning and the desire to make a difference – to make their efforts and their lives meaningful - both in the near term and in the long run. And it's a process which can't be started too soon.

Here are the top 10 "need to knows" on my list and a brief comment on each:

(1) You Get What You Work for, Not What You Wish for

In the real world, effort trumps talent and inspiration without execution means nothing. Our attitude is that, while we may not always outsmart the other guys, we will always out-prepare and outwork them.

(2) Keep Raising the Bar

Successive approximation beats postponed perfection. The fact is that you get better by getting better and you do that by constantly raising the bar and iterating like mad. In a world of fast followers and global competition, we want to always be on the move and moving forward.

(3) Shoot for the Stars

If you don't ask, you never get. Someone is gonna be first and grab the best seat in the place and it might as well be you, but not if you don't go for it. As Michael Jordan used to say: you miss 100% of the shots you don't take. And, if you don't bother to ask, the answer's always "No".

(4) Don't Sell Yourself Short

There are always plenty of people who will tell you why you can't do something – mainly because they haven't tried or couldn't do it themselves. Don't allow yourself to be defined or constrained by other people's limitations. Ya never know whether you can do it until you try. And every day the people who are doing it are blowing by the ones who insist that it can't be done.

(5) Start Now with What You Have

Waiting for the perfect moment and all the stars to align won't get you anywhere and waiting for a schedule or permission will get you left in the dust by the people who are just getting out there and getting things done. Nothing will ever get done if every objection and problem needs to be resolved before you start. The time will never be just right, but the time to start is always "now".

(6) Nobody said Life was Fair

Sometimes things just don't work out. The best entrepreneurs understand that no one makes all the right choices or decisions – the trick is to learn from all of them – good or bad – and to not make the same mistakes over again. And, while hard work is necessary for success, it's not sufficient in itself or any certain guarantee. Luck, timing, tools, the quality and commitment of your team, etc. – all of these are also success factors. And even when everything aligns, there are still too many instances to count where the world seems to have conspired to kill your dream. This is why resilience and the ability to get over the past and get on with the future are just as crucial as the perseverance that it often takes to stick with your idea through thick and thin. Fall down three times; get up four times.

(7) Never Play the Blame Game

People can always find an excuse or blame their circumstances for why things didn't happen or work out the way they hoped. But the ones who will always succeed are the ones who take whatever they are handed and make those conditions and constraints work. Hoping for something better isn't an effective strategy – it's just a formula for further disappointment. When you start blaming others for your problems, you give up your power and the ability to make critical changes.

(8) It's Only a "No" for Now

Winners keep pressing and never take "No" for a final answer – just an opportunity to try harder. Excellence and real results are always based ultimately in perseverance – sticking around long enough so that even if you can't win them over, at least you will eventually wear down their resistance. There are no shortcuts or tricks to make the path easier and there's no finish line either.

(9) Sometimes the Baby Just is Ugly

Kids who think they'll live forever (and who are frankly too young to even understand the consequences of many of their actions) have no concept of opportunity costs or the fact that your time is probably the scarcest resource you have. Sadly, it's often the same kind of problem with passionate, but inexperienced young entrepreneurs. They stick with things way too long and end up beating a dead horse when they should be moving on. They regularly forget the first rule of holes: when you're in one, stop digging.

(10) Make Something that Makes a Difference

It's hard to get out of your own head when you're young, but it's never too early to explain the value of being connected to something – a cause, an idea, a team, etc. – that's bigger than yourself. At 1871, we say that you can't be in this stuff for the money – it's just too hard and it's really not about making money or even about making a living. It's about making a life worth living and one that makes a difference and a contribution to others.

TULLMAN'S TRUISMS

ANYTHING YOU CAN MEMORIZE, I CAN GOOGLE

While VCs often talk in their peculiar shorthand about quickly figuring out whether a certain startup's customers – regardless of their species or breed – are going to eat the company's dog food (meaning a newly-introduced product or service); it's equally important for the company's management to make sure – whenever it's appropriate – that their own team members are also fully committed to the business's own offerings and that they're using them as much and as often as possible. The car guys in Detroit figured this out (sadly it was one of the few things they did) when it was made clear to every employee that it was absolutely verboten to even think of driving a foreign car to your job at Ford or GM.

This wasn't ever simply a loyalty test – it's just a fact of life that it's much easier and more convincing for someone in sales to provide his or her own testimonial and to demonstrate through examples from their own actual experience the value and benefits of what they're selling. You never want to be the shoemaker's kids and you never want to be in the position of urging someone else to do something that you haven't or wouldn't do yourself. It's just not credible. No one should ever take advice from someone who doesn't have to live with the consequences.

At 1871, we use the tools, apps and products of a number of our member companies who started out here because (a) we should and (b) because they work. Then we make it our business to spread the word. And that's why I'm so impressed with the Chicago-based branch of the Startup Institute which is located within 1871 and which is just cranking out amazing results – not only in their own operations – but, more importantly, in terms of providing a constant and growing stream of talented and excited new employees for so many of our member companies.

I think that 1871 companies alone are hiring about 10% to 15% of each Startup Institute cohort as they graduate from the program. Some of these firms have already hired 4 or 5 people from the SI program and they keep coming back for more. In terms of attracting, training and retaining talent for Chicago companies in general, over 90 Chicago-based businesses as well as major corporations have employed SI graduates and alumni so far. This is pretty big news for an operation that's only been at it for a relatively short time.

As it happens, the overall population of 1871 aligns almost ideally with the target populations which the Startup Institute seeks to train. This is why I think it's working so well for all concerned. We have newbies for sure. We have career changers. We have smart folks with real experience who need a tech and digital refresh – or better yet – a couple of partners. We have people that did one thing for a long, long time and are now looking to pursue their passion. And we have plenty of folks full of energy and passion who are looking for the right place to make a difference.

But what's most interesting about the whole situation is what it says about the kinds of employees that both our early-stage businesses as well as the companies entering the growth stage are going to need to keep adding to their teams. And, if you're running a startup anywhere, there's a lesson here for you as well.

One surprising hint: it's not just about programmers, engineers and other techies. And it's also not just newbies or people looking for their first jobs right out of school. Our businesses need (1) talented sales people, (2) serious management help as they scale, (3) domain experts to help identify real customer needs and requirements, and (4) even a little gray hair.

And that's where the unique make-up of the day-to-day population of 1871 comes in. Very few people realize just how diverse and robust a group of entrepreneurs can be when you have 1500 people a day showing up at your doorstep. Each day. Every day. One particularly interesting fact is that our largest single group of members is composed of people with more than 14 years of industry experience. Not youngsters and not newbies.

1871 today isn't just about any one group or type of individuals. It's not just for people interested in tech – in no small part - because tech is a part of everything today. You couldn't avoid being tech-enabled if you tried. Nor is 1871 limited or appropriate only just for people of a certain age or only for those interested in simply a single industry or market sector. Passion, innovation, inspiration and entrepreneurship come in every size and shape and we welcome them all.

And the most important thing that you learn about people when you're building a business – which is the very reason that the alumni of the Startup Institute make such great hires and can hit the ground running and start making a difference immediately – is that to build a great business, you need all kinds of people with different attitudes, aptitudes and abilities. Trying to hire only people who look, act and reason just like you is a fool's mission. It's the diversity of ideas and even ideals that makes all the difference.

One of the oldest clichés in business school is the statement that "customers want ¼" holes, not ¼"drills" which is a pithy way of simply reinforcing the idea that the primary focus and messaging in terms of presenting your product or service to the customer (and ultimately properly setting and then meeting his or her expectations) should be as closely aligned as possible with the results (benefits) that the customers are seeking rather than on other less critical features or concerns. People don't want copiers; they want clean, quick and inexpensive copies from machines that never break, jam or run out of toner.

Professor Clay Christensen describes this type of exercise and investigation as one where you are trying to correctly identify what the customer wants the product or service to do. In his classic example concerning breakfast beverages at McDonald's, he says the task is to figure out the job that the customer is "hiring" the milkshake to do. It turns out that that job was largely related to keeping early morning customers who were facing long commutes to the office from being bored as they drove. The milkshakes gave them something to do for an extended period of time and something to suck on while they whiled away the miles. So don't ever say that McShakes don't suck.

In earlier times, this results-oriented approach was known as "solution selling", but for me that particular phrase has taken on an interesting new meaning which grows out of a pretty fundamental change in the nature of many of the products we are now manufacturing.

In today's economy (except for consumables like toner and ink for our printers), the in-service life of all kinds of products has been so dramatically extended that the basic underlying business models of major manufacturers and entire industries have been changed. These days, (because the useful life of products which manufacturers could previously and reliably predict would become obsolete or used up in a reasonable timeframe) has now been lengthened to the point where they effectively last forever, the manufacturers have had to begin to re-envision their businesses.

No one smart thinks that they can simply sell a single product anymore. If you want to survive, you sell services and solutions – lifetime relationships and continuing connections - rather than transactional and occasional encounters. I wrote recently that the book business these days isn't about books anymore. (See http://www.inc.com/howard-tullman/the-case-for-pursuing-massive-growth.html) The point there was that the former publishers were all morphing their businesses into learning management companies which could sell protectable systems and services rather than individual books. The need for similar migratory movement is even clearer in various manufacturing sectors.

Take light bulbs for example. They don't burn out the way they used to and – as a result – the bulb manufacturers have basically improved themselves out of a major portion of what used to be their most consistent flow of recurring revenues. In any given cycle, they're selling fewer and fewer bulbs and there's zero prospect of a return to the old days. Even more importantly, after you've solved the power consumption issues and the longevity concerns; what do you really have left to sell to your customers or to differentiate your bulbs or fixtures from anyone else's?

The answer is that – and this is exactly what the big bulb guys are doing with their biggest institutional customers - you sell bundled "lighting" which is really the turn-key, all-in, "solution" that the customers are looking for rather than bulbs, fixtures, lumens, etc. and thus you avoid getting your brains beaten in and your margins crushed by price-based, foreign competitors. Lighting customers (big and little) just want to see where they're going and not worry about anything more than that. This approach is actually a return to the old days when the electric companies used to basically give you a bunch of bulbs for free from time to time as long as you'd come get them. Even back then, they knew that they were selling a solution and a service rather than a bunch of bulbs. And this is just the beginning.

Once you start thinking about the solution for a given problem like transportation – how, for example, do I most efficiently get from here to there - you start to focus on a broad range of available choices for intermodal transportation (planes, trains, buses and Ubers) rather than on the need to rent or own a particular form of vehicle. It's the same story with hotels and Airbnb – you're looking for clean, safe, inexpensive shelter – not a particular chain or brand of hotel. Utility, mobility, convenience and speed are all far more important to consumers today than possession or ownership and there's really no going back. (See http://www.inc.com/howard-tullman/why-gen-y-doesnt-care-about-cars.html)

137 – YOUR KEY EMPLOYEES AREN'T FUNGIBLE – THEY'RE INVALUABLE

You would think it would be clear that any business's most valuable workers aren't multi-colored (but otherwise uniform) Checkers pieces (although – given their varying skills and capabilities - they might be more properly thought of as chessmen) which can be swayed, swapped, moved around and motivated at will. But this fact of life is apparently not obvious to millions of managers at every level in organizations of all sizes who continue to believe that – in almost everything involving people – one size or one approach fits all.

As we try to bring innovative and entrepreneurial behaviors into all kinds of industries, we find that - especially the senior managers - functionally assume (even though we obviously know better in our hearts) that – in a world of radical and constant changes – within and outside of our own businesses - every one of our team members will accept and react to the new and challenging behaviors that these changes will require gladly, readily and in the same fashion. This approach seems to be largely because we remain stuck with the last remnants of the tired old thinking that was derived from the precepts of the industrial revolution and thereafter deployed in both our schools and in many of our businesses.

In the schools, we're still trying to teach everyone the same things at the same time. Too many schools believe that one size fits all and that a single solution and a single "sage on the stage" spewing wisdom to a room full of sleepy students is the way to go and further that everyone there will actually learn the same things at the same rate. This is the last gasp of the mechanical factory model and it's hard to kill because – truth be told – it's cheap, it's orderly, and it's a lot less work for the teachers as well.

But don't blame most of the teachers – they'd much rather be actually teaching than spending a big part of every day with bureaucratic bullshit and paperwork. This whole educational system is beyond stupid, but it's so very, very slow to change. Differentiated learning ("to each his or her own") is the only approach that makes the slightest sense and we have the inexpensive tools, tablets and other technologies that can make it a reality today if we only have the will to make it so. (See my prior INC. education posts: http://www.inc.com/howard-tullman/why-education-needs-innovation.html and http://www.inc.com/howard-tullman/chicago-teachers-and-entrepreneurs.html. Here's hoping that the schools start to improve sometime soon.

We have a different variation of the same problem in too many businesses today. We think that everyone has basically learned the identical things in school and therefore that they will – by and large – perform in the same manner with roughly the same results and outcomes. We're still judging these employee "books" by their covers (and evaluating recent graduates by their inflated grades and grandiose degrees) instead of taking the time to test and determine the real skill sets and benefits that each of them brings to our businesses and, more importantly, the real impact that each of them can have on our company's workflow, overall efficiency, other employees, and bottom line. Credentials and degrees are a long way from competencies – they're basically crutches for lazy HR people – just as org charts and job descriptions don't begin to tell you what's really going on in your company.

People (and today's typical management tools) haven't changed in a long, long time and the rules are still the same: what gets measured is what supposedly gets done. Most people do what you inspect and not (sadly) what you expect. But, even though every day our analytical capacities grow and we have more and more data available about almost every aspect of our employees' performance, it turns out that very often we aren't paying attention to the right and most important metrics. We pay way more attention to punctuality than to productivity. We've got plenty of measurements, but they don't tell us the real story. And we're drowning in data that doesn't help us determine who's really driving the bus.

In order to make a material difference as managers and change agents, and to effectively bring about the important improvements and advances needed in our organizations, we have to be quantifying and measuring our key people's individual impact and influence, rather than merely gathering stats and information about their attendance or their relative positions. Only when we have a new and clear perspective on which of our employees can – directly and indirectly – be the most helpful in promulgating the attitudes and behaviors required for the desired changes can we figure out which of them can help us get the critical messages across to the remainder of the team. And given that better than 75% of all new initiatives introduced in large organizations fail; it's beyond critical to find these people in your own organization sooner rather than later if you want to be responsive to the ever-changing demands of the marketplace and stay competitive.

The good news is that, as you might expect, there are new data and analytics-based startups which are creating the tools that the biggest and smartest companies and other institutions will use to more effectively determine how to deploy and position their best employees and how to optimize the performance and impact of those key players. One of the most interesting new companies I have seen in a while is *Syndio (*https://synd.io*)* which creates actionable analytics about people in organizations of all sizes. But in doing so, the *Syndio* folks start from a slightly different place than you might expect.

It's a simple twist, but it makes a big difference. We all understand that, in rolling out just about anything, it pays to get the "good guys" on your side including the leaders, the stars, the celebs, and even the loud (and often obnoxious) voices that people will often listen to for whatever reason. We think of these people as "influencers" and we all get that it's better to have them in our camp rather than resisting our programs or dumping on our ideas.

But it often turns out – especially as companies grow – that we only think we know who these people are and we're often wrong. Lots of these folks are "all hat and no cattle" as my friends in Texas like to say and sometimes the most effective folks are actually the "friends in low places" rather than the blowhards in the big offices. A couple of critical care nurses in a hospital can save more lives by modeling and enforcing good hand-washing disciplines (among the staff <u>and</u> the doctors) than most of the surgeons I the course of a year.

And even if and when we can identify and pick the right types of people; what the science of networks and influence says about delivering really effective campaigns and results is somewhat different than you'd guess. It turns out that, although the people are undoubtedly important – role models, change agents, information spreaders - among others, the real gating factor is their relative positions within and the strength and size of their networks within the business. It just so happens that a movement can be started or a systemic change effectively initiated and grown within an organization just as easily by a mere mortal with a strong set of internal connections (and a powerful message) as it is can be by some superstar orator, politician or other impassioned advocate. Whole governments in the Arab Spring were brought low by the selfless and desperate acts of a few individuals.

But the trick is that - without new tools and systems – growing businesses and large organizations are highly unlikely to find all of these people and properly recruit them to the cause. As a result, their new initiatives and programs are diluted and far less impactful than they could and should be. They need programs like *Syndio's* which overlay their traditional HR data with the new social and network analytics that identify and quantify the real, respected movers and shakers and the scale and scope of their influence networks within the business.

Syndio can implement these types of analytics quickly and easily for virtually everyone in a given workforce without any significant hit to ongoing operations or existing information or HR systems. And, once they are in place, they actually become bi-directional tools as well. Not only can the management's messages be more effectively distributed; these identified individuals can and do regularly become the sources for all manner of input and feedback from the field which would not otherwise be available at all to the senior management team. It's a benefit with a double bottom line.

But the real bottom line is very simple. Top down communications in business today are largely a waste of time and breath. Treating your employees as a homogeneous population to which you can broadcast a single message won't work any better for your business than it has for the TV networks of old. Peer to peer, customized communications to and from people we are directly and regularly connected with and whose opinions we value and respect are the only ways we want to learn today. People don't commit much of anything to companies today – they commit to other people.

TULLMAN'S TRUISMS

ONE RABBIT BEATS TEN TURTLES

When most people talk about how difficult and challenging it is to be an entrepreneur, they actually focus on the most obvious things which, frankly, every entrepreneur should already know – how long and hard you have to work, how risky and difficult it is to try to start something new, how unclear and uncertain things are going to be throughout the journey, etc. But honestly, you can learn about any of these things from about a billion different books which are out there dealing with the trials and tribulations of starting a business. None of these concerns should come as a surprise or as anything that the entrepreneur didn't know he or she was signing up for long before they set out on their venture. They might have been kidding themselves about how hard or easy things were gonna be, but they can't really say that they didn't know.

However, it's not these basic bumps in the road that are the make-or-break considerations and the hardest hurdles for entrepreneurs to deal with as they're building their businesses. And they're also not the ones that create the heartaches and those random gray hairs that pop up years before they should in the fullest heads of hair. The toughest and most painful parts of the process are all about two things: personal (sometimes moral) choices and decisions about people. If you haven't had to deal with some of the problems yet, just give it time because you will be dealing with some of them soon enough whether your business is going gangbusters or slipping sideways or headed south.

These really aren't matters of "if"; they're all about "when". Part One of your job is to be ready. Part Two of your job is to decide how to handle each situation. Here's a hint – there will be plenty of tough questions and hard choices as you build your company, but you've only got one reputation.

(1) Miss A Milestone

It happens to almost everyone at some point, but it still hurts. It's hard to swallow and even harder to explain to all those folks who thought you walked on water. This is one of the relatively easy situations to handle after you get over the initial embarrassment and wipe the egg off your face. Just explain the situation to everyone (insiders and investors) clearly and quickly and describe the proposed next steps (and concrete solutions) to get the business back on the right track. Don't play the blame game and don't ruin a good apology with excuses. And don't waste too much time dwelling on the past, playing "woulda, shoulda, coulda", or looking backwards. Learn what you can from the mistakes you made and keep moving forward.

(2) Break A Promise

In Hollywood, we used to say that the most important rule of all was also the simplest. It succinctly described celebrity, business and life in the movies all in a single sentence: "I'll love you 'til I don't." Similarly, when Steve Jobs would abruptly change his mind and his direction on a project or a product, he wouldn't explain or apologize. He'd just say: "I'm doing what's right for the business right now." Whatever went before was past and quickly forgotten. He had plenty of issues, but (once he was back in the saddle) he had almost no "business" baggage. In tennis or golf, it's called "in-game amnesia". If you're thinking about the last error, you're far more likely to blow the next shot as well.

The moral of these stories is a pretty basic tenet of Startup Management 101. If you're stuck in the past (or bound by your best guesses from back then), you're not going to change the future. Despite our best intentions and best-laid plans, the world keeps spinning and changing and our commitments and even our most sincere and well-intended promises sometimes don't survive the chaos of rapid change and the required responses as well as the back-and-forth that goes on in between and – as often as not – they shouldn't.

None of us has a crystal ball so we can only do the best we can in the moment. Keeping your word isn't some antiquated Victorian virtue or a nonsense notion in today's world of sadly situational ethics, but it's only one very important consideration as you balance and try to triage the onslaught of confusing challenges and "either/or" choices which your business is going to inevitably face. There are no magic solutions or easy resolutions to these dilemmas. All you can do is to do your best under the circumstances.

(3) Tell A White Lie

Sometimes a little inaccuracy can save tons of explanation and many hours of arguments and lectures, but it's a slippery slope. And the sins of omission in this department are just as bad as white lies or taking advantage of the fact that some director, investor, customer or employee just neglected to ask the right questions. It's not on them to tell the truth – it's on you and – you'll learn over time – that the truth only hurts when you don't tell it. No one likes bad news, but everyone in the investment world really hates surprises and the longer you wait to tell someone the right story and the whole story, the more damage you do to the relationship and to your reputation. It's never easy to say what no one wants to hear, but it's often absolutely essential and it's always the leader's job to do the deed and take the heat that's sure to follow.

(4) Make A Payroll from Your Pocket

Sometimes enough is enough (even for an entrepreneur) and, as obvious as it may seem to outsiders, it's still never that easy to admit. Dreams die hard, but there are plenty of times when the baby's just ugly and needs to be put out of its misery. There are rarely skid marks in a startup – you hit the wall pretty abruptly when the show is over. And yet, there are other cases when it seems that there's just one more hill to get over or one more sale to make and then the business will be in the clear and on its way. But, as you look around, you realize that you're the only one left in the room thinking about reaching into your pocket for further funding.

If you've got more cash than sense, this is usually a pretty easy decision. But, a much harder choice arises when you have limited funds and you've already bet the ranch and borrowed as much as you can and now you have to choose between competing mouths to feed and one of those competitors is your family's and your kids' futures. Business doesn't get more personal than this and you have to be VERY careful that your ego and your stubbornness don't overcome your common sense and your most critical responsibilities and obligations.

One of the skills that makes someone a great entrepreneur is tunnel vision, but when it's not just you on the cutting edge, you've got to make sure before you jump into a further swamp that it really is a light that you see at the end of the next tunnel and not a big nasty freight train coming the other way. And – like it or not – it's also not a call you get to make all on your own because it's not just your future that you're foolin' with. This is another really hard conversation to have with all of the interested parties, but you owe it to everyone who helped get you started and stuck with you through all the ups and downs to make sure that they're there when the rubber really hits the road and the business hangs in the balance.

(5) Give Yourself Some Goodies

Entrepreneurs are basically big crybabies and spend a fair amount of their time feeling sorry for themselves and grossly under-appreciated. They feel taken advantage of, conspired against, and constantly let down by people who don't share their crazy zeal. And I'm just talking about the healthy ones. You can forget about the truly paranoid ones and you'd do well to steer clear of them. A good rule of thumb is to never work for someone who has more emotional problems than you do.

So, you might ask, what does this have to do with you? Well, it turns out that it's a pretty short step from feeling victimized to deciding (in your own addled brain) that you're pretty much entitled to take whatever you can get or get away with. And it always starts small and gets worse over time. And, whether you believe it at the moment or not, you will be there one of these days. It's just another inevitable part of the process. Too much work, too little family time, too much stress, too few strokes – and one day the switch just flips – and the hard choices are staring you in the face.

Expensive meals and travel, hi-tech gadgets and gear you'd never pay for yourself, sports tickets, special events and other goodies for the guys, etc. All "justified" in the name of marketing, morale, and media among other claims and excuses. And all that's basically really going on is that you're taking your company's and your investors' money and putting in your own pocket.

And, believe me, once this bullshit begins, there's no end to the dollars that can disappear and no limit to the rationalizations and outright deceptions that accompany this kind of sick and deluded behavior. Once you start feeling like the business owes you a bunch, it's amazing how quickly that comes to include just about anything you can imagine. Redecorating your home "office", all kinds of loans and advances that never seem to get repaid, cash advances at the strangest times and places, etc.

The truth is that you wouldn't begin to believe the crazy justifications you hear (sadly after the fact and the damage has been done) to explain what any sane person would simply call stealing or worse. You may feel that this shoe will never fit you and that's great. But I'd say it still makes sense to be on your guard and watch your step.

(6) Fire A Friend

When you're all sitting around in the garage getting started, it's pretty easy to say just about anything about things to come in the future and (mostly) to convince even yourself that you mean it. And in your heart you probably do, but your head already knows better. "Friends forever" is one of those promises that (in the world of startups) are almost always made to be broken. As time passes and your company grows (and the demands of the real world start to intrude), you'll quickly discover that: (a) you don't get to make all the decisions by yourself any longer; (b) that the needs of the business can quickly outgrow the talents and skills of even the best of your friends and co-founders; and (c) that – like it or not – in building a business and especially a company culture, majority rules. If your closest friend can't cut it with his or her co-workers, you absolutely know who's got to go. That doesn't make it any less painful to disappoint and fire a friend (and you'll find yourself getting mad at the faceless others who are "making" you do it), but – in the end – it's the right and only thing to do for the good of the company. And you need to "own" the decision. Don't complain or tell anyone that "they" made you do it or that you had no choice (even if you didn't) because when you blame these hard decisions on others, you're giving up your own credibility and authority. If it's the right decision and the right call, then it's yours to make and yours to live with.

(7) Do It All Over Again
They say it's hard to go home again and I think that's probably right. But I know for a fact that it's sheer torture to have to blow up your whole business and start all over again. And most people just aren't up to the task – they give it the good old college try, it doesn't work out for them, and then they go get a day job to feed themselves and their families. And there's nothing wrong with that for them – it's just not how it works for a true entrepreneur. And frankly, I'm not sure that you can even call yourself a true entrepreneur if you haven't had to go thru one or two of these near-death experiences yourself.

People that get it right the first time and never have to re-trench or re-load might be the smartest folks around. Or they could just have been remarkably lucky – right time, right place, right investors, connections, etc. For myself, I like to bet on the ones who've been thru the Valley of Death and come out the other side (maybe not smiling), but with their energy unchanged, their passion intact, their commitment strengthened, their teams largely still together, and their eyes always on the prize. They are the scarred and battle-hardened pros that I call real entrepreneurs.

TULLMAN'S TRUISMS

THERE IS NO FINISH LINE

I wrote recently about how tough it was for most of the relatively new and highly varied coding schools which have popped up over the last year or two to cost-effectively and consistently attract sufficient numbers of students with common enough goals and expectations (and skill sets) to make their businesses viable. (See http://www.inc.com/howard-tullman/how-to-create-a-business-in-the-adult-education-space.html). Frankly, I'm not that confident that most of these newbie "schools" will even survive, much less do a great job of teaching their students anything of lasting value.

On the other hand, some of the places which have developed tightly-focused courses (especially those targeting Apple's tool sets) like those which are being offered by programs like *Mobile Makers* – the leading iOS mobile boot camp - which has been doing this kind of training for years in Chicago (and now in San Francisco) provide a real value to their students because – right along with *Apple* – they keep raising the bar and constantly upgrading and updating their materials. And this – to be precise – is exactly why the traditional schools (at any level) can't compete. They simply can't adapt and change their courses fast enough to keep up with the accelerating pace of change.

In a separate piece, talking specifically about what we should expect our students to take away from coding classes, I argued that the most important considerations weren't the particulars of the coding skills which they learned in the moment (because they would soon change), but instead they were the life skills around approximation, iteration, curiosity and confidence which would provide the long-lasting value and benefits. (See http://www.inc.com/howard-tullman/the-real-benefits-of-coding.html).

As the Apple World Wide Developer Conference wraps up this week, it's really encouraging to see that *Apple* has upped its game with the introduction of *Swift 2.0* and that 2.0 is starting to really close the gap and catch up to *Objective C* (which is plenty powerful, but woefully complicated). This, of course, is exactly what successive approximation is all about. You get better and better and closer and closer over time and you never stop. In the next year or two at the outside, I would expect that *Swift 2.0* will be the primary foundation for iPhone development going forward.

Not that *Objective C* will be disappearing any time soon, but the smart developers and folks looking to upgrade and upskill themselves need to be thinking about how to straddle and support both languages which will be important in the *XCode* development environment for the next decade at least. It's especially instructive, as I noted above, that *Swift* itself is only about a year old and it's already being dramatically enhanced and expanded. That's the autocatalytic rate of change (where each change lessens the time to its successor) which most of the traditional players in the adult education world can't remotely keep up with.

In fact, the WWDC conference and the announcements to come aren't even over yet and yet I was really pleased to see a recent note that *Mobile Makers* in particular (I'm sure there are others that will eventually wake up to these opportunities) is incorporating these new *Swift* changes into its July classes. Of course, it helps that they were at the conference and that they are part of a firm that uses these brand-new tools every day to build real-world solutions for its clients.

Even more importantly, *Apple* also announced (not unlike the same comments made in the conversation I had last week with Satya Nadella who's the new CEO of *Microsoft*) that *Swift 2.0* would be open source and that it would work on Linux. This is a further indication of Apple's direction and its plans to create the dominant development languages in the *Apple* world. It also demonstrates the broader available markets and employment opportunities which these new commitments are creating for developers trained in Swift 2.0.

So, I guess that the bottom line for me is pretty clear. Learning the newest coding skills makes a great deal of sense for a lot of people right now. If you have the necessary skills, the jobs are out there. And, if you want to be sure that – as much as humanly possible – you are "future-proofing" your educational investment, you need to find the schools (like *Mobile Makers*) and the courses that are created by the early adopters, the rapid responders, and the only ones who are able to deliver tomorrow's goods instead of yesterday's news. Otherwise, it's not worth your time or money.

140 – AN OUNCE OF INTUITION IS WORTH A POUND OF PERSUASION

There's nothing quite like the feeling you get when your intuition pays off and people behave exactly as you predicted (and hoped for or dreaded) or when things turn out precisely as you expected. You could also call these moments the result of educated guesses or extra-sensory perceptions, but however you describe the process, the exhilaration's exactly the same. It's always a rush to be right.

It's not just a game of "I told you so" (although you did), it's really the satisfaction of knowing in your heart that these kinds of outcomes aren't actually just happy accidents or good breaks – they're another example in the long line of things that happen because you worked hard to make them happen. You always want to be driving the train, not chasing the caboose.

And there's nothing that makes the selling process easier than getting a jump on the customer and getting out in front of the competition by doing a little precision guesswork. It's just human nature that we'd all much prefer to be pulled in the direction toward which we were already inclined rather than pushed into something which we're not really sure is right for us or our business. Pounds of persuasion will never make up for even a little insight into what's really important and what's driving the customers' decisions. That's why I often say that - while it's hard to push a rope, it's actually pretty simple to pull a string. Or, as The Lone Ranger used to say: it's so much easier to ride the horse in the direction he's headed.

I have come to believe in matters of both intuition and magic in the way that Penn & Teller do – they show you how the trick is being done and you still can't figure out what exactly is going on. And what you take away from the experience of watching them perform is not some mystical sense (we all still know these are tricks); instead you leave feeling that you've witnessed the highest level of professionals executing difficult tasks in a craft that takes hundreds of hours of preparation, patter and patience.

It turns out that intuition – which can make or break so many things in your business and in your life – isn't something that's given only to the few. It's a skill that anyone can develop and one that grows more powerful as you continue to use it. Everyone has the same chance to build their own crystal ball – you just have to do the work and spend the time. It's exactly like the old saying about luck – the harder you work; the luckier you get. But first you have to know what the tools and techniques are that you should use in order to turn yourself into an intuitive wizard.

Get a Calendar and Track Your Customers' Schedules

So much of the world of business happens on a schedule and yet way too many people are either ignorant of that fact or oblivious to exactly how important timing is to successful sales. If your customers' aren't ready to listen or you're pitching them at the wrong time or place, it just doesn't matter what you're saying or what you've got to sell. I'm not talking simply about Salesforce ticklers or remembering someone's birthday; I'm talking about becoming a stone- cold expert on each client's procurement process and internal timing and planning cycles so you know how to be there when the customer is ready to buy. Too many salesmen in my life have returned empty-handed to report that they just missed the boat, they got beat out by someone who was there at the right time, or they got misled or misinformed by the client about their purchase schedule. You learn in this world that, in a lot of selling situations, the client doesn't want to say "No" to your face and so they tell you it's too soon or too early in their cycles to buy or commit until finally one day when they break the bad news to you that they went elsewhere. Just remember that in sales "it's always too soon until it's too late". Do your homework.

Anticipate and Prepare for the "Second Sale"

There's really no telling what's going to happen in the room when the customer and his finance team get together to review and decide whether to renew your arrangements with them. This is the "second sale" and it's even more critical than the first. Sadly, you won't be there, but that doesn't mean you can't influence the outcome by making sure that you have an advocate in the room (word to the wise – it will never be the bean counters) and that you have provided your spokesperson with the support, the cost benefits, the time savings, and the other justifications – basically all the ammunition necessary – in order to support the idea of staying in business with you. This stuff doesn't happen by itself and the customer rarely takes the initiative to go to bat for you. It's on you to make sure that there's a compelling case and lots of reasons to renew and that you get it in front of the right people at the right time.

Listen to the Customer and Put Yourself in Their Shoes

Many of us think that our customers are really good at complaining and making their feelings known, but the truth is that they aren't. They don't want to spend their time telling us what isn't working for them (or why) and they certainly don't want to argue about whose fault that is. Anyone who tells you that the customer understands that a given problem is their fault is an idiot. There are no customer problems. By and large, unhappy customers don't typically spend a lot of time sharing and communicating because they don't think that's their job. They get nervous or unhappy and things build and develop from there, but they rarely go out of their way to let you know. When they reach their limits, they just pick up and leave. It's your job to read the tea leaves, ask the questions that no one else is asking and get them the answers before the building burns down. Sometimes no one wants to ask the critical questions because it means hard conversations, tough choices and more work for people who are already busy and otherwise occupied. But that's small potatoes compared to losing the business or the customer or the tenant.

The bottom line: renewals are just business; terminations are personal and surprises are the worst of all. But, if you do your job and pay attention to your business and your customers – meeting their current needs and expectations - and anticipating their future desires and requirements, they'll think for sure that you've got a crystal ball hidden somewhere.

TULLMAN'S TRUISMS

AN ENTREPRENEUR'S JOB IS TO READ THINGS THAT AREN'T ON THE PAGE YET

So it turns out that – contrary to both the common wisdom and our own expectations - video didn't really kill the radio star after all. We continue to re-learn the same lesson over and over again that – by and large – in the areas of media and communication – the majority of our new distribution technologies and channels are consistently cumulative rather than destructive. We're also seeing that the "second" screen – the phone or tablet that sits beside us while we watch TV these days - is also adding to and enhancing the viewing experience rather than degrading or replacing it in our homes.

Having said that, there are clearly devices and products which are well on their way to the dustbin. As an example, I definitely wouldn't want to be a fax machine manufacturer these days for love or money. There's probably still a residual space and market opportunity for document scanners for a little while longer (although the next generation will likely be single-shot, image capture devices rather than the painfully-slow, mechanical transport beasts we use now), but, for the moment, "Send me a fax right away" is pretty much right up there with "Buy me a buggy whip while you're at the General Store" in terms of comments we rarely expect to hear any more.

At the same time, from the Department of Unintended Consequences, there are a host of changes and new behaviors coming down the pike that we really didn't expect or anticipate and these are going to impact our day-to-day behaviors and our businesses in a number of challenging ways. Here are a few – mainly driven by the merger of mobile and social and the advent of constant connectivity that you should be thinking about.

(1) Whither Wikipedia?

If everyone's on their phones and other mobile devices, who's actually gonna be left sitting in front of their desktop every day editing articles for *Wikipedia*? And honestly are they the kind of people that we would want to have their hands on the levers anyway? There seems to be a real risk of seeing the Groucho doctrine of adverse selection at work. (You'll recall that Groucho famously said that he wouldn't care to be a member of any club that would actually have him.)

Turns out that nobody knows the answer to these questions, but what is very clear – from the recent *NY Times* article and others - is that (a) it's getting harder and harder for *Wikipedia* to attract and promote new editors and (b) it's obviously a challenge for even the most digital of us to do any serious editing on a 3 inch mobile screen while you're on the move. So stand by and keep your fingers crossed because it's going to be a bumpy ride. (See http://www.nytimes.com/2015/06/21/opinion/can-wikipedia-survive.html.)

(2) So Long Search

Guess what else it sucks to do on your phone? Search. Search is a big pain and getting the answers back is even worse. Try accurately typing in a long-tail, multi-term reasonable search request for anything that really matters and you get a boatload back of "stuff", but very little of substance or consequence. It's just more lists and more links and more work. We don't really want ads or alternatives on the run – we want fast, simple answers. We want to ask our phones for answers – not interact with them or be interrogated by them while we struggle to get to the right result. How about the helpful hints and shortcuts they offer? To date – not so much of either. So we need to be thinking about new solutions and new protocols for search and we need them soon.

(3) Paperless is Pretty Much a Phantasy

Anyone who thinks that digital technology to date has helped us make a big leap forward in the paperless revolution should take a look around just about any office, business or school in the country. We're still drowning in paper for a variety of reasons and it's not going to change any time soon. In fact, as we find more and more occasions when we need to convert something digital to a hard copy to share at a meeting or sign on the fly, we're actually going to see the return of more printer stations that connect wirelessly to our devices at places like airports and more paper all around.

But, in many other cases where we're being aggressively encouraged to use our phones in lieu of paper, I'm pretty sure it's still a bad trade. I especially love to watch the daily juggling acts of the digital mavens that take place in the TSA lines at the airport. You think that it's fairly easy to exhibit your boarding pass on your phone (don't let it go to sleep while you're waiting in the line), and you also need your driver's license; you've got to dump your drinks; slip off your shades so they can see your eyes; get ready to bust your laptop out of your briefcase unless you're TSA-Pre; and remember to put your little cosmetics baggie on the conveyor belt as well. Turns out it's just as easy (or more so) to have a printed copy of your boarding pass with you when you enter the gauntlet. And forget about the iWatch being that much better since it's almost impossible to contort your arm and your body to swipe the thing without dropping something else or inadvertently turning the watch display off.

I've been saying for a while now that the context in which you communicate with your customers is actually more important and material to the success of the communication than the content itself. Your pitch can be Hollywood-quality and utterly heroic, but it will only hit home with those who hear it. We want to be talking to the folks who are willing to listen (and maybe even interested in our story) and not to the accidental observers, the poor suckers who are duped into clicking on random crap, or the people who don't even see our offerings because they're positioned "below the fold" in digital terms. I pity the fools who are still paying millions of dollars for videos "shown", but not seen by any human beings. And I can't wait for the media agencies who are still selling clicks instead of real, measurable results to credulous cretins to take their last desperate breaths and disappear.

In addition, it's increasingly clear that the source of the information and the credibility and connection of the referring/sharing party matters more than brand, celebrity endorsements, bogus rankings, etc. This is precisely why social is rapidly overtaking search as the primary source of everything we want to know about and why Facebook continues to blow away Google on every possible scale. We want to hear from the people who we know and whose opinions we value and not from the crowd or a bunch of strangers with nothing better to do. In addition, people with broad connections and networks within their organizations or cohorts turn out to have just as much (or more) viral power and amplification capacity as the for-sale "influencers" that everyone has been chasing for the last several years. We just not as dumb any more as the dopes on Madison Avenue continue to think we are. We are looking for authentic, accurate, actionable and timely information to make our buying decisions and it has become a reasonable and realistic expectation that this is exactly what the best and most competitive businesses will provide.

We call this approach "smart reach" – what I want, when I want it, wherever I am, and without asking. And it keeps getting smarter as our data and our tools continue to improve. What has changed the game recently is that the degrees of possible precision in targeting have continued to become more particular, detailed and granular. It's simply no longer sufficient to use proxies, placeholders, and best guesses in order to properly target and reach your audience. In addition, just knowing who the audience is isn't enough information any longer to be the predicate for an effective communication strategy: you've got to know what they are interested in and – even more importantly – when – in terms of their behaviors – when to reach out to them in order to complete the circle.

There's a simple reason that high value products searches are almost all taking place these days on Amazon and not Google or other search engines. When I'm engaged in a defined activity, I go to the power tool for that job – the specialist, not the GP – because I'm time-constrained and I'm trying to get something specific done. I'm not browsing and I'm not bored – it's not a discover exercise, it's a task.

And it's in this mode that the more valuable assistance and offerings you can provide for me (including suggestive selling and "nudge" commerce ideas), the more real value you are providing and the more receptive I am to the pitch. This seems pretty obvious and simple – you're being helpful and additive – not distracting or irrelevant. But it's a message that being missed by the masses of marketers at the moment. If you don't incorporate the mode of my behavior into your marketing model, you're missing the boat.

There's an interesting debate developing right now that addresses exactly these kinds of concerns. It has to do with the fact that – while Facebook has now caught up with (and possibly passed) YouTube in terms of the number of video views per day (call it 4 billion plus a day for each of them) – YouTube argues that the engagement levels of the viewers with each YouTube video are dramatically different and much more substantial and that this "context" makes YouTube a much more attractive channel for video ad placements. YouTube says that Facebook's video "views" suffer from all the same complaints I mentioned above – inadvertent views, distracted viewers, drive-bys, etc. – and that – as a result – the appropriate context for delivering the right video ad to an interested viewer isn't present. But, of course, when the videos you're being shown are sent by your friends and are actually theoretically meaningful to you, you could argue just the opposite - that I'm more likely to watch and be interested and receptive to related video content in this mode – than when I'm bored and scrolling thru random video recommendations on YouTube hoping to find the next great cat video.

In any case, the more major takeaway is that we do many materially different things when we're online (and also we behave differently when we're mobile – which almost everyone is these days – as opposed to when we're sitting in front of a screen) and our attitudes and receptivity to messaging varies as well. In order to reach us effectively, you've got to know how to determine and your plan needs to take into account that my interest in your message will vary greatly depending on whether I'm shopping, gaming, socializing, or just scrolling. Messages that aid and assist me in the process are welcomed – things that interrupt or are irrelevant are ignored.

So the bottom line is pretty simple: if your audience isn't listening, it doesn't matter what you are saying or how well you are saying it. The right pitch at the right point in time and place is the only message that matters and the only one that will make it thru the confusion and the clutter to the customer.

I think we have almost completed our efforts to stamp out venture tourism at 1871, our digital startup factory, in Chicago. There's a right way to do these things, but it's not by the bus load or by constantly bothering and interfering with the busy people who are trying to build their businesses. This isn't what we mean when we talk about the desirability and inevitability of disruption. Seeing the sights is nice, but doing real work together is what gets the right things done. If it was a straightforward or easy process, everyone would be doing it instead of talking about trying to do it or pretending to do it with fancy coffee makers and free beer.

And I'm also hoping that we're seeing the last few groups of corporate executives who think that 1871 is an entrepreneurial petting zoo where they can stop by for a short visit while they're downtown before a ball game or dinner and, apparently as a result of some new form of osmosis, have an ounce or two of innovation juice rub off on them and also discover that maybe a few drops of digital disruption have made it into their own systems. Here again, success and results are a matter of analysis and application rather than attitude and artifacts. You can't win a race with your mouth and all the pretenders and the props in the world won't change that simple fact.

But unfortunately putting an end to most of this superficial stuff in our place hasn't really solved the broader problem because it's just oozed out into the world at large and you've got a bunch of bozos taking their bullshit on the road and way too many people willing (for their own reasons) to help make that happen. Week in and week out these days, there's a tech event everywhere you look and a bunch of promoters and sponsors trying to sell tickets and fill seats along with a million media outlets looking for cheap content and talking heads to wrap their ads around. It appears that they'll basically take anyone they can get to talk about tech topics whether they have anything valuable to say or know what they're talking about. And putting five no-nothing speakers on a series of panels doesn't make things any better any more than combining two lukewarm cups of coffee makes a hot drink.

I know that this isn't a new phenomenon in any respect, but it really hurts our industry in particular (where a lot of older buyers and conservative executives are already reluctant and skittish to commit to new solutions) to have a situation where (a) the real talents are head down and too busy working their butts off (often in stealth mode) to participate in these circuses and, as a result, (b) the vacuum is being filled by wanna-bes and wishful thinkers who have loads of time on their hands because their own businesses are going nowhere. I find it especially interesting that a lot of these guys are the very big talkers who've never built or exited even one successful business on their own, but they're more than happy to tell you all day long how you should be building yours.

And - the saddest thing of all - is that a large reason that their own startups suck is that they're always on the road talking themselves up and focusing on manufacturing "buzz" instead of taking care of business. All the marketing in the world won't turn a pig into a prince if there's no substance behind the smart talk. And all the "promotion" that these guys keep saying is critical to get the word out about their companies (in order to justify their non-stop trips and travel) doesn't help make payroll or get the products built.

Great buzz comes from real results and the best solutions and not from the guys with the biggest set of lungs. It's even worse when they don't know what they are talking about and end up giving their audience a brutal mixture of bullshit and bad advice in the bargain which is obviously not a good deal for anyone.

I've just suffered through 3 or 4 of these business implosions and in every case you can point to an entrepreneur who was too busy spewing this stuff and drinking his own Kool-Aid to realize that his business was slipping through his fingers and down the drain. These screw ups come in all sizes and shapes, but here are 3 primary potholes and pieces of bad advice that you want to be sure to avoid. Remember that it's much smarter to miss the pothole entirely than it is to get a great deal on the tow truck that eventually pulls you out of the ditch.

(1) Don't fake it before you make it

Recently, I read about one of these blowhards explaining to an audience that – not too long ago - he didn't have a real product or service (as if he does today), but he was out there trying to sell investors and other gullible people his unbuilt and ultimately unscalable "solution" (which he was trying from demo to demo to have his back office people pull off manually in real time) as a form of market research in order to determine if real customers would buy the actual, to-be-built, service in the future.

We actually saw this guy's "pitch" a while ago and had a really good laugh afterwards that he could seriously imagine that anyone with the slightest technical know-how wouldn't understand instantly that there was no "there" there. Nonetheless, at the talk, his sage advice to the listeners was to "fake it until you make it" which has to be the worst single thing you could suggest to anyone who was serious about building an actual business rather than just trying to raise some money from a bunch of people too stupid to look under the hood of the operation and see that there was nothing there.

And, what's worse, is that this kind of loose and ignorant talk encourages other young and eager entrepreneurs to tell investors and prospective customers just the rosy parts of their story and a few fibs and a white lie or two in the process of their pitches thinking that this is the way to get their deals done. It's never been a good idea to assume that the guys with the dough are dumber than you or that they can't see through these kinds of stories. You may feel better at the end of the meetings and think that you pulled it off, but it'll be just short of forever before you get a call back from these people so I wouldn't be celebrating or holding your breath.

(2) Nail it before you try to scale it

We try to work with our 1871 member companies and – where possible – to use their products and services ourselves. Most of the time this approach has worked out well although I certainly understand how hard it is in relationships like this for the parties to be wearing multiple hats. But, in some cases, it's been a disaster and the single largest cause has been that the entrepreneur is so focused on expansion and growth that he or she drops the ball in the base business and fails to do a first-class and reference-ready job of taking care of the existing customers who are the real bread and butter of the business. If your biggest backers and strongest supporters aren't happy and satisfied using your service, you shouldn't be worrying about how soon the San Francisco office will be up and running. The market will wait for a superior service – but if your foundation is flawed and falling apart, you're not going anywhere. Ultimately, no one remembers who the first provider was; it's the best one that wins the gold.

The second part of this particular pothole is a variation on the same theme. If the dogs are eating the dogfood, make more dog food and keep selling it until you get to a size that matters and a level of operations where you are self-sustaining and not burning cash. Taking your foot off the sales accelerator and starting to worry too soon about the next version of the product and how many killer features your tech guys can think up and add to it is a great way to lose your way. Telling prospects that you're already working on the next version of the product (because you're so smart) isn't a way to pull them into the boat; it's an invitation for them to wait until V.2 is there and ready to go. They don't want until you get things right or be your inadvertent beta testers or the victims of your learning curve – sell them what you can deliver today and then build on their real desires and demands for your future enhancements and offerings.

(3) Don't be a mile wide and an inch deep

Trying to be all things to all people is always a formula for failure. Try to do a very few things really well in your products and services and in your business. Trying to solve too many problems and serve too many masters is foolish. Feature and function elaboration (especially when it's superficial and not deep) is just an ugly form of pollution and something that is driven almost always by your tech team and rarely by your customers or serious prospects. Unserious prospects will bend your ear for hours about all the things that they would like the product to do and – just as soon as it does – be sure to call them back so they can buy it right away. This is why I always say that there's an infinite demand for the unavailable. Real buyers and especially new buyer hate feature creep – it makes it hard for newbies to get started and costs time and money in training, mistakes and adoption. Not every product or service needs email built in as well. Do a few things really right.

TULLMAN'S TRUISMS

YOU EARN THE RIGHT TO DO THINGS YOUR WAY

Startups and early-stage growth businesses need 3 critical things to succeed: capital, customers and coders. Cash these days isn't really a question. Chicago investors have plenty of investment dollars for new and growing businesses. Customers aren't that hard to come by either. The city has more large corporate customers in different industry sectors than any other major U.S. city without being dominated by any single market segment. Boston doesn't want the health care guys to catch a cold any time soon. NYC and L.A. both better pray that mainstream media still matters to millennials. But in Chicago, things are doing just fine across the board. And it doesn't cost an arm and a leg to find a place to live here either. It's a great place to make a living and a life and to start your business and your family as well.

But we can do much better in the coder department. We graduate tons of engineers and computer scientists each year from our colleges and universities and too many of them still head to the coasts. Those patterns are starting to change and 1871 and the city both have specific attraction and recruitment strategies in place, but it won't happen tomorrow. So I've been thinking about what else we can do to help re-attract and return the talent which our growing businesses need <u>back</u> to Chicago from the coasts and I have a modest proposal. We can work together to make the whole here larger than the sum of its parts.

And we can make it work because it takes advantage of a unique attribute of what makes the Chicago tech community so special to begin with – our constant and unselfish willingness to reach out and help our peers. No city has the kind of public/private and philanthropic partnerships that are everyday affairs in Chicago and which support a culture of collaboration and cooperation which is unmatched elsewhere. Sure, we're fierce competitors in many ways. And that's especially true when it comes to scarce talent, but we still don't steal people from each other like they do every day in the Valley. And we're also caring competitors who spend more time sharing, supporting and giving back to the newer folks who are just starting out than you'll see in most other cities. This attitude has been a defining Chicago trait and tradition since forever and it keeps getting stronger as places like 1871 continue to grow and expand. This is one of the reasons we have literally hundreds of volunteer mentors at 1871 every month spending their time helping our member companies.

So how can we help each other be more successful in attracting talent to Chicago? I think there's a pretty simple answer which – if we do it the right way – will help to expand and bolster the entire city's tech economy over the long term as well as helping each of our businesses get better and stronger talent.

It starts with a couple of simple facts. Attracting super talented technical people from the coasts and convincing them to return to the city or suburbs isn't ultimately about money. Frankly, a lot of them grew up here, went to school and college here, and would love to return to raise their families here. And these are exactly the kind of experienced candidates - who've lived through the rocket ship rides and seen these hockey stick movies before - that our early growth-stage companies need to help them expand quickly and avoid the typical pitfalls while they do. Been there, done that makes a big difference these days when you're moving a mile a minute in multiple directions. And many of these "players" who've been to the Valley or the Big Apple and made plenty of big bucks have also figured out that it's not the cash, but the community and the challenges that really matter. They'll readily admit that the bloom is long off the rose in their current positions, but they're still reluctant to make the move home. Not because of dollars or option grants, but because of <u>optionality</u>.

They are simply afraid of what might go wrong if they make the tough call and pick up their families and move across the country and then things don't work out. No one wants to make a career mistake like that, but we know it can happen. And the fact is that the consequences are far more severe when there's a limited local pool of fallback options and alternatives. Basically the breakage costs are higher when there's no established safety net and a host of other equally viable and attractive job choices waiting in the wings.

This is simply NOT a problem or a concern in the Valley where there is a constant demand for talented people and a multitude of different companies and jobs competing for them. But it is definitely still "perceived" to be a problem in Chicago even though this is simply no longer the case. There's no question that in the last few years we've had our share of big-name and big company recruits from elsewhere who spent some time here and then headed back West, but now we have dozens of companies that ought to provide the glue we need to grab and hold these folks even if they hit a bump in the road the first time around. Just the "G's" alone would tell you that – Google, GrubHub, Gogo, Groupon, GoHealth, GiveForward, Georama and Guaranteed Rate – just to name a few. But we have to do a much better job of getting the word out – along with the facts and figures - and here's what I think we need to do <u>together</u> to get better.

So here's my simple suggestion. When you're recruiting a techie from out of town, make it your business to tell him or her about some of the other opportunities and cool companies in our town that might also be important to check out. In fact, suggest that he or she see a few of the other great tech businesses while they're here – put a few less carbs and a few more companies in each visit – and help make those meetings happen. You know who to call. And maybe we should even start thinking about sharing the costs of bringing some of these candidates into the city. Sure, I get that you might lose one or two prospects over time to a neighbor, but – in addition to broadening the pool of talent for all of us - you will reassure and comfort every single one of these people on the only real issue that matters. Convincing them that there are solid alternative employment options and choices here is the smart thing to do for your own benefit and for the overall tech economy here as well. It's a pretty small thing in the scheme of things, but every little thing that you can do to add to the reasons to return makes the outcome that much more likely. It's never gonna be a sure thing, it's just the right thing to do.

It's like the physics of candles. When I ignite your candle with mine, it doesn't diminish my light, it makes things twice as bright. It works the same way with ideas. We can make a lot of things better if we do it together. Or as the Beatles would say: in the end, the love you take is equal to the love you make.

TULLMAN'S TRUISMS

ALL OF US ARE SMARTER THAN ANY ONE OF US

It's surprising how long it takes for even those of us who think we're fairly astute and self-aware to realize and acknowledge certain things in our lives and behaviors that, in retrospect and with the benefit of hindsight, seem frightfully obvious. I don't want to appear to be piling on here, but I have to admit that I've put my Apple Watch aside for now because – in a ridiculously short amount of time – the novelty wore off and it turned from what I thought might become a necessity into a nuisance. I've already got plenty of those in my life (along with a bunch of nightly chores and things I've already got to plug in and attend to) so taking on another chore and another device wasn't high on my list. And I know I'm not alone.

I'm convinced that my personal reaction isn't unique and that it's actually part of an increasingly common consumption pattern. I think we need to find a new term to describe this recurring phenomenon because it's only going to become more and more prevalent. The truth is that I've been talking about the problem for a couple of years now and, more specifically, the risks it poses to new businesses trying to introduce new products and services.

Early adopters turn out to be even more rapid rejecters. If we're fairly quick these days to adopt and try new things; the big recent change in our behaviors is that we're far more unforgiving and demanding and that we're dumping things that just don't cut it at an even faster rate. The abandonment curve is probably 10 times steeper than the adoption curve on new products. You've got to get it right - right away - because the world doesn't wait and you rarely, if ever, get a second chance or bite at the apple. The foolish fad of MVPs is over – trying to release a half-baked product to a voracious, but highly critical and choosy marketplace is simply suicide.

Maybe it's all about living in a world where we've come to expect instant gratification in all things, but I think it goes deeper than that. I think that, if you're going to try to launch a new product these days, even if you have the best designers and marketers in the world, you need to take a longer look at how we live these days and the 5 major dimensions/distractions of our daily lives and build those considerations into your offerings and your launch plan. If your offerings aren't properly aligned and consistent with how we behave and/or if you haven't developed a plan and a strategy to address each of these areas and potentially help change the underlying behaviors, your product will quickly move from smart to superfluous. In today's social world, you can fly from being the "belle of the ball" to being the "butt" of late night jokes in a flash.

In addition, once you do launch, you better have a team set and ready to help you authentically manage (yes I realize that's somewhat of an oxymoron) the word of mouth and the inevitable and highly-opinionated conversations that are sure to follow. There are no vacuums left in today's world of social media which means that, if you're not talking about your products and driving the discussion as much as possible, someone else will be.

We talk about free will, but the truth of the matter is that we are all creatures and captives of our habits. And our days are dictated to a far greater degree than we understand by the 5 C's: conversations, conventions, comparisons, compromises and chores. Think of these as multi-dimensional descriptors – some are more like scales, some are buckets of conclusions, some are expressions and choices, and some are points of reference and departure.

As you try to make sense of where the Watch is headed, and as you plan the introduction and rollout of your own new products or services, watch out for these early indicators:

Conversations

As surprising as it may be in this "all-talk, all-the-time" world, we still learn the most by listening (not talking) and a large part of everyone's day is consumed by conversations. In the old days, conversations were largely consensual and two-way deals. Today, not so much. There have always been braggarts, blowhards and bullies, but today it seems that everyone's their own outbound broadcaster (regardless of whether they have anything important to say) and opinions, not necessarily facts, are omnipresent whether we've asked for them or not.

We're trapped in this awful place between TMI (tiresome) and TMZ (tawdry or worse), but the aggregate direction of the conversation's flow is still important and instructive and the talk about the Watch is already shifting in tone from high-energy advocacy and endorsements ("Can't live without it") to more moderate and measured discussions about value and utility. From religious fervor to reasonable analysis is never the way you want the talk about your "gee-whiz" product to progress. It's a slippery slope and the Watch is already headed in the wrong direction. Just listen to the folks talking on the train.

Conventions

We're not exactly all sheep or lemmings, but we do still love to follow the crowd and the standard conventions in most things. We don't always color within the lines, but no one's rushing to jump off a cliff every day either. And, very often, the entire compliance process is so internalized and unconscious that we don't even realize what's going on. You may imagine that your new watch is going to be a great messaging device, but the guy sitting opposite you in the meeting thinks you're an impatient and inattentive asshole who keeps looking at his watch and wishing that the meeting can't be over soon enough. Not exactly the message you want to be sending to that important client or customer.

If you're old enough, you'll recall that a certain President named Bush not too many years ago probably lost an entire Presidential debate because he got caught sneaking a peek at his watch instead of paying attention to the discussion. The message was clear – he wanted badly to be somewhere else – and the millions of people watching on TV felt that he was disconnected and that they were being dissed. It's almost the same exact problem for younger employees who try to be conscientious and take their meeting notes on their phones while the elders in the room see them and think they're insufferable idiots who are checking their email and newsfeeds instead of focusing on the matters at hand.

And then there's the basic question of who wants or needs to wear a watch anyway these days? Certainly no one under 30. We're completely surrounded by digital devices and the time is everywhere. Telling the world to take two steps backwards to re-adopt a device that was once essential, but which is now largely extraneous, makes no sense at all.

Comparisons

We generally like to proceed from the familiar and not stray too far from the tried and true in our decisions – especially about new devices and technologies. And we never want to be the guy testing the depth of the puddle by jumping in with both feet since that puddle might just be a sewer or a well. The way we manage this process day by day is by constantly performing mental comparisons – how much is something new basically the same and how much does it differ? How big a leap of faith will the transition require and how deep is the chasm? And ultimately – and most of all – are the differences actually improvements which are worth the price of change, the costs of acquisition, the pain of the mistakes due to trial and error, and the time spent on new training and learning curves?

We are all realistic enough to know that there's no free lunch and that no new products are pain free. So we look at what we are doing and using now and how well our current tools and technologies serve our needs and then we compare the new products or services to the old ways of doing whatever. In the overall scheme of things, it's hard to say that the Watch brings much new to the party. It's a lot less clunky. It's got a bevy of nice and expensive bands. It's got most of the same apps as my phone, but only a few that have already been successfully transitioned to mini-mobile use. And not much more to set it apart for half a dozen other devices.

But really the worst sign of all is that we're engaged in measuring and comparing at all. The best and most compelling products never even get this kind of a down-and-dirty review and product proctology. They're a passion, not a process. You take them on faith. And that's the kind of connection that you can also take to the bank.

Compromises

Our lives are all about choices and compromises (very few things are perfect on Day One) and we make these coin flips every day. Unfortunately, the lion's share of them are rarely between diamonds and rubies and very often they're "either/or" selections between bad and worse. So when we do have something to say about these decisions, the analysis often goes like this:

(a)   is it going to save me time;
(b)   is it going to save me money; or
(c)   will it make me smarter or more productive? And, more recently, will it increase my status?

We're willing to make deals every day, and we're willing to invest some time and effort in making things happen, but we have to believe that there's some actual value in each transaction to make it worth our while. When you run the Watch through this calculus, it's hard to make much of an argument in its favor. So when you apply the traditional tests (time, money, and productivity), there's not a lot to hang your hat on and absolutely nothing that your phone alone won't pretty much do for you already. Ask yourself what it really buys you to have your watch tell you to take your phone out of your pocket so you can do something. And when you get to questions around status, all I can say is Glass. Just remind yourself how quickly the Google Glass went from cool to creepy to compost. It's just a matter of time before people will start to check out your Watch and quietly wonder if you didn't get the memo.

Chores

We're all beyond busy these days and things aren't gonna get better any time soon so the last thing we need is more unnecessary assignments and chores. Keeping our critical devices charged up is enough of a hassle as it is and worrying every night about your Watch as well is just too much. And I'm pretty sure that having my phone ping my Watch all day long over Bluetooth is sucking the juice more quickly out of my phone as well. And don't get me started on the question of what kind of fitness monitor the thing can be when it's sitting on your desk charging for a few hours instead of being on your wrist keeping score. I've written about battery failure and Fitbit anxiety before. See http://www.inc.com/howard-tullman/fitbit-anxiety-is-part-of-a-larger-problem.html . But until someone really makes an 18 hour watch battery, I'm just not a believer.

So that's my take. These are just my humble opinions. And while I may be lonely for a while –just you watch – I won't be alone for long.

As many times as I remind people that it's always a bad bet for any company to try to be all things to all people unless you have the technology to support mass customization solutions (See http://www.inc.com/howard-tullman/surprise-you-can-be-all-things-to-all-people.html) and that, in the vast majority of cases, this scattered and over-extended approach results in a business that's spread a mile wide and an inch deep; I'm still confronted almost every day with new examples of the same problem. No one gets anything 100% right the first time out and trying to build a product or service that is so comprehensive that it works for the world is crazy. I'm still confronted almost every day with new examples of the same problem.

This isn't a problem that's limited to new or small businesses with little or no experience. The biggest guys in the business are equally adept at repeatedly stubbing their toes in exactly the same way – they try to boil the whole ocean by biting off too much too soon and trying to address every possible part of every market and they quickly end up choking in the process. Niches are nice and a really smart place to focus as you start.

You would think that anyone with any smarts (or at least some access to any decent tech conference or publication in the last decade) would be sick of hearing and absolutely know by now that a lack of early focus (or an inability to say "no" on a regular basis to ideas that are clearly attractive, but off target) is a certain formula for failure. You can try to do pretty much anything you want today, but you can't do it all at once. This isn't new news. I've been harping on this subject myself for 20 years or more. Focus, focus and more focus – start small, nail it, then scale it.

The fact is that, when Henry Ford launched the Model T, I'm reasonably sure that the last things on his mind were seat coverings, trim options or paint colors. You could buy your new Ford automobile in any color that you wanted as long as it was basic black. He knew that he had much bigger fish to fry – matters of substance, not style – if he was going to ultimately succeed in a cost-effective manner on a large scale. So he focused on the big things first. The new car was all about function, not fashion, and it was also an early lesson for all of us on the importance of laser-like focus and tunnel-vision when you're launching not just a new product, but new ideas, categories and behaviors as well.

At the same time, as everyone knows, had he been too focused on simply incremental improvements (faster horses), he would have never made the critical jump over the chasm and into the future. See http://www.inc.com/howard-tullman/stop-focusing-see-around-corners-instead.html . So a little balance and some perspective are big advantages also.

Apple used to have the same kind of courage of its convictions in its new products - at least while Steve Jobs was still alive. Ear buds for the iPad – you can have any shade of white that you like. Model selection across several products - meager or non-existent or pre-packed at the factory. Consumer choices – not really interested. The whole marketing posture sent a clear message to the consumer that Apple had already made all the important choices for you and they'd tell you what to like. Frankly, as cool and stylish as the products were, what was really critical was what was under the cover and inside the box. In the end, that's what really matters.

White pretty much used to be for Apple what Black was to the Model T. In fact, you could argue that the eventual advent of a variety of colors at Apple (black, white and silver don't count) for the 5c as an example along with the proliferation of a dozen bands for the new Watch weren't triumphs of innovation or new ideas; they were basically fairly confusing and boring line extensions which were more reflections of just a touch of desperation rather than design. The only thing we know for sure these days is that hesitating and hedging your bets as well as halfway execution aren't the hallmarks of any great entrepreneurs.

Today it feels a lot like what was really lost when Steve died was that singular sense of unerring confidence which I thought of as his "sometimes wrong, but never in doubt" approach. A little hubris isn't exactly the worst thing an entrepreneur can have when he or she is first starting out – it's probably critical. Apple used to be all about an intensely focused effort to do a very few elegant things really well. The feeling seemed to be "we'll always be Apple and never be Android". In fact, Apple still brags about all of its products fitting on the kitchen table, but - to me - the burgeoning product mix these days looks more like potpourri than perfection.

And guess, on the other hand, who seems to have learned its lesson and who's getting it right these days? At least as to Glass. It's Google that's taking a couple of steps backwards in order to move the whole wearable computing category forward. They're doing it by (a) narrowing their focus (not chasing the consumer for now); (b) addressing a limited number of problem sets; and (c) going after target customer markets with readily-discoverable best use cases and the most obvious and low-hanging solutions. It's all about industrial uses and enterprise level solutions for now rather than trying to continue to change the behavior of consumers across the entire planet overnight.

It seemed pretty obvious to me from Day One that Glass was a perfect tool for the surgical suite (photos, narration, shared viewing, largely hands-free and sterile, etc.) and a farce for the fashionistas. And if they get it right with Glass, you can bet that we're going to see a very similar strategy with respect to Google voice search and voice recognition in general (even Siri) which has suffered for decades from the same attempts to overreach instead of focusing on the immediate opportunities to massively increase industry productivity by addressing easy needs rather than beating their heads against the wall trying to solve the last 1% of the problem.

Voice recognition is essentially more than 100% accurate when it is properly employed to interpret, capture and respond to a fixed and basic vocabulary and/or a finite set of commands. This is why it will be so central to the next several generations of the connected car where we'll never see a keyboard that makes any sense. And the opportunities are huge because millions of businesses have exactly these kinds of finite vocabularies of products, services, descriptions and conditions or instructions which could use accurate voice control systems every day to save millions of man hours which are now wasted with inventory functions, clipboards, scanning guns, etc.

The introduction of new technology is always tough and the obvious conclusion is that you don't have to make it harder than necessary on yourself by aiming too high at the outset. Focusing on immediate problem solving for customers who are willing, able and interested in buying what you've got to sell today is the name of the game.

TULLMAN'S TRUISMS

BUILD ONE BUSINESS AT A TIME

I had a conversation with a commodities trader recently about Starbucks and how their results have been so impressive over the last year or two. He said that the main reason the stock had done so well was that they were enjoying the financial advantages of depressed commodity prices for coffee. He thought their recent growth was all about their cost structure which frankly – in his opinion - was more a matter of great good luck than anything that they had actively done to manage for this outcome or to achieve these results. I guess when you're a hammer, everything looks like a nail.

I told him that he was totally missing the boat and looking at the wrong metrics and that – because his perspective was off - he wasn't giving the company and their management team anywhere near the credit that they deserved. Interestingly enough, we're drowning in data today, but the sheer increase in available information isn't improving our analytical abilities or helping us (as much as it should) to make better decisions. You can be so focused on particular numbers that it's easy to lose sight of the bigger picture. We think we know what's going on and why, but - on closer examination - it turns out that we're looking in the wrong direction or commending or complaining to our managers about things that are often beyond their control.

Just because some things may look differently these days doesn't mean that anything has actually changed. The bottom line of any good business still grows because its revenues are increased (without an offsetting rise in operating expenses) or because its costs are materially reduced without any sacrifice in the level of its sales. This is the immutable math of margins and it has been ever thus. Nonetheless, it's surprising how often confusion sneaks into this basic equation, alters the correct calculations, and results in inaccurate causal attribution. It may be math, but it's got to be good math and the right metrics to matter.

And even the sharpest managers are guilty of applying versions of the same faulty logic and erroneous explanations - especially when it's in their near-term best interests to do so. In good earnings periods, they're more than happy to take plenty of credit for benefits beyond their bailiwick and in tough times they're pretty quick to blame poor outcomes on bad actors and external forces. I remember when I was selling my computerized resume service to colleges that, in good economic times, the schools bragged on their "job placement" centers, but, in hard times, those same folks took to calling themselves "career guidance" counselors. Actual jobs weren't any longer a part of their jurisdiction.

A lot of this is just human nature, but when you start focusing on or blaming third parties and outside events for your successes or your difficulties, you give up the power to make the kinds of changes which are necessary to continue to improve the situation. Similarly, when you're looking in all the wrong locations for the explanations; you're never going to end up in the right place. The most important job is to illuminate the correct causes so you can eliminate the real problems and so you can also accelerate your commitments to and investments in the things that are actually moving your business forward.

In our conversation, I went on to say, just for starters, that Starbucks had recently raised their prices and that – notwithstanding the sticker shock (as if anyone really noticed or cared except the press) - their customer counts (and, of course, their top line revenues) were still growing. They weren't trying to save their way to success. (See http://www.inc.com/howard-tullman/saving-your-way-to-success-why-you-cant-do-it.html). Frankly, if you're going to take advantage of improved operating efficiencies or available short-term cost savings due to market movements, the smart play is generally to pass those savings on to your customers by reducing your prices to draw more customers in, not to jack your prices up and try to soak the current group. This is the approach which Walmart and Costco have clearly mastered.

And yet, Starbucks seems at the moment to have the best of both worlds. I told my trader buddy that there had to be a better explanation than commodity costs for the kind of pricing power (and price elasticity) that Starbucks continues to demonstrate. My view was that what was improving their overall results was a series of initiatives that the company continued to aggressively advance and that the commodity cost savings were simply additive to, not dispositive of, their overall earnings momentum.

I felt that there were 3 areas where they were just hitting it out of the park and that these were the kind of long-term growth drivers that were driving the continuing appreciation in the Starbucks stock price as well. These are some of the same levers and tools that every startup can also use and which every one of them needs to be addressing as early as possible in their own growth plans.

First, I said that I was impressed with the fact that the number of participants in the Starbucks reward program has grown to over 10 million people and that these "members" spent on average 3 times as much as non-members do. There is nothing better for the bottom line than growing the average ticket of your existing customers. (See http://www.inc.com/howard-tullman/why-knocking-on-old-doors-is-the-best-sales-strategy.html). They're already inside the tent and now you've just got to show them more attractive opportunities to increase their spend with you while they're there. Virtually no marketing costs and a direct benefit to the bottom line. And loyalty programs continue to pay multiple dividends beyond straight dollars – they drive powerful word of mouth, authentic endorsements, community growth, social media amplification, etc. Every new startup from Day One needs to understand that building a real business is about capturing and retaining the lifetime value of each of those customers which you spend big (and scarce) bucks to acquire and that membership is about much more than just privileges, it's critical to profits as well.

Second, purchases thru the Starbucks mobile app are now accounting for more than 20% of the daily in-store sales. Saves time, saves personnel costs, improves speed and satisfaction – what's not to love? Starbucks (and many other retailers) are rapidly heading in the direction of having their products ready and waiting for you to pick up rather than having you wait for the stuff once you get there. And, of course, it's all about connectivity and mobility. In Europe, the hottest trend ("click and pick") is to order online and then drive to the store to pick up your purchases – often from a drive-thru window. But incorporating a viable mobile solution into your order fulfillment and payment streams isn't as easy as it seems either inside your company (for obvious legacy and enterprise-wide issues) or, more importantly, outside of your company's four walls because it's VERY tough to get the typical consumer these days to add any proprietary app to their already crowded and cluttered phones. You've got to show them a really good reason or try to figure out how to fold your functions into an app that's already there. (See http://www.inc.com/howard-tullman/want-your-app-to-succeed-get-it-out-there.html). This is why Starbucks has such a leg up (with 10 million rewards members) on businesses like McDonald's, for example, who's just trying to get into the game and doesn't really understand the major barriers to adoption which they're facing. The truth is that no one these days really needs another app.

And third, Starbucks keeps adding new complementary products and services offered by on-brand channel partners (NY Times, Spotify, Lyft, etc.) who are dying to get at their affluent and highly-consumptive customers. Having made the acquisition investment, this is a great way to amortize some of their sunk and ongoing costs and still keep growing the overall pie at the same time. It's a lot easier (and much less costly and risky) for third parties to pay Starbucks for this access than it is for them to try to lay their own pipe and reach all of these customers themselves. If the bundles are well done, they can clearly benefit both marketing parties and the consumer. Any business that can become the go-to channel for already assembled concentrations of ready-to-buy customers is in exactly the right place these days to reap the rewards that inure to the gatekeepers and toll takers sitting astride the mobile web. But, here again, you have to be careful that the experience is additive and appreciated by the customers or it's not worth the incremental revenue for your business.

Everything today is about the overall experience and trying to add too much to the process can be a real buzz kill as well as a persistent problem especially when nothing matters more to the customer than getting in and getting out of the place as fast as possible. I want to grab a Venti and vamoose! There's a lot to love about that dolce latte; but my time's much more valuable than your caffe mocha.

We hear a lot of disparaging comments and complaints these days about the hyper-inclusive management style of many early-stage businesses and how it's hindering their progress and growth. I'm sure you've heard some of these statements as well and they're not all simply cases of unhappy whiners or sour grapes. In many cases, it's a serious issue and, as the workforce continues to get younger, it's going to become a bigger problem. It's fixable in most cases, but only if it's addressed, explained, clarified and resolved in a straightforward and honest manner. People like to know who's actually leading the charge in their company, what their roles are, what's expected (and not expected from them) and where the business is headed. But, in some young and fast-growing companies, because so much of the organization is in flux and constantly in transition, it's hard to determine who's actually running things and who can make a binding decision that will stick. If the finality of decisions turns on who was the loudest and who was the last to get in the face of the CEO, the place is doomed.

A lot of this carping may just be background noise, but I think that there's also some substance to these discussions that's definitely worth thinking about for a bit. You hear wisecracks about founders letting "the inmates" run the asylum in the name of equality or democracy and that, as a result, those businesses are headed right into the ground. Or you read angry rants about the need to "get the amateurs off the field" so that the real professionals can take over. I don't really think that this is just an age thing or purely the province of people who are fundamentally resistant to change. It's more philosophical than that and it has much more to do with figuring out a good governance strategy for your company than it does with gray hair.

And, as easy as it would be to write these conversations off as just the latest manifestation of the generational conflicts that are seemingly rampant in so many businesses today, it's a much harder argument to make when you're talking about startups where there really aren't as many age gaps as you might find in larger and more established businesses. Just because most of the people in your business are roughly the same age doesn't automatically mean that they're in accord about how and who should run the show and who should be included in what decisions.

It's less an age thing and more a culture thing which depends largely on where they've been and where they're coming from and actually how they were raised. There are plenty of people these days who buy into ideas like radical transparency and complete information sharing or participatory management at all levels because they heard it in school or from others without having seen how wrong some of these experiments have gone or having tried to manage systems like this. You can be totally sincere and very passionate about your feelings, but still be completely wrong about what's good for the business. And the sooner you get straightened out, the happier and more productive you'll be. Or, if it's not for you, you'll be gone. Organizations can grow through adoption or attrition – either way works. You can get with the program or you can go elsewhere.

And frankly, it's not really your call anyway. Good businesses aren't run by majority rule. You may all be in the same bed, but everyone's got their own dreams and their own obligations and responsibilities. Collaboration and community and Kumbuya are all cool things, but – in a crunch or a crisis – it's the CEO's job to make the hard calls and everyone else's job to line up behind the decision and execute the plan. Period. Full stop.

At a certain point, even for the CEO, seeking more input from more people is as much about putting off the tough calls as it is about further informing yourself or arming yourself with more ammunition. Expanding the decision set and waiting to decide almost never results in a better outcome. Better the best decision you can make at the time based on the data you have available than delaying the decision until it becomes a crisis where your choices and options are fewer and less attractive.

And, as it turns out, the data acquisition and evaluation issues are actually the less challenging parts of the problem. The bigger and more difficult issue has to do with managing the expectations and the emotions of your people. This is where the wickets can quickly get sticky and where no good deed ever goes unpunished. You can repeatedly explain things to people, but you can't understand for them. It's very hard to tell someone that their participation isn't required (or that their input isn't being solicited) without essentially telling them that their opinions don't matter and yet that's basically the exact truth – at least as to some areas of the business. This is especially difficult today because (particularly in a new business) everyone considers themselves an expert on almost everything.

Bottom line – it's always going to be hard to tell people what they don't want to hear and it's never going to get easier, but it's essential to the integrity and effectiveness of your decision-making and your company's operation. And while no two situations or businesses are exactly alike, I think there are a few critical considerations that you – as the boss and the one ultimately accountable for the final decisions and the consequences - need to take into account.

(1) Democracy in decision-making is diverting and delusional.

If everything that's up for discussion is also up for grabs because it's subject to further changes, second-guessing, and unending debate and everyone in the place is entitled to not merely an opinion, but a vote on everything; nothing worthwhile will ever get done. This creates major roadblocks (both inside and outside the business) to getting the right things done in a timely fashion. As I wrote in an earlier *INC.* piece, it's pretty clear to anyone with any real management experience that not everything in any business is everyone's business. See http://www.inc.com/howard-tullman/with-this-much-help-youll-never-get-anything-done.html . Not everyone's opinion is necessary or valuable; not everyone's ideas are great or need to be considered; not everyone knows what they're talking about; and – in any event – consistent unanimity is never essential to a strong and effective decision-making process. It's just another fantasy from the four guys who started in the garage. All for one and one for all is fine for a slogan, but having too many cooks in the kitchen makes for some very sorry soup.

(2) Democracy in meetings is demoralizing and debilitating.

Meetings don't run themselves unless they're being run by morons. There needs to be a meeting leader and the leader needs to be a good listener, but even more than that, he or she needs to be a good chooser and a great editor. It's also not a popularity contest. It doesn't have to be a rude process, but it does have to be ruthless in protecting the purpose of the meeting, moving things along, cutting off people who are off track or off message, and managing the outcome of the discussion in the time allotted. Democracy in meetings is not a value in and of itself and trying to pretend otherwise is a waste of everyone's time and dysfunctional as well. Business meetings are neither occupational therapy sessions nor venues for free expression. If they have a valuable purpose at all, it's about getting things discussed and decided and not about giving everyone in the room scrupulously equal air time to express themselves and to share whatever thoughts may have serendipitously popped into their heads. Just because something occurred to you doesn't necessarily make it interesting or valuable to me. In meetings, it's a lot better to make one person unhappy than to suck the life out of the entire group by making them suffer through someone's enthusiastic, but stupid, suggestions.

(3) Democracy in design is dumb.

Style and design talents aren't things that are remotely equally distributed in the general population and certainly not among the employees in your company. There are people who are really good at these things and that's why you find and employ them. You need to commit to and trust a talented design team and express a simple vision and set of objectives to them and then get out of their way. This isn't a class project where everybody gets to try their hand. I've concluded that design committees are the singly most useless entities in the history of collaborative enterprise and - without exception - result in wasted time and money as well as a crappy outcome because they operate on two equally stupid principles: (a) the design which is least objectionable to the most people on the committee will be the best design; and (b) if each committee member gets something incorporated into the design which is near and dear to his or her heart, then everyone on the committee will be happy and that's all that really matters. The quality of the design is subordinated to the comfort and convenience of the committee.

(4) Democracy in dollars is demotivating and destructive.

People aren't stupid and trying to paint them all with the same brush or compensate them all in roughly the same way is the easiest and quickest way to lose your best people and demotivate even the good ones who stay while they're looking for their next job. (See the very unhappy experiences of Dan Price, the founder of *Gravity Payments*, who tried to scale up the pay of everyone in his company to at least $70k a year for a very cautionary tale.) We used to call the folks who stuck around, but stopped caring "people who quit without leaving" and they are super-bad for your business. You've got to pay people what each of them is really worth to the business in terms of both their value and their contributions (as well as their judgment and experience) and you've got to make it clear to the rest of the team that this is exactly how the world should work. The people who contribute the most (not necessarily those who simply work the most) are the ones who will earn the most. And even more to the point – people with highly-specialized and valuable skills are often worth a multiple of what you might be paying other team members – especially in our highly-competitive talent market. If people don't think that's fair, they're free to go work elsewhere.

There's a reason that democracy rhymes with mediocrity. Compromise and consensus are at the core of democracy, but they have almost nothing to do with creativity or with supporting and promoting the kinds of singular visions and ideas that are most likely to change the world.

Customer segmentation has been around as an essential business practice for ages. In fact, the age (or range of ages) of various customers has always been one of the more obvious ways in which merchants and other service providers could slice and dice their potential consumer and business targets into theoretically distinguishable clusters whose needs and interests could be distinctly and differently identified and addressed in bulk. Gender, geography, graduation levels, etc. were other basic criteria which fed into generalized profiles and composites. Credit, race, political views and other less politically correct characterizations also made their way into the calculations as often as not.

But, as with everything else today, new and better personalization data and other measurement and location-sensitive identification tools are rapidly changing the game and the ground rules for sales success. It's not enough to know who I am and what I'm interested in although that's a decent starting point. Mass customization is the minimum goal and very little will be left to deal with in grossly simplistic terms or in bulk because every consumer today wants to believe that they're being treated as individuals and they want to make their purchasing decisions by the bite or the byte on a one-off basis. One size no longer fits almost anyone and the greatest sin of all is to take any of your customers or prospects for granted.

At the same time, what is still somewhat surprising in this all-digital, all-the-time, world is that - in addition to the new learnings which the data can now provide about almost every customer's desires and objectives which will further increase our ability to individualize our offerings and responses - many of the consequences, strategies and prescriptions growing out of the latest research are primarily physical in nature rather than digital.

Think of this as the latest version of "retail revisited" - not as a fad or even a trend, but as a major shift in the ways that traditional retail space will need to accommodate new customer concerns and requirements. See http://www.inc.com/howard-tullman/the-future-of-self-service.html . We'll be building new and different spaces containing smaller, more personal, environments which will best suit the new mobile and constantly-connected customers whom we expect to attract and also permit us to adapt on the fly to the desires of each and every entrant – new or returning – based on their needs at the time.

Comprehensive use of demographic data will be useful, but no longer a competitive differentiation. And even basic "interest" and social information (far more critical today than mere customer attributes) won't be sufficient to win the battle because the new behavior drivers won't be uniform or consistent even on an individual basis. Some expected, routine and consistent behaviors which are fairly reliable will be ascertainable, but the real winners will understand that - each time a customer now appears - it's essentially a brand-new day dictated and determined in the moment by the customer's then-dominant and most pressing desires.

Customers will continue to fall into new distinct categories, but the categories will vary over time in significant ways. My shorthand for these variable behaviors is to think of them as "objectives". What's the customer's goal and how can the environment and the staff best facilitate the success of the customer's quest to achieve it? See http://www.inc.com/howard-tullman/whats-wrong-with-retail-and-what-does-it-mean-for-you/html.html . In a sense, this is simply an effort to peel the consumer onion a little more and get tighter and tighter views of the customer, but at the moment, no one is even thinking about looking at the customer through this new lens.

And while some "goal" creep and overlapping or inconsistent desires are certain to occur for some customers, once you start organizing your approach and your thinking around this new perspective, you're going to find that it's fairly easy to understand and appreciate its importance, but very complicated to implement an in-store program to address it. It's simple to see because it's absolutely applicable to you and me as well as to everyone else, but it's hard to address all the different requirements of the various individuals.

Here are some of the competing profiles and customer expectations which the retail environments of tomorrow (which actually means right now) will need to accommodate. Now's the time to start thinking about how your business or service can address them.

(1) Mission (In and Out) versus Discovery (Time to Explore & Learn)

Time is the scarcest resource of all today and mission-driven shoppers want to be in and out of the store as quickly as possible. We live in a world of instant gratification. The shoppers like express checkout lines manned by real people and they hate self-checkout systems which they know will take them twice as long to use for the few items they have purchased. ATMs are a whole lot faster and easier than tellers, but scanners are still slow and difficult. Explorers, on the other hand, are there with a different purpose – they're willing to commit the time it takes to find new and unusual offerings – to experiment with new choices and to learn about new alternatives. They're the pioneers of the entertainment economy where the experience is the most important aspect of the encounter. These are the ripest targets for in-store sampling, demo stations, special offers and even videos. They're in the food lane and not the fast lane and they're in no hurry. And it's a phenomena that's by no means limited to groceries. You know the times are changing when the quality of a new car's sound system and its Wi-Fi connectivity are as (or more) important to the purchasing decision as the car's performance.

(2) Choice (Super Selection) versus Convenience (Front and Center – Grab and Go)

A significant amount of research over the years has gone into the paralyzing effect on choosers of too many choices – it often results in no action at all - and this problem sets up another challenge for retailers. Overwhelming the consumer with massive displays and innumerable choices and emphasizing selection works for some folks, but it can be very off-putting to the customer who knows just what he or she wants and is brand-loyal as well. We're going to see mini-stores within the bigger boxes, but not ones dedicated to marketers like Microsoft or Samsung or P&G. The minis coming soon to stores near you will be choice-constrained and filled with the most frequently and consistently purchased items so I can grab what I need and get out. Using the back walls of the big box for dairy products in order to pull the shopper through the stores is a strategy that just won't work any longer for a significant segment of the audience. In fact, more and more customers will be ordering bulk items and commodities that they would typically buy every week online by subscription or fulfillment services and not trying to drag the same stuff home from the market every week.

(3) Click and Pick (Drive-Thru) versus Park and Party (Time to Kill)

Same day delivery is coming soon (one hour delivery for Amazon Prime customers is already rolling out in major markets), but it still may not be fast enough to beat what's exploding all over Europe – click (buy online) and pick (drive to the store to get it) has become amazingly popular – especially with Moms – who'd rather throw the kids in the car and make three quick pickups (without ever even parking) at her favorite stores instead of sitting at home and hoping for the delivery guy to show. More than 30% of several major retailers' holiday sales last season were in-store pickups of goods ordered online and the trend continues to accelerate. But again, that approach only serves some of the shoppers. A different group of people goes to the store because they have nothing else to do. They're anxious to lose themselves in the store for as long as possible because they've got time to kill and nowhere else important to be. They'll be quick to grab a bite at in-store food service operations – not because they're famished - but because they're anxious to get off their feet. Having the snack shops at the front of the store – beyond the registers and post-checkout – is another design idea whose time has come and gone.

There are plenty of additional examples and there's not a business around that won't do far better if it adapts its facilities to accommodate all these variable demands and - at the same time - adapts its sales approach to each customer's specific goals. It's not that hard to quickly figure out what's driving each customer, but if you aren't focused on finding this out, your customers will quickly find someplace else that has and do their shopping there.

I spoke recently on business basics at the Chicago Startup Summit which was put together by the terrific teams at Virgin Unite and RM72 as an educational and networking experience for entrepreneurs (and wanna-bes as well) with a particular focus on socially-conscious businesses. The day-long event was held at Chicago's new Virgin Hotel which is especially near and dear to my heart because: (a) it's pretty much a startup itself - being that it is the first Virgin Hotel in the world with 20 more to come and (b) the core team which put the new property together did their initial ideation and development as active members and residents of 1871.

When I ordinarily talk about The Perspiration Principles, I try to focus on what I regard as the 5 main requirements for success in business and, of course, in life as well: passion, preparation, perspiration, perseverance and principles (or values). The sessions at the Summit were an opportunity to broaden the conversation and add three more P's to the pot: a focus also on people, purpose and planet.

The central idea was how we can change businesses for good either by creating businesses that specifically focus on doing good or helping existing businesses think about (and actually implement) cost-effective and innovative ways that they can do their business in a better fashion which takes into account broader concerns and the idea of a double bottom line.

The diverse group of speakers and presenters I joined spanned the entire social spectrum so much so that I felt from time to time that - while I was talking about bedrock basics - super-smart people like Mats Lederhausen were talking about concepts and ideas that sounded a lot more like rocket science. But based on the reactions and comments of the crowd, everybody found something to help them make sense of this crazy and exciting new world of constant change and disruptive innovation.

In any event, I was grateful for the opportunity to review with the group some of the basic ideas and strategies that have been the foundation for almost half a century now of my practice and of The Perspiration Principles as well. While some of the ideas have been expanded and adapted, it is amazing how little the fundamental premises have varied. Many of them are self-explanatory and where they aren't I've just added a short summary.

Here are the Top 10 from my ever-growing list:

(1) You Get What You Work for, Not What You Wish For

Hard work always wins. In the real world, effort trumps talent. Hope is not a strategy. We may not outsmart them all, but we'll certainly outwork them.

(2) Keep Raising the Bar

Constant iteration is the key. You get better by getting better. Successive approximation beats postponed perfection. There's no finish line – ever.

(3) Shoot for the Stars

Always ask for the best seat in the house. You miss 100% of the shots you don't take. If you don't ask, the answer's always "no".

(4) Don't Sell Yourself Short

Feasibility will compromise you soon enough. Don't allow yourself to be defined by the limitations of other people. Fueling your fears is a waste of imagination.

(5) Keep Moving Forward

Excellence is always anchored in perseverance. It's only a "No" for now. Over every hill is another hill. The only easy day was yesterday.

(6) Start Now with What You Have

Waiting doesn't necessarily get you to a better answer.

The time will never be "just right". Elaboration in planning is a form of pollution. A good plan executed today beats a perfect plan next week. It's easier to ask for forgiveness than permission. Only the winners decide what were the war crimes.

(7) Nobody Said Life Was Fair

In the world of startups, there aren't rewards or punishments, there are only consequences. Some win, some lose, but those who don't constantly change, die for sure. There's no such thing as a good excuse. Make smart mistakes and don't repeat them.

(8) Never Play the Blame Game

People who blame their circumstances for their situation will never change things for the better. The ones who succeed look for the conditions they need to succeed and – if they can't find them – they make them.

When you continually blame others, you give up your power to make things better.

(9) Sometimes the Baby is Just Ugly

Time is the scarcest resource. Opportunity costs are everything. If you're digging yourself into a hole, the first order of business is to stop digging. Don't be reluctant to change your mind. Don't try to do things cheaply that you shouldn't be doing at all. Stubborn on vision; flexible on details.

(10) Make Something that Makes a Difference

Focus on making a difference and making a life rather than just trying to make a living.

TULLMAN'S TRUISMS

REPETITION IS A CONVINCING ARGUMENT

We hosted a tour and an hour-long fireside chat for Dr. Brene Brown at 1871 this week as part of our WiSTEM program which focuses on 1871's female entrepreneurs. The event was attended by about 300 excited members of the *Rising Strong* community. Brene was careful at the outset not to call them "fans" although you couldn't prove that from the emotion and energy of the crowd (which started gathering an hour before the sold-out doors even opened) or from the rousing reception and standing ovation she got when she walked on stage. She pointed out that - while her process was a shared experience, a collaborative conversation, and, most importantly, a two-way street – fandom was a fundamentally passive, one-sided, and static state. Simply buying any book won't make you better – it's in applying the lessons and learnings from the book to your own life and circumstances - and then doing the hard work of taking responsibility for and true ownership of your stories - where the change starts and the results begin to show. You've got to put your heart where your mouth is and let yourself be seen.

To say that the crowd was present and "in the moment" would be an understatement. They were absolutely hanging on her every word. But, interestingly enough, at least in Brene's terminology, they weren't being "mindful" which she said was a fuzzy and fussy word that she'd done her best to successfully expunge from her vocabulary. We agreed that a better and more concrete phrase would be that they were "paying attention" which I believe is the newest and most meaningful form of currency today – especially given our noisy, cluttered and confused world. The truth is that, if your audience isn't listening and paying attention, it doesn't really matter what you're saying or selling. And, of course, it turns out that whatever it is that you pay attention to in your business and/or in your relationships are the only things that matter anyway in the final analysis.

Dr. Brown joined us to talk about *Rising Strong*, her newest book (which – a week after publication - is already on the *New York Times* best seller list), and also to talk about a major new online learning and sharing initiative (called *COURAGEworks*) which she will be launching in a few months with Oprah and others. And she was gracious enough to spend some time listening to testimonials and answering questions from the crowd. We covered a lot of territory in our talk, but a few key concepts and ideas stuck with me which I think are particularly relevant to entrepreneurs who are starting new businesses in uncharted waters where the perils are high and the prospects of failure are great.

The most fundamental idea, of course, was the whole basis for the research and the new book itself which was an attempt by Brene to discover what the common qualities were among those who had set out on a journey, failed once or twice, sometimes spectacularly, but who had then picked themselves up, started forward again, and ultimately succeeded. What did it take for them to make it and what attitudes and characteristics did they share? I'm not going to try to answer a book's worth of inquiry in a brief blog post, but here are 3 of the main things that I took away from our talk which – not entirely surprisingly – aligned pretty nicely with some of the central *Perspiration Principles*.

(1) Failure's Just Another Word for Education

I've said for a long time that failure sucks. See http://www.inc.com/howard-tullman/who-said-failure-was-fashionable.html. People who pride themselves on their record of repeated failures are sadly deluded and just kidding themselves. They need to face the facts and face reality so they can get on with their real lives. See http://www.inc.com/howard-tullman/what-nobody-tells-you-about-failure.html. And Brene also made a very interesting comment early in her remarks. She said that "failure is an imperfect word" because, if you take the time and have the patience to learn from your failures, then they aren't failures any longer – they're lessons. See http://www.inc.com/howard-tullman/failure-happens-four-ways-to-do-it-well.html. And once you've gone through the ringer, and learned your lessons – good and bad – it's highly likely that you're a better bet for the next time around. Not a sure thing – but a decent bet. See http://www.inc.com/howard-tullman/should-you-hire-failed-founders.html. What you learn finally is that, if you really own your own stories, you're the one who gets to write the happy endings.

(2) It's Ultimately All Up to You, But You Can't Do It Alone

No one does anything important these days by themselves and having a team to support you and a community to surround you are both critical. And you'll need someone in particular to connect and share with as well. Brene suggested that in her case all the breakthroughs involved a therapist (which we can't all afford although she noted that there are low income programs and practice requirements). And she said that regardless of who you select, there were two more very important caveats: (a) make sure that your happiness and healing doesn't depend on or require their response and/or approval; and (b) make sure that the relationship is truly reciprocal if you expect it to and want it to last. It can't be a one-way street and you can't really open up to someone and share your feelings if the feeling's not truly mutual.

But it's equally critical to remember that – in the end – it's still on you alone to get the process started and the right things done. I tell entrepreneurs all the time that they shouldn't try to convince themselves that they're doing what they are doing for someone else. It's just too hard and long a journey. You need to own the entire process – all the ups and downs – and you need to do it without reservation – putting your whole self out there - because there are no guarantees and there's no halfway way to do what needs to be done. You need to own it and own up to it. All the advice and wisdom in the world won't help until you internalize and take on the task. You can explain things all day to people, but you can't understand for them.

(3) It's Not Always Nice, But It's Always Necessary

The truth is that it's never easy to say what people don't want to hear. But it's an essential step in the communication and sharing process. A leader needs to tell the team what he or she expects of them, what they're trying to accomplish, why it matters, and what sacrifices the journey will entail. Only then - with the requisite knowledge and understanding in place - can everyone sign up and engage with a whole heart. People don't necessarily care that they aren't certain where things are going, but they know for sure that they don't want to go there alone. They want people by their side who share their vision, their passion and their commitment.

But – at the same time - no one can climb the mountain for you and it's critical to understand where you stop and where the others begin. Brene said that empathy is a valuable and important emotion, but it's not an instance of feeling <u>with</u> someone else, it's about your non-judgmental feelings <u>for</u> someone else and their circumstances or situation. And it's that stepping back and creating a bit of distance that makes it possible to help without falling into the pit (or swallowing the problem) yourself. Getting mixed up in the mess isn't going to help anyone. This is why clear limits help to make for a clear conscience and a happy heart.

It's important to be very direct about boundaries (even with family) and, frankly, as Brene said: vulnerability without boundaries – without telling even those you're closest to – what's OK and what's not – isn't vulnerability at all. In the startup business world, everyone wants to help and their enthusiasm is a blessing, but too many people in the process makes for a big mess. Some people just don't get to dance every dance and make every meeting even if their feelings get hurt. See http://www.inc.com/howard-tullman/with-this-much-help-youll-never-get-anything-done.html. That's just another part of the leader's job – ultimately someone has to decide and only that vote counts because it's not a democracy and it's not a popularity contest either. See http://www.inc.com/Howard-tullman-four-reasons-democracy-ads-up-to-mediocrity.html. There's no question that how you do it matters a lot, but you've got to do it for sure.

Join the 24 million other people who have watched Brene's TED talk on The Power of Vulnerability: https://www.youtube.com/watch?v=iCvmsMzlF7o.

I moderated a HR panel last week with Shawn Riegsecker, the CEO-founder of Centro (http://www.inc.com/profile/centro) in Chicago, and two of his senior tech talent recruiters. Centro is an ad-tech firm which already has over 700 employees in some 37 offices spread across the country. They've been ranked as the city's Best Place to Work for 4 or 5 years running in the *Crain's Chicago* survey; they've almost doubled their headcount in the last 18 months; and they don't see any end in sight. Like everyone else, the team at Centro is trying to hire all of the top tech talent they can get their hands on in order to support their continuing growth and the expanding demand for their services. And, of course, they're competing for that A-level talent with 100-plus other Chicago-based technology companies which are growing just as fast or even faster. Great news for the city's tech scene – not so much for the recruiters on the hot seats to get the job done.

But even considering how much pressure they're constantly under to grow, and as crazy as the talent competition all around them is, their strategies and the ideas that came through in our discussion were extremely thoughtful and long-term. The four main concepts - which I think are relevant to any fast-moving and fast-growing business today - were: (a) their personnel energies are primarily focused inside their business – they believe that building and maintaining their company culture is the key to recruiting and retaining the best people – not worrying about the competition; (b) they're in a hurry, but not hurried – they have a lengthy, multi-person, and quite diverse interview process and they're sticking to it - especially because it sends the right messages to their current employees and to prospective hires as well; (c) they understand that the things that worked for them in the past and got them this far (like a hugely impactful internal cash bonus program for new employee referrals) aren't sufficient to keep them moving forward and ahead of the pack, so they're constantly looking for new tools and better ways to get the job done; and (d) they're struggling – right along with every other tech firm – with how they can make their workforce more diverse even though – in terms of gender – they're already as diverse as any firm in the city.

(1) You Didn't Find Me, I Found You

The only thing better and more rewarding than finding and recruiting a super-talented new employee is learning that the prospect in question actually sought out your company and found you. Forget that this is highly efficient and cost-effective, it tells you that your culture is spreading beyond your four walls and that you've succeeded in developing an authentic, word-of-mouth (not manufactured) reputation as the one of the right places to be. You can't make this stuff up – you've got to live it every day and model the behaviors that matter. But as you do and as the critical attitudes and actions spread from the CEO throughout the entire company, you'll quickly learn that nothing is more contagious than a shared vision and a set of sincere and compelling corporate values. In the best companies, people don't come for the job, they come to be part of the vision and to spend their time in a place that values and appreciates them doing work that makes a difference.

(2) If I'm Not Growing, I'm Going

A definite key to successful retention was the idea that all of the employees needed to feel cared about and listened to by the company's senior management and especially by the CEO. An important part of all great companies' cultures are the (sometimes apocryphal) stories passed down over the years of special efforts, extraordinary gestures, and honored commitments by the founders and senior management as well as instances where they put the welfare and concerns of the employees ahead of their own. Centro has plenty of those tales especially during the 2008 recession when the first people to take pay cuts were the senior executives. But, even more important, has been the ongoing need for each employee to feel and believe that the company was committed to their own continued education and growth. Centro pays 100% of its employees' tuition costs for educational courses each year. Bottom line: if your key employees don't see a commitment, a path and a future full of promise, they're unlikely to be sticking around.

(3) Doing Things the Same Way Doesn't Make for Better Results

Centro has a reputation for promoting from within and it's another important element of the overall company culture. But if you're looking only at your existing employees for new management, you're not likely to be introducing the numbers of change agents and alternative thinkers that you'll need to drive real innovation. Companies and systems get stale without new blood and people with different perspectives being added regularly to the mix. Similarly, Centro has an amazingly successful employee referral system which pays their team members a cash bonus for each new hire they refer. This in-house program has historically accounted for well over 50% of their new employees and it's working like a charm, but it's not sourcing a diverse enough population of leads because the vast majority of the folks the employees know tend to be like them and look like them and that hasn't helped the company identify the kind and number of qualified minority candidates that they need to broaden their overall workforce. So they're looking into other channels including outside recruiters. But the most important thing they are doing is focusing on rapidly advancing their qualified minority employees into higher levels of management so that there's increased visibility and concrete demonstrations of the company's commitment to this goal.

(4) I Can Make You Better, But I Can't Make You Care

Centro prioritizes skills and character in their hiring. You've got to have the right skills to make the cut, but you're not really welcome if you don't have the character and the values that the company was built on from the beginning. I don't care how much you know until I know how much you care. You can fix a bad fit by changing someone's position or responsibilities or upskill a motivated and committed worker so he or she can do a better job and that's the kind of commitment that a great business makes to its people; but there's no cure for a crappy character except the door as soon as possible. Keeping someone around who's destructive or corrosive (however productive or talented they may be) is a cancer for the company and it's never too soon to tell these folks to take a hike. Hire slow, fire fast.

TULLMAN'S TRUISMS

PEOPLE ASK FOR CRITICISM, BUT ALL THEY REALLY WANT IS PRAISE

A new business can't dodge every bullet and not every point of failure is foreseeable. But that doesn't mean that you have to put your head in the lion's mouth or make things much harder for yourself than they need to be. If you're willing to make the effort, you can learn from the mistakes of others and the errors and bad choices of those who have gone down in flames before you and - at the very least - you can hope to avoid making the same mistakes. You're gonna make your share of mistakes for sure, but just try to make them your own. I like to say that ignorance is curable, but stupidity is forever. If you never listen, you'll never learn. And if you're so pigheaded and arrogant that you think you can pull these things off all by yourself, you're in for a very rude awakening and an even tougher ride.

Over the last year, I've seen an interesting behavioral pattern develop which I share with you as a clear and cautionary tale – people who otherwise seem fairly rational - are leaving incubators like 1871 way too soon for their own good. And what we're seeing is very clear. If you leave the nest too soon and leave your support systems behind (including those whose impact and value you don't even fully appreciate), your business is much more likely to fail and fail quickly. Going it alone - whether it's because some desperate landlord offers you a great short term deal on space or because some investor has a brother-in-law in the business - is simply stupid if you and your team and your business aren't really ready to function as a fully-independent entity.

Don't just take my word for it, but do consider these trade-offs, risks, and other considerations in making a move so that you can at least say that you looked hard at the issues before you leapt.

(1) Focus

The very last thing the founder of a startup needs to do is take his or her eye off the ball and lose focus when the company is just getting to the cusp of some modest success. Fooling around with fabrics, worrying about who sits by the windows, and trying to be your own architect instead of beating down customers' doors are all bad uses of your time and distractions from the main business which is taking care of your business.

(2) Friends

Absence might make the heart grow fonder in some romance novel, but in the real world of building a business, it's hard enough to find time for a social life to begin with and frankly "out of sight" is very often "out of mind" notwithstanding the most sincere promises and the best of intentions. You don't know how important even those casual friends were to your mental well-being or just how lonely it is to be out there on your own as you're going through these things and you're no longer surrounded by people who "get it" and who are living the same dreams and nightmares every day.

(3) Feedback

You'll never get a straighter story than directly from your customers, but right behind them in the line of straight shooters are your fellow entrepreneurs, the volunteer mentors and – most of all – the seasoned and experienced managers of the best mega-incubators like 1871 who are there mainly to help you make your business better. 1871's a non-profit with no agenda other than job creation and the only way that jobs happen is by helping to build businesses that stick around and become self-sustaining. Even your best employees aren't going to regularly tell you that you're just blowing smoke (even if you are), but you can count on your peers and the people who've been there before to tell it to you like it is. A true friend always stabs you in the front.

(4) Food, Facilities and Other Freebies

If you're typical, you take a lot of the food and other freebies at your incubator for granted, but these goodies feed your team (which isn't inclined to stop eating any time soon) and – by the way – these things aren't really "free" in the first place. They're there because the providers want their offerings to be exposed to the thousands of people who pass thru a place like 1871 every week. Once you're out on your own (and I want to be gentle in telling you this), none of these major vendors will give a damn about you or your people's preferences and you can expect to be paying your own way. Tasty tacos and perpetual pizzas aren't cheap and your people aren't interested in paying themselves when they read every day about other businesses going whole hog on freebies. Same deal with providing your own receptionist, security, conference rooms, cafes, projectors, white boards, tele-conferencing hookups, and high speed Wi-Fi. It's all on your dime now and those dimes add up pretty quickly to a pile of cash that you'd be foolish to spend of stuff like this - even if you had it to spare.

(5) Funds

And speaking of cash to spare, I can't begin to tell you how really excited your investors are gonna be about tying up a big chunk of change in security deposits and fancy furniture which could be used in a million better ways to keep building the business. And prospective new investors will be even more put off to look at a balance sheet with a bunch of restricted funds and capital assets. The winners in the game today are "capital-lite" businesses who figure out how to rent or share resources rather than using scarce funds to furnish fancy facilities. And, by the way as you looking for new funds, don't expect that the dozens of VCs, serial entrepreneurs and angel investors walking around 1871 every day to meet with companies will be dropping by your new digs anytime soon. Doesn't happen.

(6) Friction

As gross as it may sound, the team that sweats together stays together and, in most startups, things rarely get better once the guys leave the garage. Sitting on top of each other all day long may be smelly, but it makes for instant communication and builds lifetime bonds; struggling to find a space to put your stuff reminds everyone that space is expensive and money is scarce and you need to grow your way out of the box; and sweating or freezing when the building air turns off each night just becomes part of the company culture that gets passed down over the years just like your folks always claimed they chopped wood all night to keep your family warm. Move into new comfy digs with windows and doors and all the trimmings and you can watch your culture start to change and dissolve right before your eyes especially when the security guards at the door of your new corporate tower give all your best employees the "stink eye" on their way in and ask them which floor they're delivering the package to.

I've seen it all happen too many times to count and I don't expect it to end any time soon, but I'm hoping that you won't be the next one to make this kind of mistake. And if you do, I'll just say two things: (1) I told you so; and (2) how can I miss you if you won't leave?

1871

We had the opportunity recently to host Bill Rancic – the first winner on Donald Trump's *The Apprentice* television program – for a keynote speech about what he's learned from several important mentors (he didn't mention The Donald which wasn't really that much of a surprise); how he's started and built his several entrepreneurial ventures; and finally a very important lesson that he took away from his triumph on the TV show in 2004 which, as he noted, seems like light years ago.

I thought that his explanation for how he won the *Apprentice* competition was very enlightening. He didn't say he worked the hardest. He didn't say he wanted it the most. And he certainly didn't say he was the smartest guy in the room. What he said made all the difference was something that we talk about every day at 1871 as well. It's the idea that nobody does anything important and worthwhile today all by themselves. You need a team to make the dream come true.

Bill said the key to his success was that he tried to "be the conductor" just like the main man at the symphony and that he used his talents to bring everyone together so they could make beautiful music. He knew – just like in the case of the orchestra - that he didn't personally have the special skills or the same abilities that each of the other members of his team had, but he was able to get them all moving in the right direction and to bring out the best effort that each team member had to contribute.

And he also knew that the most amazing things get done when no one cares who gets the credit. Harmony trumps hubris – no pun intended. It certainly wasn't easy – he had some confrontations and some hard sledding, but he always kept in mind what Robert Schuller said: "tough times never last, but tough people do!" And he never spent his time blaming others when things went wrong. That would have been a waste of breath and energy.

After the show, when he started working in the real world, he said he was fortunate to have some great people to learn from and whose examples he follows to this day. And he was smart enough and modest enough to know that, until he really knew what he was doing, it was a mistake to try to do things on his own. He needed to play a role for a while before he tried to roll his own even though one of his first ventures was in the mail order cigar business. See http://www.inc.com/howard-tullman/entrepreneurship-will-you-sink-or-swim.html. Bill had a very clear idea of where he wanted to end up and even how he thought he would get there, but he was smart enough to know that these things were going to take some time and that the smartest thing he could do in the meantime was to concentrate on learning something from someone every day on the journey. It's important to have a mental roadmap, but patience is also essential. See http://www.inc.com/howard-tullman/why-you-need-a-reverse-roadmap.html

He also noted that his father was a source of both instruction and inspiration. Bill said that one of his father's principal rules was that "practical execution" was what really mattered in the end. All the talk was simply that – results and actions were the things that made a difference. His Dad used to say: "show me, don't tell me" or as I like to say: "you can't win a race with your mouth". Less talking and more typing is how things get done. And it won't ever happen if you don't get started. There's no simple playbook or set of rules for how you invent the future – you've got to get the ball rolling, keep your eyes on the goal, and be agile and flexible all the time.

Bill said that when we're born – we're only afraid of two things – falling and loud noises. We're the ones who learn to be afraid of other things and who too often let those fears keep us from stepping out and taking the kinds of risks that are essential for entrepreneurs to succeed. He quoted Emerson as saying that you needed to do what you are afraid of and that – if you do – success will find you. And as far as risks, he said that the key was to recognize and manage reasonable risks so that you could convert them into opportunities and rewards – not to try to avoid every possible risk. The ship that stays in port is always the safest, but it rarely accomplishes anything.

And finally he talked about the business with the bumblebee. He said that for years scientists have been saying that bees were never supposed to be able to fly because the ratio of the size of their wings to their body weight was all wrong. According to the "laws" of physics that meant that they could never have enough power to lift themselves into the air. Bill's point was that – just like so many entrepreneurs who do every day what others thought was impossible – no one ever told the bees that they couldn't fly and, accordingly, off they went.

But there's an important sequel to the story. Today no one says any longer that the bees are defying the laws of physics or nature because we have finally figured out that – just because the bees don't fly in the same way that fixed-wing airplanes do – doesn't mean that rules of gravity have been suspended for them. The fact is that bees – just like entrepreneurs – have figured out (with a little help from Mother Nature) a different way to solve the problem. They fly by rapidly rotating their flexible wings and that's how they get themselves off the ground.

Every day entrepreneurs are doing the same thing – we look at the same problems that millions of others have observed from new and different perspectives – and come up with novel solutions which are often obvious in retrospect. This is because we don't ask why; we ask why?

I try to be open and receptive to every new idea for a product or service that's presented to me because it's part of my job to be a good listener and to evaluate new business ideas and because you can learn something valuable from almost every pitch – sometimes it's exactly what you should also be thinking about (and maybe already doing) in the context of your own business – and sometimes it's something that you wouldn't consider doing in a month of Sundays. I learned long ago that you can have the very best of intentions and still have a really bad idea.

But, in any case, it's generally a good investment of the modest amount of time it takes to pay attention and be polite unless the people pitching haven't done their homework, don't appreciate or want to hear about the magnitude or difficulty of what they're setting out to do, or just aren't really prepared to effectively present and defend their ideas. No one these days has time to waste listening to half-baked businesses or fever dreams. Everyone's entitled to their own ideas (good or bad), but not to their own reality. And another hard-learned lesson is that there is virtually no consistent correlation between great talkers and great ideas. Ideas are driven by enthusiasm, but success depends on execution – you can't win a race with your mouth.

And lately, I feel like we're having another unfortunate run of what I call "slice it and dice it" disease. The premise of all these pitches is that you can take any good idea for a product, service or network (typically someone else's idea who is already hitting it out of the park) and shrink that business down to a narrower target population or a specific niche or a certain kind of consumer and instantly turn the process of serving that smaller segment into a big business as well. Messaging apps just for Moms. Social networks strictly for softball players. Reward programs restricted to redheads. You name it.

I do often say these days that - because of the Internet - niches are no longer necessarily small, but that doesn't mean that they're any easier to address and conquer or that – in fact – while the barriers to entry are deceptively low, the barriers to success aren't even higher than ever. You still need a compelling reason for people to use your product or service and to change their behaviors to do so. Even relatively new habits are hard to break. And while it's true that one size never fits all, it doesn't follow that there's an infinite demand for things in every possible size, shape or variety. Different isn't always better.

And frankly as pervasive as the idea is that we can monetize everything that any of us has in excess (I call this "the emerging surplus economy"), I don't see the whole world being Uber-ized any time soon. We'll see hundreds of variations on this theme, but very few valuable businesses will survive after the novelty wears off and the difficulties of delivering these types of programs at scale becomes increasingly apparent. Uber everything is pretty much a pipe dream.

But if you insist on slicing the salami and heading down this long and winding road and if you're intent on building the next luxury linen outlet just for little people or something even more exotic and esoteric, ask yourself these three questions first:

(1) Who Really Needs Another Whatever?

We've all got more stuff than we need. More friends and followers than we could ever keep up with. More apps and programs on our devices than we can even remember. And more devices than we know what to do with. And you want to add your pony to the pile? I don't think so. I'm afraid that most of the boats have sailed, most of the folks have decided what they're interested in, where they spend their time, and what they pay attention to, and it's gonna be really hard to explain to them why they need another anything.

And your offering isn't even another anything exactly – it's sort of a particular piece of what they already have a bunch of in several variations. It's like offering someone a new email address. Most people would rather poke their eyes out than have to start checking another mailbox and that's even assuming that you could convince them that the effort was worth the time. What exactly are you offering that isn't redundant and duplicative – even if it's slightly more targeted and focused? Most folks have figured out the basic filters that help cut down on the crap they're seeing every day and all the big guys are already adding built-in (and often default) ad blockers to try to delay the inevitable and ongoing migration from websites and email to messaging services which is accelerating every day among the mobile millions and putting a critical damper on online web ad sales. It's really hard to see how you'll even get your message out there to these targets who are doing everything in their power to shut down the volume and turn off the spigot. The most likely outcome is that you'll be left in the dust at the starting gate or trampled by the crowd because you don't have a clear and concise answer to why anyone needs what you're selling.

(2) Who Could Do the Same Thing in a New York Minute?

If it's a remotely good idea, there are hundreds of businesses much bigger and more established than you with millions of existing users who are exactly the people/prospects you want to pitch. All of these competitors (and potentially very fast followers) are searching every day for more products, services and solutions to offer their users since they are under tremendous pressure to constantly engage and retain them. They have no new acquisition costs. They have already built the necessary pipeline and technology. And they are just waiting to steal your idea if it's any good and serve it up to their customers. Nothing you have is gonna stop them, but if you stay small enough, maybe they won't notice you. And the thought that they will swoop in and buy your baby business instead of ripping you off and building their own is another bad bet which happens roughly once in a blue moon.

(3) Who Will Pay Anything for It?

Your friends and family may think your idea is terrific and you might easily recruit a talented team to take on the challenge with you since everyone wants to be an entrepreneur today, but remember that there's an infinite demand for the <u>un</u>available and you won't know a thing for certain until you have something to sell that lots of people want to buy, be part of, or otherwise support. Nothing happens without customers and sales. We buy things because we think they are worth more to us than we are paying for them and – more importantly – when we are convinced that they deliver something we don't now have, but definitely want. Businesses need to be built first on revenues from real people and then they can expand their model to incorporate advertising and other income streams. But the dream of building a large population first (and basically for nothing) so it can be marketed and sold to advertisers who will pay to access these folks is simply a nightmare today. It's an old story (and an even older movie) – it's not clear that it ever worked over the long haul for anyone (Twitter seems to still be looking for an answer while their user base continues to plummet) - and I can assure you that you will also run out of money and starve long before your attempt to crack the code goes anywhere.

Nirvana is that moment of insight and stillness of mind – of perfect clarity - when all the passions, all the delusions and all the frenzy have been driven away. When you have to look in the mirror and face the facts. And when you do you'll see that not every niche leads to nirvana.

TULLMAN'S TRUISMS

NEVER INVEST IN AN IDEA THAT YOU CAN'T ILLUSTRATE WITH A CRAYON

I have been talking for a while now about an important distinction between the content (message) of an attempted communication and the context (channel and timing) in which that content is delivered. The main objective of smart marketing is to successfully engage the customers/consumers at the right time in a useful dialogue, which has become increasingly two-way and interactive, and not to engulf them in a continual and indiscriminate flood of inappropriate and irrelevant material.

If you get all the elements correct (right time, right place, and right message), you're golden. If you blow it, it means nothing but grief for all concerned. And yet, this basic idea apparently hasn't dawned on millions of marketers who just keep mechanically shoveling their shit our way and who think that there's still some value in sheer velocity and volume. They're dead wrong; they're consistently antagonizing and alienating their audiences; they'll eventually be barred and shut off from these channels, and their clients and companies are paying a heavy price for their ignorance. If they don't quickly change their rationale, their approach and their direction, they'll be left in the dust.

The truth these days is that – given the noise, the clutter and the fierce competition for our fleeting and precious attention – the basic rule of thumb is quite simple: if I'm not listening, it doesn't matter what you're saying. You should save your breath and your bullets for smarter, better and more cost-effective targets. I have previously called this approach the need to focus on "smart reach" and you can catch up on the concept here: http://www.inc.com/howard-tullman/to-sell-more-your-marketing-must-embrace-smart-reach.html. Basically, you've got to provide each customer with what he or she wants, when he or she wants it, wherever he or she is, and without asking. Otherwise, all bets are off.

But the idea of "smart reach" alone is yesterday's news for those of us who are focused on keeping ahead of the game as well as the competition. The expectations of the consumer are ever changing and progressive (constantly rising). We all know that what may have worked well for us in the past (and, in fact, most of our prior experiences and successes) aren't likely to be relevant to creating tomorrow's triumphs. Just doing the same old things isn't going to make for better results – especially as the competition all around us continues to mount. Experience, in times of radical disruption and change, can be much more of an albatross, a constraint, and a problem for growing businesses rather than something they can comfortably rely upon. See http://www.inc.com/howard-tullman/navigating-the-information-superhighway.html . And so the moving finger keeps writing new stories and it's those new stories that will create and build the critical connections to the consumer in the future.

And, as smart and aggressive a focus on "smart reach" still may be for many businesses that haven't even begun to advance their thinking; I'm afraid that the bar is jumping up again and that smart reach's time has come and gone as a "be-all, end-all" strategy. This is in part because it's a uni-directional concept (a remnant of the old broadcast "one-to-many" era rather than reflective of our new networked economy) and that's no longer the two-way world we have to operate in. Today all 3 of the main nightly network news broadcasts reach only about 22 million viewers while every day more than 160 million people in the U.S. check in with Facebook. This is the new "many-to-many" environment in which we learn as much or more laterally from our peers as we do from any top-down sources.

Smart reach is all about customized mass communication and individualized messaging, but today we need to think more about our interactions with the customers and consumers as multi-directional conversations: conversations with us, discussions and interactions between interest groups, and third-party sharing among consumers and their peers and influencers as well - in which we will never be direct participants. We know that we couldn't be everywhere the consumer is today even if we tried. And we also acknowledge that we can't service and control every channel to the consumer even with unlimited time and resources. But being there when the buyer is ready to buy is the most critical objective of all. If you can't be found, you will never be chosen.

So the best new strategies have a lot more to do with conversations than simple communications and a lot more to do with advocates and influencers than with advertising and infomercials. This isn't easy for a lot of folks to swallow, no good marketer ever wants to trust his or her fate to others and give up some degree of control over the messaging, but it's easier than you might imagine once you understand that it's no longer about you or your products and services – it's all about them. It's their agenda, they want to drive the process, and you need to figure at least how you can hitch a ride.

If we can't be there ourselves (directly or indirectly), and that's increasingly a given, when these critical conversations and decisions are taking place, then we need to have our messages convincingly and consistently carried forth by authentic and motivated messengers – prompted (but not paid) proxies if you will – who will make it their mission to passionately promote our products and services. Make them care – create a dream that they can adopt and make their own – and let them go forth and spread the word.

Consumers today don't really care to hear anything more about the features and attributes of your products; they want to know how those products will directly benefit them (value) and how they will make a difference in their day-to-day lives (impact). Today we trade our attention for offerings which we believe to have real and specific value for us. Just adding more information to the conversation has no intrinsic value unless it is

(a) effectively and credibly communicated,
(b) resonates with the target audience, and ultimately
(c) impacts and drives the desired behaviors. If you can't make me care about what you have to say, I'll quickly move on to the next best thing. I call this the "show me or see ya" problem.

We really don't have the time or the inclination to do the heavy lifting of learning about new things or ideas these days, but we are willing to briefly listen. And who exactly do we listen to? Some things (like word of mouth) never change and we're still taking the lion's share of the guidance we seek on product and service selections from our friends and peers. But our universe of "friends" has expanded dramatically (and mainly artificially) to include a lot of influencers and others whose opinions and ideas we've come to trust and value even though they would never meet the traditional definition of a friend. Brands used to serve this purpose – as shorthand for quality, value, safety and reliability – but now – given the limited time we all have and the vast amount of choices and the frightening lack of quality decision-making data - we look to loudmouths (not in the pejorative sense), mavens and other mock and manufactured experts to tell us what they think we ought to know. And realistically, to reach these new audiences, these are the folks that you want to deliver your messages for you. And keep in mind that these aren't - by and large – hired guns, flacks, media people or celebrities; they're the ordinary, feet-on-the-street, every day denizens of the web, who are living the new technologies every day, and who the crowd has selected, endorsed and designated as the ones worth listening to.

These folks are a curious breed – passionate about being in the know – passionate about being ahead of the crowd – and most passionate about being in front of a crowd at all times. They live by the doctrine that nothing is real until you've shared it and that everything is better when it's shared. For some it's mostly ego, for some it's a desire to educate, and for the truest believers, it's an almost moral obligation that they feel to share something that has benefitted them with the masses. This is largely their lives (it's definitely <u>not</u> about the money) and they are at it as close to 24/7 as they can possibly be. Here again, in today's short-cycle world, you need people feeding the beast 24/7 on your behalf and these are the ones who seemingly can't help doing just that and couldn't stop doing it if they tried. I call them WOMbots. Word of Mouth "robots". And as peculiar and different as they may seem to us at the moment; they're a lot more likely to have both an immediate and a lasting impact on your business and our future than all the old-line ad agencies and all the new-line social media marketing businesses combined.

TULLMAN'S TRUISMS

THE FUTURE ISN'T SOMETHING TO BE FEARED; IT'S SOMETHING TO BE SHARED

Straight from the heart of the Startup Nation, this very frank and realistic film is an important cautionary tale for everyone who imagines that they want to start a business or be an entrepreneur.

The clear and consistent message is that it's very hard to do this kind of work and that it's not just hard on the entrepreneurs, but it's equally as difficult (or more so) on their families as well. Before any wanna-be starts down this path, you need to ask yourself (as well as the people you care the most about) the very same question that you should ask before you loan money to a close friend – which is the most important – and which are you prepared to lose? I tell all our entrepreneurs that there's always more work, but you've only got one family. Building a new business is a 24/7 job and there's no way to leave anything at the office at the end of the day because the day never ends.

The second important message from the film is that it's pretty easy to convince yourself of just about anything – convincing investors and customers that you have something real and different and important is a much more challenging job. There are only a few people who will care enough to tell you the truth and that's especially true when the truth hurts. But the truth only hurts (as you'll see throughout the film) when it ought to. It's never easy to say what no one wants to hear.

You'll also hear a recurring refrain from Yosi as he explains how his idea for Fiddme came to him. This really bothered me. He keeps saying that he thought to himself in that moment: "I think we have a startup." But no one who knows anything wants to hear that. Saying "I think we have a business is good." Saying "I think we've found a pain point and a solution" is better. And saying "I think we have lots of people willing to pay for our product or service" is best of all. We've got tons of startups today – what we're looking for are sustainable businesses. Cash is important, but customers are king.

And, if you listen closely, you'll hear the venture capitalist David Blumberg explain a very critical concept in the startup world. Being a little early is OK, but being too early means you die. And here's a little known fact – the largest single determinant of startup success is timing – not the idea, not the team, and not the funding. You've got to be in the right place at the right time for lightning to strike. And it also helps a whole bunch to be lucky.

I wasn't crazy about how one of the stories ended (no spoiler alert is required here) because it confirmed one of the worst possible messages in our business which is that it's better to be lucky than smart or hard-working. In fact, there's a great new book out by Randall Lane called: "You Only Have to be Right Once" which tells the stories of our latest crop of a dozen tech billionaires and leaves you with the exact same impression – that with the possible exception of Mark Zuckerberg – the rest of the new breed of super-hero entrepreneurs could just as easily have been driving a cab these days or working as a computer technician.

And the final, very instructive, message (mainly for Israelis rather than U.S.-based entrepreneurs) is that it's a stupid waste of time and effort to go from Tel Aviv to the Valley looking for your pot of gold. Cash is everywhere in the states these days, but much more than capital, businesses need customers to succeed and there are NO customers on the Coast. If you want to build a real business, you need to be where the buyers are and that's in places like Chicago and not San Francisco.

One last thought which I think the film also makes clear – it's a hard life and a bumpy road for sure – but for a certain breed of person – it's the only way to live. We spend a great deal of our lives working and the greatest privilege and joy there is .. is to be able to get up every day and do something that you can be excited and enthusiastic about.

SILICON**WADI**

I t seems today that we need to find an apt acronym or a pithy phrase to describe the latest new idea, development or tech craze in order to make these things (which aren't exactly rocket science to begin with) real and understandable for the masses or at least for the mass media. Everything seems to be about buzzwords and jargon and the critical need to have a catchy log line or two. The name game is as much a part of the norm now as the novelty of the idea and owning a killer URL or app name is worth at least as much as your highly-polished elevator pitch because the name itself might be the thing that gets you in the door in the first place – long before you have a chance to extol the virtues of your business.

But sometimes the pundits' rush to find a fitting formulation (or to rudely jam something into a framework or structure that they're already hawking) leads to a characterization or description that's more "high concept" than helpful. Simpler is almost always better, but sometimes it's not sufficient to get the story told. Right now, I think we're seeing this process operating on a daily basis with the world' newest fetish – the "sharing" economy. Sharing may be a part of the story, but it's not the whole answer or enough of an explanation to really help us understand what offerings are real (for the long term) and which are here for today and likely to be long gone tomorrow because they're mainly just way stations or transitional solutions. There's a fairly obvious reason why Reed Hastings called his business *Netflix* rather than *Mailflix*. It's never really about who's first – it's always about who's best and who's the last one standing.

So, while it's true that in some cases part of the new economy relies on the sharing of certain common assets (we "share" the use of individual Divvy bikes in Chicago and timeshares of all kinds have been around forever), the real significant changes are better described as products and services (and, of course, applications) that are increasingly permitting millions of us to monetize (not share) our excess capacity or our surplus assets. And that's why we need a broader frame of reference for these new economic ecosystems.

Initially, I was convinced that a far better and more descriptive term for at least the transactional part of this new phenomenon was to call it the "Surplus Economy" wherein each of us would be permitted to market and exploit our underutilized assets and resources - these could be skills, talents, time, labor, property, knowledge, etc. - by using our new connectivity tools and the ability to immediately and cost-effectively reach global marketplaces - to sell and distribute our valuable properties and abilities to others largely without regard to (and generally free of) the time and place restrictions which have historically made such widespread and hyper-efficient marketplaces impossible on the kind of scale that we are already beginning to see across a number of different industry sectors. We weren't trying to share our talents – we were quite clearly trying to sell them to as many takers and interested parties as possible as quickly and easily as we could.

However, this primary concentration on the seller-side demands and desires of these new marketplaces and on the technical nature of the transactions which they enabled turned out to be insufficiently broad to fairly describe what was going on because this characterization failed to account for the buyer-side actions and objectives as well as the very critical temporal (time-based) component of these new services. The sellers clearly wanted to sell (as sellers always do), but the buyers' demands were more complicated.

First, they needed to efficiently discover the availability of the opportunities being offered in the midst of the immense noise, clutter and confusion of our online world and to connect with the parties on the other side of the prospective transaction. Interestingly enough, as important as being global is to the providers of these services, hyper-local solutions have the most appeal to the end-users on both sides of the deals.

Second, they needed to authenticate and validate the offers being made. (This is a topic all of its own and suitable for a separate piece.) But surprisingly this requirement is becoming less and less of a concern to substantial numbers of consumers. They don't want to be defrauded or otherwise ripped off or cheated, but – at least until they've been burned once or twice - they're more concerned with other elements and aspects of these transactions.

Third, they needed established and credible systems for payment which – for all intents and purposes – are a given these days.

And finally, and most importantly to understanding the entirety of what's going on, the buyers want it when and where they want it and - most of the time - they want it NOW. Time is the scarcest resource in our lives today and these businesses across the board are selling us time and convenience every bit as much as they are providing whatever product or service we're seeking. You can call this the "on-demand" or the "on-time" economy, but because the expectations of all consumers are progressive and constantly rising, I'm calling it the "Right Now" economy because (a) that's where we are all headed; and (b) if your business or company isn't operating in this new real time, right now, competitive world, you can be sure that someone is coming up right behind you to offer a better, faster, cheaper and more attractive service than yours and to offer it right now.

The implications, challenges, opportunities and problems (especially from a regulatory perspective) which these new economic ecosystems present are almost beyond calculation and the new kinds of businesses which they will spawn are enterprises that we are just beginning to imagine. When you consider the degree to which (at least at the outset) these new systems (a) require little or no capital, (b) utilize modest and readily available technologies, (c) build upon existing consumer skills and behaviors, and (d) basically free-ride on stable and well-established distribution systems, it's easy to understand how quickly and globally the "Right Now" economy is growing with no end in sight.

I've been saying for a while now that there's a problem with the classic definition of insanity which basically maintains that - if you insist on only doing things the ways you have always done them, it's crazy to expect better or different results. Otherwise stated, it's simply an acknowledgment that "to get what we've never had, we're going to have to do what we've never done." We hear a lot of this talk, but – especially in larger businesses – it's mainly just that – a lot of talk and wishful thinking and not much else. And part of the reason may be that the traditional formulation itself has worn out its welcome. It's not enough to simply be a new or different way of doing the same old things; the new solutions need to be bigger, broader and better all-around in order to make a real difference.

One simple solution for the perception part of the problem may be for these traditional businesses to look at the way the smartest startups view the world. To the guys still sitting quietly in the C suites with their fingers and toes crossed who are hoping that this web/digital thing will just blow over like some many other fads before it blows up in their faces or seriously beats up their bottom lines – especially during their time in the hot seat - I would simply say: if you really want things to stay the way they are, they're gonna have to change. And change dramatically and change soon.

Simply looking at past actions, present plans, capabilities and resources, and/or the actions of direct and obvious competitors isn't a sufficient inquiry any longer. Incremental improvements may change the results by a few cents or goose this quarter's market share by a point or two, but they're not going to alter the game anymore. Looking for tweaks and short-term improvements is just too narrow a perspective and far too limited an approach to succeed in the new world of global competitors – many of whom aren't saddled with your legacy systems or the need to support the old enterprise offerings while the customers want tomorrow's technologies.

In today's disruptive and discontinuous world, this constricted view isn't especially helpful or instructive because it has us all looking backwards or laterally instead of looking ahead. Our job today is to desire, expect and demand more than what others - and the world at large - thinks is possible. At 1871, we like to say that, if you don't know it's impossible, it's that much easier to do. And, of course, things always seem impossible to the naysayers until they get done and then they belatedly seem obvious.

So, if we limit ourselves to what has come before or benchmark ourselves solely against the known competition, we are bounding our opportunities by the limitations of those around us. That's simply too low a bar. Just because they can't or haven't done something doesn't remotely suggest that we should take on those boundaries or that we can't do much more. The ways things have always been done aren't the upper limits of what's possible or achievable - they're just what's come before - supported and calcified by the tired and conventional wisdom.

There are countless ways that we fall into this mindless way of thinking, but one that seems to be uncommonly common is the way we have historically regarded and identified our competition and, more importantly, how we organize ourselves to address and deal with them.

Large businesses have traditionally regarded their primary markets as zero-sum environments with the attitude that it was their job to take as much market share away from their competitors as possible. Basically, a "what's mine is mine and what's yours we can talk about" attitude. AT&T executives used to joke that they weren't a monopoly, they just enjoyed 100% customer loyalty. All these executives saw their world as a see-saw or a teeter-totter with compensating adjustments being made over time among the players. It was a "nice" world – things were predictable – things were consistent – things were reliable – and often it was a world governed by overt or indirect understandings and agreements as to price controls or price level maintenance arrangements which served the players' interests in maintaining high prices and avoiding price wars, but rarely, if ever, benefitted the customers or end users.

Today, almost every aspect of that world has changed. The customer is in the driver's seat and if you're not meeting his or her needs, they'll be gone in a flash. And those needs continue to regularly expand with a constantly rising bar. Good enough no longer is – the way you stay in the game is getting better all the time. And the competition looks a lot more like dodge-em cars than the see-saw because: (a) they're coming at you from every direction, not in a linear or direct fashion – and (b) their numbers, approaches, offerings and multi-channel delivery systems are exploding. It's not a fixed set of folks – it's not a gentlemen's game anymore – it's every business for itself and everyone wanting your business as well.

I've described this new world of opportunities – especially for new and nimble businesses – as one where there are so many new and different areas for aggressive and innovative companies to conquer that the real challenge is more about focus than anything else. You can extend your business into new areas – you can "slide to the side" into adjacent markets – you can offer alternatives to existing solutions – cheaper, faster, more accessible, etc. and you can create entirely new markets and products and services based on the new tools, mobility and connectivity which we now have. See: http://www.inc.com/howard-tullman/five-reasons-your-market-is-bigger-than-you-think.html .

None of this is remotely good news for the big guys, incumbents and the powers that be. In the absence of immediate action and changes in their own businesses, the best they can hope for is a slow and painful slide into oblivion. Or they can recognize that maintenance (or trying to just hold on) isn't a vision or a strategy for today. Today, you can't sit back and let things happen to you – you get better by getting started and getting better every day thereafter. It's fairly easy to understand, but ridiculously hard to consistently execute.

At 1871, we try to do it every day and we keep 3 objectives constantly in mind:

(1) Set Impossible Standards;
(2) Expend Extraordinary Efforts; and
(3) Achieve Remarkable Results.

Expect nothing less from yourself and your team and you'll be surprised at how well things will work out.

TULLMAN'S TRUISMS

THE BEST WAY TO GET AHEAD IS TO GET STARTED

In a recent fireside chat, Dennis Chookaszian, the long-time CEO of CNA Insurance and more recently a substantial angel and early-stage investor and advisor to numerous public and private companies, departed from the usual plethora of pompous pieties and platitudes that seem of late to comprise the primary content of far too many typical technology panel discussions and got down to sharing some concrete and very specific advice for startups, some concise rules of thumb and formulae which he uses to evaluate the likelihood of a startup's success, some thoughts about the criticality of scaling swiftly, and a few closing comments about the importance – early on – of paying attention to matters of ethics and the core values of the business you're trying to create. As I like to say, you can't build value if you have no values. See http://www.inc.com/howard-tullman/how-far-will-you-go-to-be-loved.html In terms of sheer content, straight talk, and take-away value, this was one of the best talks and Q&A sessions we've ever had at 1871.

Dennis is a guy who – as much as it's ever possible to do so – has really refined his investment strategy and approach and made a science of how he looks at prospective investments. In addition, it was clear that he's thought long and hard about exactly how he advises young entrepreneurs on what they can realistically expect on their journeys and the best ways to prepare themselves and their companies for the very bump roads and precarious paths ahead. He noted that he's often approached by folks for help in raising early stage capital or providing senior level introductions for them to large firms and – as often as not – he says that while he could help, he won't - because he doesn't think that it's the right time for them to raise capital or that taking in investment capital (even if it's abundant and readily available) is the right approach for the development stage of their businesses. In the startup business, you eventually learn that a quick and honest rejection is a lot more helpful in the long run than a grudging or half-hearted favor that ultimately does neither party any good.

As you might expect, the discussion started with what he called the "rule of three" which is a simple way to think about the need to focus the scarce resources and bandwidth of the entrepreneur on the most critical and pressing issues for the business. He said that – as a general proposition – it's almost impossible to pay attention and devote your energies to more than 3 or maybe 4 critical concerns at a time. As Confucius probably should have said: "Man who chase too many rabbits end up with none."

The three most important areas that Dennis felt every startup needed to concentrate on were:

(1) Substantial and Sustainable Revenue Grow

If you can't determine early on who is going to pay you for your new product or service and you haven't demonstrated that the dogs are gonna eat the dogfood, then it's highly likely that you don't have a viable business. In addition, your business model and your actual results need to realistically demonstrate an achievable market size and a path to securing market share sufficient to show early exponential revenue growth. Dennis's shorthand for this criteria was T2D3 which meant that your year-over-year revenues were expected to triple in each of the first two years and then to double in each of the next 3 succeeding years of the business.

Dennis shared some very specific and detailed criteria with the group about how each business should look at the nature and quality of its revenues in order to determine whether they were on the right path. The four critical factors were: (a) businesses building recurring revenue bases are far better than ones dependent on constantly securing new business especially because renewals are much easier and less expensive to secure than new sales; (b) the customer retention rate of the business was absolutely critical – all customers are very costly to acquire and very easy to lose today in a world of almost infinite choices and alternatives; (c) businesses based on products or services having a steady stream of new customers or ones that required constant replacement or renewal (the "razor blade" model) were much more attractive than durable goods businesses (like selling refrigerators) where the products had very long repurchase or replacement life cycles and could even fairly quickly reach points of substantial saturation; and (d) businesses offering products or services which had a predictably high rate of obsolescence were much more attractive than those where the products had long useful lives.

Finally, Dennis was also brutally frank with the audience about how frequently startups fail. While he believes (as noted above) that the most recurring cause of early business failures is a lack of sufficient and rapidly-expanding revenues, he also noted the problem with pointless perseverance. He said that very often the biggest mistake an entrepreneur can make is trying to stay the course and waiting too long to bite the bullet and either pivot quickly or decide to shut the business down if it's not making the necessary progress. I like to say that there's nothing worse than profitless prosperity where your top line keeps growing, but there's no bottom line in sight. He pointed out that establishing some milestones or benchmarks for measuring your business's success over a fixed period of time and then sticking to those metrics either way – in good times or in bad times – in deciding your next steps is a form of management discipline that is essential. See http://www.inc.com/howard-tullman/the-future-of-tech-metrics-not-moonshots.html .

(2) Resisting Raising Too Much Capital Too Soon

Dennis is a bootstrapping hardliner. He doesn't agree with the "appetizer rule" to wit: that the time to eat the appetizers (or raise new money) is when they're being served or available. He believes that you should raise as little as you can for as long as you can regardless of how easy it might be at a given point in time to secure new funding. For a contrary view, see:

http://www.inc.com/howard-tullman/tech-startups-take-the-money-and-build.html . He also said that you should only seek outside investment (and only as much of an investment as you realistically will need) once it's clear that you have an actual business with provable revenues that is going to grow and prosper. Otherwise the outside money will cost you too much and – probably worse for you and the business – conceal the fact (or defer the unhappy realization) that you haven't really figured how to operate and scale the business in a profitable manner. He noted that mega-incubators like 1871 are great places to get started because they enable entrepreneurs to avoid all kinds of costs and commitments that are bad uses of their scarce capital and – at the same time – to secure access to enormous amounts of "free" resources, education, networking and mentoring that will all be crucial to their long-term success.

(3) Leadership and Ethical Values

The smartest investors bet on the jockey and not the horse and nothing is more important for the success of the business than the strong leadership skills of the senior management team. And, because the required skills sets will change dramatically over time as the business grows, it is also critical that the management be sufficiently flexible that they can grow and adapt to the new requirements of the business. Dennis noted that this is a _very_ rare outcome and that it is unusual for the CEO of a startup to survive in that role beyond a certain point in terms of the company's revenue growth, market(s) size and share, etc. It's very clear that entrepreneurial and managerial skills are quite different and specifically the CEO's role and involvement in various functions and parts of the company will need to change materially as the years go by or the CEO will need to be changed.

What cannot change and what is critical from the outset are the values that the company develops and builds upon as it creates its own internal and external culture and, here again, it is the CEO whose behaviors and attitudes are the most critical in providing the essential role model for the rest of the company. Mission statements are a dime-a-dozen these days and all the talk doesn't mean a thing if your actions and behaviors aren't aligned with your professed beliefs and values. Over time, the values of each business will develop and the priority of certain concerns and considerations may change somewhat, but it's a very slippery slope that needs to be jealously guarded because it is very hard to ever recover from the damage that results from broken promises and commitments. By and large, values don't abruptly break; instead they crumble a bit at a time. I like to say that it's much, much harder to live up to 99% of your values than to honor them 100% of the time.

Dennis said that each of us needs to determine which values are most important and that we all need to establish an ethical framework. Once you have established those ground rules, it's crucial that you also make it clear that there are boundaries and bright, red lines which simply cannot be crossed. While people are people and we are all fallible, there are just some behaviors which no business can abide or afford. In other situations, some understanding and forgiveness and a second chance might be the most appropriate response.

In his view, everyone has a three tier ethical framework and the critical issues in each case are what behaviors are in each tier and then which tier a particular case of questionable behavior falls into. The three tiers are

(1) Zero Tolerance;
(2) Possible Rehabilitation; and
(3) Everything Else. Behaviors which fall into the first tier are (1) honesty/integrity breaches and (2) any kind of abusive behavior. There is simply no way back from these kinds of problems and any proven violations must result in immediate termination. Violations that impair the core values of the business cannot ever be tolerated.

Other issues which fall into the second tier – personal problems, substance abuses or performance problems – can potentially be remedied by giving the offender a chance to correct the problem. But these cases must strictly a one-shot opportunity to get things straight and any repeated behavior needs to be swiftly dealt with and the person must then be terminated.

Everything else can and should be dealt with through the normal management and HR processes. By and large, these cases should not involve the senior management team. Only those instances which impact the business's basic culture and mission are serious enough, central enough, and important enough to be reinforced and reiterated through the involvement and behaviors of the business's leaders. People, since time began, have paid attention not to what we say, but to what we do. Some things never change.

I t may be the season to be jolly and it's always great to celebrate our successes, but as the end of the year draws near, it's also a time to reflect on all the things that didn't get done; the ones that didn't go the way we planned; and even those dashed dreams that turned out to be more about heartfelt hopes than high-value ventures. As frenetic and frazzled as the holidays can be, they're also a great time to take the time to catch your breath, take stock (no pun intended) and look ahead.

During the rest of the year, when you're up to your ears in alligators and everything's a fire drill; it's easy to lose sight of the long game and the real objectives of the business as well as the goals that you've hopefully set for yourself as well. Those personal goals are every bit as important as anything you've got planned for the business. Your greatest fear should never be that you might fail in a given business – there's always another one of those around the bend just waiting to be started – it's the fear that you might spend a significant part of your life working on something that doesn't really matter or make a difference.

You've only got a certain number of "at-bats" in life and it's important to make sure that you make each and every one count for something and that – in the process – you become someone to be counted on as well. (See http://www.inc.com/howard-tullman/to-succedd-be-the-one-everyone-can-count-on.html .)

All of this – the ups and downs - the good news and the bad – are part of the deal every entrepreneur makes when he or she sets out to change things. Change is never easy and overcoming the resistance to change is a lifetime job. But like everything else in life, it's all about what you make of the situations you find yourself in and how you move forward that ultimately makes the difference. (See http://www.inc.com/howard-tullman/so-youve-got-problems-thats-probably-great-news.html .)

This can be a time of rebirth, re-dedication and renewed commitment or you can waste your time and energy doubting yourself, blaming your circumstances (or the folks around you), and fearing the future. Things aren't ever as good or as bad as we imagine and the things we imagine are always worse than the things we face up to and take head on. You can let yourself get down or you can get busy.

I expect that you know where I come out on that question. So I've got three simple suggestions of things to do when you're getting down.

(1) Get Past the Past as Soon as Possible

Don't waste a lot of time looking backwards. There's not much you can do today to change the past, although you can certainly learn from it. Just don't get stuck there because it's almost always an invitation to spend your time navel gazing, making excuses, and bemoaning bad breaks. That's absolutely not where you need to be focusing your energies. In addition, by this late date, I'd expect that whatever lessons there were to be learned from past triumphs and pratfalls have already been incorporated into your going-forward plans. Sitting around worrying about missed chances and blown deals won't help you move the business ahead. You can't build your future on regrets and "shoulda, woulda, couldas." And finally, looking in the rear mirror is distracting. It makes it easy to run off the road or smack into something big and ugly that could have been avoided if you had been looking straight ahead.

(2) Call on Your Customers While You Still Can

Get off your butt and get out there and talk to your customers before they find someone else who's demonstrably more interested than you are in what matters to them. Listen carefully to what your customers are doing and saying about their own pressing needs and their current desires. Customer expectations are progressive. If you're not on top of these needs, you'll soon be at the bottom of their list. Business plans and strategy sessions are great, but if all that effort is taking place in a vacuum uninformed by real customer feedback, then it's a waste of time. There's a great big world outside the four walls of your business and you need to get out there because that's where your future will be found. Remember, you'll never get straighter answers to your questions than the ones you get directly from your customers because they're the ultimate users of your products and services.

(3) When You're Thinking About Quitting, Remember Why You Started

There was an important reason you started your business and a problem or problems you set out to solve because you thought you could make a difference by doing things that hadn't been done before in new ways. When times get tough, you need to remember that it's a marathon and not a sprint and the most critical thing you can do is to keep moving.

I'll bet those problems haven't dried up and disappeared although your approach to solving them may have changed – ideally for the better – and that's O.K. – as long as you're still addressing concerns that remain important to your customers and so long as they're still willing to pay a fair price for you to solve their problems for them.

And I'll bet that there are new competitors coming at you from every direction and competing with you in a variety of ways – price, speed, access, ease of use, etc. That's O.K. too and totally to be expected. Your job is to make it as hard on those folks as possible and the best way to do that is to do your business better than anyone else and to do it that way every single day.

But at the end of the day, when you're feeling as low as you can go, you just need to remind yourself of one simple fact: there's nothing in the world that a true entrepreneur would rather be doing than just what you're doing every day. Coming to a place, working on a dream, and doing it with a group of people who are as excited and enthusiastic about what they're doing as you are is the greatest privilege anyone can have and it's <u>you</u> that's making it possible for yourself, but also for all those other folks who are looking to you to lead the way.

It's O.K. to get down – just don't let it show – and don't ever let them down.

TULLMAN'S TRUISMS

IT'S NOT EASY TO SAY WHAT NO ONE WANTS TO HEAR

Not every solution or app needs to set the entire world on fire or to be built on a platform just slightly less grand than the Taj Mahal. It's not always "smart" to build your app to run on the hottest and newest smart phone and nowhere else. You might get some buzz and some early adopters, but being in the shiny new thing biz isn't the path to building a big business in many cases where ready access and broad availability trump haptic feedback, VR capabilities and other gee whiz features. Mass ultimately always matters and when the real value and design of your business is to touch and impact as many people as possible, the lower the bar to use and adoption, the better.

I'm not talking about MVPs or lean anything. I think the whole lean startup spiel is way overblown. (See http://www.inc.com/howard-tullman/busting-the-lean-startup-myth.html) In today's rapid-fire economy, you rarely get two bites at the apple and it's very hard to skinny down a complex and resource-heavy app on the fly because the market isn't going to wait for you to get it right. The market just moves on – abandonment curves are many times steeper than adoption curves – so you need to take your best and simplest shot first and then build up from there as your users tell you what else they need and what makes sense to them.

Sometimes the most creative aspect of an idea (and the key to its ultimate success) isn't how radically different it is from the way we've always done things, but how much it's the same - with just the slightest tweaks that make all the difference. Riding on existing track and/or piggy-backing on someone else's pipeline is a lot less costly and quicker than trying to build your own. The truth is that the closer you can stay to "business as usual" and the more you can rely on previously learned actions, current channels and the ways that customers, users and consumers are already behaving, the easier it will be to get your new product or service adopted and incorporated into their day-to-day lives.

People only think they always want the neatest and newest thing on the block until they remember that "new" also means changes, anxiety, training and learning curves, mistakes, resistance, incremental costs, discomfort, etc. Better to make things as quick and easy as possible if you want to get a lot done in a short time and make a real difference. Start low and grow.

This topic came up recently at a meeting where everyone was bemoaning the funding cutbacks in social services in many cities and the fact that outreach efforts, awareness campaigns and other marketing initiatives were among the first things to be dropped so fewer and fewer folks were even learning about the availability of possible support programs and various other services which they and their families might desperately need.

Of course, I said that we had a startup at 1871 (mRelief) which was already working with the city on "an app for that" which lets just about anyone quickly and easily figure out exactly which Chicago and/or community-based programs exist that might have benefits applicable and immediately available to them – especially in the current environment – and further that the app was designed by the 3 female founders to serve and provide information from a multitude of different services and agencies all in a one-step, one-stop fashion. This meant that a single promotional campaign for the mRelief app (which was supported by all the concerned agencies and city services) could get the word out to everyone in the city who needed to know at a fraction of the cost of each organization or department trying to do anything on its own with little or no available funding to do so.

Interestingly enough, their overwhelming response was to say that this all sounded great BUT they pooh-poohed the suggestion because they believed that none of the targeted populations would have the kind of fancy phones they'd obviously need to use the mRelief service. And that's when the discussion got really interesting because anyone and everyone with any phone can use the service. That was the beauty of the original intent and the original design. They went as low technologically as you can go (SMS texting) and built a system that works at that level for all comers. The analytics and the back-end are where the weight of the system is – the front end's as light as a feather and just as simple – you answer a few questions and you're good to go. It's up, it's operating and – with any luck at all – it'll be coming to a city near you soon and literally saving lives in the process. They have just released a version (https://build.mrelief.com/) which can be used by other cities to adopt the program. Pretty happy news for the holidays.

And the bottom line – an old rule of design – complexity is the enemy. Make your solution as simple as possible, no simpler, and get started right there.

As the bogus unicorns start to crumble into unicorpses (as per no less an authority than *The New York Times*), our more modest and meaningful metrics – focused on building viable (cash positive) businesses and creating real job growth instead of voodoo valuations and media hype – are starting to look positively prescient. Relative capital constraints (or at least capital that resists flocking like lemmings to the latest shiny story) make for stable businesses run by reasonable operators who understand that the race (before the spigot shuts off) isn't always simply to size; it's at least as important to get to sustainability which means that you're burning less than you're bringing in - from contracts and customers – not new investors.

In Chicago, we've got a growing stable of solid businesses providing real products and services and real benefits to millions of users across the country and the world and – at the same time - they're creating concrete enterprise value for their backers and investors as well which isn't likely to dry up and blow away when the first headwinds and competitors arise. These aren't businesses that aspire to be the first on the block; they're aiming to be the best in the business. Does it better always beats did it first. And we're seeing similar growth and prospects in other cities throughout the Midwest as the "rise of the rest" continues unabated while the fantasy stories on both coasts continue to crumble. You can only win a race with your mouth (and your media) until you have to take your next breath. And that's very, very tough to do if your business is under water and a long way from shore.

I wrote a while ago about one of our EDtech companies at 1871 (*ThinkCERCA*) rolling out new programs to schools to help students learn to think about and actively engage in their learning instead of passively sitting back as the old wisdom from the "sage on the stage" washed over and right past them. Today they're leaning into this new tech-enabled world where they take control and responsibility for constructing arguments and building the foundations for their own education. Tell me - I might listen. Show me - I might learn. But let me do it myself and I own it for life. Watching the kids using *ThinkCERCA*'s tools to build their arguments step by step starting with their <u>Claim</u> – then gathering the <u>Evidence</u> for it – then explaining their <u>Reasoning</u> for it – next addressing the <u>Counter Arguments</u> – and doing it all in <u>Language</u> appropriate to their audiences is an amazing experience. You can just feel the difference – they're taking charge and ownership – and it shows in their posture and in their faces.

But the proof is always in the pudding and that's the best news of all. The measured and validated results are starting to come in from across the country for a number of 1871 businesses including *ThinkCERCA* and the momentum and traction are continuing to build. Apart from sheer multi-year jumps in capabilities and other material growth in reading and other skills (especially in schools that started as under-performing at grade level), the systems worked consistently in diverse environments for learners at every different level <u>at scale</u>. This meant that differentiated learning could be ongoing without consuming enormous (and scarce) amounts of teacher time and resources which had been spent in the past attempting to locate and provide useful materials for each student.

The technologies alone wouldn't have succeeded without substantial preparation and without creating a receptive cradle of culture which also supported the change initiatives. But, once in place, it became clear almost immediately that there was no turning back and that these systems were game changers for everyone involved – students, teachers and parents as well. And of course, success breeds support, adoption, and further successes as well. This is how and what it means to build a real business – Chicago-style. Real people. Real progress. Proven results.

And frankly, it's just way more important to be improving the education of the next several generations of kids in this country than it is to be building the 14th take-out delivery service or the next nichy social network that only a nerd could love. Building a business that makes an impact and a difference is just a better way to spend your time. Technology isn't an end in itself – it's a tool that benefits us all, but, more importantly, it permits us to build products and services which will enable and continue to improve the lives of others for decades to come.

Sometimes you just smack yourself in the head and say to yourself "why didn't I think of that?" It's so obvious and so right. But, of course, that's what makes great entrepreneurs. Entrepreneurs don't know what's impossible or what they can't do. They don't color within the lines or stay stuck in their silos. They see what everyone else has seen (and lamented for years); they think about it differently; and they bring a new perspective/approach to the problem. And then – in retrospect – it's blindingly clear to all of us. As Nelson Mandela used to say: it always seems impossible until it's done.

For years, I've been depressed by the fact that millions of people are trapped in crappy, dead-end jobs (yearning to be free to try to do something meaningful and important) because they are imprisoned by their need to preserve their company-based health insurance coverage for themselves and their families. It's hard to imagine the economic impact and the creative forces that would be unleashed if the futures of so many weren't fettered by the bonds of the bozos who run the health insurance scams in this country. (See http://www.inc.com/howard-tullman/why-wiki-work-is-the-future.html) This is in part why 1871 became the first mega-incubator in the world to offer health insurance programs for its member companies although – truth be told – almost all of our entrepreneurs think they're immortal and indestructible as well so they're more concerned about innovation than insurance in their day-to-day lives.

Now I'm not naïve and I do realize that "portable" health insurance and increased employee mobility isn't exactly a high priority on the lists of any of the major corporations in this country who are plenty concerned as it is with (a) motivating and hanging on to their good young people and also with (b) trying to figure out how they can attract the next several generations of smart, skilled newbies to their big, old and somewhat tired businesses. I don't see their HR departments rushing any time soon to get rid of the insurance handcuffs.

But, there's actually good news out there for everyone and a new solution that will serve both the existing young employee workforce and also be a sure-fire attractor for new talent. Forget free Frosty Melts, gym dues and mid-day massages – the new great employee perk – for businesses big and small – is right before our eyes. And the best news is that it's something you can get started on tomorrow whether your revenues are billions or bupkes. So even the big guys can do some good for a change by doing good for their employees.

In my daily conversations with dozens of techies in their 20s and 30s, it turns out that the real problem for almost all of them is not insurance, it's their substantial student debt. Frankly, no one cares about their 401(k) when they're worried about foraging for food on a weekly basis. In fact, a staggering number of young workers these days don't make any 401(k) contributions even when their employers are willing to match them.

So a new company based at 1871 (*Peanut Butter*) has come up with a simple, straightforward way for businesses to help their employees (new and old) get this brutal burden off their backs. Keep in mind that 40 million Americans have student debt right now and it averages over $30,000 a person. So this isn't just a new employee recruitment tool; it's also a powerful and proven retention tool to help keep your proven people around the place years longer.

And believe me, in this competitive recruitment market (where only a few companies can afford ridiculous signing bonuses and other incentives), you don't want your company to be the last one on the block to be offering this important helping hand to your best employees and hottest prospects.

Talk about a magnet for Millennials – this is the real deal – and these kids in particular are saddled with more student debt than any generation that came before them. Over 70% of the Class of 2015 graduated with student debt.

By 2020, Millennials will represent almost 50% of the total U.S. workforce. Surveys already indicate that most of the major employment decisions that new graduates are making are informed by the impact of their choices on their student debt including industry selection, job acceptances, and relocation options. If, as an employer, your benefits offerings aren't in the competitive set; you can bet that you'll be on the outside looking in at the competition as the best candidates head elsewhere.

Peanut Butter (www.getpeanutbutter.com) is a benefits administration business that makes it easy for employers of any size to make contributions to help their employees pay off their student loans. It's all online and everything from establishing the plan, signing up qualified employees, confirming loan amounts and determining contribution amounts, and even routing, tracking and documenting the payments being made are all incorporated with detailed real-time reports. Treasury management services are provided by a large and long-established Chicago-based financial institution.

Needless to say, this is an almost impossible task for an individual company regardless of their resources to undertake (even with the best of intentions) because every single employee's story is different and there are literally tens of thousands of different lenders, payers, borrowers, etc. It's an ideal use case for a one-stop, cloud-based platform business where all the investigation, standardization, documentation, payment programs and infrastructure are already built and in place so that it becomes a turnkey solution for each of the businesses who want to provide the service to their employees.

You could always try to do this yourself, I guess, but it would be a stupid use of your energy, time and resources when the solution is already sitting there. And an even dumber thing to do would be to wait until everyone else is already offering the benefit to their people. Just remember the old adage – when it's obvious that you need to change; it's probably already too late to do so.

I mentioned in a recent INC. blog piece about *Peanut Butter*, a student loan repayment service for employers (www. getpeanutbutter.com), that one of the most compelling reasons I expect their startup to be successful was that they were creating a solution that virtually all of their future customers would eventually desire, and, at the same time, solving a problem which none of those prospective customers would or, for the most part, could solve for themselves and their own employees.

Interestingly enough, this dilemma wasn't because the customers (large or small) lacked the technical abilities to take on the problem of documenting, servicing and helping to pay down millions of unique student loans for their employees all across the country. It was due to the fact that it wasn't remotely worth the time or effort for any one of them individually to devote the necessary personnel, funding and other resources in an attempt to solve the problem. And yet, it was a very desirable competitive offering with obvious pent-up demand, a low-cost (and possibly pre-tax) incentive that they would love to offer to their employees, and it was clearly an attractive recruiting and retention tool as well. (See http://www.inc.com/howard-tullman/making-student-debt-less-sticky.html)

The most striking fact was that it was the very uniqueness of each loan and each employee's situation which made it inefficient and uneconomical for any one business to take on the problem. But, at the same time, in the aggregate, this problem was a large source of growing concern for more than 40 million student and parent debtors (as well as their employers) and a wide-open and lucrative market for the entrepreneur(s) who could provide an effective remedy.

I like to say that a bunch of tiny little problems (seemingly nuisances not worth anyone's time or trouble) can very often roll up into quite a substantial opportunity. And, believe me, there's nary an industry out there where you won't find similar aggregation opportunities if you take the time to look.

We see this kind of widely-distributed, but unaddressable pain in all kinds of political and community situations where the powers that be just can't or won't be bothered to try to build a solution and no individuals have enough of a stake (or enough at stake) to take on the larger problem for the good of all. Everyone suffers, but no one typically cares enough to step up and try to solve the problem.

Of course, at least in the area of tortious business conduct, and but for the fact that most class action lawyers are scumbags, this was exactly why the vehicle of class litigation came into being so that a few representative and committed plaintiffs could act on behalf of the interests of an entire class of injured parties. Unfortunately, the overwhelming outcome in 99% of all class action cases is that it turns out that the only parties whose interests are being served are the lawyers. The bad guys may sometimes be modestly punished, but the good guys who are the actual victims generally get squat. But I digress.

The real moral of this story is that there are a couple of underlying principles at work here which have universal application and value and, if you can identify how they present themselves in an industry that's of interest to you, and you can quickly build a low-cost solution (at least at the outset) that can massively scale as demand grows, you can ultimately create a very large and profitable business. The principles and the patterns are there in every marketplace. At 1871, we have companies (in addition to *Peanut Butter*) dealing with similar issues in education (*Learnmetrics*), funds transfers (*Pangea*), social services (*mRelief*), etc.

More and more of these kinds of problem situations are being created every day as the flow and volume of mission-critical data accelerates and the complexity of all data-driven marketplaces grows exponentially. The confusion in formats, inconsistent language and terminologies, conflicting or competing vendors who refuse to adopt common conventions and methodologies, and similar problems which preclude straightforward and efficient communication and the rapid transmission of critical information have created Towers of Babel in dozens of industries. These present nothing but great opportunities for clever and ambitious entrepreneurs to build one-stop solutions. It's their job to find and address the pain points in new marketplaces and to do it before someone else does.

What are the basic market characteristics that you need to look for?

(1) There are no industry standards, common measurements, or terminology, but effective normalized communication between the parties is increasingly critical.

(2) There are no central hubs, channels or clearing houses to locate and access the vast amounts of data being generated and the data exists in multiple, inconsistent forms and formats.

(3) Individual industry members aren't incented or otherwise motivated to act on their own either independently or in concert and/or may be legally prohibited from doing so.

(4) The industry desperately needs consistent data and objective documentation to authentically and accurately measure and report its progress and performance to multiple regulatory and funding constituencies.

What are the components of the solution you need to build?

(1) You need to aggregate, translate and standardize the diverse data and different inputs so you can accommodate all the alternatives out there.

(2) You need to be the one-stop shop and the simple solution that all the players can share regardless of their levels of sophistication and technology.

(3) You need to invest in the infrastructure and build the broad and scalable backend that no one else has the bucks or the balls to build.

(4) You need to build it before any of the big guys finally figure it out so that you're the benchmark for the business and their best bet is to buy you.

This is one of those rare environments and moments in time where the *Field of Dreams* isn't a dream. If you build it right; if you're just a little patient; they will come.

TULLMAN'S TRUISMS

DON'T DEFEND YESTERDAY - BUILD FOR TOMORROW

Starting and growing a new business has much more in common with a tornado (and some would say a marriage) than you might expect at first glance. They both begin with a lot of sucking and blowing and, if you're not careful and lucky as well, you could end up losing the house. And while it's never a good idea to bet against Mother Nature or gravity, the good news is that many of the things which are most likely to bring your business down are man-made and sometimes the product of your own actions or – more likely – inactions.

It's increasingly clear that the costs today of true inaction far outweigh the risks of just about anything you're willing to try to do. Keep in mind though that refusing to do things cheaply or quickly or too broadly or before you're fully prepared isn't inaction – it's good decision-making. The things you say "no" to - in the long run - will have a far greater favorable impact on your ultimate success than any quick hits or shortcuts you get sucked into pursuing before you're ready or it's time. Two easy ideas to keep top of mind: don't say "maybe" when you should say "no" and don't try to do something cheaply that you shouldn't do at all.

In addition, these days everyone is an expert on everything and a million people are willing to give you advice – especially when they have no responsibility or liability for the outcomes. (See http://www.inc.com/howard-tullman/expert-advice-is-overrated.html .) Their advice almost always sounds the same: "do something now"; "go big or go home"; "if you snooze, you lose"; "be the first mover", etc. But sometimes the best decision you can make is to say "no" and that's not because you don't want to act – it's because you want to act when and how you choose and when the time is right. It's not always the popular choice or decision, but it's almost always the smart one.

There are certainly going to be some unavoidable risks and existential threats to your company that you'll need to respond to and you're not going to end up anywhere worth going if you try to keep your head in the sand and just creep carefully forward. Things are just moving too rapidly in the global marketplace to act defensively and a go-slow strategy of risk avoidance can be a death sentence for a startup.

But, at the same time, there are also some bumps in the road and some obvious pressures and problems that you can sidestep if you keep your eyes open, pay attention to the signs, and know where to look. The trick is not to let any of these influences (the need for speed, the gospel of scale, the ecstasy of expansion, etc.) and/or influencers (analysts' and media's musings, competitors' and critics' complaints, investors' own agendas, politicians pushing for publicity, etc.) pull your business apart. Screw up your courage, stick to your guns, do what's right for the present, and be ready to flex in the future.

It's really a simple matter of physics. Critical mass actually is critical and it's your job to build or assemble it and to hang on to it. You're pulling everything – all the time – toward the center of things (you're a centripetal "force" – focused, attentive, deeply involved, etc.) trying to hold a lot of things together and the outside (and sometimes the inside) world is constantly conspiring to pull things away from you (they're centrifugal forces – "trying too much too soon", "spreading yourself a mile wide and an inch deep", "trying to be all things to all people", etc.). But as any good entrepreneur knows in his or her heart, you can't have it all. So the trick is to not get tricked into trying.

While many of these concerns are external and market- or competitor-driven, the most insidious ones are from the folks you think are your friends and who technically should be looking out for your best interests. Here's a flash – if they're human and they're breathing, they're looking out for their own interests first. That's just human nature and not a bad thing per se, it's just something to keep in mind as you consider their suggestions and thoughts. A grain or two of salt doesn't just make the soup tastier.

Influencers come in several recurring types, sizes and shapes – watch out for these:

(1) VCs and Aggressive Investors

Most of these guys never met a farm they wouldn't bet and your business (in their minds) is no different. Full speed ahead is the only speed they're interested in and, if you don't make it, they'll be long gone when the layoffs begin. Only moonshots matter and being in the middle of anything is mediocre at best and boring which is even worse. You're trying to build a firm foundation for a sustainable and profitable business and they're trying to find stories they can promote and sell to the next round of greater fools. It's not easy to tell these people to cool their jets from time to time and that your pace doesn't reflect the depth of your passion or your commitment. The best advice I can give you is to try to make sure that you've got some Board members and other advisors (not investors) who've actually run businesses to help take your side in some of the silliest of these arguments. They can help you push back. (See http://www.inc.com/howard-tullman/why-its-better-when-board-members-back-off.html .)

(2) Politicians

Politicians also love big winners, but they love patronage more and so their primary goals are favorable publicity (no surprise) and spreading the wealth around. As soon as they see a roaring success in the city, they want to put you and your business on the road and have you build copies and clones throughout the state or the country – whether it makes the slightest sense for you to do so or not – because their focus isn't on your progress, prosperity or profits, it's on the populace at large and they see it as the more sites and stories, the merrier. This is a great way to over-extend your business and end up spread so thin that nothing works anywhere and then – of course – it's gonna be shame on you when it all comes tumbling down and they'll be over the next hill chasing the newest shiny story. Rapid expansion is always exciting until it isn't and it's looks easy to everyone who doesn't have to execute the plan.

(3) Media

The media operate on a simple principle – they'll love ya 'til they don't and they're always waiting for you to slip on that banana peel and take a tumble. I realize that they're a necessary evil, but you need to be very careful that you're not saying things or doing things (even worse) to "prove" something to these people because (a) it's never enough to satisfy them in any case and they won't believe you anyway; and (b) it's a fool's errand to waste your time trying to impress people whose livelihood is much more about finding the warts and shortcomings in your story than in celebrating your successes. The best thing I can say about your interactions with most of the media today is the advice I heard long ago about why it makes no sense to wrestle with a pig. Only the pig enjoys it and you just eventually end up covered in mud.

The bottom line is simple: these are all distractions that do next to nothing for your business and are best avoided as much as humanly possible. Keep your head down, keep your eyes on the prize, keep moving forward and all the rest of this stuff will take care of itself if and when it matters at all.

> TULLMAN'S TRUISMS
>
> # THERE'S A REASON IT'S CALLED "CRITICAL" MASS

Everyone knows that Illinois has serious financial woes. Of course, these days it would be hard to find a state that doesn't have money problems of its own so there's plenty of misery to share. Sorry state finances these days are as much of a "bitter sweet" oxymoron as jumbo shrimp, military intelligence or exact estimates. The more interesting part of this situation is what the best state managers are trying to do about the problem. We all acknowledge that they can only address the parts of the crisis within their control and that they can only access those funds and resources available to them. But notwithstanding these limitations, Illinois's Treasurer, Mike Frerichs, is leading the way in a fashion that couldn't be better or more timely news for entrepreneurs, startups and the overall tech community.

I would expect that you will quickly see other states in a hurry to jump on this business-boosting bandwagon and follow our leaders' lead. I'm hopeful that – as an entrepreneur - when the conversations and the arguments start in your state that you'll have the ammo to hold up your end of the discussion as well and – if you're so inclined – even help to lead the charge.

As the state's chief investment officer, he has just announced the creation of a new $220 million growth and innovation fund (drawn from existing investments and not tied to the state's budget stalemate) which will drive innovation and job creation in the state by supporting investments in emerging technology companies. These funds will not be directly invested by the state (thank goodness for that), but will be distributed to 15-20 existing, experienced and successful venture funds which will in turn make the specific selection and company investments. It's expected that this action will attract another $400 to $500 million in private-sector money as well for young and growing Illinois startups. Sounds pretty positive to me.

But, much to my surprise, and to a certain extent because of an overall lack of understanding of the fact that the funds in any state's coffers aren't fully fungible, a lot of people (including some of our own VCs and entrepreneurs at 1871) have been critical of this new initiative. While there are legitimately two sides to parts of this argument, I think that it is really important for all of us to understand what really isn't open to argument. Then - at least - the discussion can proceed on the merits instead of based on simple misunderstandings.

What's not open to argument?

If you're the chief investment officer of any state and you're charged with earning the best possible return on all the state funds that have been entrusted to you (including, for example, thousands of families' 529 college investment funds), then you simply have to invest. There's really no choice. You can't save your way to success by sitting on the sideline. In addition, you can't spend a dime of these "trust" funds to help the state solve its general operating problems and deficits because that's completely against the law and the very detailed and complicated rules governing these specific funds. It would be nice to see some of these dollars spent to save critical programs, feed and care for folks, and address other pressing needs, but it's just not possible. So the choices are pretty clear – sit on it or invest it smartly.

What's debatable?

Venture capital investments are risky. Startups fail every day. Maybe the last place that the state should invest even one fiduciary dollar is with early-stage and growth stage businesses, but I personally don't agree. This topic we can debate all day long and there are certainly multiple viewpoints, but almost every fund (professional, institutional, family offices, etc.) understands the idea of diversification and the need to have some exposure to the various parts and sectors of the new economy. In addition, we know that the only real job growth in our economy for at least the last decade has come from the hiring spurts of new businesses (not small businesses) and frankly it's very much in all of our interests to keep that ball rolling.

What's really smart?

As often as this idea has misled us in the past, I firmly believe that the smartest part of this investment strategy has been the state's decision to leave it to the professionals. The beauty of the VCs is that they have only one simple agenda – other than paying themselves a lot of money - and that is to maximize the returns for their investors. They don't have to deal with the media. They don't have a million competing political concerns. They don't have to try to be all things to all people. They just have to do their jobs the very best that they can and make a lot of money for the state on the funds that it has invested with them.

Bottom line: as long as you know what you're talking about, you can argue the merits of the program any way you like. Just don't tell me that by encouraging the growth and expansion of hundreds of new businesses and the creation of thousands of new jobs that the state is taking the food from any families or helping the "haves" to the detriment of the "have nots" 'cause that ain't happenin'.

Whew! We're thisclose to getting our new 1871 3.0 build-out project done where we're expanding our Chicago facility by more than 50% to create more space for startups, schools and sponsors. It's typically a mixed bag of relief and euphoria when you bring one of these big budget babies in on time and on the money. And right now, before the next wave of activity and the next crisis rolls around, I'm just happy to take a breath once in a while, push out my blog posts, and wait for the fresh paint to dry.

Growing your business is always a challenge regardless of what stage you're in and it can be a blessing and a curse all at the same time because one thing's for sure – more isn't always better by a long shot. And not all motion or commotion moves your enterprise forward. I believe that construction projects (they're virtually unavoidable at some point in your business) are among the most painful parts of the company growth process. They're all non-stop, on the fly, mission-critical streams of big and small decisions - all of which are time- and money-sensitive – and most of which are harrowing and tough cases of "either-or" choices where you're usually trying to build the Taj Mahal on a Taco Bell budget. It's the old sad story of "Pick Any Two": your project can be (1) done well, (2) done on time or (3) done on budget – totally up to you. Of course, if you're a good entrepreneur and you're like me, you simply say that you don't have to make these false choices and bad decisions – you would simply like to have it all. Not easy, but essential.

And – regardless of the pain in the middle of the project - when the drywall dust finally settles and the last of the painters packs it in, you'll discover that the whole adventure has taught you some very important and basic lessons that you will put to use in building your business for many years to come. Everyone learns (and earns/deserves) their lessons in their own way (and in their own time) and everyone's lessons are a little bit different based on their circumstances, but after building out more than a quarter of a million square feet of new space over the last few years with some very important help at my side, here are a few hard-earned notes that I'm happy to share with my fellow entrepreneurs.

(1) Nobody cares as much as you do.

Entrepreneurs need to take this stuff - every last bit of it - personally and to heart. I always say that the one who cares the most wins. That will never change and the people who tell you "it's just business" are the ones who always end up eating dust and watching the doers fly by. Caring enough and being willing to show it - without apology or embarrassment - and insisting that there's always a right and best way to do even the hardest things without compromising is hard, every day work. It's easy to get down at times and worn out as you keep pushing those big ugly rocks up the hill, but it's the perspiration and the perseverance that separates the great ones from the also-rans and the people who are willing to settle for second best. If you continue to consistently insist on the best, you'll be amazed what you end up with. In the end, people commit to other people and sign up for their dreams – not only because they want to be a part of something great and bigger than themselves – but also because dedication, enthusiasm and caring are the most contagious things around. You'll also find that you can't do this all by yourself and so it's absolutely crucial to have people on your team and at your side whose "take no prisoners" attitudes are the same as yours. But they're not gonna be the most popular people in the place and so another part of your job is to run interference for them and have their backs when they go to bat for you and the project because a whole boatload of folks will have it in for them from the beginning. You want people who soar, not people who settle, at your side.

(2) No one pays attention like you do

It turns out that - if you're out of sight, you're out of mind. Being there - in the moment and in the thick of things - is always better. Paying attention is an art and you can't phone this stuff in. As the Chinese say: All things flourish where you turn your eyes. It not only shows that you care a lot - it shows that you're also willing to roll up your sleeves and do whatever it takes to get the job done. Most architects don't get this concept and - as a result - instead of nipping things in the bud and in the moment because they're on the site and on the job - their attitude is that - if something is done wrong, we'll just waste precious time, a lot of energy, and someone else's money on finger-pointing, extensive CYA documentation, and then they order "do-overs" instead of concentrating on "do-rights" the first time around. It's a disgusting and wasteful approach and it makes the guys who matter - the client and the contractors - very unhappy. Enough "do-overs" can suck the contractor's profit and enthusiasm right out of the project and then you – the owner-client – are really screwed because no one wants to be working for nothing. If you want people to care and try to do their best, your best bet is always to be there right beside them and – at the same time - to do whatever you can to keep the "professionals" from messing up the program. Very often, in the end, that means that you have to do their job (or rather the job they should be doing) for them.

(3) No one sweats the small stuff like you

If you always sweat the small stuff, the big things tend to take care of themselves because they're built on a solid foundation where the details make all the difference. Compromise is a crafty beast and shamelessly sneaks up on you whenever you take your eyes off the ball - even for an instant. It's a very slippery slope and it's easy to lose your way because the first cut turns out to be the easiest not the deepest and then it's all downhill from there. The people who complain about micro-managing have never built anything special in their shabby and second-rate careers and their shortcuts always show in the end. It turns out that it's easier to be 100% on the program than it is to settle even slightly for less than the best. And you will be totally amazed at how easy it is to make the right calls and decisions - however many there may be - when you stick to your guns and your values throughout the process.

(4) No one is a bigger noodge than you
People certainly need instruction from time to time, but what they really need is to be reminded constantly of the central goals, the key directions and the main chance because - in today's short attention span world - even the people who are listening aren't necessarily hearing what you're saying or remembering what's most important when the chips are down and the going gets rough. It's your job to make sure the messages are getting through and that means being obsessive, being overly and redundantly communicative, being omnipresent, backstopping everything, and always being attentive. And, of course, doing it that way every day.

In service businesses today (and, by the way, every business is a service business today or it won't be a business for long), you don't get a chance to consult the manual or a second chance to make a first impression. Your people are on the firing line from the get-go and the idea of a rule book and standard operating procedures is a joke because nothing's standard any more. Trying to set up rules and responses for every case is a crazy waste of time and doesn't remotely relate to the pace and the extent of the disruption that every business is facing every day. The days when you could "set it and forget it" or let anything run unattended for any period of time are long gone. And your people have to react right now wherever they are and whenever the client or customer wants answers and doesn't want to wait. This isn't an easy environment for anyone and mistakes are bound to be made. No one hates mistakes more than I do, but what you learn over time is that it's more important to be a constant and constructive coach for your people than to constantly be a judge or an umpire.

TULLMAN'S TRUISMS

ALL GOOD THINGS COME FROM DETAIL

For me the Super Bowl had so many of the unfortunate characteristics and reminders of the kinds of struggles that every startup goes thru that - by the game's anti-climactic end - it felt surprisingly like just another day at the office. It was more like an obligation than an opportunity. You had to watch it, but no one really expected that you would enjoy it. And the commercials were not much better. The game was much more of a sideways shuffle than a spectacular show and there certainly wasn't a lot of "joy in Mudville" for anyone on either team. It wasn't a thrilling competition between two super-closely matched competitors – it was more like a contest to see who could make the fewest mistakes and still put some points on the board. There's no passion in playing to avoid the potholes rather than shooting for the stars.

Building a business can feel like a similar grind for days and months on end, but those are the times that it pays to keep your head down and keep plowing straight ahead since that's what will make all the difference in the long run. Playing it safe – trying to straddle the middle – going for maintenance rather than majesty – all leads you to the same sorry state. This startup stuff is hard – it's not for the faint-hearted - and not everyone gets a trophy for trying really hard or a salute for showing up. You've got to set the bar high – model the necessary behavior every day – and never let them see you sweat. Anyone who tells you that being an entrepreneur is a lot of "fun" hasn't been there and is most likely lying to you. It can be thrilling and super satisfying; it can be exhilarating and enervating; it can also be downright lonely and depressing, but it's always work – not fun. Fun is what you theoretically do on your own time – as if there was such a thing in the startup world.

On Sunday the good news was that everyone survived - not too many injuries or concussions – but also not many points on the score board for long stretches - not a lot of glory plays or great stands or saves - and not exactly an inspiring contest likely to stir men's blood. It felt like the winners were more relieved to escape with their modest victory and some dignity than ecstatic about how they triumphed. And sometimes in the startup world, you can get to the end of a week where you wonder how you even made it through and ended up still standing only to discover that you didn't really accomplish a damn thing in terms of moving the business forward. The truth is that today it takes more than baby steps and incremental improvements to change the game and move the needle. The future isn't going to be incremental – it's going to be explosive. What we don't know is just whose efforts are going to be the ones that make the real differences – the hustlers, the hipsters or the hackers. But whatever the team consists of, it's headed nowhere without a leader that the rest of the folks can believe in.

I think in a way that some of the disappointed feeling that surrounded the conclusion of this grossly over-hyped "big game" is an unfortunate commentary on how hard it is in our stupid celebrity-soaked system to root for a great defense rather than celebrating an amazing offense. Just like in a startup, the sales guys get all the kudos for bringing home the bacon while the coders just catch a lot of crap when the system shuts down. No one said that life was fair, and the linemen always come last, but who honestly really remembers that the most important touchdown in Sunday's game was scored early on by the defense. If you're in it for the credit, you're in the wrong place. To win, on game day and in business, everyone has to show up and do the very best job that they can – regardless of their responsibility or position – and know that they helped make a difference. No one does anything major these days all by themselves.

I guess it just goes to show you that you and your own team had better learn to appreciate and take your everyday satisfaction from all the preparation, perspiration, passion and hard work that you put into what you're building together (which you desperately hope will be special) regardless of the near-term outcomes and results because the world in general doesn't really care and no one gives you any points in the end for trying. "Almost" counts in love and horseshoes, but not so much in the real world of business.

Worse yet, just as we saw in the game on too many occasions, what you've put together and pushed painfully forward in your business can also be pissed away in a matter of seconds. There were mistakes and mishaps galore, foolish errors and omissions, sacks and stupid choices, taunts and other bad behavior that killed critical drives, and wastes of hard-to-come-by momentum throughout the game - virtually everything we also see in the startup world every day.

Now I can pretty much forgive a fumble or a missed field goal because those almost never arise from a lack of trying. As often as not, the main cause of a fumble is because the runner was trying to press for a few more yards and gets stripped or hit so hard that he loses the ball. But a lack of commitment or a failure of leadership is something that no team or business can accept for long. It's corrosive and contagious. For me, the saddest thing about Sunday's Super Bowl wasn't Cam Newton dropping the ball; it was that he stood there (while America and the world watched with bated breath) and didn't throw himself into the fray. He was deciding, not diving. Looking, not lunging.

And we were all sitting at home on the edges of our seats screaming "go for it", "get the ball" and he didn't do a thing. In fact, I'd say that the key to the ultimate moral victory in the game (forget what the score ended up being) really came down to that single play - a few painful and probative seconds - which may not have changed the final outcome, but that forever changed my impression of Cam Newton. And I'm willing to bet it changed the impressions of millions of other viewers as well.

When the moment arose and he was tested, he didn't step up – he hesitated – or worse, he took a pass. Maybe it was heart that he didn't have. Maybe he was saving himself for next season. Maybe he just didn't want it as bad as we wanted him to. But, whatever the reasons or the excuses, it wasn't what we expect from our leaders, and it was a sobering lesson for any startup.

You can't lead from the back seat or the bleachers. You've got to be in the moment – all-in – showing your people and your team that you care more than other people think is smart or safe. That you demand of yourself and them more than others think is practical or possible. And that when the window is there and the opportunities arise; you'll be the first one through to take the chances and seize the moment.

TULLMAN'S TRUISMS

DON'T LEAVE IT TO OTHERS

If there are two critical things that the "loners" – the boy in the basement or the girl in the garage – are lacking (apart from cash, company and commiseration) in trying to build their businesses by going it alone or sitting mainly by themselves in some stripped-down coffee shop/co-working space, it's: (a) the value, impact and influence of the entrepreneurial environment which they're missing out on with its almost tangible atmospheric benefit of contagious energy, excitement, and osmosis, and (b) the aggregated power of connecting with the people assembled in an amazing and enormous place who could be surrounding, supporting and sustaining these guys and girls as they build their companies – including especially the ones they're specifically going to need to meet and hire (sooner rather than later) if they really want to see their startups grow and succeed.

Seeing others succeed around you is often the single most powerful spur to your own success and a powerful tool to help you model your own behavior. Looking and listening is how we learn – as Springsteen says – he learned more from a 3-minute record than he ever learned in school. Lateral, high-speed learning is a critical skill for digital startups right now especially as technology keeps quickly leaping from applications in one industry to the next and across markets. Seeing not only becomes believing – it also becomes the shortest path forward if you can see it and share it – you too can be it. And constant copying of along with design drafting on others' ideas and innovations aren't just forms of flattery, they're essential business strategies and skills. See http://www. inc.com/howard-tullman/when-to-steal-from-other-founders.html .

There's a reason that vacuums suck and almost no chance at all these days that anyone is going to build a real business by themselves. It's what you learn after you know it all that makes all the difference and you can't learn all this stuff by yourself. I'm also pretty sure this isn't something you can be taught in school. You can only effectively expand your knowledge beyond your own experience base by learning directly (mentors and coaches) and indirectly (instances and examples) from qualified others who've been where you're headed and who've done successfully and repeatedly what you're trying to do. One hit wonders may be super smart, but it's an even money bet that they were just lucky and in the right place at the right time. Not a lot of worthwhile and transferable lessons in their experience.

And frankly, no one can actually teach you to be an entrepreneur, but – at least at 1871 – we know we can show any entrepreneur how to be better, smarter, more effective and more likely to be a winner. And that's what we do every day. All of your learning is a matter of your own timing and – while you can only really learn when you're ready – you learn nothing if you're not where the opportunities arise to do so. You've simply got to be there.

People who think that incubators and accelerators are all about coffee, beer or real estate really don't know squat. At the end of the day, the best of breed mega-incubators like 1871 are all about a community focused on ongoing learning and shared experiences. We say "learning" because – while "education" is something supposedly done to you; real learning is done by you. One of the earliest things you learn at a place like ours is that the closer you sit to the action, the better the view and the more rapidly you learn. There's just no substitute for paying careful attention. You learn a whole lot more by observation than you do from conversation and you never learn anything important by talking. And today what you will ultimately earn depends entirely on what you learn.

One of the most powerful aspects of the hyper-active and serendipitous environment at 1871 are the hundreds of planned, programmed and accidental interactions, intersections and connections that are constantly taking place between the 1600 plus members, mentors, sponsors, investors, partners, educators, government officials and just plain-old visitors and guests who spend their days – every day – here at the fast-beating heart of Chicago's technology ecosystem.

Now I suppose, to be fair, that if you've never known and enjoyed the benefits of being part of a special place, you don't really know what you're missing and what you could be learning or who you're likely to meet and the roles they will play in your future. If you think you can't afford to be part of such a place, all I can tell you is that you really can't afford not to be and if you think education is expensive, try being ignorant in today's competitive world and see where that gets you. The truth is that you can't learn anything unless you're willing to risk something.

And it's only after you choose to leave a place of such aggressive and ferocious learning that you really come to appreciate what you had and what you largely took for granted because the benefits were so much a part of just being there that they blend into the overall environment. We used to say (in the game business) that you never knew the real value of a brand or celebrity endorsement until you no longer had one. It's very much the same kind of thing when new entrepreneurs are embedded in the kind of all-encompassing bubble that we've built for our member businesses. See http://www.inc.com/howard-tullman-6-reasons-to-stay-in-the-incubator.html. In this life, you often don't really know what you got 'til you lose it.

At 1871, we've made startup success into an actual science. We've learned a great deal over the last couple of years which lets us continue to set the curve and raise the bar for what really matters if you want to help hundreds of entrepreneurs build better businesses. And we've learned – apart from the foregoing – that it all comes down to four critical considerations which are a part of everything we strive for:

1. It's critical to learn to be fast first – then you can take the time and have the luxury to work on being the best at what you do. Successive approximation always beats postponed perfection.
2. It's critical to develop the ability to continually learn and then to constantly re-learn the essential skills in your business and to expand those skill sets as well. You and your team can never be reluctant to do so.

3. It's critical to be able to rapidly draw on the talent, resources and funding that you will need to immediately scale your startup as soon as the moment is right. You'll never be able to do this fast enough by yourself and you need to make yourself part of a complete ecosystem where all the necessary tools and solutions are readily at hand.
4. It's critical to develop the ability to learn faster than your competitors since this is the only clear and sustainable competitive advantage from here on out. To do that successfully, you need to be in a place where you're surrounded by challenges, changes and new solutions and not stuck somewhere in a cellar or a silo.

Sounds pretty simple when you say it. Doing it well is a lot harder.

TULLMAN'S TRUISMS

YOU GET BETTER BY GETTING BETTER (EVERY DAY)

Thank God I'm just a grandparent these days without grammar or high school kids of my own who are trapped in an increasingly bizarre and irrational world run by adults – mostly parents and otherwise unemployable administrators (with the unfortunate teachers sadly caught in between and desperately trying to please everyone) where the rules, the procedures, and the approved behaviors vary from day to day and the changes come so rapidly and abruptly that the characters in *Alice in Wonderland* would be totally jealous.

As a grandfather, I don't have to regularly attend parent-teacher conferences or get pedantic notes sent home with my son or daughter addressing the latest concerns of a bunch of thumb-sucking, politically correct idiots who are completely out of control, but I do have to live with the increasingly depressing prospect that our future workforce (and our economic and social future in general) are being mucked up by these morons who – by default and our own inattention – we've regrettably left in charge of the education and futures of our kids. I don't think things are going to get better any time soon unless the vast majority of the people (who have their heads screwed on straight) get actively involved and try to knock some sense into these zealots who are all worried about everyone's feelings whatever the facts may be. These people practice and promote a bogus/DYI brew of pop sociology and psychology and shared "wisdom" that only the folks at Fox News could love.

Our kids are being victimized by a bunch of crazy, granola-heads and "procto-parents" who are systematically ruining our kids' respect for rigor, sucking the stuffing right out of them (traits like grit and a thick skin which we used to believe you'd need to succeed are now passé), demanding that we dumb down every class, and slowly killing our country's competitiveness. I mean "victimized" in old-fashioned, dictionary sense of the word and not in today's BS double-talk where everyone gets to be a victim and terrible "triggers" abound. And when I say procto-parents (from the root word "proctologist"), I mean parents who are totally into minding their kids' and everyone else's business, but don't know their asses from their elbows, or the first thing about effective education or how to build the kind of self-sufficient, self-starting students that we actually do need to compete in the global marketplace.

We have to be preparing our kids for the path ahead, not spending all of our time preparing the path for our kids, smoothing the road and softening every blow, and running interference for a bunch of pampered princes and princesses who won't be able to cope with the real world if they ever even get there. I'm pretty sure that it's only a matter of time before what few Phys Ed classes are left in our schools will have a separate cohort of kids resting comfortably on massage-ready, La-Z-Boy loungers because they brought a note from home saying that they're entirely "allergic" to work while – at the same time – the rest of the class plays games where no one keeps score, everyone's a winner, and there are trophies to take home for Mom and Dad to proudly display on the mantle.

We're seeing a world where awards and acknowledgments are replacing actual achievements. Schools across the country are eliminating academic excellence recognition in favor of bullshit attendance awards. They are commending punctuality instead of performance. Last year, a high school in Ohio named over 200 kids in the graduating class "valedictorians" because they didn't want to hurt anyone's feelings. This stuff sucks and must be stopped. We need to challenge our children and give them at least a little look into the real world where there are winners and losers every day. When everyone's a winner, we all lose in the end.

There's a very good reason that we establish examples and role models and behaviors to be emulated – it's because we want our kids to aspire to greatness – not to just getting along and making ends meet. And if you can't "see it" – if you can't watch and want the success of those around you (and the accomplishments of the many who went before you as well), you can't ever hope to "be it".

The idea that "trying" is what counts – regardless of results – is a sad commentary and a cheap excuse foisted on the real doers and the winners by sad sacks and also-rans who just can't cut it. Of course effort matters – you accomplish nothing by wishful thinking and half-hearted attempts at anything. But we demean and diminish the standouts and the ones who will really make a difference in our lives when we insist on lumping them with the rest of the mediocre pack and pretending that the world doesn't care about outcomes. We keep score and we measure in our lives and our businesses because ultimately what we measure and what we care about is what gets done.

I realize that, if we were only dealing with the conventional wisdom, the simplest and most straightforward answer to the textbook question of when a company's CEO should stop his or her day-to-day selling of the company's products and services would typically be "never".

It's not exactly the ABC rule ("Always Be Closing") from *Glengarry Glen Ross* (You can watch the classic Alec Baldwin speech here: https://www.youtube.com/watch?v=Q4PE2hSqVnk.) but it's pretty close. Maybe today we would call it the ABS rule. Always Be Selling. If you're not excited about your business and your prospects, why would you expect anyone else to be?

In a way, you can just think of it as the need for the management of any startup to be perpetually pitching and it always starts at the top. It doesn't matter who the target is (customers, prospects, investors, employees, etc.), there's always a story to be told and sold. Telling and selling. And the CEO (so the experts tell us) should always be out front succinctly selling the story, deliriously describing the dream, and rigorously rallying the troops. It's a basic part of the boss's job description and not one that anyone gets to delegate. No one knows your business better than you.

Now, as a general proposition, I would say that it's hard to disagree with this idea. If you're not out there and constantly on the case, you can be sure that a competitor will be happy to take your place. You can't sell anything sitting on your ass in your office and nothing today sells itself. And the truth is that the best CEOs are also great salesmen (or women) who could sell shoes to a snake, but that may not be their highest and best use for the business after a certain point in its development. That's really the key question – when does it make sense for the CEO to stop?

There's actually a pretty good answer to this question – one that's especially relevant for startups – and a pretty simple guideline which can help you determine exactly (a) when it's the best time for the business to start hiring some qualified sales managers and (b) whether the time is right for the CEO to take a step or two back from the front line, hand off the ball to the sales team, and bench himself so he can be doing better things for the business.

Timing is everything in building the right team for a new company and, notwithstanding the fact that most of the time people are too slow in bolstering their business with some seasoned seniors, it's just as bad to be too early as it is to be too late. Getting some "grown-ups" in place and up-to-speed before you really start to scale the business is a key success factor in your growth and the best possible insurance that you won't stumble along the way. You want people who could sell muzzles to dogs on your team, but not too soon. It's too costly to have them just sitting around while the product guys try to get things right and they hate it as well. The very best sales people take it personally and want to be out there selling every day.

So the proper timing to add some professionals to your team is not an easy or obvious decision. I like to say that, in cases like this, it seems that it's always too soon until it's too late. However, the good news is that I can definitely tell you (with some degree of confidence and certainty) when it's definitely <u>too soon</u> for a startup to add dedicated sales talent to the team.

There are two simple rules:

(1) You don't need a sales team until you're ready to scale; and
(2) You're not ready to scale until you've sold a LOT of the SAME stuff to a bunch of SATISFIED customers.

We all know that there's no real business without sales and satisfied customers, but not all sales are the same for all purposes. You've got to nail it before you scale it (confirm both product and market fit) and big businesses are never bespoke. That's why it's critical that the successful sales which stick be of the same basic product or service without costly customization, without one-off incentives or add-ons, without a whole lot of handholding, and without spending more to get them than you're ultimately putting in your pocket.

But what does this have to do with the CEO being out there selling? He or she needs to be out there selling <u>until</u> the concrete sets and the product or service is locked down and secure. Until you've had a dozen serious sales (with happy customers) and it looks like things are sticking and the dogs are eating the dogfood. If there are still open questions, if there are changes or mid-course corrections that must be made, if there are pricing concerns or additional critical features to be added; there's really only one person who can make those calls and it's critical that the inputs to the decision-maker be direct and ideally face-to-face from the market and the customers. No one will ever tell it to you straighter than a customer and you need to hear the unvarnished truth to ultimately get your offerings just right. But you can't fix things from afar – only from the field.

Salesmen who don't make sales are especially good at coming up with excuses and offering explanations and reasons why your stuff doesn't sell. The worst of them are the best at this because that's mainly what they do all day – they make excuses instead of sales. And in startups, especially in the early stages when everyone pitches in, a lot of people are trying to sell who aren't even "sales" people and who have little or no training. They try to "sell" because there's no one else around to do it. That's not a good place for any business to be. "Trying" doesn't drive "buying" in the real world – selling is a skill just like many others and not something you pick up in your spare time. See http://www.inc.com/howard-tullman/bring-back-the-peter-principle-please.html.

So it's easy for an entrepreneur to lose patience and rush to get some skilled help in this area. But it's smarter to make sure that you've got something real and solid for these folks to sell before you bring them in and turn them loose and ultimately that's a call that only the CEO can make.

There's no question that there's a power and many advantages to being the first mover in a new market along with almost as many downsides which require careful navigation to avoid. I've written about both sides of this specific "advantage" previously and it remains a complex area and one which is highly dependent on the specific circumstances of each situation. See http://www.inc.com/howard-tullman/first-mover-advantage-maybe-but-be-smart-about-it.html. And I also appreciate that the conventional wisdom suggests, in almost every tech-based or tech-enabled business, that the markets over time will tend to become "winner take all" environments where a single player will emerge who grows more and more dominant. See http://www.inc.com/howard-tullman/future-of-content-marketing-simplereach.html .

But it's equally important to understand that in certain types of markets, especially those of enormous size, it's perfectly acceptable – in fact – it's highly advantageous to "settle" for being second. Not only can you go to school on the market leader and see everything that works or doesn't work before you build your own model and your go-to-market strategy; you can actually build your business specifically to fill a gap, offer an alternative, address an unmet need, or just concentrate on serving a large and accessible portion of the target customers whose priorities differ from those served by the big guy in the space.

I've been watching one of these technically David and Goliath stories start to unfold over the last year or so and – for my money – it's starting to look a lot more like a Cain and Abel contest which is gonna be much more interesting and a lot more competitive than I think anyone expected. I'm talking about *Jet.com* taking on *Amazon* pretty much head-to-head and beginning to carve out a very sizable business in a very short time. My best guess is that their first full year gross sales may hit $1 billion. As I noted above, it helps *Jet.com* a whole lot that we're talking about a marketplace – retail – that is not only huge, but which has never been a "winner take all" world. Even *Amazon* owns only a modest fraction of the whole market.

While scale is very important in terms of the creation of a viable backend for its business (*Jet.com* estimates that it will require $150 million worth of infrastructure investments for it to be competitive on a national stage – it's raised over $800 million so far); the complexity, geography, diversity and volume of the retail industry (so so many small and dissimilar items spread across millions and millions of unique customers) has pretty much made it impossible for anyone including *Amazon* (even after more than 21 years) to capture more than about 20% of the opportunity.

So enormous upside remains for other players like *Jet* especially if they can crack the critical code in ways that are distinctly different from Amazon's approach. It's much much harder for the market leader to respond quickly and competitively to new entrants whose approach is different and oblique rather than head-on. It doesn't help even the smartest player to just step on the gas (add more marketing dollars, offer more discounts, create more bundled services, etc.) if the competitors aren't playing the same game. And sheer size as well as deeply embedded code and ingrained business habits and operations are all impediments to any kind of rapid response to new players offering alternative solutions in the market. See http://www.inc.com/howard-tullman/whats-wrong-with-retail-and-what-does-it-mean-for-you/html.html .

For openers, *Jet.com* has completely changed up the transaction model. You still pick the goods but (unlike Amazon), they pick the dealer and the delivery method and – with your permission – the time it takes for the delivery. The differences these modest details make in (a) the ability to optimize (minimize) the overall costs of the entire transaction and (b) the ability to share the realized cost savings in real time (in fact in advance) with the buyers are pretty amazing. Breaking up the Bezos "bundle" into its many component parts and transparently creating and offering alternatives and better economic choices for the consumer is going to completely change the game. Everything's about the buyer's bottom line: waive free returns – save money; use a debit card rather than a credit card – save money; wait a few days for delivery – save a bunch; etc. And those are just the most obvious areas.

What exactly has *Jet.com* figured out and what are they doing that's so smart?

(1) One Size Doesn't Fit All

Henry Ford got away with offering one version of the Model T in one color, but those days are long gone. Consumers want to drive the deals and they believe that they should have unlimited options and choices. And frankly with today's technologies, they're not entirely wrong. See http://www.inc.com/howard-tullman/surprise-you-can-be-all-things-to-all-people.html. But, needless to say, these desires and the growing expectation that this is "business as usual" are a nightmare for companies looking to grow by delivering basically the same set of services for millions of satisfied shoppers. *Amazon's* entire model is based on a bundle rather than a basket – you get a lot of value and a lot of service and convenience from Prime – but you don't get much choice and you have only the most modest ways to adjust the price of the package. *Jet.com* is all about having it your way – every day – any way that works for you. And when you're purpose-built for that kind of flexibility from the start, it's almost impossible for the "old" guys in the business to match your agility, flexibility or responsiveness.

(2) Everyone's Best Deal Differs Every Day

It turns out that the best deal for me today may not be the same as yesterday's or tomorrow because my concerns and objectives will change frequently. The systems we build going forward will have to suit the users, not the other way around. Consumers don't want to conform today – they want to choose. I say all the time that time is our scarcest resource, that attention is the new currency, and that increasingly we will only make time for what we're interested in, but not everyone's in a hurry every day. Not everything is critical at this very moment; not all things are urgent or important in the scheme of our lives; and – in a lot of cases – if we're offered a reasonable choice and some (financial) incentives, we're perfectly willing to wait for a variety of things as long as (a) the choice is ours and (b) the choice isn't irrevocable.

(3) One Item Shipments are a Waste

When you think about it, *Amazon's* methodology is the poster child for the wretched excess and the indifferent and wasteful wave of selfish consumerism that is slowly sinking our society in so many ways. We've been trained by the Prime movers that it's perfectly acceptable to order single items from multiple sellers across the country and expect them to arrive this afternoon on our doorstep. It's all about the IG culture – immediate gratification – and not wanting to wait for the marginal marshmallow. It doesn't really much matter how wasteful and ultimately expensive this whole approach may be. No one complains too much about the excess packaging that piles up everywhere. Everyone ignores the environmental costs of multiple shipments; etc. But *Jet.com* believes in building a smarter basket – asking folks to be just a little patient – saving a bunch of money – and not letting the inmates run the asylum – although they wouldn't be likely to own up to the last observation. They aren't doing this – by the way – for the good of the country (although that may be a nice by-product), they're doing it because it makes good business sense.

(4) Money Matters Much More than We Imagine

Too many of us techies today live in an insulated and isolated world which is basically a shiny, buffed-up bubble that completely ignores the day-to-day concerns and the financial realities of the people who make up most of the world. Sometimes our biggest blind spots come as a result of our own behaviors. If you live your life at Starbucks and move thru an Uberized economy where an extra buck or two (for access, speed or convenience) is a drop in the bucket, it's hard to imagine the daily struggles of millions of Moms who are trying to make ends meet and who desperately care every day about saving a few dollars to help make sure that they can feed their families. *Jet.com* is all about building a business to serve the millions to whom money still really matters and who are absolutely ecstatic about consciously saving money every time they order from *Jet.com*. Not only do they feel that they're more in control of their own destinies; they feel that they have a new range of intelligent choices that is equally important to today's consumers.

There's a lot to be learned by looking very closely at how *Jet.com* is taking on *Amazon* – both in terms of your own company's offensive strategies and in terms of the defensive preparations you should be making to respond to the inevitable competitive threats that you can expect right around the corner especially as you grow. By the time everyone else figures this stuff out, it will be too late to make a difference. So now's the time to get moving.

In running any business today, it's almost a moral certainty that you won't have all of the necessary information that you need in time and in a form and place sufficient to permit you to make all of the critical decisions you're likely to be confronted with on a daily basis. It's a given that waiting too long today and the indecision and inaction associated with such reticence are far more costly choices than the downside of any decisions you might make or any actions you might take. If we knew all the answers and how things were gonna turn out, we wouldn't call our sometimes fruitless attempts "experiments". There are no guarantees in the startup world except one: standing still will get you run over sooner or later. The way you build a successful business and the way you get better every day is by getting started and improving every day. And every new day gives you more data, more insights and more to work with as you struggle to figure things out.

Intuition, great guesses, pattern recognition, experience, research, homework – all of these things help to fill the data gap, but it's still the case that you're going to come up short some of the time and that's just how it goes. Eventually all the models stall out and all the formulas fall short and then you've got to make that leap of faith. That's why you get paid the big bucks. The good news is that – over time – most ignorance is curable if you make the necessary commitment and do the hard work entailed in getting on top of the situation every time – even as the situation(s) continue to quickly and sometimes radically change. Your job is to steer the ship and keep things on course through a sea of changed conditions and circumstances without ever giving up on the goal. You can trim the sails from time to time, but you can't lose sight of the shore or water down the vision.

The right attitude and the consistent application of serious effort including a fair amount of false starts and a bunch of trial and error will eventually overcome the initial absence of the facts, figures and results you need. But only if you do the work. Today, far too often, not knowing actually means not looking or not caring enough to look long enough and hard enough to find the necessary answers. We can fix ignorance over time with research and education; but indifference and not caring will eventually kill your company. See http://www.inc.com/howard-tullman/why-whatever-will-sink-your-business.html .

One of the deepest and darkest data holes these days in terms of willful ignorance is the actual value of traditional advertising as compared to the billions of dollars being spent on it. I'm surprised and even a little impressed to see the remarkable amount of creativity and ingenuity that you find in larger companies when it comes to figuring out how to hide their stunning degree of indifference and their continued reluctance to change their old ways of doing things. It's still a Mad Men world; it's still "business as usual" with a little less alcohol; and the clients (as compared to the agencies and the MSM networks) are still getting the shaft. There are better tools, there is better data, but no one – even on the client side – really wants to rock the boat and do the hard work of getting better and more accurate answers. Everyone wants to change the world, but no one wants to change themselves or be the first one to move things forward.

We need a lot fewer Mad Men and a lot more Math Men (and women) today if we're going to get things right. The most critical attributes of the Internet and the new digital economy are not the speed, immediacy or low cost of the network; it's the heightened direct access to Individuals, the ability to accurately measure their engagement and their resultant actions, and the remarkable degree of accountability that is enabled as a result. We can discover and measure reach, resonance and reaction in real time in ways that simply were never previously available. But none of this capability matters if no one in charge of spending the money cares. Or worse, they might theoretically care, but they're not willing to do the extra work of finding out the actual answers.

A few smart people are starting to figure this stuff out – they're totally focusing on performance-based marketing, not wishful thinking or last year's news – and they are going to change the competitive game. But the truth is that they're not gonna spend any time educating the rest of us because they have realized that the people with the deepest pockets don't really want to hear what they have to say. As a result, what we're seeing – and what the digital economy now enables and can deliver – are more and more cases where the smartest customers are becoming their own media buyers and building their own tools to get the job done. They've figured out that this new competency isn't just a competitive necessity; it's a sustainable competitive advantage.

So what can you do for your own business to make sure that you don't get left behind or foolishly spend your scarce resources with people still using broad gauge, shotgun strategies – "spray and pray" style – which are remnants of the old TV network game instead the new price- and value-based discovery tools which are available today to help you reach the right digital audiences for your message? If no one is listening, it doesn't really matter what you're trying to say.

Here's the bottom line: today only bozos buy eyeballs. It's not about volume or tonnage anymore; it's about smart reach. See http://www.inc.com/howard-tullman/to-sell-more-your-marketing-must-embrace-smart-reach.html . Ask your people and your vendors the hard questions. Are you engaging real people or robots? How do those consumers react and respond? Are they clicking through and buying something from you? Can you invest more dollars (in viable and actual inventory) and improve your results based on what's working for you? And can you do this in real time before the moment passes? Can you be there when the buyer is ready to buy?

To win today, you need to do three things:

(1) Your entire ad spend will need to make economic sense for your business and provide real measurable metrics (and demonstrable results) which are now available if you know where to look and who to ask;

(2) Your agencies and other vendors will need to justify their recommendations and rationalize the dollars they are asking you to commit – not on the come – or based on the distant past – but based on concrete and current data; and

(3) You'll need to develop or acquire the right tools (or the right partners) to permit you to monitor and adjust your ad and marketing spends in real time so you can be proactive rather than simply reactive – feeding your winning initiatives and shutting down the losers as soon as possible.

Nothing today in the digital economy is "set it and forget it" anymore. We live in a "real time, right now" world and no one has the luxury any longer to ignore these changes, to wish them away, or to sit back and hope that someone else will do the hard work for them that it's gonna take to get ahead.

TULLMAN'S TRUISMS

IT'S MUCH WORSE TO BE IRRELEVANT THAN TO BE EXPLOITED

An interesting recent article written by Farhad Manjoo for the *New York Times* (See http://www.nytimes.com/2016/03/24/technology/the-uber-model-it-turns-out-doesnt-translate.html?_r=0) argued that the UBER model doesn't translate very well to other cases and that it can't be reliably applied to explain or justify the existences of the thousands of businesses which have rapidly appeared in virtually every industry claiming to be the "UBER" of whatever. He thinks these companies are being started and run by people who are either irrational or sadly deluded and that a massive shakeout is on its way if not already underway. He says there's one UBER and that's UBER – end of story. He's not entirely wrong, but his view is too simplistic.

Now, of course, to hear tell from the "right now" industry mavens, no old-line business today is safe from aggressive and disruptive innovators planning to mobilize the masses to do the biddings of others on demand and – albeit over time – they'll be working for a relative pittance. Manjoo notes the inconvenient fact that, in some of the most visible cases, the soaring costs of delivering these small-scale, bespoke services on a hyper-local basis with quickly growing volume has in fact already brought about price increases – not savings – for the end users. He argues that it's pretty clear, if you can't fairly rapidly achieve mass consumer pricing, your EON (Economy of Now) business on its best days will be a niche nicety for the folks with more money than time or brains and never break out of that box. (See http://www.inc.com/howard-tullman/four-rules-of-the-now-economy.html).

But judging by the conventional wisdom in too much of the current media, many people still believe that these EON guys have got a better plan. And, in the time-honored tradition of cockeyed optimists around the world, their plan (which they feel should be painfully obvious – at least to the uninitiated) is to make up the per-unit losses on the soon-to-be-realized, just around the corner, and miraculously scalable volume. Sales and volume will cure everything over time. Just ignore the hemorrhaging losses for now and let us keep spending that readily-available VC cash while the spigot's still wide open. And, to date, the venture capitalists – a depressingly "me-too" crowd of sheep and fashionable followers if ever there was one – have been more than happy to pile on and be energetic enablers of this idiocy. It looks like they'll keep funding clones, copies, competitors and even some clowns until there's so much noise and confusion in the marketplace that the whole construct comes tumbling down.

To Manjoo, it looks like the first cracks are already appearing in the pipe dreams that are barely holding these stories together. The time of reckoning may be a lot nearer than these folks think. Too many of the also-ran players are already stuck in the proof point pudding (moving sideways instead of forward) and finding that they can no longer sell the same old "just wait and see" story as easily to the guys that totally fell for it the last time. Fool me once, shame on you; fool me twice, shame on me.

Businesses that continue to lose money on every transaction are ultimately not businesses at all – their continued revenue growth with no bottom line is simply profitless prosperity. UBER benefitted by taking advantage of the unique circumstances in the cab industry and Manjoo claims that there are virtually no other major industries where those same characteristics (crappy customer experience; high, regulator-protected prices; oligopolistic markets; huge numbers of daily users; lack of viable alternatives; etc.) apply – ergo no more UBERs. But this is too narrow a view.

The fact is that there are a number of other industries and opportunities which have completely different conditions and attributes than the cab business, but where the circumstances and the underlying motivators which drive rapid adoption and growth are nonetheless such that they will also support the same type of solution that UBER offered for commuters. You just need to know where to look and what to look for. It's not a matter of a bad or non-extensible model; it's all about finding the right services to offer to the right customers in the right markets.

Let's just take one case and apply some alternative criteria to look ahead. I would argue that not one of these five statements describes the pre-UBER cab industry in any material way.

(1) The individuals supplying the service are highly skilled, hard to find and specialized.
(2) There is unmet/growing demand in every business and marketplace.
(3) There is no single supplier (of any size) presently able to meet the new demands.
(4) When you need the service, you need it now and there are very few alternatives.
(5) Price is almost completely immaterial and controlled entirely by the seller.

Now let's find an emerging problem of immense proportions for millions of businesses on a daily basis that needs a solution. There are plenty – here's one of the most obvious: IT. An UBER-ized solution for IT professionals is inevitable and just around the corner and here's why:

(1) Unlike cab drivers, IT professionals are highly-skilled technicians and not easy to find or hire. But the much more critical concern is that increasingly, of necessity, they need to be area and product specialists just to stay up with the technologies which are of the most immediate relevance and concern to their current positions. The truth is that there's no such thing as an IT generalist any longer. And, in addition, because outages are sporadic and unpredictable, these expensive experts are both bored and under-utilized most of the time if they are full-time employees of a single organization or worse because they're being used for tasks and support services that are a waste of their training and expertise. A solution that let them become freelance, independent providers and which provided enough demand for their services to fill and fully utilize

their talents by engaging them on demand to address the varying needs of multiple businesses is clearly the smart way to go.

(2) And, at the same time, from the perspective of millions of businesses, almost every one of which cannot possibly afford a multi-person IT staff with the capabilities to support and repair the dozen or so different technologies being used in a typical business today, there is a growing exposure and risk that they are simply unprepared to respond in any timely fashion to major problems or system interruptions which may occur in any of a number of mission-critical parts of their overall business operations. And, here again, this concern doesn't even begin to consider the exposure presented by malicious or criminal cyberattacks and other forms of industrial and corporate espionage which increase in frequency and severity every day. An interesting question – and one that will plague many companies in the next few years – is what level of unpreparedness will be deemed in hindsight to have been sufficiently negligent to invalidate your business interruption insurance even assuming that you have been conscientious about buying and maintaining such coverage? Assuring that your business has ready access to 24/7, on call and on demand, IT support across all of the necessary technical areas is going to quickly look like a very prudent form of insurance and risk abatement.

(3) While some of the major consulting and accounting firms and a few software operations are starting to make some noise about the need for additional levels of business protection and support, the fact is that, as of now, there's simply no viable supplier or solution – regardless of what a business might be able to afford to pay – which can support all of the diverse IT support needs that continue to grow and to grow more complex and more broadly distributed throughout entire organizations. Even more to the point, none of the big guys can actually afford to build teams of these professionals and employ and pay them full-time while they sit on the bench waiting for the next fire alarm to ring. Realistically, only an on demand, distributed marketplace of technical professionals can really solve the problem in an economic fashion so long as the market can be constructed in a way that efficiently allocates opportunities and optimizes the time and talent available from each individual. The big consulting firms are much more likely to help engineer the marketplace solution than they are to hire and provide the underlying personnel and other resources to support it. A perfect void and an amazing opportunity for a new player.

(4) Who ya gonna call? Killer IT pros are scarcer than plumbers when you really need them and, when you need them, you need them right now because increasingly if your computer systems are down, your business is down as well. Your in-house team can help somewhat, but – as often as not – the thing that's busted is something they've built in the first place and have been bandaging rather than rebuilding for years – (See http://www.inc.com/howard-tullman/build-a-bridge-over-your-old-code-not-another-band-aid-.html). And it's going to become quickly apparent that they're going to need some outside help and some specialists to really get things up and running as soon as possible and to minimize the damage not only to your business, but to the businesses of all of your customers who are also dependent on your systems. Here again, the pros are the ones who are likely to avoid the quick fixes that end up costing you ten times more in the long run because no one remembered that resetting this particular program also wiped out the year-to-date billing data for the last year or two. But the real pros are never the ones who are on your day-to-day payroll because you can't afford them.

(5) When your business is burning down, no one gets bothers looking for a bargain. Just like your heat or hot water in the winter or the AC on a hot summer day, you don't know how much you'll miss it until it's gone and you'll pay pretty much anything to get it back as soon as possible. Price is simply no object in cases like this.

So there you have it. I can't tell you when for sure, but I can tell you for sure that there will be UBER-like providers of outsourced IT support for companies of every size and shape because the explosion of diverse technologies in every industry and our businesses' complete and utter dependence upon these tools means that there's simply no choice and realistically no other viable solution.

And who wouldn't like to serve a huge market connecting millions of customers having urgent technical needs, limited alternatives, and little concern about price with millions of highly skilled professionals who would love to be their own bosses, fill their days with challenging and diverse problems instead of bullshit make-work jobs, and have countless opportunities served up to them on a regular basis which they can pick and choose as they wish. Sounds like IT heaven to me. And a lot like UBER as well.

I can't tell you how many times I'm in a conversation or strategy presentation with the senior management team of a major corporation and one of the first topics which comes up is their frustration with the lack of effective internal communication and information sharing in their own company. I'm not talking about mushy mission statements or internal HR "touchy-feely" messaging; I'm talking about the hard core, operational data which you need to drive the business and – even more crucial – the kind of anecdotal material and other market inputs which often get talked about at the water cooler, but never make it upstream to the people who can react to the information and change things. Information has no value unless it's successfully communicated.

These execs literally say that they (as well as other critical in-house decision makers) don't know what their own organization knows and – try as they might – they haven't been able to devise an effective solution to make the current situation better. They acknowledge that – even in the best of businesses – the quality of information deteriorates as it rises in the organization. And again, this covers every kind of information that's important to the company – we're not just talking about critical research or new discoveries; it can be as mundane as meeting menus or engineers needing more microwaves in the café – it's anything that bears on and impacts the overall productivity and success of the business.

This system-wide breakdown results in: (a) missed opportunities, duplicative efforts and misdirected expenditures; (b) inappropriate communications, false starts and other initiatives which eventually need to be walked back from the brink; and (c) the old standby where "the left hand doesn't know what the right hand is doing". It's inefficient, it's unprofessional and beyond embarrassing, and frankly it's a growing competitive disadvantage for any business. Data is the oil of the digital age and, if you're behind the curve or only seeing part of the story, you're in serious trouble which is only likely to get worse. Data alone won't do it of course because more data isn't the same as better information. You need a system that turns data into information and information into knowledge. Knowledge only becomes power when it's used and – unlike every other part of the creation and production process in any business – growing knowledge isn't subject to the law of diminishing returns.

As the information flow in the outside world becomes more and more streamlined and comprehensive, not having timely and accurate data about your own internal operations, issues and activities is an enormous information gap which consistently results in wastes of time, resources and energy. It can demoralize your people; anger your customers; confuse your partners and vendors; and give aid and comfort to the competition. I tell our member companies at 1871 that only two words matter today – transparency and efficacy. A fair assumption is that everyone everywhere will know what you're doing and how well you're doing it and, if you don't, shame on you. You'd think that addressing this kind of shortcoming would be a priority, but the lack of existing tools or technologies to help address the problem has pretty much remitted it to being a known concern with no known solution. Apologies for the slightly Rumsfeld-esque reference.

There are several reasons for this persistent problem (which I would note is by no means restricted to "big" businesses) and this seems to be a recurring issue for millions of businesses regardless of how "open" a business claims to be. Some of the practical impediments to timely sharing are structural and logistical issues including cases where surveys may be manual, where the respondents are multi-lingual or where employees are widely distributed, in different time zones and/or in distant locations. Others are procedural or hierarchical where there may be a reluctance to confront more senior managers, sensitivities around relationships with other groups or departments, a culture that prefers peace to progress and quiet to confrontation, etc. And then there are the "kill the messenger" concerns where no one wants to be the one to deliver the bad news. Last, but not least, are managers who don't want to know. Even though confusion is a higher state of knowledge than ignorance, these are the folks who say: "don't confuse me with the facts". (See http://www.inc.com/howard-tullman/3-things-you-need-to-know-about-advertising.html .)

But there's good news on the horizon. An 1871 company, *Baloonr* (www.baloonr.com), has built a simple, self-serve, system that enables rapid-fire, company-wide, anonymous (but trackable) information, idea and feedback gathering from sources inside the company (as well as outside if desired) on a prioritized and confidential basis. Any group of any size can be accommodated at any time. Talk about a "right now" solution. It's already being used by a variety of large organizations – ranging from startups to universities to Fortune 50 companies – and the results have been impressive. My favorite quote from one of the early users was "it was like putting on glasses for the first time".

As proposals move through the system, advancing and being enhanced at the same time, they gain support and weight from various quarters and eventually they can be claimed and properly attributed to their authors. Credit ultimately goes to those to whom it is due and no one is penalized or stigmatized for suggesting ideas that didn't make the consensus cut.

As you might expect, the most immediate organizational advantage of the *Baloonr* system is actually the simplest. It's like a "secret ballot" on steroids. The initial cloak of anonymity makes it possible for everything to be shared without reservations (or personal consequences) and for the best suggestions and thoughts – regardless of origin or authorship – to be floated up to the top of the pile. (Pun intended.)

In addition, while we keep hearing about how the introverts are a great untapped resource at many companies, this system permits even the most reticent to participate and contribute for the greater good. All of the constraints relating to status, authority, gender, position, etc. are effectively removed and true collaboration is possible.

And finally, and even more importantly, high-speed iteration and building on the best ideas is enabled (again without positively or negatively "considering the source") with participants from across the entire enterprise joining and adding to the conversation.

If knowledge is power, *Baloonr* may hold the keys to the kingdom. Because today it's what you don't know that you don't know that can kill your business in no time at all.

For the last year or two, it's been fairly easy for the naysayers to continually predict the imminent demise of *Facebook*. The latest rants have been based on some factoids from unattributed persons focusing on the alleged slippage in the sharing by FB users of their "personal" news and details. For me, even if proven to be true, this falls somewhere between "who really cares anyway?" and "TMI" to begin with. There's plenty of this kind of crap to go around and we should all actually be grateful to hear that the over-sharing is abating even if Kayne and the Kardashians are still killing us with just their shameless alliteration alone. The KKK has nothing on this "family".

And still, as far as I can see in terms of actual metrics, the FB juggernaut continues forward largely without a hiccup notwithstanding some bumps in the road and a few false starts (search on *Facebook* even with 1.5 billion requests a day continues to be – at best – a work in progress) which, given the aggressive, but forgiving culture which Zuck and Sheryl have built, are treated – not as catastrophes or career-enders as they might be at *Amazon* – but simply as the likely results and costs of the typical trials and tribulations of building any new business.

Facebook (after a dozen years) isn't exactly new, but they've managed (to an amazing extent given their rapid growth) to preserve a day-to-day culture of constant innovation and experimentation that's virtually unheard of in other companies of their size. If we all knew in advance how these kinds of constant tests and experiments were going to turn out, we wouldn't need to try them in the first place. But at FB, the code is never set in concrete and it's ever-changing. There's no such thing as business as usual. And while it clearly helps to be brilliant; it's far more important to be fearless.

And, in terms of the stock market, the bears and the shorts also haven't really been any more successful in laying a glove on the continued consistent rise in the company's stock price. Even downticks in FB's stock for Q1 were almost non-existent. All this talk about *Facebook* being a voracious vampire which needs to be put down with a stake in its heart before it ruins all of our lives and poisons the minds of our children is just junk. The professional pundits are finding that attacking *Facebook* is just about as hard and as sloppy as trying to nail *JELL-O* to a tree.

The reasons we're regularly offered for the impending FB disaster come in basically three flavors:

(1) The kids no longer think it's a cool place to be and are rapidly moving in large numbers to the hottest new app or service – whatever that might be. The truth is that this simply isn't happening because – apart maybe from *Snapchat* to a degree – there's really not a lot of other places to go for all the functionality of *Facebook*. And God forbid, your friends might not even follow you there. New sharing services continue to pop up and come and go and their numbers never remotely resemble the reality of *Facebook*'s size and scale. As an example, and to almost no one's surprise (except maybe Marissa Mayer's), one place the new destination definitely isn't is *Tumblr* although – not too very long ago – it was being touted as the next big thing and the morons at *Yahoo* quickly paid a bundle for a bunch of ad-free nothing.

(2) *Facebook* is fast becoming a "business" (Surprise!) and that can't be good for its business because it's not cool to be perceived as trying to make money as opposed to being mainly mission-driven. This is just another version of the "kids will be kids" BS. The people who matter have always known that – social aside – *Facebook* has been in the performance marketing business since the start and is now demonstrably the absolute best in that business – bar none. *Google*'s grasp – on the other hand – continues to slip as more and more of the action on the web has less and less to do with websites and everything to do with apps. If you can't see into the silos, you can't show me where to sell my stuff. And don't even get me started on the growing threat of ad blocking apps which are impressively effective against browser-based ad targeting and virtually useless to date against ads served within apps.

(3) *Facebook* played a nasty trick on us – we all helped to build their massive social sandbox – and now they've closed the gates and want to charge us for playing (read: marketing and advertising) there. Grow up people – this shouldn't be news to anyone who's been watching this movie for a while. It's never been a question of "if"; just a matter of "when" *Facebook* would start charging for effective access. While *Twitter* continues to wander in the wilderness looking for a monetization model, FB has been focused on the bottom line for years. I'm not exactly sure when the idea of "paying to play" fell out of favor – especially for emerging media companies like FB – and it's clearly becoming the base case just about everywhere you look as publishers try to hurriedly re-erect pay walls and resuscitate their subscriptions systems without completely strangling the golden goose. One important difference is that the publishers know that (in reducing free and easy access to their content) they are acting at their peril whereas this is just a logical extension of *Facebook*'s plan from the get-go. Honestly a lot of this particular flavor of whining just seems like sour grapes from folks who didn't get there first.

Overall, many of these conversations feel like wishful thinking mixed with a little dose of *Schadenfreude* being foisted on anyone willing to listen by tech talkers and media mavens who missed the boat and who are now sitting on the sidelines watching their futures sail away. Others are spurious spews by negative know-nothings, failed competitors, or also-rans whose own launches went nowhere or whose paper sailboats are getting steadily soggier and slowly sinking as the sun sets on the old ways that the MSM used to do business.

Having mastered the people part of the platform business, we're seeing *Facebook* turn its attention increasingly to the publishing part of the process and the fact is that today all the major platforms out there (*Apple*, *Google*, *Amazon* and maybe *Microsoft*) are also trying to successfully manage the same migration. The main difference – as platforms continue to grow into publishers – is that *Facebook* alone among them doesn't seem the slightest bit interested in creating its own content. Maybe they've been watching some of the others stumble along the way (See http://www.inc.com/howard-tullman/three-lessons-from-youtubes-programming-disaster.html .) or maybe they just prefer managing and distributing the milk to owning the cow.

For decades, traditional media was either owned (newspapers and radio and TV); paid (marketers and advertisers); or earned (news, celebrity and notoriety – good or bad). All of these channels had a single end in mind (apart from selling us something) and that was to help generate word of mouth (WOM) which – in the best of cases – was what I used to call "Triple A": active, affirmative and authentic. WOM is basically what we hear directly and honestly from friends, family and co-workers. It has always been the prime driver and the most effective and consistent influencer of consumer behavior. We knew that strong, positive word of mouth was critical to the ultimate success of any product or service, but managing and growing it was always much more of an art than a science. You paid your money and you kept your fingers crossed and hoped for the best. A lot of what was paid (and it's still the case today) was wasted (like vitamins), but we never really knew or could accurately determine what worked.

Facebook came along in 2004, completely changed the game by making the web personal so we actually knew who we were talking to, and made the WOM process scientific because word of mouth became social sharing and sharing in *Facebook*'s world is a science. Make me care and make me share became the mantra and social sharing became the 4th leg of the media biz. (See http://www.inc.com/howard-tullman-make-me-care-and-then-i-will-share.html .) Social sharing was simpler than owning and operating the presses; cheaper than paying for the privilege of getting your story out there; and much easier than having to earn the world's attention by doing something special, important or otherwise noteworthy. Social sharing quickly became WOM on steroids.

And the real "secret sauce" for *Facebook* was that virtually all of the content creation and all the heavy lifting was being done by the users. This continues to be the basic FB economic model today and also the central reason for the impressive margins that FB manages to maintain. It's also the reason that *Facebook* poses such an existential threat to traditional publishers and media makers.

Owning 4 of the fingers in the fist out of 5 ain't bad and that's always been *Facebook*'s plan. The initial two digits in the platform strategy were (i) curation and (ii) distribution and these have essentially been in place since the beginning. *Facebook* and the other platform players simply seized control from the publishers of the distribution of their products and never looked back. Today massive distribution platforms like *Facebook* are the primary ways in which the world gets its news and information. We're fundamentally lazy people and creatures of habit (we spend 50% of our mobile time using a single social app) and we're basically gonna keep going where we've been going – only more so – as the noise, clutter and confusion continues to mount. Decision fatigue is a drag for all of us. We're more coasters today than explorers.

Publishers may still be feeders (if they make their news "fit" the new formats), but *Facebook* is the force and the power in the new equation, and frankly, the publishers don't really even know where their stuff is being sent or seen these days. They basically have to take *Facebook*'s word for it. And yet, no publisher today can afford any longer to try to go it alone – it's all about aggregation – and if your content isn't front and center somewhere, your business will be nowhere soon enough – and you'll be breathing in the other guys' exhaust.

Most of the math that I've seen suggests very clearly that the publishers who are riding on FB's coattails are doing much better than the guys still trying to do anything themselves. The audience is huge and the traffic they're seeing is a multiple of what they were pulling previously to their own destinations. We can expect more and more of the remaining outliers to throw in the towel and join the crowd pretty soon. If you don't make dust, you eat dust. And the dust never really settles because *Facebook* never stops building.

The next two steps in the roadmap to global domination were around (iii) hosting and (iv) monetization and this, of course, is precisely what *Instant Articles* is all about – it delivers control to *Facebook* of every part of the media publication process except the costliest and most challenging component – the actual creation of the content. This is also why *Instant Articles* is both a tremendous attraction and an enormous threat to the very publishers and media companies who are already racing to be a part of the new program. The old line players are simply turning over the keys to the kingdom to *Facebook* and hoping for the best. And you can expect precisely the same kind of frenzy around the relatively new *Facebook Live* feature – live streaming video generated directly and instantly by the users. Massive amounts of new content at little or no incremental cost to *Facebook* and complete control of curation, distribution, hosting and monetization.

This is the fist of *Facebook* closing around the throats of the last standing, old line publishers and media companies and telling them basically to stand aside while *Facebook* robs the train and then everyone can talk politely about splitting up the new loot. "Trust me", they're saying – we'll talk soon – and here's how the talk will go: what mine is mine and what used to be yours, we can talk about.

These days we're constantly rushing from one thing to the next. All of us – all of the time. The days are ever longer and the nights are even worse. I call it a life of "playing the entire game in overtime". You might be kidding yourself and calling it masterful multi-tasking, but I'd say it's mostly just a mess. We're constantly trying to make time for everything and we're discovering that, not only is this an impossible dream, but – what's worse – is that we're ending up spending too much of our time on the urgent – rather than the important – things in our lives and in our businesses. More every day, we're losing sight of what really matters. Our inboxes (calls, emails and especially texts) are driving us instead of the other way around. The fact is that you'll never get into the flow if you're fighting non-stop fires all day long.

It's also abundantly clear that, as the speed of our days increases, we're losing the one-on-one people time necessary to connect with the others in our lives and in our companies whose thoughtful input we need to make smart decisions as well as the right choices for the future. I'm talking both about accessing crucial company data as well as not cutting off the far more critical access to the personal and emotional feedback we all need from those we work with in order to succeed. Sadly, with the rate of change in our lives accelerating every day, I don't see things getting better for us any time soon unless we start to take back some control, have a little patience, and slow the entire process down.

It starts with making time to listen. People will tell you the truth – which only hurts when it ought to – but only if you make it clear that you're interested and paying attention when they try to talk. Entrepreneurs all pride themselves on being great talkers with the "gift of gab", but it's much harder to sit still and listen. Even better, no one's ears ever got them into hot water.

Taking on and trying to do too many things at once makes for an unendingly stressful life and – even worse – mediocre results across the board for your business. It never pays to be a mile wide and an inch deep in anything. It might be worth the pain and the sacrifices if the bottom line results were there, but the evidence is all in the other direction. Trying to be all things to all people or please all of the people even part of the time is as impossible as trying to be in two places at one time. No one expects this of you (except maybe you) and – if you give them a chance – they'll tell you that and they can even help you get over some of the hardest spots. It's never smart to try to do everything. It's not remotely practical to try to do it all by yourself. And, in the end, it's a losing proposition for everyone because you inevitably find yourself trying to do a bunch of things poorly or cheaply that you shouldn't be doing at all.

"Hurry sickness" is definitely an occupational disease of entrepreneurs, but it's not incurable. Slow down, catch your breath, ask for some advice and help, and let your people do the talking. Wisdom and smart decisions are the rewards you get for listening when you would have much preferred to be talking.

There are two main reasons (apart from a continual lack of enough time and a constant lack of enough money) for the persistence of this particular problem and both can be addressed – maybe not entirely eliminated – if we just keep a couple of simple ideas in mind.

The first reason for the constant frenzy is because no one wants to slow down and be run over by their competitors and/or be left behind by their customers. Fast followers are lurking behind every bush just waiting to go to school on your example, create a faster, easier or cheaper solution, and quickly try to take your place. Customers' expectations are perpetually progressive – the bar never stops rising – and their demands will only continue to increase and ratchet up over time. You've got to be rapid and responsive, but not rabid.

It still pays to be paranoid and to try to keep constantly moving your products and services ahead (while iterating all the while), but speed alone isn't all that helpful if you're headed in the wrong direction. Not all movement (however frantic) is progress or even forward motion and too much trying can sap precious energy, waste critical and scarce resources, and take your eyes off the main chance. There's a right way to handle and prioritize these things, but a successful approach rarely starts with acting in the moment or reacting to the surrounding circumstances. It starts with listening and taking stock.

Looking for effective solutions without taking the time to carefully listen to your customers' problems is like working in the dark without a flashlight. A lot of coding and other activity may make your engineers feel better (it's a somewhat effective antidote for anxiety), but it's not likely to be moving the ball up the field or leading your business to a better result for your clients unless it's informed by actual and timely customer input. Making the time and taking the time to listen closely is not only smart business; it's the safest way to proceed because no one ever listened themselves out of a job.

The second reason that drives a lot of entrepreneurial excess has more to do with managing people's imagined perceptions rather than reality except that – in the intense context of a startup – perceptions and impressions are often long lasting and can quickly harden into unpleasant realities.

I'm a major advocate of leading by example and modeling the behavior that you expect from your team, but many entrepreneurs take this idea too literally and push it too far. They believe that, if you're too calm, too collected, or too unconcerned with today's crisis, your team members will think that you don't care or that you're not all-in. Ya gotta let them see you sweat so they'll know you've got some skin in the game right alongside theirs. And, to prove the point, they think they need to run around like crazy people all day long. They worry that, if they slow down or sit down, people will be suspicious of their commitment.

But the truth is that these are the very people trying to get your attention and also to get a word in edgewise. They'd line the floors with flypaper if they thought that would slow you down for a few seconds. They want to be heard and they want to be helpful and it's all up to you. Listening is the highest form of courtesy.

So give yourself a break, take some more time to listen, and – when you're drowning in a hundred contradictory suggestions and ideas – remember the cardinal rule: most of the time, it's far more important to listen to people's advice than it is to heed it.

TULLMAN'S TRUISMS

LOOKING FOR THE SOLUTION WITHOUT LISTENING TO THE PROBLEM IS LIKE WORKING IN THE DARK

The bond between the best entrepreneurs and their businesses is often so tight and all-encompassing that they can make the easy mistake of confusing who they are as people with what they do for a living. They lose sight of some of the more important things that distinguish making a living from having a life. And because they take their business's ups and down so personally, there's virtually no separation between their everyday work and what little time is left for the rest of their life (not to mention family and friends). Everything suffers as a result.

If their business takes a hit (which startups do on a regular basis), they feel like they're failing personally as well and that they must be fundamentally worthless. If that sounds overly dramatic or simply overwrought; come live in my world for a few weeks and you'll change your mind in no time at all. The external stresses of building a new business are nothing compared to the mental beatings and recriminations we administer to ourselves on a regular basis. It's not healthy, it's not smart, but it's a fact of the life we've chosen.

Having said that, I want to be clear that I believe that there's no such thing as "just business" and that it's essential to take your business personally if you want to have any chance of real success and of building something that matters and makes a difference. But, at the same time, I don't think that you can let your identity itself (and your sense of self-worth) be entirely subsumed by the day-to-day crises and fire drills and the many bumps in the road and temporary (we hope) setbacks that we all deal with. While the ups and the occasional wins are nice; it's the downs and learning how to deal with them that makes all the difference in the long run. The highs may be high, but the lows are a lot deeper.

We all get depressed from time to time because – as it happens – and I hope this doesn't come as a complete surprise to anyone – life isn't fair. Even the nicest people get knocked in the head from time to time. The very best of intentions are scant protection from the vagaries of the startup world. And especially in this business, not everything ever works out the way you've planned. Sadly, and far too often, it turns out that being in the right time and place (or just catching some other lucky break) beats out a lot of better ideas, a bunch of long hours and hard work, and even much better technology and solutions. That's just how it goes. But where things go after that (and where your business ends up) is up to you and how you handle the bruises and blisters that are all an essential part of growing any business.

I've watched hundreds of entrepreneurs handle every kind of adversity (and lived through more near-death experiences myself than I care to recall) and I've concluded that there's a right way to proceed and a lot of ways that are wastes of time which will lead you nowhere. Some of these approaches are just common sense ideas, but it's easy to lose sight of them when you're feeling down and troubled. That's when you need a friend and a helping hand. So here goes.

What Won't Work

(1) Playing the Blame Game

There's always someone or something to blame. Usually it's the people not in the room or the circumstances beyond your control or the weather which we can't do a thing about. It doesn't help to whine and worse – by putting your fate in the hands of circumstances or third parties – you give up your own power to change things. Sitting back and feeling sorry for yourself isn't ever a viable solution.

(2) Settling for A Situation that Sucks

Nothing I know gets better by itself. If you want a better outcome or result, you have to take control of the situation and make things better. Standing still means you're slipping backwards while others are racing ahead. When you settle for less than you deserve or for less than your best; it's a very slippery slope and – as often as not – you end up with even less than you settled for.

(3) Trying to Ignore the Problem

If you don't want to believe or accept something, there's no amount of evidence that will change your mind. But, if you ignore a serious problem long enough, you'll have a crisis on your hands eventually and then you'll have no choice but to take action. It's makes much more sense to be proactive and get on the problem now and get started on a solution before things get out of control and you end up just reacting to the latest fire. Ignoring the unhappy facts doesn't make them go away; they just fester.

(4) Trying to Be Superman

Nothing much gets done today by one-man armies or super heroes – your business's important problems are complex and it takes a competent team to address and resolve them. You can't solve these things all by yourself regardless of how many all-nighters you pull. Putting a team together distributes the burdens and some of the stress and makes for a much better result.

(5) Trying to Distract Yourself

You may think that you can focus on other more trivial things – see a show or a movie – take a run or work out – have a few drinks – and magically stop worrying about the elephant in the room, but that's not the way your entrepreneurial brain works. It never shuts down completely. Convincing yourself that you don't care isn't as easy as you might imagine – regardless of what a great sales person you may think you are. And even if you get your head momentarily out of the game; your stomach will still be keeping score.

What Will Work

(1) Doing Something Now to Fix the Problem

Nothing beats "now". You may still not get it totally right, but you won't get anywhere at all if you don't get started. Better to be doing something constructive and moving the ball forward than to be sitting in a pile of pity feeling sorry for yourself. The people who work hard and still can't find the right answers or circumstances don't come to a screeching halt – they bend the world to their needs and desires – and they create their own solutions and make the conditions and circumstances that they need to succeed.

(2) Raising Your Sights and Expectations for Next Time

At 1871, one of our favorite mottos is: "It's Only a "No" for Now." The most critical skill of any successful entrepreneur is perseverance. Get knocked down – get back up – try again harder. But also – while you're at it – aim a little higher the next time because selling yourself short or settling for half a loaf is stupid – regardless of all the people who are more than happy to tell you why things can't be done. When you shoot for the stars, you'll be amazed at just how far you can go. There's always a best seat in the house; your job is to go for it.

(3) Focusing on What is Working and Building from There

I call this "eating the elephant one bite at a time". Not every problem can be solved at once and you can't generally get across the chasm in a single leap, but you can build off the foundation formed by the accomplishments and successes that you've had to date and then break the remaining barriers down into manageable and bite-sized challenges and then take these tasks on one at a time. It may require a little more time, but eventually a lot of small steps, pushes and the occasional shove – as well as a little bit of patience – will get you there.

(4) Acknowledging that Things Could Be a Lot Worse

Serial entrepreneurs will tell you that it's never as bad or as good as it looks. People who aren't living this life think that all entrepreneurs are cock-eyed optimists who view everything through their rose-colored glasses and believe that trees grow to the sky. But we know better. Whatever brave and excited face you have to put on every day and show the world (and your team as well), deep down inside, it pays to be paranoid. But it's also essential – in the privacy of your own mind – to be proud. Proud of what you set out to do; proud of how far you've come when so many others never could; and proud of what you've built so far and of all the people you've benefitted along the way. There are a lot of much worse ways you could be spending your time and your life. Admit it and get on with it.

(5) Remembering Why You're Doing This in the First Place

We didn't come this far to quit or to only come this far. We didn't come to play; we came to win. And we wouldn't be doing this at all if it wasn't important and likely to make a difference to a lot of people in addition to ourselves. That's why we come to work; put our noses to the grindstone; and try to get better every single day. If it was easy, anyone could do it. It's not.

It's getting to be graduation season again. Every year I'm asked to speak and the temptation to save some time by resurrecting and reusing versions of my prior talks is substantial especially because I'm personally convinced that those prior words of wisdom were not only invaluable, but timeless as well. But being consistent (or lazy) requires you to be just as ignorant today as you were a year ago and I'd like to think that – even at my advanced age – I've learned, re-learned and unlearned a few new and important things.

In addition, the world is moving much too rapidly (and not necessarily forward) for anyone to look back as little as a year in time and not feel that there's been so much water under the dam and so many radical changes in our lives that we need to take a fresh look at what things are really going to matter and make a difference in the lives of this year's graduates. So many of them want to be entrepreneurs and start their own businesses that I feel uniquely qualified to give them a bit of advice.

I'm not talking about philosophy or politics – I'm just trying to make sure that there's at least one contrarian and maybe one voice of realism among this season's many purveyors of touching truisms, pious platitudes, and bumper sticker BS – all of which feel like they were written by either Hallmark or the hack speech writers whose prior Republican clients and "candidates" are now sitting on the sidelines sucking their thumbs and watching The Donald drive the bus off the bridge.

The costly privilege of getting a Master's, an MBA or a JD these days changes the way you look at the world – mostly – I would argue - in a good way – and the rigor, the arguments, the grit and the perseverance that it takes to survive the process prepares, distinguishes, and sets new graduates apart from the millions of less fortunate folks in whatever endeavors they choose to pursue. Their first and most important job is to choose an initial path wisely so they can put all their new abilities to good use.

They possess powerful skills – not to be wasted – not to be withheld for fear of failing - and, mostly importantly, not to be frittered away. In my world, failure is an everyday occurrence and an accepted part of the landscape. The best entrepreneurs aren't afraid of failing – their greatest fear is spending a significant part of their lives doing something insignificant that doesn't really matter to anyone.

Today's graduates don't have to and they shouldn't settle for a day job or anything less than doing something important and making a difference. It pays to aim high even if you occasionally miss or stumble. There's always a best seat in the house – a best row at the show – and while you may not always get it – shame on you if you don't go for it.

So here are a few things that I've learned which I hope will help on the journey.

(1) Not Everything Worth Doing is Worth Doing Well
Even if you're not a Marine, it's still great to try to be the best that you can be. Striving every day for excellence is stimulating and rewarding. It's a good goal and a worthy objective. On the other hand, shooting for perfection is neurotic and will simply drive you crazy. No one and no business can afford to be perfect even if it were possible and it's a waste of time to try.

In most things today, good enough is enough to get started – then you can start to grow. You want to concentrate on doing a few things really well and saying "No" to a million others. Focus is everything - you can do anything you want, but not everything. Pick your spots and take your best shot.

(2) Successive Approximation Beats Postponed Perfection
Iteration in our world is everything and it's an unending process whereby you keep getting better by getting a little better every day. Any professional knows this – the minute you stop going, you stop growing. It's like ironing (i think) – you keep going over and over again – until it's done. Of course it's never done because there's no finish line today – only the next mountain.

(3) The Name of the Game is to Win, Not to be Right All the Time
Growth is inherently embarrassingly – mistakes are inevitable – skinned knees and bruises are part of every business. Going in, it helps to know that you'll never have all the data you need for certain decisions so you'll learn to draw sufficient conclusions from insufficient premises and try to make the best decisions you can. There may be better answers out there, but there's rarely only one right answer and any reasonable answer is better than waiting while the world passes you by.

(4) No One Does Anything Important Today All by Themselves
Technologies quickly become commodities while dedicated, motivated and passionate people who can work together effectively are the only long term, sustainable competitive advantage any organization can really have. Today is the slowest rate of technological change that you will experience for the rest of your life, but human nature never changes.

Teambuilding, collaboration and listening skills trump pure talent today and it doesn't help to be creative if no one cares what you have to say. The only thing more important than teamwork is a willingness and a desire to do the hard work that it takes to build a real business.

(5) Life's Too Short to Be a Bore or a Chore

We act as though comfort and luxury were the chief requirements of life when all that we really need to make us happy is something to put our mind to, put our heart and soul into, to be enthusiastic about, and to be proud of. Maybe that sounds like a plateful (and it is), but it's within our reach.

At 1871, we're lucky enough to go to work each morning joined by excited, energetic and enthusiastic people who are setting out to change the world in important ways. They will face plenty of bumps in the road, but we've learned that when you're surrounded by other people on the same path as you, it makes you up and improve your own game.

My fondest hope for every new graduate is that they can find a similar place, a special kind of environment like ours, and similar challenges. There's no better or more worthwhile way to spend your days.

TULLMAN'S TRUISMS

THE LESSONS THAT COST THE MOST TEACH THE MOST

181 – PRESENTATION PROFICIENCY – A CRITICAL SKILL FOR THE NEXT CENTURY

As we - especially anyone under the age of 25 - continue to read less and less and watch (and listen) to constantly increasing amounts of content (for better or worse and often unwittingly and unwillingly), it's becoming clear that new types of communication skills are going to be essential for any kind of success in our schools, our businesses and our lives. Not to mention our politics because – say whatever else you will about his messages – The Donald is a master communicator and it's no accident that he swiftly left the dirty dozen and a half in the dust.

I think there are some critical lessons here for all of us and especially for our future. In our sound bite-obsessed and media-driven world today, it's not just WYSIWYG – "what you see is what you get" – it's pretty much what you see and hear is <u>all</u> you get - whether you like it or not. And the people who develop the ability to tell their stories and deliver their messages clearly, quickly and in ways that connect with us emotionally are going to be the <u>only</u> ones heard. In the future, it'll be much more important to teach your kids to sing than to fish. I don't mean literally to sing, but they'll need to know how to aggressively "sell" their ideas in a swift and succinct fashion. Low energy is for losers.

Every day, our world is becoming more about form and less about substance. It's about delivery, not details. Activity rather than accuracy. And speed above all. If you're not quickly and effectively connecting with me, you have no hope of communicating anything of importance to me. If I'm not listening, it doesn't matter what you're saying; if I don't care about what you're saying, it doesn't matter how smart or important the message may be; and, if I can't find you in the noise and clutter, you'll never be chosen.

Sadly, in addition, we're also seeing more and more of a trend where media is sliced and diced and siloed and where each listener is seeking affirmation and not information – we are basically looking and listening only to the people who are telling us what we want to hear – it's not about discovery; it's all about dogma. An echo chamber made of mirrors instead of windows on the world. And it's not likely to get any better any time soon so it's on each of us to make our way through the morass and figure out how best to function in this frantic and fractured new world.

The good news is that there's a little encouraging light at the end of the tunnel. Some savvy and talented people have spent a great deal of time studying what works in this new world and what it takes to get the word out successfully and effectively to your "audience" – whomever that may be. Chris Anderson is one of the good guys.

We hosted Chris, the "Head of TED", recently at 1871 for a short lecture about his new book *TED Talks* and for some Q&A with our member companies and other guests. Chris modestly pointed out that - contrary to people's expectations – he himself wasn't a great speaker at all which was fairly surprising because he has selected and prepped virtually all of the TED conference speakers for many years and there's no better forum than a TED talk to get your ideas across. It turned out that that was about the only thing he said which was totally wrong. He was terrific.

He showed us some short video examples of great (and not so great) TED talks from the past and then shared some specific suggestions about his conclusions as to what goes into crafting a memorable presentation – especially an 18-minute masterpiece – to be delivered in front of one of the toughest and most accomplished audiences in the world. And he also made it very clear that these ideas weren't just specific tips about what it takes to be a top talker at TED – they applied to every kind of opportunity you may have to present any ideas worth sharing.

I'm not going to try to cover everything he mentioned (I'd suggest that you get his book for all the details), but here are some of the key concepts that seemed especially important to me.

(1) Tell A Story
The right story sets up the idea you are trying to share. Our whole world revolves around storytelling and metaphors/analogies are some of the best shortcuts.

(2) Start Strong
If you don't hook them at the beginning, they'll be gone in a flash. Their smart phones are lethal weapons in the attention war.

(3) Talk Your Way
Authenticity is everything and if you're uncomfortable or forcing it or trying to be someone you're not, the audience will know it instantly. They have great BS detectors.

(4) Explain on the Way to Persuading
The world won't take your word for it. Give me a reason or two to go along and show me why it matters to me. Convincing yourself is easy – selling others is much harder.

(5) Put Some Passion into It
Chris called this "unleashing your voice". Heart helps. No one really cares what you know until they know how much you care. This is why celebrities shilling for the latest shiny object so often suck.

(6) Connection Precedes Communication

Eye contact is essential – we learn by looking deeply into each other's eyes. You've got to make that human connection. Connect with your audience – however small or large – by focusing on them as specific individuals and addressing your comments to them directly.

(7) The Pros Rehearse More than Anyone – So Should You

Making it look easy is very, very hard. Rehearse, rehearse some more and then do it a few more times. If you do it right, you won't be stale, you'll be successful.

Cleaner and dramatically more fuel-efficient cars make a lot of sense to me. Electric vehicles (once we master the concerns around economic battery life and thereby effectively eliminate range anxiety) are going to be omnipresent in the central business districts of our cities within a few years. Charging kiosks will be on every corner and in every garage and the vehicles we end up driving from place to place won't necessarily even be our own as shared fleets of every form of transportation (bikes being just the beginning) multiply.

OnStar and similar emergency notification services which can rapidly and automatically summon and precisely direct roadside assistance to disabled vehicles will clearly help save lives. Route guidance, parking apps and wayfinding systems have already become an essential part of our hyper-mobile lives and something that we increasingly can't live without. Apps which solve for and facilitate inexpensive inter-modal transportation solutions will be the newest forms of Frogger – letting us leap quickly from bus to train to plane all seamlessly. See http://www.inc.com/howard-tullman/how-ridescout-demonstrates-the-power-of-the-platform.html .

And nothing I've seen lately remotely compares to the joy of triggering your tailgate with a swipe of your toe when you're holding a ton of packages - unless it's the ability to beep your horn and flash your headlights while you're staggering around a dark parking lot after a Bulls game trying to find your ride home.

But when it comes to in-dash video displays, heads-up windshield indicators, touch pads and screens, etc., the slope quickly gets quite slippery and I'm not such a big fan. And when the car guys shamelessly tell us not to text and drive – out of one side of their mouths - and then endlessly tout new audio-enabled features which will read my emails and texts out loud – and let me dictate answers as well - and then they go on to pretend all the while that I'm not going to be terribly distracted in the process - I have to take a few giant steps back. Just because we can do these things doesn't necessarily make them simple, safe or smart options.

But the much bigger issue going forward is the fantasy of millions of self-driving cars hitting the roads any time in the next several decades. It's just never going to happen – even though it's one of Detroit's newest and most persistent pipedreams. The car manufacturers are hoping to save their bacon (or at least reach retirement age before the impending deluge) by shifting their current production activities to comparable numbers of new, technologically-advanced, "smart" cars even though there's no one under 30 who really wants to own a car at all. See http://www.inc.com/howard-tullman/why-gen-y-doesnt-care-about-cars.html . And even though Uber already has more daily riders today than the public transportations systems in Boston and Chicago combined and has jumped ahead of the cab companies in San Francisco, Los Angeles, Dallas and Washington, DC. And also because it takes just short of FOREVER to turn over any significant part of the cars on the road in the United States.

There are about 250 million cars on the road these days and – notwithstanding the fact that we buy about 17 million new cars a year and about 40 million used cars a year – the overall age of the cars on the highways today is increasing and now averages about 11.5 years of age. 14 million of those cars are more than 25 years old. Not a one of these is "smart" and every one of them is capable of smacking right into your self-driving super car for the next 20 or 30 years. Of course, President Obama could make all the cars older than some cutoff age illegal to drive before he leaves office. But if you think it's hard to get a gun owner to part with his piece, try taking a car away from a Californian if you want to see a really nasty battle.

So I wouldn't be holding my breath any time soon for the tsunami of smart car sales which the car guys are praying for every night. Because, even apart from the fact that building the steel in cars as opposed to creating their software controls and smarts will continue to be less and less valuable and more and more of the ass-end of the industry, the truth is that we don't need smart cars, we need smart roads to handle millions of relatively dumb cars. The cars won't be as dumb as today, but millions will be easy to retrofit because the tasks they'll need to independently perform will still be mainly mechanical (starting, accelerating, slowing and stopping) and not too much more. These functions are already onboard (think cruise control) and can be easily updated and controlled by dongle-based, Wi-Fi-enabled units accessing the vehicle's OBD (onboard diagnostics) port which will receive directions and instructions from road-based markers, sensors and transmitters.

We live in a world where the best winning technologies are built on powerful platforms. See http://www.inc.com/howard-tullman/the-primacy-of-the-platform.html . And the truth is that we need to start think of our roads and highways as precisely that – a transportation platform much like a railroad system - which will efficiently, safely and securely control the movements of millions of vehicles – without the necessity of equipping every single vehicle with hundreds of omni-directional, multi-function, expensive sensors and cameras and other devices. Smart roads are a lot smarter than millions of not so smart cars.

Yes, we will have to upgrade the miles and miles of roads, but we are already doing that throughout the country anyway. And, while this is a daunting task, it wasn't so many years ago when none of us would have believed that Waze and Google and Navteq would have mapped out almost every road in the world and put that data in our cars and on our phones for free.

We can start with the interstate highway system which you will be amazed to learn is less than 50,000 miles of roadways. All we need to do is to develop a comprehensive plan to do it, figure out how to pay for it, and get started. Not easy I'm sure, but a lot easier than replacing 250 million individual vehicles over several decades and chasing a constantly moving goal line.

I've been struggling for a while now in trying to make some sense of how we should regard and manage social sharing as a viable marketing tool and also as another critical communication channel for our businesses. Content marketing is here to stay, but – notwithstanding the myths of virality - it doesn't happen by itself, no one can make it happen for you (it's like pushing a rope), and it almost never happens overnight. (See http://www.inc.com/howard-tullman/the-trouble-with-social-media.html .) Nonetheless, while no one knows what makes a mega-viral hit, some players have emerged who can help you press your winning bets, amplify the impact of the "stories" that sell, and use your always finite resources in ways that will get you the most bang for your buck.

Surprisingly, the folks who are best at it right now aren't the biggest guys or the most experienced ones – it's the fast, flexible and scrappy mid-sized players who are mastering the new tools and tricks of the trade. And – while you might think that the PR firms would have a real edge in managing messaging in this area - it turns out to be the digital agencies and not the old-line flacks who are turning in the results that matter.

Of course, the best players of all right now are the complete newbies who don't know any better and don't know what they're not supposed to be able to do and – as a result - they're just doing it and killing it as well. If you want to see the future, keep your eyes on the "kids" creating content on the leading visual platforms like *Snapchat* and *Instagram*, but even more importantly, watch what's happening with all of the new live streaming services. One thing that jumps out of the jumble is that polished and professional material is almost worthless, that edits interrupt the vibe, immediacy and flow of the best stuff, and that the rawer and more direct the footage, the fresher and more authentic it appears.

In our new "right now" world, the closer you can come to "real time", the better your bottom line will be. And speaking of bottom lines, it's also significant that these new channels are finally offering producers (previously held hostage by *YouTube*) serious audience volumes and financially attractive alternatives which are letting them make a living doing what they love.

We spend so much of our time these days sitting alone in front of some screen that sharing has become the default way that we make things real. It's not sufficient to "get a life" any more, we have to show the world – or at least our world – that we "have a life" and we evidence our existence digitally by sharing.

Selfies are the new autographs not simply because they are self-authenticating (unlike that LeBron James jersey sitting on your shelf which was certainly signed by someone), but because in addition selfies make our lives real in that they show that we were there – in the moment – doing the deed – and that's what matters most. If you can't prove it, most likely you didn't do it.

It's not an easy process to get a handle on all of this and it's even harder to get clear metrics so that you can accurately measure actual performance in economic (rather than "feel good") terms because so much of traditional advertising and marketing has been single-threaded and uni-directional (one brand or business to many customers and consumers) for so long that it's a real challenge to make this shift in mindset and come around to accepting and dealing with the reality that in this new media world the customer isn't interested in a single channel of anything. It's truly an omni-channel world and the more paths you have to reach the consumer, the merrier.

Tech channels today (in part because of their broad scope, targeting ability and relatively low cost) are additive, not redundant, and the cumulative impact of well-crafted messaging (delivered in the right context and at the right time) across multiple channels may be the only effective way to break your messages thru the clutter and noise in order to reach and engage your customers.

But in trying to determine exactly how to take advantage of this peculiar place where the brands and the marketers no longer control the conversations and where at best – and only if you're very good and very quick – you may have a fighting chance at shaping some of the new narratives, there is a very substantial cognitive tension between creating and delivering real meaning (value and authenticity) on the one hand and securing effective monetization (costs and actual benefits) on the other. The entire social sharing space just continues to get more complicated and more difficult to decipher every day and very few players have demonstrated any consistent end-to-end success.

I think it's only going to get worse as the lines between content creators and content consumers continue to blur and merge into one another. In addition, this is not a concern or an issue that's going to fade away any time soon because it's too appealing (certainly on a superficial level at least) for any new business to ignore or to avoid this easy, low-cost and largely "outsourced" method of creating substantial quantities of content to "feed the beast".

Of course, there's a major issue about the quality of the third-party content that's being created, but once you've gotten over that issue (loving the circus, but hating some of the clowns), the fact is that you've got to have a presence in these discussions about your marketplace and – more particularly – about the place of your products and services in those markets - whether you like it or not. These conversations are being carried on whether you choose to listen and participate or stand idly by. Ultimately, listening is a great start, but listening alone won't get you to the head of the pack and, if you're not noticed (or discovered), you'll never been chosen.

So, in the same spirit as we have talked in the past about "smart reach" (See http://www.inc.com/howard-tullman/to-sell-more-your-marketing-must-embrace-smart-reach.html.) being essential to overcome the glut, noise and clutter of the traditional marketing channels, right now the most critical discussions center on the need for "smart sharing" and precision targeting rather than the kind of random regurgitation and rapid redistribution of content which we're seeing far too much of today - often without regard to its relevance and value to the recipients.

Sharing without caring and sometimes without even reading the shared material has become an ingrained and knee-jerk process for too many people and one which just exacerbates the identification problems, the acquisition costs, and the difficulty of reaching and successfully engaging the right audiences. (See http://www.inc.com/howard-tullman/three-ways-to-put-more-sting-into-your-social-media.html.) Volume and velocity aren't as important to real impact and ultimate success as are the nature and quality of the connections which your sharing programs are designed to create and build over time. (See http://www.inc.com/howard-tullman-make-me-care-and-then-i-will-share.html .)

There are basically four buckets of social sharing today and three of them aren't worth spit. This doesn't mean that they won't continue to draw eyeballs – some morons never get tired of wasting their time - it simply means that those eyeballs are basically useless to your business. To build real connection and value, you need to attract and engage people who are highly influential, not the ones who are easily influenced. Too many agencies are just selling tonnage today and what it takes to win is a light touch - not a heavy hand.

So be smart and tell your people to skip these guys. And if they offer any resistance, just remind them that guilt by association is alive and well and that when you associate with dogs, you also end up with fleas.

(1) Shameless Sharing

Frankly, it's no easier to understand or explain the continued popularity of the Kardashians than it is to understand how The Donald is now the presumed nominee of the Republican party. But it's clear that they've both been aided, enabled and enthroned by a clueless MSM which is in its own desperate financial struggle to drive eyeballs, clicks and views from who knows who so they can try to make their mortgages. You have to wonder who imagines that these kinds of audiences and followers have the slightest value. They're the dregs whose main prior pastime was watching daytime television. And they're only as loyal as the next new thing.

Of course, the media guys aren't alone. They're running these scams with the connivance of the TV networks and the big ad agencies which continue to push big-budget TV advertising while the whole world increasingly looks at everything but the nightly network news. (See http://www.inc.com/howard-tullman/3-things-you-need-to-know-about-advertising.html.) As the smart people who run real businesses and actually pay the bills wake up to measurable, performance-based marketing, these ruses and standard routines – based on the theory of greater fools - will end and end badly. Best to stay far away.

(2) Stupid Sharing

If celebrity, fashion and pitiable personalities aren't your thing, there's still a ton of other clutter and crap – made-up news, phony courses and cures, medicine based on miracles – which is constantly foisted on all of us along with the thousands of cat videos, singing parrots, dancing dogs and music videos from the dark ages.

I'm not exactly sure when the major brands just threw in the towel and decided that any visibility (regardless of the context or the accompanying associations) was better than being left out, but things today are totally out of control.

If you put your brand and your business's good name out there where you can no longer control the content, the context, or the conversations, you're jeopardizing years of credibility and hard work for a "benefit" that's uncertain at best. It's better in many cases to wait it out rather than to wallow in the muck that passes for online media.

(3) Solicited Sharing

I've been pretty hard on solicited social sharing services – whether it's users of free samples, in-kind or cash payments for pictures, blog posts or other excited write-ups that are bought and paid for, etc. It seems to me that you have to consider the source, the motivation, the integrity, and the value of this kind of content before you decide if it makes any sense to listen to what these "endorsers" have to say about anything.

It's the same question we all have about celebrity endorsers who exceed the scope of their experience and their actual qualifications and lose all their credibility in the process. And how many of us find the professional advice of the "doctors", "nurses", and even "sufferers" in TV ads to be valuable when the FDA makes these mopes reveal in big bold letters that they're actually all actors just hired to sell the stuff to sick suckers.

But I've been giving this particular bucket a second look because it turns out – much like the battery of psych and employment tests which we all think we can game, but we can't – that it's completely shocking how much people today will inadvertently share in their tweets, shares and selfies without even knowing it. And smart data mining companies like *Pay Your Selfie* (one of the more advanced businesses at 1871) are learning how to aggregate and analyze shared images and then identify, extrapolate and provide these very useful insights to brands and manufacturers.

Pay Your Selfie was featured in a recent *New York Times* article (See http://www.nytimes.com/2016/05/08/business/media/what-do-consumers-want-look-at-their-selfies.html.) about uncovering consumer desires and the article identified three aspects of their particular program which really set them apart from the crowd and makes them look much more like a next-generation digital market research firm. These parts of the program are in addition to the fact that they actually initiate and launch their own custom surveys to their panels as rapid-fire focus groups.

First, the participants don't have to have large social followings or be "professional" posters so there's a reasonable chance to get some real and diverse people participating and to avoid some of the risks and biases typically associated with self-selection surveys. In addition, done right, you can attract and facilitate the behavior of actual and credible influencers who honestly want to endorse the product or service. There's never been a better example of this kind of action than the millions of *GoPro* videos.

Second, the participants' selfies can be kept private and they don't even have to be willing to publically share their selfies so there's an improved likelihood that the information being gathered is somewhat more open and honest than we have come to expect from standard media and other polls where the world says they wouldn't touch Trump with a 10-foot pole and then turns right around and votes him in.

Third, as noted above, there's a tremendous amount of ancillary data which can be extracted from the experience – whether the user knows it or intends it – and this kind of circumstantial and contextual data is probably much more important in the long run. So who, what, where, how and when these activities are taking place are all bonus learnings for *PYS*'s customers. The *Times* article even suggests that the users get so accustomed to the process that over time they lose any self-consciousness or desire to control and edit the content which makes for more accurate and authentic results. So maybe this particular bucket is on its way to being half full instead of full of it.

(4) Smart Sharing

Encouraging and amplifying smart sharing, on the other hand, makes sense for everyone because word of mouth (whether it's analog or digital) is still the most important and prominent way that we learn almost anything. Smart sharing has four basic elements: (1) immediacy; (2) authenticity; (3) personalization; and (4) credibility. I'll be covering these in detail in another post, but - for the moment – if you can concentrate on avoiding the bad solutions, you'll be way ahead of the game. It's so much better to avoid the potholes entirely than it is to get a great deal on fixing your flat tires.

TULLMAN'S TRUISMS

A LITTLE BAD PUSHES OUT TONS OF GOOD

It seems like nary a week goes by these days without my having an intense and well-intentioned conversation about someone's fear of his or her business's bubble being burst by baby-faced disruptors. Most of these talks are initiated by mid-level and middle-aged managers at large firms whose businesses for the moment are usually comfortable incumbents in various large and complicated marketplaces. But they're running a little scared because they know that new levels of competition and new kinds of competitors are clearly on the horizon.

Their companies typically have yet to be roiled or wholly upended by new entrants wielding the latest cloud-based SAAS solutions to address long-standing and often glaringly obvious industry shortcomings and inefficiencies. It turns out that not every industry is as toxic and easy to topple as the taxis. (See http://www.inc.com/howard-tullman/not-every-industry-can-be-uber-ized.html .) But they have nonetheless been charged by their own managers and bosses with attempting to anticipate and get ahead of the problem as well as their looming competitors by identifying the likely candidates, tracking their progress, and carefully watching their latest actions.

As a result, they spend great gobs of time and energy pouring over product portfolios and new releases; they try to analyze every article and media mention as well as all available tea leaves; and they obsess over alleged lost opportunities even when these are often modest at best and largely immaterial given their scale. But everyone's read about the innovator's dilemma and knows that the most devastating types of disruption start at the bottom of the food chain and slowly work their way upwards – often before the incumbents even take notice of their presence.

So it's always smart to be on the lookout. But I would argue that even the most conscientious scrutiny is much more effective when you're looking in the right places. You don't want to be like the drunk looking for his lost keys under the street light – not because that's where he thinks he lost them – but because the light is better there.

And, as often as not, those places are as likely to be <u>inside</u> your business as outside the four walls. So you might really need a proctoscope to look deeply inside rather than a periscope to look out over the turbulent seas trying to see what you can see. Focusing your attention and efforts on emerging external threats which you basically have little or no control over ignores the much more obvious internal areas of your business where (assuming that you can overcome the inertial resistance to change and the company turf and political issues) you can make changes that can quickly and cost-effectively anticipate new threats and blunt or entirely eliminate them. You can do it to yourself and your organization before someone does it to you.

Looking hard in the mirror is a lot closer to home and a much clearer view than staring out the window and wondering when the sky will start falling. Keep in mind that this is exactly what the little people looking to eat your lunch are doing every day anyway. They are scrutinizing every aspect of your operations looking for weaknesses, gaps, shortcomings, etc. that they can address and exploit. But in this particular examination, you have a huge edge.

Unlike your prospective competitors and others on the outside, you have the advantage in the analysis of having all the facts and figures about your business at your fingertips. The guys on the outside looking in have a fist full of FUD and not much else. But to make this approach really work, you have to act like an outsider yourself at the outset in order to get the right perspective. It's absolutely critical to avoid taking too many things for granted which can quickly get you into trouble. Everything needs to be on the table and up for grabs or you won't get anywhere. The good news is that it's a lot easier than you would think to start with a blank slate and take stock of your business.

The first step in the process is to put yourself in your customers' shoes and ask yourself: first, how you can materially improve the customer's experience across each of the following dimensions, and, second, which improvement will have the biggest impact without regard to the cost of implementation. Cost is ultimately important, but in the real world, things that make a great deal of sense tend to pay for themselves pretty quickly in dollars and cents.

The basic dimensions are as follows:

(1) Simplicity and absence of transactional friction
(2) Speed
(3) Convenience
(4) Accessibility
(5) Affordability

Keep in mind that these are the exact same attributes of your business that the competitors are looking at as well and they're asking exactly the same questions as you. I'm sorry if this seems pretty simple and straightforward, but the truth is that it absolutely is just that easy and yet, very few of us take the time to step back and – starting from scratch – see clearly what we can do better.

There's very little magic to this process and – as I tell all our big corporate partners and sponsors – apart from a willingness to do the work and to accept and implement the results of the investigation – there's absolutely no reason why any company – large or small – new or old – can't do precisely the same thing.

In addition to the "defensive" ammunition which this analysis will help you develop as well as with identifying the actions you will need to take, there's another upside to the discovery process – the prospect of a great deal of new revenue from changes, channels, customers and other low-hanging fruit and opportunities that were sitting there – unappreciated, undervalued and unexploited – right before your eyes. (See http://www.inc.com/howard-tullman/five-reasons-your-market-is-bigger-than-you-think.html .) It's a double-edged sword which cuts both ways – adding to the upside and protecting against the downside risks as well.

You'll note one other important feature of my list. There's really no reference to <u>new</u> products, services, etc. That's not an oversight or accidental. You don't have to invent anything new to pull this off – you just have to figure out how to do what you're doing a lot better.

And it always starts with taking a hard look at your business. As Michael Jackson used to say: it's all about the man in the mirror.

TULLMAN'S TRUISMS

MAKE SURE THE DOG WANTS TO EAT THE DOG FOOD

I believe in lifelong learning and I'm also absolutely certain that a great deal of what each of us learns going forward (man, woman or child) won't be in a traditional classroom setting or even in (or through) what we think of today as a traditional "school". New channels, new delivery systems, and new technologies are all emerging to broaden the resources available to us and video – in every size and shape – is leading the way. But I hope that we're not raising generations of kids to believe that you can get all you ever need to know from a 5" screen held a foot in front of your face.

In the real, grown-up world, we ultimately learn best by doing - first by listening; then by trying; and finally by succeeding and moving onward and upward. And, interestingly enough, more and more of us are taking direct responsibility for this process and doing it ourselves (DIY). It seems to me that there are a variety of different reasons. It could be because we're cheap, or we're impatient, or it's because we want our ongoing "education" to be ala carte – when, where and how we want it. But whatever the drivers, it's clear that today we're totally engaged when we're learning thru "hands-on" activity and we're totally turned off when we're being lectured to. We all want to be in charge and in the driver's seat.

The truth is that the DYI gene is also an integral part of the DNA of every good entrepreneur. Sometimes it's driven by a thirst for knowledge, a lack of patience or a lack of resources and sometimes it's all about ego and arrogance and that's where things can quickly run off the wrong side of the tracks. There's an unfortunate tendency today to degrade and devalue practical experience, prior results and real expertise. It's never smart for someone starting a new business to automatically assume that you know better than the people who've been there and done these things before. They call these people experts for a reason. Patterns do matter, history always helps, and gray hair sometimes signifies patience and wisdom rather than simply advanced age.

I'm convinced that part of this attitudinal problem is the MSM's insistence on offering up an instant "expert" on any subject on a moment's notice just to keep feeding the 24/7 media beast and to keep us from changing the channel. Every retired anybody is apparently qualified to pontificate on whatever today's topic happens to be whether they have the qualifications, the credentials or even the credibility to do so. I guess that saying this stuff just makes it so and style certainly trumps substance. When everyone's an expert, it's increasingly easy to believe that no one really knows anything and that you might very well know just as much as they do. Or that you can look it up.

And while it's true that everything anyone needs to know may be out there somewhere, it's more than a little naïve to believe that it's that easy to figure everything out on your own. I put part of the blame for this idea on simple youth (about 50%) and the remainder on YouTube where it is apparently written that by watching enough videos, you can eventually learn anything all by yourself. I'd also assign a little slice of the blame to my friend Sal Khan as well. Democratizing access to better explanations of complex concepts is undoubtedly a social good. And there's no doubt that the ability on your own time to watch (and re-watch) these materials is a major advantage. But, until we can prove otherwise, it always comes down to the same concern for me – it's not what you're being "taught"; it's what you learn and master that matters. I often say that I don't want a surgeon who's watched a hundred operations; I want one who's done them – over and over again.

We also know that we can learn a great deal by observation and from others around us – I call this lateral learning. (See http://www.inc.com/howard-tullman/when-to-steal-from-other-founders.html.) This is one of the reasons that I love the new Maker Movement with its core of contagious community and its constant sharing and celebration of craft and artistry. We want to do these things ourselves, but not necessarily by ourselves. It's just as lonely to be a maker as it is to be an entrepreneur and maybe there's no real difference between the two. So there's solace, support, and substance in being surrounded in your journey (whatever it may be) by like-minded others.

These desires and motivations are similar and just as important for our kids as for the rest of us. And they may represent the best hope that we have to pry their little eyes away from their screens for even a short while. You may think they're just playing games, but the reasons these games are so compelling and addictive is that the players are, in fact, (1) progressively building skills which will serve them well in their digital futures even while they're failing 80% of the time; (2) gaining a growing understanding of the power of process, trial and error, and iteration; and (3) developing an appetite for concrete achievements and skilled-based rewards which are often more accessible and socially/emotionally valuable to them than any diluted recognition or shared and politically correct acknowledgements which they might receive in school. (See http://www.inc.com/howard-tullman/stop-promoting-mediocrity-in-our-schools.html .)

Very few things in their school activities can compete with the engagement and adrenaline rush of these games. But hands-on, immersive, maker projects where they have both ownership and control can get the job done. All you have to do to see this at work is to visit any school with a robotics lab. The truth is that they have to make these kids go home at the end of the school day. And frankly, it doesn't really matter what they're making. Robots are nice, but so are a million other projects. The magic in the process is in the making, not necessarily in the end result. Just as any entrepreneur would tell you as well.

There's a pride, an ownership and an authenticity to something that you create with your own mind and your own hands that no hardware or software will ever replicate. Technology can augment almost everything we do, but it will never replace the emotional content of the creative process. This is just the newest, tech-enabled, version of traditional constructivist learning, but it's critical that we bring it back into our schools. (See http://www.inc.com/howard-tullman/the-real-benefits-of-coding.html .)

We need to make our kids into problem solvers, coders, builders and makers – not mechanical memorizers - and we can't start too soon.

As anyone who reads my weekly INC. Magazine blog can attest, I'm a diehard blogger. INC. is one of the great business communication platforms and an important channel for us to regularly get the word out about our member companies, track the expanding tech scene in Chicago, and distribute new ideas about what's happening with startups and disruptive innovators across the nation. It's an important resource for thousands of entrepreneurs and a quick way for us to share what we're learning every day at 1871 from and with hundreds of companies and thousands of people who are going through the very same (and sometimes scary) process of starting and building their own businesses.

And although the media world continues to change radically all around us, I don't plan to give up my seat at the table any time soon or stop writing and publishing my thoughts even as the time frames shrink, the production pressures grow, and the desires to have everything be bite-sized continue to mount. As hard as it may be for most people (and even for some curmudgeonly editors) to understand, certain things worth saying simply can't be said in a sentence or two. Sound bites and snippets basically suck – whether we're talking about the nightly news or the newest nasty politician – and they don't add anything important to the meat of the conversations that really matter.

Now I realize that we're all short on bandwidth and attention these days, but that's no real excuse to stop learning or to settle for fictions and factoids instead of facts and real substance. And I also understand that reading and/or listening does take some time, a little work, and patience as well. There's a reason they call it "mastery" and not Minute Rice. And it's abundantly clear that all of these important parts of the puzzle appear to be in increasingly short supply. But it's not just that we're all busy or even the onset of the "right now" economy that's the juice that's pushing this movement forward. The largest villains in this story are the dream of "viral" videos and the cameras embedded in every cell phone. It's just become too easy to make a message and a mess that masquerades as something meaningful. Every clown is now a cinematographer and we're all stuck in their circus.

We're smack in the midst of a "tidbit takeover" and it's making it increasingly difficult to find a place, a home, or an appreciation for the long form of just about anything. Velocity is all that matters now – value is an afterthought at best. We're turning the classics into CliffsNotes. Novels into pithy nuggets. And broadsides into listicles and bullet points. And this is why I'm afraid that the blog business is basically busted for anyone who's trying to make a buck from it. (On the other hand, the alliteration industry is alive and well.)

We're all too willing to settle for short, speedy, second-rate stuff – especially videos - instead of insisting that people take the time to say or write something that really matters. The fact is that, if no one's really reading or listening, it doesn't much matter what you're writing so a bunch of bozos with no lives and nothing better to do are taking over. If we want things to get better, the first step is to clearly understand the problems and then to start thinking about what we can do to shut down the click-bait con artists, viral vultures, and other BS artists who are constantly clogging up the critical arteries of the Internet with their cheap tricks and phony features. (See http://www.inc.com/howard-tullman/the-trouble-with-social-media.html .) We all need to be a lot smarter about how we're each spending our own time online because if we don't object to how these clowns are constantly sucking us into wasting our time, they'll never have any real incentive to stop.

And by the way, don't imagine that this is just some goody two-shoes stuff or a cathartic philosophical diatribe. It's ultimately about your business's bottom line. If you're concerned about cost-effectively getting your company's message out to the right prospects, consumers and customers, you need to make sure that you're not spending your scarce resources in passé places and on cluttered channels that are getting you nowhere.

Take it from me that your ad agencies, social sharing "experts" and/or marketing companies aren't gonna be the ones to give you the straight scoop on this situation. They're all in the same bag with the media and the publishers and they're a big part of the problem. No one wants to mention the Emperor's clothes or admit that no one's seeing or hearing your story as long as you're foolish enough to keep footing the bills. (See http://www.inc.com/howard-tullman/3-things-you-need-to-know-about-advertising.html .)

So as you try to make some business sense of what's going on, here are a few critical considerations to keep in mind:

(1) Video isn't a virtue by itself.
It's quick, it's visual, and it's immediate, but none of these attributes make it necessarily better, more informative, or even more effective in getting your message delivered. In fact, it's harder and much more time-consuming and costly to create and edit a good video than it is to write a great blog post. Stream of consciousness vlogs are just as often instances of verbal diarrhea as they are cases of memorable communication and unedited webcast videos of events and panels are even worse. (See http://www.inc.com/howard-tullman/your-streaming-video-sucks.html.) Claims of immediacy, rawness and authority aside, random rants are rarely relevant and juvenile junk is still just junk.

(2) Not every shooter is Scorsese or Spielberg.
We're in the mist of this crazy democratization of content where the distinctions between creators and consumers are blurring, and often, disappearing entirely. Speed and quantity – not care and quality - are the name of the game. Technology may keep improving and the capture process continues to become easier and easier, but the truth is that talent, creativity,

preparation and production values are still essential to turning out something that matters. Just because you made and shared it doesn't make it interesting or important to me. If you look around, it's amateur hour all day long and apparently everyone now thinks they can create content that's just as good as we now see on TV or online. UGC (user-generated content) is all the rage today because it's plentiful, cheap and created for free by third parties. And who are the publishers to complain? After all, they're under enormous pressure every day to feed the ravenous beast and they'll sell their ads against whatever garbage anyone wants to watch. And frankly, even what passes for "professional" creative sets a painfully low bar, so it's not like they're offering a host of better alternatives.

(3) It's All About Affirmation, Not Education or Information.

Media and political success today (if you can call it success) is too much about telling people what they want to hear rather than what they need to learn or to know. It's unlikely to get better any time soon because you don't see much of the world around you when you're staring into the mirror or watching some slanted cable news show. Today, it's no longer an aspirational "be like Mike" world -- it's all about being free "to be just like me." YouTube users aren't looking for instruction or excellence; they're looking for confirmation that they're just as capable of creating crap as the people whose videos they're so faithfully watching and they can't wait for their turn to generate box office numbers working out of their bedrooms or basements. Surprisingly, it took YouTube itself quite a while (and $300 million) to figure out this distinction. (See http:// www.inc.com/howard-tullman/three-lessons-from-youtubes-programming-disaster.html .)

None of this is remotely encouraging and it certainly doesn't bode well for the businesses with real products and services to sell and a real message to get out there. But it's not like you can take your ball and go home either. So when it's up to you to make the call on how to swim in this swamp, you'll find that there's no rule book or roadmap on how to do it right. The best advice I can give you is: (a) to make small consistent bets with people who can give you real time feedback on exactly what's working (engagement and execution – not eyeballs and bots) and then have someone stay constantly on top of the situation so that you can kill off the bad spends and double down quickly on what is driving actual results and purchases; and (b) use these channels and your content to drive traffic from the big guys to sites you own and control so that all your efforts and all your dollars aren't wasted just working to make money for Zuck.

TULLMAN'S TRUISMS

IF YOU DON'T PUT THE WORK INTO SOMETHING, YOU DON'T KNOW THE WORTH OF IT

On the occasion of the 20th anniversary of his venture capital group, Pritzker Group Venture Capital, I had a lengthy fireside chat with JB Pritzker at 1871 (JB led the group that founded 1871 in 2012) which was held before an enthusiastic crowd of entrepreneurs, investors, and several hundred others interested in hearing the gospel straight from the horse's mouth. When you're JB and have more than 20 years' venture experience and roughly 160 investments behind you, there's a whole lot to say that's well worth listening very carefully to. It was especially refreshing to be able to steer away from the standard clichés and get into some very practical tips and suggestions about what he and his team look for in considering a deal and how that differs from many other venture firms which are constrained by the requirements of their limited partnership agreements and other considerations like IRR (as opposed to ultimate return on capital) as well.

As many times as I have done sessions like this – being on one side or the other of the microphone – I find that there's always something for each of us to learn and a few key take-aways which I believe are worth sharing with your own people and with the startup world in general. We discussed a wide range of topics (while trying to stay as far away from politics as possible); spoke specifically about some of his more recent deals as well as his firm's particular investment criteria and objectives; and then took some questions from the audience. One of the things that was clear throughout the conversation was that the value for the audience in sit-downs like this is less about the novelty of the information we hear and more about the need to continually be reminded about the pretty basic basics of the business of raising money.

Among the very first things we covered was the necessity of "warm" introductions. Unsolicited business plans tossed over the transom are just as quickly tossed in the trash. I was reminded as we spoke of a great old piece of Chicago advice for patronage jobseekers which has been attributed to various politicians and goes: "We don't want nobody that nobody sent." It's the same story for your pitch and your proposal. If no one cares enough to vouch for you and your idea and make the right introductions, you'll never get to first base. And these aren't courtesy intros from the guy next door or someone's brother's brother – they're from highly-regarded business professionals whose time is precious and whose advice and opinions are always being sought. It's a small club and getting in the door is the first step to getting anything done.

Next on the short list was the need to temper your confidence with a little humility and a fair amount of listening. This, of course, is a life skill – not just a fundraising tool. (See http://www.inc.com/howard-tullman/leaders-learn-best-by-listening.html .) JB said that no one knows the answers to every question and, even if you think you do, there's more to the investor courting process than simply demonstrating that you are right all the time. Investors want to be wanted, needed, and heard (as we all do) and they want to feel that their input, guidance and assistance will be invited, appreciated, and even listened to from time to time. They're looking for a long-term partner, not a game show contestant, or the best college debater. Building a big business is a long, painful process and, while speed and skill are important, so are collaboration and team-building and building that team is as important with your investors and in the board room as it is with your partners and employees.

Without any question, the largest single cause for startup failures (more than 40% of the cases) is no market need. JB noted that it's absolutely critical that your pitch: (a) identifies a deep, existing and acknowledged pain point; (b) demonstrates that the "sufferers" are willing to pay serious money to have the pain addressed and remedied; and (c) shows that you have a viable and deliverable solution to the problem. No one wants to pay anyone to develop the cure for no known disease or try to fund and launch a solution in search of a problem. And while you're at it, you need to show that there's a lot of these folks and that the market (and reasonable add-ons and extensions to it) is big enough to support the expected growth of your business and, more importantly, to include a couple of bigger players as well as potential buyers for the business. *SMS Assist* (the newest Chicago unicorn) was cited as an example of a business that started out serving 3 basic service and maintenance needs of retailers (floor care, lawn maintenance, and snow removal) which – even at scale - wouldn't have amounted to a very large and interesting opportunity until you added in the revenues associated with the 45 other kinds of needs and requirements these customers also had which *SMS* could grow to address.

Almost 25% of startups fail because they don't assemble the right team and – in our technology-drenched world today – JB noted that it is crucial that your E suite (engineering, design and programming talent) be at least as robust and strong as your C suite is. VCs bet on the jockey, not the horse, but increasingly they're betting on the whole team and not just the boy or girl wonder. Things today are so complex that it's rarely if ever a one-person show and – as often as not – the real meat of the new business is not the smiles and the sizzle and the showmanship of the CEO; it's the steak and the substance of the people in the pit making the programs sing that makes the difference in the long run. As I like to say, you can't win a race with your mouth. Nothing speaks louder than code. JB said that his ultimate decision to make a commitment to and an investment in *Signal* (Number 1 fastest-growing company on *Crain's Chicago Business* 2016 Fast 50) was largely based on his confidence in the experience, talent and prior successes of the CTO they had recruited to the founding team. It's almost always a good bet to go with the people who've been there before and are looking to do it again rather than the folks who say they can get you there.

Finally, right behind market fit and team problems in terms of fatal failings for a startup, comes the substantial risks associated with strong competition (either existing or emerging) which drives about 20% of the new companies out of business. JB noted that competition is a complicated conversation to have with any entrepreneur. On the one hand, it's obvious that your new business is always going to be replacing or enhancing or improving upon something that is going on now because nothing exists in a vacuum. And, in addition, if no one else in the world was doing something similar or interested in what you were hoping to do, you might have to ask yourself why. And finally, those potential competitors (large and small) may also turn out to be very helpful in determining and demonstrating the size of the opportunities and the markets you're looking at taking on. In fact, they may also be potential channel partners, strategic investors and, ultimately, acquirers as well. The point is that they can't be ignored and your pitch and your plans have to have plenty of provisions for how you expect to deal with them. And, by the way, it's perfectly OK to argue – as the guys from Netflix often say – that you're not trying to do things differently, you're just going to do them well.

The final thought that JB left us with was pretty simple. He said that it was critical to know what you don't know and – having acknowledged and accepted that – to get busy every day figuring out how to fill those gaps. (See http://www.inc.com/howard-tullman/common-communication-mistake-destroying-productivity-success.html .)

Pritzker Group
VENTURE CAPITAL

This year's Global Entrepreneurship Summit was held last week on the campus of Stanford University with about 1200 delegates from more than 170 countries/territories including almost 700 entrepreneurs. Packed into 2 intense days were dozens of presentations and conversations ranging from Alphabet (GOOGLERS galore including Sergey and Sundar) and Airbnb all the way to Uber and Zuckerberg with a dash or two of Obama, Kerry and Pritzker crammed in between.

Even the cast of HBO's *Silicon Valley*, the white hot tech satire, stopped by to briefly entertain the crowd although it was abundantly clear that these guys definitely need a great writers' room and strong scripts to actually have anything clever to say. Their shtick was too little, too loose and too long. Part of the problem was that there weren't enough Valley VC fan boys in the audience to fawn over their every word hoping to be the next in line for a guest cameo on the show.

Overall, GES2016 was a fact-filled feast and an FOMO frenzy where it was almost impossible to choose which sessions and master classes to attend and which to skip given the amazing array of speakers and the very broad and diverse range of topics. The good news was that it was hard to go very wrong with whatever you chose since almost every panel and every class had several must-see speakers. And the organizers actually built in enough time for some reasonable networking assuming that you weren't committed to running from one end of the campus to the other trying to get from session to session. Bottom line – lots to see and lots to learn from the stages and from each other.

As I reviewed my notes on the way home, I tried to find the 5 ideas/remarks that especially struck me and which I felt hadn't already been tweeted to death. I was going for profound rather than pithy (if that's even possible in conferences like this where everyone's going for the triumphant and tweetable turn of a phrase) and for substance rather than sound bites. I also tried to stay away from scripted statements or concepts and pronouncements that I had heard the same people say or write 47 times before. And finally, I was looking for comments that rolled several related thoughts into more overarching and general observations. Personal anecdotes are OK, but they're less broadly relevant and applicable than the accumulated experiences of the entrepreneurs who're in the trenches successfully doing the hard things right now.

Here are my top 5:

(1) Innovation is Inevitable and Unstoppable. It's a Global Race and the Rest of the World Isn't Going to Wait for You
You can't hold back the inbound waves of innovation with a white picket fence or a million different laws. All the impediments, regulations, tariffs and other obstacles which the politicians hope will postpone or entirely avoid the impending and highly disruptive changes are – at best – only temporary barriers to the coming storm. But that futility wasn't the most insightful observation. Innovation isn't a bubble, it's a massive expanding balloon and when you press against it locally or impede its progress, that action doesn't stop its forward motion, it just shifts and migrates the progress which continues to move forward elsewhere and other players, parties, countries and competitors grow, gain and benefit while we fall further and further behind the curve.

(2) Get the Story Straight from the Source and Be Shameless While You're at It.
The best entrepreneurs are quick studies and good listeners, but the vast majority of them are also arrogant lunatics (I say that lovingly) who think that they can rapidly learn to do just about anything. This simply isn't true. Great programmers don't morph or grow into great salesmen over time because they read a lot of books and blogs. The smartest business builders know: (a) that they are very good at some things; (b) that by applying themselves they can supplement their skills and knowledge in certain other important areas; and (c) that they simply suck at a bunch of tasks and roles which they shouldn't ever go near. (See http://www.inc.com/howard-tullman/how-to-make-smart-hires-even-if-youre-a-ceo.html .)

Apart from knowing what not to try to do at all, the next best thing is to master the art of asking the right people for help. Mentors are the key – not manuscripts or lectures – and getting to the top of the pile of possible mentors is essential. There are plenty of mentors who simply aren't worth your time. (See http://www.inc.com/howard-tullman/how-to-deal-with-marginal-mentors.html .) So, as Brian Chesky said, be shameless and shoot for the stars. What's the worst that can happen? They can only say "No". And, truthfully, as we like to say, it's only a "No" for now, so keep asking.

(3) As Good as We Think We Are, Your Ideas Might Just Be Better
Year after year, GOOGLE wins honors for being a great place to work and for their HR policies. It's an impressive accomplishment and the result of years of thoughtful commitment and hard work. So you would think that, as they grew and created new entities, they wouldn't "mess with success" or try to change the things that were working so well for them. But that's not how things have turned out. Rather than imposing all kinds of HR rules and requirements on the new businesses, they have basically told them to figure out what works best for their companies and their people. The underlying thought – notwithstanding years of prior experience and great outcomes – was that there's always a reasonable chance that someone's new ideas and suggestions may be improvements on the status quo. Facebook has taken a similar approach with Instagram and WhatsApp. I call it the one-way door theory – you can ask for any upstream corporate help

or resources that you need at any time – but no one from corporate or HR will be "helping" you run your business without a specific invitation.

(4) The Grander Your Goals, the Easier It is to Avoid Wasting Time and Resources on Things that Won't Move the Needle.
Almost every decision you'll need to make becomes clearer and far more black and white when you're talking in terms of box car numbers and off-the-charts growth. If everything's a stretch, the process itself opens up a pretty clear gap between what's critical and what's not. When you set "10X" targets, there's just no time for "nice to haves" or frankly for anything in a minor key. It's all-in, all the time, and everything needs to quickly clear the "bang for the buck" bar. If the magnitude of the outcome isn't obvious, it's obviously a waste of breath to be arguing about the need to do something or the likelihood of its success. If the attempt still results in a "so what" success, it's just not worth the trip. Start small, aim high, scale quickly.

(5) The Business Only Dies When the Founder Gives Up – Everything Else is Just Business as Usual
Everyone from Steve Case (one of his 5 P's) to President Obama talked about the value of perseverance. Building a business is brutally hard work even when most things go well and it's clearly not for the faint-hearted. But what really stuck in my mind was Adeo Ressi's simple statement that it all comes down to the mental mettle and the mindset of the entrepreneur. You're either "in it to win it" or you should get out of the game entirely. There's always another way to go until you give up.

New businesses can fail for any number of reasons. The top 3 reasons are pretty consistent across hundreds of cases: (1) there's no demand or need for your product or service; (2) you don't have any more cash; and/or (3) you don't have the right team. There's no shame in any of that.

The only sins in the startup world are to stop caring and/or to stop trying. I'm not sure which is worse, but my money's is on not caring because it takes away from your soul when you do what you no longer believe in. (See http://www.inc.com/howard-tullman/why-whatever-will-sink-your-business.html .)

The truth is that people are rarely willing to walk over you until you lie down.

I've written recently about how unfortunate it is when businesses don't know what they don't know. Whatever their particular organizational biases (age or gender) or structural barriers (hierarchy or bureaucracy) may be which interfere with open and effective company-wide communication, the bottom line is that they're flying at least partly blind and it's actually an easy fix. (See http://www.inc.com/howard-tullman/common-communication-mistake-destroying-productivity-success.html.)

The only worse sin in my book is not effectively using materials and other assets that you've already bought and paid for. Waste not, want not. I'm sure this all started in my childhood with the "clean plate" rule – especially when the family occasionally went out to eat – and I'm also sure that there are fancier formulations for this philosophy, but, down on the farm where I'm from, the basic rule with purchased goods and services was "pay once, use often" until you used up the very last drop. Sorta like *Maxwell House* coffee.

This economical disposition is also probably the main reason that I love all platform businesses – you build these babies one time and, if you do it right, they pay you back almost in perpetuity. (See http://www.inc.com/howard-tullman/the-primacy-of-the-platform.html and http://www.inc.com/howard-tullman/why-platforms-is-the-new-plastics.html.) My first grown-up business (CCC Information Services) is 36 years old this year (still going strong with about 1900 employees worldwide) and it's all based on my plan to build a computerized vehicle valuation platform (as well as a national network) which quickly became the de facto standard for the entire insurance industry. Of course, it didn't hurt that CCC was aggressively well-managed and ranked first in profitability among all of the companies listed on the *Inc. Magazine* 100 Lists for 1986 and 1987.

So when I first heard about Chicago-based Knowledge Hound, (www.knowledgehound.com), I was pretty excited because I saw it as a SaaS startup which was addressing a large and important problem (the inefficiencies in the way corporations were spending billions of dollars on market research and surveys) with a pretty basic solution which had two compelling attributes: (1) it was going to save its customers (and their clients) millions of dollars as well as enormous amounts of valuable team time while increasing productivity; and (2) it had all the makings of a powerful platform both in terms of its basic service offerings and in terms of its ability to morph into a marketplace as well.

The Problem – Corporate Amnesia

Major CPG companies and other corporations spend hundreds of millions of dollars each year constructing, assigning and fielding market research projects and then summarily reviewing and incorporating the survey and research results into proposals, pitches, and other internal presentations to a variety of audiences. And then they file and/or stuff the research reports into a folder or a drawer somewhere and promptly forget all about them. Days, weeks or months later, someone elsewhere in the company with the same or a similar kind of inquiry has absolutely no idea of what research is already in the company's hands/files and – given the usual time constraints – authorizes a new and often completely redundant research job. This wasteful and costly process goes on constantly throughout the year and no one (no pun intended) is any the wiser. There is simply no simple way to know what's there.

If you ask someone about the problem, they will usually offer you one of two common excuses – the research is off point or the research is out of date. Even apart from the fact that they don't know what they're talking about because they don't know what's out there, the bigger issues are that; (a) almost all of these reports come back with a variety of related findings which may be precisely on point; and (b) the very age of the prior research may be invaluable if the new questions and inquiries have to do with trend lines, changes in attitudes or different behaviors.

The Solution – An All-Seeing Eye System

Knowledge Hound offers a very simple answer. Its system permits the rapid retrieval and reuse of relevant research which is already owned and paid for by the client – wherever it may be located – and without regard to who initially authorized it or to what prior uses it has been put. Every report is located, tagged and flagged, and then added to the master indices. After an initial (and admittedly somewhat painful) intake, conversion and organization process, the client will now have direct and immediate searchable access to all of the research results (both direct findings and adjacent/tangential observations and conclusions as well) that are located anywhere in the company's files and archives through a KH dashboard which virtually anyone in the company can quickly learn to use. In addition to a powerful search engine, the KH system provides analytics and a straightforward visualization tool as well so that the retrieved and repurposed results can be quickly and clearly presented to all interested parties inside and outside of the company.

The Platform and the Marketplace

And here's where the Knowledge Hound story gets really interesting.

First, while it's a bit of an uphill slog to get all the old research reports at each firm categorized, input and discoverable; once that task is completed, the worm turns and each participating firm (with KH's help) can start to impose new submission criteria and formats on its vendors as well as some process and increased discipline both internally and externally so that all future reports go quickly, clearly and very efficiently into the retrieval system. The KH template could readily become the industry standard for submittals and reports. In addition, each company can require prior inquiries and research into the existing KH database of reports as a condition precedent to initiating new research requests. This is all in the interest of saving the companies time and money in many ways and increasing the speed and responsiveness of their businesses to client requests for information as well.

Second, who says that the only subsequent users and "buyers" of all of this prior research have to be within the company itself. Once the overall and aggregated database of research reports and their component parts and findings reaches a certain critical mass (and with the permission of the participating firms), KH can offer up these reports and their conclusions to other firms and third parties in an anonymized knowledge marketplace much like Amazon offers individuals' and other book sellers' used books right alongside its new editions. This marketplace has the further potential to help each participating company offset some of the internal costs of its own research efforts by participating out and reselling the results after the fact.

Here again, in the winner-take-all nature of the platform world, there won't be numerous places to go to search for these reports. Knowledge Hound could quickly become the biggest dog on the block.

We had the rare opportunity last week to sit down at 1871 with Joe Mansueto, the founder and CEO of Morningstar, for a fireside chat. Having known Joe for more than 30 years now, and given the astonishing growth and success of his various business ventures, I'm always amazed at how modest and accessible he remains and what a great booster of Chicago and its entrepreneurs he has always been. When we finally wrapped up our own conversation, he made time to chat with more than a dozen of our member companies, to answer their questions, and pose for a few selfies as well.

In fact, when I had asked him earlier in our conversation about how he came to acquire *INC. Magazine* and *Fast Company* (eleven years after starting Morningstar) which seemed at the time like such traditional, old-line, media properties, he said these were personal investments and that he had decided to do the deal (which was completed in about 30 days) because he believed so strongly in the missions of those magazines (both of which had been languishing under their prior ownership) and he wanted to help make them grow and prosper. He smiled and pointed out that his wife said at the time "at least he hadn't bought a sports team" although, in retrospect, it seems like that might have been a better financial investment.

We covered a lot of ground in our chat (including the fact that the name Morningstar came from the last line in Thoreau's *Walden*), but there were a few of Joe's observations and comments that were somewhat surprising and really stood out for me. Here are the 5 that I think are valuable for every entrepreneur to keep in mind.

(1) He's Still Solo

While he regularly makes outside investments with a group of other investors for his own personal account, he made it clear that – even in this day and age when everyone is looking for strategic partners, joint ventures, and hoping to use OPM – when it's his own business, he prefers to own 100% of the opportunity and go it alone mainly for two reasons: (a) to avoid conflicts and different agendas or inconsistent views on how to move the business forward sometime down the line, and (b) because, if you're all-in, the rewards (when they're there) are much greater than if you hedge your bets and share the risks, but (by doing so) limit your upside which then has to be shared by co-investors and partners.

(2) He's Still Selling

When I asked him if he still believed that mutual funds were the best investment vehicle for 90% of the investing public, he said that – as the CEO of Morningstar which tracks fund performance – what else could he possibly say? Of course, he also invests directly in stocks which he says he does because it's fun. I asked him for some investing tips and – with appropriate disclaimers - he went on to talk about what he looks for in companies and investments and – highest on his list – were businesses with sustainable competitive advantages (if there's any longer any such thing these days) including effective barriers to entry or "moats" as he called them which made the companies' market positions defensible. Examples he cited included high switching costs, strong brands, patent protection, etc. (See http://www.inc.com/howard-tullman/to-keep-your-customers-build-more-moats.html .)

(3) He's Still Scared

Taking a page from Andy Grove's preaching on paranoia, Joe said that when he is looking at new businesses, he always asks himself the question: "how is Amazon not going to kill this business?" As we have all learned, it's not about how you start the race that matters, it's how the race ends up that separates the winners from the crowd of wanna-bes. It's great to invent something new and be the first mover, but you've got to keep looking over your shoulder for the fast followers running right behind you and make sure that you have a plan to keep ahead of the pack. (See http://www.inc.com/howard-tullman/first-mover-advantage-maybe-but-be-smart-about-it.html.)

(4) He's Still Hiring

I was a little surprised to hear that – even with all of his other responsibilities - Joe is still actively involved in doing college recruiting for the company. I've said before that I'm not even sure that most CEOs should be doing any hiring for their businesses, but he says that there's nothing more important to the future of Morningstar than attracting and retaining top talent. I agree with the goal – my issue in many cases is with the guy or girl doing the job. (See http://www.inc.com/howard-tullman/how-to-make-smart-hires-even-if-youre-a-ceo.html.) Just like everywhere else in life, it turns out that the best person in the business isn't necessarily the best person for a specific job or for every job. (See http://www.inc.com/howard-tullman/bring-back-the-peter-principle-please.html.) Of course, I'd be happy to have Joe doing the hiring for me any time.

(5) He's Still Strategic

When I asked him about his role as CEO and especially what his priorities are right now (and whether they've changed over the years), he said he was focused on 4 areas. Talent, as noted above. Culture and creating an environment supportive of his people and conducive to their doing great work. Allocation of capital among competing priorities. And, top of the list, strategy which, of course, is a critical determinant of all of the others as well. If you get the strategy and the values of the business right, the execution – while no less challenging – is at least a little easier to pull off. Strategy in cases like this is as much about saying "No" to things as it is about embarking on new initiatives. I got the impression that setting the course and then stepping back and letting his team get the job done was the basic philosophy which had clearly served him well.

As we wrapped up, I asked Joe about how strongly he relies on market research, focus groups, and other third party tools and input in evaluating and determining whether to launch new products. He said something that should ring true for every entrepreneur who's ever had to overcome the "wisdom" of the crowd or the mediocrity of the marketplace. He said – and I'm paraphrasing here - the next great American novel (or next great business) won't be written by a focus group or a committee, but by a committed and passionate individual writing <u>from</u> the heart and not <u>for</u> the herd. Thoreau couldn't have said it better.

We need a better, smarter solution for all of the problems we're having (far too many of which are basically of our own creation) with the myriad different ways in which our personal information is being used and abused, shared and stolen, distributed and dumped, and otherwise hijacked for novel and nefarious purposes far beyond our intentions and almost universally without our permission or consent.

I'm always struck by how little thought we give to exactly how much critical information is an essential part of our everyday lives and how little we know about the care and control that is being exercised over it. Take a minute or two and try (before you read on) to think about the major data buckets that describe and define your life and your daily activities.

As an obvious example, financial comes readily to mind, but it's not simply a compilation of the information we need to have readily available in order to enable our purchases. There is an enormous pool of data about our assets and property – our various portfolios – and whatever other property – tangible and intangible – we may own or control. And this analysis then extends into and determines our financial condition – creditworthiness – borrowing capacity – current and prior debt and repayment histories. And finally, there is all of the information regarding our every purchase and act of consumption and how vendors, brands, marketers and others can employ that data to direct, influence, and ultimately even change our expectations, desires and real-time behavior.

Other major buckets include demographic and psychographic data, medical information with all of its complicated intersections with insurance and medical care, interest data across every dimension of our lives, political, religious and gender preferences, social materials including the non-stop flow of newly-created and forever archived content in all formats, etc. Here too, as more and more consumers of content become creators as well, the glut of mineable material will continue to grow exponentially. In addition, there are additional mountains of data (ultimately valuable to each of us) being accumulated every day on the opposite side of each activity and transaction by the counter-part parties. This is the bi-lateral aspect of information. Much of this data has considerable instructive and educational value for us in terms of tracking our own performance, behaviors, activities, health and consumption, but none of it is currently available to us.

Securing, managing and protecting all of this data is a global crisis that's already out of control and a situation that's only likely to get more critical over time especially because the next generation or two are so generally indifferent to these concerns about data and information security. I'm not sure that they even understand the concept of privacy these days when nothing is sacred and everything is shared. Worse yet, it seems likely that this is one of those problems which each of us is incapable of or otherwise unable or unwilling to solve for ourselves.

We're all contributors to the problem (whatever our ages) because we're impatient suckers for speed and convenience and we decide every day to share our personal information in more and more diverse kinds of digital interactions where we'd rather save a few minutes in our day instead of painfully re-entering our basic stats and identity into the umpteenth terminal or browser or mobile app in order to complete some purchase, connection or other transaction.

I wouldn't hold my breath for any help from the government and I wouldn't have any confidence in anything created and offered by those bungling bureaucrats in any event. It may be that some anti-theft and fraud progress will be forced on us by the credit card guys (the "chip in the card" revolution is well underway) whether we like it or not and regardless of how it extends the time and increases the friction in each purchase. Biometrics and facial recognition technologies may also help.

But ultimately I believe that the solutions which will make the critical differences are going to be developed by innovators operating outside of and independently from the current industry players. In part this is because we have so little trust and confidence in the traditional systems that we are far more likely to adopt new solutions and approaches. One of the amazing aspects of the Internet has been its constantly increasing ability to enable us to trust and do business with people we have never met whether we're talking about an Airbnb house guest, an Uber driver or a EBay seller.

This type of environment, of course, is exactly the kind of situation that creates great opportunities for entrepreneurs. We've got wallets and we have a variety of password "safes" and other vehicles but, in their very design and implementation because of the emphasis on security, they defeat the ultimate goal of being a constantly-refreshed and updated personal data node on a worldwide network where every element of your data profile can be stored and accessed in real-time - all of the time.

We need a new object and here's an idea that I think is worth taking for a spin. A SPIN (Secure Personal Information Node) would be a repository for all your information and also bi-lateral because it would not only provide you with output at the point of sale, but it would also accept and incorporate input from every source that you uniquely authorized and permitted. Every transaction would be two-directional and each action would increment and enhance the core profile and the aggregate of all the data. A simple dashboard would permit you to change and update consents and permissions on the fly and to vary the depth and the amount of information and access you wanted to be able to securely provide in each type of transaction.

It won't be easy, but it's coming because it's inevitable. Maybe you'll be the one to make it real.

From time to time, I think it's useful to try to get rid of some of the persistent, tech-flavored, factoids which sadly are increasingly found everywhere these days in our media-saturated and overly exposed, but woefully under-informed hurry-up culture. These convenient "facts" are foisted upon us by the everyday experts and the bogus business bloviators who make a living telling us what we want to hear – not information, but mainly abject affirmation – and repeating the same old tired story lines that we've heard for years.

Of course, it's also easier and much less costly for lazy or ignorant news readers (talking heads) and their writers to parrot the old news and the standard company lines than it is for them to get qualified reporters out there in the real world and to ask them to try to figure out what's really happening. Some of the "social media" reporting and crowd-sourcing we're seeing in the MSM these days wouldn't pass anyone's smell test. They pass this junk reporting off for gospel and conventional wisdom at a time in our new disruptive and digital world where virtually nothing that made sense in the past is a smart course of action for the future and where experience and past practices can be your worst nightmare instead your best friend.

The useless stuff they spew isn't as critical or troublesome as the half-truths and outright lies that make up so much of the political conversations today, but it's still problematic because the aggregated noise makes it harder and harder for us to find anything helpful or useful among the clutter or for new businesses to break through the chaos and the confusion in order to bring something different and better to the marketplace. Their blather creates unnecessary and wasteful barriers to progress and especially to the introduction of novel technologies into traditional venues and industries.

I've picked just a few of these which are especially off base to talk about in this piece.

(1) **People are using their phones in-store to price shop and then buy online from other vendors.**
This is about as far from today's reality as it could possibly be. The fact is that "showrooming" not only doesn't suck for the bricks-and-mortar stores; in-store use of mobile increases conversion by numbers north of 25%. And when the in-store shopper did his or her homework online before coming to the store, they're more than 40% more likely to convert into real buyers. The most interesting change in consumer shopping behavior these days is "click and collect" - driving huge jumps in the number of buyers ordering online and then going to the store to pick up their purchases.

(2) **Online shoppers are the world's ficklest folks because they have unlimited choices which are just a click away.**
More make-believe from the media. Here's the truth – we are and we have always been creatures of habit. There may be 500 channels out there, but – to the extent that we're still watching network television at all (a rapidly diminishing activity largely limited to specials and other live events) - we still watch only our 4 or 5 favorite channels at the most – not up very much from the Big 3 that used to be everyone's only choices. And – in addition - we are constant victims of decision fatigue – show me or offer me too many choices and I will just disappear. We don't want or have the time to consider more – we want quick, easy and convenient. And we want it now. Here's a dirty little secret – shopping carts are very sticky. And I'm not talking about the ones in the stores themselves which are covered with all kinds of mystery substances and which no one ever seems to clean. I'm talking about the fact that once your product makes it into a consumer's online shopping cart – especially if it's basically a commodity – it would take a stick of dynamite to dislodge it. We're still trying to ascertain whether this behavior is a result of excessive loyalty or simply downright laziness, but whatever the cause, you want to get there first while the getting good because that buyer isn't in a hurry to go anywhere else, choose any alternative product, or do much of anything beyond clicking the same items on the same weekly list. Inertia is most likely the best barrier to entry and competition ever invented.

(3) **Everyone's "cutting the cord" and Netflix is killing the cable biz.**
Cable isn't just a cord any more that's readily snipable; it's a gigantic and largely unavoidable pipe that's the most reliable connection you have to the world outside your windows. And you need it desperately to stay connected – not simply for social, sports and other entertainment purposes, but – more and more – to make sure you keep your job and your business. The mobile phone's fine for lots of things, but it's still not remotely how the lion's share of business gets done. As we all spend more and more time working at home, we're still counting on cable for the critical connections. Comcast, for one, is doing a great job of stemming the fall-off in video customers by adding internet users at a greater rate. And, in fact of late, while cable companies in general continue to steadily increase their revenues, Netflix is seeing its subscriber growth slow significantly. And interestingly, you might ask how exactly does Netflix find its way into most people's homes these days? OTT? Not really. It comes right thru the cable connection and now – belatedly, but from a position of strength, not acquiescence - Comcast has even decided to add the Netflix app to its X1 cable-box platform. Frankly, Comcast has much bigger fish to fry and more important things to sweat than Netflix. And so does Netflix. The ride for Netflix is getting bumpier all the time because there are more and more, better entrenched and established players like Amazon stepping all over its toes. The bottom line is this – if Netflix is killing anything – it's killing traditional TV advertising as more and

more affluent viewers abandon the traditional networks and avoid commercials entirely through new viewing behaviors and time-shifting strategies especially binge viewing which is already up to about two hours a day.

Advertising today – by and large – is a penalty that only poor people pay. The rest of us are looking and watching the other way.

TULLMAN'S TRUISMS

MADE-UP METRICS MEAN ABSOLUTELY NOTHING

The Sage Summit for 2016 was held in Chicago and featured keynote interviews with an impressive number of technology celebrity/entrepreneurs including Sir Richard Branson, TV "Sharks" Daymond John & Robert Herjavec, Ashton Kutcher, Gwyneth Paltrow and Yancey Strickler (CEO of Kickstarter).

Frankly, you never know how these things are going to turn out although I was pleasantly surprised that both the business observations and the jokes were much better than expected. I mean when Gwyneth starts talking about KPIs and multi-year business plans, it's a moment. And she had a great quote from a friend about intentionality, aiming high, and not letting the naysayers get you down. Her friend said: "where you look is where you go." And truer words were never spoken.

Sir Richard Branson told a great story about buying his first plane for Virgin Airlines from Boeing. The salesman was willing to make the sale, but he suggested changing the name of the airline from Virgin because he said that otherwise the passengers would think that the airline wasn't willing to go all the way. He is always worth listening to and a class act as well. (See http://www.inc.com/howard-tullman/a-day-with-richard-branson.html .)

And when Yancey Strickler said that Kickstarter had helped create more than 8800 new businesses and non-profits since it began in 2009, it was fairly amazing, but when he added that Kickstarter users have pledged over $2.5 billion for more than 110,000 projects, it was astounding. I was also amazed to hear that he has NO social media applications on his phone (he fessed up to adding Twitter the night before so he could follow the goings-on at the DNC convention).

Strickler said that he fears that the interruptive nature of our mobile devices is very bad for our sanity. He said that: "social media is doing to our brains what smoking used to do to our lungs – it's mental sugar – and it's addictive." Ashton said that he turns off all the notifications on his phone and that it is always on "do not disturb" (except for calls from his wife) because that's the only way he can get anything done. He said that otherwise you're working for all the people who call and want you to do things on their schedule instead of setting and controlling your own agenda. On social media, Ashton also said that it was stupid and a waste of resources to chase every new social app or trend. Notwithstanding the Kardashians, he noted that celebrities go where the fans are while fans don't necessarily go where the celebrities are or want they to go. Trying to pile on to this week's latest bandwagon or hottest download is a great way to go bust. (See http://www.inc.com/howard-tullman/1465913643.html .)

When Ashton focused on what it takes to scale your business from a people perspective, he talked about a very important consideration that's a real challenge for companies as they grow especially given the "can do" attitude of the startup world. He noted that, when you begin, everyone pitches in and does whatever it takes, but as you grow, this approach no longer works because no one has all the skills to be really good at everything and so it becomes critical for "people to stay in their lanes" and focus deeply on what they can do really well. New and different people will need to be brought in and added to the team to cover more specialized skill sets as you expand the business. I called this "sticking to your knitting" in a piece I wrote a while ago. (See http://www.inc.com/howard-tullman/with-this-much-help-youll-never-get-anything-done.html .)

Daymond John said his mother was quite the negotiator – she borrowed $100,000 to help him in his business by mortgaging her home which couldn't have been worth $75,000 max. He wasn't really sure how she came up with the cash, but he was sure glad that she did. Daymond made some very interesting observations about the need to know what your strengths, weaknesses and interests are and to change and adapt your businesses accordingly. He found out that he doesn't want to have hundreds or thousands of employees ever because that kind of scale makes it impossible to have any kind of real personal connections to the people working with and for you. And he said that a critical skill for success was the willingness to ask for help and to admit to what you don't know.

Since a number of these folks are active investors themselves, they were all asked about what they look for in a deal and – as you would expect – it was much more about the entrepreneur than the idea. As Daymond noted, they all looked for people with the humility to ask for help and a willingness to learn from anyone and everyone they encountered. Ashton pointed out that the winners had a sense of generosity about them and a willingness to share and to help others that was contagious and readily apparent. And he said that it was critical that successful entrepreneurs learn to manage and contain their emotions.

Making a difference and giving back was a part of everyone's comments although Ashton said that he thought that people who spent time worrying and talking about their "legacies" were assholes. When he was asked what he'd like people to say about him in 50 years, his answer: "Is he still alive and building shit?" totally brought down the house and was clearly the best line of the day.

194 – ASK ME MORE QUESTIONS AND I'LL TELL YOU NO LIES

I think we're almost at the bitter end of the "I Talk; You Listen" world. If no one's listening, you might just as well save your breath and your advertising/marketing dollars as well. Top-down lectures, sages spewing from the stage, one-way mass communications, and indiscriminate broadcasts (rather than carefully targeted pitches and programs) are all increasingly tired products of the past. The future of digital communication will require new consumer connection tools that are personal (interest-based), interactive (immediate and responsive) and credible (peer-based and authentic). They're on their way and it's pretty exciting.

The fact is that it actually doesn't seem to matter which industry or marketplace you're in. Everyone will be impacted by this transition to conversations and those that don't or can't make the move to the new two-way world will be left behind. This is mainly because - with the comprehensive personalization of the web (thank you Facebook) - the entire social fabric and the ways in which we communicate and share information with each other are quickly changing. There are important lessons in these changes for all of us who are focused on and measured by our performance and by the results we achieve. And, as always, when we need new tools and solutions, this means that new opportunities are being created for entrepreneurs.

Of course, it seems unfortunate that our schools are always among the last to learn and adopt anything new and – as a result - there are still loads of laggards in the land of learning. Educators love to hear themselves talk just as much as any politician and these days it seems that they have only marginally more of value to say than your average alderman. They're also among the world's worst listeners. They're still way more concerned in some respects with what they're teaching rather than with what their students are actually learning. And the people teaching digital marketing in our universities are several generations behind the curve and still headed in the wrong direction. They need to get out and see what's happening in the real world.

Even more importantly, and sadly, our schools are one of the last union-driven holdouts and bastions of BS which continue to resist true measurements and performance-based evaluations of the faculty's work and results. The entrenched administrators, professors, teachers, lecturers and other bureaucrats are happy to excessively test, minutely document, and regularly judge their students' test scores, but they're not willing themselves to be held accountable for much of anything. And the last people they want to hear from are the students and their parents who are paying for their alleged "services".

In the rest of the real world, however, and quite thankfully, things are changing radically and rapidly. Everything that's smart today is built on a dynamic, data-infused, two-way or multi-party conversation – not a static presentation – and, most importantly, every campaign or initiative that's going to have any value and/or ultimately succeed in building connection and engagement needs to anticipate and build an effective plan that incorporates a feedback loop and a real-time response capability as well. This sounds great, but the technology for millions of businesses to do this in a simple, straightforward and cost-effective way – largely by themselves – and without layers, buffers, interpretations and other intermediaries – really hasn't been readily available up until now.

Your customers want and need to be an active part of the conversation and your strategy needs to enable and actively encourage that interaction because that's ultimately what drives actual engagement. The only thing worse than not asking your customers and prospects questions about their needs and desires is to fail to respond in a convincing, informative and timely manner to their questions and comments.

And just as bad for business are inquiry systems that are so painful to use and so full of barriers, detours and friction that no one in their right mind would waste the time and energy that they require. (See http://www.inc.com/howard-tullman/how-to-optimize-your-web-site-for-users-not-just-for-you.html.) What we need are new cloud-based tools like *SquareOffs* (www.squareoffs.com). *SquareOffs* lets any publisher (novice or professional, large or small) insert context-sensitive polls, surveys and quizzes (with virtually no code required) which capture answers, display results, and also facilitate the consumer's ability to instantly share the poll and the results with others who can then join in the process and the conversation and invite their friends and followers as well.

Sample Poll:

You can try the poll yourself here: http://tullman.blogspot.com/2016/08/sq.html .

Apart from providing a relatively simple and cost-effective new polling tool for capturing customer comments, sentiments, and concerns which almost any content creator can readily employ (pretty much DIY), *SquareOffs* delivers on the five most important attributes of any new digital media solution.

(1) Amplification

It's almost impossible these days for a business acting alone to directly break thru the noise and clutter in order to get its message to the right target audiences and to learn anything of value from them in a timely manner. And it's way too expensive to try all by yourself to reach the gross number of consumers which your business needs in order to net the volumes and revenue numbers necessary to yield the sales results that would justify the costs and the effort. No one does anything today without help and the trick is to enlist and recruit others to help you do the heavy lifting without having to pay them to do so. The solution is enabling smart social sharing which amplifies and expands your reach far beyond anything that you could hope to accomplish yourself. True influencers are automatic and authentic sharers – not because of incentives or payments – but because it's in their very nature and it's something they actively want to do. *Square Offs* makes it easy.

(2) Authenticity

The only content that gets effectively communicated these days is authentically shared material (often user-authored) and *SquareOffs* encourages and accelerates that behavior by helping publishers and authors provide current and compelling bite-size choices and content (suitable for sharing) which triggers our natural (water cooler) inclinations and behaviors to share something new, something timely, something political, something we're concerned or passionate about, etc. with those around and closest to us. And, here again, the *SO* system helps the customers and consumers pitch in big time as they select and sort just the right (interested) target populations from their own networks based on connections to and common interests in the topics and materials so the word gets spread and sent to the right people at the right time. Something, by the way, which the initial publisher as an outside third party couldn't hope to ascertain or act upon. Now I realize that I've written recently about the scourge of stupid and knee-jerk sharing, but in these kinds of specific instances, smart sharing gets the job done right. (See http://www.inc.com/howard-tullman/1465913643.html .)

(3) Accuracy

Big media businesses and ad agencies lie to us every day about their ability to identify, target and reach the right consumers and audiences for our messages. The truth is that they do a miserable job on all three counts – reach, resonance and reaction. (See http://www.inc.com/howard-tullman/3-things-you-need-to-know-about-advertising.html.) But particularized, peer-to-peer sharing is a whole different kettle of fish and one which is surprisingly efficient. And when the system quickly reports results back to its users, it confirms the immediacy of the communication and validates and reinforces the individual's effort. Sharing simply begets more sharing. Interactivity and feedback loops (along with the need for self-expression) are growing into essential components of any communication programs which want to build and maintain consistent and continuing connections with consumers and customers.

(4) Analytics

By and large, especially in today's crazy world of politics, standard surveys suck. There are too many reasons to count, but consider, just for openers, that the people who are running most of the polls in this country are still using antiquated lists of landline telephones for their survey calls. When's the last time anyone you knew used a landline for anything or even still had one in their home? These bad news phone boiler rooms use the world's cheapest labor to reach a terribly skewed (and largely screwed) population of old, rural and home-bound people who are also the only ones with the time and any interest in talking to them. The "results" they obtain are the worst kind of anecdotal rather than analytical data and they're basically worthless. On the other hand, the digital world and services like *SO* offer levels of data, demographics, and other direct and behavioral measurements that provide meaningful and useful inputs as well as the ability to optimize spend, make real-time adjustments to ongoing campaigns, and reinforce the most effective messaging.

(5) Accountability

Keeping score (leader boards, result tabulations, rankings, etc.) and comparing ourselves to others are natural human behaviors which social media and the global and ubiquitous connectivity of the web have exploded to dimensions we never anticipated. Everything today is out there – to be tracked, measured, reported and shared – and every business, source, publisher, supplier and vendor will be held to new standards of measurement and accountability as users and customers increasingly demand concrete results and performance metrics to justify their outlays. They will expect to know how you're doing for them and, if you're not getting the job done, they'll simply go elsewhere.

Ad tech firms are out of favor these days – too many players, too many unmet promises, too little transparency, too few successes, and too much money for nothing much to talk about in the way of results. But it doesn't have to be that way going forward. Simple services like *SquareOffs* can solve many of the shortcomings of the old methods and provide real results at reasonable costs for businesses of any size.

Some of the best ideas I've ever heard from eager young entrepreneurs never seem to see the light of day. There's plenty of passion at the beginning of these conversations and the energy and enthusiasm are there, but as time passes, their interest in making it happen dissipates, their momentum fades, and at that point – for many of these folks – it's on to the next great idea or "story". Selling futures is always easier than dealing with today's realities. It's also a lot cheaper and requires less work.

And, in fairness, you can only tell the same story to the same people so many times before they stop listening and you run out of breath. Passion is great, but it's no substitute for an actual plan and intensity is like using a lot of salt and seasoning on cheap food – it helps to hide a lack of preparation and proficiency – but it won't change hamburger into haute cuisine.

I thought that I understood everything there was to know about this "building a business" business – the classic emotional peaks and valleys – the constant stream of higher hurdles and repeated rejections – and even the internal feelings of simple embarrassment; the anxiety of disappointing friends and loved ones; and the flat-out fear of failure. But you learn something new every day in the world of startups.

One of the things you eventually learn is that spending your days talking about your ideas and what you're gonna do is a waste of time and breath – it's a lot like talking back to the guy on the radio or TV: it may make you feel a little better, but it doesn't change a thing. Woulda, shoulda, coulda gets you nowhere. Talking about running with the bulls has nothing to do with getting out there in the street and scrambling for your life and limbs. It's important to believe in your idea – if you don't, why should anyone else? But, as I always say, you can't win a race with your mouth.

It's really difficult for a lot of outsiders to understand and appreciate how hard it is (and has forever been) to get a new idea funded and successfully off the ground – especially when it's your first time around the track – and then to keep it up, alive, and moving forward until it becomes a self-sustaining and reasonably respectable business. Building a business is tough, it's painful and it's lonely. Nothing starts out as a great idea (whatever you might have heard from those speaking with the benefit of hindsight) and without a lot of grunt work, blocking & tackling, and perseverance; there are no brilliant achievements or overnight successes.

In fact, one of the absolutely best things about being in a massive mega-incubator like 1871 is that you have the support, the mentors and resources, the regular reassurance, and the certain knowledge that there are hundreds of people surrounding you every day who are going through the exact same process and that some of them are at least as clueless about what's coming next as you are from time to time. (See http://www.inc.com/howard-tullman-6-reasons-to-stay-in-the-incubator.html .)

Everyone also knows that a major downside to the startup life is that there are always plenty of people (sitting safely on the sidelines) who are willing and just waiting patiently for the chance to tell you why your idea won't work or to offer a knowing "I told you so" after the fact. Tolerating the talking turkeys and the annoying know-it-alls is just a necessary part of the journey that's almost a given these days and since we're primed to expect it, it's fairly easy to develop a thick enough skin to let this stuff just roll right off your back.

But what I never really appreciated that the backslappers and supporters and cheerleaders – the people who seem to be totally on your side - can be just as damaging and destructive in some ways as the naysayers. If you're not careful, their compliments can inadvertently encourage you to talk your idea to death. They're just trying to be helpful and supportive and – as friends and families go in general – they mean well and they're pretty enthusiastic listeners, but talking to them isn't going to move the train down the track.

There are a couple of specific reasons to watch out for this type of time and energy sink.

First, they don't actually know anything. I understand that everyone's a consumer and a creator today and also an expert on new businesses, but here's the thing about cheap applause – it's OK to enjoy it just as long as you don't quite believe it. Novices add nothing but noise to the critical conversations.

Second, there's an infinite demand for the unavailable and people will tell you all day long that they'd be happy to buy your product or service "if only" and you can fill in the blank. If only it came in a different size or color or it ran on Android or the batteries lasted forever. Boosters are miles away from buyers and – especially for a startup – only customers ultimately matter.

Third, these kinds of constant conversations really keep you in the dark – you can't learn anything of consequence from anyone but a customer. In the long run, hearing the good and bad news right from the horse's mouth is the only way to go. The upside of hearing the often painful truth is a lot greater than the cold comfort of remaining blissfully ignorant of the facts.

Bottom line. If you don't break out of the bubble of babble and blandishments, and get busy in the real world, you can quickly run out of gas and oxygen and talk yourself out of business.

Walt Disney said it best a long, long time ago: "The way to get started is to quit talking and start doing." If it worked out that well for that scrawny little mouse; just imagine what it can do for you.

I never knock clichés. They wouldn't be repeated for decades by millions of people if there wasn't at least some grain of truth and inherent value in most of them. Even Yogi-isms (the "philosophical" observations of New York Yankee catcher Yogi Berra) always provided some genuine guidance. There's no stronger call to action than Yogi's famous advice: "when you come to a fork in the road, take it". Or, as we might say today: "don't just stand there, do something". And there's never been a clearer explanation of pattern recognition (which is so critical to making smart investment decisions) than when he opined: "it's like *déjà vu* all over again". And my favorite – as a former restaurant owner and operator – was his comment about the perils of excessive popularity. He noted that: "no one goes there nowadays, it's too crowded".

I was thinking about Yogi in a slightly different context recently when someone told me that a specific situation we encountered was the exception that proved the rule. The more I thought about it, and how he used the phrase, the more I wondered if he even understood what that expression actually meant. I'm not sure that most of us do.

It's like young lawyers who say "for all intensive purposes" when they mean "for all intents and purposes" or worse in cases where people butcher the lyrics of classic songs. Wrapped up like a douche (instead of deuce) was always my Springsteen example from Blinded by the Light. I realize that the lyric was actually written by Manfred Mann. But it will always be Bruce's song to me.

As it turns out that part of the reason for the confusion around the significance of exceptions to the rule is because we don't even reference the full phrase these days – we've dropped a critical part of the original language – because I think it seemed on its face to be so circular. The complete expression from ancient Rome actually states: "the exception confirms the rule in cases not excepted". This reminds me a lot of Humpty Dumpty saying to Alice about a word that: "it means just what I choose it to mean – neither more nor less." Whatever that means.

Still another part of the difficulty is that there are a number of different "accepted" understandings of the concept which vary (according to the scholars) in degrees of accuracy and correctness.

But what really interested me was a different concern which is important for every entrepreneur and that was the traps we can fall into when we make the bigger mistake of thinking that a single rule governs all of the cases in a given situation.

It turns out that there are rules that are common and applicable to regulating behaviors in industries that we think of as being quite diverse (like medicine and manufacturing) and then there are other <u>different</u> rules (rather than exceptions to the same general rule) that apply to govern other types of behaviors. It's not about good or bad apples – it's about being careful not to treat apples and oranges as if they were the same.

As you create your business's culture and identify and communicate the behaviors you want to encourage in your company, it's essential to start from a clear understanding of which rules make sense for the kind of business you're building and the industry you're in. And you need to understand as well that all the rules in the world won't ultimately get the job done unless you want robots inside of real people working for you.

The best businesses are organized around expectations of performance and not based on rules of behavior in large part because even the best managers can't be there all the time and you need your people to make the right calls in the moment – not run to or hide behind some massive rule book. Just like one size never fits all, your core beliefs have to closely and specifically align with what makes the most sense for you, your team, and your company. (See http://www.inc.com/howard-tullman/are-your-values-costing-you-too-much.html.) This is a process that's actually a lot easier than it sounds.

Let's take a simple example of what's pretty much understood as a "universal" rule/proposition which, I would argue, has next to nothing to do with the way that millions of entrepreneurs should run their businesses. The simplest way to state the basic concept is this:

Preventing Errors is Cheaper than Fixing Them

Hard to argue with this pretty conventional piece of wisdom. It's always cheaper to do everything right the first time. Not possible, but theoretically cheaper.

Of course, almost every car manufacturer would disagree with you. At least until they get caught lying about what they knew and when. Like poorly positioned exploding gas tanks or shrapnel-spewing airbags. Then they have no choice, but to fix the errors regardless of the cost. And, at that point, they rationalize it as a PR and marketing cost and not the result of a design or process problem or – worse yet – the end product of some stupid cost-cutting move that put profits above people.

But leaving the car guys aside, here's the crux of the question: in some businesses the smartest and most conservative course is error avoidance and, in others, it's the worst way you can proceed. Your job is to determine which is the right course for your company and – just to make things rougher – it may be that different strategies are right for different parts of the same business. Simple shorthand – we want new and faster bullet trains being built (innovation), but we want today's trains to run safely and on time (operation).

So how do you determine what's best for your business? Here are a couple of simple questions to ask yourself:

(1) What is the fundamental deliverable of my business?
   (a) <u>Goal A:</u>
   Is it providing a consistent and dependable outcome? Each and every time and as regular as rain. This would describe industries like manufacturing and professions like medicine? No one wants a cowboy for their cardiologist. Let them experiment and learn on someone else.

   (b) <u>Goal B:</u>
   Or is it providing new, unexpected and innovative results? Are my clients and customers looking for completely different ideas and game-changing creativity? This would describe industries like advertising (at least in the old days) and high-end fashion. Everything about successful fashion these days needs to be inspirational and definitely not institutional. Frankly, no one could wear the latest Parisian fashions even if they tried because – for the runway shows – they're mostly stuck together with tape and safety pins.

   Once you have figured out whether you're basically building an A or a B business (and yes I know that every business will have elements of both), then you need to ask yourself:

(2) Am I building a system with controls and a bunch of procedures and processes to help my people deliver a fixed and expected result?
These are primarily businesses dominated by operational and managerial concerns. Error-free execution is essential. Process changes, innovations, and system improvements are normally outside of the day-to-day scope of operations. You will also need people to help you get better, but every day you need to take care of business.

(3) Am I creating an environment that encourages experimentation, risk-taking and new approaches with all the errors inherent in that process that you would expect?
These are primarily businesses dominated by creative and developmental concerns. Leaps, not layups, are what it takes to succeed. Trying to avoid mistakes, avoiding embarrassment, and playing it safe is a formula for failure.

Once you know where you're headed and what you are building, you can decide how to focus your time and attention most effectively. It helps a whole lot to have a roadmap – especially if you care a lot about where you end up.

There's more to this discussion. But the critical thing is that the demands, the designs and the drivers of these two very distinct types of businesses are very different, and it's easy to confuse your objectives and commingle your approaches if you're not totally clear. No one business or single approach can be all things to all people.

If you're running a "factory"; rules, regulations and restrictions are your best friends.

If you're running an operating room; protocols, checklists and sterilizers will save lives.

If you want new ideas and novel solutions; you need stronger people, not more structure.

If you're building the future; you can't steal second base with one foot on first.

TULLMAN'S TRUISMS

PROCESS CAN QUICKLY BECOME A PRISON

Even though every major city in the U.S. is suffering from similar problems with significant increases in gun-related violence, Chicago has sadly become the media poster child (hopefully just for the moment) and the go-to TV, cable and web whipping boy specifically for gang-on-gang shootings and the related and random violence which continues to take innocent lives in its wake. While this is clearly a mounting national crisis and by no means limited to Chicago, one ray of local sunlight is that Chicago may have some of the best heads, analytical tools, and technology in the country for figuring out how to get ahead of the flood of weapons, wounds and widows which is swamping certain parts of the city almost every day.

It's clear that recent cases of police misconduct have certainly intensified the attention being paid to Chicago and the nature and volume of the ongoing conversations, but instances of officers' illegal actions don't explain and are certainly no justification for the new levels of violence which are primarily a result of hundreds of cases of a known and relatively small number of gang members shooting members of their own and other gangs. A city of more than 2.7 million people is being plagued and terrorized by the actions of a few groups of thugs and criminals primarily located in 5 geographic districts in the city. And about 80% of the criminal action is centered in just 3 of those 5 problem areas. But the reputational damage to the city and the psychological impact on its residents is far more broadly distributed and felt.

According to our new police superintendent, Eddie Johnson, who spoke recently to a group of senior business leaders, while Chicago may have as many as 100,000 individuals who self-identify as gang members, there are only about 1400 real thugs, criminals and felons who are doing almost all the shooting. Superintendent Johnson also pointed out that the CPD's proprietary Strategic Subject List (SSL) – now in its 5th iteration and developed with support from the University of Chicago Crime Lab – directly identifies the bad actors and scores each one on a scale from 1 to 500 in terms of propensity to commit and/or otherwise be involved in violent crimes. 85% of the expected gang shooters and gang shooting victims over the next reporting are already specifically identified on the SSL list. The remaining 15% are the innocents who get caught in the mayhem and wounded or killed by these morons.

Certainly, the ease of access which the thugs and felons have to cheap and readily available guns (largely from unregulated gun shows held in states adjacent to Illinois like Indiana and Wisconsin with lax gun laws and little enforcement) has increased the likelihood that there will be more and more actual shootings (rather than simply fights and beatings) in the course of gang confrontations. Chicago's police force confiscates more illegal weapons each year than the total guns taken off the streets of New York City and Los Angeles combined.

There are many other opinions being offered by every talking head in town and elsewhere as to additional contributing causes, but only the most modest amount of real data and concrete, actionable information. Stupid judges who prematurely and repeatedly release gang members and convicted felons with rap sheets full of prior gun offenses certainly don't help the situation. Jail and prison officials who promptly push out parolees (with only a small fraction of their sentences having been served) are demonstrably prioritizing creating space in their cellblocks over citizen safety. Shoplifters on average spend more time behind bars than shooters. And we certainly can't leave the task up to the media which always prefers to lead the nightly news with whatever bleeds. That sad and sick situation (where ratings rather than reason or any sense of responsibility rule the roost) is unlikely to change any time soon.

It's clear that we all need to take a breath and work on improving the substance of our arguments, and the effectiveness of our tactics, instead of simply raising our voices. Having some actual facts and figures available to all of us which we can use to move the discussions forward productively will also help us to identify and start working in the direction of some viable solutions. As the old saying goes, anyone's entitled to their own opinion, but there's only one set of facts for everyone.

Progress is being made. Under Superintendent Johnson's direction, the Chicago Police Department is using new data-driven analyses to help develop and drive alternative approaches to the community (including the known criminals) in a number of ways.

First, there is an increased emphasis on conversations, rather than confrontations. Less immediately visible police presence at events and demonstrations actually leads to less likelihood of escalation and violence.

Second, there are more and broader opportunities being identified for communication efforts that get ahead of the possible problems rather than crisis management actions that are entirely reactive in nature. Always better to avoid the pothole in the first place than to get a great deal on the cost of the tow truck.

Finally, active advance intervention and direct involvement with especially vulnerable SSL-identified gang members (accompanied by various offers of support, employment and other relief) are showing real results in reducing the likelihood of those individuals' violent behavior.

You can't ultimately answer the questions for these kids, and some will always choose the wrong path, but at least we can show them some concrete alternatives to losing their freedom or their lives or, worse yet, accidentally killing someone else.

I was recently asked what productivity tools, handy tips or other strategies I have used over the years to help me stay on course – focused on my most important goals and primary objectives - in the midst of the messy multitude of ongoing emergencies, unavoidable distractions and regular interruptions that make up my typical day. I wish I had a good answer or a magic wand to solve the problem, but I've yet to find a single approach or solution that works even most of the time. It's a constant battle and it only gets harder as your business and your responsibilities and the demands on your time grow.

I do think that it helps to ask yourself many times a day a simple question: is what I'm doing or about to do moving my business forward? If not, do something else. And I also think that it can be destructive and a very bad idea to ask yourself a different question - whether what you're being asked to do in the moment is the highest and best use of your time. That question is an ego trap and it becomes way too easy to quickly convince yourself that you're too good or too busy or too important to do some of the very mundane things that need to be done.

It may not be your specific job and it may not be the best use of your time in some purely economic sense, but some things just need to get done and it's important that people feel that you're more than happy and prepared to pitch in. This is not solely because critical work can't be left undone; it's also because the even bigger risk to your business is that the message which this kind of bad and arrogant behavior often sends is a culture killer. I pick up the trash all day long. I run the lion's share of my own errands. I answer my own phone. If I'm too good to do these kinds of things, why should anyone else care about getting them done?

Now I do think it would be nice to be King and simply get to set my inviolable schedule and stick to it like clockwork, but my business life is really no different than anyone else's and that's just not the way an entrepreneur's world ever works.

The best entrepreneurs try to steer a steady course forward through constantly changing and challenging circumstances. They fiercely protective of their time and they try to keep anyone else from controlling their calendar or their inbox. (See http://www.inc. com/howard-tullman/slow-down-it-might-save-your-business.html .) And they do have one more trick in their bag that makes all the difference. They know that they don't have to finish what they start. And you don't either – at least for right now.

But that's rank heresy you say. Even the Bible insists that we finish what we started (2 Corinthians 8:11) and I'm sure Shakespeare and Ben Franklin had a thought or two on the subject as well. Bear with me for a moment and think about the most productive people you know. They're absolute masters of constant triage – re-prioritizing things all the time and on the fly - and that's what keeps them rolling in the right direction.

They don't worry so much about square corners, neat piles and getting everything done exactly on time and to a T – they're focused on paying attention to what's most important for the business in the moment and that always taking precedence even if other tasks get left undone. Punctuality is much less important most of the time than productivity. It's a given that there's never enough time to get everything done and done well – part of the trick is that understand that not everything worth doing needs to be done to perfection. Good enough is often good enough and sometimes – left to their own – things will even take care of themselves.

Now I'm sure that it's more than a little frustrating to all those folks waiting in the wings or right outside the office – hoping that their request or project is still on the top of the pile – or worse yet – getting ready to dump some new problem in their boss's lap, but they're not the ones driving the train or setting the schedule and the best bosses make that distinction abundantly clear – early and often. It's OK to ask and it's even OK to push once in a while, but nagging is a no-no. For the moment, it is what it is. Down the line, we'll make it into whatever it will be. It's all about doing the right things and not worrying about doing things right.

So if you find yourself in a fix from time to time and feel a little like you're drowning in too many tasks, give yourself permission to give yourself a break and put the things that can wait to the side (even if they're not finished) so you can focus your energies and attention on the things that matter most at the moment.

It seems that a week doesn't go by these days without my hearing a version of the same startup struggle over and over again. The companies may change, but the song remains basically the same: we couldn't find it so we had to build it and now it's a bigger business opportunity for us than the business we set out to build when we began. Interestingly enough, it's not usually a product or service change that they're talking about – it's almost always an instance of their core technology infrastructure creating new value propositions and offerings for third parties.

An activity tracking system, new programs that help to cost-effectively automate basic and/or redundant functions, measurement tools which permit real-time adjustments in response to market conditions and consumer reactions, etc. all fall into this category. They start as internal tools and end up being white-labelled and sold/provided to third parties (as often as not existing customers of the business) in order to make everyone's lives easier and all of their businesses more productive and profitable.

Now this isn't a simple pivot tale – we encourage the occasional pivot, but no rapid twirling please (See http://www.inc.com/howard-tullman/you-can-pivot-but-you-should-never-twirl.html). This is more along the lines of "we built this thing and then it ate us". And that turns out to be not a necessarily bad thing – just a different direction than anyone expected or anticipated. Just as an aside, this is NEVER something that you want to spring on your Board or surprise your directors with – it's critical to get out in front of the discussions about changes like this because they represent alternate uses of the business's resources which everyone needs to get comfortable with in advance.

Since more and more of this seems to be happening all around us with greater and greater frequency, it's worth keeping an eye out for in your own company before it sneaks up on you as well. As the late Jerry Garcia was fond of saying: "Somebody has to do something, and it's just incredibly pathetic that it has to be us." And it's not as easy as you might think to get this stuff right.

We live in a world that we think typically and pretty clearly dictates a simple answer to the "buy it or build it" question. The conversation and the analysis usually goes like this:

(1) Unless (a) it offers an essential and sustainable competitive advantage for your business and (b) you have some particularized skill sets and resources that make your organization uniquely qualified to build whatever it is; the obvious answer in most cases is to go out into the marketplace and buy that necessary part of your product, service or solution from someone else; and

(2) Make sure that the someone else is someone who (a) does it for a living and does it well and (b) will keep doing it, investing in it, improving it, and delivering it less expensively and more efficiently than you can - at least for the foreseeable future. Not necessarily forever, but certainly for a lot longer than you can or should be paying attention to it at the time.

Things (however appealing and au courant) that aren't mission critical - wanna haves rather than necessities - can't be allowed to consume bandwidth or scarce time and resources in a new business because that strategy simply wastes crucial focus and momentum and diverts your team's attention from the main chance.

The old joke used to be that eventually every app and program would have email built in whether it was needed or not (your dog actually doesn't need email) - today you don't have to look any further than everyone's rush to incorporate live video capability into their mobile offerings to see the same kind of fast-following frenzy. No question that, for some of the players, it is an essential add-on and the sooner the better. But for others, it's a distraction that will be disappeared or dumped by them by December.

The trick is to keep the two ground rules listed above in mind as you set out to decide how your business needs to handle the "build or buy" decision each time it arises. It's a case-by-case situation and one rule won't work as a general management proposition because, apart from the strategic part of the analysis, there are cost considerations (given the continuing decline in the prices of new technologies) which can sometimes make it so attractive and inexpensive to try adopting an outsourced solution (at least as a pilot) that it just doesn't make sense to take the time (and waste the time) that it would entail to do any prolonged strategic analysis.

Cheap is sometimes the easy way out for people who can't figure out how to do things better, but, in other cases, cheap may just be the best way to proceed in putting a toe in the water without making a major commitment until you determine whether the initiative makes sense. Not everything worth doing is worth doing well right away – you don't test the depth of a puddle by jumping in with both feet.

I'm sure that there are plenty of examples that come readily to mind. Here are 3 descriptive buckets that seem to cover many of the cases where these kinds of questions and opportunities are likely to arise.

(1) Improved accountability

You can't get the right information from your partners and vendors about how you're doing or what dollars you're really spending and why (either because they don't have it or because they won't share it with you for their own reasons) and so you start to develop and build the internal ability to measure and track these things and – very quickly – you find that there are a staggering number of others equally in the dark about these things who would love to have access to your new tools and pay for the privilege. You have to decide – among other things – whether letting your proprietary technology out there is worth the risk of eventual sharing and some levels of disclosure which may improve your competitors' abilities to keep up with you in these areas. Machine Zone's Realtime technology (https://www.mz.com) grew out of its own frustration with efficiently managing its massive ad spend and now it makes some of its tools available to others – but it never shares the secret sauce.

(2) Improved efficiency

It turns out that many businesses today have: (a) access to the basic CRM tools (like Salesforce) and (b) also (at least theoretically if they're prepared and able to spend the required amounts of cash to buy the necessary access) to the required data pools and other sources of transaction tracking material which they clearly all need to most effectively translate all those data streams into actionable information, but they don't have the in-house people with the smarts to integrate all these things into the kinds of reporting systems (dashboards for short) that the majority of their employees need in order to use the information to better do their own jobs. Of course, you can farm the job out like Caterpillar has done with Uptake (no pun intended), but there may be a few too many babies in that particular bathwater.

A better solution is to find a team that has already built the integrated tools <u>and</u> made the considerable investment in accessing the critical data streams and have them provide a SaaS-type dashboard service to your people. This gets you much the same results, but doesn't outsource the learning and the skill sets that will make up your competitive edge. Companies like McNabb Technologies built tools like their TouchCR relationship management system (http://touchcrsolutions.com) and integrated it with Salesforce in order to first address their own selling and service needs and now they make the platform available to others.

(3) Improved productivity

One of the best ways to make your new business hum is by getting your customers to do more of the work themselves by shifting as much of the transaction responsibility (selecting, ordering, payment options, timing, pick-up or delivery arrangements, etc.) to their side of the equation as long as there's less, <u>not</u> more, friction as a result of the changes in the process. If you can make their lives easier, save them time and/or money, help them avoid re-entries and redundancies, and even anticipate their needs, they'll be more than happy to pitch in. And they can help across a pretty broad spectrum by doing things and supplying personal information that ultimately saves you time and makes your offerings to them more targeted, more compelling and easier to say "yes" to as well. (See http://www.inc.com/howard-tullman/we-need-to-take-charge-of-our-data.html.)

The smartest web marketers do this by "pushing through" their in-house technology to their partners' sites so that the end consumer ends up dealing directly with the ultimate vendor even though it looks like their transaction is occurring on some intermediate site. This reduces response and fulfillment time, increases the accuracy of inbound orders, and permits the back-end vendor to aggregate data and transaction histories to improve recommendations, side offerings, suggestive selling, etc. which might be beyond the abilities of the middlemen. As the complexity of our technologies continues to grow, fewer and fewer small merchants are going to be able to make the necessary investments in the systems that will keep them competitive in the high-speed, rapid response world of e-commerce and they will come increasingly to depend on their back-end partners.

This is good news for wedding apparel marketing companies like Chicago's Brideside (http://brideside.com/) which is finding that more and more of its consumer-facing partners are asking to have Brideside's front-end ordering systems run their website's e-commerce interfaces as well. This approach helps Brideside justify and amortize its continued technology investments and gain more immediate access and selling opportunities to the ultimate buyers. A separate issue that may arise down the road is when major players and big suppliers start to insist for competitive reasons on limiting access to the shared-out technologies. (See http://www.inc.com/howard-tullman/a-big-customer-wants-exclusivity-now-what.html .)

The bottom line in all of this is pretty simple. As you're building a better mousetrap to help run your basic business, you may actually also be building a path to a bigger and better business at the same time. Just make sure that you're driving the process and making the right choices for your company all along the way.

The Chicago Cubs are having a spectacular season (so far) and, without taking anything for granted, it's clear that their talent strategy and their commitment to rebuilding the whole team with young, healthy impact players have begun to pay serious dividends. For a team that feels like it's been around forever and waiting to win big for almost as long a time, the Cubs also look an awful lot like a scrappy startup and a work always in progress where everything is up for discussion (and change) if it's likely to move the mission forward.

We had a chance recently to hear a lot of "inside baseball" talk from a couple of the management players in the Cubs organization and there were a few key takeaways from their experience that I think will be just as valuable for whatever business you're building. Keep in mind that these are simply my observations about what's going on and what's behind the rebirth and their improving fortunes. There's nothing "official" about what follows, but it does come directly from a few of the horses' mouths.

Creating the right culture and reinforcing the commitment of everyone in the organization to winning the World Series were two of the higher level and very central themes of the conversation. This reminded me of the early days of 1871 in some important ways. When we began discussing and defining the culture of 1871 and the special community which we hoped it would become, we spent a substantial amount of time on issues of governance. As you would expect from a group that included a number of successful and outspoken entrepreneurs, there were plenty of competing ideas and lots of loud opinions. Entrepreneurs don't always color within the lines or act like grownups and – of course – that's part of their enduring charm. But – if you're not careful - it can also make for a messy environment which is disruptive in all the wrong ways.

I'd say that ultimately we ended up opting for a basically Miesian "less is more" approach with just a few red lines. If things worked out well, 1871 would be a place driven by the right attitudes rather than by rigorous authority. I like to think that my biggest contribution to the whole process was a single sentence. I said that "a great culture has to be built on expectations of performance, not rules of behavior". We couldn't have written a master rule book even if we wanted to for an enterprise which was very much a grand experiment that we fervently hoped would become a self-sustaining and organic ecosystem. The Cubs have some of the very same challenges - to pull the broadest possible community into the park - to change the surrounding neighborhood for the better - and to make the entire country sit up and take notice of what is happening in Chicago.

As I listened during our meetings to the details of the Cubs approach, I was struck by the similarities to our own 1871 philosophy – the Cubs way was all about building a winning team for sure – but the foundations and the manner in which the ultimate goals would be achieved were all about the individual's responsibility for (a) controlling their own behavior; (b) improving their own performance (there would be plenty of help, but they needed to provide the heart); and (c) contributing to the greater good which meant specifically the players putting the team's success ahead of their own.

I came away having identified 5 basic strategic steps that I think are working for the Cubs and which are a helpful framework for anyone building a new business as well. Keep in mind that these things don't propagate themselves and that consistently communicating them to the members of your team and the broader world of third party stakeholders is a crucial and ongoing part of the success of the system. Everyone wants to know where they're going and how they're gonna get there and also wants to be sure that they won't be going alone. Equally important today for the younger players and team members is overt recognition and reinforcement - delivered authentically all along the way. Silent gratitude doesn't mean squat. Money is always nice, but acknowledgement and appreciation are the real drivers for young people these days.

So here are the 5 "simple" steps.

(1) Set the Team (Talent)

The up-and-coming ballplayers are the building blocks of any business's future and you're got to get and/or grow the best possible raw material for your team as cost-effectively as possible which - in the major leagues - actually means as early as possible. It's too bad that there's not a farm club system for every industry and this is a real issue for startups because you have to manage a mix of energetic young people and experienced older folks when you're growing quickly since not everyone can be learning the ropes of your business as they go. OJT is great, but too many people with too much rope can hang your company out to dry.

One really important thing to note is that the Cubs aren't just looking to recruit and grow their own talent on the field – they're applying the same approach to every part of the organization. In a business like baseball that is so people-centric throughout the whole organization, the gap in impact and effectiveness between a good team member and a great team member isn't 2X; it's more likely 5X to 10X because, in a service business, everything happens every day on the front line and there's no time to consult a rule book or a manager – you've got to go with your gut (and with what you've been taught, seen and internalized) and you've got to use your best judgment in the moment since you won't get a second chance to make a first (very critical) impression.

Initiative, creativity and empathy are force multipliers and the hardest challenge in an expanding and rapidly-growing people business is to keep these qualities alive in your team members as they age, grow and progress in your organization.

(2) Set the Table (Tools)

If you don't give your team the best available resources, tools and technologies which they will need to be successful (within whatever your realistic cost constraints may be), you're asking them to work with one hand tied behind their backs. This won't get you very far. The Cubs are spending over $600 million just on bricks and mortar in order to leapfrog the entire league and move from a sorry last place to the number one position in the country (if not in the world) in terms of athletic facilities, training and rehab resources, technology, nutrition, etc. I've seen the new spaces and they are astonishing.

Here again, there's an underlying element that is critical. My good friend, Harper Reed, who is awesome always says that – contrary to popular opinion - building a great corporate culture isn't about snacks, hammocks or foosball – it's about creating an environment where talented people who respect each other can work together to take on important challenges and make a difference. Respect is the key word.

The Cubs set aside a substantial empty space in their new clubhouse digs for the players' lounge, but then the designers stepped back and let the players decide exactly what screens, games, instruments, etc. would be in their lounge and how it would be set up. This wasn't about toys or technology – it was about respect for the players' opinions, their downtime, and their desires and giving them some ownership in the overall process and the outcome. The players' pride in "their place" is palpable.

(3) Set the Schedule (Timing)

Nothing this big or this costly happens overnight, but something happens every day and everyone notices. In our world today, if you're not moving forward, you're losing ground to someone. Momentum means more than size or scale. An ounce of momentum is worth a pound of acceleration. So it's critically important to put some concrete stakes in the ground and then to hit those targets. They don't have to be moonshots – they can be small, solid steps, but they need to point people in the right direction and show them that the wind is at the business's back and that things will only get better from here. And these milestones need to be recorded and celebrated throughout the business on a regular basis. Lastly, it's death to overpromise and under deliver. If you want people to believe your promises about tomorrow; it helps to have kept your word from yesterday.

(4) Set and Manage the Metrics (Thermostat)

What gets measured is definitely what gets done. Even more importantly, there's no sway and no confusion when you're talking about performance against previously agreed-upon goals and standards. You make your numbers or you don't. And there's really no such thing as a good excuse in a well-run business. Or getting by by blaming the other guys or laying it off on circumstances beyond your control. You take your medicine and you move on, but you also take away and apply the lessons going forward.

If you're gonna sit by and watch things happen to your business, you might as well be sitting in the bleachers. It's not enough to be the thermometer and just passively record the results; the best managers are thermostats whose actions raise the heat and improve the outcomes.

This may seem a little easier to do in a game that tracks at-bats and hits and runs than in your industry, but every business needs to develop effective and relatively frictionless ways to keep score for everyone's benefit and also to establish and implement these criteria at every level and for everyone in the business. The continued emergence of new and inexpensive measurement technologies is making this responsibility easier and more essential all the time.

(5) Step Back (Trust)

Once you've put everything in place, there's another critical element in the process that really separates the winners from the copycats and the folks who are just going through the motions. You can't "ape" your way to a winning culture. You can't buy a mission statement that means anything real down at the mall. You need two-way trust. You have to take a step back and trust your players and your people to get out there and get the job done.

You can't do it for them. In fact, you can explain things to them – over and over again – but you also can't understand this stuff for them. You can talk your way into their heads, but it's what's in their hearts that makes all the difference. They have to know three things: that you trust them; that the system is objective, not subjective; and that you've got their backs – rain or shine – as long as they give it their all.

There have been a lot of prescriptive articles written over the last few years (mostly by academics and other people who haven't been there themselves) about the critical (and often ignored or overlooked) need for succession planning in large companies – especially at the level of the most senior management. I've seen massive notebooks at some big businesses that detail the candidates and the replacement process for practically every member of the senior management team.

On the other hand, apart from the occasional VC who insists on key man insurance as an investment condition, there's been very little discussion or literature about this issue in the startup world. Given how single-threaded so many startups are, you'd think this topic would be much more top of mind than it is.

It's clear that there's never a perfect moment to talk to the founding CEO of a startup about replacement, succession or making a prompt and graceful exit (even when everyone basically agrees that it's essential to moving the business to the next plateau) or about him or her being "kicked upstairs" to a board position or an advisory role, but treating the entire issue like it's a taboo subject doesn't make any sense at all. And yet, it's pretty much the ways things are and have always been. As many businesses as I have been a part of and as many times as I've addressed these issues as a Board member, it never seems to be a clear or easy process.

I think this is mainly for three reasons: (1) the incumbent CEO never wants to discuss stuff like this – it's just like talking about your will or your funeral plans with your wife or kids; (2) most VCs would tell you (if they were being remotely honest) that, in 75% or more of the cases where the company is wildly successful, they totally believe that they're going to have to fire/replace the CEO anyway so they'll worry about it down the road; and (3) it's too early in the company's brief lifetime to date to be discussing these kinds of "negative" ideas and concerns. We don't want to scare the troops or the investors. I call this last consideration the "let's rob the train first before we worry about splitting up the loot" mindset.

But the truth is that - no matter how unpleasant the topic may be - it's a good idea for the CEO when the time is right to get ahead of the pack and actually try to initiate and direct some of these discussions before they take on a life of their own and he or she becomes – at best - an interested bystander to the process. Boards rarely directly broach subjects like this without a precipitating event or a firm push or incentive from someone and it's almost always better to be the one making things happen than the one watching things happen – especially when they're happening to you.

But of course the hardest question in this process really isn't "who's next?" – the critical question is "when is the time right?" to start thinking about making at least a plan and maybe even a change. Interestingly enough, INC. Magazine's owner, Joe Mansueto, just stepped out of his CEO role at Morningstar – a company that he founded more than 30 years ago. He didn't wait to be asked or to be pushed – he knew that for him (and I imagine for the business as well) that the time was right. I've known Joe for decades, but – just to be clear – I haven't spoken to him about his decision and none of the considerations I discuss below should be attributed or assumed to have had any role in his choices.

How will you know when the time is right to at least start talking about the subject? Even if you think it's early (or never gonna happen to you), it's a good idea to know some of the internal signs and some of the emotional signals that will help you decide whether and when it's appropriate and smart to think about succession issues and your eventual (and hopefully consensual) decision to move on. I've talked to maybe a dozen serial entrepreneurs over the last couple of months specifically on this subject and, of course, I've been through the process many times myself and it's pretty clear that the inventory of emotions and concerns is fairly common. Here are the ones that I've seen and heard time and time again.

(1) When it feels more like an exhausting job than an exciting journey.

I've always thought it was stupid to ask an entrepreneur whether he or she is having "fun". Building a new business is a whole lot of things, but anyone who's lived through it won't tell you that it was a lot of fun. It's challenging, stimulating, overwhelming at times, and certainly satisfying when you succeed, but it's not a lark. When you're actively unhappy at the end of a long day instead of just being beat, it's time to think about beating it.

(2) When it feels more like pulling the wagon than leading the charge.

Leading people is always a challenge and it helps a bunch to have the right people on your team. But after you've shown them the vision and the path, in the best businesses, the burden's on them to move the ball forward. Trying to drag a disinterested division down the road or carry a "care less" crew on your back is just too much work for anyone to try to do alone. Begging your people to believe is a waste of breath. Find new people or a better place to be. You can't push a rope.

(3) When no one, but you is interested in what's new or what's next.

Businesses that don't keep raising the bar and getting better every day start dying. It's that simple, but that doesn't mean that it's easy to encourage everyone to keep one eye on the future. People inside your business are always reluctant to change or to part with what they see as working "just fine" for them. But meanwhile the rest of the world is trying to eat your lunch. This isn't about some fixation on always seeking the newest shiny object or buying the best new whatever – whether you need it or not. It's about living in a world where change is the only constant.

(4) When the process becomes more important than the business's progress.
Nothing is more heartbreaking for a true entrepreneur than watching bullshit bureaucracy slither its way into the business. Punctuality comes to trump productivity. Rules and regulations get in the way of real results. People prefer peace and quiet over progress. Hurt feelings are more important than hard facts. And too many crave consensus and the lowest common denominator over the chaos of creativity and new challenges.

(5) When the conversations are about imitation rather than innovation.
If the best your business can do is just a little bit better or cheaper or faster, you won't be in business much longer. Thinking small and aiming low are self-fulfilling prophecies. And if I can write down a simple set of rules and instructions to do the lion's share of your business, a machine or a robot will be taking your place a couple of weeks from tomorrow. The future isn't going to be incremental – it's going to be radical - and the businesses that want to grow and survive will need to make a demonstrable difference in and add real value to people's lives. Design will be important, but not protectable or proprietary, because the web lets the whole world know what you're thinking and doing in an instant. Speed, impact and exemplary execution will be everything.

(6) When everyone's talking about better safe than sorry.
If all the talk is about saving the business's bacon and securing the status quo instead of the setting the curve and shooting for the stars, you're on the wrong escalator and headed in the wrong direction. You can't save your way to success; you can't steal second base with one foot on first; and, if we knew in advance how all these things were gonna work out, they probably wouldn't be worth doing in the first place. The caterpillar is safe in the cocoon, but it's the butterfly that's beautiful. The best businesses are richly rewarded for taking the greatest risks (not gambles, but calculated risks) and playing it safe today is the riskiest thing you can do.

(7) When you spend more time looking over your shoulder than over the next hill.
It's important to cherish and celebrate the past as long as you don't live in it. You can't change it; you won't forget it or get over it; and the very best that you can hope for is to avoid making the same old mistakes again. But the worst mistake of all is to use the past as an excuse for not moving forward or as a place to hide from an uncertain future. The best entrepreneurs run toward their fears, not away from them.

And, just to be clear, since the most critical choices are the ones we make with our hearts rather than our heads, you'll know it's time to go when your fears are greater than your dreams.

TULLMAN'S TRUISMS

TRY TO HAVE MORE DREAMS THAN MEMORIES

I'm so tired of regularly reading about and constantly being lectured on the virtues of failing fast that I'm beginning to wonder whether the phrase is an embedded Swift Key on mobile keypads or a built-in slide which is automatically inserted into PowerPoint and Keynote presentations. But, as I've said many times in the past, there's no fun in failing (See http://www.inc. com/howard-tullman/who-said-failure-was-fashionable.html) and it's no badge of honor to lose although I don't think that - for young entrepreneurs - it's really a case of losing in any event – because, even if you don't win, you learn a great deal as long as you're willing to listen.

Just remember that there's nothing noble about noble failures and that even the grandest failures aren't really fatal – they're just opportunities to start again – better and smarter. The truth is that you'll absolutely learn much more from your failures than your successes although it won't feel nearly as good. And, you never want to quit too soon because, in the startup world, almost everything looks like a failure in the middle. This is why perseverance is so crucial. Things always look grimmest right before success breaks through.

So, I'd like to retire the phrase "fail fast" and replace it with something that to me is a lot more descriptive of the whole experience and the smart way to look at the process. It's not ultimately about how quickly you fail, it's all about the education, the take-aways and specifically about the mistakes you hopefully won't make again. So instead of making sure that you are failing fast, my suggestion is that you try to "fail forward" when things are headed downhill. Learn and gain in the process. Brene Brown says failure is an "imperfect" word because it's never the end of the story if you're smart. Failures turn into lessons and lessons make you better going forward and somewhat more likely to succeed the next time around as long as you're a good listener. (See http://www. inc.com/howard-tullman-3-tips-from-brene-brown-about-failing-brilliantly.html)

Failing forward has all the virtues of failing fast - an awareness of opportunity costs - the ancient wisdom of "stopping the digging" when you find yourself deep in a hole - and an understanding of how seeking the cure for no known disease or working desperately on solutions for non-existent problems is such a sad waste of your energy and scarce resources. But an important distinction is that the idea of failing forward always looks ahead - gets you right back up on the horse again - and builds on the useful and valuable experiences of your prior attempts. In addition, if you handle the wind-down like a pro, you will actually make it much more likely that your next deal will be easier to get done because even failing well is an art. (See http://www.inc.com/ howard-tullman/failure-happens-four-ways-to-do-it-well.html)

It's almost never about a clean sweep or a complete restart - there are too many babies in the bath water to just toss the whole thing out the window. It's always an iterative process with lots of triage included. You want to preserve what worked (remembering that someone spent a lot of time and money on your last adventure), you definitely want to hang on to the people who put their hearts and souls into the program, and you want to be humble and smart enough to carefully determine what went wrong and why. Just a word to the wise about that last idea - in the vast majority of cases - it will emerge that what bit you in the ass wasn't just something you weren't good enough at or something that you found out that you didn't know how to do - it will be something that you didn't even know that you didn't know (or hadn't thought about) that made all the difference.

The lesson here is that it's the careful research and the customer investigation - the stuff you do before you start – that, in the end, will turn out to have the greatest impact on the success of the business because real demand and customers are the whole ballgame. Everything else you can hire, fire, fix or improve as the battle progresses, but, if no one wants what you're selling, there's no there there.

I have been saying for at least 30 years now that the most attractive (and profitable) customers any business can have are the ones that you already have in house. It's more important to deepen your connection to your existing customers than to spend a lot of time and money trying to figure out why certain customers left. After all, while you might learn some things from the process, you can't really water yesterday's crops and, in any case, it feels a little too much to me like crying over spilt milk. Extract the necessary lessons, fix what can be fixed, and move forward.

Good existing customers get better and more valuable over time (increased spend, referrals, lower maintenance costs, etc.) and they represent the absolutelylowest-hanging fruit for additional incremental business (product and services add-ons, extensions, new offerings, service plans, etc.) as well as the greatest and easiest opportunity to increase your share of their total spend. (See http://www.inc.com/howard-tullman/why-knocking-on-old-doors-is-the-best-sales-strategy.html.)

So it's absolutely critical to do everything you can to hang on to your good customers and clients. Nothing is more important to your bottom line than preventing customer attrition and avoiding churn. If you can't do this, and you're spending a fortune on the front end to pull in new customers while you're losing them out the back, your company's going nowhere fast. It's like kissing your sister or as Yogi Berra used to say about his road trips: "We're lost, but we're making good time." The truth is that, if you're losing existing customers as quickly as you adding new ones, you're not making or building anything – you're just treading water – and once you run out of money, they make you go home.

The name of the long and winning game is to "own" your customers for life and to exceed their expectations throughout your relationship with them. Today we have the tools and the data concerning virtually all of our customers which should permit us to totally manage our relationships with them if we invest the time and money to look at the available information and – most importantly – if we know what we are looking for. Everything in life happens on a continuum (or a series of cycles) and your job is to monitor your customers' timelines and jump in at the appropriate junctures (long before the competition is even in the game) to make the next connection and the next sales.

When you're already in their wallet, you can absolutely work wonders. And when you're already connected to them through low-cost digital marketing and communication channels, assuming you haven't abused the privilege or their patience, you have an inexpensive and very direct channel to reach out to them with customized, personalized and timely offers consistent with their prior activities, past purchases, and interests. It's a marketer's dream scenario and it's the very essence of what I call "smart reach". (See http://www.inc.com/howard-tullman/to-sell-more-your-marketing-must-embrace-smart-reach.html.)

Part two of this process is making sure that you stay out in front of the customers and aggressively anticipate their desires, demands and requirements so that the offers you make to them make sense. As Steve Jobs used to say, they may not even know what they want and it's your job to entice, excite and encourage them in those next directions. If you do it well and consistently, the customers may never re-enter the competitive marketplace since you are effectively and pre-emptively satisfying their needs. (See http://www.inc.com/howard-tullman/keep-your-customers-by-thinking-ahead-of-them.html.) Today, I think there's probably no better example than the Amazon Dash buttons which permit on-site, as-needed, immediate re-ordering capability right in the consumers' homes at the place and precise time when they need to replenish or replace essential supplies. Be there when they want to buy.

The job of staying ahead of your customers is equally true whether you think you are selling a product or a service. The smartest operators know that every business is really a service business today because the real nature of every business is that it's always about making the next sale, managing the next interaction or event, delivering an uninterrupted stream of service, etc. You never want the customer "to come up for air" because if he or she does re-enter the marketplace and starts shopping around, your job becomes a million times harder.

So the ongoing task and the critical questions are always the same – how do I know when to act and how do I pre-empt/ intercept the customer at exactly the right times in our relationship? The answer is actually easier than you would think because - even though the start and stop points on the cycle may vary by customer - at some definable and determinable point, every customer will move through the same cycle. You just have to understand and learn how to measure and manage the cycles.

The basic cycles are pretty much just extensions of human nature. It's a process that we are all already familiar with and living through every day ourselves. The five primary phases are:

Desire Leading to **Decision**
Action Leading to **Satisfaction**
Boredom Leading to New **Desire**

We want it, we buy it, we love it for a while, we get tired of it, and we want something new. Sound vaguely familiar. Well, here's a flash, this is a process that every single one of your customers is going through right now. Your job is to figure out who's where in which phase of the cycle. It's important to understand that the cycles are going to vary dramatically depending on a variety of important considerations and they will vary from industry to industry as well.

Some of the variables which will impact the types and durations of the cycles (but not the fundamental stages or phase within the cycle) include:

(1) how large and financially/emotionally important is the transaction;
(2) how often is a transaction likely to occur and what other connections/interactions with the customer will take place between transactions: and
(3) how easy is it for the customer to change vendors, services or products and how readily available are competitive offerings?

But, regardless of a given cycle's duration, there are similar cycles to be identified, tracked and managed in <u>every</u> business and properly managed, these cycles are the keys to keeping your customers for life.

TULLMAN'S TRUISMS

KNOCK ON OLD DOORS

There's no polite or easy way to say this, but winter is on its way in more ways than one. It's getting tougher and tougher for startups caught in the lukewarm limbo between ideas and invoices to get their early backers to up their bets especially when it's not clear that they've found a viable business model and/or a way to stop the bleeding sooner rather than later. Too many pivots with too little to show for the dollars down the drain and pretty soon no one wants to hear your "someday soon" story or your next grand plan. (See http://www.inc.com/howard-tullman/you-can-pivot-but-you-should-never-twirl.html.) And if you're not even breaking even, no bank will look twice at your business or your balance sheet. This change isn't restricted to the unicorpses in the Valley; it's going on in every village where waves of wishful thinkers are starting to wonder what hit them.

My sense is that the smart investor conversations taking place today aren't very often about the company going big for the gold or about the current investors doubling down so some startup can shoot for the stars. These increasingly cranky chats are less about excitement and enthusiasm and much more about ennui and possible exits. Because the two things that some early investors and every VC understands are sunk costs and opportunity costs. While the entrepreneur is sweating survival; the investors are trying to decide whether their incremental dollars would be better spent on a new deal elsewhere. These are the days when the easy money gets hard. Those great gluten-free sugar cookies (from the hip new bakery down the block that just shut its doors) are tasting more like ashes in their mouths and they're asking themselves how they ended up sitting in a room with no doors feeling like some sucker after the circus left town.

The unhappy folks who are still sitting at the table (more likely associates now than the partners who got the ball rolling) aren't talking about how much more money they can put to work; they're trying to figure out how little additional cash they've got to put up in order to preserve what's left of their position. Everyone is telling you that they're really not inclined to do much of anything at all if you can't drag some new money from outside players to the table to help set the price and get the next round started. Flat valuations in times like this are the new "up" rounds and there are down rounds galore. (See http://www.inc.com/howard-tullman/tech-startups-take-the-money-and-build.html.)

This is a Plan B world at best and the down and dirty talk on the limo ride to LaGuardia almost always includes whether to also shoot the CEO while they're in the process of trying to clean things up and save a little face. So if you're the one on the bubble, forget Plan B, and get started on what I call Plan C. You need to get a head start on talking about the tough choices and critical changes that need to be made. It's about figuring out what immediate actions you can take that will make a difference before they turn the lights out. You can have results or excuses, not both. Focus on facts rather than futures if you want to be around when things turn around. And forget about playing the blame game – no one cares.

Plan C is all about choices: contraction, consolidation, combination, conversion, and concessions. The last C is closing the doors and that's not a sight that anyone wants to see. So see which of the C's makes the most sense for your startup.

(1) Contraction

Just suck it up and admit it. You can't be all things to all people and no one ever has been. Focus on what sets you apart and what represents the best prospect of a long-term sustainable competitive advantage for your business and forget everything else. Don't apologize, don't try to explain, just buckle down and get the job done. The recent launch of UberEats in Chicago (as an "instant" meal delivery service) and its almost immediate abandonment of that commitment is a good example of knowing when to hold 'em and when to fold 'em. It doesn't take a genius to figure out that it's pretty stupid to open the umpteenth home meal delivery service in Grub Hub's hometown.

Businesses that scale too soon and which are a mile wide and an inch deep are doomed for many reasons, but the clearest and most telling is that they can't cost-effectively engage with, support, or connect to their customers because the customers are simply too few and too far between. It's critical to nail it before you scale it and, if you're grossly over-extended, your business is going nowhere.

(2) Consolidation

Shut down the stupid San Francisco office sooner rather than later. You had no business being there in the first place and the fact that you're doing no business there ought to speak for itself. San Francisco may be the most overheated and least representative market in America. Everyone there drinks the Kool-Aid for about 10 minutes and then moves on. Building a new business there is as slippery and unstable as trying to nail Jell-O to a tree.

New York should be next on the list. NYC isn't a city – it's 5 or 6 different marketplaces all mashed together – with a million people just waiting to eat your lunch. Your business expansion needs to be driven by actual demand, feasibility and real opportunities – not by some investor's fantasies and/or by fables about life in the Big Apple foisted on the public by the media and promoted by people barely making it in Brooklyn.

(3) Combination

Take a careful look around and see who else in your space (or adjacent to it) is doing things right and see what the prospects of some kind of combination may be - especially if your market itself continues to become more cluttered and competitive.

We hear constantly that the shared/surplus economy or the "Now" economy continues to grow fueled by millions of millennials holding multiple jobs. But tracking the gig economy isn't quite that easy. While the number of multiple job holders has in fact grown dramatically, the percentage of the number of people so employed as compared to the total number employed has been flat or down over the last decade. No one knows for sure what the new world of work will look like in a few years.

We had a great example of a timely and smart combination recently in Chicago where *Shiftgig* (www.shiftgig.com) and *BookedOut* (www.bookedout.com) got together and decided that there were all kinds of economies and opportunities in a merger as well as the sheer relief in knowing that they could stop trying to beat each other's brains out in the market. They are both players in the increasingly-crowded space which the Commerce Department is trying to define as "digital matching firms". *Shiftgig* was bigger and better established, but *BookedOut* had a lot of momentum and was gaining important traction in the experiential marketing sector. Now instead of spending time building duplicative back ends and other redundant systems and offerings, they can bring a single story to the market in a cleaner, more efficient and less costly way. This is exactly the kind of story that all of their investors wanted to hear.

It's not easy in any market to attract the technical talent, the motivated sales people, and the operations folks that you need to grow quickly. A well-planned and thoughtfully executed combination can demonstrably accelerate the process. You need to be careful to make sure that the companies' visions are aligned and that the problems they're addressing are similar and that the cultures of the businesses (and the leaders in particular) aren't in conflict. These things aren't made or broken in the board room when the papers are signed; they rise or fail in the implementation and the execution. But in today's world, it's often a lot better and smarter to combine than trying to go it alone.

(4) Conversion

Sell some of your stuff to someone else. You may be great at lead generation and lousy at closing the sale once those prospects show up at your door. Or you may be a great sales organization that sucks at fulfillment and customer service. When you look at your skill sets and your customers, users, clients, etc. through a different lens – looking at them as potential assets to be converted or sold to some other enterprise - it helps you see more clearly exactly what kind of business you're building. It may make the most sense to look at your company as a conduit or an intermediary and not as a one-stop shop trying to meet all the needs of the marketplace. You've got to play to your strengths and build on those if you're planning to stick around.

(5) Concessions

Maybe your pricing made sense in some early fever dream where you were the best and only player in the space, but now there are fast followers and clones everywhere you look and their offerings (at least on the surface) look a lot like yours. Once your customers start talking about price, you're on a very slippery slope. (See http://www.builtinchicago.org/blog/no-one-wins-race-bottom.)

Here's the bottom line. In the long run, you can't save your way to success and it's no fun to fire your friends or postpone your pet projects. But if you don't survive during the difficult times, you and your business won't be around to savor any success down the road. Do what needs to be done and do it now.

I must have heard the story about the tortoise and the hare a few million times in my youth and you'd think I'd be sick of it by now. But - and this is amazing to me in today's "everything in a hurry" world - the basic lesson - that slow and steady progress wins the race in the long run - is still remarkably relevant and applicable - especially to new businesses. It sounds a little old fashioned and even a bit boring and it's rarely something that you'll hear any VC say - especially when the topic on the table is how quickly to scale the business, but it's something that the very best entrepreneurs always take to heart and keep top of mind. Rushing to roll out your business nationwide (and being a mile wide and an inch deep) may make the boys in the board room happy, but it's bad for your business if you aren't ready.

One of our recent Chicago success stories is *SpotHero* (www.spothero.com) which helps drivers find off-street parking spaces and owners fill their parking lots and garages. There couldn't be a better example of the "go slow until you get it right" approach. While competitors, copycats and other knock-offs attempted rapid geographic expansions across the country, *SpotHero* hunkered down and stayed in Chicago for the first two years of its existence. They figured out that you've got to nail it before you can scale it.

Today, 5 years later, they're still <u>only</u> in about 20 cities (with 5 major cities contributing about 98% of all their revenue), while one of the few competitors who are still standing is "doing business" in more than 150 cities. I say "doing business" because *SpotHero* earns more parking revenue in one of its cities than those guys do in all 150 of their cities combined. *SpotHero* is larger and growing faster than its remaining competitors (notwithstanding having raised less capital) because they continue to focus on deeper and better connections to each of their markets and customers rather than simply trying to be everywhere at once. Doing a lot of things is not the same as getting things done and done right.

Adding marginal inventory (or any other kinds of commitments) in new markets without assuring the presence of matching demand is an easy trip to the toilet. It's like the busted-out guy who takes an Uber to Bankruptcy Court and then invites the *Uber* driver into the proceedings as a creditor. Similarly, the kind of parking you're identifying and booking for the consumers who are using your services matters as well. Events parking is relatively easy, but it's also infrequent and a relatively small part of the overall market. *SpotHero* targeted the biggest and best parking concerns and locations in the country (with massive numbers of consistent- often daily – users) from the get-go and now works with 9 of the top 11 players including all 5 of the largest parking companies in the U.S.

It's never easy going after and trying to sign all the big guys. They're tougher and smarter and more demanding, but they're also the best businessmen. What you can learn from them and what they can help you accomplish is priceless. (See http://www.inc.com/howard-tullman/a-big-customer-wants-exclusivity-now-what.html .) If you can lock these folks in and deliver the right results for them, there's no better place to be and no easier way to scale. Let the other guys drive themselves crazy chasing Mom-and-Pop lots all over the place. What they're missing is that every new lot they add reduces the yield to the guys who came before and that Ponzi-ish approach can't make anyone very happy over time.

There are almost always at least two economic sides to any marketplace (regulators, legislators, etc. don't count for these purposes). When you're growing your new business, you need to be very careful in the process that you don't leave the early adopters and your beginning boosters behind. They were there for you when the whole thing got started and they're critical references, foundational supporters, and concrete demonstrations that your product or service is sticky. Tracking and driving improvements in same store sales are the best and easiest way to measure stickiness and the best way to keep score as well especially when those critical numbers keep ticking up year over year in your oldest markets. This is because, if the older customers lose interest or cashflow and they're leaking out of the back door, it doesn't matter how you're doing in terms of growing or buying new customers at the front end of the funnel. (See http://www.inc.com/howard-tullman/why-your-best-new-customers-are-your-old-customers.html.)

Good business isn't usually about beating the other guys - there will always be new and different competitors - and there will always be people pitching cheaper and even better solutions. Chasing someone else or trying to quickly copy their plans and trying to outdo them assumes that they know what they're doing and are a lot smarter than you. I don't think there's any good reason to believe that. Sustainable businesses create real, demonstrable value for their clients and customers and they keep upping the ante.

No one new gets to rest on their laurels or their past performance even if they have a track record to point to which most startups don't. Customers' expectations are progressive. It's NOT about how fast you're going (but never slow down), it's about how fast you're getting faster and better. It's all about acceleration, not simply velocity. And it's about innovative techniques and technologies rather than tonnage as well. Precision trumps sheer volume. Your pitches, programs and proposals must be better, not just longer or louder.

It's not always a discussion or a conversation about a specific contest, feature, function or challenge. As often as not - it's about making this discipline of "always trying to be a better you" a part of your company's culture and embedding it in the ways that you do business whether you're selling products or services - widgets or wisdom - or whatever.

Having a great product isn't enough. No one sells just a product these days. We're all in service businesses trying to secure not a single sale, but to grab and hang on to the lifetime value of each customer. Creating a business that will last is about building long-term relationships and compounding customer trust. Connection and continuing engagement coupled with constant improvement and innovation are what keeps you in the game. I wouldn't be surprised to see them developing some new tools soon which will let their lot owners dynamically price parking in their lots based on all the same kinds of variables that so many other services are now using for surge pricing.

Startups don't have an established following or a brand to rely upon as shorthand for their promise to deliver and/or as a way to overcome the decision fatigue that plagues all of us these days in a world of infinite choices. Startups make a future promise and then it's directly on them to deliver on their commitments and to keep raising the bar. It's your business's job to earn and retain my loyalty. Loyalty today means nothing more than the absence of a better alternative.

Over-promising and under-delivering is obviously fatal over time. And even the coolest technology alone won't get the job done. *SpotHero* stuck with old-fashioned paper documentation until they precisely figured out the needs, comfort levels and the concerns of their customers (for the moment) and – only then – did they build a killer mobile app that now handles more than 80% of their reservations. The other players are still using websites.

Bottom line: People don't long remember who was first; they only know who's best. *SpotHero*'s the best in the biz.

TULLMAN'S TRUISMS

DON'T MAKE THE MENU LONGER, MAKE IT BETTER INSTEAD

D o they still let kids play the "Musical Chairs" game or is it no longer politically correct? You know, that's the game where the players walk around a group of chairs to music and try to sit down quickly when the music abruptly stops. The challenge is that there is always one less chair than the number of players and the one left standing is eliminated. I've always loved it because of its metaphorical power as much as anything else. Building a new business (or a career) is a competitive race in many ways and – especially as you progress – you quickly learn that there's not always room at the table for everyone. I like to say that it's lonely at the top, but at least it's not crowded. Having our kids get a little slice of real life experience early on and come to understand that occasionally you might have to push or shove your way to a seat in order to succeed isn't the worst thing in the world for anyone.

My position on schools, teachers and parents who promote the "everyone's a winner and trophies all around" view of the world is very clear. I think they're killing our country's competitiveness and mortgaging our kids' future with a bunch of fake, feel-good, psychology that mainly lets everyone save face. And I'm not talking solely about the games they play – it's the same problem in the classroom as it is on the playing field. It's so much easier to administer and grade a useless multiple choice test and to inflate every kids' grades for their college applications than it is to create challenging course work and content that excites and engages them. (See http://www.inc.com/howard-tullman/stop-promoting-mediocrity-in-our-schools.html.)

Most teachers today are doing a crappy job of teaching our kids the critical thinking and problem-solving skill sets that it's going to take for them to succeed in the new digital and global economy. And too many parents are just too busy or otherwise occupied to take an active interest and role in their kids' educations. It's much simpler to just pat your kid on the head for "trying" than it is to sit and pour over his or her homework to see what they're learning. (See http://www.inc.com/howard-tullman/startup-lessons-for-kids-and-entrepreneurs.html.)

So, you can readily understand why I would wonder if Musical Chairs is just another "too real" contest whose time has come and gone. But, for me, it's also an everyday reminder of a very critical fact of life for startups that we all need to keep in mind. Most startups aren't going to grow up to be stand-alone big businesses. A few of the best ones will find a way to get there. (See http://www.inc.com/howard-tullman/protect-your-startup-from-big-competitors.html.) But most young businesses are going to need some serious shelter from the coming storms and they're going to have to plan to fold their product or service into someone's else's success story.

There's always a lot of talk about how technology is a "winner take all" business and it's not wrong, it's just a tad overstated. Because there's so much money sloshing around these days to fund competitors and because I think we're going to see a likely return to more government antitrust oversight, we're much more likely to have strong oligopolies (2 or 3 main winners) rather than monopolies in most tech-driven markets. This is slightly better news for growing startups because it increases the pool of prospective buyers. But it's still going to be a tough road. And the early signs are already starting to show.

(1) **We've had it up to here with additional apps.**
Downloads of new apps are dropping every month and the trend is accelerating. The glut is growing and - for a new entrant - it's virtually impossible to be found among the 50,000 new offerings pouring into the app stores each month. And, in case it isn't obvious, if you can't be found, you will never be chosen. In addition, we're lazy and we're digital creatures of habit so we barely use the vast majority of the apps already on our phones. If we were better housekeepers and tossed some of these unused apps, our screens would be a lot cleaner and we'd save tons of time that's now lost searching for specific icons lurking somewhere in the mess. At best, we're using maybe 5 to 7 apps a month on any kind of consistent basis and, according to *comScore*, 50% of our activity is concentrated on a single (usually social) app. If you're a standalone app, you'd better start looking for a home.

(2) **We're gravitating to do-it-all gateways, not dedicated gadgets.**
Fitbit is flailing. Retailers are flooded with product sitting on their shelves and that makes huge Xmas orders for additional product highly problematic. How many wrists do they think we have? How many measurements really matter to most of us? And how many dedicated devices does anyone want or need when each and every day the basic functionality (steps, heart rate, BP, etc.) is being built right into all of our other mobile devices? And *Fitbit's* caught in a classic squeeze from both ends of the price spectrum which is likely to persist. *Apple* wants to own the high end and *Xiaomi* is chipping away at the lower end of the range. But there's a much bigger structural problem facing all the gadget guys.

We are a country of one-stop shoppers and it's the folks that control the gateways, the channels and the top-of-mind interfaces, not the gadgets, who are increasingly becoming the only games in town. No one is better at this game right now than *Facebook*. (See http://www.inc.com/howard-tullman/facebooks-fabulous-future.html.) Honestly, it's only a matter of time before it becomes clear that all the tracking devices, all the navigation devices, all the data-generating wearables of whatever stripe (just like all the content created by professional media publishers) will need to knuckle under and feed their results thru Facebook's front door to the consumer because that's where the consumer lives and that's where the data needs to be. Facebook's phone was a bust, but guess what? They figured out a better and far more profitable way to serve their users and they shifted all the risk, pain and costs of production onto the backs of the gadget guys. If you're a dedicated device, not made by *Apple*, or in bed already with *Facebook*, you're toast.

(3) We've decided that good enough is more than enough for most of us.

GoPro is gasping. Competition is up, diversification into drones is going nowhere fast, Christmas looks lousy, and the forecast for the year is down. And they're having a hard time manufacturing the next new thing. Sounds just like the litany of *Fitbit*'s woes. The truth is that most of us are mere mortals and we don't need the newest and greatest anything - we just need something in our price range to get the job done. And the competition is pushing the prices down and the basic quality up. In almost every tech sector, the players keep raising the bar and upping the average so that, in most cases, good enough today is plenty for the vast majority of customers. *GoPro* has burned through the pros, the enthusiasts, and the super-picky (and price-insensitive) people and now they're staring into the consumer chasm and facing a world of competitors (including all the phone manufacturers) whose offerings keep getting better, cheaper and more waterproof. It's hard at this point to imagine what they would call their sustainable competitive advantage. If you're the price and quality leader in your space, you need to start working on Plan B.

And overall, regardless of where you feel you fall, now's the right time to take a hard look at just what you have and what you've built and to sit down with your team and your advisors and discuss what the best alternatives are to capture and extract whatever value you've created in the business before it goes away. It's already past time in most cases (and largely a waste of time) to talk about how anyone is going to recoup their prior investments as opposed to their pro rata share of today's value. No one who's interested in moving forward spends much time looking in the rearview mirror. They call these kinds of dollars "sunk costs" for a very good reason. They're long gone and they're not coming back.

TULLMAN'S TRUISMS

DON'T TRY TO DO SOMETHING CHEAPLY THAT YOU SHOULDN'T DO AT ALL

Recent newspaper headline: "How Data Failed Us in Calling An Election". Here's a flash – it wasn't the data's fault – it was the media's mess. I realize that the search for someone or something else to blame is always successful; but I think it's abundantly clear who was really responsible for the situation. It was the prognosticators and the professional blowhards who got it so wrong. The truth is that the data doesn't know or care. It's like the Dude in *The Big Lebowski* – it simply abides. What you do with it and how it's used makes all the difference. If you let a monkey drive your car, it's not the monkey's fault when the accidents and crashes come.

So let's not dump on the data and data-driven decision making (which is essential to the future of almost every business) just because a bunch of over-eager media messiahs ignored the science, misapplied the mechanisms, and tried to manufacture a true miracle out of a mess of mixed messages which were never going to accurately predict the ultimate voting behaviors of millions of people who weren't prepared to share their true feelings with anyone and especially not with paid political pollsters with an agenda and the answers they claimed to be seeking already firmly fixed in their minds.

The most basic breakdown in the "research" process this time around was the fact that the pollsters weren't looking impartially for information; they were simply seeking confirmation and affirmation of what they wanted to see and hear using a deeply-flawed system and a methodology that everyone knows is meaningless in today's mobile and digital world. Just another ugly byproduct of the world of cable news where we only watch and listen to the people who tell us what we want to hear. It's the worst possible combination of an echo chamber in which you sit drinking your own *Kool-Aid*.

If you use a screwdriver to slice your roast beef, who exactly do you think is to blame for the chunky cuts that result and which end up looking totally disgusting and pre-chewed? Is it really the tool's fault? Maybe you should have used a Phillips instead of a flathead for a more presentable platter. Or maybe you should have taken a moment to think about whether the instrument you chose would ever be up to the task that you set out to accomplish. The heaviest hammer still can't nail Jell-O to a tree. We should really know by now and freely admit that no amount of historical information is likely to accurately predict certain kinds of human behaviors. Voting isn't the same as buying a vacuum cleaner – you never know what the voters will do until after they've done it.

In much the same way, if a major part of your prospective voter polling methodology is predicated on calling large parts of a population that no longer answers their phones or which has a substantial cohort under a certain age that doesn't even own a land-line phone any longer; what would lead you to believe that you had any real basis to believe your results or that they were probative or predictive of anything that mattered?

And this is the situation even before you factor in the really depressing fact that the people desperate enough to waste their time talking to strangers on the phone are as likely as not to tell those folks exactly what they think they want to hear or what passes for the politically correct answers of the day rather than how they really feel or plan to vote. The telephone is maybe the worst possible tool for eliciting the truth about anything. Political research calls are the second most dreaded calls you can get these days – only PBS pledge drive calls are worse.

But based on the self-serving and misguided <u>mea</u> <u>culpas</u> that we're reading and hearing these days in and from every major media outlet, they did their very level best to bring you the correct stories and you'd think that those rascally polling numbers underlying the breathlessly reported trends that seemed to change from minute to minute must have had a mind of their own and gone way way off the reservation and miles from the last remnants of reality. The people who can't dance always blame the band for playing the wrong music.

The truth is that the numbers are neutral at best (except when they're just dead wrong as in some of the state polls) and the data's not to blame when it's tortured and twisted in support of answers and expected behaviors that it was never capable of predicting in the first place. It reminds me of a thermos – it doesn't really know whether it's keeping some beverage hotter or cooler for a period of time – it just sits there and does its job.

If we want explanations or excuses for the fact that the folks who were supposed to know didn't know anything in the end – we have to look at them (the number crunchers) – not the numbers. They're happy to have all of the responsibility; it's only fair – given the results - that they have a full share of the blame as well.

I t's not possible these days to read any new or old material about organizational behavior without coming across a screed or two on the general subject of how too many meetings simply represent a waste of time, energy and resources. I've also written here on aspects of the same issue. (See http://www.inc.com/howard-tullman/how-to-deal-with-time-wasters.html.) These sessions rarely accomplish anything except maybe some pseudo-bonding; they don't have a logical and clearly-understood endpoint so they seem both pointless and endless; and, most often, they sorta drool to a conclusion without agreed-upon action items and/or documented next steps for at least half the people in the room.

Maybe holding meetings for meetings sake makes the miserable managers feel more productive, but they don't do much of anything for the business but waste a bunch of time. If the people in the meeting really had a choice, they'd rather eat dirt than sit through another moment of time in their life that they'll never get back to help justify someone else's job security. Managers who don't already (and always) have a pretty good idea and a solid handle on what their folks are doing or about to do (and why) aren't doing their own jobs.

Unfortunately, every business these days - regardless of age or size - seems to suffer from this syndrome and it doesn't appear to be getting any better. I even see it every day walking around 1871 and peering into our many conference rooms where two seconds of checking peoples' postures will tell you the whole sad story. Are they engaged and leaning in, are they actively contributing to the discussion, or are they just leaning back and shooting the breeze? And, of course, the worst cases of all are those where you see the alleged leaders of the meeting (who're supposed to be running the show) sprawled all over the place like a bag of spilled and soiled laundry. Watching the last remnants of any energy seeping slowly out of these unwitting captives sitting sadly in their chairs is truly depressing. I'd rather watch paint dry.

These kinds of make-work meetings are a menace to every company's momentum. They swiftly suck the oxygen and the urgency out of whatever initiatives and good ideas might be floating around. They're poorly planned, badly organized and run, and grudgingly attended by most of the participants who sit slouched in their seats trying to look engaged or trying to sneak a peek at their phones. The only people who really enjoy these sessions are those seeking a respite from doing any real work and - as a result - they're more than content to sit silently in some corner and just focus on keeping their eyes open. (See http://www.inc.com/howard-tullman/trying-to-motivate-your-employees-forget-it.html .)

Frankly, any recurring staff or team meetings (especially kick-off meetings for the week) that take more than 30 minutes are probably over-populated; attempting to cover a bunch of unnecessary stuff; giving everyone a chance to chat so we don't hurt their feelings; and otherwise driven by some foolish need to justify the time spent by the attendees in getting to the meeting. Here's a flash – the shorter the meeting, the more people that will thank you – regardless of the length of their journey. Everyone's got better things to be doing.

Sharing important and timely information in regular update sessions only makes sense if every participant consciously edits their input and if some of them - from time to time - are smart and courageous enough to pass entirely instead wasting everyone's time with a useless report or a compulsory comment. Not every department is doing something every week that honestly matters to the whole team.

Here's a simple rule of thumb for when to keep your own mouth shut – don't say a thing unless it's going to help someone else in the room do their job better. Otherwise, stifle the urge and save us all from hearing how you spent your weekend or plan to spend the week ahead. Trying to keep everyone in the loop on everything is a game for losers and a major time suck. You want your people turned on - not tired out - especially as you start out the week.

I think the key is to keep the meetings that you absolutely must have as "CRISP" as you can.

Concise: More than a couple of topics is simply too much – focus on a few important things.

Rigorous: Keep everyone on the case - start with questions – end with answers and action items.

Immediate: What needs to be done well right now – push off the stuff that can wait a while.

Short: Not one minute more than you need – no need to fill the time with fluff or folderol.

Prompt: Start and end on time – every time – and let the latecomers watch from the wings.

Who would have thought that there would be some worthwhile words of wisdom coming from Glinda, the Good Witch, in *Wicked*? I saw *Wicked* again recently for the umpteenth time and I was struck by how relevant some of the lyrics from the song "Thank Goodness" were to the entrepreneurial mindset and to the ways many entrepreneurs behave. These pithy but poignant phrases were words that any struggling entrepreneur would recognize. And they were so timely as well, given that Thanksgiving is right around the corner, when we're all supposed to be so aggressively appreciative.

One of the things that we entrepreneurs don't do well is to say "thank you" fast enough or often enough to so many of the people that matter in our lives and who make our achievements possible. Not just thanks to our peers and team members, but to our friends, family, investors, advisors and mentors as well. Why is that and why can't we do better? Of course, this could be a function of busy schedules and the fact that we're all in a hurry these days – although it's not actually that hard to be thankful and to take a minute or two to let someone know that you are – so that seems like a somewhat inadequate explanation. Praise and recognition are quick, easy and cost-effective ways to acknowledge and reward your people's contributions. And worth making time for. Success is definitely sweeter when it is shared.

But the truth is that there are some deeper-seated startup psychologies at work and, while these aren't offered as excuses, at least they're a plausible explanation for some behaviors that don't otherwise make much personal or business sense. Frankly, entrepreneurs just aren't that conscientious about taking the time to say "thanks" to the people who helped them along the way. But I honestly don't think that this behavior is because most of us are unappreciative or simply ingrates.

I think it's more that we're uncomfortable and don't quite know how to handle these circumstances when we're thrust into the spotlight. Celebrations are so yesterday. They make you feel like your goals are behind you and that's just not how entrepreneurs look at the world. So we tend to clam up and try to soldier through the ceremonies, but our heads aren't really in the game. We're somewhat awkward, completely stuck in our own minds, and maybe a little tongue-tied in these cases because – in some respects – we just don't believe or buy into the whole process and we're a little surprised to find ourselves in such a spot. It's a little hard to be gracious when your principal goal is to get off the stage.

In the *Wicked* play, Glinda is supposed to be joyously celebrating her engagement, but, as things progress and she sings about how "happy" she is, we hear more and more of a tone that suggests that she's got some very mixed feelings about what's going on around her. According to the crowd and the conventional wisdom, her "dreams" have all come true, but she's not so sure. She says that "**it is, I admit, the tiniest bit unlike I anticipated**".

And, instead of being a happy and <u>simple</u> time, "**getting your dreams – it's strange, but it seems a little – well – complicated.**" She knows that she should be overjoyed and grateful, but she's not quite there yet. We've all been in similar circumstances – waiting for someone to pinch us to make sure things are real. And it's also a bit of the "dog that caught the car" syndrome. You finally grabbed the brass ring that you've been chasing for a while. Now what? And maybe even more importantly, you find yourself – just like Glinda - wondering what you had to give up in the process to get there.

Most of the best entrepreneurs I know would tell you that they do a lot better in tough times and in dealing with adversity than they do with success and when things are working out well. Success is a little like wine. It's just hard for a true entrepreneur to believe in it. You don't believe in wine. You drink it, enjoy it for a moment, and then you try to get on with your life. Entrepreneurs are superstitious and they want to get back to work before anyone notices and before anyone can snatch the moment away. For a lot of us who are confirmed paranoids, these "celebrations" are rarely joyous occasions. At best, they're waystations on what we expect to be a much longer and harder road ahead.

It also has something to do with authenticity as every returning vet will tell you. Only the guys actually in the trenches – the entrepreneurs themselves – really know how close to the line things got – how near to the edge they came – and how much luck (and even a little fear) had to do with the outcome. And only the entrepreneur knows all the sacrifices that it took to get there and how quickly these things can turn around and race in the wrong direction. Glinda says: "**There's a kind of a sort of a cost. There's a couple of things get lost. There are bridges you cross you didn't know you crossed until you've crossed.**" These things are hard to share with folks who haven't been there.

And then there's this crazy idea that has you asking yourself exactly how big a deal it could be if you (of all people) were able to pull it off. It's a little hard to congratulate and thank your teammates when you're not sure whether you even deserve the credit in the first place. The battle's always far from over, there's no finish line – just another hill, and it's a lot more like sitting on tacks than it is resting on your laurels.

The world thinks that most entrepreneurs are beyond confident, if not arrogant, but the truth is that they're mostly scared little guys running full speed ahead, jumping over the potholes, and trying to look over both their shoulders to see who's coming up behind them to take their toys away.

Is it any wonder that they forget from time to time to say thank you for the honor?

I used to feel bad for the guys in our IT department because they had the same lifetime problem that the heads of Homeland Security have. As we all know, the terrorists and other scumbags only have to get it right one time and horrible things can happen while our counter-terrorism teams and other law enforcement personnel have to try to be right every time and then – when nothing happens – no one bothers to give them any thanks or other recognition. People just whine about the costs, the delays, and the stupid rules and figure that protecting us is what we're paying these folks to do. The best the good guys can hope for is a tie. No harm, no foul and sadly no credit for keeping us safe.

I think that the IT departments in almost every business have been similarly taken for granted (or given the Rodney Dangerfield "no respect" treatment) and they get little or no recognition from anyone even though the complexity, significance and risks associated with their responsibilities in our companies' operations have multiplied geometrically in the last decade. You basically can't do anything intelligent today in almost any business without solid, timely, reliable and accurate data – it's the oil of the digital age – and the IT guys are the ones with their mitts on the meters, mechanisms and measurements – the IT infrastructures – that are the make-or-break gates, tools and tunnels through which everything critical in our data-driven world passes. If they don't get it right, your business simply doesn't get done and – relative to your competition – you might as well be back in the Dark Ages.

So I've been spending a fair amount of time talking to and coaching IT teams (as well as working with smart startups which are developing new approaches to help cut through the clutter in big corporations so the data can efficiently get through to the people and places it needs to be) and I'm encouraged to see a few positive signs and a slowly-growing acknowledgement of the importance, the criticality and the severity of the problems to which under-investing and under-appreciating the centrality of your IT team exposes your entire company. We humans only understand the degree of our dependence on these machines and systems (which dictate so much of our lives today) when the devices shut down, the data disappears, and the systems stop delivering the information we need to proceed.

And while you can say that time eventually changes everything, the truth is that time only changes (usually for the worse) what you don't change first. I tell all the IT people that I meet that they have to be their own best advocates and change agents and act on their own behalf if they really want to see meaningful improvements and add real value to their businesses. This is no easy sell because these folks aren't really built that way and "selling" their ideas is the last thing they ever thought they'd be stuck doing. The waves of change are coming – you can swim with the tides or sit still and be submerged.

I've found that there are three specific ideas and approaches that senior-level IT folks need to focus on if they want to make a serious contribution to the future of their firms.

(1) Be a Weapon, not a Shield

Playing great defense isn't enough these days and the smartest IT players are the ones turning the data they're developing and extracting from the deluge of connected devices into "weaponized" information and decision tools that move their businesses ahead by providing better and more timely solutions to both internal users and outside customers and clients. What gets measured is what gets done and comprehensive measurement – that tracks installation <u>and</u> adoption <u>and</u> improved outcomes – is all a necessary part of getting smarter. Helping your team optimize every aspect of your operations by giving them real-time decision support puts them in a position to make the most critical calls – like when they should double down on their winners and how soon to ditch the dogs – quickly and correctly. Triage is crucial because no one has unlimited resources today and enabling cost-effective execution by providing increased metrics and visibility is what the best data-driven IT strategies are all about. Money is just expendable ammunition – data is power – and guess who's in charge of the data?

(2) Focus on the Future, Stop Patching Up the Past

Everything is about the future and we need bridges forward and not just more bandages. (See <u>http://www.inc.com/howard-tullman/build-a-bridge-over-your-old-code-not-another-band-aid-.html</u> .) The network is the name of the game and helping your team exploit the extensive resources outside of your own shop is essential. Connecting your company to the critical partners, collaborators, and new technologies that are outside your four walls (and doing so securely without sacrificing speed, accuracy or ease of access) is the most pressing challenge. Equally crucial is to make sure that your people are an active and effective part of all the "social" conversations that concern your business (but don't necessarily invite or include you) because these new channels are changing the way we all confer, compare, communicate and consume. If your products and services are part of the ongoing conversations and apart of the decision set when the buyers are ready to buy, you're nowhere. Finally, holding down the fort just isn't enough; you've got to do more than simple maintenance because your business needs a vision and a path forward – not another Mr. Fix-It.

(3) Make Sure You're in "The Room Where It Happens"

If you don't ask, you don't get. As a senior IT professional, you've got to step up and insist that your presence and your input is central to securing the best solutions for the business. There's a great song in the play *Hamilton* about the importance of being in "the room where it happens" – where the decisions are made that impact us all – and if you're not there – if you don't have some skin in the game – if you just a spectator standing around and waiting – then the changes that do happen will happen to you – not through you. It's not always safe to step up – it's never about security or the status quo – but it's the smartest bet you can make. If you don't believe in yourself and your abilities, who else will? And take my word for it, waiting never gets you to a better result because the world is just moving too quickly to give anyone the luxury of time. Just like in racing, you need to understand that no one waits for you.

If it's any consolation in these tough and troubling times, just remember that they're going to blame you for anything and everything that goes wrong anyway. So, if you're already walking on thin ice, you might as well dance.

TULLMAN'S TRUISMS

BE IN THE ROOM WHERE IT HAPPENS

Visitors to 1871 are always surprised to see so much gray hair on the heads of folks zipping around the place. (No one here saunters – everyone's in a hurry.) It turns out that a significant portion of these older folks are our mentors and, while gray hair is sometimes simply a sign of age and not necessarily of wisdom, that hasn't been our experience, and we couldn't be happier or more blessed to have hundreds of experienced business builders (most of whom are senior executives from various industries) regularly volunteering their time to help coach our new companies.

They certainly do this to aid and support our startups and to give back to our community, but they also get an extraordinary look over the horizon at the kinds of disruptive innovations that are right around the corner in their own businesses and marketplaces. It's a wide-open and welcoming window on the future. Everyone today lives in some kind of bubble and it's essential for all of us to try to get outside of our own environments and our comfort zones from time to time and get some exposure to new people and new ideas if we want to keep going and keep our companies growing. Our volunteers get a real kick out of the chance to spin out some of their own new ideas and to be innovative in their own right in ways that just wouldn't, couldn't or haven't worked in their own corporate environments where peace is often more important than progress. It's an energizing, if temporary, escape from the echo chambers and the smothering silos that they operate in from day-to-day in their own firms.

At a certain age, in the grown-up world, ideas and ideals are largely replaced by more conventional concerns and goals. Age is a horrible price to pay for "maturity". There's an unhappy concession to business as usual and, in so many of these places, it doesn't feel any longer like they're doing something new and special – reaching a top speed or setting a personal best – it feels like something they're giving in to like going bald, gaining weight or getting old. It doesn't have to be that way. We're still dreamers at 1871 and it's a totally contagious disease which hits you the moment you enter our electric and energized ecosystem.

There's a certain freedom of thought and action at 1871 (not knowing what you're supposedly not able to do is a huge advantage) and there's a compelling sense of urgency because, for entrepreneurs and innovators, the right time is always right now. There's never going to be a perfect time; the stars will never totally align; and you'll never have everything you need to be certain of anything. But that's all part of the deal and what makes things so exciting. We don't take time for granted at 1871 – it's the scarcest resource we have – and we don't believe in waiting for some perfect moment to get started because waiting never gets you to a better result. Doing is what gets things done.

This year our mentors will provide more than 7500 hours of one-on-one advice and support for our members through our workshops and "office hours" program. These face-to-face meetings are the ultimate in entrepreneurial education delivered by people who have been there; people who speak frankly and directly with no hidden agenda or ulterior motives; and people whose own innovative suggestions and ideas often contribute as much to the business's ultimate success and direction as any other member of the startup team. In addition to being people who know what they're talking about (which regrettably is not always the case with some mentors – See http://www.inc.com/howard-tullman/how-to-deal-with-marginal-mentors.html), our veteran mentors are a ready and consistent source of leads, customers, network introductions and even investments for our startups. It's a total win-win deal.

But the more important observation is that there is, in fact, a significant part of our membership who are building their new businesses every day and who aren't remotely like the Silicon Valley newbies that you might expect from the persistent media descriptions and your favorite cable shows. In fact, our members under 30 years old aren't even the majority (by age or industry experience) of all the entrepreneurs in our place.

Innovation, it turns out, has almost nothing to do with age. Innovators come in every size, shape, color and age. Being an innovator is all about your powers of observation, your openness to new ideas, and your willingness to accept and embrace change. The entrepreneurial bug and the desire to make a change that will make a difference in many people's lives can strike at any time and at any age. And we've got hundreds of examples to prove it.

We've got really smart serial entrepreneurs who are here because they see no need to make sizeable infrastructure investments and lease/equipment commitments before they know whether their new idea is as good as their last one and whether the dogs are gonna eat the dogfood this time around. It pays big dividends to "know before you go" and we make that possible.

We've got career changers who've put in their 20 years at the grindstone and now they want to do something new, different and maybe a lot more meaningful and do it in an environment where they're surrounded by individuals on a similar journey who are driven by like passions instead of sitting around somewhere where their family and/or their peers keep asking them politely whether they're having a breakdown or a midlife crisis. There are always plenty of people happy to tell you why your dreams can't come true – it's much smarter to surround yourself with people who can help make those dreams happen. It also makes sense to stay far away from the people who have a problem for every solution.

We've got Moms with kids finally in school and other eager empty nesters who are all looking for an effective on-ramp back into the workforce (along with the necessary programming, training, resources, funding and support) to help them jumpstart their re-entry into the business world with an idea or two for a business that they've always wanted to build. They don't really care to be the odd duck out at some cheap co-working space for adolescent amateurs with great coffee and beer blasts, but not much in the way of content or companionship. They like being somewhere where people know their names and share their hopes and dreams.

And then we've got a whole collection of seasoned professionals (in their 40s, 50s or 60s) who know their businesses like the back of their hands and know what new management tools and other information and resources they're going to need in order to maintain and, in fact, grow their businesses going forward, BUT (and it's a very big BUT) they don't know the first thing about the desktop and mobile technologies that it's going to take to build the solutions they need. And they couldn't build these sites, apps and/or dashboards even if their lives (and not simply their livelihoods) depended on it. So, every day we and our in-house team of recruiters act as matchmakers and connectors working to pair these domain experts with technical resources, programmers, and engineers of all ages who can work with them to design, develop and build exactly the apps and answers that they're looking for. These are marriages that are more made in hard work than in heaven, but the key is that they work well for all concerned.

What's the bottom line? There's room for everyone in the pool. It's never too early or too late to get started. Entrepreneurs have no expiration date. You're only "old" when you let your regrets take the place of your dreams

TULLMAN'S TRUISMS

THE OLDER YOU GET, THE MORE IT MEANS

If you love Springsteen songs for the lyrics like I do (not that there's anything wrong with the music, of course), and if you're not just sayin' that (like the people who used to claim that they read *Playboy* for the articles instead of the anatomy), then you know what I mean when I say that there's a line or a poignant phrase from some Bruce song that seems perfect for just about any and every occasion. I can think of dozens of time – staring down into one abyss or facing up to another impending disaster - when Springsteen was the only solace I could find. Even in the worst of times, his music has always been a touchpoint and an anchor to hold on to and, even when you may be at a loss for words, he speaks to all of us.

In *This Hard Land*, he asks a stranger: "can you tell me what happened to the seeds I've sown…..can you give me a reason, sir, as to why they've never grown?" We've all been there – as entrepreneurs and founders - asking for answers, reasons, or even just explanations to the same recurring questions. And the ultimate answer, of course, is that there aren't any answers – only the road ahead and perseverance. Two ideas which couldn't be more central to Bruce's canon.

An entrepreneur's life is a constant struggle – you're caught each day between sadness and euphoria – teetering between crazy confidence and debilitating doubt – and cranking up one of these ancient anthems is as good an antidote for the everyday angst and the anxiety which we all face as anything I have ever known. The best music takes us to another, better, place – not forever – but long enough to catch our breath, hunker down, and hit it hard one more time.

The truth is that – even if you can't recall the exact language (although a frightening amount of this stuff is stuck permanently in our heads) - you won't have to look very hard to find the specific lyrics on Google which succinctly suit each situation. What's better than chanting the mantra: "no retreat, baby, no surrender" when the going gets really rough? No metaphors required – the meaning couldn't be plainer or more direct – yes, Travis, he's talkin' to you. And it feels pretty good to know that you're not alone in the struggle. There's always someone standing there if you should falter. Crank up the live version of *If I Should Fall Behind* and say no more.

Bruce is, without a doubt, an oracle for the ages (past and present), a master storyteller for our time, and an entrepreneur as well. Every entrepreneur knows in his or her heart exactly the kinds of battles, compromises, and heartaches which he speaks of in his music. His songs describe and fit our feelings (and our failings) like a glove. The connection is similar to (but more emotionally powerful than) the way we interpret the text of every fortune cookie and each day's horoscope so that it feels like it was meant just for us. Listening to Springsteen lyrics is like re-reading a specially-meaningful verse of gospel, an inspirational letter from a long-time friend, or a final farewell note from an old flame.

The Boss can sum up in a few authentic and heartfelt words what it seems as if we've spent a lifetime living and are living every day as well. The songs skip right over all the filters and all the defenses and get right down to the fundamentals. They're perceptive and pithy without being patronizing or pretentious. Philosophical without ever being pathetic. Wise, but never whiny. Short, but oh so smart. And, as he hopes in *No Surrender*: "We learned more from a three-minute record, baby, than we ever learned in school." He's written the uber-text for our lives. And, it's virtually inescapable.

As 2016 draws to a close and we meet each week with dozens of the entrepreneurs who are building their businesses at 1871 to review their progress and their prospects, the Springsteen songs often act like shorthand in my head for the different (and often difficult) stories we're hearing. The successes we're seeing are easy to categorize and to deal with – up and to the right – double down on what's working and kill the dogs - and let's see a lot more of the same. They're - *Born to Run* – all day long.

But the much harder conversations are with the folks who are just treading water and trying to keep their heads above the waves; those whose businesses are going sideways with no positive changes on the horizon; or, worst of all, the ones running out of cash, customers and runway. It's never easy in these talks to say what no one wants to hear. But telling the truth comes with the territory and there are only a few ways – none especially kind or polite – to deliver the bad news.

A product that doesn't sell or a service that no one wants or needs isn't the basis for any kind of successful business. It may be a good feature, an attractive add-on, or a lot of other things, but it's clearly not a company in the making. And the sooner that message sinks in, the better for all concerned. It's always about time, alternatives and opportunity costs and the clock is always ticking. (See http://www.inc.com/howard-tullman/protect-your-startup-from-big-competitors.html.)

At times like these, the entrepreneurs' own frustrations and disappointment are also more than obvious — they're palpable. And these folks feel like they've let the whole world down. Bruce said it best in *Jungleland*: "…they reach for their moment and try to make an honest stand but they wind up wounded, not even dead." But the very best entrepreneurs, the ones we'll hear from again, rise to the challenge. They're dangerously honest and, at the end of the day, they don't argue with the facts or the truth. It's as hard to tell the truth as it is to hide it – maybe harder.

It takes a great deal of strength, confidence and courage to stop the frantic, full speed ahead, charge (with you in particular running willy nilly down the road) so you can honestly take stock of where things in your business actually stand. It usually takes a lot more guts to pull the plug at the right time (for everyone's sake) than to keep beating a dying horse. And make no mistake – it's also an obligation you may owe to a lot of other people. (See http://www.inc.com/howard-tullman/failure-happens-four-ways-to-do-it-well.html.) Startups don't stop until the founders give up, but sometimes stopping and moving quickly to salvage whatever you can is the smartest thing to do. Even in the darkest hours, Bruce would say that you gotta believe that there are *Better Days* ahead. Leaving the past behind is the first real step to a brighter future.

And now's a very good time to ask yourself the hardest of questions.

The process starts by acknowledging a pretty simple reality: that ultimately the marketplace decides everything. It's not what you want to sell that matters; it's what the world wants and is willing to buy from you that makes all the difference. Businesses aren't generally paid to change or reform their customers; they're paid to satisfy their needs. There are a million excuses, explanations, and other ways to avoid the question, but ultimately customers buy for their own reasons, not yours. They may say they love you – but they vote with their dollars, not their hugs. It's actually pretty easy to keep score and know the difference.

So if your stuff's not selling – even if you are the greatest salesperson in the world and could sell shoes to a snake – or talk a dog off of a meat wagon - then you have two choices: sell something else to the customer or stop selling to the customers entirely and start thinking about selling or shutting down the business. Tech startups and digital businesses in general don't typically have a lot of hard assets to sell (especially in distressed circumstances), but there's still plenty of potential value to be realized (for you and your investors) if you go about the process correctly and so long as you don't wait until it's too late. Knowing what you've got to sell is just as important as knowing when it's the right time to sell.

But it all starts with being honest with yourself. I think of a line from *The River*: "Is a dream a lie that don't come true or is it something worse?" I realize that dreams die hard, but living a lie is harder still. If you tell the truth, it becomes part of your past. If you lie, it becomes part of your future.

TULLMAN'S TRUISMS

HELP YOUR CUSTOMERS THINK PAST THE SALE

In my last blog post (See http://www.inc.com/howard-tullman/what-the-boss-can-teach-us-about-loss.html .), where I talked about when it's the right time to shut down an unsuccessful business, I said that - especially in the context of a "fire sale" – most tech startups and digital businesses don't usually have too many hard assets to offer, but that, if the entrepreneur goes about the process correctly and doesn't wait too long, there is still plenty of potential value to be realized. Sometimes, it turns out, that the sum of the parts is greater than the value of the whole.

I've gotten several inquiries and requests to detail the sale process a little more and specifically to describe in greater depth the kinds of residual assets which can retain some of their value even as the business itself slowly circles the drain. Knowing what you've got to sell and how to present it in the most favorable light is just as important as knowing when it's the right time to sell. I've described a bunch of these "assets" (tangible and intangible) below, but it's also very important to appreciate the overall context, some of the basic ground rules as you get the whole program started, and some of the complex psychology involved.

It's critical for everyone (especially the founder) to be open and willing to approach and pitch as wide a population of possible buyers as the team can identify even when some of those meetings will entail eating a healthy helping of crow and other assorted and sundry humiliations. Having an outsider (with less emotional skin in the game) represent the business in any negotiations or discussions with prospective buyers makes a lot of sense as well. This is especially essential when the pool of prospective purchasers includes former competitors because, when you're winding your business down, you can't let the conversations get all tangled up in discussions about who won, who lost, and why or they'll never go anywhere. The only goal is to get the relevant deals done – as quickly and painlessly as possible – and then to get on with whatever is next. Blame, anger, revenge, disappointment and everything else needs to be put aside.

And, as obvious as some of this may seem to outsiders, I've found that, when you're stuck in the middle of the swamp and sinking, it's hard to look objectively at the situation and try to make the best of where things actually stand. Entrepreneurs – by their very nature – regularly vacillate between the highest highs and the lowest lows and - when the end of the dream is in sight – they tend to get really down, to paint everything black with the same brush, and to undervalue some of what they have built and actually accomplished. It helps to have someone else (from the industry, but not the company) take a fresh look at all of the possibilities and evaluate all of the various assets.

And finally, specifically for the founder, even if you've made some kind of peace with yourself about the shutdown and you're ready to throw in the towel and just walk away, that's rarely the best action for all of the others concerned about and invested in your business. You don't want to throw out too many of the babies you've built with the bathwater - even when that seems like the easiest and least painful course. So, what are all these valuable assets?

(1) Sell Your Systems and Your Software

This pretty much goes without saying., but it's rarely fertile ground. And there usually isn't that much to actually sell. In the world of the cloud and SaaS, most startups don't "own" the administrative programs and systems they use (like Salesforce, etc.). So, there's nothing to sell even if they have built custom tools that operate on top of these platforms because – as often as not – those adaptations and customized enhancements are very specific to the business itself, often rift with spaghetti code and poor documentation, and held together with digital duct tape. Most acquiring competitors aren't interested in paying up for or maintaining dual systems that perform essentially identical business functions. On the other hand, if you've really cracked the code and built some special, black-box, technology that competitively sets your business apart, then stand your ground, set your price, and don't sell yourself short.

(2) Sell Your Customers and Your Supporters

By and large, customers want painless, cost-effective, and uninterrupted solutions to their problems. The clear emphasis is on maintaining business as usual. They are frighteningly indifferent to who actually supplies the tools and technology needed to meet their needs and, as a result, so long as midstream transitions can be made seamlessly and as invisibly to the clients and customers as possible, getting paid to switch your customers to a competitive platform is an attractive and common outcome in cases like this. Pretty much the same deal applies to social media assets like followers, etc. although the big social media sites haven't made this process easy. Of course, the whole migration will be much easier if you have been careful not to spend a great deal of your time knocking the competition to your own customers. Transitions that entail transfers between arch enemies are never that appealing to customers. This is why it's always safer to toot your own horn than to spend time raining on the other guy's parade.

(3) Sell Your Sources and Your Suppliers

Every business has sourcing and supply chain issues and, in many competitive markets, suppliers have agreed over time to restrict their business dealings to only some of the players in their marketplace. You may have some of these exclusive or protected connections and relationships and providing access to them to someone not already in the inner circle is a highly valuable commodity. Endorsements and most favored nations deals are similar areas as are channels where suppliers have anointed only a few players to make direct connections to their resources with everyone else being required to deal with the designated gatekeepers.

(4) Sell Your Leases, Your Locations, Your Permits and Your Licenses

Putting your business where you did and securing favorable terms and leases may turn out to be among the very smartest things you actually accomplished. Certain businesses are mainly about "location, location, location" and you may be sitting on some of the best places to be in town. Sometimes it's just as bad to be too early in your business as it is to be too late, BUT the early birds do tend to get great leases in parts of town that are still in transition, offer below market rates, and thus have substantial embedded value. In the same fashion, because regulators in new areas of disruptive innovation are constantly playing catch-up, you may have permits and licenses that are grandfathered or which were otherwise secured before the city or state or other governing body tried to pull up the drawbridge and shut down the approval process. These can be invaluable aids and assets to well-financed latecomers to your market.

(5) Sell Your Sponsors and Your Partners

Sponsors of B2B businesses are generally in it for the PR and the exposure and, as long as they're seeing the prospect of increased opportunities in that area, they're likely to ride along. Technology partners are in it for the products and services they can ultimately sell to you or through you to your clients and customers and, here again, those relationships and connections should be relatively easy to transfer. In the startup world, however, the tech players in particular are a very small set of companies and it's a better than even odds bet that they're already connected to most of the other players in your sector.

(6) Solve Someone Else's Problem and Sell Them Your Secrets

You may have lost the overall battle to competitors in other parts of the country, but, in your home town, you may be the best there is and there are plenty of people elsewhere trying to figure out a quick and easy way into your market as they look at how best to expand their businesses. You can save them a lot of time, money and mistakes by smoothing the path for them. And don't forget also that, in parts of the business, you may have figured out a better, faster, cheaper and more effective solution than the competition ever will and that's a major asset to put on the block as well.

(7) Sell Your Staff

They're not chattels, but they do need jobs and they also know almost as much about the business as you do. So, do them a favor and help find them a home. They may want to follow you loyally to the next great adventure, but you don't have one at the moment so don't let your ego get in their way. Loyalty is great except when it's a liability.

(8) Sell Yourself

Suck it up and go to work for the buyers for a period of time. If you can pull this off convincingly, and not drive yourself crazy while you're doing it, it will make all the other assets more valuable. And you might even discover that you're better at doing simply what you love to do in your new role (like selling or designing) than you were at worrying about a million details and W2 forms at the old place. And a lot happier too. Not everyone needs or wants to be the boss.

A little patience and some crucial perspective (usually gathered from people who've been there before) can make a great deal of difference in how the whole thing ends up. As surprising as it may seem, it's really not all about you. On the other hand, as you do walk away, keep in mind that your work is just what you do, not who you are – it's easy for entrepreneurs to confuse the two.

Making it too personal is a great way to make sure that it's not productive. Being honest with yourself and living with the ambiguity and very mixed feelings is crucial. As Death Cab for Cutie says in *The Ghosts of Beverly Drive*: "You wanna teach, but not be taught and I wanna sell, but not be bought". Selling isn't easy – especially selling yourself – but it's all part of the grand bargain you make when you sign up to start something up. This is the business we've chosen. What you're selling may change from time to time, but you're always selling something.

It's a little depressing at this late date to find that I still have to sit through too many strategy sessions and lengthy lectures with various academics and other "experts" (all of whom are - by the way - sitting safely on the sidelines with no skin in the game) about what tentative investors we Midwesterners are. They insist on patiently telling those of us (who are sadly forced to politely listen to this rubbish) that the definitive difference between East and West Coast investors and us is that we're way too conservative in our investments and too hesitant in our risk-taking. They also conveniently ignore the recent reports that almost half the venture investments in Chicago yielded 10x returns.

Apparently, we still haven't learned the wisdom of failure and we're frankly way too afraid to fail. Better to play it safe than to be embarrassed by a bad outcome. Imagine that. 8.2 billion dollars of successful exits last year in Chicago alone and I guess we still haven't figured out that it takes a few falls, some badly skinned knees, and a lot of other disappointments before you get to grab the brass ring. The fact is that there's nothing that hard to figure out about failure and we get it. It's an easy knock on the world outside the Valley, but it's no longer one that relates to the new realities and the Rise of the Rest.

The fact is that I've written several pieces in the recent past on how to deal successfully with different kinds of failure (See http://www.inc.com/howard-tullman/who-said-failure-was-fashionable.html.) and how failing (and learning from it) are essential parts of the startup world and of every decent entrepreneur's life (See http://www.inc.com/howard-tullman/failure-happens-four-ways-to-do-it-well.html.) and so have about a million other people. And those of us who pay even the slightest attention to these questions have pretty much read all the material that's been written on the subject. So, it's not exactly a mystery waiting for old Sherlock to come along and set us straight.

But the old and traditional assumptions and the tried and true, but very tired stories die slowly especially if you're a writer who's too lazy to look around and see what's actually happening these days all over the country and especially in the Midwest. So we continue to hear the same old stuff and the conventional wisdom from the same stale sources. Apparently, these people don't believe that we can read or that we've actually observed anything in terms of what it takes to build a successful business or what approaches have really worked over the last decade or two. Honestly, the way that some of the Unicorns of yesterday are quickly becoming unicorpses might even suggest that revenue first investing and a wee drop of caution and due diligence might not be such a bad bet.

The fact is that we farm boys (and girls) know a lot more about failure (and its attendant emotions and painful responsibilities) than the feckless frat boys on the coasts who fail happily on a regular basis as long as they're burning through someone else's money. The list of coastal unicorpses (*Quirky* or *Kitchit* anyone?) continues to grow as their VC backers casually write off hundreds of millions of dollars from grossly overfunded deals. After all, it's not like it's their money really. To make things even worse, these deals look increasingly like desperate copycat bets that would never get done elsewhere.

These "go-go-gone" deals wouldn't get a second look in Chicago - not due to some abject fear of failure – but because even the most amateur analysis would tell you that being the 4th or 5th player in a space that was a marginal business to begin with is simply a stupid idea. But, as Gene Kleiner used to say, venture capitalists will go to any lengths to try to copy someone else's success.

But the Left coast, in particular, still does have a very clear and specific edge in the "go big or go home" sweepstakes and that is all about the appetite (and, in fairness, actual skill) for rapid-fire scaling and the willingness to make big (some would say crazy) bets. Reid Hoffman wrote about this distinction a long time ago, but his observation that, in tech-enabled businesses, "first-scaler" advantage consistently beats "first-mover" advantage still rings true. It's not about failing, it's about scaling.

And it's not simply a one-dimensional equation – the momentum and excitement generated by the player who gets big quick has a clear flywheel effect – it pulls talent, funding and other critical resources to the venture and, even more importantly, takes a great deal of the oxygen (and cash) out of the marketplace that would otherwise be available to copycats and other potential competitors. (See https://www.inc.com/howard-tullman/future-of-content-marketing-simplereach.html)

There's no other place in the world where a kid who's still wet behind the ears can order 2,000 servers for immediate delivery with a straight face (along with a bankroll from some of the bluest-chip bankers out there) and actually be taken seriously. Until a lot more investors elsewhere in the country develop a willingness to commit resources at a level which is a full quantum more substantial than anything they've done to date – not millions, but hundreds of millions – it's entirely likely that the fabulous moonshots (and the monstrous flameouts) will remain a phenomena peculiar to the Valley – inexplicable (and sometimes irrational) excess combined – from time to time - with previously unimaginable levels of growth and success.

But here in the heartland, we're OK with that. The truth is that money doesn't lead, it follows and the true capital in new businesses isn't money, it's ideas. If refusing to run through someone else's money like it's water while you figure out whether you're building a real business or backing a bozo makes us conservative or too wary, we're proud of the label and don't mind a bit being painted with that brush. In the end, it's never really about the money anyway. Money is just what people without talent or passion use to keep score. In Chicago, we prefer revenues and results.

215 – LOOKING FOR LOTS OF IPOS THIS YEAR?
DON'T HOLD YOUR BREATH

Hope isn't really much of a strategy these days. I hear a lot of cheap conversation and a fair amount of wishful thinking about this year's expected abundant crop of initial public offerings, but – at least to date - there's not much to show for all the talk. I'm sure we'll see a few brand-name (and bloated valuation) deals come thru the pipeline this year (although Q1 is already in the books with little or nothing other than *Snap* to arguably brag about which is a little tough because as of the moment it's trading down 3 or 4 bucks from its opening price). You can expect to see some aggressively manipulated and short-term upward bumps in the opening sessions for some of these "winners", but overall, it's gonna be another very slow and painful season for IPOs regardless of how much hype the Street and the financial media try to manufacture. Why?

I'd say that it was for one or more of three pretty clear reasons. It's either because (1) they're a good solid and growing company that doesn't need or want the help, the heartaches, or the hurrahs of being public (they'd rather continue to focus on building their business); or (2) they're one of the bogus unicorns which have been largely hoisted on their own financial petards and now they can't figure out a way to get their deals out the door and sell their story to the public suckers without the embarrassment of a downward valuation adjustment when the underwriters actually start writing up the book on their deal; or (3) they're already a dead dog living on borrowed time and trying to prop up a tired tale which should never see the light of day, but the greed-crazed brokers and bankers are reacting to that old Wall Street maxim that "when the ducks are quacking, you better find something to feed them" (or your competition surely will) and so they're pretty much willing to try to sell anything they can get on file with a semblance of a straight face. Anything to make a buck.

You'd think that most of us had learned our lessons at least in the case of the dog deals, but there's really no evidence to support that. My Dad used to say that, if you were offered an oil and gas deal in New Jersey or a share of a thoroughbred in Toledo, you should flee as fast as you can. If these things couldn't get done in Texas, Tennessee or Oklahoma, they weren't worth doing and it wasn't a question of "if" you'd lose your money, it was just a matter of "when". To me, for several reasons, that's what the market looks like today. When I hear some of the folks talking about the IPO "window" being open for business, and I look at the junk that people are promoting, the only window I'm reminded of is in the Beatles song *She Came in Through the Bathroom Window* and the lyric: "Didn't anybody tell her? Didn't anybody see?" Apparently not.

As far as the Unicorns go, there's an internal set of obstacles and some market issues as well. Internally, they have been hyping and promoting these crazy valuations and then using them for follow-on fundraising and now when they have to justify these nutty numbers to some third-parties (even as shameless and short-sighted as most brokers and underwriters are), they're finding that the numbers just won't stand up and they're having to go back to their investors and talk about "public" valuations which may be less than the last couple of rounds of capital injections. These aren't easy conversations, but the saving grace may be that everyone in the pool at that point is part of the same bullshit bandwagon and no one really wants to mention the Emperor's lack of haberdashery. In some ways, this would be like having Ronald McDonald criticize your taste in clothes.

The second bigger problem is that the ongoing private valuation inflations have so jacked up the numbers that there's really little or no bump left for the public even if the sellers can get the offering out the door. This is why *Snap* is already flatlining. Where can you really go when you've already sucked all the sex and juice out of the story? This has pretty much been the case basically since the LinkedIn offering in 2011, but it has reached insane levels now where the comparisons between the private value return multiples that have been created and the public value return multiples are downright disgusting. Take a look at any of the following: LinkedIn, Yelp, Facebook or Twitter; and you can see the tiny fractions of the overall value that ever accrue to the public investors. There's probably no clearer demonstration of how and why we're constantly hearing about increasing and massive levels of wealth concentration in this country. We knew it was happening, but we probably didn't realize that we were some of the most active enablers.

But the most interesting discussions relate to the reasons that the good companies with great prospects don't want to go public, don't need to go public, and, most likely, shouldn't go public. There are at least half a dozen clear concerns which the management teams of these businesses consistently allude to in detailing their reluctance to go public:

(1) We don't need the money. Cash isn't an issue and we don't need public paper to do acquisitions.
(2) We don't want to incur the substantial costs – both of getting public and being public in terms of compliance, filings, etc. - and we don't need the management distractions.
(3) We don't need the additional media scrutiny and the multi-agency regulation that being a public company brings.
(4) We're not excited about the mandatory disclosures which simply serve to assist and inform our competitors and other copycats and fast followers about our activities, results and plans.
(5) We think M & A is a better exit in many cases ("we're building to be bought") and a lot more manageable and controllable than the vagaries of the public markets. It's always better to be bought than sold.
(6) We don't want to be the next whipping boy for POTUS. Bottom line: an IPO is no longer the brass ring for anyone with a brain and a real business – it's more likely to be a bunch of sad sacks and oversold salesman walking around with tin cups.

In case it's not abundantly clear to just about everyone, starting a business from scratch and then growing it into something with some decent traction, modest momentum, and a real reason for being is plenty tough. And, of course, that's just the beginning of a long, often painful, and assuredly bumpy ride. But here's the deal: you don't have to make things even harder on your business or build yourself a bigger mountain to climb than you absolutely must.

Don't try to be or to own everything – no one can afford that approach these days. Don't be too proud or stupid to ask for help, find smart partners, ride the rails that someone else already built and put in place at great cost, or use a platform that's already reaching the markets you're aiming for instead of trying to build your own. The latest and greatest case of not reinventing the wheel is how *Instagram*'s *Snapchat* clone after only 8 months already has more daily users than *Snapchat* did at the end of 2016. Snapchat is 6 years old. The message is simple. Take the path of least resistance as long as it moves you forward and plan to fill in the missing pieces down the line (if they are still necessary) when you can actually afford them.

Do what you absolutely have to do right now and do whatever can wait when you get a chance. It turns out that a lot of things, equipment, investments, marketing campaigns, etc. that were absolutely vital and mission-critical in the moment turn out to be unnecessary, outmoded, or just wrong if you give yourself a little time and space to see what happens in the meantime. (See https://www.inc.com/howard-tullman/the-beauty-of-backing-into-a-business.html .) As you develop and build out your company, you should take every chance you have to shed the stuff that doesn't matter or simply makes the struggle tougher or more expensive. Every marginal cost and capital investment that's avoidable needs to go. Spending money is easy; making money is hard. Here's the basic rule: dump the dumb stuff and double down on what can make a real difference in your destiny. (See https://www.inc.com/howard-tullman/five-keys-to-effective-outsourcing.html .)

And when the world is sending you a message or giving you a golden opportunity, you need to go with the flow. That's why The Lone Ranger used to say: it's so much easier to ride the horse in the direction he's headed. Find the fastest bandwagon out there and jump aboard. Inertia is very tough to redirect or overcome – but it's a real blessing when it's working for you.

Habits are hard to break for a good reason – they're based in what has worked well for us in the past and we're reluctant to part with them – but we're happy to expand and enhance our ongoing experiences if you can give us a solid reason and a convincing argument for why we should. The closer you can align your "asks" of the consumer/customer to existing actions and behaviors, the happier everyone will be and the quicker people will adopt your solution and incorporate it into their day-to-day lives. Why try to hurdle the fence when the gate's wide open.

On the other hand, if it's student body left and you're the only one headed in another direction, you can scream all day at the top of your lungs, but it won't make much difference or move the crowd your way. And if the technology has already advanced to the point where no one needs your help or your product or service, you might just as well pack it in and try something else. No company can produce, pivot or innovate fast enough to outrun a future that's already miles ahead of them and preordained. Our smart phones (and eventually our smart watches although it won't be any time soon – See https://www.inc.com/howard-tullman-five-reasons-the-apple-watch-failed.html?cid=search.) are already comprehensive trackers and capable of any measurements critical enough to matter to us and in our lives on a regular basis. We just don't need another dedicated device.

I wrote a piece here recently (See https://www.inc.com/howard-tullman/where-will-your-business-be-when-the-music-stops.html.) about how Fitbit doesn't have much of a future and how it really wasn't anyone's fault other than the guys who failed to realize that we need another rechargeable pain-in-the-ass device on our wrists (or tacked to our t-shirts) about as much as we need a third elbow. In fact, there are already activity-tracking t-shirts on the market. So, a product with a very, very short remaining shelf life and really no next act isn't much of a business and it's not even a novelty for much longer.

But there are smart examples of companies going with the flow that I think are worth thinking about. One, for sure, is the Chronos Disk (https://wearchronos.com) which is a thin, smart device that attaches to the back of your watch and instantly adds Bluetooth enabled fitness tracking, music controls, and a "find my phone" function. Takes a couple of minutes to attach (or remove and switch to another watch) and you're good to go. An hour into the process and you completely forget that it's even there. So, for you folks who love your fancy watches (yes, I know you're all over 30), you can have the best of both worlds in a minute. Habit? Check. Existing behavior? Check. Barriers to adoption? None.

It's pretty straightforward. Build your business to capitalize on someone else's capital investments – like TV monitors already installed in every venue imaginable. Plan your product or service so that it rides right along with existing activities – no new learning curves – no new apps to download (even if you could find them in the clutter) – no hurdles to overcome. And then it's off to the races.

Warren Buffett said it all: "I don't look to jump over 7-foot bars: I look around for 1-foot bars that I can step over."

I'm always amazed at how few technology-focused entrepreneurs understand the power and value of the calendar (maybe the lowest tech tool of all) which has been around for at least 5000 years. You'd think that everyone had figured out how it works. And it's even more depressing to learn how even fewer managers and executives use the calendar effectively to help plan and manage their businesses. So much in the business world happens on a schedule, and yet, too many sales and marketing "experts" are either ignorant of that fact or oblivious to exactly how important timing is to successful sales. If your customers aren't ready to listen or if you're pitching them at the wrong time or place, it just doesn't matter what you're saying or what you've got to sell. (See https://www.inc.com/howard-tullman/three-keys-to-becoming-a-sales-wizard.html .)

And actually, I'm not talking about just one central calendar that's critical to this task; I'm talking about developing a consistent "discovery and triage" process (updated quarterly throughout each year) to identify and incorporate the events, activities and opportunities found in <u>all</u> of the calendars that bear on your business and doing it without fail at the beginning of every new year.

<u>Discovery</u> because there are always new and relevant events (albeit way too many) beyond the recurring and basic ones and even the old standbys get refreshed, rebranding or repositioned over time. There's no upside in taking any of this stuff for granted or assuming that what may have worked or didn't work in the past for your company is the case going forward. If you don't make it someone's business to look up and carefully track these things, they'll be over and gone before you know it and you'll be sucking wind while someone else is taking advantage of the opportunities that they offer. (See https://www.inc.com/howard-tullman/do-your-customers-love-you-more-than-yesterday.html .)

<u>Triage</u> because, even though we all suffer from FOMO (fear of missing out), the truth is that even Fred Astaire couldn't dance every dance, play every stage, or be in 2 or 3 places at once. So, once you have all the data and dates on hand, you will always have to make some hard choices. Some involve time, resources, available staff, etc. and, of course, they all involve dollars. But at least when you consciously decide to play or pass, these will be your choices and not oversights, omissions, accidents, etc.

<u>All</u> because, to do this right, you need be get outside your little CRM program and track the obvious as well as the esoteric haunts of all the likely prospects and suspects that you need to get your story in front of before the competition does. If the rate at which things are moving and changing outside your business exceeds that of your own actions, plans and activities, you're on a downward path and headed to the exits. To compete and remain at the top of your game, you need to map and manage the entire ecosystem – not simply your little corner of the world. The big calendar buckets are as follows:

(1) **Universal calendars:** Annual Events and Holidays, Elections, Recurring Celebrations and Anniversaries, Film Releases, Award programs

These calendars provide obvious and easy opportunities to free-ride on and otherwise tie into available media, promotions, and content that is being generated regularly and consistently by other providers. In addition, millions of engaged eyeballs are already focusing on these outlets and channels and – if you're smart – you can "hijack" some of that volume and interest as well. I'm not talking about stealing.

I'm talking about sitting down with a national events calendar and building a full year of piggy-backing your content and linking your messaging to the constant and recurring flow of annual activities, promotions, releases and other communications that will eventually beat a path to your door throughout the year.

And – to be very clear – none of this prime traffic will include your stories unless you get ahead of the curve and make it your business to build the links and connect their content and their communities to your own media, messaging and commerce. Done well and in a timely fashion, you'll be enlisting the entire entertainment, news and media world in promoting a regular stream of your content ideas. How much easier and cheaper could it be?

(2) **Industry calendars:** Conferences, Events, New Product or Technology Announcements, Publications, Effective Dates of Significant Legislation or Regulations

This is pretty obvious and most companies do a decent job here, but they don't cast a wide enough net. Too many businesses today think that because they know a great deal about their own company and a fair amount about their direct competitors that they're on top of the situation.

But that's not where the industry disruption, the new products and services, and the most threatening competition is gonna come from. It's at the edges, the intersections and the adjacent industries where the new solutions and the biggest risks to the status quo lie.

So, you've got to have a plan to see what's going on in those verticals and other industry sectors as well and, frankly, it's the fastest and easiest way to get a boatload of new ideas on the cheap as long as you've got good shoes and a couple of days to spare.

(3) Customer Calendars: Businesses are no different from trains. They stay within some pretty clear rails and they run on schedules, cycles and procurement systems which - to a large extent - you can get your hands on if you spend the time and know what you're looking for.

Do your homework. Make damn sure that you and your sales team understand the budget and buying cycles of your top target customers and prospects. These things are set in concrete. And bad timing can be the quickest deal killer of all. Plus, if you show up at the wrong time, it's pretty obvious to the customer that you don't know much about their business, their calendars or their requirements. Don't make this amateur mistake.

There is one exception to this rule, and it depends entirely on your relationship with your buyer. It is possible that, on occasion, you will tumble into an *Alice in Wonderland* scenario where the buyer lets you know that, instead of their budgeted funds being totally spent, they have excess funds which they need to spend in order to avoid having their budget cut the next year. Make a compelling offer, sign the deal, take the money and run.

(4) Other Calendars: Educational, Government, Political, Regulatory & Administrative

Here's the bottom line. There's nothing sadder than a salesman who returns empty-handed to report that he or she just missed the boat. They got beat out by someone who was there at the right time, or they got misled or misinformed by the client about the purchase schedule. You learn that, in a lot of selling situations, the client doesn't want to say no to your face. So, you're told it's too early in the company's cycle to buy or commit, until one day the potential customer finally breaks the bad news to you that it went elsewhere. In sales, the rule of thumb is: "it's always too soon until it's too late."

There's never a perfect time for the customer to buy because most of them would just as soon not buy anything if they had the choice. It's the sales person's job to control the clients' calendars; to always be in their faces; and to be there whenever the customers are ready to buy. It's all about "at-bats" and always asking for the order. Lots of important things are lost for lack of asking. You never want to be at the airport when your ship comes in.

I've always admired the engineers at Mercedes-Benz for many reasons. But their most consistently admirable quality is their restraint. By and large, for at least the last decade or two (with the notable exception of the utterly useless Touchpad introduced in the last couple of years which looks like the horn on a western saddle and adds nothing of value to the vehicle), the guys at Benz never "gilded the lily" or added technology purely for tech's sake. Maybe that's because they have the maniacs at AMG to add that kind of crazy stuff for them, but I like to think that it's because they reject the "too much is not enough" attitude of some many of the other car manufacturers. Anyone who has suffered through the multi-year nightmare of BMW's iDrive system know exactly what I'm talking about. The only thing the oxymoronic iDrive system wouldn't try to help you do was drive the damn car because you could never figure out the controls.

The simplest example of doing things the right way and the one that I have cited for years is the inside rear view mirror. At one time or another almost every luxury car group – except Mercedes – felt that it was absolutely essential that the rear-view mirror be powered and remotely controlled for adjustment purposes just like the side view mirrors. The guys at Mercedes thought that it was stupid to add a feature like that when you could simply reach up with your hand and make whatever adjustments were needed. Quick, easy, and accurate with no time wasted trying to find the right button or control. Now, of course, with the advent of the rear-facing cameras in almost all of the higher-end cars, some of the utility of the rear-view mirror has gone away, but it's still the first thing that a smart driver adjusts in an unfamiliar car so some things never change.

The moral of the story for startups is simply this – it's increasingly possible when you're building new products and solutions to overshoot the need, the utility and the demand for a certain degree of technical support and assistance and end up with simply too much technology for your own good. This can add complexity, costs and confusion to the equation without increasing the value or the utility for the end user even a little bit. Think of this as the vehicular version of *Occam's razor*. The simplest solution is most often the smartest. And, as I wrote recently (See https://www.inc.com/howard-tullman/dont-slow-up-your-startup.html.), it's always easiest to go with the flow. And, when you add long-standing consumer behaviors, habits and preferences to the calculations, the case for building easy-to-access and even easier-to-use solutions becomes more compelling. The best technology disappears into the solution.

As I have watched Amazon (with the amazing Dash buttons) and others (like Samsung with its new "connected" refrigerators) increasingly establish beachheads in the kitchen for ordering and replenishing just about anything, I 've been struck by two facts: (1) they are building off what they have and the systems and equipment they've already invested in instead of looking for the best solution for the end user (an inside out "Steve Jobs" focus ("we'll tell you what you want") rather than outside in – finding out and designing what the customer really wants); and (2) they all seem to have overlooked a most basic fact of life and a relatively primitive tool that we have all pretty much taken for granted for years now. I'm talking about the bar codes that appear on virtually every non-perishable product in the world. None of these high-tech systems takes advantage of the decades that the food and consumer products industries have spent in building massive databases and a ubiquitous classification and identification system even as we – the world's consumers – are being re-introduced to this very fact by virtue of the self-service checkout aisles, counters and machines which are being deployed in almost every major retail chain. I made very similar observations just recently (See https://www.inc.com/howard-tullman/the-most-underrated-planning-tool-in-business.html .) about how smart it is to use something as simple as a calendar to manage your business and how often we overlook that tool. So, you might ask, why don't we have a simple and similar solution in our homes. Of course, the vast majority of folks (tens of millions of homemakers) are still using pen and paper to make their lists and praying that they won't forget the list when they hit the market.

But if you want to take a small step toward the digital future, what could be a simpler way of building your grocery store list (or reordering commodity goods on the spot) than swiping that empty can, package or container past a simple bar code reader that lived in your kitchen. It beats the daylights out of the best phone app because you don't have to stop doing whatever you're doing while you wash your hands and find your phone and open the right app and – sorry Alexa – the simple barcode also has all the detail and specificity that you really need for this kind of order built right in so that you don't have to spend time teaching Siri or Alexa the entire taxonomy of the Safeway snack aisle. Swiping takes a few seconds and is virtually flawless. And, as you might imagine, the retailers and marketers out there would love nothing better than (and be happy to pay for) to get up-to-the-minute demand reports from millions of homes on exactly what homemakers were purchasing without having to what for the largely-antiquated in-store POS systems to crank out the data.

The good news is that - at 1871 - it's just a matter of time before someone walks up to you with just the solution you're looking for. One of our current WiSTEM companies (Lystr Technologies, www.getlystr.com) is building exactly this gadget right now. And it's a bifurcated solution as well – you can swipe any barcode – or, if you wish, just speak to the device and the product will be added to your smartphone grocery shop list. It's clean, it's relatively tiny (no one needs another clunky anything on their kitchen counters, and it's pretty much foolproof. I'm excited to see just how long it takes for all the major grocery chains to start coming around our place to check this baby out because it could be a down and dirty Amazon killer which the bricks and mortar guys are clearly dying for.

And, by the way, there's no reason that every restaurant in the world wouldn't think this is a no-brainer as well. Stick it in the pantry, store room, cooler or back of house and train the entire kitchen staff to keep track of what's 86'd from day to day so your supplies and inventory are always current. Hospital supplies – pretty much the same deal. In fact, any organization that regularly uses and consumes disposables should get on this kind of a program.

It's not "high" tech, but it beats the heck out of running out of essentials when you need them or forgetting half of what you need when you run to the store. Just sayin'.

219 – IT'S VERY HARD TO BE IN THE HARDWARE BUSINESS

I talk all the time about the battle raging in Detroit (for the moment) between "smarts" and "steel" and how every day the hardware guys are losing more and more of their share of the actual value in each vehicle as the software and the sensors take over and the user's experience (what's going on inside the car) takes on increasing importance and significance as compared to the mechanics (what's under the hood and what gets you to where you're going) of the journey itself. If you wonder why there's so much conversation and noise about the entertainment centers, video displays, cameras as well as the connectivity being built into the new cars and trucks, it's because pretty soon we'll all just be sitting quietly and passively in a comfy seat while the car takes us where we need to go. And your insurance company will be happy to insure you and your car in the near future as long as they're sure that you're not actually driving it. I'm not really sure at the moment whether I think that smart cars or smart roads (like they're building in Atlanta) are the best bet (See https://www.inc.com/howard-tullman/why-smart-cars-are-stupid.html.), but, take my word for it, within 3 years, some of us won't have to drive ourselves anywhere.

And don't think for a moment that it's only the car guys who are under the gun. I think everyone who makes stuff is gonna have to get more aggressively into the content/software part of the game pretty soon or they'll be left behind. If you want to see an early warning sign of the trend, consider that Apple's just reported iPhone 7 sales declined and, while Tim Cook blames it on the advent of the iPhone 8, that seems to me to be only a modest part of the explanation. I think that - for a growing part of the population who religiously buy the latest and greatest - we may be reaching an incremental demand saturation point where good enough is actually good enough and we conclude that there are plenty of other things to spend our discretionary dollars on. It's hard to justify to your CFO (from a financial perspective) buying an expensive new phone with at best imperceptible functional improvements when the device you have is more than sufficient to get any and every job done that matters. Call me when the battery life actually lasts a full day and I'll be the first in line.

I'm getting the feeling that more and more of us are increasingly focusing on the function rather than the form of so many things. We want the hardware to do its job and get out of the way – we're tired of celebrating the box and now we're paying far more attention to the beef. Only engineers and designers care about whether the edges of my new phone have disappeared. The camera is definitely the new keyboard and capture/communication device, but I'm into its speed, ease of use, and functionality rather than its good looks since pretty much every phone that matters today looks about as good as the next one coming down the line.

But it seems that a lot of folks apparently haven't gotten the memo yet and it's depressing to watch these slow-mo crashes as they're happening or to see someone who's about to run into a brick wall. My favorite new commercial catastrophe is the upcoming Fitbit smart watch which is intended to compete with the Apple offerings in that space. Keep in mind that last quarter Apple moved past Fitbit to become the market leader in wearables. Of course, that's not much to brag about and I'm not sure anyone really noticed or cared especially since Apple doesn't break out stats on the watch. But regardless, winning this category isn't much to write home about; it's a little bit like being Dolly Parton's shoes.

I've already said my piece already about Fitbit and the living dead syndrome (See https://www.inc.com/howard-tullman/where-will-your-business-be-when-the-music-stops.html.) which is how I see their future. And I made my position clear on the Apple watch a while back as well (See https://www.inc.com/howard-tullman-five-reasons-the-apple-watch-failed.html.) So right now I feel like FitBit's latest smart watch initiative is anything but smart and it's even more reminiscent of the old college adage that: "when 3 different people tell you you're drunk, it's time to lie down and take a load off". These guys need a prompt and radical pivot, but it seems to me that they're knee-deep in fast-setting concrete and unable to get out of their own way.

The move away from building physical goods for all these guys can't come soon enough. (See https://www.inc.com/howard-tullman/six-reasons-not-to-manufacture.html.) If you're Apple with a cash hoard exceeding $250 billion, you've got to be looking at how really well your services business (iTunes, Apple Music, App Store, etc.) is doing (just for comparative purposes, Apple's business is almost 3 times the size of Netflix and twice the size of Amazon's AWS) and saying how do I accelerate this part of my business even more rapidly? This is the world today - not how fast am I going, but how fast am I getting faster?

Even with the stock setting new highs seemingly every day, you've got to be looking over your shoulder and asking one crucial question: why is Apple getting its ass kicked in streaming media? They're not even on the leader board (along with Facebook which is also not a player yet) while YouTube, Netflix, Amazon and Hulu keep growing their shares. Remember the iPod? These are the guys who made mobile music/media a reality and today – at least for the foreseeable future- they're nowhere.

But things may be starting to change. It looks like yet another iteration of Apple Music (based obviously around branded and bite-sized video offerings) is stirring and we may see the first offerings (already oft-delayed) in the near future. Honestly, I hope so because otherwise the Beats acquisition will continue to look almost as bad as Yahoo!'s purchase of Tumblr which still holds the decade's dumb buy title. Of course, no one will ever retire Time Warner's lifetime stupidity title for the AOL acquisition.

I'm good. No mas. In fact, I'm up to here in unused apps and mystery buttons that, at best, are befuddling because I no longer have any idea of what they do or what they're for. It's great to have a cool-looking button for your app unless no one can remember or figure out what it means or does 3 or 4 days later. I'm sure that when I downloaded each and every one of these mission-critical apps, there was a very solid reason and a crucial need (hah!), but today I don't have a clue. It reminds me of the days when you'd automatically accept every LinkedIn or Facebook request to connect because – after all - who could have too many contacts or friends? Be the first on your block to download the newest app whether you need it or not.

The truth is that I'm starting to worry about whether I can spare the space on my phone any longer for these rusty and remnant placeholders from the near and distant past. And it's a little depressing each week when the App Store reminds me that I have 87 updates to download as well. So, thanks, but no thanks. Please do me and my mobile a favor and don't bring me your newest app to add to the vast array of orphans already sitting unloved and long untouched on my phone. We have jumped the shark and reached the apex of apps. It's all downhill from here.

Even if I could find your new app in the App Store among the 40,000+ new entries each month, I'm basically not interested because my plate is more than full. Of course, the very fact that it's so noisy, cluttered and expensive to try to launch a new app and get the word out to the marketplace and especially to the likely users is the second reason why it's pretty much a waste of breath to bring me your new breakthrough productivity product or umpteenth social media solution. (See https://www.inc.com/howard-tullman/want-your-app-to-succeed-get-it-out-there.html .) The one exception to this rule is that – in the case of company-developed internal and proprietary connectivity, communication and productivity apps – where the company can mandate and control distribution, installation and usage by its employees (and measure these criteria as well), then new apps can still be very important and powerful tools.

If I wasn't such a lousy housekeeper, 70% of these tired and tiresome things would be gone and no longer taking up the very precious parcels of real estate which are the screens on my phone. In fact, while some of the buttons are vaguely familiar, I'd say that I have no concept whatsoever of what about 25 of these things were even supposed to do. And you and what's happening on your phone are no different. Whatever these things were supposed to be doing to us or for us, they're not doing squat today.

It seems that we're all digital hoarders for no good reason. I'd say that it's just another instance of the persistence of the path of least resistance. Honestly, it takes about two taps on an icon and a simple press on the little "x" to make these things disappear, but we can't bring ourselves to do it. Is it because we got them for free and we love hanging on to a bargain? Are we saving this stuff for a rainy day – just in case there's a pressing need for some conference event app that you last used in 2012? Maybe. Too bad there's not a Task Rabbit to come take care of this torture for me.

The real explanation for the problem is actually older than time. It's mostly about custom and utility. We are completely creatures of habit, loyal or lazy (you decide) and we get set in our ways, sheer inertia takes over, and we're reluctant to budge because what's working now is fine (or at least good enough) for us. (See https://www.inc.com/howard-tullman/keep-it-simple-stupid.html.) The numbers we're seeing from ComScore and others don't lie and they are frighteningly consistent. We might "touch" a dozen or two dozen apps a month (I think that estimated number is way too high), but, even if it's accurate, it's a fleeting affair at best. We stick with the stuff that works and dance with the one(s) we brought to the party.

Right now, we are spending almost half of the time we engage with our phones on a single app (usually our primary social network) and we spend 90% of the time on the 5 apps that we use the most. This doesn't leave much running room for any of the new kids on the block and when you see how quickly the Instagram knock-off of Snapchat Stories blew right by it, you can also understand that – even if we're willing to take a quick look at something new – we're suckers for the tried and true. There's a lot to be said for one-stop shopping. As I've said, the power of the ubiquitous platform (See https://www.inc.com/howard-tullman/why-platforms-is-the-new-plastics.html.) is the heart of Facebook's continued dominance. Facebook remains the Number One app for anyone 25 and older. (See https://www.inc.com/howard-tullman/facebooks-fabulous-future.html.)

Bottom line: No one's looking for new places to go. And we don't need a newfangled app to tell us that.

GrowCo was great again this year and there's no place like New Orleans to let the good times roll. I had a chance to catch up with a bunch of old friends and get up-to-date on where their businesses are headed and what they see as major issues for their companies and for their continued growth going forward. The future isn't really clear for a lot of us, especially with the uncertainties in D.C. these days, but it's also not going to wait for any of us – so we need to keep moving forward. Overall, I thought the tone was upbeat and optimistic, but, of course, what else would you expect from a gathering of great and upcoming entrepreneurs.

It was cool to hear some very encouraging news from Steve Case about his new book and the Rise of the Rest; Sheryl Sandberg provided some real insights into new, simple and cost-effective tools that Facebook is deploying to help startups and growing businesses compete effectively with much larger firms and far more precisely direct and target their scarce marketing dollars; and Kevin O'Leary is always good for a few laughs, but also definitely tells it like it is. It's clear that we can all learn something new at sessions and gatherings like these and there was plenty of valuable content and a lot of tips and information that I thought could be put to immediate use by almost every attendee – speakers included.

The room for my talk on "future-proofing your business" was packed (I'm happy to report) and afterwards I had a chance to answer specific questions from about a dozen attendees. I also did a Q&A video for the INC. website which should be up soon. Many of the folks I spoke with said that they wished their whole team had been there for the presentation and a few suggested that it would be great if I could put a blog post together which hit on at least some of the major themes in my presentation so they could share them (along with their thoughts and notes) with the other key individuals in their own shops.

It's tough to compress 200 slides into 1200 words, but I'm willing to take a shot at it. So here goes.

(1) Time is Scarce, Choices are Many, Speed is Everything

If you're not in a big hurry, you're probably too late. Every business today needs to compete along the various dimensions and vectors of time – speed of access, inquiry, response, service, delivery, payment – you name it. The desires, demands and interests of consumers and customers, partners and vendors, and even regulators and government agencies continue to grow and accelerate and, if your focus on an everyday basis isn't on how fast your business is getting faster, you'll be out of business soon enough.

(2) The Future is Here Now, It's Not Incremental, It Won't Wait for You

Playing it safe and waiting for near certainty and relying on processes that used to deliver the degrees of visibility and precision which were typical in the decision-making of all organizations is actually a risky strategy today because far too many competitors (both large and small) are out there who are willing to move immediately and suffer whatever the consequences may be. Jumping off the cliff and fixing things on the way down is business as usual these days and the truth is that – once you've taken the big leap – a lot of the imagined impediments and serious concerns just fade away. What we're seeing over and over again is that baby steps and incremental changes and improvements are comforting in the near term, but they aren't going to change the game or move the needle in the long run.

(3) Constant Change is "Business as Usual", Iteration is Essential, Cannibalize Yourself

If you don't keep raising the bar and outmoding yourself, you can be sure that someone else will promptly come along and do it to you. I like to remind people that, if Zuck is worried about Facebook being replaced by the latest and greatest new kid on the block, then we (mere mortals) should all be quaking in our boots. Change is the only constant today and you need to make yourself into a moving target – always trying to move your business ahead – and ideally being over the next hill before the competition even figures out where you're heading. Technology will help you along the path and speed is crucial, but take the time to make a thoughtful plan first – even if you know that you'll need to change it a million times thereafter – because, if you don't care where you end up, any road will take you there. But if you want to build a real business and make a difference, make a plan first.

(4) Better isn't Enough, New and Different is Essential, Loyalty is a Crutch for Losers

There are a million "me too" products in every market today and making yours a little bit better isn't a formula for success or a way to build a sustainable competitive advantage. You need to be thinking about how these new technologies can help you to do new things and to do things differently in ways that will set your business and your products and services apart from the pack. Consumers today have almost infinitely choices and very low, if any, switching costs. Their only loyalty is to themselves and they're only loyal to you as long as you keep delivering real value and as long as they haven't found any better alternatives yet.

(5) Mass Customization, All Things to Each Person, I Want What I Want When I Want It

Everything today is about me. I want it my way all day. That used to be an impossible task at scale for almost any business. But the good news is that we have tools and technologies available now that are accessible to almost any business regardless of size (as Sheryl said) and reasonably cost-effective. These new data-driven solutions permit you to be all things to all people and to deliver the right content at the right time and place in a customized and individualized fashion to millions of potential customers.

Bottom line: We have plenty of content, activity, data, demands and noise and not remotely enough time, attention, focus, engagement and information. The most successful businesses of the future will help us master, organize and intelligently deal with the vast choices, inputs and resources now available to us in order to permit us to live fuller, better and more productive lives. It's gonna be a bumpy and frightening ride in many respects, but well worth the trip.

In business, as in life, at the end of the day, your good name is all you've got. Reputations and brands can take a lifetime to build and only moments to mess up or destroy. The list of examples is endless and too painful to recount. I still believe in the value and efficacy of a good brand name (although my enthusiasm is waning), but then I'm an old guy and a pretty traditional buyer. And yet, even I have changed some of my ways. I can remember only a few years ago when I would happily pay a ridiculous premium to buy Sony products (especially big screen TVs) and now it's hard to even find Sony equipment in most big box retailers.

Samsung seems to have just come along and killed Sony (while no one - including Sony - was looking) and honestly no one to date has taken the time to figure out how and why and/or especially how quickly Sony's demise devolved. And you can relax because I'm not gonna be the one to waste your time or mine in trying to suss it out today mainly because that boat has clearly sailed and no one needs to read more old news.

I'm sure there's a lesson or two in that pitiful pile (all the ponies are long gone), but they're most likely to be either frighteningly obvious or not really worth learning. So, if you care, you can go there, but for me, the sad Sony saga is at best a simple and instructive footnote in the changed ways in which we need to think about the value and impact of strong brands. If you take your customers for granted or believe that you own them for life, they won't be your customers for long. Nothing is the future forever.

I wrote about this issue a while ago (See https://www.inc.com/howard-tullman/does-your-brand-matter.html) and I said at the time that a strong brand can be a form of shorthand to help cut through the noise and the clutter for consumers who are clearly suffering every day from decision fatigue and definitely need a helping hand as they choose between so many available options. But investing more deeply in pure brand-building today only works if your current and potential new customers willingly buy into your brand's promise(s) and believe that you can deliver the underlying value in the transaction. You can't push a rope or drive a customer to do much of anything these days – the best you can hope for is to lead them gently and authentically toward the right decision. Brand used to be the last line of defense against an educated consumer and product parity in the marketplace. But it's no longer capable of getting the job done alone.

We're seeing that overall trust in brands is constantly diminishing (by now, it's just under 50% of all adult consumers who simply don't believe in the claims of traditional advertisers and, of course, the millennials are even less credulous) which means that everyone who's out there trying to sell something needs to look specifically at their company's offerings, the channels they're employing to reach their targets, and their own competitive circumstances in order to determine whether their ongoing and/or expanded brand investments will continue to provide meaningful protection and reasonable returns. I'm not too optimistic.

I still believe in the basic brand proposition. It's a little like having a powerful celebrity endorsement. You don't know how much it's worth (or how much it adds to your story) until you no longer have it, it ages out, or someone else takes it away from your "heroes". Jordan will always be Jordan, but Curry and Kayne are the new, hot guys on the street and they're killin' it. No self-respecting kid today - except for a few smart-ass sneakerheads – would willingly be caught in a pair of Jordan kicks. The trains keep movin' down the tracks and nothing stands still for more than a moment. What's red-hot today is ho-hum tomorrow. And your brand alone is not going to be enough to keep you in the game.

It's a lot like TV these days. For now, it's still laying those golden eggs, but the eggs are getting smaller and less attractive every quarter. In limited cases, the numbers and the eyeballs are still there, but in most instances, no one cares because they're old folks and coach potatoes – not today's active and mobile consumers. The conversation is headed in the wrong direction and, for the networks, there's really no going back. CBS is for seniors and proud of it (or maybe settling for it). Fox is for fascists and perverts. NBC is like Nutella. Looks like chocolate – tastes like crap. And ABC is an also-ran that isn't even in the consideration set any longer. Whatever the names and brands of the traditional networks used to stand for, the jig is up for good. Today they stand for mediocrity, mendacity, money uber alles and the triumph of the lowest common denominator, which is a pyrrhic victory at best.

The die is cast. The next several generations of viewers have already made the switch to multi-modal digital media consumption and they're not coming back. And this is at a time in the revolution when the two most critical players (Facebook and Apple) are only belatedly awakening to the virtues of streamed media. Traditional TV is toast – someone just needs to tell those guys to lie down and die.

Real value today isn't being attributed to brand assets to the same extent it previously had been – now it's all about customers. Customer connections, customer engagement, customer retention and customer word of mouth (WOM). If you aren't getting better and faster at what you're doing, you won't be able to compete much longer in this "what have you done for me lately?" world of progressive and constantly increasing consumer expectations.

If you're not constantly raising the bar, you're on the way to going broke and your brand's not much of a barrier to the relentless onslaught of social media which has basically seized control of these crucial conversations. If you're not easier to do business with than the next guy, you'll be the last guy pretty soon.

It's not enough to say you don't suck or that you're no worse than the next guy, you need to be something special – stand for things that matter and make a difference – or you'll get lost in the shuffle. The best brands are a sacred promise, but just saying it doesn't make it so.

Social media is an ongoing and basically 24/7 production process feeding an expanding set of digital channels that need to be understood, rationalized, and managed - at least initially by you as the CEO in terms of creating the "voice" and direction of the communications and in determining the objectives being sought – because - whether you like it or not and/or choose to stick your own head in the rapidly shifting sands – your social presence is increasingly the first look at, the first impression of, and effectively the digital front door of your company as well as a bunch of windows into what's apparently going on inside. Take my word for it, if you're not out there and in control of your story (to the extent that it's even possible any more), the vacuum will readily be filled by any number of other people (employees, ex-employees, competitors, advocates for a million causes, etc.) with their own good and bad axes to grind.

SM is such a critical part of every business's business today that it really can't be left to the alleged professionals (hired guns at old-line agencies who generally know almost as little about this stuff as you do) or simple delegated to those of your employees who have the attitude, aptitude, and interest in creating some of this material. If your own people are active and willing participants in this parade of good and bad news (and everything in between), it's also likely that, in some cases, whether you know it or not, they've been encouraged by their managers and peers (theoretically within the bounds of reason and good taste) to create some of this material on their own (without supervision or review) in order to "authentically" help to tell your company's story. Not only is it unlikely that anyone asked your permission, it's also most likely that no one bothered to tell you much of what's going on. So, as sad as it seems, you don't really know what's being said out there about your company.

And, if your business is like most of the SM newbies out there who are running to catch up while wearing concrete sneakers, you've got a lot of otherwise productive time and energy being spent by your people (and possibly a pile of money as well on outside vendors) in the unclear pursuit of who knows what. And, in case it wasn't obvious, if you're asking your own amateur employees to do the job on their own time and dime, you can count on getting what you pay for. Don't even get me started on the questions of who "owns" the stuff that's being spewed.

I'd suggest that it's time to take stock of the situation and figure out if the prize at the end of the path is even worth the time and effort it's taking to get there. In most cases, the way things are being done today, the answer is that it's demonstrably not. (See http://www.inc.com/howard-tullman/the-trouble-with-social-media.html) Just doing things to keep people busy because you've been told that you need to do something is not the same as getting things done that matter for you and your business. And, for sure, paying the professional panderers for the privilege of reaching an audience of idiots and other click-bait bozos isn't worth the trip. But it's nothing something that's going away so it's on you to figure out what to do.

Even some of the smartest publishers don't know (or maybe they just don't care that much about) the difference between tricked traffic which isn't worth squat and actual active attention which is the golden fleece. I regularly see leader boards celebrating the success of various headlines in capturing viewers' clicks (although not necessarily actual readers) without the slightest reference to whether the underlying articles were even worth reading. (Tip to headline writers - numbers under 5 in listicle headlines and the use of celebrities' names are big draws.) I guess traffic will always trump teaching moments in the new media world where monetization means more than meaning.

And clearly video assets will forever more triumph over verbiage. It appears that a central and largely unfounded fantasy of the new gig economy is the get-rich-quick idea that imagines cadres of kids (and plenty of grown-ups as well) creating homemade videos in their bedrooms or basements which are launched into the cloud and then magically reach millions of viewers. As an aside, the creation of podcasts is a branch of this behavior which is almost exclusively reserved for adults (both as producers and consumers) because apparently listening is much harder to do than looking and the kids today just can't be bothered to pay that much attention to much of anything.

The second phase of this fever dream is that the world immediately reaches out to these amateur auteurs and fervently demands more of the same as well as offering princely sums of money for the privilege. Hefty influencer contracts, product endorsement opportunities, peer and brand recognition, and ultimately maybe even "real" employment quickly follows and all is well throughout the land for the new media maestros. And, so as not to miss the bandwagon, suddenly every business is in the video business as well and there's a video crew (generally composed of otherwise unemployed film school graduates from the area's colleges) trying to spin the day's every activity into something golden which they think the world wants to see.

Now, I wouldn't really care if this was mainly an academic discussion about loads of people with little better to do than watching lots of videos of charming cat musicians and/or infinitely less entertaining compositions where we see morons inventing new ways to fall off of things or otherwise impale themselves. But the viral virus keeps spreading and it will inevitably impact your business. The overall glut of this garbage has advanced to the point where it's important for every entrepreneur to at least understand a little bit more about what's really going on because the increasing noise and clutter just keeps making it harder and harder to get your messages through and to reach and effectively engage with your current and prospective customers.

Social media – well done and well-managed – can help you break through and connect with the right audiences if you make it your business to get smart about it. If you think it's a fad or something that's going away, you don't get the way the marketing world has changed forever.

It's just like in poker. If you don't have a clue about who's in the game or the pool and what they're doing, the patsy at the party is most likely you (or it will be soon enough) and that's an unhappy and ultimately untenable situation that never ends well for the ones who end up with the short end of the stick. Get busy or get left behind.

TULLMAN'S TRUISMS

PEOPLE UNDERSTAND ENERGY BETTER THAN FACTS

I'm not sure that, in the last year or, honestly, in the last decade or two, there has been a single deal (assuming that it closes as planned) which will be regarded as a more impactful transaction across multiple industries (and the entire omni-channel economy) than Amazon's recently announced acquisition of Whole Foods.

In addition, I don't think, going forward, apart from one of the Big 3 auto guys (or maybe Daimler AG) buying Tesla, that there will be another deal of this game-changing magnitude. So many of the other deals being discussed are "so-what" stories at best and, as I always say, two warm cups of coffee don't make a hot drink. So, I wouldn't waste a lot of time or breath on what's next, the question for today for grocery chains and independent markets across the country and, frankly, for <u>all</u> retailers is what do we do now?

And you can believe me when I tell you, as I suggested above, that this isn't just a concern for the guys who sell cantaloupes and kumquats. In case it escaped anyone's attention, Amazon is well on its way to becoming the nation's largest apparel merchant as well and that's even before the rollout of its just-announced Prime Wardrobe business which provides an at-home, try-it-before-you-buy-it, clothing service. And, because it's Amazon, the new offering comes with a special and very appealing little twist, the more of the ordered and inspected items you decide to actually buy, the cheaper the whole order will be for you. I like how this "bundle before you buy" incentive approach has you mentally accumulating and acquiring more and more things in your head before they even arrive on your doorstop.

I don't have any special sauce or secret solutions for the nation's merchants, but, if I was going to start trying to plan my increasingly bleak future, I'd want to be sure that I at least understood all of the dimensions of the deal and all of the different levers that this acquisition affords Amazon. My sense of the general media coverage has been that it's a little long on hype and hysteria and fairly light on helpful information and analysis.

So, I thought it would be useful to try to briefly outline the 3 very distinct legs of the strategic stool and how each element enhances and extends Amazon's position in the marketplace.

(1) Distribution/Access

Yes, the Whole Foods deal is an aggressive bump (over 425+ stores will remain for sure – at least for a while – and they can be delivery depots and mini-warehouses as well – and not merely for groceries of course) in Amazon's distribution channels (but WF's systems are almost certainly not up to Amazon's performance levels or expectations). The much more salient point is ready access to affluent parts of the population. Whole Foods stores aren't uniformly spread across the country – they are highly concentrated in upscale areas – and, as a result, provide access to an enormous number of exactly the kind of customers Amazon loves right along with their disposable income. Almost half the U.S. population that matters (probably not a politically correct thing to say) is within a hop, skip and a jump of a Whole Foods market.

(2) Replenishment/Cross-Selling

Shopping for our groceries (especially staples and commodity products) is basically a chore – not a pleasure and the less of it we have to do, the happier we'll all be. There's a reason that across the country we now spend more on food outside of the home than inside. No one needs to go anywhere any more to replenish the basics that they buy over and over again. We estimate that 70% of what you purchase each week at the grocery store is the same old stuff. So why wouldn't you have it automatically shipped (for free of course) by Amazon to your door. They spoiled us with a single click solution a long time ago and now we're moving toward no clicks at all. As their systems get smarter and smarter, we won't even have to press the Dash buttons any longer, they will know when we're about to run out and we won't have to run out any longer.

Even more compelling from a "getting to know us" standpoint is the fact that about 60% of the current Whole Foods customers are already Amazon Prime members. The cross-selling opportunities and the data-driven incentive plays are off the charts. Prime members are already princes and princesses online and in the Amazon stores (which is to say they pay less for just about everything) and it's only going to accelerate as they are increasingly identified and linked while they're in the WF markets. Special pricing, coupons and rebates on your phone, deliveries that beat you back to your burrow, etc. It's going to be a whole new level of omni-channel communication and it's going to make shopping elsewhere a complete time-wasting drag.

(3) Engagement/Trial

And it's not simply the productivity and efficiency savings that will make the new shopping experiences so special. Remember that it was the guys from Whole Foods who changed the entire supermarket experience for the better in the first place. They turned the mundane into the magnificent and made it fun once more to go to the store. Costco figured out how to get Dads back into their stores (tech, tools and TVs), but Whole Foods made it fun for the whole family. Hopefully, this is an area where the general Bezos bloodletting ethos won't overdo it. Save me money for sure, but don't turn the place into an Aldi where you feel like you've gone colorblind because every generic package looks like the joy and the excitement were actually drained out before the products ever hit the shelves.

The good news is that the opportunities in the stores are so additive and important (from an experience, repeated trial and data standpoint) to Amazon's ever-increasing accumulation of behavioral information and ultimate objective of knowing everything about us that I think they'll leave things alone for a while. Having 400+ living labs to try a little bit of everything has to bring the purest joy to Jeff's little beating heart. And, if he drives the crazy WF prices down to some realistic level over time, I'm sure none of us is going to be unhappy either.

I'm discouraged with the underlying quality and delivery problems of the vast majority of the new on-demand services. I think many startups are killing the golden goose before they even get a chance to start growing. There's a lesson here for everyone. You can't scale with slugs and snails. Regardless of how cheap and plentiful the labor force may be or how receptive the market is to trying new ideas, you can only rely on novelty (and on "buying" loyalty with discounts and other breaks) for a limited amount of time if the underlying fundamental value of the service isn't there or when the way that the service is delivered consistently fails to meet the realistic expectations of the customers.

The new app adoption curve is high (assuming anyone can find a new app amidst the noise and clutter), but the abandonment curve (how quickly we dump or discard these new offerings) is 10 times steeper and only getting worse. The still-born IPO of *Blue Apron* last week is merely the latest indicator that "buying" customers with promotions and marketing dollars is an expensive and ultimately futile way to build a real and sustainable business. The people on Main Street who ultimately have to pay for these things are a lot less interested in hype and broken promises than the hustlers on Wall Street who are trying to sell shares in these "story" stocks to the newest suckers. But that's another story for another day.

And, to be clear, I'm not blaming the apps themselves for the service results and the outcomes to date. If it's a smart and productive app, with a useful and well-designed interface that's easy, and you have a decent plan to get it out there to the market so someone will see it, then I'm all for it. (See https://www.inc.com/howard-tullman/want-your-app-to-succeed-get-it-out-there.html.) At the same time, I think in general that the apex of apps is upon us and, in recent posts, I've done more than my share of dumping on the future prospects for the app economy. (See https://www.inc.com/howard-tillman/we-have-reached-peak-apps.html .)

However, the real problem now isn't that we are drowning in new apps or that the apps are crap, it's the people behind the apps who are increasingly the problem. Not the coders (they're just fantasists building the slick front doors and fancy interfaces for the apps); not the marketers (they're lying about the efficacy and consistency of the underlying services, but it's likely (unlike car salesmen) that they don't necessarily know that they're lying yet) and it's not even the young entrepreneurs who have never had to deal with the day-to-day realities of getting ordinary worker bees (and, worse yet, gig workers of all ages) to clean up, show up, buck up, and do their jobs the right way - all day - each and every day.

Here's the truth. If you're in a "hurry up" business today (and, frankly, who isn't?) and building your business in the economy of now, you can't build your operation and scale it with indifferent people who just don't care. (See http://www.inc.com/howard-tullman/why-whatever-will-sink-your-business.html.) This is the hard lesson that we're learning every day in the everything-on-demand economy. It's easy to build an app to let people ask for anything - it's really hard to field a team of trained and talented people that delivers the required service and support every day. And this is a big challenge for companies which are mounting and launching product and service delivery businesses based - not primarily on their tech - but on the people they rely upon to get the job done. It only looks easy from the outside.

Almost none of the entrepreneurs I'm seeing even have a path to a viable solution because they don't realize how hard it is to motivate people these days and, more particularly, to keep doing it each and every day. Motivation is exactly like bathing whether we like it or not. If you don't make it your business to do it daily, pretty soon your body and your business will start to stink. And, here's another flash – by and large – none of these folks care about the business or the company you're building, they mainly care about themselves. And, if you think you're gonna get them to simply sign up for your sacred crusade and walk through walls for the greater good with sweet talk and option grants, forget it. The "right now" economy works for them as well – they want to know what it is that you're doing for them (and paying them for) right now.

You need a strategy and a solution that speaks to them about them – their interests, their needs and their objectives. You won't be able to "sell" them anything, but you can show them plenty and help them to understand. It's all about PROPS.

My particular PROPS are **P**ride, **R**espect, **O**wnership, **P**ower, and **S**tyle. If you want your people to commit and put their hearts and souls into their work, you need to help them understand that - in the end - it's all about them and the choices they make. To work well for you, their work has to also work for them: (a) they've got to like themselves, (b) they've got to like what they're doing, and (c) they've got to like how they're doing it. You can help them in this discovery and education process, but you can't push them. These are "new" collar jobs and they require some adjustments on everyone's part. The process always starts from the same point: any job can be a creative and satisfying endeavor if you put some thought and energy into making it one and anything you routinely do in an unthinking stupor will eventually bore you out of your mind.

Here are a few ideas to share with your people to help them get to the right place.

(1) Pride
No one comes to work to do a decent job. Everyone wants to get better. And no one is hired to sit around and eat chocolate cake all day either. It's important for every team member to be proud of their work and to understand that the work they are doing makes a difference. People never forget how you made them feel. You should appreciate and recognize effort, but ultimately the respect and the rewards need to go to the ones who deliver the demonstrable results. Your business should be built on your people's pride in their exacting execution and consistent craftsmanship.

(2) Respect

You will never go wrong betting on the best in your people. If you don't respect your people, you shouldn't expect much from them in return. Make it clear that no job is too small or so unimportant that it's not worth doing well and that no job is beneath anyone in the business. Everyone is there to get the work done and expected to help. In some cases, it may not be the best (or highest) use of someone's time to pitch in, but it's always important to the company's culture that the underlying message be delivered. You're all in the boat together – sink or swim.

(3) Ownership

It's critical that each team member takes ownership of and responsibility for making their job into something worth doing and then getting their particular job done as well as it can be done. Nothing in business today is more critical than careful measurement combined with strict accountability. Without effective, real-time measurement, it's not really possible to keep score. Especially in creative businesses, getting the most out of people isn't necessarily getting the best out of them. Your main metrics have to be rigorously aligned with your mission. You owe it to the best of your people to make sure that when it matters the most, you'll know exactly who measured up and got the job done.

(4) Power. A shared and noble goal is an enormous source of power. An important purpose which is understood and adopted by all is a more effective driver of any desired behavior than rules, regulations or any other exercises of simple power. Ideas may bring people together, but it's ideals that hold them together. When new people enter a culture with a powerful work ethic, it quickly becomes their norm. Being surrounded by people on the same path as you makes you up your own game. Enthusiasm and pride are both highly contagious and informed enthusiasm (not blind faith) is not only a force multiplier, it's one of the most powerful engines of success.

(5) Style

How you do the job is almost as important as the job you do. Attitude trumps aptitude in today's collaborative and team-based businesses and determines your altitude as well. You want to be the one that everyone knows they can count on in a pinch. (See https://www.inc.com/howard-tullman/to-succedd-be-the-one-everyone-can-count-on.html .) A different world can't be built by indifferent people. The truth is that you can work with someone to improve their skills and make them better, and that is almost always worth the investment, but there's no cure for a lousy attitude and the sooner you remove the problem, the better your business will be. Not giving a damn doesn't make them bad people; it just makes them bad for your company.

Bottom line: successfully building and scaling a business has always been (and will always be) about the quality, commitment and the talents of the people you're able to attract and retain – at every level of the company – as you grow. There's no standard handbook, approved organizational structure, or simple set of rules and instructions that you can rely upon because every new business is unique and no one's been exactly where you're headed. But you'll never succeed by yourself so the main goal is to find other strong people to join you who are willing to help set the course, steer the ship, and counsel the crew as the journey progresses. They need to have two specific qualities above all – highly motivated to do something important and never satisfied with what they've accomplished to date.

Many years ago, I realized that there were enormous advantages to developing new data-driven services and solutions which provided real-time access to comparative corporate intelligence in ways that could overcome the barriers to effective information flow which existed within many large businesses. Too many companies didn't know what they knew or what they had and did a poor job of sharing and communicating the knowledge they were aware of. Today, we have newer companies like Knowledge Hound (See https://www.inc.com/howard-tullman/how-knowledgehound-sniffed-out-a-new-platform.html.) and 1871 alum Baloonr (See https://www.inc.com/howard-tullman/common-communication-mistake-destroying-productivity-success.html?cid=search.) helping companies address specific aspects of this problem.

It was also clear way back when that the same kinds of issues existed within entire industries where groups of competitors operating independently needed to have certain kinds of critical information made available to each of them which they couldn't efficiently accumulate or practically/legally share easily among themselves. These were often oligopolistic markets with very large players operating essentially in their own vertical and narrowly-focused silos who couldn't even see what they were missing much less come up with a solution. Basically, they needed someone independent from outside their industry to build a common, shared (call it "horizontal"), and broader data platform for them.

One of the simplest examples of this type of solution was the development (in my first business in the auto insurance industry in the early 80's) of a computerized service which I called *VINguard*. Initially, it was simply a program that let insurance adjusters validate and decode the 17-digit VIN (Vehicle Identification Number) for any car that was involved in an insurance claim for a theft or a total loss. Embedded in the VIN number by the manufacturers was a bunch of descriptive information about the car in question which could save the adjusters considerable time in data entry and which would also make sure that they were dealing with the properly-described insured vehicle.

But that wasn't the only problem which the auto insurers had. It turned out that the costlier problem was that crooks and other con artists would take the VIN number from a single wrecked car and then use it to obtain insurance coverage from and file false claims with multiple different insurance companies for the same allegedly destroyed or stolen car. Amazingly, the insurance companies at the time never talked to each other or exchanged information about suspect VINs that should have been taken out of circulation.

And, of course, this situation was the opportunity we saw at CCC and which *VINguard* addressed by creating and constantly updating a VIN database built from information drawn from the claims departments of all of the large automobile insurance companies which was then provided back to them as an anti-fraud tool. We broke down their silos and created a horizontal data platform that spanned the individual insurance companies and solved a problem that they really couldn't solve themselves. In essence, we sent them back their own information and charged them for the privilege. But, in so doing, we saved them time, resources, and unnecessary payouts as well as increasing the productivity of their people - all at the same time. So, no one complained.

This, of course, is all part of the power and value of building an industry-wide platform which I've written about in the past. (See https://www.inc.com/howard-tullman/how-ridescout-demon-strates-the-power-of-the-platform.html.) You make the investments and do the hard work of building it once, it's used by many who couldn't justify the time or investment to do it themselves, and you take the money to the bank.

A more recent example of the same idea is Rippleshot. Rippleshot (www.rippleshot.com) is a company started several years ago at 1871 which is a provider of fraud-deterrent services helping merchants and card issuers help protect themselves from stolen credit card numbers in ways they can't do alone. Other examples abound.

Bottom line: In today's global and inter-connected world, shutting yourself off in what seems to be a safe and secure silo offers little real advantage or protection. You probably know what your own business is all about and you may even have a fairly clear idea of what your direct competitors are doing and planning. But that's not the problem.

You need to access and understand the criticality of everything that is going on around you and especially outside the four walls of your own business. The coming changes, disruptions, and new technology solutions as well as the changing demands of your clients and customers are not simply head-on challenges – they're lateral attacks, competitive entries from adjacent markets, and newly-enabled ways of doing business that never existed before.

Uber wasn't a better taxi company – it was a harbinger of the new world.

These aren't the best of times for the tech industry where every day it seems like another jerk emerges in the news as the latest poster boy for ego and entitlement who can't figure out how to keep his hands to himself and/or his ugly mouth shut. And, seeing so many feeble attempts and faux justifications made in the name of the need for speed and scale doesn't really advance the discussion or help to improve or explain the situation.

It's as if we're saying that because we're in such a hurry to be huge, we don't have the time to be decent human beings. But, come on, there have to be some basic behavioral ground rules and also a little more substance to the culture of the tech and entrepreneurial community than simply the celebration of cash, cars, and creepy/chauvinistic CEOs chugging Cristal. I get that money doesn't care whose pockets it ends up in, but morals and menschkeit actually do matter.

And I realize that - apart from the obvious and easy cases of gross and overt behavior - it's not quite as simple as you might think to create some guidelines and guard rails for these situations because – as much as we don't like to admit it – many of these businesses are being built and run by beginners and – as often as not – they're no more advanced and informed in terms of their people strengths and skills than they are in any of the other areas of operating and growing a business. You can tell people things over and over again until you run out of breath, but ultimately you can't understand for them. If they don't get it and take these ideas to heart, the job just doesn't get done.

And, it gets even more complicated when you try to put a stake in the ground and commit your team to certain important ideas and values because - in the real world – even the most sacrosanct values are somewhat mutable and, in the context of a new and growing business, some of them actually do have to change to some extent – at least from a priority perspective - as time passes and the business grows and hopefully matures. There are concerns and necessities that drive the operations of a startup (like making payroll and keeping the doors open) which aren't the same as those which a larger and more established company can "afford" because survival in the short run sometimes trumps the desire and ability to secure other social goals. Even if your heart is 100% in the right place, it's hard when you're in a hurry to serve too many different masters or to try to be all things to everyone.

Democracy in decision making is a good simple example. (See https://www.inc.com/howard-tullman-four-reasons-democracy-ads-up-to-mediocrity.html .) It's absolutely clear that whatever the "deal" was when the startup got started about everyone being consulted and having a vote on everything important to the business doesn't usually last beyond the first fundraising. There's just not enough room at the growing table for everyone to have a seat. And, more importantly, too many things become time-sensitive to let you take the time to take everyone's temperature on every question. There are solid business reasons, as the size and complexity of your business grows, to avoid inviting everyone to every party. (See https://www.inc.com/howard-tullman/with-this-much-help-youll-never-get-anything-done.html .)

But none of these legitimate considerations are intended to excuse the plain old boorish behaviors or worse which we're reading about today and the truth is that no entrepreneur can afford to create a company culture which isn't based on certain fundamental beliefs which are established right at the start of the business. It's a lot easier from Day One to live up to 100% of your values than 99% because there's no end to that slippery slope once you begin to move in that direction. And you never know how deep your commitment really is until those values are stress tested. Talk is cheap.

If you build a business based exclusively on speed and shortcuts – even if you claim to be acting in the best interests of your customers – you'll eventually end up with a second-rate solution. If your best idea is always to blame the customer and never take responsibility for the cause and the remedy, your products and services will surely and shortly suck. Worse of all, if you encourage your people to embellish the truth or flat out lie to your customers, they'll also eventually lie to you. Fish and businesses rot from the head down. There's a right way – not necessarily an easy way – to do these things, but it starts at the top of the organization.

And when you do get it right and your culture is clicking on all cylinders, it's a beautiful thing. That's why it's especially encouraging for me to occasionally stumble upon a story worth sharing that suggests that there are still people in our business who actually give a damn about the things that really matter. This is one small such tale.

We were in a board meeting for one of our EdTech companies and talking about the usual KPIs and basic business stuff and about how various aspects of the company's product development and enhancement efforts were progressing and especially how quickly we were moving to bring some of these new and critical features to market. And July's an especially tough and stressful time in the EdTech world because the start of the new school year is just around the corner and, if you're not there when the doors open, you're nowhere.

You spend a lot of time in these meetings trying to deal with the "nice to have" versus the "need to have" issues. There's often a lot of jargon and abbreviations in these "technical" conversations, but it appeared to me that one major set of fixes and updates (which had been a gating factor for a lot of the work to follow and consumed a lot of time and resources) were finally done (or almost done) so that the developers could move on to some of the next changes which were clearly revenue and student acquisition drivers.

And here's where the conversation got really interesting. The just-finished changes weren't gonna add students any time soon. They weren't going to drive new monthly or quarterly revenues. They weren't even being requested or required by current customers who were basically happy with the status quo or ignorant of the requirements. And, under the best of scenarios, the changes were addressed to the needs of only a tiny portion of the potential user population. This didn't feel like either "need" or "nice" to have – it felt like the last place the team should be spending scarce resources or critical time.

In fact, it turns out that there's another category in the consideration set for companies that care about what they're doing and why. It's called "right to have". What were the changes all about? They all related to upgrades in ADA-compliant accessibility. Keyboard capabilities, screen readers, and captioning – all necessary to make the company's products available and workable for everyone. Changes that were anticipatory and miles and miles ahead of the market, most of the competition, and even their own users. And, make no mistake, this was heavy lifting and a lot of thankless hard work.

Bottom line: Not necessarily the place that the numbers or non-stop notoriety would ever take you, but the right thing to do if you're trying to make an important difference in people's lives.

TULLMAN'S TRUISMS

COMMITMENT, NOT AUTHORITY, PRODUCES RESULTS

Not everything worth doing is worth doing to the Nth degree. Just like you can overthink and over-engineer your technology (See https://www.inc.com/howard-tullman/can-you-have-too-much-technology.html.), you can foolishly try to achieve levels of immediacy, proximity and/or precision that frankly no one really needs or cares about (except maybe a few of your geeky engineers) and burn through lots of cash, waste a lot of time and energy, and frustrate your own people in the process.

It turns out that in the real world good enough is often good enough (See https://www.inc.com/howard-tullman/keep-it-simple-stupid.html .) and that trying to be better than that (or perfect) is more about your own neuroses (or bragging rights) than an attempt to address the actual needs, requirements and desires of your people, users or customers. Six Sigma needs to take a step or two back because, while it's a great goal and a significant standard to shoot for in some businesses and contexts, it's a foolish fantasy and a false formula in the majority of cases.

Constant observation and measurement, ongoing review and iteration, and continuous improvement are essential to your long-term success, but getting out too far ahead of your skis, spending more than you can afford shooting for levels of unnecessary precision, setting standards that make no sense and add no value to your offerings, or trying to address too broad a set of needs and customers are all formulas for expensive failures. Worse yet, these ever-elusive objectives distract you and divert attention and resources that need to be focused and applied to far more critical needs.

It's way too easy in our metric-driven digital world to fall in love with stats and factoids and to pursue the numbers while losing sight of the desired end game. (See https://www.inc.com/howard-tullman/the-curse-of-microsoft-excel.html.) I remember long arguments with clients in one of my first businesses where we tracked customer satisfaction by making millions of phone calls each year to consumers at home to determine how satisfied they had been with a recent experience. It might have been a service visit, a sales encounter, a meal or a hotel stay.

The clients (and their internal bean counters) were always worried about the numbers – how many interviews had we done – how many were fully completed – how many customers were happy or unhappy. And, believe me, I know those were important considerations. But what they never understood was that the most important measurement – the real goal of the effort – was to successfully connect with and, if necessary, "fix" the customer. It was critical to show them that the reason for the call was because we cared about them and their satisfaction – not that we needed to be sure that our CSI or NPS scores were up to snuff. And, even more importantly, that we would try to correct and resolve any problems or issues which they had. If we were interrupting something important, if they just didn't have time to talk, if they didn't care to participate – the critical action was not to push them or browbeat them into participating so we "completed" the interview – it was to politely apologize for bothering them at a bad time and hang up. Getting it right (not pissing the customers off) was more important than getting one more incremental interview done.

We see similar problems when IT departments exceed their brief and try to achieve levels of company-wide information access without balancing the potential risks to the business against the actual (not imagined or assumed) users' needs. Trying to create and maintain ubiquitous data solutions can create unnecessary exposures from a cyber security perspective for your organization without adding any incremental operational benefits. The truth is that all of the people almost never need access to all of your data and especially not all of the time. This is the constant tension between "real time" and "right time" access that too few companies take the time to understand and manage.

One of my favorite examples which exposes millions of businesses to peril is permitting real-time access for employees working outside of the office to inventory, shipping and billing records on the company's main computer systems. While email and collaborative work groups are obvious instances, these are relatively well-understood problem areas and - although overall employee compliance and security diligence generally still sucks – this isn't where the kinds of catastrophic business invasions, data and financial manipulations, and ransom lockups and accompanying demands are likely to come from.

The more common exposures and most serious breaches come thru the most mundane of access points which the entire business tends to take for granted and assume that there are no exposures of consequence inherent in the activities around such basic business processes. The facts are clearly otherwise and we hear every day about outside penetrations where company and customer data is stolen, company funds and materials are misdirected and diverted, and millions of dollars of false receipts and invoices are created and fraudulently paid. All right under the noses of the company's financial and audit teams.

But there are some fairly simple solutions and I think that almost every business can figure out a method within their SOPs to take a step or two back from the newest frontier and focus on protecting your basic business instead. And here's a flash – you need to worry about this because your IT guys are all about the latest and greatest and fastest and whatever. They know that it only takes one security hiccup to bring the house down on their heads (and they know that it's fairly inevitable and that, at best, they can only play for a tie anyway against the bad guys) so they spend their time focused on the things they can control like access, speed and response times even these are the most likely gates to cyber Hell. When all you have is a hammer, everything looks like a nail.

But you can do better than that (and greatly improve your company's odds of avoiding a data disaster) and you can do it quickly and without spending a lot of time or money. There are a bunch of approaches like air gaps and sneaker net systems, but I'm just going to focus on the one I've used successfully in the past which I call the DMZ.

To build your own DMZ, you start by asking who outside your four walls needs access to your internal data and servers, why they need it, and how immediately they need it – both in terms of access and in terms of the timeliness of the data they are trying to get. What you will find is that a lot of people need little or no immediate access (if they ever need it at all) and that a lot more people can live very happily with levels of access and immediacy that get the job done for them without exposing or jeopardizing any of the company's critical servers and systems. Once you scope and scale the problem, building a straightforward solution is simple.

In our case(s), we knew that we had hundreds of sales and support people in the field all across the country and they needed to make regular inquiries, BUT they rarely needed the information they were seeking to be real-time data. It was totally acceptable for more than 95% of the inquiries for specified data to be delivered same day data – not last minute. And so, we built the DMZ which was just a disconnected data repository into which we dumped (and regularly refreshed) relatively current data (up to 8 times in a 24-hour business day) which everyone in the field could access any time, BUT those inquiries were never connected or attached in any way to our in-house servers. They had sufficient and timely information to respond to their needs and their customers and we had a one-way, bullet-proof system that never let the outside world directly access our systems. Everyone in the place slept better and no one was really any the wiser or missing anything they really needed to do their jobs.

Bottom line: even if we could give everyone on the team perfect information in real time and at all times, we couldn't afford it and it's not worth the attendant risks. Good enough to get the job done is good enough.

TULLMAN'S TRUISMS

PERFECT IS NICE, BUT NO ONE CAN AFFORD IT

We were honored and excited last week for 1871 to host Anna Catalano (See https://www.linkedin.com/in/annacatalano/) to speak to our members (and especially the past and present participants in our WiSTEM program for female entrepreneurs) about successful leadership. It's actually quite a pleasure and a relief to hear from someone with years of experience who built a substantial and multi-decade career in a major industry at a global corporation (BP/Amoco) instead of a wet-behind-the-ears "expert" who's had about 15 minutes of startup success and actually had no clue about how he or she got there or what to do next. Luck and plentiful VC lucre are no substitute for a lifetime of learning and a lovingly-presented litany of lessons (good and bad).

There's a lot to be said and a great deal to be learned from people who have actually been there before and done what you're hoping to do rather than from newbies who are inventing their "careers" as they roll along and hoping at the same time to get their businesses built and scaled before they run out of time, cheap money or good ideas. And, it's fairly rare to find great mentors who have melded their business activities and successes with enough thought and analysis to actually extract something more than just the same old war stories from their past. Not every mentor is a good deal or a good use of your time. (See https://www.inc.com/howard-tullman/how-to-deal-with-marginal-mentors.html.) Anna's analysis was invaluable. Even more importantly, she made it her business to talk about some of the areas that rarely get addressed in polite panels and other discussions.

She covered a number of important topics (including unwritten rules, lifelong networking, making your way in your own way, and not hiding your light under a bushel basket), but I was especially interested in the last section of her talk which focused on what she feels are the factors which consistently (and often abruptly and surprisingly) derail great leaders (without regard to gender) who looked to the outside world to be cruising along at the very top of their game. Her very frank and thoughtful comments were extensive and she expanded on her basic ideas during the Q&A session. There was a lot of important content and I just want to summarize her five key bullet points on the leadership issue and add a couple of comments of my own. I'll take full responsibility for any interpretations that don't make a great deal of good sense since Anna's comments were right on the money.

Needless to say, all of her comments are ways in which any leader can easily lose his or her direction and they're everyday risks and concerns for all of us. But they're especially important – given the news these days – for the young and inexperienced leaders who are sitting in the scary (and somewhat shaky) catbird seats on top of fast-moving and rapidly expanding startups. (See https://www.inc.com/howard-tullman/theres-no-excuse-for-being-a-tech-jerk1500059719.html.) Only in Hollywood these days do they still believe that you have to "be" 15 years old in order to understand what a teen wants to see and hear or spend their parents' hard-earned cash on. Age, maturity and relevant experience are slowly creeping back into the equation. I wouldn't hold my breath for any wholesale housecleaning any time soon, but some of the signs at least are hopeful. More unicorns are cratering into unicorpses every month.

We're officially at the end of the "fake it 'til you make it" era and I say that its expiration is long overdue. (See https://www.inc.com/howard-tullman/three-ways-to-put-more-sting-into-your-social-media.html.) Go big or go home is also getting to be a pretty tired tale because it turns out that real sustainable businesses not only have customers, they've got revenues and profits as well. And everyone is getting over the media's fleeting fascination with the latest Boys Wonder. These "little" leaders who are drinking their own Kool-Aid and who think you can fool all of the people at least some of the time (while you're trying to figure things out) are on their way to a rude awakening and an abrupt collision. There are rarely skid marks when a startup business blows up because in too many cases no one who mattered was looking, listening or cared about that big ole locomotive coming down the same track from the other direction. Or they weren't paying attention to the many little cracks starting to appear in the sides of their rapidly sailing ship.

In her presentation, Anna focused on 5 specific shortcomings that are most likely to cause problems. These were my main take-aways.

(1) Leaders who stop listening

Listening is a critical leadership skill and the highest form of courtesy as well. Leaders who don't listen end up as losers and their companies become laggards. (See https://www.inc.com/howard-tullman/shut-up-and-listen-will-ya.html?cid=search.) And it's not just listening to the people around you – it's listening to your customers as well because no one will ever give it to you straighter than the story you'll hear right from the customers' mouths.

(2) Leaders who don't stay grounded

You'd think that – even in these crazy times of radical change – most people would have learned to stick with what has worked for them in the past (at least until it doesn't work any longer) and also to hang on to the advisors, the tools and the techniques that got them to where they are, but they haven't. It's still too easy to lose touch with your roots, to get too big for your britches, and to think that you've become endowed with some superhuman powers. We're all human and – if we're smart – we're also constantly learning from everyone around us because you never know who's going to bring you your future.

(3) Leaders who let problems get worse.

Nothing except some wines I suppose get better all by themselves, but problems that start out small rarely disappear – they grow, they fester and they get worse if you try to ignore or minimize them. We see this every day as businesses that should clearly know better do a lousy job of controlling these problems while they're small and instead let them get totally out of control. You can blame social media and cellphones for amplifying the scale of these things, but it's not a new issue and the best companies have always known that it takes just short of forever to build a great brand and only a few highly-visible boo boos to jeopardize the crown jewels. And the truth is that great leaders look at problems not as nuisances, but as opportunities to get better. (See https://www.inc.com/howard-tullman/so-youve-got-problems-thats-probably-great-news.html .)

(4) Leaders who don't see change coming.

The list of losers who didn't see critical changes coming to their industries – from Blackberry and Blockbuster to Borders - just keeps growing as the rate of change and the emergence of new technologies keep accelerating. Today the question is no longer how fast you are, but how fast your business is getting faster in delivering whatever your product or service may be. No one can afford to stand still and the best companies spend a lot of time and energy looking over the horizon to see what's coming their way. This is precisely why so many of them are engaged now with startups at 1871.

But, as I told Anna after her session, I think that the companies that <u>did</u> see the changes coming - like Kodak which invented digital imagery, but didn't want to bring it to market and kill their own film business – or the Swiss who created, but shunned, digital watches, and let the Japanese come into the market and put 50,000 Swiss watchmakers out of work in two years (1979-1981) – and instead of reacting – turned a blind eye or tried to ignore or bury the risks - were actually the worst offenders because they were afraid to face the facts.

(5) Leaders who don't manage their impact on others.

I always say that no leader should expect his or her people to listen to their words and ignore their actions. Leaders are everyday role models (like it or not) and – in their daily interactions with team members - can cast light or shadows, but they can't escape the impact and the impressions they make on everyone around them – often without even knowing or appreciating just how substantial those might be. And, in the broader context, where we're all so intimately and continually connected, the statements and the brand "promises" that your business makes bounce all around the globe and, here again, even the best of us can only control a small portion of the stories being told. But the fact that it's harder these days than ever and that it's a 24/7 job to try to say on top on doesn't excuse anyone from trying or relieve anyone of the responsibility for and the consequences of what they say and do.

Bottom line: there's no magic bullet or mystery to this stuff. It's not so much a case of being instructed as it is one of needing to be regularly reminded that (a) nothing good happens by itself and (b) you are the person primarily responsible for making the right things happen. Come to play every day, pay attention to the details, don't take anything for granted, and keep raising the bar. However high you've risen, it's still always about attitude and not altitude.

I've been thinking for some time about the need to remove the social and economic stigma from vocational training - starting in our high schools and community colleges where it's largely disappeared - but especially at the college and post-college level including particularly the kind of high-end training which we provided at Tribeca Flashpoint College for students who wanted to work in the film, game, broadcast and media industries and who were in a hurry to get started. We're beginning to see some increase in the volume of discussions and even some recent commentary on the subject, but the progress has been too slow and sporadic to make much of an impact or any real difference so far.

And frankly the overall situation isn't as simple or straightforward as it might seem because - while everybody wants to get better and get ahead and thinks they should - these things don't happen by themselves and even the best solutions are only suitable for a small segment of the population. You've got to want it, be willing to work for it, be right for the job you're seeking, and not get too far ahead of yourself or too far out over your own skis. This isn't a cure-all for the world's problems or an overnight panacea, but it's very clear that, if we don't get started on addressing the problem, things will only continue to get worse. I'd rather see a serious solution to a portion of the problem than a bunch of folks sitting around bemoaning the absence of a perfect answer.

There's no longer any question that education and training which equips a new graduate with the tools and technologies that it takes to join today's tech- and data-centric workforce is far more likely to lead to solid earnings and long-term employment in our new digital and global economy than an expensive and traditional 4-year program which leads nowhere and creates - at best - so-what social "skills" at a time when the marketplace is increasingly looking for meat-and-potatoes, hit the ground running, value-added players who can be additive on Day One and make an immediate impact. People still looking to find themselves are going to find fewer and fewer places willing to hire them and pay them while they struggle down the path to career nirvana. This just isn't the way the world works any longer.

But an even bigger concern and a much greater exposure for our entire economy relates to what efforts we're making across the board in our businesses to upskill our existing workforce - especially the folks in their forties and fifties - who basically lack the digital skills and smarts that they will need to be valued contributors to their businesses in the next few years. We know, they know it, and we're basically doing nothing about it. This is really where the rubber will hit the road and where we're gonna need new commitments and training programs for significant portions of this currently-employed, but severely at-risk, population rather than the newbies who at least are largely digital natives - not digital immigrants like all of the rest of us. These people (millions of them) aren't going to age-out in time or just disappear and no business will be able to retain them as they continue each year to become less and less effective.

But - even if a company is ready and willing to make the right moves and commit the time and treasure that it will take to get the program started - it's a tricky process. As I noted above, there's not enough room for everyone on the new ark and it's going to require some hard decisions and many difficult conversations. Some of these areas are highly politicized and will require elaborate dances around claims of ageism and other forms of discrimination. Others are subject to contractual impediments such as union work rules – or company policies regarding long term (or even lifelong) employment. But it's abundantly clear that the best protection that a business can offer its under-trained or unskilled workers is a path toward better training and new skills suited to the "new" collar jobs of the future and the opportunity to pursue it.

There's no single right way to get started or one-way approach that suits every situation, but there are a few important ground rules to keep in mind so that you get started in the right way. And let's be clear that these aren't necessarily politically correct observations, but they are the facts of life today.

(1) There isn't enough time and there aren't enough resources to go around.

Every business has financial constraints and priorities including – above all – the need to keep performing <u>while</u> you're transforming the workforce. Someone has to mind the store and no business can afford to have too many members of the team otherwise occupied. So, it's crucial to design and develop your programs to initially accommodate a realistic and reasonable portion of your employees and not try to serve everyone at once. Some people will need to be patient, some people will opt out of the whole program, and some people will need some convincing. You don't need to beg anyone to get better, but some folks may misinterpret the effort or think that they won't be successful and, if they are valued employees, they're worth the time and effort it will take to convince. them

(2) You can't help all of the people and you shouldn't even try.

There are people who just aren't good candidates for this kind of program. Plain and simple. If they've gone as far in the business as they can go, they aren't worth the investment. If they don't value the opportunity, they aren't worth the expense. If they aren't willing to make the necessary effort, they aren't worth the time and they probably won't be around for that much longer anyway. You can only show people the path, you can't take the trip for them. You have to be willing to make these difficult calls and to live with the consequences, the hurt feelings, and even the departures. Otherwise, you're doing a disservice to your company and to the people who are really into the program. It's not easy, but it's essential.

(3) It's hard to turn even the smartest scholar into a super salesman.

Some people are just best suited for certain roles and professions. Maybe it's genetic, maybe it's their upbringing or education, or maybe it's just their personalities. A few can reinvent themselves, but that's not the high percentage bet. One of the mistakes that companies make is trying to append digital skills to the wrong people. As much as your marketing guys want to learn data science, here's the truth: it's much, much easier to teach a data scientist the rules and business basics of marketing than it is to teach even a marketing guru the equivalent of years of university data science training in his spare time. Teach him everything there is to know about social media all day long if you like, but don't try to make him into something he'll never be.

(4) You don't learn or "grow" into certain skills no matter how long you've been on the job.

This is wishful thinking or worse. Left to their own devices, most people simply don't take the time or make the effort required to get better. They don't take extracurricular courses, attend optional lectures, read the literature on their own time, etc. They're happy with what works for them now and they've already got plenty of their plates so they aren't gonna go out of their way to add to the pile. But, the only direction that things go by themselves is downhill. If they're not getting better, they'll slowly (or not so slowly) get worse.

Bottom line: If I accept you as you are, I make you worse; if I treat you as what you can become; I help you become better.

TULLMAN'S TRUISMS

NOTHING IMPORTANT HAPPENS BY ITSELF

231 - WHY BENCHMARK SUIT AGAINST UBER'S EX-CEO WAS A BRILLIANT MOVE

For the umpteenth time, especially in the last few months, we are seeing why the Valley isn't just hyper-insular; it's often flat-out ignorant of how people think about and react to things in the real world. They're so out of touch with basic commonsense considerations that they fail to see or recognize things that seem frightfully obvious to us mere mortals. I guess, as the old Simon & Garfunkel song goes, we sometimes hear what we want to hear and disregard the rest. Still, and notwithstanding the SV community's phony protestations to the contrary, it's hard to ignore the fact that Benchmark's suit was a brilliant move - not a blunder – but a strong opening gambit to pull off something that was increasingly looking like a distant and faint hope. It's a classic strategy cross which melds market manipulation and a variation on Brer Rabbit's briar patch pitch where he begged Brer Fox not to toss him in the brambles. I see Benchmark – having bitten the hand that has theoretically fed it billions - hoping and praying that someone will "shame" them into selling their position in Uber. What a classy way to bail on a bad situation (their investment's value is sinking daily and they have no easy way to exit) while claiming that you were trying to be the bigger person or at least a good sport under trying circumstances.

Benchmark's suit to unwind the not-so recent steps by Uber's former CEO to expand the Uber Board with additional seats under his control is just the latest example of the willful suspension of belief and reality that it takes to try to operate with a seemingly straight face in the Alice in Wonderland world of the Valley. It's clear that Benchmark has failed to convince SoftBank or anyone else to buy even a decent portion of their Uber position (as its putative value continues to plummet) and that they can't really go flat out in public admitting that they're trying to dump their stock and lock in their enormous profits without triggering yet another spin or two in the downdraft that keeps sucking at the stock's price. An announcement like that might very well trigger a wholesale run on the Uber piggybank and a wild whirlpool of lost billions circling the drain. So, they've set things up where growing numbers of well-intentioned 3rd parties are "demanding" that they sell their Uber position and get off the Board. How clever and great for them is that? Talk about dodging the Tar-Baby.

Forget about the fact that the bozos at Benchmark would have agreed to the terms of the new deal they made (and are now trying to renege on) regardless of what or when they knew about the ongoing behavior at "Boober" because, for years now, greed has totally trumped governance in all of these "unicorn" companies where the little boys have all the control and the different classes of votes to run the show in ways and with degrees of freedom that would never have been acceptable to any prudent investor in the past.

It's even more remarkable to hear that the SV community at large is so allegedly upset and utterly unnerved by Benchmark's radical failure to follow good form and just swallow hard and "suffer" in silence. I'm talking about all the handwringing and "oh my goodness gracious" teeth-gnashing over the fact that - in the simplest terms - a VC firm sued an entrepreneur. And, worse yet, the fact that the guy initiating and directing the suit was a director of the company up until about 15 minutes ago (and Benchmark still owns about 13% of Uber) when he replaced himself with a younger guy from his firm. This is just not cricket and it's no way for a grown-up VC firm to act because it could spoil the likelihood of deals coming their way in the future.

None of this behavior is ever supposed to happen in the Valley because who would want to do business with such a litigious venture firm in the future. VCs are supposed to be good-natured gentlemen who simply suck it up when they lose hundreds of millions of dollars and - in this even crazier case - when they are literally more than eight billion dollars ahead of the game on their piddley $27 million-dollar investment. The common wisdom is that the Valley is a very closed off little world and the word would quickly get around to all the best entrepreneurs and - lo and behold - those Benchmark guys would never get a good deal done again. To this canard, I say bushwhack.

Benchmark has/had a very big problem. They had a winning net position valued at around $8 billion, but they had no way to get off the sinking ship and liquidate that position before things got even worse. The truth is that almost any action by them would drive the value of the business even further down and cost them even more money. So, they sued over a relatively insignificant Board matter (everyone knows that Travis is not coming back) and said a lot of nasty things about TK and now they're sitting back and watching other people try to convince them that the best thing for them to do "for all concerned" would be to sell their position. The irony alone is amazing.

And, of course, the jury is still out because of that old adage: that the value of anything ain't what you say it is; it's what someone else is willing to pay you for it.

We've talked and worried for years about the potential harm to businesses that unforeseen results and unintended consequences can cause especially when the companies involved are new and relatively immature. When you read the typical after-action analyses, which try to make sense of these "abrupt" changes or the "surprise" upsets (which probably shouldn't have surprised anyone), they are almost always directed toward studying how well or poorly the particular actor, entity, business or other originator of a series of decisions and actions fared as a result of its inability to anticipate, forecast or mitigate the nasty changes brought about by its own deliberate actions. The academics and other analysts rarely look beyond the primary participants to examine the ripple effects and the impact on more remote third parties which can often be even more problematic.

The truth is that cases where someone could or should have known what might happen if they had fully done their homework and taken the time to carefully look ahead and plan accordingly aren't all that interesting. If you don't know or care what road you're on, it's shouldn't come as a big surprise when you end up in a ditch somewhere. A "plan" without a roadmap is nothing more than a daydream. (See http://www.inc.com/howard-tullman/why-you-need-a-reverse-roadmap.html.) Folks in a hurry to get started without much of a care where they're headed basically get what they deserve.

For startups, it's more interesting and far more valuable to look at the risks and consequences of the kinds of changes that are much harder to see - even with Superman's X-ray vision and a crystal ball - because they're outside of the traditional scope of inquiry and investigation. This is why the big guys so often miss the boat and what provides at the same time a continuing stream of exciting openings and opportunities for new businesses. Too often, when large, established players look at their markets and their direct competitors, they only see what they're looking for and what's pretty much right in front of them. But in today's world of immediate and radically disruptive innovation and overnight shifts in supply and delivery chains as well as the constantly-escalating demands of consumers, you can have the best in-market research in the business and all the competitive intelligence a business can buy and still get bit in the butt by a newcomer from nowhere.

More and more, the existential risks and the primary threats of abrupt displacement come laterally from new entrants, from unrelated businesses expanding into your space, from leapfrog technology advances, and from changes in the customers' needs and requirements. These can provide clear opportunities for your own business if you seize them (See https://www.inc.com/howard-tullman/five-reasons-your-market-is-bigger-than-you-think.html.) and serious challenges to your company if you're asleep at the switch.

Starting from the publication in 1997 of *The Innovator's Dilemma*, we've become increasingly aware of the risks of ignoring the new kids on the block. I don't regard this as much in the way of breaking news. In fact, the far more interesting questions relate to the increasing instances where changes and new behaviors in a given vertical or marketplace have enormous consequences in other sectors of the economy which we would never have imagined. We've always understood this in the context of nature where a material variation in any basic ecosystem could inadvertently harm countless other and different lives, but it's been underappreciated in the business world.

For sure, some of this proliferation is a product of our hyper-connected world, but it's also the case that the availability and ubiquity of new technologies at lower and lower costs is accelerating behavior changes across markets in ways that make it critical for every business to be far more aware and spend much more time looking increasingly far afield on a consistent basis. There's very little chance of fully insulating any business from these oblique challenges and consequences, but you can develop a practice which at least helps you discover and potentially anticipate the more distant results earlier than your competitors. It's all about anticipation, exploration and vigilance.

And, for a startup, if you want to get ahead of the pack and look for open fields and unexplored spaces, you've got to think even further downstream than the obvious cases and start considering the demands for new kinds of products and services that the more remote "ripples" will create in the near future. Some of these implications are pretty clear. There's not much hope for cabbies and truck drivers. Amazon's cashier-less stores will soon imperil the 11 million cashiers in this country. We have far more cashiers in this country than teachers which is a sin of a different stripe. And as voice input and video output continue to explode, I'd hate to be manufacturing keyboards much longer. But that's just the head of the stream.

Between online ordering (less store visits), automated home replenishment of commodities (ditto) and in-store pickup combined with self-service checkout aisles and kiosk deliveries, the chewing gum business is in the toilet and impulse sales at the register (candy, necessities and sleazy magazines) overall are plummeting. Bubble gum sales are off more than 40% over the last few years. Who'd a thunk it and why is this happening? Because we are no longer standing trapped with our carts in the "transition zone" and subjected to the constant temptations stacked conveniently right at our fingertips. Amazingly, over $5 billion in grocery store sales each year used to originate in the checkout line. So long spur-of-the-moment Snickers and Spearmint. What's the next delivery channel or mechanism?

Every day on-site assembly and on-demand 3D printing becomes less of a stupid and wasteful novelty and more of a business necessity eliminating inventory and transportation expense and providing just-in-time supply solutions. Thousands of plastic parts in millions of businesses cost more to transport than they cost to produce or sell for. Sadly, it's more bad news for the transportation industry. The pressure to push everything closer and closer to the perimeter – basically to the point of purchase and delivery – is ripping apart all the elements in the traditional supply chains. The 3D machines are still slow and costly, but the future is clear.

And voice commands are gonna take an even bigger bite out of and be even a bigger threat to brand equity than online purchasing which has already almost entirely eliminated the pizzazz and tactile impact of packaging. Whichever tool or voice assistant you use, you'll find early on (as the current stats are clearly showing) that it's a pain in the ass to give incremental details (like brand names or product sizes) to the machine and, as the machine increasingly knows what you already ordered, you'll be ever more inclined to just ask for the usual. Amazon already has Alexa default whenever possible (and sometimes whether you like it or not) to the Amazon versions of many commodity goods. You can override these things, but who wants to go to the trouble and who really cares what brand of batteries you're ordering anyway?

Maybe these guys at *Brandless* (www.brandless.com) are really onto something?

TULLMAN'S TRUISMS

YOU NEVER KNOW WHO'S GOING TO BRING YOU YOUR FUTURE

I have been talking about the increasing power and economic value of building and aggressively deploying proprietary platforms for several years now (See https://www.inc.com/howard-tullman/why-platforms-is-the-new-plastics.html and https://www.inc.com/howard-tullman/the-primacy-of-the-platform.html) and it has become clearer and clearer - as we see the growing dominance of the major tech players - that this oligopolistic trend will continue largely uninterrupted unless and until the government (unwisely I would argue given the AT&T and Microsoft debacles of the past) decides to interfere and possibly try to break up some of these businesses.

Whether you call them FAMGA or FANGA and regardless of which of the 4,5 or 6 tech giants you include in the current mix (does Google get a second slot for Alphabet? - do you prefer Netflix or Microsoft?), the impact that these monster entities are already having on our businesses and our lives and especially going forward is more than a little frightening. Frankly, our best hope is probably that the big guys are so competitive that they will keep each other in check and relatively honest although there is little evidence of that happy outcome to date. Right now, Google still owns search, Amazon dominates e-commerce, and Facebook and Google have pretty much split digital advertising down the middle.

Nonetheless, as an encouraging example at least in the short term, you might take some solace from Amazon's immediate actions to reduce many of the product prices at Whole Foods. Google's teaming up with Walmart to help them both compete more effectively with Amazon is another ray of hope. Fed Ex using Walgreen's stores as depots is further instance of what I have called the PxP (platform to platform) program which basically amounts to paying someone (in some form or other) who has already built a platform or other effective distribution channel to send your goods and services down the same pipeline.

This shared channel strategy has extremely compelling economics. Players avoid the costs and risks of trying to reinvent the wheel; they're able to move into the market much more quickly than if they had to build things themselves; and the platform provider on the other side gets to amortize and offset some of the costs that were initially incurred and invested in building out the system in the first place. A nice deal if you can get it and basically a win-win deal for both parties. Of course, if it's just the big guys partnering up in cross-industry strategic alliances, it doesn't really help us peasants. As I like to say: when the elephants dance, the grass (that's us) takes a beating. But the real question is how does a startup play in this space?

The answer may be an interesting new development that offers some very exciting opportunities for smaller and newer companies which grows out of a different view and a new perspective on the platform theory. Instead of looking at a specific platform as an attractor - extended by the creator/builder out to new potential users in the marketplace - which I call the inside-outside approach, I'm seeing more and more small startup companies approaching bigger organizations with an outside-in pitch that seems to be gaining considerable traction in a number of areas.

These new businesses almost all make the same pitch to the big, old, tired and traditional businesses: a) we built a clean, new system from scratch (no spaghetti code or hair on our baby) to solve specific, known problems; b) we move much faster than you can because you're lugging all that legacy load along with you; c) the people who built your systems won't break them or blow them up - they're believers in band-aids and duct tape - not clean, new solutions; d) we have the access to the necessary talent and skills in critical new areas (machine learning for one) which you can't buy, hire or otherwise afford to add to your already enormous IT departments; and e) solving this particular problem is Number One on our list (in fact, it's all we do) and – in your company - it's lost somewhere in the pile of problems that your CTO and CIO are trying to triage and manage. I'd say these are all pretty accurate observations and very convincing arguments. So how does it work in practice?

Two recent examples which I've seen - both in the human capital space - are each instances of taking the existing resources, skill sets, and technologies of a startup and extending them into a larger entity to expand, enhance and eventually replace their existing and badly antiquated systems. It's outside-in and eventually, in many industries, it's the most effective way for startups to win.

The basic idea is to seamlessly integrate: (a) incremental gig economy resources which were previously (and principally) thought of as being exclusively outside the big business – additive and supplementary creative talent or additional skilled and technical workers – which were callable on demand with (b) the internal resources and talents of the big business which – as often as not – the big business itself did a lousy job of identifying, organizing and utilizing because their HR systems simply failed to capture the necessary details, workloads and skill sets of their own personnel.

In many respects, this situation is another version of the old problem of a company which doesn't know what it knows. (See https://www.inc.com/howard-tullman/how-knowledgehound-sniffed-out-a-new-platform.html .) In these cases, the big businesses aren't able to marshal and organize their internal resources quickly and effectively so they end up unnecessarily turning to 3rd party outside vendors on a project by project basis and pay for talent and services that their own people could and would more cost-effectively provide if they had been "visible" to the individuals responsible for staffing the particular projects.

In one cases, the staffing was literally bodies needed to staff events and in the other case it was creatives needed to execute and complete projects in a timely and professional fashion. In both instances, the costs to the big businesses were secondary considerations – not because that made good economic sense – but because the demands of the moment and the absence of good information afforded them little or no choice but to pay up if they wanted the jobs done on time.

While the outside 3rd party startup vendors were happy to take their money, that was a risky short-term bet and a bad long-term strategy. The far better bet was to suggest to these "buyers" that the same outside software solutions built and employed by the startups to manage their talent and workforce descriptive data and scheduling could be used inside the larger companies to organize the same analytical and organizational capabilities for their own employees and – by melding the internal and external workforces into a single and readily accessible database – each time there were specific personnel requirements, the buyers could quickly look over all the available talent inside and outside the business – optimize their selections to minimize incremental costs and utilize all of their own people first – and then seamlessly supplement any jobs with the outside talent available through the startups' own workforces.

Not only could this solution be implemented easily and quickly without disrupting any of the big companies' existing systems, the startups were happy to add the internal employees to their systems for free. Why would the startups do that? Because it set up an easy and immediate way to demonstrate the superiority of their solutions and it was also a trojan horse because it gave them access to thousands of additional (albeit currently employed) creatives and other skilled workers who might very well be interested in outside or incremental work or even in new employment opportunities. Obviously, there are some ethical issues in this sensitive area, but the main objective was the first – for the startups to quickly show how effective their systems could be in better allocating resources, reducing outside costs, and actually being more responsive to both internal and external customers.

These kinds of shifts and penetrations from the outside in won't happen overnight, but because they initially operate in parallel to the status quo systems, they are far more attractive to the change agents in these big businesses who are trying to make things happen because they don't really require anyone's permission and they basically can't be effectively blocked or stymied by the IT or HR departments. Even more importantly, the financial results are immediately apparent and indisputable.

TULLMAN'S TRUISMS

YOU GET PAID FOR WHAT YOU DO, NOT WHAT YOU KNOW

Another thousand startups will shut down this September. Will yours be one? Should yours be one? Now's a good time to ask yourself those questions. Winter's on its way and it seems to me that things start to get more serious as the summer slips away. Labor Day weekend offers an excellent break in the day-to-day craziness of starting a new business and the ideal time to ask yourself whether all the work is worth it. It's not an easy conversation to have – even if you're just talking to yourself – especially because there are so many other interested parties. You don't want to disappoint them or let your team down, but sometimes the best thing you can do is step back and take a hard look at where things stand.

It helps to remember that, in most instances, you're spending other people's money - often close friends and family - and they didn't sign up to lose their shirts. In fact, if they're like most amateur investors, they didn't plan or expect to lose anything. They all believe that trees grow to the sky. There's not much you can do about the already spilt milk and the funds that are long gone, but you can be responsible and realistic about what to do with the resources you still have and what makes the most sense for all the stakeholders. This is part of the job. (See https://www.inc.com/howard-tullman/failure-happens-four-ways-to-do-it-well.html).

And, maybe it's time to admit that there's no end in sight to your "profitless prosperity" and that that elusive break-even point keeps receding just like the horizon. Revenues (bought and paid for with borrowed marketing bucks) may be growing, but you're just treading water and there's no demonstrable bottom line or end game. Worse yet, you've learned that the minute you stop goosing the top line revenues with flash sales, deep discounts and shipping spiffs, things slide backwards quicker than you can say *Blue Apron*. People get tired pretty quickly of hearing tales of tomorrow. And smart investors have even less patience after a while.

Sadly, it also appears that even your most supportive sidekicks are starting to look at you a little bit sideways and think a lot about their next opportunity. It's getting harder and harder to put on a happy face in the face of the impending doom. People on the inside know too much and watch your every move much more closely so it's very hard (and not really fair to anyone) to keep living a lie. Taking a break from time to time to take stock (no pun intended) of your situation makes a lot of sense. And the right time is always now.

I've done this kind of baseline review regularly for decades for my own businesses and for hundreds of others where I've been an investor, director, advisor or just been recruited to give my unvarnished (and only somewhat informed) opinion. And, while it's not quite a science as yet, pattern recognition still pays off more often than not and it's become pretty clear to me that there are five simple signs that things aren't going your way and that the odds are pretty strong that they're not likely to get better anytime soon.

So, if you're up for a quick reality check, read on.

(1) My Products Don't Sell

Businesses certainly need capital and talent to succeed, but they need recurring customers most of all. You can make up any number of excuses or think of a million reasons why the register doesn't ring, but all the explanations in the world don't really matter at the end of the day. Money talks and bullshit (and wishful thinking) walk. Entrepreneurs fall in love with their product or service and forget Rule Number One: it's not what you're selling that counts; it's what they're buying. Businesses that don't sell don't survive.

(2) My Business Doesn't Scale

If you're content to be a small business and just get by and your investors are happy that you've got a nice hobby even though they'll never see any return on their money, then be my guest and keep struggling for spare change. But, if you're trying to build a real business, it's got to be one that can scale; one that doesn't depend solely on you; one that has readily replicable products or services; and one that isn't bespoke. If everything is one-off and handled by hand, it's hard to see a happy ending. (See https://www.inc.com/howard-tullman/when-should-the-ceo-stop-selling.html?cid=search). No one is Superman and starting startups is increasingly a team sport and not a place for one-man armies or solitary geniuses.

(3) My Story Doesn't Shine

As crazy and committed as you may be to your business, your excitement and enthusiasm may not be that contagious. If the idea doesn't catch fire after a while, you need to understand that the market is sending you a message. Maybe there's a pivot in the making, but that's often just a way of postponing the inevitable. (See https://www.inc.com/howard-tullman/you-can-pivot-but-you-should-never-twirl.html). Early indicators of a lack of pizzazz are difficulty in attracting and hiring experienced people; finding it hard to secure follow-on funding; and hearing all too often that your solution is "nice to have" but not "need to have". If there's no light in the customers eyes, you're not long for this world.

(4) My Metrics Doesn't Matter

I'm often surprised how often even good managers fail to track the really consequential metrics of their business. They focus on factoids and fantasies while their customers are looking for real results. Maybe they know better, but they don't want to admit it. (See https://www.inc.com/howard-tullman/the-curse-of-microsoft-excel.html). The truth is that it's not simply about deploying a new solution and it's not even about utilization of a new product or service, it's ultimately about moving the needle and making it matter for the end user. If your business isn't delivering concrete and measurable improvements that enable your customers to upgrade their operations in some material fashion, it won't take them long to discover that you're wasting their time and money. Don't believe your own press – or your own marketing facts and figures – if the impact isn't obvious to the customer, all the hype in the world won't get you to the home stretch.

(5) My Service Doesn't Suck

Life would be so much better if everything was just black or white. The worst nightmare for an entrepreneur or an investor is a business that goes sideways and doesn't have the courtesy and good grace to just die. The truth is that in today's hyper-competitive world, and notwithstanding that noted philosopher Joe Maddon, it really isn't enough to say that your product or service doesn't suck or that you're no worse than the next guy. If your business is just getting by and not growing or going anywhere, it might be time for everyone's sake to put the beast down for good. It's always about opportunity costs and what you and everyone else on the team could be doing more meaningfully and more profitably with the rest of your lives.

Ultimately, if no one has an appetite for your app and no one is swooning for your service, it's time to think about doing something else. In this life, we look backwards to learn and we look forward to succeed. Now's a great time to take a good look.

TULLMAN'S TRUISMS

THERE'S A DIFFERENCE BETWEEN FASTING AND STARVING

There's an old Haitian expression which translates roughly to: "beyond the mountains, more mountains" which I think should be the every-day motto of all good entrepreneurs because it's a spot-on description of the basic fact of life in a startup. The battle never really ends, iteration and constant forward motion are critical to any real success, momentary "success" is just a way station in the struggle, and there's absolutely no finish line. In fact, I've found that every time you think you can take a break, catch your breath, slow the pace a bit, or that you've reached the top; it turns out that that's actually the time when the real climbing begins. It's not exactly a Sisyphean exercise because it's neither pointless, eternally frustrating, or free of any real progress – it's just that it can feel that way sometimes.

But every once in a while, you actually do pull off a huge win, a game-changing triumph, or the sale to end all sales and then the question of how you and your people handle those highs will be just as critical to the ultimate success of your company as your ability to handle all the bumps in the road and hard times that also come with the territory. What you do after you win a big one is even more important to moving the business ahead and keeping the team together (and focused on the next few hurdles) as is how good you are at picking yourself up off the floor and getting back in the game after getting punched a few times in the nose by a client or a competitor or even one of your own folks. Especially when, as Steely Dan said, you've got to *Do It Again*.

In Chicago, no one's had a bigger recent win than the Cubs winning the World Series after 108 years. I had the chance to sit down recently with several senior members of the Cubs organization to ask them how they've tried to handle this situation in their own organization. Some of the basic ideas and approaches we discussed were certainly worth sharing. I've said in the past that the Cubs' turnaround journey was like the trials and tribulations of a startup in many ways and the resemblance remains clear even in the new season. (See http://www.inc.com/how-the-cubs-a-140-year-old-baseball-team-operate-like-a-startup.html .)

Here are a few of the most important ideas to keep in mind:

(1) Take Some Time to Celebrate and Say Thanks

Entrepreneurs generally enjoy the process and the journey more than the celebration and the hoopla at the end of the path. This is due at least in part because they always retain the knowledge (and the stomach-churning fear) that any success is fleeting and can disappear or be overtaken just as quickly as it is sometimes secured. As a result, they're not likely to kick back and rest on their laurels and they also don't understand that not everyone in the place is like them. So, they focus on getting right back to work. (See https://www.inc.com/howard-tullman/why-entrepreneurs-are-really-terrible-at-saying-thank-you.html .) The truth is that, however far you've come, the trip has been tough on everyone (with sacrifices being made in varying degrees all around) and it's important to acknowledge the win (and also the effort that it took to get there) and to give everybody and their families a little time to bask in their share of the spotlight and the glory before getting back to business and starting to climb the next mountain.

(2) Don't Move the Goal Posts Too Far Too Fast

It's easy in the heat and excitement of success to get too full of yourself, too aggressive in your plans, and too far out over your skis. It never hurts to aim high because feasibility will compromise you soon enough, but no one gets to heaven in a heartbeat these days. Everything in this life takes longer than you think (although the long run is often shorter than we expect given the accelerating rate at which technologies are changing our lives) and good things simply don't happen overnight. A baseball season (especially at the start of the year) can look like it's gonna last forever and so it's not a bad idea to set some early, modest hurdles, before everyone starts talking about going for the gold. A little caution and some patience and maybe walking a bit before racing headlong ahead into the mist makes a lot of sense and leads consistently to better outcomes. (See https://www.inc.com/howard-tullman/slow-down-it-might-save-your-business.html .) "Does it better" always beats "does it first". And the last thing you want is a disaster on your way to building your dynasty.

(3) New Numbers Are Not Enough – People Need a New Vision

The right metrics always matter, but no one ever invested financially or emotionally in a set of numbers – they need to believe and buy into a story about the next journey and be shown a realistic path to get there if you want them all to sign up for the ride. Pie in the sky doesn't win pennants. The path doesn't have to be certain or easy (and you can talk as much about the individuals' contributions and commitments as about what the team is going to achieve), but the message has to come thru loud and clear. One thought driven home is better than three left on base. True motivation comes from inspiration which comes from within. (See https://www.inc.com/howard-tullman/trying-to-motivate-your-employees-forget-it.html.) And while the message is gonna vary in every case – the fundamental content is almost always the same and it always has a lot less to do with more and much more to do with better because better beats more every time. It's not enough to be good if you could be better and it's not enough to be very good if you could be great.

(4) Don't Play It Safe – Failure is a Fundamental Part of the Process

I've talked about every aspect of failure over the years in this blog and how it bears on startups and – in baseball for example – even the best hitters in the business fail 7 out of 10 times. So, failure is a given and a necessary evil that everyone needs to get comfortable with. The key is to build a resilient culture that gives your team permission to fail without accepting failure as a given. Playing it safe – trying to avoid making mistakes or being embarrassed isn't a formula that works for anyone these days. In many young businesses (and in businesses with young players and employees), too many folks start out depending on their talent alone. You can do that in the minors, but as you "grow up" in sports or in any other line of work, it turns out that the mental game is every bit as important as the physical skills and talents and only the players who master both sides of the equation become real successes in the long run. Failing early and figuring out how to handle it is a much better approach than risk avoidance which basically limits your upside opportunities without really providing any downside protection. Playing it safe today is risky.

TULLMAN'S TRUISMS

ANYONE WHO THINKS HE'S ALMOST THERE DOESN'T UNDERSTAND HOW LONG THE JOURNEY IS

I've talked in the past about how businesses need to look beyond the known (basically what they're currently doing and what their direct competitors are up to) and try to imagine, discover, and exploit those less obvious opportunities which are lateral to or adjacent to their markets because: (a) that's where many new customers may be found; and (b) if you're not careful and observant, that's where your next best competitor is likely to come from. (See https://www.inc.com/howard-tullman/five-reasons-your-market-is-bigger-than-you-think.html.)

Having done these kinds of cross-sector analyses on a regular basis since I was in law school – this is what the doctrine of Section 7 potential competition is all about in antitrust law – I find both parts of the process to be almost second nature. First, I spend hours every month just looking over and beyond the local marketplace activity for discovery purposes and second, I've developed some simple rules of thumb which help me in deciding which of the adjacent projects and potential new products and services make the most sense for whatever the business in question may be. But I've learned recently that there are a lot of companies – large and small – and plenty of entrepreneurs who could use some help in this area and particularly some fairly simple guidelines for what makes the most sense under their current circumstances.

Too many times I'm seeing companies lurch into uncertain or unknown territories on what looks like no more than a hope and a prayer or – worse yet – the whim of some internal executive wiseman or board member. If they had taken even the slightest bit of time to determine what they brought to the quest and what the realistic likelihood of success would be, they would have never left the starting gate. This isn't a complex process. It's basically 4 steps.

(1) What are our core competencies? What are we good at?
    (a) Customers
    (b) Distribution
    (c) Size and Scale
    (d) Domain Expertise and Intelligence
    (e) Platform
    (f) Networks

It goes without saying that you can't be good at everything and that the most important initial calculation has to be determining in which areas you have an unfair competitive advantage (if any) which you should aggressively pursue. In the areas where you have no edge whatsoever, you either want to avoid them entirely or farm them out to third parties provided you can do so at a reasonable cost.

(2) Where are we headed?
    (a) New Products or Services
    (b) New Geographies or Markets
    (c) New Channels or Delivery Systems
    (d) New Customers/Consumers
    (e) New Partners/New Competitors
    (f) New Opportunities for Margin Expansion

(3) How close is the target to our core competencies?
    (1) Directly In Our Wheelhouse
    (2) A Stretch, but within Our Competence and Capacity
    (3) New Applications or Approaches, but Employing Known Technologies
    (4) New Offerings Dependent on Previously Unused Techno-logies
    (5) New Across the Board – New Product or Service with Technologies to be Created

It's a little obvious and embarrassing to point out that, in this particular category, the further down the list you start, the less likely you are to succeed. And yet, it happens every day that deluded dreamers and wishful thinkers charge off into the clouds chasing pots of gold without the slightest clue as to how they will reach the end of the rainbow.

(4) What are the Relative Levels of Risk and Reward?
    (1) Is There Substantial Upside and Additional Expansion Prospects?
    (2) Is It Too Far Beyond Our Core Competencies to Pursue?
    (3) Do We Have the Skills and Resources to Successfully Undertake and Deliver the Project?
    (4) Is the Nature of Competition in the New Market Greater or Less than that in Our Current Markets?

(5) Is the Market Mature or Expandable?
(6) Is the Market Currently Regulated or Likely to Be Regulated in the Near Future?

These are not exclusive or exhaustive criteria or considerations and any such lists need to be adapted to the nature and specific characteristics of your business. But it's committing to and regularly undertaking the necessary investigation, internal audits and analysis that will eventually separate the winners from the losers.

It's rarely the size alone of the bet that makes or breaks the bank. It's the people who don't understand the size and scope of the risks that they are taking who wind up in the poorhouse.

TULLMAN'S TRUISMS

NOBODY OWNS THE CUSTOMER, BUT SOMEONE ALWAYS OWNS THE MOMENT

In today's "right now" economy where no one wants to wait for anything, we're seeing more and more instances of businesses pushing the delivery of their products and services to the perimeter – to the edge – or what might be called the closest boundary to the customer. This, of course, becomes infinitely easier as digitally-enabled consumers are increasingly seeking virtual products and services rather than physical objects. But it's an equally valuable and important idea for virtually every kind of business as well. Delivering what I want, when I want it, and wherever I am has always been the end game and as we continue to be more and more connected, our desires in this regard and the competition to respond to them continue to accelerate.

For the individual end user, books, games and music are just the beginning. Why travel downtown to see your physician when your phone can bring the doctor to your digital door? Telemedicine is on the way and it's becoming clearer and clearer that time-wasting trips to the doc don't add anything to the efficiency of the ultimate treatment in the vast majority (more than 70%) of cases. Let your fingers and your phone do the walking. You save time, avoid the costs of getting to and fro, and, in most instances, get a better, faster and more satisfactory result. And, if you still crave that human touch, urgent care facilities – with better hours, shorter lines, and customer-centric practitioners – are popping up ion every neighborhood right next to the nail salons and the futon and mattress stores.

For businesses, the potential savings in time and costs are even greater because of how large a portion of the overall expense of various products and services is composed of the embedded transportation charges imposed by multiple parties throughout the supply chain. My favorite example is the cost of hundreds of different plastic and composite parts at any given car dealership or repair shop. The math is simply amazing – the costs to ship and deliver the parts to their destination are substantially more than the costs of the parts themselves. If ever there was a clear and compelling use case for distributed 3D printing – on site and on demand – with basically NO transportation costs, this is it. And again, this is just the beginning of the analysis. Inventory costs are also dramatically reduced, waiting times for critical parts which often delay the overall completion of many repairs are largely eliminated, and mistakes in the parts specified and required can be remedied in the moment rather than after delivery of the wrong pieces.

The compelling combination of constant connectivity and complete mobility is also freeing up large portions of the workforce who were previously constrained and/or tethered to offices, desktops, proprietary environments, etc. Not only can examinations, inspections, evaluations and even transactions now be done almost anywhere – in the field, in the home, in the factory – but they can be supported, supplemented and improved with resources, decision-support tools, and even visual supervision from afar. Forms of augmented intelligence like these will change our businesses far more quickly than artificial intelligence. Just as our phones let us be better and smarter shoppers, they will increasingly help almost every enabled worker perform their tasks faster and more accurately.

Even more significantly, many businesses will push the process and the "work" out to their customers at the edge and let them take advantage of the same tools and systems to do a better job of serving their own needs. We can expect to see more and more instances of streamlined self-service like JP Morgan Chase's mobile check deposit service coming down the pipe. Every major automobile insurer in the U.S. will quickly copy Allstate's example and encourage insureds and claimant to use their own phones to document and report of damage to their vehicles using variants of the technology developed years ago by a Chicago-based startup – SnapSheet – which is already working with a number of the major insurers across the country. (See http://www.inc.com/howard-tullman/put-your-new-business-idea-to-the-three-question-test.html).

And so the question for your business is pretty simple. How easy is it to do business with you? How can you simplify the process – push the tools out to the end user – speed up the transactions – and ultimately end up with far more happy campers as customers. If you don't do it and do it now, you can be sure that someone else will.

Nothing beats one-stop shopping and I doubt that anything ever will. It saves us time, often money and it's ridiculously convenient. But, if I had to guess at what might eventually get us headed in a new direction, I would say that robotic replenishment may take us most of the way there. And, of course, Amazon is already out there leading the way. When more than 70% of the stuff we buy religiously every week at the supermarket (or thru online ordering) are the same commoditized items, and the machines that watch and track our online purchases (with increasingly accurate bricks-and-mortar attribution) keep getting smarter and smarter, it's only a matter of time before "one-click" becomes "no-click" for most of us. Amazon will know before you do that your pet's vitamins are about to run out and ship you a refill before you ask.

And the truth is that the more comfortable we get with ordering or re-ordering the "usual" and having time-based standing orders, the tighter the hold which the automated fulfillment guys will have over us. It's hard to imagine how any competitor interrupts an automated transaction (even with a better offer) when there's no window to get in front of the customer. (See https://www.inc.com/howard-tullman/why-you-never-saw-it-coming.html.) At the same time, in the good news category, once we're free of the drudgery of dragging all the usual stuff home, our actual shopping to the market may once again be an awesome experience rather than an unavoidable chore as well as an opportunity to discover and try new things.

In the business world, we're also constantly on the lookout for tools and technology that can save us time, help us avoid reinventing the wheel, and, most importantly, create solutions that will attract and aggregate enough users, capital and technical resources to enable and justify the continuing development efforts required by the "owner" to invest and keep growing and enhancing the platform. We're more than willing to reward someone else for doing the heavy lifting for us and doing it better than we ever could as well. I've explained before that this is one of the reasons why platforms are so powerful. (See https://www.inc.com/howard-tullman/the-primacy-of-the-platform.html.)

But the truth is that it's just becoming more and more obvious that a few key players and central platforms (in search, social and e-commerce) are getting to the point where they will be controlling significant segments of the entire economy and our lives as well. You can describe this phenomenon as the result of successfully building a flywheel or as a dramatic demonstration of the power of momentum (See https://www.inc.com/howard-tullman/future-of-content-marketing-simplereach.html.) or simply attribute it to the "winner take all" world of innovative and disruptive technologies, but whatever you call it, it comes down to our desires to do as little as possible in the way of redundant and repetitive efforts and to simple math as well.

It doesn't matter who was first; it always comes down to who does it best and commits the dollars and the effort to maintain and even extend their edge on an ongoing basis because the competitive bar never stops rising. These essential and substantial outlays of time and money simply aren't the kinds of expenditures that individual users – regardless of their size – can support and it's demonstrably a bad allocation of their scarce resources in any case because someone dedicated to the task will always be doing it better than they can. An inexpensive third-party platform that helps your employees service and reduce their student debt is a great example and a lot smarter than adding more expensive bodies to your HR department even if they were up to the task. (See https://www.inc.com/howard-tullman/making-student-debt-less-sticky.html.)

If your own internal effort (however well-intended) is a sideline or a sometime thing instead of being laser-focused and constantly top of mind, it's gonna lead to a second-rate result. This is exactly why startups can inject better and more focused products and services into large organizations than the big guys can usually develop and implement on their own. The startups bring purpose-built solutions provided by businesses trying to do one thing really right while there a million things that need to get done on the plates of the IT guys at the corporate giants. (See https://www.inc.com/howard-tullman/outside-in-is-the-new-way-to-win.html.)

But it's also the case that large, established providers can also design and develop aggregated solutions that are right in their wheelhouse and then help to amortize and distribute some of their own investment by licensing or otherwise making these tools available to others in the marketplace including many of their own customers and even in some instances competitors. Getting customers to adopt these new tools is a great way to have them do more of the necessary work on their own and saves you time and money.

In the platform business, almost any incremental volume is good volume and users are users regardless (in most cases) of who or where the traffic is coming from. ComScore's new Activation solution suite creates audience segments which can then be deployed internally or thru third-party ad tech platforms. To save their clients time and money, ComScore has already forward-integrated its solution into over 15 different vendors' offerings including products from Centro, Salesforce, Adobe, etc.

Some of the smartest big guys (like KeyBank and Hertz) have figured out how to partner with super tech-savvy startups like Snapsheet in Chicago to create systems that will change the way whole industries (like banking, insurance and vehicle rental) do business in short order. Whether it's photo documentation, aggregated payment walls for multi-channel remittances, or delivering better, smarter and faster customer-centric experiences in the field – Snapsheet and its corporate partners continue to lead the way and develop new answers.

Of course, there are clear competitive exceptions which we are starting to see especially in the race to dominate and control the media expenditures of consumers. Amazon's Echo Show product won't play YouTube videos. Wonder why – especially when Amazon is GOOGLE's largest customer? Keep in mind that Amazon is now dominating search for high-value items with a share almost twice that of GOOGLE. This is also clearly why Disney is pulling its offerings from Netflix and starting its own streaming services. And, it's why CBS is carving out its sports offerings from ESPN. Facebook and Apple are still trying to figure out how to move more aggressively into the exploding streaming media space and who they decide to cooperate with and who they decide to crush will made for a great soap opera. Frenemies forever I guess.

The bottom line really hasn't changed – it's just repeating itself in different industries at an accelerating rate – and the message is clear. Until human nature radically changes, and don't hold your breath waiting, we'll always gravitate to the one-stop shops, the easiest and most accessible solutions, the pre-built answers and already in -place tracks and, in fact, we're much more productive in our own businesses as well when we stick to our knitting, focus on what we can do best, and let someone else build the massive infrastructure and platforms that will eventually connect us all.

We'll all end up paying the platform "pipers" for the privilege and sometimes being gouged by the gatekeepers (like Netflix which is raising their rates again), but honestly most of us won't really mind.

TULLMAN'S TRUISMS

THERE'S A TIME WHEN PANIC IS THE RIGHT RESPONSE

I realize that it's a little frightening for many of us when we hear some of the intimidating statistics about the immediate headcount reductions in more and more industries which are being driven by the growing deployment of what we're generically calling "bots". But I don't think bots are so bad for business. I realize that – while the major shifts are just beginning - we're already talking about the future employment of thousands of analysts and adjusters in the insurance and finance industries and hundreds of highly-paid attorneys and associates in various sectors of the banking business. But, on an individual business basis, regardless of your size, the sooner you figure out how to incorporate and deploy these little time and money savers, the better off you and your business will be.

And honestly, at least for some of the folks who will be displaced or replaced by these efficient and energetic little guys, it will be a break for the better. No one in their right mind will miss any of the boring, repetitive and utterly useless tasks that are a painful part of too many of our jobs. If your tasks can be reduced to a set of instructions and rules that need to be repeatedly and flawlessly executed; we'll soon enough find a program or a machine to do that work better, quicker and more accurately than you and to do it all day long as well. No one argues with that part of the equation. We'd all love to be freed up from our chores and be doing exciting, creative and constructive work.

The rub comes in the rest of the story – the ratio and the scale of the jobs being eliminated as compared to the new jobs available to replace them. To quote Bruce Springsteen, in *My Hometown*, "Foreman says these jobs are going boys and they ain't coming back." Take a look at the hospitality business just as a simple example. Airbnb is closing in on Marriott's market cap (it's already worth about $10 billion more than Hilton), but their employee headcounts are in different universes. Marriott employs over 225,000 people and Airbnb has about 3500 – yes 3500 – employees. And I'm not just picking on Marriott, Hilton has about 170,000 team members. You can nitpick the numbers and argue that some of those people are doing different and allegedly irreplaceable functions – but, in the end, the real question is whether the end user – the customer/guest – whose actual needs are being more than met – really cares about whatever it is that fills the day for those extra 400,000 workers. I'm not even sure that most of their managers know what makes up their day.

When you couple the substantial reductions in the workforce with the readily-demonstrated and clearly impressive gains in terms of enhanced productivity and lowered operating costs that we're also seeing and documenting in multiple markets, it's clear that there are major bumps in the road ahead and significant disruptions in the ways business has traditionally been done especially because the vast majority of these changes are neither complicated in regard to the necessary technologies nor costly in terms of the required capital. Low-hanging fruit abounds. JP Morgan Chase reports eliminating over 350,000 hours of legal document review time per year by employing bots and smart contacts.

When I use the term "bots", I'm not talking about anything as challenging as truly intelligent agents or even anything autonomous. I'm talking about simple lines of code – and not that many – which can successfully execute instructions and directives or commands which are well-established and documented by humans. I hate to call any of this stuff artificial intelligence – at best it's augmented and extended intelligence – and the intelligence being extended is ours and the folks being augmented are us. We're talking about systems and tools that will help us perform routine tasks with minimal supervision or ongoing direction and essentially automatically upon request. Every business still has some of these pockets of obvious inefficiency and it's mainly ignorance of better options and inertia that keeps them from realizing immediate improvements and significant cost savings. Your business does too and the sooner you do your own audit and analysis, the better off and more competitive you'll be. (See https:// www.inc.com/howard-tullman/use-a-mirror-to-mind-your-own-business-first.html .)

There are opportunities everywhere, but the sweetest spots for almost any business seem to fall into 4 recurring buckets. Forget about chatbots and retweeters. Focus internally first where you can get the biggest bang for your buck and where you can ride on existing rails. The people providing support and resources in this emerging space are few and far between right now, but they tend to target these critical areas: HR, Finance, Operations and Sales. I know, you're already saying "well duh, that's just about the whole business", so trim it down to HR and Finance and start there. Eat the elephant one bite at a time.

One of the best providers is an 1871 alumni organization called Catalytic (www.catalytic.com) whose tagline says it all: "Do more of what you love, and less of what you don't" and they are smart enough to understand that they are in a "rinse and repeat" business so that each time they build a new process bot; they create the ability to provide a version of that same solution to thousands of other businesses more efficiently, more rapidly, and less expensively. They talk about concrete client results delivered in days, not months or years. They're worth a look.

And, to be successful, you need a plan that's ongoing and iterative and that's always targeting and attacking the dumbest things you are doing. In many cases, it's an approach that follows the same basic steps: digitize and dump the paper; speed up the flow and the inter- and intra-departmental handoffs; automate as many steps in the process as possible; measure the results; and do it again. It needs to become a habit and a mantra of your business – always moving to raise the bottom and improve the average.

It's an interesting thing to watch the adoption cycle as well. It's both competitive and contagious. The more you do; the more your people will want to do and, interestingly enough, you'll have them bringing suggestions and ideas to you for next steps – forward integrations into other programs like Word and Excel, for example – instead of sitting on their hands and bitching about the bots.

The dashboards and the flow charts which you now have access to provide levels of actionable information and data that were never available before and frankly these are the exact tools that you need to move your business forward. Managing by exception rather than brute force is the only way to spread your scarce and costly resources around.

It's been coming for a while now and, like most momentous shifts, it's one of those things that seems impossible until it happens and then, looking backwards with the benefit and precision of hindsight, it appears that it was pretty much inevitable. And then you start to wonder why it took so long for all of us to catch on and see what was happening literally right before our eyes. I think we're at the cusp right now of a comprehensive collapse of the traditional television experience across a much broader spectrum of the population than anyone anticipated and at a much more rapid rate than anyone thought was possible. TV is toast.

Some common behaviors are still shielding the scope of the collapse. TVs are often turned on in many homes and in other venues with no one watching. They serve as inexpensive comfort companions and white noise machines, but no one in their right mind would pay to reach these phantom viewers. It's the old media version of the tree falling in the forest which no one hears. And many of us clearly remain victims of our own inertia and laziness. We can't bring ourselves to cut the cable even though we know in our heads and our hearts that there's no reason to continue to pay for 500 channels crammed with nothing worth watching. And finally, there are the sports nuts who are captive of the ESPN bundles, but even with them, we're also seeing these full-line forcing deals continue to break down as sports-specific and carefully curated streaming services proliferate.

Streaming media is exploding – 73% of millennials are currently using some form of streaming service – Netflix's subscriber base is already bigger than cable. We're getting closer and closer to the world of "OTT and you and me" and it really can't come too soon. In a world where time is the scarcest resource, choice is an imperative and smart time-shifting is the newest superpower. Appointment TV is an albatross soon to be completely discarded.

Frankly, to the extent that anyone's still watching the tube in real time, they're old and tired and no one with any marketing savvy or limited advertising dollars cares about reaching them anyway. This aging and graying marketplace has been a topic of strained and uncomfortable conversations with media execs for a while now, but here again, we're seeing the discussions picking up and the trends accelerating.

Over the last 6 years, the only 2 age groups whose share of watched TV minutes grew were people aged 50-64 (up 5% or so) and those over 65 whose numbers jumped to over 26% of the total TV pie. In terms of live TV versus digital, viewers over 55 watch twice as much broadcast as viewers under 35 and the disparity continues to grow. 500 hours of video is being uploaded to YouTube every minute (Facebook is facing another flood of inbound content) and we're watching over 4 million videos a minute in the U.S. at present.

But what actually brought the seriousness of the situation forcefully home to me and provided some indication of what sad shape the tube is in was a recent announcement from the cigarette guys that they'd be running a year's worth of new disclosure ads on TV. Dollar wise, it's like old home week on Madison Avenue – a clear cause for celebration – and no creativity or client approvals are required since the painful content is specified by the government. But I think of this development as the icing on the TV corpse's cake or casket as the case may be.

Remember that cigarette ads were banned years ago from the networks for obvious reasons including, but not limited to, the fact that these are advertisements created by the creepy people who are consciously continuing to try to poison us and our kids every day. Disgusting for sure, but their latest and most flagrant caper is a testament to a level of manipulation and shamelessness that boggles the mind. They've been required by the courts to make and publish some seriously negative ads and blunt disclosure statements admitting to making cigarettes more addictive and citing stats on deaths from smoking.

But the way they're going about it is a first order fraud that's being foisted on the courts and regulators (and indirectly on the public) and the vehicle for this scam is - wait for it - the Big 3 TV networks who couldn't be happier to take tens of millions of dollars in new advertising from these people. What will the networks be paid for? Running black and white mea culpa ads.

And here's the beautifully awful and wonderfully cynical part of this whole deal. They're running these court-mandated ads 5 days a week for a year on the Big 3 nets in the prime-est of prime time because they know that the people who are going to be watching those ads are the people least likely to need to be talked into buying their cancer sticks. Either those viewers are already lifelong smokers slowly killing themselves or they're people with at least half a brain who concluded long ago that they'd prefer to live a longer and healthier life and dumped the nasty habit.

After all, who is really stupid enough to still smoke these days or, worse yet, to start smoking? The most obvious marketing targets for the tobacco companies are young people and millennials, of course. Kids who think it's cool. 13% of kids under 25 are still smoking and, God forbid, we give them any reasons to quit. So, let's do everything we can to keep them from seeing these stark mandatory messages about disease and death.

How do you do that? You stick all the message smack in the middle of prime time. Hiding in plain sight. And why is that so smart and so cynical? Because today most of the kids and millennials aren't watching TV at all. In fact, 47% of millennials and Gen X'ers watch NO media on traditional TV. PSAs in prime time are about as effective and useful as a phone booth to a moose.

I say all the time that it's just as hard for an entrepreneur to slow down, catch his or her breath, and take stock of the current situation as it is to keep constantly running full speed ahead 24/7/365. This is because I learned long ago that speed isn't of any use if you're running in the wrong direction. We keep insisting that "speed kills" in a good way and that everything today is about rapidity and response time (and for sure these are tremendously important considerations), but too much speed can also be terminal. And honestly, the real competitive question in terms of building and maintaining a sustainable advantage isn't even how fast you are moving today, it's how fast your business is getting faster across all the essential vectors of delivery – time, location, access, convenience, etc. You don't have to beat the bear, but you always have to stay ahead of the guy running beside you.

I realize that this isn't theoretically as much fun as aggressively pursuing the newest, hottest and coolest new thing. There's a lot less to brag about when your peers and fellow YPO-ers ask you what you're working on and what's new. And I appreciate that directors, investors and especially VCs hate to hear things like this, but a little patience, timely infrastructure enhancements, and an actual ongoing plan to look inside as well as outside your business are what pay off in the long run. (See https://www.inc.com/howard-tullman/slow-and-steady-still-wins-the-race.html.) If you get too far out over your skis, you're cruising for a bruising and it's just a matter of when, not whether. The trick in this business is to focus on building a foundation for long-term and sustained success. If you're simply aiming to take the money and run, you'll end up doing just about as well trying to rob a few neighborhood banks.

When you do take the time to look, you often find that there are plenty of opportunities for improvement right under your nose. (See https://www.inc.com/howard-tullman/use-a-mirror-to-mind-your-own-business-first.html.) Typically, these immediately-available and quick-hit adjustments and process or procedural changes are low-hanging fruit, with modest implementation costs, and very little, if any, downside risk versus fairly obvious rewards. In addition, they're substantially easier to get down in a timely fashion. This is because no one turns you down when you offer to make their jobs easier and their efforts more productive. No one really likes to change unless they have to (or you can show them clear and measurable benefits) and it's always hard to give up what worked for you pretty well in the past for the uncertainty of something new, but the things that got it done in the old days just won't deliver tomorrow.

Of course, if things aren't working for you or haven't worked for you in forever, then you'd think that it would be a lot easier to get the ball rolling and to make the necessary changes happen. But it's not. It still takes a special kind of leadership, a lot of preparation and perspiration, fierce perseverance, and a willingness to be the most hated guy on the block for what seems like a painfully long time. If you were really unpopular in high school, you have some idea of what you're signing up for when you take on one of these campaigns.

I found myself thinking about how hard it is (in the context of most startups) for any entrepreneur to have the discipline to live with the short-term hits, complaints and criticisms – from inside and outside the business – and to take the longer-term view as I watched the Houston Astros win the World Series for the first time since 1962 when the team began. And, of course, in Chicago last year, we saw the Cubs pull off the same kind of miracle after more than a century of waiting. (See http://www.inc.com/how-the-cubs-a-140-year-old-baseball-team-operate-like-a-startup.html.) In each case, the management opted for near-term sacrifices and a lot of grief (but no compromises) in order to build a club (and a business) for the long term. There's no question that they were each "going for the gold" and that they didn't have much choice. Tom Ricketts set the bar for the Cubs the day he took over the team and *Sports Illustrated* put a target on the Astros' backs and a media spotlight on every step they took with a flashy cover story that ran more than 3 years ago.

But they both got it done and the lessons for every entrepreneur looking to build his or her business are pretty clear. I'd list the key lessons as follows:

(1) It takes time and a thick skin. Nothing happens overnight.
(2) It takes a team willing to sacrifice for and support each other. Sluggers who are only out for themselves have to go.
(3) It takes character and a culture that cares about more than just winning. There are things more important than money. Making a difference matters most.
(4) It's about managing the terrible tension between consistency and flexibility. Agility is essential, but no less important than a long-term vision.
(5) It's about finding, nurturing and growing talent – mostly homegrown – and being ruthless about the ones who aren't reaching their potential. It's better to make one person miserable than to have a hundred unhappy people and a mediocre business.

It seems that there's always time to do things over (because we often have no choice), but it's a whole lot smarter and much cheaper in the long run to take a little more time at the outset and try to get things right the first time. As the tailors all say: measure twice, cut once.

In the case of your new hires – the inbound talent which will ultimately make or break your business – if you get the messaging and the training wrong at the beginning, these are generally unrecoverable errors and things will only get worse over time. And keep in mind that "newbies" come in all sizes and ages. Gray hair is a sign of age; not wisdom, experience, or knowledge that is specific and relevant to your business.

If you mess things up at the start, you'll soon enough get to that awful and uncomfortable conversation where someone will ask you about one of the new hires and you'll say "I don't know" or "the jury's still out". But here's the truth, when you say "I don't know", the fact is that you <u>do</u> know. And now you have to make a much harder and costlier decision.

Churn kills a lot of young companies because it keeps them from building the core team that will take the company to the next level. And, getting a reputation as a place with a revolving door and constant turnover will make it harder and harder to attract the best talent and the cream of the crop. But keeping people around who aren't cutting it is the worst thing you can <u>ever</u> do. It kills your culture and it will eventually drive your best people away. It's not the people you fire that make your life miserable; it's the ones you don't. Good managers will always tell you that they never fired someone too soon. But the best managers try hard to avoid these situations entirely. (See https://www.inc.com/howard-tullman/three-employees-you-need-to-fire-now.html .)

Investing more time and training in your people in the early days doesn't always work out – even when you have the best of intentions – but, as I look at so many of our startups, they're not even making a reasonable effort to address some very critical concerns which are fundamental to the foundation and future of their companies. You've got to make a commitment early on to giving your newest employees the background, the context, the tools and the training that they will need to succeed. And it helps to build in a few prescriptive guardrails just to make some basic things abundantly clear.

Everyone I ask about their onboarding processes gives me all the usual excuses – "we're just too busy to take the time", "we all went through the same process and we survived", "it's a sink or swim world", etc. Here's a flash – welcoming and training key new hires isn't some hazing process and "surviving" these days isn't the same as thriving – in fact, it's a formula for failure. Ultimately, the only long-term sustainable competitive advantage that your business will have is your people – concerned, committed and dedicated to making a difference. But they won't thrive if they get off to a shaky and wrong-footed start. And this stuff doesn't take place by some process of osmosis or by itself. If you want it to work and to matter to your people, you've got to make it happen. Clear, consistent and constant communication and regular reinforcement is the key. It's just like bathing, if you forget about it for a few days, things start to stink.

And the most important elements of the process don't have anything to do with how the coffee machine works or where to sign up for the spin class; they have everything to do with the company's culture which is the hardest thing for a new person to pick up on and the hardest thing for any business to put into words. I'm not talking about mission statements; this is the meat and potatoes stuff where the rubber meets the road and the real work gets done.

And remember that these folks are under a lot of stress from the organization as well as pressure of their own making. As the Eagles said about the New Kid in Town: "Great expectations, everybody's watching you. People you meet, they all seem to know you. … Everybody loves you, so don't let them down." Also, in case things in a new position weren't confusing enough, these days the basic behavioral ground rules keep shifting as well. A rose may still be a rose, but a hug today is a whole 'nother thing. Every place today has its own rules of the road and norms are a thing of the past.

So how can you help? Here are a few suggestions.

For the Management:

Define the Job/Position and the Time Commitment
Explain Your Expectations in Terms of Behavior and Results
Establish and Share the Job Evaluation Criteria
Make Sure Everyone's on the Same Page
Give Each Newbie a Buddy and a Mentor

For the New Employee:

Hold off on the Hugs.
Hold off on the Humor.
Bag the Beers for a Bit.
Stay Away from Social Media Sharing. (TMI is Trouble)
Be the First to Listen and the Last to Speak.

Way back in April of 2014, I wrote a short cautionary piece for Inc. about some of the good and bad aspects of the cloud and how startups in particular needed to make certain that they didn't end up prematurely spreading their businesses a mile wide and an inch deep which was frightfully easy to do with the many charms and exciting enticements of the cloud. The cloud was cheap, it was relatively easy, and it was everywhere you wanted to be (just like VISA) - all at once. That, of course, was both a blessing and a potential curse if you weren't careful about how you rolled out your offerings. Trying to support and service from here to eternity isn't easy for anybody. (See https://www.inc.com/howard-tullman/in-cloud-we-trust-dont-bet-your-business-on-it.html.)

At that time, especially for new entrants, the main reason that the cloud was so easy and accessible was because there was really only one reasonable and cost-effective on-ramp and that was Amazon Web Services (AWS) which really created the cloud for us civilians who simply didn't care to learn about or pay for any more infrastructure than what was absolutely necessary to get our companies launched. AWS was an inexpensive, ubiquitous and utterly scalable ("buy" the byte – pun intended) solution that seemed to become the industry standard overnight. Google and Microsoft were basically nowhere and IBM wasn't even in the game. Watson was playing chess while Amazon was cashing checks.

I sat in many tense meetings when the guys from Microsoft tried to give people amazing deals on Azure (which Microsoft eventually offered as a cloud alternative) and it was like they were offering to give these people a bad case of acne. They were discovering that they couldn't even give it away and, for my two cents, I didn't see any realistic prospect that things would get better – not because it was a bad service – but because the last thing growing startups can afford (regardless of the "learn as you go" myths and whatever else you've been told) is OJT (on the job training) because no one wants to pay for someone they're paying to learn on their dime. The brutal reality was that – even if you were inclined to try Azure, you couldn't find and hire anyone who knew how to work with it because everyone else you knew (and also every newish business in your neighborhood) was using AWS. If you can't find the horses to hurdle the next hill, you stick with the herd and go with what's tried and true – even if it's relatively new.

So, for several years, I basically believed, once again (just as with the web, with search ("Binged" anyone lately?) and with mobile), that Microsoft had missed the boat. And frankly, when I would continually see that Microsoft still ranked among the most valuable companies in the world and hear that its stock was at all-time highs, I couldn't really understand or explain why that was. I had met Satya at 1871 and he was a terrific and committed technologist, but he wasn't a magician. There had to be more to the story.

Ultimately, whenever I was asked about it, I attributed it largely to the last vestiges of the inertia which kept Windows and Office entrenched for some many years. No one I know is getting any less lazy and it's awfully easy to stick with what has worked for you in the past even though it's very clear that it's not gonna get the job done going forward. Habits and installed bases are hard to break.

But it turns out that I hadn't really picked up on a much bigger boat and a far more material movement. I was so entrenched in our startups and small businesses that I missed how quickly the cloud was transforming the enterprise-level solutions. The biggest businesses in the world can't get to the cloud fast enough. And frankly, this space is Microsoft's home ballpark and increasingly it's once again Microsoft's business to win or lose. I like their odds these days because I learned long ago that, if you want to beat Babe Ruth, you better be playing something other than baseball. (See https://www.inc.com/howard-tullman/forget-about-the-wisdom-of-the-crowd-figure-out-who-matters-most.html.)

However, the real psychological driver – the thing that even Amazon (and certainly GOOGLE as well) will have to eventually overcome - isn't simply the reliance on the breadth and stability of Microsoft's technology (by definition it's almost never cutting-edge); it's that - in our new connected world - where we get into strangers' cars and we invite strangers to stay in our homes and we buy things from people all over the world that we will never meet, nothing matters more than trust and, lo and behold, the big boys trust Microsoft a lot more with their data and their security than they may ever trust the new tech kids on the block. This is what is likely to make Azure a winner in the long run. If you're looking for someone to hold your hand while you're crossing the chasm, it's more than reassuring to be guided and supported by Microsoft who's already there with its legacy customer base. Just as an example, Microsoft's Active Directory service has over a 90% market share in the enterprise.

As hard as it is to believe, Microsoft – an ogre for decades in the past – has become the trusted OG and, most likely, the keeper of the cloud for the future.

W e're on the cusp of some radical changes in how and where we'll be working – driven largely by the introduction of new players and suppliers, new business models, new automation technologies and new connectivity tools – which together are changing the face, the composition, the size and the future of our workforces.

How and how rapidly these new forces will change everything you do in your own companies isn't clear, but it's inevitable. These changes aren't going to be slow and incremental – that's no longer the way the world works – and, as a result, the sooner you start thinking about them and planning for them, the more prepared you're going to be and the more likely you are to be surfing the waves rather than drowning in the floods.

Today, we're all connected by powerful and fully-portable devices which are increasingly intelligent and sentient – we're prepared and we're expected to work anywhere and everywhere – we're on call – like it or not - 24/7 and 365 days a year – and because these are the requirements of our work world today, we readily extrapolate and extend them well beyond our own day-to-day lives into the broader workplace as well. What's good for the goose is equally good for the gander. We're all in a hurry these days and time is the scarcest resource of all.

And, in fact, once we've experienced these hyper-speed services – either as providers or recipients - once we're an active part and a participant in the "right now" economy – it takes no time at all for us to mentally up our own expectations and anticipate exactly the same levels of speed and service throughout the rest of our lives. Why would anyone wait for anything?

If Walgreen's can give me a walk-in, one-minute flu shot, why would I wait three weeks to make a pain-in-the-ass appointment - with my regular doctor's nurse – to get the exact same shot and pay a lot more for the "privilege". And, oh by the way, while I'm at Walgreen's, I can drop off my Fed Ex packages as well since every Walgreen's is now a Fed Ex hub as well.

No business or industry is going to escape these kinds of changes and the smart money is on the people that are thinking today about what they will need to do differently tomorrow in order to not just survive, but thrive in the new mobile and digital economy. The question that you need to be asking yourselves is not simply how do I use some of these new-fangled technologies to do my business better – the critical question is how will I use these new tools to do things for my clients and customers that I never imagined that I could do before. A Chicago startup called LISA has an app (https://lisaapp.com/) which provides easy tenant access to all kinds of onsite personal services. It's like an automated concierge service for office buildings and it's just one good example of what's coming down the line.

These changes (which are coming at a faster and faster pace all the time) will have significant and disruptive impacts on the workplace and on the demands that tenants will be making on their landlords. It's not going to be enough to say that you are fairly responsive and pretty quick – you need to have a plan that is focused not on how fast you are today, but on how fast your business is getting faster and becoming more adept and – most importantly – how capable you are of anticipating and exceeding the needs and requirements of your customers. You need to learn to skate to where the puck is headed, not chase it down the ice.

The expectations of all customers are perpetually progressive and the movement is always up and to the right. What was great yesterday – even things that were miracles of speed and service – are just "so whats" today and business as usual. It's increasingly a "what have you done for me lately" world and – if you're not meeting the demands, you can be sure that there are plenty of others waiting in the wings to step in and fill your shoes. The idea of parity – that "we're no worse than the next guy" is being blown up by new entrants with new business models that aren't held to the same old standards and aren't doing business in the same old way. Traditions these days are – by and large – just excuses offered by people who don't want to change.

Now I understand that almost no one likes change, but it's really not change that's the problem. Changes – when they come – take place in an instant. It's overcoming the resistance to change – the reluctance to leave behind the old ways – to abandon the things that have worked "pretty well" for you in the past – that keeps us from moving forward.

But here's the hard news – what worked for us in the past – simply won't cut it in the future – things aren't going to be a little bit different – the shifts in the ways we do business will make a lot of the old methods and programs – not simply slower or less effective – but essentially meaningless. And, if you don't do it to yourselves, someone else will promptly come right along to do it to you. So, now's the time to get started.

Customers and clients are increasingly fickle folks these days and their definition of loyalty is also new. Today, loyalty doesn't mean much more than I haven't seen anything better – YET. I realize that that's not encouraging, but that's life in the fast lane. No one really owns the customers or clients any more…you can own the moment and the experience, but you have to deliver the goods each and every time.

Everyone knows that Steve Jobs once said that asking customers what they wanted in the way of a new product or service was a waste of time because he said: "customers don't know what they want until we've shown them". There's been a lot of discussion about whether this means that market research is basically useless or whether it means that the way market research has been used by many businesses isn't helpful, instructive or productive. I'd say that it's clearly the latter.

I don't think Steve was condemning an entire industry although he didn't have any great love for gathering or relying upon numbers for numbers sake. I think his basic disinterest was because it's clear – way back then and right up to today – that too many companies use market research like a drunk uses a lamppost – for support rather than illumination. Or worse yet, they approach it like the guy looking for his lost keys beneath the street lamp because that's where the light is best. Convenient, but not constructive. Comforting, but not convincing or compelling.

And, basically, that's what you're doing if you're designing and deploying your market research in order to support foregone conclusions and to justify assumptions about the customers that you've already built into your offerings. If you know what the answers are going to be because you "fixed" the game, then it's not research – it's redundant window dressing – and it's not worth the time, money or effort. It's not an experiment if you already know how things are gonna turn out. And if it's mainly a CYA exercise, to satisfy someone else's fears or anxieties, there are quicker, cheaper and easier ways to deal with their needs. Even medication and mixed drinks are better cures for corporate "concerns" and bureaucratic BS than throwing money away on silly surveys.

On the other hand, if you want to make a sincere effort to use the available tools to get better and smarter about understanding the needs and desires of your existing and potential customers (and to even build on those foundational beliefs to create new needs and drivers), there are some effective ways to go about it. The right field research is absolutely essential when you're focused on incremental and iterative improvements because committed customers are relatively adept at identifying the margins and in describing and detailing adjacent adjustments and tweaks. Please don't leave these things up to your engineers or you'll be adding useless features and added functionality that no one needs. Leave the development of bloatware to the big guys.

When you're looking into "new" as opposed to "next" and when you're trying to cross the chasm and change the game, defining the scope and objectives of your market research efforts is harder and many experts would tell you that it can't be done by asking your customers. I'd say that it depends on what you ask them and what you're looking for in their answers. If your inquiries are oblique rather than obvious and contextual rather than confrontational (not in the aggressive sense of the word, but simply meaning too direct), I think you can learn a great deal.

I like research that focuses on the 4 C's. Conditions, circumstances, concerns, and community. You're looking laterally and you're trying to learn more about the customers' lives than about their expressed likes and longings. These are different, longer range lenses and they're likely to return data relating to longer term, but much more valuable and substantial opportunities as well.

The innovative products of the future (and the ones creating sustainable and valuable new offerings driven by behavioral changes) aren't going to be predicated on new flavors or even fabulous new features as much as they're going to address fundamental needs that are often apparent from the outside, but which consumers and customers are often reluctant to address or admit. I saw an interesting example of this entire process recently in Japan.

I don't know whether to primarily blame office cost savings and cutbacks; the fact that no one wants to make and wait for an entire pot of coffee; or the ease, convenience and ready access provided by the new abundance of coffee shops, but all over Japan, they are eliminating coffee makers in offices. This has basically killed the coffee break and, much more importantly, the conversations, the collisions, and even some of the social interactions and community that used to be a part of these places. Maybe they still gather at the water cooler for chats, but I doubt that as well. It was clear from Nestle's research that the employees in these businesses missed the breaks and the chatter far more than just the coffee.

So, the CEO of Nestle Japan decided to build a single-serving coffee maker for offices without their own machines which used one-shot cartridges, but his rollout plan also took into account the real pain point for the target consumers which was actually the loss of connection and community. The new machine has been a huge success, BUT not for the reasons that you might expect. In fact, if Nestle had simply tried to sell the machines (and the cartridges) into the many offices which had just gotten rid of their previous machines, the whole project would have been a bust. And giving away simply the machines for free (planning to sell the "razor blades") wouldn't have worked either because the aggregate weekly costs of the cartridges are not insignificant.

Nestle's plan enlisted individual advocates and influencers in each business office and these people "work" for Nestle for free by collecting payments from each employee weekly for their coffees and then remitting the sums to Nestle in order to replenish the cartridge supply. Not only has the connection point been restored, and the community reinvigorated, but the very acts of the collection process have increased the inter-personal interactions and engagement of all of the participating employees in the program.

Needless to say, there's no way that any traditional front-facing research would have elicited the underlying drivers and real desires of the customers. Even more importantly, it turns out that the real "customers" weren't the businesses themselves, but the individual employees who were consuming the coffee. A standard survey of the employers wouldn't have uncovered any part of the problem or helped to determine an innovative and immediate solution to the issue of funding the program.

Customers can't tell you what they don't know – especially if they're not actually the customers who matter.

These days the old HR rules and the standard practices and behaviors (which never meant much anyway in the startup world) are changing so rapidly (just like everything else in our lives) that the management approaches and motivational strategies which used to work may or may not get the job done. There's no longer a simple rule book that's worth anything in a world where no one knows what's politically right or wrong from day to day and the sands keep shifting. I'm not talking here about the current conversations regarding sexual abuse and harassment. Those are black and white cases of stupidity or criminality and have no place in any business.

But when you're trying to build your company culture from scratch, along with everything else, ambiguity about how you and your team members treat each other is the last thing you can afford. Language, lectures, liquor, looking at someone the wrong way - these are all potential land mines and I guess we're gonna need new signs saying "huggers beware" in our lounges. Thumper used to tell Bambi to say nothing if she couldn't say something nice, but the best advice today seems to be to say nothing period if you want to stay out of trouble. Of course, that makes it tough to run your business. So where do we go from here?

There have been debates among business consultants and corporate shrinks for centuries over whether the carrot or the stick is the most effective motivation tool for your people. As far as I can see, the jury is still out. And it's getting harder all the time to determine how to move things forward in your company without going too far. I'm talking about everything from how you talk to your team to trying to "tell it like it really is" to people inside and outside your shop. It's increasingly an eggshell world and things that were common practices and words that used to be "aw shucks" are now likely to cause some awful anguish and some very unhappy people.

Part of the problem is that a lot of the effectiveness of the approach you pick depends on the particular context of your communications, the relationships between the concerned parties, and even on the type of business or industry itself. For example, we see both approaches in politics every day. One politician threatens his opposition (and even the people in his own party) with all kinds of grief and retribution - funding new primary opponents - pushing them to vote publicly for unpopular bills or initiatives - badgering them from his bully pulpit - etc. Another one takes the exact opposite tack - he'll always have your back if you're in his party - he'll never put you between a rock and a hard place with your constituents - and he'll do everything in his power to make sure your seat is safe. And as we know, keeping your seat and your job is what it's actually all about for these guys. As my old friend Bill McGowan (founder of MCI) used to say: "these guys have great loyalty to their businesses, but their number one loyalty is to their own tush." In your own case, you've got to decide what's likely to be the best way to deal with your people, your partners and vendors, and the public at large.

It's also becoming clear that there may be significant changes in what will be effective depending on the ages of the people you're trying to influence and/or incent. We keep hearing about young people who want to work for a company with a cause and one that's more than just building the bottom line. The incentives that will matter to them and, in fact, their own goals are likely to be a lot more complicated than those of your longer-term team members. And there will be a sub-section of these newbies that haven't really decided what their own goals would or should be and that makes them into moving and very difficult targets. They're clearer on what they don't want to be a part of than on what's important or how they plan to weigh and balance the life challenges and choices we all have to make. It's just like looking at art - easy to tell what you don't like - hard to know what's good and likely to last and matter over time. And if you think it's hard to evaluate inanimate objects, getting an accurate read on the folks you work with is much more difficult.

It's just so darn easy these days for a supervisor or manager to inadvertently "disrespect" someone when he or she is only trying to suggest to them that there might be a better way to do their job. I say "suggest" because it seems that no one today actually gets to "tell" anyone how to do anything. It's hard to see how things can be improved and how businesses are going to get better when we spend more time tap dancing around people's feelings than we do focusing on the facts of their performance. We can't all be winners and wonders all day long. (See https://www.builtinchicago.org/blog/we-all-lose-when-everybody-wins.)

And, as I wrote a while ago, there's also a pretty convincing school of thought that - in the best companies - motivation is not something you do to people - it's something that comes from within them provided that (a) you do a good job of setting the stage and creating the right environment and culture and (b) you do an even better job of not demotivating them. It's all bi-directional. As I used to tell my faculty when I ran Kendall College and Tribeca Flashpoint, it's not what you teach, but what they learn that matters. And no one learns much of anything if they don't actually care. (See https://www.inc.com/howard-tullman/trying-to-motivate-your-employees-forget-it.html.)

I think we're at an important crossroads right now because there's no more important determinant of the likely success of a new business than the passion and the emotions of the people driving it forward. If we're all increasingly afraid of our own shadows, scared to reach out to others and share our feelings, and afraid to connect closely to the people we work with and care about, we're not going to be building the kind of businesses in the future that anyone can be proud of.

As we are about to begin the new year, I was reminded of the old adage that the biggest mistakes in business are made in what we think of (at the time) as the good times, not when the going gets rough. And, although it may just be me and Taylor Swift who think this, I'd say that from the perspective of the stock market and its reflected glow which has certainly made it easier for millions of startups to come by cheap capital and especially easy for a bunch of really bad ideas and crappy businesses to get funded, these are pretty heady days and a fair number of financial folks are feeling pretty fat and happy. So, I'd say now's the time for a word of caution or two.

First, do whatever you want to do about investing in cryptocurrencies, but if you insist on doing it, do it directly and for your own account. Don't be stupid enough to hire or pay someone to help you become a bitcoin miner (whatever you think that means these days) or let anyone convince you that there's anything easy or trivial or even well understood in the entire process. Stick to something you know something about. And, if you're still on the fence and your greed still threatens to overwhelm your good sense, there's another rather simple test you can use when these bozos try to foist their "farms" on you and rent you a piece of the future. Just ask them how come they're still hawking this junk if they're so prescient and far ahead of the crypto curve. Or, more simply stated, if they're so smart, how come they're not already rich. The guys who made the most money in the Gold Rush didn't strike gold, they sold deeds to the dopes and shovels to the suckers. Try not to be either in the year ahead.

Second, on the same subject, don't do your friends and especially your family the favor of helping them into this particular swamp. FOMO fever is rampant, but just remember that you barely understand what's going on and you have absolutely no business trying to talk someone else (who clearly can't focus on the likely prospect of or afford the eventual losses) into jumping into the puddle with you. I get that misery loves company, but you'll have to live with some of these people for the rest of your life (if they don't kill you first) and the pain of all those future lectures isn't worth the few moments of pride you get for being "in the know". I've already said my piece on the merits of the whole bitcoin subject (See https://www.inc.com/howard-tullman/why-i-bailed-on-bitcoin.html.) and I sold my bitcoins a while back (once I figured out how to find them and re-gain access to my account) when I was reminded of another old market adage that every smart trader knows – you never lose money taking a profit too soon. Sure, you may leave some shekels on the table, but unlike the pigs who will eventually get stuck holding the empty poke, you'll have plenty of dry powder for next time.

Third, nobody you know actually knows anything about artificial intelligence and, notwithstanding that fact, 99% of the startups you'll see business plans and proposals from over the next year (along with all of those painfully pivoting to the proposition as well) will tell you that they do. The truth is that they don't and the last thing you want to spend your time and money on is funding their OJT (on-the-job-training) while they try to figure things out. A.I. is not business process automation. It's not predetermined pattern recognition. It's not accelerated data retrieval. Building a behind-the-scenes bot or a series of macros or tagging a bunch of pixs as a library for future image recognition isn't A.I. and the fact that your CRM program knows my shoe size isn't machine learning.

This is another one of those conversations where it's hard to know where to start complaining because - in so many of these cases – even if they had the remotest idea of what they were talking about – the tools and technologies that they're bragging about have little or nothing to do with the business they used to say they were in and maybe even less to do with where they say they're heading. They spew all these annoying acronyms and exaggerate their exactitude with a bunch of assertions that are really fantasies of false precision.

We used to say that, notwithstanding what your engineers think, it's clear that not every product, service or application needs to be larded up with an email function for no good reason. Your dog doesn't need email and it's not really clear to me while we're just talking here that an 8-year-old needs a Facebook account either, but sadly we're very likely to see these things happen. And, today, I feel that we are seeing the same bad behavior and all the associated BS with virtually every company (young and old) which is now claiming that their product or service incorporates powerful machine learning and AI systems. Here's a flash – if you have to tell it what to do, it might be augmented intelligence or a good supplementary tool for decision support, but it ain't A.I. when the primary "I" in the equation is you.

Some of these claims may be real and accurate, but a bunch are just smoke and mirror stories which are likely to give us all the bad name. Can we put a stake in it before the conversations go completely crazy? It'll save us all a lot of headaches and heartaches down the line. My barber needs predictive A.I. tools like a fish needs a bicycle.

Finally, while you are changing your smoke alarm batteries, change your passwords to something secure (or get a password security system like Keeper (www.keepersecurity.com) in place for your business) because getting hacked these days isn't a matter of "if", it's just a question of "when". Happy Healthy New Year.

The end of the year is always a tough time for entrepreneurs. There are several reasons for this and you'd think that, after a few years, it's a time of year that even a first timer starter-upper would get used to suffering through, but that's not how things work in the business of building new businesses. Even the very best entrepreneurs are "glass half empty" folks who are always focused on what didn't get done in the year just ended and - even more importantly (or depressingly) - what remains to get done on the long, winding and bumpy road ahead. The pressure never lets up and everyone eventually learns that there's no finish line.

I've said before that entrepreneurs are lousy at graceful gratitude and even worse at saying "thank you", not because we're ingrates, but because we barely believe in our own successes and good fortune and because we're forward-focused - always climbing the next hill or facing the newest challenge instead of reflecting on (or celebrating) the past. (See https://www.inc.com/howard-tullman/why-entrepreneurs-are-really-terrible-at-saying-thank-you.html.) This isn't always a bad thing and it's part of the psychology (or pathology if you prefer) that also makes it possible for entrepreneurs to quickly get over their past hiccups and get on with their main job of making history and changing the world.

It also turns out that it's not a condition or circumstance that anyone else can really help you get over. Friends, family, faculty and even most "mentors" aren't gonna make much of a difference. Mentors especially can be a mixed blessing. You won't actually know if a one-timer winner was smart or just lucky to be in the right place at the right time. And it's especially hard to gain much great guidance from someone who "sold" their startup six minutes before the sheriff came to take away their keys and shut the doors. You never want to ask for directions from someone who hasn't been there and, with too many mentors, it's very hard to effectively convert their particular experience into something that means much to you in the moment. (See https://www.inc.com/howard-tullman/how-to-deal-with-marginal-mentors.html.)

It's not that all of these folks are unwilling to help (or try), it's that, if you haven't been there and/or you're not living through it right at the moment, you really just don't understand, and all the empathy, good will and best intentions won't make up for the fact that you're in the soup and they're sitting on the sidelines. You learn in this business that money doesn't really care who makes it and that having a bunch of bucks says basically nothing about your brains or your business sense.

So, if there's no help elsewhere, you're pretty much stuck with looking inward. That's not the worst thing in the world because – at least when you're alone – you're with someone you love. I think about this a lot every year when New Year's Eve rolls around and I'm making a command appearance at any place that I'd rather not be which is basically every place you can imagine. Yes, I know that it sounds like an inverse testimonial ad for Visa. And, if this admission cuts down on my future NYE invites, it's a price I guess I'll just have to happily pay.

O.K. You're stuck with talking to yourself and what can you say to help get over the year end blues and back to business? I wrote a pretty good piece on this a while ago that's worth revisiting (See https://www.inc.com/howard-tullman/holiday-resolution-get-past-the-past.html.) and, in case you're too lazy to link back, the 3 main suggestions were: (1) Get Past the Past as Soon as Possible; (2) Call on Your Customers While You Still Can; and (3) When You're Thinking About Quitting, Remember Why You Started.

But it was the last few lines in the post that were the most important to me – then and now. I wrote:

"...there's nothing in the world that a true entrepreneur would rather be doing than exactly what you're doing every day. Working on a dream, and doing it with a group of people who are as excited and enthusiastic about what they're doing as you are is the greatest privilege anyone can have. And it's you that's making it possible...."

It's hard and lonely to be a leader – it always has been – and it's an enormous responsibility that you have taken on – to yourself and your family, to your investors and your employees, and to your customers and clients – all of whom look to you and depend on you – day-in and day-out – to make their lives different and better in important ways.

It's a journey that you take on and that you take all by yourself – even as you find yourself constantly surrounded by others. You may go fastest by yourself, but you go furthest with a strong and dedicated team beside you.

And ultimately you will find that, even when and if your faith in yourself falters from time to time, what really matters and gets you thru is the faith, the confidence, and the trust that you place in others that makes all the difference. You aren't a real leader until others believe that you are putting them first and serving a purpose greater than yourselves.

Great leaders don't create followers, they create new and better leaders. Make that your most pressing project for the New Year.

Every year around this time, I try to remind my team about a few basics – half a dozen simple rules of the road – which have served me well over the last 50 years. I do this not so much because I think they need instruction (we all definitely "know" what we're supposed to be doing), but because each and every one of us needs regular reminders since it's just too easy in the heat of battle and the stress of the day-to-day to forget, skip over, or just plain ignore some of the business fundamentals which will ultimately separate the winners from the also-rans. So, here's my short list.

(1) Pay Attention and Write It Down

Focused attention facilitates learning and retention. Take good detailed notes in every meeting. The dullest pencil beats the sharpest memory. Don't sit there pretending that you can simply take it all in. You can't. There's absolutely no substitute in life for paying attention and making it a habit to capture the essential information during each meeting is the best way to keep your head in the game and your eye on the ball. If you're gonna be present, make sure that you're all there. (See https://www.inc.com/howard-tullman/what-i-learned-from-my-waitress-and-what-you-can-too.html.)

And, as an aside, lawyers who advise you to keep only brief minutes of critical meetings are morons who are just trying to make their jobs or lives easier. Finally, the goal is always the same: try to be at least a little smarter by the end of the meeting. If you can't honestly convince yourself of that, then maybe going to the meeting was a waste of time. (See https://www.inc.com/howard-tullman/make-your-meetings-crisp-or-forget-them.html.)

(2) Use A Calendar and Start Your Planning Yesterday

Start right now and scope out the whole year to the extent that you can and keep doing this all year long at least monthly. There's a lot going on all the time and it's hard to keep up. If you do this right, it's a lot like having your own crystal ball. It's not magic and there's no mystery – it's all about good preparation and research. In fact, it's like owning a slo-mo machine in our sped-up world. You get an edge on the competition because you've already been there.

This simple process enables far better planning and preparation; avoids embarrassing conflicts which might bury you (you'll never get noticed if you build your campfire next to a conflagration); assures fewer surprises and last-minute emergencies; and makes for many less missed opportunities. Doing your homework ahead of time avoids headaches and heartaches all year long. (See https://www.inc.com/howard-tullman/the-most-underrated-planning-tool-in-business.html.)

And, especially for a startup, it's a great way to save time and marketing dollars. Parades are very expensive – go find an event or someone else's parade (who's headed in the right direction for your purposes) and run right alongside of them or even race to the head of their conga line. A lot of the big guys have plenty of money to stage great parties, but they're slow as molasses. Trying to lay your own track – build your own pipeline or highway – or even just bust through the noise and clutter that's out there is crazy when you can just hitch a ride on someone's else railroad and ride for free on their dime. Hop on board before the other guys even know what's happening. But understand that you can't do it if you don't make it your business to know what's going on and what the world around you is doing.

(3) Do More Reading and Less Tweeting

Let your fingers do the walking, but not the talking. Give your phone and your peeps a break and shut up for a while on social. The smartest people I know read something relevant to their business every day – as often as not (even these days) it's in print - in a book or a magazine – or even in a newspaper. I'm not talking about the shit on social, but real substantive material. Some of it may be internal business reporting; some of it may be competitive intelligence; some may be customer inquiries and feedback, and some of it may be blue-sky, but it all adds value and improves outcomes when it's coupled with intelligent action. You can't win a race with your mouth or your social media meanderings. (See https://www.inc.com/howard-tullman/dont-talk-your-idea-to-death.html.)

And keep in mind that you're not being paid to waste your time and your company's money churning for hours though irrelevant newsfeeds and random tweets. Here's a flash: if you aren't being paid, you're not the producer or the driver of the engagement or even in control of the show; you're the product whose eyeballs and alleged mindshare are being sold to the highest bidder – just like the patsy in the poker game – if you don't know who the sucker is, you're the sucker.

(4) Ask Questions Until You Understand the Answers

Someone said: "better to remain quiet and be thought a fool than to speak up and remove all doubt", but they were dead wrong. The truth is that virtually all innovation these days comes from asking the right questions and it's absolutely an iterative process. If you're afraid to be embarrassed or to admit that you don't know it all, join the club and then get over yourself. We're all just bumbling through this stuff and no one has the secret formula or has figured it all out. As long as you've done your homework, there really aren't any dumb questions and anyone who's ever run a tech startup will tell you that: (a) the most important thing is to know all the questions rather than to have all the answers because (b) no one ever knows either all the questions or all the answers, but that shouldn't stop us from asking. And the most critical question to ask is the one that you need to ask yourself every day: How badly do I want it?

(5) Remember to Regularly Review Your Reverse Roadmap

It's frankly depressing to see how many young entrepreneurs are basically working for next to nothing and just don't know it yet. Of course, if you don't care where you end up, then any road will take you there. But if you do (and especially if you're also looking out for the members of your team who are also working their butts off), then it makes sense to take the time to figure out where you actually stand and where you're likely to end up in terms of dollars and cents. I realize that it's supposed to be all about the journey and the joy of building something, but it doesn't mean you can't be a little mindful of the math that ultimately matters. This stuff isn't easy, but understanding it is essential. Take the time to get smart about it or be smart enough to ask someone who knows to give you a helping hand. (See https://www.inc.com/howard-tullman/why-you-need-a-reverse-roadmap.html.)

(6) Raises Aren't Revenues

Too many folks are focused today on the fundraising process rather than on building sustainable businesses. It's a problem that's aided and abetted by the media which celebrates every new round because it's easier than digging into the merits and the mechanics of the actual businesses and it's a simple way to keep score.

But, all the cash any business raises don't mean squat without satisfied customers and serious sales. Paid invoices are a much more reliable indicator of whether your business is going to work than additional investments. (See https://www.inc.com/howard-tullman/bury-the-unicorpses-and-get-real.html.)

And then there's that little thing called profits which turns out to be the most important thing of all. Spending money is easy; making money is hard. Just because you killed a cow doesn't mean that you're gonna eat steak for dinner. There's a lot of difficult work and nasty details to attend to and none of it is easy.

TULLMAN'S TRUISMS

THE FAINTEST INK IS CLEARER THAN THE SHARPEST MEMORY

Now that we're past the holidays and hopefully beyond all the talk, stress and angst of the always painful year-end compensation discussions, I wanted to discuss a far more important conversation that also takes place right around this time of year. It's usually one we have at home immediately prior to the time when we all solemnly make those annual "work less and spend more time with the family" resolutions along with the accompanying promises and commitments to our partners and our kids.

Every entrepreneur (and everyone else building a business) knows how these things go especially today when we're all working longer and harder, spending less time with our families and loved ones, and feeling somewhat rotten and very guilty about it. And, by the way, it doesn't make it any easier or less emotional just because there are really good reasons for the extra time away or because the jobs we're doing are actually that important not just to ourselves, but to plenty of others as well. As I usually say: there's always more work, but you've only got one family.

So it is that in these family meetings and other conversations, we find ourselves explaining and excusing and generally trying to justify our efforts and our absences to our families and especially to our kids. And, unfortunately, for lack of a better or more straightforward explanation, we often seize upon a particularly unfortunate turn of a phrase and a pretty lousy excuse. We say (in so many different ways and words) basically that:

I work to make money: to buy you (*fill in the blank*); or

I work to make money: to provide you with (*insert here*); or

I work to make money: so we can do or go (*destination please*).

You get it, right? Sounds familiar doesn't it. Maybe it's a spouse, but most often it's our kids. And just what are we telling them? We're telling our kids that we work for money - that money is what matters - and that money is to buy things, places, people, etc. - that "getting" is really the be-all and the end-all. And that's too bad. Because it's a bad explanation, a dishonest excuse, and a bad message. In fact, it's probably the worst message possible. But it's quick and easy and we all fall into this trap from time to time. But we can do better and, frankly, we better do better because our kids are already drowning in media messages that say – a million times a day - it's all about the bucks.

So, I have a modest suggestion for the next time you find yourself in this particular fix. Let's try to change the context - change the conversation - and tell our loved ones the truth (or maybe just what we hope the truth should be) whenever we're asked about why we work. But, of course, it helps to spend a little time thinking about a better answer before the fat's in the fire.

What is the truth? What's the honest answer? It helps - by the way - to start by being honest with yourself. When you're dragging, feeling a little sorry for yourself, can't take another day of work (and it's only Wednesday), and you find yourself mumbling and grumbling to yourself that "we need the money" or "I have no choice" or "I've got bills to pay", you're just kidding yourself just like we've all been kidding our kids for years.

If you don't know (or admit to yourself) why you're working and what you're working for or you can't think of a good reason to come to work, then do yourself and everyone else a favor and go find something else to do. I tell all our 1871 companies the same thing: "we act as though comfort and luxury were the chief requirements of life when all we need to make us really happy is something to be enthusiastic about." If you don't love it (most of the time), leave it.

O.K. you say, but what is the right answer when the kids ask (as you're sneaking out the door on Saturday morning to spend the day at the office): "Hey Dad, how come you never come home?" Or maybe: "Why is work so important all the time, don't we come first?"

I think the truth and the best answer is that we work for two basic reasons: (A) to make ourselves proud and (B) to help other people. We don't really work for money. We work to be productive and creative. We work to make a difference in our lives and the lives of others. We work because we secure real satisfaction from what we achieve with our hands, our hearts and our minds.

There's no price tag on the stuff. Money isn't even a good way to keep score. Does anyone really think that a rock star's contribution is millions of times more valuable than a teacher's? That's just more media bullshit. We work to accomplish things that move our lives forward, that matter in material ways, and that we can feel honestly and sincerely good about it. There's no shame or false pride in that. There's nothing to be embarrassed to tell your kids about. If you love it, let them know and pray that someday they'll have a similar experience and privilege.

Is it foolish (or do we sound selfish) if we admit that we work because it makes us feel good and fulfilled? I don't think so and I think it's a much more constructive, effective, and appropriate answer for everyone - kids and grownups too. Don't tell your kids you work because you have to, or worse, that you work to buy them Christmas toys or other goodies. We work because it's important and that's what grown-ups do. It's something to be unashamedly proud of and to share with our kids and others. We're building things to make the world a better place.

And that's where Part b comes in. We're not isolated islands and in this thing all by ourselves. Everything we do or don't do impacts many others - especially those of us who teach. So, it's just as important to understand, acknowledge and have our kids appreciate that - apart from the selfish motivation of making us feel good - we all work as well for a greater good and to help others by making their lives better and fuller as well as our own. Hard work and commitment is how life moves forward and how the world gets better. A lot of tiny steps by millions of people - a little bit at a time - and mountains move.

And that just leaves the matter of money. What should we say about money? I hope that the message I've shared with my kids is pretty simple. Money, beyond life's necessities, is for charity and for giving back. It's not an end in itself. It's not a game of running up the score. It's not a worthwhile goal because there's no finish line and there's always someone with more. At best, it's an enabling and an ennobling tool to make valuable, important, and charitable things happen.

The bottom line: work hard and be proud of the work you do; love what you do or do something else; try to make a difference in this world every day in large and small ways; and use all of your talents, energy and resources to help others to better their lives. And lastly, hug your kids much too much, far too often, and until they squeal.

TULLMAN'S TRUISMS

WHEN YOU BLAME OTHERS, YOU GIVE UP YOUR POWER TO MAKE THINGS CHANGE

A dark "secret" from my past is resurfacing in the form of businesses that are selling nonsense and calling it artificial intelligence. I'm embarrassed. I feel a little bit like Frankenstein's father. The "monster" I built is somewhat more mundane than the big guy of fiction. On the other hand, my creature is real - it's alive! - and taken on a life of its own, morphing into something that's just as evil and mendacious. Worse yet, my creation is spawning a whole new generation of artificial intelligence impostors and other simple macros masquerading as intelligent machines.

I wrote briefly about this problem and the rampant confusion in a recent post, but I think it needs some further explanation so we can all try to get on the same page and set some basic ground rules about this A.I. stuff.

About 40 years ago, I built a relatively simple system that I named the "consultant in a box." The system linked specific numerical scores and behavioral rankings with phrases and texts, which were then combined by a word processor into what appeared to be evaluative paragraphs prepared by a sociologist or psychologist. We sometimes jokingly called this glorified Wang program our "shrink on a stick" because it created frighteningly convincing formulations that could fool most readers and reviewers into thinking the reports were the product of thorough research and thoughtful analysis. They were instead *pro forma* pap being poured out of a production line.

On its very best days, my little monster machine would put out dozens of slick little synopses that ranked and rated sales people and jobseekers. These rankings were no better than, and about halfway between, horoscopes and fortune cookies. But they were completely convincing because we had figured out how to quickly, easily and inexpensively tell a whole lot of people in a hurry just what they thought they wanted to hear.

In the years that followed, I incorporated my evaluation engine into a variety of different technical and mechanical environments. It even eventually directed the way various characters reacted and responded to choices made by each player in one of my more successful CD-ROM computer games, called "ERASER TURNABOUT" and published by Warner Bros. Interactive. The way the player initially responded to a detailed "interactive" video conversation with the psychiatrist in the game determined the ways in which the game progressed and the player's journey as well as his or her likely success. The system essentially produced a different variation of the game every time it was played. These days-; literally decades later-; companies like Narrative Science turn baseball box scores into newspaper stories and stock stats into portfolio analyses, albeit with a touch more science and a little less schmaltz.

But my shabby past came painfully back to haunt me just recently during a board meeting, as we sat reviewing reports on prospective candidates while trying to find a great new head of sales for one of my portfolio companies. One of the participants started trying to parse and analyze a couple of the boilerplate comments buried in a bogus report that was put together by the company's HR team. She might just as well have been reading tea leaves. Turns out the HR guys used some outside consulting/recruiting firm that was in turn using a system just like my old one to crank out this crap and try to convince some clients that what they were reading had even the slightest connection to reality.

If it hadn't been so ludicrous (no offense to Ludacris), it would have just been pitiful to see such a waste of time and money. I wouldn't rely on a program like this to pick a horse in the fifth race at Pimlico much less to select the person you were trying to hire to help you build your business. But there we were watching someone trying to make sense out of sentences arranged by a software program that had about as much substance as the server aligning the silverware brings to the task of setting the table. The server knows exactly where to place the spoon, but hasn't the slightest idea of whether you're going to use it to eat your soup or your spumoni. It's all a matter of placement and proximity - location and language - and not about performance or personality. Just because you know where to stick a fork doesn't mean that you understand what to do with it.

And that's what got me thinking again about what's so wrong about the way too many people are talking about artificial intelligence. As I've said before, true A.I.-; when it arrives-; won't be about business process automation. This is the easy stuff that bots ought to be doing already in a bunch of big businesses. A.I. is not as simple as predetermined pattern recognition (or tagging a million pix for future matching), which is really all about accessing memory. Simply asking a machine to find and match text in a database that aligns with the content of queries initiated by a user isn't moving the needle forward. It's certainly not to be confused with "reading" or as exhibiting any actual intelligence. And finally, there's nothing to get all excited about regarding accelerated data sourcing, which is nothing more than rapid recall and retrieval. So, what's a simple test for the real A.I. of the future?

I think A.I. comes down to two simple words: Extraction and Extrapolation. A true A.I. system will perform both functions without supervision or ongoing direction. It will have procedural rules, some data management protocols, and guard rails, but no *a priori* restrictions or limitations.

Extraction in this context means that the system will continuously review the flow of data (which is basically unstructured) and from the data flow it will derive and identify behaviors, frequencies and trends-; not by comparing them to pre-existing models or patterns, but instead by finding new ones that were previously unknown, unbounded or otherwise unidentified. The determination of the ranges and boundaries of these new "objects" will be among the most critical chores of the new systems, which will need to ascertain the extent, perimeters and parameters of the new patterns and objects by applying new measurements of power, density and frequency to the data flows. As the power and presence of the new objects diminishes at the margins, the boundaries of the new phenomena will be ascertained and locked in.

Extrapolation in this context means that the system will have the independent capacity to capture these new patterns and objects. And beyond that, to rationally build upon them, expand them and-; most particularly-;generalize their patterns and behavior into other areas, both adjacent and remote. Critically, the fundamental activities will not be the incremental expansion of prior experiences and analytical results, but instead create and develop new projections and anticipatory expectations of future behaviors and activities.

The bottom line: if you already know why, it ain't A.I.

Recent revelations about phony Twitter followers are the latest twist in an old game of audience amplification. You need to make sure that you're always locked in on the right metrics. And more importantly, that you're always acting on the information.

It's never too soon when you're starting a new business to take a break, catch your breath, look around, and make sure you're heading in the right direction, doing the right things in the right way, and chasing the right rabbit. Chasing too many rabbits at once is a formula for failure. Doing things just to keep busy (or because you can't sit still) is both debilitating and dumb. And it doesn't matter how fast you're going if you're on the wrong road. So, do yourself a favor and slow down occasionally. This isn't anything you don't know. What matters is having the discipline to stop and take stock of where you are and to "course correct" mistakes in a timely fashion before they become unrecoverable failures. Left to themselves, problems will fester and only get worse-- they rarely go away. Fixing things doesn't happen by itself. I've developed a simple set of steps to guide you in the process. I call these the 5 A's:

Audit: figure out where to look for opportunities/exposures and what to look for;

Analyze: determine what's going on--right and wrong--and when changes need to be made;

Act/Adjust: bite the bullet and do what needs to be done, but don't take on too much at one time;

After Action: see what happened, good and bad, and,

Anticipate: get started on what's next.

Keep in mind that tweaks are fine-- not everything is a teardown or a complete redo. You don't test the depth of a puddle by jumping in with both feet. As we like to say, start small and scale. Importantly, don't plan on stopping, because this is an ongoing, constant, and iterative process where you get better a little bit at a time all the time. But only if you get started and keep at it. Not all the time-- not every day-- but in a regular and systemic way. Just like innovation, continuous improvement is not a department or a part time thing or a chore. Always striving to get better at what you do is part of the culture of the best businesses.

The second and equally important part of the process is proper metrics. What gets measured in your business is what ultimately gets done because that's what you are paying attention to. Of course, watching and measuring the right things is paramount.

Metrics are all the rage today because Americans love nothing more than keeping score. All kinds of folks-- well-intentioned and also awful people--play off that desire every day. I can remember in the simpler times when we thought that clickbait headlines and listicles for losers were about as low as you could go in the corrupt competition for eyeballs. I warned then warned then that tricked traffic, vicarious visitors, and the kind of morons attracted to the latest news on Momma whoever›s new diet weren›t worth reaching or pitching to in any case because they weren›t buying anything worth selling-- but at least we thought they were living, breathing human beings. I said:

> "...if you're advertising on a web site, and its primary traffic drivers are hacks, tricks and clever pet pix, what are its visitors really worth? Even assuming that those visitors are people and not tracking robots?
>
> I›d argue that they›re not worth your time and certainly not worth your money. Instead of attracting people who might be interested in your products or services and also highly influential, you can end up spending money to attract mobs of easily-influenced people who probably couldn›t explain how they got to a given website if they were asked.»

How naïve I was: things can always get worse and more disgusting. Because the race to the bottom never ends, and lowlifes can be innovative, too. The latest craze of fraudulent exaggeration allows you to buy bots to tweet your site and acquire fake robotic followers to build up your alleged "audience," a service provided by shady scumbags in foreign lands. Duping people into thinking your social media voice (your megaphone) is much bigger and broader than it actually is isn't much different from the many ways that marketers seeking to monetize their media have lied about their metrics, viewership and reach since the beginning of time. But that's a swamp for another day.

For the moment, what's critical as you review your business is to be sure that you're measuring the right behaviors and results in the right way. To do this correctly, you've got to go all the way. Too often we settle for part of the story or fall for the form and forget the substance. I see this all the time in software and solution implementations. Too many IT professionals think they are keeping score, but they aren't really asking deep enough questions or looking hard enough at what's going on in order to actually know the score.

Effective software rollouts are a three-step process and every step counts. First, you have deployment -- getting the stuff on everyone's machines and devices. You can't stop there. Second, you have adoption-- are people using the new tools and solutions-- are the dogs eating the dogfood? That's a good next step, but you're not home yet. Finally: results. Is the whole big hairy deal making a real difference in your operations and your bottom line? If not, it wasn't worth the trip. This is the hardest and most uncomfortable question because no one might like the answer. The rule here is simple: if you've made a mistake, you've got to acknowledge that bad news and make the necessary changes. You should never stick to a mistake just to try to justify the time and money you spent making it.

Metrics are messy, but they're the keys to the kingdom; you've got to master the ones that matter. And they're fluid. Smart businesses are flexible enough to shift the ways they keep score (even when this may be unpopular with their customers) if the new approach makes more sense and is a better and more representative way to track the behaviors that drive the bottom line. A very relevant example is the recent shift that Starbucks made to its rewards program. Instead of simply tracking store visits, Starbucks shifted to tracking what the visitors/customers actually spent which, of course, makes so much more sense. The airlines figured this out a while ago and adjusted their frequent flyer programs to emphasize dollars spent over miles traveled or segments flown.

Part of your review process should focus on the same kinds of questions and concerns. Maybe you're measuring what's easy to measure. Maybe you're measuring things that don't matter and wasting time and money doing that. Maybe you're too focused on squeaky wheels and not on long-term loyal customers. There are a lot of ways to get this wrong and only one way to get it right. Get started.

TULLMAN'S TRUISMS

DATA IS THE OIL OF THE DIGITAL WORLD

253 – WHY YOU SHOULD NEVER LET KYLIE JENNER ENDORSE YOUR PRODUCT

I'm sure that it was a major PR and ego blow to the team at Snap -- and apparently to Snap's market cap -- when, to the utter surprise and amazement of the social media morons who breathlessly track and «report» on all this commotion and noise, one member of the hyper-alliterative Kardashian family (does it really matter which one?) abruptly decided to abandon her stupefying Snapchatting in favor of some equally superficial and petulant posturing on Instagram. This news somehow disturbed the social media universe and the stock market at the same time. More importantly, it also confirmed once again that having your product or service in Facebook›s sights is never a good place for any young business to be.

I'd say that you can really begin to believe the end of the world is near when the allegedly rational and arguably analytical stock market reacts instantly, if thoughtlessly, to trivial and wholly manufactured "news" like this and immediately erases a billion dollars of value. True, this is a stock that was and continues to be grossly overvalued. I guess, in that respect, you could say, "no harm, no foul," since this was a business which deserved getting its just rewards. Or maybe the better way to put it is that, if your whole business is built on social media hype and fundamental lies from Day One, then it›s entirely fitting that your future fortunes should live or die based on the same artificial factoids and frenzied reliance on the feeble functionaries who make up this make-believe world.

But the good news is that I think we may finally be coming to the belated realization that the vast majority of the world -- including most of the people who pay attention (engagement, not eyeballs), really buy things (actual revenues), and matter materially to marketplaces (making money, not made-up metrics) -- just don't care about celebrities any more.

Movie stars don't matter much when movie theater attendance is at a 20-year low. Traditional TV is in the toilet, with half the millennials now totally disconnected and cutting the cable so TV "stars" are also toast. And since so many of us no longer believe what we see on the tube anyway, the credibility of our newscasters is colossally low. Amazon is now the most trusted brand in the U.S. and because we all get our news from social media channels -- not TV -- the traditional networks' "brands" are busted -- most people couldn't tell you the actual source of any news they know, but they can typically tell you where they saw it on social media.

We just don't care what any of these people do or say; their inauthentic product endorsements and touching tributes are increasingly ineffective and not worth the inflated costs of securing them; and as their recent, and massively counter-productive, political involvement convincingly demonstrated, we certainly don't care what they "think," if that's what it can be called. YouTube lost about $300 million learning these new realities a couple of years ago when it tried to launch 100 celebrity-based channels and no one showed up to watch.

And when you move downstream from the arguably talented film folks to the cretins that pass for reality-TV celebs, things get even worse. It's hard to imagine that anyone could care about the actions, antics, attitudes and altercations of these C-level, no-talent bozos who are unceasingly foisted upon us by the people who program cable and curate the new digital media channels. If the people in the control booths think that we identify with these idiots (rather than laughing at them), they're even more out of touch than anyone suspected.

Humiliation TV jumped the shark years ago, but clearly not everyone got the message. The current cast of characters on most of these shows are people we're much more likely to pity than to regard as peers. Ignorance in action is never attractive when we're trying to learn something of value. Interestingly, if you track the evolution of *Shark Tank*, the shift is very clear. The balance of featured businesses has moved dramatically toward winners and celebrations of success, and no longer do we see anywhere near the number of clueless creators who used to be a big part of the program.

Peer-to-peer programming, people we can relate to and respect, and enhanced mediated connections are where we're headed. There's a very good reason that Netflix, which is totally data-driven and responsive to our demonstrated desires, is now bigger than cable. We're looking for substance, not sparkle. Live streaming media -- whether it's interactive education, practical conversations, or group exercising -- are the models for the future. We want a sense of community, we want shared experiences, we want real and valuable content, and we want authentic communication and sharing.

The Kardashian krash tells you that most of the media guys still haven't gotten the message. That's why the medium is such a mess.

I t's not your strength, or maybe be even what you enjoy doing. But being on hand to show the flag--and close the deals-- isn't something you can simply hand off to the sales team.

I wrote a while ago about when and how the founder in a startup should decide that he or she no longer needs to be making every sales call. My focus then was on the importance of understanding and quantifying your product's state of development and relative maturity. The idea is that until you know exactly what you're selling --by doing it over and over again and not as a one-off-- and know that it can be sold consistently by others, you'll need to stay in the field and keep selling.

That›s because your product is still being developed on the fly and continually redesigned/reconfigured to better suit the real requirements and demands of the customers. And, the fact is that ultimately only you can make the critical design and development decisions and you›ll do a much better job of that if you are hearing it directly from the end users and not from a bunch of whiny salespeople. But once you do reach that point, you need to kick yourself upstairs and focus on other things. I encouraged CEOs who spent too much effort selling to better use and optimize their time. I suggested that they needed to find competent sales managers and others who could tee up just the right meetings for them - not «opening» meetings which are a dime a dozen - but «closing» meetings where the deals got done.

Finding these sales meat-eaters isn't easy; they are the hardest hires for any startup, but it's absolutely critical to have them onboard if you're going to build a viable business. There's no more challenging job than being the person who has to fire people. Everyone else gets to talk about what a tight-knit, stick-together group the company is (just like a "family" of friends), but the sales manager is the one who has to deliver the bad news over and over again. This essential role doesn't win any popularity contests and - just to be clear -most CEOs suck at it. They're more focused on leading the charge forward and being the business's biggest cheerleader rather than handing out the monthly pink slips.

When you're hiring sales talent, you need to also be careful to avoid the empire builders. There's a whole generation or two of sales management types whose experience is in large organizations. I have found fairly consistently that they are the wrongest guys possible for a startup because they grew up in a system where they measured their value and their success by the sheer number of people they managed rather than the results that those folks delivered. Nothing kills a young business faster than bloat and bureaucracy and having too many sales people sitting on their hands and not selling is the worst kind of poison. So be careful what you wish for and who you hire for this critical job.

And, at the other end of the spectrum, I'm also seeing more and more startup CEOs who discover way too soon that they don't like the wear and tear, the travel, and the rejection that are all crucial parts of selling a new product or service. So they retreat, thinking they can run their businesses while they're sitting on their butts behind a desk back in the office. That's not how this game works; that behavior is a formula for failure. You may not be an extrovert, you may not be the world's greatest storyteller or presenter, and you may not even know the technology that underlies your business as well as half the other people in the company. You are, however, the boss and today that fact alone means a lot, at least to the people who make the final purchasing decisions. Remember that these buyers are typically older than you, they grew up in strictly hierarchical systems where titles count, and they need to be made to feel important and respected if they're gonna sign off on your deal. No offense to any of the members of your team, but they don't want to deal with the monkey-- they need to see the organ grinder. That's you.

Why? For all the obvious reasons. (1) People don't really care how much you know until they know how much you care. Showing up shows them that you actually do care. (2) Startups are notoriously scattered and in a hurry. Focus and attention to detail are scarce commodities and the customers want to know that you personally are connected, paying attention, and directly engaged with their business, their concerns and their problems. And finally, (3) they want to hear it from the horse's mouth. Not second hand. They want commitments and assurances from you (since they know that the sales guys will tell them anything and promise them the world) that you will stand up for and stand behind your product or service and make good on whatever they've been promised. The buck always stops with you.

None of this is very tough. You just have to say what you're going to do and do what you said you would and everything will be hunky-dory.

Young companies get too caught up in trying to lure high-profile types to their boardrooms. But you don't need hood ornaments; you need time, expertise and an ability to help you drive the company forward.

Budding builders of businesses and big-city mayors often seem to have the same problem when it comes to putting together boards, whether they're boards of directors, advisors, or industry experts. They tend to go for the gold and the glitz and they end up getting too little time, no real help, and nothing else of any actual value in the bargain. They consistently emphasize and over index on people's titles and credentials and forget that-; unless you're only concerned with window dressing and PR-;the object of the board-building exercise is to get some regular help, a sympathetic ear or two, and some people on your team who've been there before, who will tell you the truth when necessary, and who share your vision for the business. Having a couple of board members who have your back is the best feeling in the whole world and makes for a much better business as well.

Being an effective board member is a serious job, not a sinecure, and selecting the right people for these roles is just as important as any other hire you might make. You don't want planners and report writers; you don't need performers and pontificators; you want doers who can help drive results. I realize that some of these guys can end up coming with the deal, being a necessary part or necessary evil as the case may be in securing your funding or for other historic reasons. The trick is to make the smartest possible choices in those cases where you actually do have a choice.

Don't confuse someone's credentials with the kind of proper concerns and concrete commitments that it takes to do this very critical job correctly. Some people collect board seats like they were baseball cards or souvenir buttons. Stay away from these professional self-promoters because, in the end, it's always about them and not worth your time or wasting a seat that could go to someone with something real to contribute instead of some blowhard looking to bulk up his or her resume. We see the same kinds of issues with some of the unsuccessful mentors at 1871. You just need to invest the time to do this crucial job right.

There's no single or simple way to get the process going, but as you begin to evaluate the various candidates-; some you'll seek out and some will appear or be suggested and introduced by people you trust-; there are six basic questions/concerns that you should be addressing in your evaluation. There may be others and special circumstances may dictate additions, but the ones that I have found always to be relevant are the following:

(1) **Do they have the time to do the job and will they make the time?**

Some of the busiest people you know still make the best board members because it›s a matter of their commitment, not their calendar.

(2) **Are they willing to show up and not just phone it in-; figuratively and literally?**

It's very easy to lose the energy and momentum at a board session when half the group isn't paying attention. If they can't really be there, in the moment, they shouldn't be there at all. Posture is actually pretty important and you want the folks leaning in and engaged, not sitting back, looking at their phones, and contemplating their cuticles.

(3) **Are they able to do the work-; board materials reviews, meeting preparation and participation, job candidate interviews, your spur-of-the-moment conference calls, etc.?**

Entrepreneurs aren't patient people and spending a day a month or a quarter in a board meeting is almost always a painful process, but it's made unbearable if the board members don't take the time (and give management the courtesy) of doing their homework and coming to the meeting prepared. We're all busy people, but the real value of bringing the board together is the interactivity and the exchanges between smart and successful outsiders with important perspectives that might not be represented within the business. The worst board meetings are repetitive dog-and-pony shows by management where the biggest challenge isn't a corporate conundrum, it's trying to stay awake.

(4) **Are they engaged and passionate about your business?**

It›s just as bad to be a sycophant as it is to be a sarcastic know-it-all. It›s important for board members to tell it like it is and to tell the harsh truth to the CEO and others when necessary, but it›s even more important that they come from the right place-; a sincere and heartfelt desire to see the business succeed for the right reasons. These aren›t smooth or easy journeys, but a little heart and a lot of good faith makes the medicine go down more easily.

(5) **Are they good and additive collaborators-; team players?**

A good board leaves its own desires and its selfish concerns at the door and works together to reach the best decisions for the company rather than pushing or promoting choices that serve other outside interests-; including, sometimes, a board member›s own investment objectives.

(6) Do they have a relevant something? It might be:
  (a) Skill;
  (b) Knowledge;
  (c) Experience;
  (d) Network/Connections; or
  (e) Money

The bottom line is the same rule as in football. You don't want the 11 best people you can theoretically get. You want the best 11 people who can come together to help you build a better business, through thick and thin, and with only that desire, that agenda, and that goal in mind.

TULLMAN'S TRUISMS

LEADERSHIP IS NOT A POPULARITY CONTEST

I feel really bad for Bruno Mars because he's stuck in the middle of one of these stupid, click-bait driven, social media debates about whether he's grateful enough and vocal enough about the influences which "black" music has had on his own work. Apparently, no matter how much or how often you say "thank you" these days and prostrate yourself to the memories of those gone before, it's never sufficient for the trolls and the haters. So, we're subjected to a 140-character debate about cultural appropriation by a bunch of know-nothings and two thumb typers who can barely spell it - much less understand what they're talking about. I'm just glad that Mick and JT have never had to go through this kind of knee-jerk noise. And Elvis would be rolling over in his grave if there was room in the casket for him to move that bloated body around.

However, these people aren't entirely worthless because they can always serve as a bad example – a stirring demonstration of exactly what not to do. And, the truth is that you can still learn a lot even from Luddites. I think there's an important lesson for entrepreneurs buried deep in their trivial and utterly immaterial observations about how quickly and easily concepts, ideas, language, thoughts - and especially expectations – can jump around from person to person, place to place, and industry to industry in today's hyper-connected and high-speed digital world.

My takeaway is all about customers and competition. We see this same kind of behavior in every kind of competition. Many years ago, every high jumper laughed at the crazy Fosbury Flop technique until he cleared those amazing heights and then everyone jumped into the pool and copied his style and the rest is history. (See https://en.wikipedia.org/wiki/Fosbury_Flop.) I always say that the expectations of customers are "perpetually progressive" which simply means that they (we) can't help themselves from continually raising the bar which means that you've got to keep getting better and better in your business (product, service, support, speed, etc.) all the time because what was yesterday's miracle is tomorrow's "so what?". (See https://www.inc.com/howard-tullman/keep-your-customers-by-thinking-ahead-of-them.html.)

We're all living - whether we like it or not - in a "what have you done for me lately?" world. And to make things even worse, your competition never sleeps and they're ready, willing, and able to step right up and grab any unhappy customers if you lose a step or two or start taking anything or anybody for granted. No one owns the customer today; switching costs, if any, are minimal; people's choices are virtually unlimited; and locked-in and loyal consumers are a sure thing only as long as you keep delivering the goods.

But the new news is that the state of the competition has changed and you need to make sure that you aren't spending too much of your time looking through the rear-view mirror or trying to measure your performance and success against the wrong bars (traditional and too low) and the wrong ball players (too few and too narrow a view).

The most important competition today for the time, attention and dollars of your customers isn't in your own backyard. It's not in your silo or limited to the set of standard competitors that you have always benchmarked your business against because that's simply too low a bar and too modest a target. The competition today for the hearts and minds of your customers - listen closely - is the last great experience (sales or service) that they've had - whenever and wherever that took place - and whether or not it has anything directly to do with you or your business. That's how the consumer keeps score today.

You need a new mindset and it starts with a simple acknowledgement. Like it or not, in today's one-stop world, you're competing against the likes of Amazon even if they aren't yet selling the same stuff or services that you are - if that's even possible anymore – given that they have virtually everything at the Everything Store. You're competing against the most trusted brand in America and you're competing with the ways (every way) that they do business.

Speed, access and convenience trump everything else and once we experience this hyper-speed anywhere in our lives, we immediately bump up the bar; raise our expectations; and apply the same new standards to everything in our lives. It's a case of appropriation uber alles and every one of us is guilty of it because it's just basic human nature. Who doesn't want more and better anything and everything.

And it's not just Amazon setting the curve in the "right now" economy. You can get an on-demand flu shot at Walgreens in 15 minutes these days - at your convenience - and you've got to ask yourself why you'd ever again beg some receptionist for an appointment to go see your internist downtown three weeks from now and then take 3 hours out of your day and spend several hundred bucks to accomplish essentially the same thing. And you'll probably catch the flu before you get around to the date of your appointment anyway.

The bottom line: if you treat your customers as if it's business as usual, they won't be back or be your customers much longer. So, my advice is to "Be like Bruno" (with apologies to Michael Jordan). Change up your game constantly, get out of your comfort zone, look beyond your own four walls and your own marketplace, see who's hit it out of the park (last week or last century), rip them off politely, and then do it better than they ever did.

Good artists copy; great artists steal.

I have written in the past about certain structural aspects of markets – especially concerning players who capitalize on the relative scarcity of prime assets or highly-desirable partners - which permits a limited number of those players with early access to, or control of, these kinds of assets to exercise an overwhelming competitive advantage in their marketplace and to withstand the attacks of even far larger and better-funded entrants for extended periods of time.

The base case for this market condition which most easily demonstrates the necessary pre-conditions (and the consequent impact on the players which get shut out) took place many years ago in the airline industry at the very beginning of the era of frequent flyer programs. (See https://www.inc.com/howard-tullman/five-steps-to-navigating-your-toughest-prospects.html.) I analogized the situation at that time to a highly-competitive game of musical chairs with cross-industry partners taking the place of the chairs. The winners got dates and the wallflowers got screwed.

In that case, American Airlines quickly and quietly linked its rewards program to regular purchases which their members made using their MasterCards. In the points acquisition frenzy of those early days, this new source of credits was immediately perceived and appreciated by the AA program members as an additional and painless way to accumulate incremental frequent flyer miles without doing anything different in their day-to-day activities. United promptly responded by entering into a deal with VISA and here's where things got very interesting because American Express – probably the best and highest-value card marketer around at the time – found itself without an airline marketing partner and thus unable to respond with a comparable competitive offering.

Over the next several years, AMEX lost millions of cardholders and billions of dollars in terms of spend as even its most loyal cardholders shifted their expenditures to the cards that provided frequent flyer miles as an additional perk. Turns out that not many AMEX customers were interested in accumulating miles on Midway or Southwest airlines or getting travel credits on Greyhound bus trips. And, as a result, VISA's growth exploded, and it blew by AMEX which topped out at about 1/3 of the number of VISA cardholders.

I call these arrangements "cross-industry blocking alliances" and we see similar kinds of behavior in the more physical world as well. In the early 2000's, UPS bought the Mail Boxes, Etc. chain of some 3000 stores intending to turn them into UPS outlets. A couple of years later (probably having little choice at the time), FedEx acquired the Kinko's chain of about 1200 stores and these days all we see is the FedEx name on these locations. Just recently, FedEx partnered with Walgreens to further extend their physical locations and depots and, of course, CVS buying Aetna is another version of the market extension strategy.

Interestingly enough, we also just saw a related, but more modest physical example in Chicago involving the same two airlines. *American Airlines* threatened to not renew its operating contracts at O'Hare Airport with the city's airport authority because *United Airlines* had been assigned more new gates than *American*. Dedicated and assigned gates are a finite and relatively scarce asset at any airport and the more gates you control, the more flights you can offer, the more passengers you can serve, the timelier your departures, etc. So, this was a highly-sensitive competitive issue for *American* which was resolved fairly quickly by allocating a few more "shared" gates to *American*.

The basic rule of thumb is that, as soon as a marketplace becomes effectively oligopolistic (dominated by a few channel providers – either buyers or sellers), you can expect to see a growing number of these kinds of exclusionary deals and partnerships. The frightening thing today is how quickly the digital world is being locked up and dominated by a few players.

So, you might ask, what does this have to do with you? In a word, the domination of the digital gatekeepers is going to be far worse and more pervasive than what we've seen before and, as more and more digital marketplaces become oligopolistic, and more and more industries are dominated by one or two massive platforms, we can expect to see a world where you – as a digital seller/provider – will no longer control the front door to your own store. Amazon's Marketplace is a fairly obvious example of this new approach. How much would any vendor have to spend to try to pull customers to their stand-alone e-commerce website when more than 2/3rds of all the high value product searches in the U.S. now originate at Amazon – and notably no longer at Google? And, even if you got the customer to your site, how realistic is it for you to try to manage the delivery back end of the transaction when Fulfillment by Amazon (FBA) can handle the whole thing (including inventory storage) for you automatically?

This new competitive environment isn't about building B2B or B2C businesses, it's all about P2P – platform to platform – and the platforms (basically the places the customers live their online lives these days) are getting fewer and fewer. Your job is to figure out how to get in and stay in the game. If you're fast, desirable and in the right place, you might get to ride along with the big guys, BUT they will increasingly control the consumer experience (the "front door") and you'll be Door Number 2 at best. This shouldn't come as new news – it's a FAMGA world – and we just live in it these days.

So, this is your wake-up call. If you aren't thinking about this issue and how you'll play in this new environment where someone else controls the primary customer experience and owns the principal connection to the consumer, you'll wake up one of these days when the music stops without a seat at the table or a business. If you aren't developing open APIs and deep links and working to be sure that they are readily and easily accessible from within these other social and commercial environments, you are in for the rudest of awakenings and sometime soon to boot.

It's a race that no one running really wants to win. And while we continue to say that rapid, technology-driven change is accelerating in virtually every industry and that speed kills, the truth is that, in certain sectors these days (many comprising principally what I would call the "nuts and bolts" low paying jobs), the trend is readily apparent, but the pace of "progress" is painfully slow and it's a little bit like watching a slow-motion, multi-car pileup on a black-ice covered highway.

There's an oppressive air of inevitability because we all know it's coming, we've all seen this movie before, and sadly no one has the faintest idea of how to stop it. Massive job losses – whole lines of work which will no longer be relevant or economically viable – and millions of people looking for a better life, but lacking the skills needed to get them and their families there. I realize that you can't spend your whole life preparing for future catastrophes, but that doesn't keep many of us from worrying as we look ahead at a very uncertain future. It's like sitting on a bed of tacks – it's pretty hard to focus on much of anything else.

And, as the media monitors and regularly reports on the latest slow and soul-crushing slide of some industry sector into oblivion, we also know that we're talking about major structural and fundamentally irreversible changes which will adversely impact the livelihoods of tens of millions of employees. And while everyone is happy to blame the technology boogie man, no one is suggesting any concrete solutions to offset the coming displacements.

And, to be brutally honest, it's not just the technology that's causing the trouble. The main driver of many of these seismic shifts isn't simply the implementation of new and powerful combinations of big data, technology and automation; it's also the fact that we're seeing that the center will no longer hold.

Consumers' behaviors and expectations continue to change at an accelerated rate and the need to push the delivery of everything to the perimeter – all part of the "right now" economy – makes it increasingly clear that there's no longer a need to be "there" wherever "there" used to be. Today, to compete, you've got to be everywhere – all the time – or you're nowhere.

In more and more cases, strategies based on concentration, centralization, and critical mass mean less and less because – through connected combinations of technology and mobility - we can distribute and decentralize functions in ways that are more localized, far more fluid and flexible, easier to staff, and considerably cheaper than trying to bring zillions of people together in overlit, sterile and sweaty places to spend 8 hours staring at a screen and trying to sound cheerful on the phone.

Call centers largely grew out of a single invention – the 800 number – which enabled national, toll-free, inbound calling that didn't become ubiquitous until around 1980. You could basically call anywhere for "free" if you had a question, needed service, or wanted to buy something from a mail order catalogue. At its peak, there were several hundred million 800 calls being made every day. To handle the call volume, huge physical facilities were built in certain parts of the country (and eventually in other parts of the world) which housed thousands of operators.

But today, no one wants to spend more time sitting on their phone waiting for an answer for anything and most cellphone users don't even understand the concept of a long-distance call. Just like we no longer want to waste any time standing in a line at the bank or supermarket. Everyone's in a hurry today. And it's clear that the race is on. Who really wants to talk to a human when you can text? And who needs a teller when your phone's a wallet and an ATM?

I'm not sure whether the first victims at scale will be those millions of retail cashiers who may have largely disappeared by the time we start to see the call centers in this country (yes, they are back in this country, but that's another story) become empty shells of themselves. Or it could be that it's the call centers that will fold first. We'll have big sheds with rows after rows of desks, chairs and monitors and no one sitting there to answer the calls which no longer come. The big credit card companies are already reporting that inbound calls now make up less than 10% of their daily inquiries.

But whichever sector sinks more quickly, we know that it's simply not good news for anyone and that the unforeseen consequences of these changes may be even more draconian and have a far wider impact than we expect.

Just some other simple examples – self-service machines and automated checkout aisles at the grocery store (not to mention online shopping and automated fulfillment programs) are killing the gum/candy business (and the sleazy tabloids as well) which depend greatly on the impulse purchases we make to reward ourselves for standing patiently in line while Mrs. McGreedy scans her 46 coupons at the supermarket.

Why would anyone go see the doctor for a flu shot at his offices in the big old hospital building when you can get the job done at your neighborhood drugstore faster and for little or no money and at your convenience?

Who needs to drive out to the suburban auto mall when there's a Tesla dealership sitting on the main high-end luxury strip right between Tiffany's and Tommy Bahama? And frankly, who wants to go to the mall at all? This is why 90% of the malls in this country are in trouble and why a small number of extremely well-located ones represent almost all of the valuable real estate.

The bottom line is that bitcoin and the ideas around distributed everything are only the tips of the iceberg of decentralization which we will see changing every part of our lives as the growing centrifugal forces generated by the promise of constant connectivity and limitless mobility conspire to pull whole worlds apart.

Everything about building a new business comes down to people in one way or another. If you don't get the right people and, more importantly, get the people right, the foundation and the future of the business will be suspect from the start. And, because you can't always find or afford the perfect people when you're beginning, you take what you can get, and you try very hard to make the best of the situation and to do the best with the team and the resources you've assembled. As your business grows, nothing will be more important than attracting and retaining the best talent. (See https://www.inc.com/howard-tullman/3-things-you-need-to-know-about-superstars.html.)

But, for openers at the outset, the smartest thing you can do is get started. The risk is that in the frenzy to get busy, you'll overlook some of the basic rules and end up somewhere you never hoped for or wanted to be. Cultures in startups are like fast-drying cement, they take root quickly and once they're set and firmly established (basically in stone), they're almost impossible to alter or improve. You set out on a great mission, with a set of values that Gandhi himself would be proud of, and then you make a few missteps and you discover what a slippery slope it can be. Values rarely break; they usually crumble slowly if they are aggressively enforced and reinforced. It's like they used to say at NASA about rocket launches: "Off by an inch at the start, miss the target by a mile".

So, there are a couple of important things to learn right away and to keep top of mind.

First, since there are only a few of you, the impact of each person's contribution, performance and attitude is far more consequential than it would be in a big business. One bad apple can spoil the whole bunch. If someone's not working out or getting with the program, they've got to go. You'll find, as often as not, that the people who are early problems are the ones with a bad attitude or those who are treating their team members poorly rather than people who are deficient in their smarts or skill sets. If they don't fit the culture you're trying to create, they're a cancer to be cut out. (See https://www.inc.com/howard-tullman-4-hr-strategies-you-should-own.html.) Personality problems aren't like fine wines – they don't improve over time – they suck from the start and don't get better. The truth is that you have to hire <u>and</u> fire fast when you're starting out. (See https://www.inc.com/howard-tullman/three-employees-you-need-to-fire-now.html .)

Second, since everyone at the outset is doing multiple jobs and since you can't be everywhere at once, you've got to trust your people to do the right things in the moment since there's no rule book, no time for extensive preparation and instruction, and there's rarely a second chance to make a great first impression with a lot of new and prospective customers. Very few startups have the luxury of OJT (on-the-job training). This need to let go a little and let your people do their jobs isn't ever easy for anal-retentive entrepreneurs - which I guess may be oxymoronic. Tell your people what needs to get done and how it needs to be done, get and give them the tools and resources they need, and then get out of their way and let them do it. Continual and consistent communication is critical to make sure that everyone is headed in the same direction. Do it until you're sick of hearing yourself talk and you might just have done it enough to get the job done.

Third, not everyone on your team to be is going to be a crazy, driven entrepreneur or as neurotic and paranoid as you are. But this doesn't make them bad people and it certainly doesn't make them bad employees. Some great contributors just want a steady job that they can do well and then go home and have a life. They don't want to be part of your crazy campaign or macho mission. And that's actually OK as long as they show up and do their jobs every day. You can't build a team that makes sense if you're trying to make everyone look and act like you. A very important part of your job is to make room for all kinds of people and to run interference for the risk-takers and the real pioneers. Talent comes in strange and wonderful packages and – while we're happy to have the upsides – we are all too often not willing to understand that there are going to be trade-offs that come with the deal. You don't get to pick and choose, and you've got to make sure that there's a place for everyone (including many who don't speak, act or look like you) in your business whether or not they believe that bathing is optional or prefer working all night long to showing up before the bell rings in the morning. Productivity and results are what you're looking for, not punctuality.

And finally, I've tried for years to figure out why some seemingly smart (and arguably perceptive) people never rise to the highest levels of trust and responsibility even though it's pretty clear that they are hard workers who are definitely trying to get ahead. And, of course, that turns out to be the answer. They're working hard, but they're in it mainly for themselves – not for the business; not for the cause; and certainly not for you. Maybe it's a little naïve in these days of rampant narcissism, but for me it all still comes down to one word: loyalty. In the struggle for a startup to succeed, when no one has time to look over their shoulder to make sure that someone's got their back, an ounce of loyalty is worth a pound of cleverness. If your heart's not in the right place, having a huge brain won't help.

Consumers and customers may be feckless assholes – always looking for the next best thing and anything better or cheaper – but the people you rely on to help you build your business have to be loyal beyond reason. They have to be the ones willing to walk through the walls and get the job done. The ones who always show up and stand up. (See https://www.inc.com/howard-tullman/to-succedd-be-the-one-everyone-can-count-on.html .)

And while a fierce commitment is necessary, it's not sufficient for success. The kind of character that really makes a difference is the combination of commitment and loyalty. It takes a bunch of both.

260 – NEGOTIATION 101 – DON'T SAY "MAYBE" WHEN YOU MEAN "NO"

I've been spending a lot of time lately talking about how our fastest-growing startups should negotiate when they are trying to hire experienced, relatively senior talent (especially in the sales area) for their companies. Lateral hires are hard for all kinds of reasons (especially when you're bringing people in to manage and direct folks who have been with your business from the start and helped to build it) and the vast majority of these hires fail for 4 main reasons:

(1) a quickly-emergent and readily apparent lack of energy (stamina) and/or little enthusiasm for the day-to-day aspects of the business;

(2) a weak connection to and empathy for the rest of the employees;

(3) an early tendency to criticize the way you have run the business pin the past; and

(4) a focus and excessive interest in and emphasis on financial and compensation issues.

But make no mistake, tough and risky or not, to grow your business beyond the grocery store, you will need to hire some grown-ups. In the process, you can evaluate, tease out, and control for some of the primary failure causes, but the biggest exposure isn't what you don't learn in advance, it's what you do or don't do in the course of the negotiations that will have the most important consequences further down the line. In many negotiations, people care less about where things ultimately ended up and a lot more about how you behaved and the way that the parties reached the final arrangements.

So, if you're heading down this path, there's one crucial <u>fact</u> and one absolute <u>rule</u> that I tell every entrepreneur involved in these kinds of discussions to keep firmly in mind.

The **fact** is that this new person is going to need your backing 110% of the time without any second guessing; without any interference or micro-managing; and without permitting anyone in the business to go around him or her and come to you with their problems or concerns. Once you've put that person in place, it's gotta be full speed ahead – no retreat and no surrender – and everyone in the place will be watching you to see how you are handling the situation.

And, believe me, I know how hard this "hands-off" approach can be when it's your baby and when you find yourself biting your tongue because you might have done a bunch of things in different ways. Rolling your eyes or shrugging your shoulders is just as strong a statement as anything spoken and just as unhelpful and, in fact, damaging to the new hire and to the whole onboarding effort.

So, you'll have to learn to turn a deaf ear to the complaints about how the new guy or girl doesn't "get it"; doesn't know every single thing on Day One; isn't fitting into the system or the culture, etc. If you're not all-in and fully supportive, then the odds against his or her eventual success move dramatically in the wrong direction. Reservations are OK in the restaurant business, but not when someone desperately needs you to have their back – rain or shine – and all the time.

But the **rule** is even more important. Just as you can't be a little pregnant, you can't afford to be half-hearted in these decisions or not fully convinced yourself that you made the right choice. "Almost" only counts in horseshoes and hand grenades. The rule is that "you should never say 'maybe' when you need to say 'no'". And that rule applies in spades when you're talking about new hires.

And don't kid yourself or try to talk yourself into these things either. When you say, "you just don't know", the truth is that you do. Doubts and concerns are rarely abated with the passage of time – trust your gut – and go on from there. Things and attitudes that you didn't like during the interview aren't going to go away – they're more likely to be intensified and amplified under the stress of real battle conditions.

Money is always a big hurdle to get over, but not necessarily in the way you might expect. The absolute dollars will matter for sure and sometimes there's just too much distance between the parties to get the deal done. The parties can part friends – no harm, no foul – and get on with their lives. But what most outsiders don't understand (along with a lot of prospective hires on the other side of the conversation) is just how personally the entrepreneur takes the compensation negotiations.

I've seen entrepreneurs work for days trying to come up with a fair offer for someone they'd love to have onboard – sweating the numbers – comparing the offer to the comp of other key players – checking with outside advisors – doing every bit of homework possible – in order to get to their best proposal. They become heavily invested (financially, but even more psychologically) in the offer and the outcome because they believe it's fair to everyone and the absolute best they can do.

And then, I've seen the same entrepreneurs crushed (and/or pissed off) by some candidate who summarily rejects the proposal because (a) he read in some know-it-all book that you're supposed to always do that with initial offers and (b) he thinks it's just an opening salvo and not a first, best and last offer. These people rarely understand how much time and emotional energy a really good entrepreneur puts into these things. And they also don't understand that each counter-offer they make sucks a little more joy out of the whole deal. It's the same kind of resentment that builds up when you've borrowed money from someone and you know that you can't pay it back.

In these cases, eventually you get to a bad result – either because (a) no deal gets done or – far worse – (b) because the entrepreneur grudgingly and half-heartedly accepts a deal that he's unhappy with and angry about for what he thinks is the good of the business. The truth is that it's the worst thing he can do because he's just lit a fuse under the whole relationship and most likely doomed the new hire as well. Taking one for the team – bidding up and against your own best offer – sucking it up and accepting a deal that you're not sure the company can afford, these are bad choices and consistent signals that there're bigger issues and problems coming. You may not want to admit it, but it's gonna be a lot harder to support and stick up for someone when, in your heart of hearts, you think they were a pig in the negotiations and overdid it.

The funny thing is that they probably don't even realize that there's a problem. It only recently dawned on me as to why the guys you're trying to hire from the corporate world don't get emotional about this stuff or understand that it's not simply an interesting exercise or some kind of a game of back-and-forth bargaining. The reason that they don't get it is because, in their world, it's never their money. If they have to hire someone, HR gives them a number (or more likely a salary range) and their job is to get a deal done with someone. Paying a few bucks more, changing a bonus or some performance targets, adding a few vacation days – who really cares? Just get the deal done.

But for the entrepreneur, it's a completely different world. Every dollar is hard-earned. Every buck makes a big difference, and nothing is taken lightly because – in the world of scarce resources – you're always stealing from some Peter or Penny to pay Paul. And, as the boss, the buck stops with you and you owe it to everyone in the business to make the best and smartest decisions you can. It's not just "business", it's your business, and it's very personal. If you haven't been in this particular hot seat, this may sound a little overly dramatic, but ask anyone who has been there, and they'll tell you that there are few harder decisions that the CEO has to make.

TULLMAN'S TRUISMS

DON'T SAY "MAYBE" IF YOU WANT TO SAY "NO"

Could it be that we're turning a critical corner where the next important group of startups won't be addressing superficial concerns of comfort and convenience or devoting their energies to all the drama around dating, mating and which watches to wear? How about if we start paying attention to stuff that actually matters to someone other than our immediate family and the few folks we were able to finagle into joining us on the journey to nowhere? Social is so yesterday. We need more trivial apps pouring into the Apple store like a fish needs a bicycle and it's hard to imagine a B2C business plan these days that has any realistic prospect of a viable exit. The image that I can't get out of my mind is of a little boat made out of paper that you push away from the shore and watch the waves move it forward as it slowly get soggier and soggier until it sinks below the surface.

And honestly, by now, doesn't everybody with a brain get that the opportunity to start the newest niche social network is long past; that it's more a question of deciding which platform you need to be on than of deciding to try to invent your own (See https://www.inc.com/howard-tullman/whats-behind-door-number-two-it-better-be-you.html); and that "sharing" your innermost secrets with a bunch of bots and trolls is a sad excuse for a social life and really just having a small sliver of your already-diluted attention span sold to the highest bidder? As they say in what's left of the ad biz, if you're not paying something for what you're getting, you aren't the buyer, you're what's being sold. Doesn't all this frenzied activity seem costly, frivolous and really tired in light of the actual problems and challenges that we're all facing?

So, how cool would it be if the next killer companies were started by a group of hyper-technical entrepreneurs directing their efforts and energies to matters of real consequence which might make concrete contributions to the ways we do business and the ways we live our lives. I sure hope we're heading in that direction because, if I never have to see Zuck's painful and placid puss (as he's being tortured by a bunch of troglodytes on the tube) while he's trying to explain that he's just running a platform (not a media business), it will be too soon. We understand that he doesn't want to be a pariah and that he (and Elon) can't really figure out what all the fuss is about, but honestly who really cares about this anyway or any longer?

Personally, I'm pretty sick of seeing a constant stream of puffed-up proposals to provide slick solutions to problems that no one really gives a crap about. Please save your breath and your stamps (remember those?) and don't send me any new ideas for social networks, this week's newest tool for teams to collaborate, apps to help me remember to brush my teeth, or sites you're planning to build to quickly connect me with others suffering from the curse of incontinent cats. We used to call these kinds of deals clear cases of "the cures for no known diseases" or "the greatest software never sold" and frankly I was beginning to fear that there was no end in sight to this obnoxious onslaught of irrelevance.

But I think that there's a glimmer of hope emerging. And the reason is that the next wave of real businesses is going to have to be built from the inside out on solid technologies which require smart, trained engineers and scientists and not from the outside in where some marketer sells a story and then the race is on to try to find some folks somewhere in the world who can build the backend and try to deliver in a timely fashion on the promises that he made. It's possible that there will need to be one more nail in the coffin of the creative bullshitters before the truth sinks in and my money's on all the companies pretending that they have something real to contribute to the AI race. (See https://www.inc.com/howard-tullman/dont-be-frightened-or-fooled-by-the-ai-monster.html.) As soon as the investors listening to these stories start looking under the hoods and learn that there's really no there there, I expect that hundreds of these businesses will find that the going gets really hard when you're "all hat and no cattle" as they say in Texas. This isn't the best news for the few companies that are spending the time and the money to build something that actually works, but eventually the good guys should win the day.

They key to the whole equation is that there's simply no way to tap dance yourself around the blockchain, augmented reality, IOT, machine learning or the burgeoning businesses building bots. You've either got the beef or you don't and to pull this off, you need hard core programmers, technical and engineering talent, smart UI and UX designers and data scientists or you're simply kidding yourself and anyone foolish enough to give you their money.

And putting together a team like this isn't something you do after the fact or once you're funded. In fact, I'm not sure that you can even buy these kinds of resources any more. They're too much in demand and increasingly aware of the fact that they've got the keys to the kingdom to come. The core of your company and the heart of the idea has to be good science and great technology from the get-go.

I want to thank you for the opportunity to speak with you on this glorious day. As the former President of two Colleges, I deeply understand exactly how important a rite of passage this is for each of you (and for your family and loved ones as well) and I'm honored to be a small part of this very special occasion.

Many of you are the first in your families to attend and graduate from college and, as the eldest of 6 children and a lifetime entrepreneur, I know in my heart just how hard it is to be the first at any new enterprise. To take that leap and that gamble. To put yourself out there with no net and no turning back. To leave the comfort and security of the way things have always been done and to believe instead that you – and you alone – can make things different and better. For yourself, and for those close to you, but also for many who will follow in your footsteps and hope that you will take a moment and look back to lend them a helping hand just as so many people made it possible for you to be here and to reach this exalted station. Friends, family, mentors, faculty, sponsors, supporters, and a host of others as well. No one does anything important today all by themselves.

And, of course, that's why you're never really alone. You're surrounded and bolstered by friends and family who are the most critical supporters. We're all fortunate to have them in our corners, but ultimately, we know that no one else can do the heavy lifting for you. You carry not only all the weight of your own dreams, desires and fears, but also the aggregated expectations of friends, family and even the members of your community in many ways.

And you have the additional responsibility of dealing with the naysayers. The ones who know what's best for you even as they sit squarely and safely on the sidelines. And the ones who are happy to tell you in great detail what's above you, or beyond you, or too big for your britches (whatever those are), or forever out of your reach. And finally, the ones who take great joy in pointing out all the reasons why things won't work – even though they've never had the courage to try. They can find a million problems for any solution.

But, to build a better world, we have to keep moving forward and we can no longer afford to be afraid to fail – we can all expect to fail from time to time – that's just part of the game, but – the key to the future is that we can never be afraid to try. Scrapes, scratches and skinned knees are all part of the process. Being brave means working to find things that are more important than your fears. You learn to focus your time and your energies on your desires (and the things that need to be changed) and not on your fears. Your faith – especially, but not exclusively, in yourself - needs to be stronger than your fears. And one day – not too distant from now – all those doubters will be bragging that they knew you when.

Today you and your grand achievements are the very best answer and testimony to all those doubters and a convincing demonstration as well of exactly what each of us can achieve if we set our hearts and minds to it. We never know how much weight we can carry until we try or what burdens we can bear until we are really tested. And this day you showed us all. You met the tests and the challenges and you overcame them to reach this special moment.

Finally, I want to assure you that the investment you've made in your education is a wise one. Education today may be costly, but ignorance is far more expensive.

A great education changes the way you look at the world – mostly in a good way – and the rigor, the arguments, the grit and the perseverance that it takes to excel have prepared you, have distinguished you, and will set you apart as you enter the working world and in whatever you choose to do with your lives. This is a special privilege and a sacred trust and your most important responsibility as well as your first job will be to choose wisely.

You've gained powerful new skills – these are not to be wasted – not to be withheld for fear of failing - and, most importantly, not to be frittered away. Every one of you is better than that – you shouldn't settle for anything less. Your careers will be very different from ours – not a linear path or a single employer – you'll move as you choose from job to job – gathering experiences – gaining additional skills – learning from good and bad role models – and ever-expanding outward as you grow toward what makes your life most complete.

And, as you move forward on the journey, please keep one thing firmly in mind. There's always a best seat in the house – a best row at the show – and, while you may not always get it – shame on you if you don't go for it. It pays to aim high.

The world is full of new and different opportunities everywhere you look. The rate of change in your lives will never be slower than it is right now – so hang on to something solid - and be prepared for the ride of your life. Entrepreneurs learn early on that – just like in racing – the world doesn't wait for you. The future isn't something that you wait and hope for – it's something that you grab hold of and make your own. You don't get what you wish for, you get what you work for.

Now I want to leave you with 3 more quick rules.

(1) Focus is Everything.
You can do anything you want, but you can't do everything. Do a few important things in your life very well. The future will be all about difficult choices and constant triage. Too many opportunities and too little time. And be honest. Commit wholly to your choices. Don't say "maybe" when you mean "no". And remember that the hardest choices are those we make with our hearts, not our heads.

(2) There is No Finish Line.

We all need to be lifelong learners if we want to make a difference and a contribution. Your education just <u>started</u> here. Iteration – constantly examining, adjusting and improving every part of your lives – is the way that we will all remain competitive, valuable and relevant in the global economy. It's easy to say. But it's a hard way to live. We get better by getting just a little bit better each and every day.

(3) There's Always More Work.

Work is like rabbits. If you let it, it can multiply to fill all the hours in the day. This is called Parkinson's Law. And it's easy – especially when you're starting out – to confuse your work with who you are. But it's not your identity – it's just what you do. And, even more importantly, while there's always more work, you only have one family and it's critical, but not easy, to remember to make time and room for them in your soon-to-be very busy life. Creating, supporting and nurturing your family will <u>always</u> be your most important work.

So that's my story. My hopes for you are simple. I want the <u>rest</u> of your life to be the <u>best</u> of your life.

We often act as though comfort and luxury were the chief requirements of life, when all that we really need to make us happy is something to be enthusiastic and proud about.

I've been lucky enough for many years to go to work each day surrounded by excited, energetic and enthusiastic people who are setting out to change the world in important ways.

My fondest hope for each of you is that you can find a similar path, a similar place and similar challenges. There's no better way to spend your days.

So now it's up to you – go forth – go always forward – and go make us and your parents proud. God bless each and every one of you.

TULLMAN'S TRUISMS

WHAT YOU PAY ATTENTION TO IS WHO YOU ARE

If you had to pick the largest single change in the day-to-day social and psychological beliefs and behaviors which we adults exhibit (forget trying to explain what's going on with the kids today) because of specific changes brought about by the digital and social tools and technologies we now use every day, what would you choose?

Would you say that it was the advent and emergence of the "gig" economy? The fact that millions of people across the country now have a completely different and, in most cases we are sadly and quickly learning, a far less satisfactory relationship to the work they attempt to find and do every day. They live fragmented and piecemeal lives in every way – absent the comfort, security and predictability of those old, staid, stable and often boring jobs – which most would say that they'd gladly return to – given half a chance –if only those jobs still existed. But, as the Boss says in *My Hometown*: "Foreman says these jobs are going boys and they ain't coming back" and so we have more and more "freelancers" (over 50% of U.S. workers by 2020) whose employment choices are far from free. It reminds me of one of the best Kris Kristofferson lines ever from *Me and Bobby McGee*: "Freedom's just another word for nothin' left to lose". I'd put the gig scam along with all the functionally-indentured freelancers in the top 5, but not at the head of the list.

Maybe you're taken by the explosive growth of the "sharing" economy even if - most of the time - it's really a one-way street that has little or nothing to do with true sharing. It's just a slightly nicer way of saying I'm selling you something. When I first started talking about these questions, I called this type of transactional model the "surplus economy", not the sharing economy, because what we were seeing was the development in many industry sectors (and in other marketplaces as well) of low or no-cost aggregation platforms that would permit consumers to monetize (sell or trade, not share) their excess capacity – be it space, expertise, talent, labor, etc. by connecting them to a wide and broadly distributed audience without the need to incur the traditional marketing and sales costs associated with reaching those "customers" in order to offer their spare or incremental services and resources to them. (See https://www.inc.com/howard-tullman/four-rules-of-the-now-economy.html.) As far as I could see, this type of activity had very little to do with sharing as it was commonly understood, but the name has persisted.

Communes are actually about sharing certain resources and "barter" more properly describes the exchange between peers of various services and benefits; the car (and bike and scooter) services – especially Uber and Lyft - that we can't seem to live without today – don't actually share much of anything. They just take our money – "share" as little as humanly possible with the poor suckers who are driving day and night to make ends meet – and pretend that they're not killing the fluid flow of traffic in the center of every major city in the world. At least Airbnb can make a slightly better argument that you're "sharing" that extra empty bedroom for a fee with some stranger you don't know from Adam.

And, of course, it's the very idea of not knowing your boarder "from Adam" that's the best answer to the question. Because, as Billy Joel is fond of saying: "it's always been a matter of trust". The very nature of new technologies and tech-enabled services and solutions is that they are often abruptly presented to us (others sneak up on us more incrementally like AI-enabled services) and we slowly move along a fairly consistent path which starts with resistance to any change (inertia) and initial distrust and then moves to a level of experimentation and grudging acceptance and then ultimately(for better or worse) some serious adoption, regular reliance and actual psychological dependence. And, if we were honest, we'd all admit that we're just a little bit afraid of being so dependent on these technologies and knowing, at the same time, that we can't entirely control them.

If you don't think you're constantly caught somewhere in this vicious and virtuous cycle, try losing your phone for a few hours or having your internet connection go down for an evening and see how quickly the fear sets in and the withdrawal symptoms start. Some of these interactions are even more invasive - they go from being a job or an obligation - a duty if you will - to an integral part of our days and something we look forward to and desire. On Amazon, reordering the dog food is a job, but scoping out the flash sales and time-sensitive offers is all about greed and desire. But I digress.

The truth is that the biggest, boldest and - at once - the most pervasive and inexplicable change in our lives in the last decade has been the emergence of the "trust economy". It's not just that we let strangers sleep in our bedrooms. We put our kids in cars with drivers whose training and credentials are mostly a mystery. Their principal qualification is showing up - usually on time. And we buy goods and services from sellers all across the world without a moment's hesitation. Why? Because we trust the technology and the system. We trust the "reviews" which we think are objective evaluations from the crowd. But, when you think about it - the "plumbing" and infrastructure aside - both the gig economy and the sharing economy couldn't and wouldn't exist without the development of the trust economy. It's that fundamental to the way the web works.

But there's a real problem. The cruel irony and the disconnect is that - at the very same time that the trust economy continues to expand - our trust in each other - in the people we deal with daily - is plummeting. We trust the rideshare guys more by far (over twice as much) as we trust our neighbors. I'm not just talking about lying politicians and crooked government employees. I'm talking about our friends, neighbors and co-workers. The surveys are consistent and depressing and they don't lie. And the results really suck and they're all headed in the wrong direction. Today only 31% of us think that most people can be trusted.

So, is there anything any of us can do to stem the tide of distrust. Is there anything encouraging in the latest findings (Edelman, Harvard, et al)? Well, as it happens, consumers these days actually do believe in the business community. Not necessarily in the old guys (brands are dying left and right because they didn't live up to their promises), but we love the new kids in town (maybe not Facebook these days) and we see the possibility that they might get it right.

There's a reason that Amazon's become the most trusted brand in America. Jeff delivers. Actions and results matter if you're trying to restore people's confidence and their belief that it's even possible to get really big without getting bad. The lesson is very clear. It's up to us to make it real – to spend less time and money on marketing and manipulation and social media – and much more on taking care of our customers and taking care of business.

It's a lot harder to be trusted than it is to be loved.

TULLMAN'S TRUISMS

ENTREPRENEURS HAVE NO EXPIRATION DATE

No business today – large or small – has any business (or any real excuse) for being stupid about their media buys. The smartest players today know that their resources are finite and that they have to be strategic and smart about their spends or they will be left behind in the dust. Smart reach (getting to the right people at the right time and place with the right message) is still the only game that's gonna grow your business. (See http://www.inc.com/howard-tullman/to-sell-more-your-marketing-must-embrace-smart-reach.html.) But to a certain extent those tools and technologies are now just the most basic requirements. Because the tech keeps charging ahead and the bar keeps rising and yesterday's miracles are just today's "so what's".

What's left of the ad biz these days is much more about science and measurement (transparency and efficacy) than it is about someone's speculation, smell test or best guess about what will work. And, by the way, the revolution isn't limited to ads – if fact, we've already seen the whole game change in music and movies – the "Mad Men" are still just mostly stuck in yesterday's mud. The best sets of "ears" in the music business (apologies to Ahmet's memory and condolences to Clive) are simply no match for *Spotify*'s statistics and Pandora's playlists. And while it still helps to be "creative", the content directions at *Amazon* and *Netflix* are much more likely to come from calculations and computations than from Spielberg and Soderbergh. *Ready Player One* was a C+ piece that was more about the numbers (and trying to play to the new masses) than about any coherent and compelling narrative and it sucked accordingly. Data today is trumping drama and even Steven seems to be running scared.

Honestly, it sure seems that every time you start to believe that you're getting close to getting on top of this stuff or almost reaching the finish, they move the goalposts and kick you in the teeth a couple of times just for good measure. You've got to have new strategies for dealing with the noise, clutter, confusion and sheer fatigue that everyone out there is experiencing, and you've got to capture what little slice of my attention you can and really hit hard when your moment arrives because it couldn't be more fleeting. It's not enough to be in the room, you've got to catch me when I'm in the zone and interested or you'll end up just talking to yourself. (See https://www.inc.com/howard-tullman/communication-multitasking-and-distracted-audiences.html .)

And then, you better show me something special – something that I care about – and that represents real value to me. If you don't, I'll be gone in a flash, but if you do, you get me and my buddies as well. The deal is simple: if you make me care, I'm gonna share and do it actively and willingly – and you can't buy that kind of authentic recommendation and direct influence for all the money in the world. (See https://www.inc.com/howard-tullman-make-me-care-and-then-i-will-share.html .)

Seems straightforward, but millions of marketers still don't get it. They're into tonnage and pushing paper. But they're just pissing people off and it's only going to get worse for them and their clients. The pressures from consumers and regulators for permission-based access and new affirmative disclosure and consent rules are growing. Congress is still sound asleep, of course, but that may be the best thing for us. In any case, the remaining bad actors will eventually be barred and shut off as their results continue to crater and their people still stuck doing business with them end up throwing their money down the drain.

But this is just the start of tomorrow's story because – even if you get to the right time and place and target customers, your pitch, production and product better be as close to perfect as possible because the stakes for screwing up have never been higher. The list of companies burned in an instant on social media for transgressions that seemed too trivial to even talk about just keeps growing. Ask the *Gap* about their China T-Shirt, *Dodge* about RAMming MLK Day, *Pepsi* about handing a pop to a policeman, *Nivea* about "Whiter" deodorant or *Heineken* about "Lighter" beer. The message is always the same: "Who Knew?" or even better yet, "Who Would Have Imagined?" and yet, in retrospect, the stupidity seems obvious and the anger and eruptions inevitable. These guys all whine about needing a crystal ball to do business today.

And you know what? There is one. It can tell you if the right audience is interested and listening. Where to put your money and your media. It can tell you what won't work. And it can even help you figure out what to say. Amazed? Flabbergasted? Dumbfounded? Nope. The answer is *Dumbstruck* (www.dumbstruck.com).

Dumbstruck is a Chicago and New York-based business that already working in the background with some of the biggest brands and agencies in the world. They built a machine that reads minds and emotions. On the fly and in real time. They're "coming out" at the Cannes Lion 2018 – International Festival of Creativity in France in June. I think they didn't want to steal any of Meghan and Harry's thunder. And they're gonna make a big noise and some huge changes in the ad biz and the momentum is already building.

That's all I can tell you at the moment, but their moment is right now. Check 'em out.

I've spent too much time recently in sessions with talented technical people (who already have more than enough on their plates and on their to-do lists) wasting too many hours talking and worrying about trolls. Trolls, for those of you lucky enough not to have had to deal with them, are social media-enabled nobodies who spend their days making trouble online for legitimate businesses. They write strident screeds filled with empty assertions about alleged system flaws and security holes and threaten to "publish" these mostly misleading and always provocative commentaries if their "concerns" and comments aren't immediately addressed. Having to deal with these people could be just my own misfortune, but it seems more than just my problem and that, in fact, there's a real concern here – especially for startups - which don't have the luxury of dedicated resources devoted to breach and security issues.

It's not so much about the alleged flaws and security issues that these trolls and fake "researchers" report or threaten to publish (using click-happy and equally craven "reporters"); it's because (a) they waste tremendous amounts of what could otherwise be productive time on the part of your technical people and (b) they specifically target those technical people who are consistently the brightest and most naïve; the most committed and the thinnest-skinned; and the most conscientious and diligent members of your team. These attributes may make them great coders and developers, but they absolutely make them the worst possible people to deal with trolls because (1) they think it's a fair contest and (2) they take every criticism and complaint about their work to heart and much too personally.

Sadly, they think that, if they can simply explain things properly to the trolls, everything will be better, and the problems will go away. It's a lot like hoping that the hungry lion won't eat you because you're a vegetarian. The truth is that there really isn't a polite or politically correct way to say this but there simply are NO good trolls. Not a one. The thought that you can feed and engage with the good trolls (or that you can even figure out who those might be) is basically and badly deluded.

These are fundamentally damaged people who can't help themselves just like the scorpion that stings the turtle which carried him safely across the river – why did he do it – because it's his nature – so what else would you expect? These guys have no one's best interests in mind other than their own. And, in fact, it's not totally clear that they even know what their own motives might be since this is no way for even asocial morons to spend most of the waking hours in their sad little lives. Nitpicking and scab scratching – day in and day out – for no good reason and to no good end.

I admit that it can be a little confusing because some of these people can actually (but not consistently) carry on what appears to be an intermittently rational (albeit usually anonymous) email or text conversation – or a Twitter storm – for periods of time until the "crazy" breaks thru, their Mom calls them up for dinner, or the tin foil hats come back out. You have to wonder why the ones of a certain age don't have day jobs that might actually give them a chance (and pay them) to employ some of their skills and analytical abilities in a productive – rather than an abusive and erratic – fashion. But this crazy world doesn't work that way.

When you deal with them over and over again, you discover pretty quickly that - in most cases (forget the real crooks and the ransom assholes) – you actually can't pay them to come to work for you or to go away. It could be as simple as the fact that many of these people couldn't function in a business environment, don't know how to conduct themselves in polite company, or have just spent too much time alone in their basements talking to themselves and their pet whatevers. Needless to say, these aren't your typical dog and cat owners. They're much more likely to keep a couple of slimy snakes and a few rodents around their place. And it seems that making your tech people miserable is what they do for fun.

So, I'd propose a couple of simple ideas which will help save you a lot of time and money and also help you curb the good-natured and well-intentioned, but foolish and dangerous, instincts of your tech people. Give them my five little rules.

(1) If you assume the worst motives possible, you'll almost always be right.
(2) Send all the trolls to Tom (or Biff or Bob) so he's the <u>only</u> one wasting his time.
(3) Don't explain, don't complain, don't share, and don't commit to do anything. It's a slippery slope and an endless deluge of demands.
(4) Threats and deadlines are a dime a dozen – don't be bullied or bluffed into doing something dumb.
(5) Fast fixes and shortcut solutions always screw something else up.

Save yourself all the headaches and the heartaches by not getting started in the first place. There's no upside to wrestling with a pig – you get dirty and the pig enjoys it. You've got much better things to do and the pig has nothing but time. Trying to get a fair shake from a troll is like trying to find the clean end of a shit stick.

I think that we're headed for some difficult times for young companies that have scrambled for a year or two to keep their heads above water, but who are now reaching the point where the rubber better be hitting the road, or their ride may be over. It's gonna take a lot more substance and a lot less "story" to keep these boats afloat. (See https://www.inc.com/howard-tullman/no-dont-need-your-pointless-app.html .) And, because it's the way these guys play the game, it's going to be a lot easier for the newest kids on the block (or the blockchain) to raise a bunch of money than for the ones who've been at it for a while and whose stories have lost a lot of heat and grown a lot of hair. Being yesterday's news or "just about to turn the corner" is almost as bad as being Yahoo! these days. No one is interested in profitless prosperity or forever chasing the horizon. "Almost" only counts in horseshoes and hand grenades.

And, I'm getting a sense that the "easy money" is starting to get harder (even the doctors are starting to ask to see the data) and that, as the time to reload those cobwebbed coffers rolls around again, it's not going to be a lack of interest or available funds that slams a lot of the doors, it's going to be a lack of concrete progress, traction, real results and a path to profitability that puts the final nails in the coffins. The money's always there; it's just the pockets that change. There's plenty of Series A money to go around; it's just that they think your business isn't serious.

So, as the boss, you're going to come to the point where you have to write the memo. You've come to that point where it's time to go – to shut the doors and turn off the lights - even though no one is certain where they're headed or what comes next. We've all been there, but, as always, Springsteen says it best: "you don't know where you're going, but you know you won't be back." Hopefully, you've prepared the path and won't be leaving everyone (or anyone) high and dry. There aren't a lot of skid marks when a startup shuts down, but there is a right way to do these things. (See https://www.inc.com/howard-tullman/failure-happens-four-ways-to-do-it-well.html.)

And there's a right way to tell your team that the dream has turned to dust. They were there for you in so many ways and thanking them for their hard work and commitment is a great place to start the conversation. It helps to be honest and to make clear that the last few months of a failing business are never fun. It's a lot like being pecked apart and beaten to death by ducks. The truth is that some experiences don't make you tougher, they just wear you out. But the key takeaway and what still makes even the wind-down process worthwhile is that you hung in there and did it together. You had the opportunity to work with some great and talented people under the worst conditions and circumstances and see them continue to come through and deliver the results for the customers and clients that were depending on them. That's a life lesson. Giving up is easy; gutting it out is hard.

I'd suggest that there are four other important messages that you might want to weave into your story. No pride of authorship here – just some ideas to throw into the hopper. Ultimately, the story's gotta be your own or it won't be helpful to anyone.

First, you should caution everyone to be careful to extract from the whole process only the education and wisdom that's in it and nothing more. Each deal, every business and all the many opportunities you'll be handed are unique and it's easy – but not smart – to try to generalize and carry your experience forward. But it's very rare that the situation's the same or that the shoe fits twice. It's like the cat who sits down on a hot stove. She won't do that again, but she'll also never sit on a cool stove either. You don't want to forfeit the future because of bumps in the past. It's up to each member of your team to be one of those people upon whom nothing is lost or wasted. They should take all of the lessons with them (good and bad) and use them to make something better and stronger the next time around.

Second, it's important not to either romanticize or ceaselessly mourn the whole thing. The truth is that things were never as great or as horrible as it might seem in retrospect and in the selective retelling. Some poet once said: "when one door closes, another opens, but we often look so longingly and so regretfully upon the closed door that we do not see the one that has opened for us."

There's no question that your team has lived thru some of the best and most exciting times of their young lives and it's possible that what comes next may never take them to those emotional heights again (you really are only a virgin once), but it's not inevitable that everything from now on will be a pale imitation of the past or a disappointment. We're all products of our pasts, but no one has to be a prisoner of it unless they're willing to settle for that. No one can step over you unless and until you lie down.

Third, nobody ever said that life was fair. After years of hard work and plenty of grief, things didn't work out exactly as you expected. No surprise there. They never do. Real life's just like that. The fact is that neither life nor nature ever care if justice is done. Every action has both intended and unintended consequences. The intended consequences sometimes happen. The unintended consequences, whatever they may turn out to be, always happen. It turns out, as Casey Stengel used to say: "that baseball is the only place in life where a sacrifice is really appreciated." It's important to always keep moving forward and to remember that, in tough times like these, there are really no winners - only survivors. The trick is to be sure to be one.

And one last thought as you all look forward to your next whatever. It really takes away from your soul when you do what you don't believe in. And even if the right song is playing, no one is going to tell you to get up and dance. It's all on you. Find something that you passionately care about, throw yourself into it with all your heart, and let the new chips fall where they may.

Any entrepreneur or road warrior who travels on a regular basis hears some new horror tale about hacks, scams and identity thefts just about every other week. Interestingly enough, these are usually fairly-credible, peer-to-peer conversations rather than media scare stories. Most recently, I've heard half a dozen versions of complaints and some serious instances of financial losses based on the porous and insecure nature of hotel and airport Wi-Fi. In fairness, all of these providers couldn't make it any clearer or disclose the risks more directly on their websites (these are not the usual disclaimers buried in the T&Cs), but the truth is that we don't really have much in the way of connectivity choices when we're on the road. Of course, you can carry your own hotspot or use your phone and run down your battery, but the vast majority of us aren't gonna do that. So, the trick is to figure out what you can do, realistically and practically, to protect yourself.

As we're forced to rely more and more on third-party-provided Wi-Fi and it becomes increasingly ubiquitous, the scale of the security problems and the prospective losses are only going to continue to grow. And honestly, as long as it's not happening to a family member or a relative, we've gotten so accustomed to these commonplace tales of woe (and worse) that they just seem to be some of the risks of the road. In addition, I have to admit that we stupidly assume (and often think smugly to ourselves) that the victims must have been lazy, sloppy or careless and that this kind of stuff could never happen to us <u>until</u> it does and then, of course, it's too late.

My humble suggestion is that now's the time to start thinking about how to be <u>smart</u> about the situation before you have to be <u>sorry</u>. My thought is simple: if you can't control the pipes, try to control and protect your passwords. Yes, I know that you've heard these lectures a million times before and yet the vast majority of us are too "busy", too lazy, or too uninformed to actually invest the modest amount of time that it takes to substantially boost the odds in your favor. In this context, I'd say that being too busy is, in fact, just another word for being lazy. There's not much I can do to help anyone unwilling to help themselves.

It would take about an hour to follow a few basic steps to improve your password protection while it can take weeks to repair and try to restore your credit and financial identity if you get hacked. You should take the time to do the math. And, for now, I'm just going to focus on the facts of life these days and then you can decide how to proceed.

First, the guys on the other side are getting smarter, faster and a lot nastier. They're growing in numbers, the hacks are easier to accomplish, and they're better equipped - especially because the tech and capital requirements to take your money are trivial. In addition, ploys and scams are spreading and being shared across markets and even countries at a very rapid rate because of the increased communications and connections across the dark web.

Second, we suckers continue to make it easier and easier for the bad guys to break in. The most frequently used password today is still "123456". Number 5 on the list is "111111" and Number 8 is "password". It takes most brute-force hacking programs less than a few seconds according to a recent survey to figure out any password of 6 characters or less and more than 40% of all passwords today are 6 characters or less. Other very popular passwords are equally infantile including: "qwerty" and "123123". And more than half of us use the exact same password on multiple sites so once the hackers are in, they can move quickly from site to site.

And finally, the middlemen (hosting services, connectivity providers, social platforms, etc.) aren't doing jack to help us help ourselves by requiring us to be smart about our personal security. They don't care if you get ripped off as long as you can always get right back on their service or network with the least possible friction and in the shortest amount of time. Every six months, some of these services make you change your password, but they don't insist upon or enforce even the most basic complexity requirements.

What should you do?

The best and smartest thing to do is to use a password manager/vault which is a single location for all your passwords and requires only remembering one password which hopefully will be at a minimum 8 characters with a number, letter, capital letter and a symbol as part of it. There are several players in the space, but Keeper Security (<u>keepersecurity.com</u>) has one of the biggest user bases and is the best for my money because they provide both individual and enterprise-level solutions and they employ a zero-knowledge approach which means that even they have no idea what's in your vault or any ability to get at it. You spend less than an hour and build an Excel spreadsheet with all your stuff (which you probably already have) and then it's imported into your Keeper vault and the next time you visit one of your regular sites, the Keeper system will automatically supply the appropriate sign-in data.

The next best thing to do is to bite the bullet and adopt two-factor authentication (2FA) which I admit can be a pain in the butt on a plane or if you're not connected somehow, but otherwise it's as easy as pie. This is another simple way to deploy an additional layer of protection and just requires that you take an extra minute to enter a security code sent to your phone which will confirm that it's actually you trying to get into your site. For sure, this is an essential fix for your primary social media sites because they are the connectors and links to many other sites where you used Facebook Connect or something similar for Twitter to sign into a bunch of third-party sites.

Both of these steps are quantum leaps in de-risking your online exposures and a very small price to pay (in terms of time and treasure) to avoid major headaches. And, if you're like everyone else and somewhat intimidated by the length of your password list (or never heard of Excel), at least work on the top five sites you visit all the time and get those fixed and protected. It's a 99/1 world in terms of anyone's web activity (we go to the same, very few, places almost all of the time) so, if you at least pay attention to the most important sites, you've got a fighting chance of dodging a bullet. But the smart money is still on the hackers and it's not really a question of "if", it's just a question for most of us of "when". I'd rather be safe than sorry.

Today the best businesses – in retail, in hospitality, and even in health care – aren't simply selling products or services – they're selling the whole package: the experiential journey; the feel-good buzz; and the "be-back" soon. It's increasingly critical to swiftly move the consumer along this path from connection to engagement and attachment and from there to a continuing commitment. Loyalty and "locked-in for life" are the dream and the desired state. But these days, it's a lot easier said than done.

More and more affluent consumers no longer have a "favorite" or preferred product or service within an increasing number of verticals. And Alexa is the next nail in the coffin of the big brands because consumers just want their cornflakes and buyers just want their batteries and it don't much matter anymore who makes the stuff as long as it's delivered to their home the same day.

It seems to me that millions of merchants, marketers and managers just don't get it. Loyalty only lasts as long as you deliver – each and every time - and no one owns anything more than the moment you've got to earn my business. Loyalty programs are everywhere these days, but for that very reason, they're losing their impact and their perceived value unless they're backed up and enhanced by the way your people and your procedures operate. Your programs need to incent and reward regular and continuous engagement and repeated transactional activity.

This is especially essential these days because the world of one-off customers is over – it's too costly, it's too hard, and the resultant and constant churn can kill any company. In a world where you've got to focus on keeping the customer coming back, and where the customer cares less and less about owning anything and more and more about utility, convenience, speed and ready access, you and your team have to manage every part of the path and every step in the journey to be successful.

It's a journey that begins before we even get there – with often inflated expectations and sometimes unrealistic anticipation – and then moves to the delivery of the "thing" itself – and finally (provided that you don't manhandle the mood or snuff the satisfaction) on to fond memories lasting long after and, most importantly and far more precious than gold, favorable WOM (word of mouth) and authentic, heartfelt recommendations. Your best promoters and influencers aren't the paid shills and cynical celebs; they're the passionate people who lived their dream and can't wait to share their stories with others.

But even your favorite fans will tell you that they're not prepared to pay up for your products simply because they buy into your story (brand promise) unless your offerings meet all of the other components of their constantly morphing consideration set. We're talking about assembling and purveying a bundle of bargains, behaviors, and benefits that are consistently better than the alternatives.

The truth is that if you disappoint me when I walk through the door or beat me up when I'm about to leave – you can be sure that I won't be back. But as obvious as this may seem, every day we see actions, processes and systemic shortcomings that are designed that squander customer satisfaction. You can give me all the points that are possible, but if your people or your procedures piss me off, that's the impression I'm coming in or going out with and you're not likely to turn me around with special discounts, package deals, special show access, or anything else after the fact because in customer service, you don't get a second chance to make a first impression. If your staff and services don't sync up with the really swell promises you've made, you're sunk.

How hard can it really be to do these basic things right? My shoe salesman knows my shoe size and preferences the second time I'm in the store because he keeps track on his own little 3x5 customer cards. But I feel that he cares about me and also about not wasting my time. I'd call that really small data, but it matters, and it works. Businesses can't afford any longer to assume that one size fits all – we know that it doesn't, and the data are there to enable differentiation and mass customization. But I can go into some of the most expensive hotels in any city (where I've stayed a dozen times before) and be treated like a stranger every time. Wouldn't it be nice if they "knew" me, even just a little bit? And that's just the beginning of the BS that the business traveler suffers.

How about the "our check-ins aren't until 3 pm" story? And, of course, if you make a fuss or scream loudly enough – wonder of wonders – they suddenly find a room for you. But why should you have to shout and get upset. And why should it be so hard to figure out that a certain number of rooms need to be turned over and cleaned up and ready to go by 10 or 11am – maybe not for the tourists – but for the road warriors. What's at work here is pretty simple – the entire process is designed to suit the schedules and the needs of the housekeepers and maids, and not the customers. It's all inside out and tough on you rather than customer-centric and responsive to a recurring, regular and simple-to-solve issue.

On the other hand, when you use the increasingly available data to combine and drive the in-store and the online connections with your customers and you build powerful loyalty programs that offer both monetary and experiential perks and advantages, the impact on the bottom line couldn't be clearer. My favorite story for some time now has been Ulta Beauty (www.ulta.com) whose whole business is hyper-personalized and where more than 22 million members of the rewards programs account for over 90% of sales. They use their information and back office tools to augment and improve the in-store engagement and create the very clear message that you, your presence and your time are both valued and much appreciated. The seamless combination of "hurry" (time sensitive) and "heartfelt" (sincere and authentic) is a wonder to watch. It's a one-on-one feeling delivered on a massive scale and no one does it better today.

What's the bottom line? The lowest hanging fruit and the absolute best customers to have are the ones you've already got. But if you don't show me a little love, I'll leave you in the lurch and find a new lover.

There's an old adage among short sellers who prey on companies with the hope that the value of their stocks will drop dramatically based on rumors, lies and/or the occurrence of anything nasty, but rarely as a result of actual changes in the real fundamentals of the business. They pray for fake news, customer reversals, security breaches and any other apparent "problems". Once they see a crack in the target business's armor, they promptly tell the media that: "there's never only one cockroach in the ceiling". This, they insist, is because history has shown again and again that problems - just like deaths and bad luck - come in clusters. The shorts swear that there's always some more bad (but undisclosed) news about their victims coming right around the corner. And then the man-made and media-fomented avalanches and the runs on the bank begin.

Of course, in some cases, it's a real public service to out the crooks and warn the investing public or those others soon to be sold a bogus bill of goods. Certainly, the recent case of the larcenous lovebirds at *Theranos* is a good example of the cascade of corruption that starts with a quiet leak and turns into a flood and a PR nightmare that is still pouring out as the long overdue criminal indictments are finally made public. As far as the VC investors, insiders, and window-dressing board members, they can fend for themselves and they probably deserve a fair amount of the grief they have gotten or will soon get. But you've got to feel bad for the hundreds of thousands of patients who these phony pukes lied to about their tests and the test results and grateful that millions more – equally unsuspecting - weren't also victimized.

Now, the truth is that even good companies are always going to have problems and, in many cases, that's not even a bad thing - it's to be expected as a part of any new business growing and maturing and stumbling from time to time along the way. (See https://www.inc.com/howard-tullman/so-youve-got-problems-thats-probably-great-news.html.) The trick for the guys running the show is to make sure that they see and hear about all of the problems and concerns as soon as possible so they can be dealt with in a timely fashion instead of letting them fester and get worse. Bad things don't get better by themselves and nothing moves by itself unless it's going downhill. And, the bigger the business, the less likely that bad news will make it all the way up to senior management without being smoothed, sweetened or smothered along the way.

If you want the straight scoop, you've got to make a dedicated effort to go out and get it. And, because even Superman can't be everywhere at once, you've got to build a culture that promotes truth-telling and doesn't try to hide the rotten fruit. (See https://www.inc.com/howard-tullman/five-rules-for-truthtellers.html.) It also helps to actively encourage your people to bring you the bad news right along with the morning coffee. It may not be good for your digestion, but it's a very smart strategy for your business.

Ultimately, this is about the core culture of your company, but you can give things a big push in the right direction if you develop a methodology and an approach to team-based problem-solving that you can push out and extend throughout the whole company. No one thinks that there's one approach that works for everyone, but there are a few basic ideas that you should incorporate in your plan if you want to get the best results.

So, you've got a serious problem. What do you do?

(1) Focus first on fixing the problem and coming up with a solution that isn't just a band-aid or a short-term fix. Take the time and spend the money to do it right the first time so you don't have to fix it over and over again.

(2) Separate <u>what</u> caused the problem from <u>who</u> caused the problem and who's responsible for it. Those personnel conversations can come after you extinguish the immediate fires.

(3) The truth is that, once you get in the habit of fixing these things effectively and quickly, you discover that people just want to get over the hiccup and get on with building their business and they don't have a lot of time to sit around pointing fingers at each other.

(4) Everyone on the team needs to own a piece of the process and accept personal responsibility for helping to come up with a concrete solution. Trying to pass things off to others – superiors or subordinates – or pretending that it's not your problem isn't an acceptable position. It's everyone's problem until it's solved. All hands need to be on deck.

(5) Once the remedy is agreed upon, everyone gets going and is responsible for implementing their part of the plan and the solution. Waiting to be told what to do and how to do just won't do anymore. If you need specific authority, or resources, or personnel, go ask for what you need instead of sitting around and hoping that these things will take care of themselves.

(6) When it's time to look backwards, make sure that it's not all about the blame game. The idea is to learn from the mistakes and to apply that learning going forward to prevent reoccurrences or similar problems.

If you do this right and do it consistently, you'll build a business that learns from every step and stumble in the journey as it grows. But even more importantly, you'll keep the inevitable slips and sprinkles from turning into storms and strife.

I got a note recently from a colleague who had previously written me a short email commenting on my last INC. column. He shared with me a simple phrase that his father often used to describe a situation similar to the one I had written about. When I didn't promptly respond to his missive, he followed up with another note saying that he hoped that his brief note and comments hadn't offended me.

I was reminded of Pascal's great line: "I didn't have time to write a short letter, so I wrote a long one instead". Or, in today's parlance, "If I had more time, I'd be briefer". I wrote him that I actually appreciated his taking the time to react to what I had written and to think about it. And I assured him that – with my exceedingly thick skin – the only thing that really offended me was waste.

Wastes of words, time, resources, opportunities, and especially wastes of breath - like apologies (without coincident changes in behavior) - or basically anyone wasting their time (and mine) in trying to make cheap excuses. Explanations and investigations are fine, but make no mistake, there's no such thing as a good excuse. You learn early on in the startup world that you can have results, or you can have excuses, but rarely both.

Honestly, I never mind anyone who does me the favor of getting right to the point and telling it like it is. In a world of blowhards and BS-ers, this is a joy and a relief. Frankly, what you can't say in ten minutes about your business, your problem or your idea probably isn't worth saying. We're all time-starved and in a hurry, so feel free to make it short and sweet.

The truth is that sometimes the hardest thing to do is to tell a simple story. If it's a pitch, make sure I can tell right away whether what you're saying makes sense, whether it's a real business or opportunity, where the warts and the pitfalls are likely to be, and whether you're the right one with the requisite passion, persistence and smarts to make it happen.

If it's a problem, it's a slightly different challenge. In the pursuit of pithiness, you still need to make sure that you tell me the whole tale and the whole truth. (See https://www.inc.com/howard-tullman/five-rules-for-truthtellers.html .) And, if you're bringing me bad news, make it the headline so we can get right into it; there's always plenty of time down the line to pat yourself on the back.

But assuming that you've got good news to share, don't hide your light under a bushel basket and – especially if you're looking for money – do everything you can to make it easy to say "yes". Too many new entrepreneurs make it easy to turn them down because they're so unprepared to take their best shot in the moment when the opportunity is there and because they don't really understand how to make the most of that short window of time.

As we used to say when I was in the music industry, it's really easy to tell when a song is bad, but only the public and the market will ultimately decide what sells. Note that I said "what sells", not necessarily what's good. The music business today is all about making money, not making great music. Always has been; always will be.

And it's the same situation when you're describing a new business. If you're all over the place; if you're trying to be all things to too many people; if your story is so complicated that it's hard to even follow; or if you've got a solution in search of a problem, it's going to be pretty easy to say "thanks, but no thanks". You've got one shot, one moment, and one opportunity to get right to the heart of the matter and the most crucial part of the entire process is simplifying the story.

How simple? Your story should answer 3 simple questions about your company which, by the way, are the very same questions that will inform and guide your company for its entire existence. These answers are also every bit as significant for each and every employee as they are for any investors.

So, it's pretty important to get the answers right at the outset. The answers might change over time, but the fundamental questions never do. Here they are:

Who are We?
Management and team members' relevant experience and credentials

Where are We Going?
Short and long-term objectives and goals – abbreviated milestones – timeframe

Why?
What problem is being addressed and solved – time, money, productivity, status

Short, sweet and to the point. You've got to be a ruthless editor and there's no question that the toughest choices are about what to leave out, not what to include. You need to think of detail and elaboration as forms of pollution. Cut to the quick. And stick to your story.

Tell the story you need to tell, be relentless, stay on point, keep it short, and make the limited time that you have count. Everything else can come later. Bottom line: don't waste my time or yours - tell a simple story

I always say that change is easy. It takes place in an instant. What's hard is overcoming inertia and the resistance to change which grows out of a simple fact - we're creatures of comfort and habit - and this means that we'd always rather keep doing things the old way if at all possible especially when they've worked pretty well for us in the past. The problem (and the risk) is that they aren't going to work for us in the future and if we don't change and sometimes even cannibalize ourselves, someone else will quickly come along to do things better, faster, cheaper or more easily and we'll be left behind. So, in today's global and super-competitive world, you can change, or you will most assuredly and eventually die.

But what do you do when your customers are basically "fat and happy" and don't want to change? We've all seen examples in the past where a company attempted to simply impose a new change on their customers and - even before the days of massive social media - the customers quickly revolted and rejected the move. If social media has done anything, it's mainly upped the ante and the pain and costs associated with getting these things wrong. And what do you do if you know that the necessary changes are going to actively drive existing customers away? Nobody wants to sign up for a near-term revenue hit even if you know that you'll come out ahead of the game in the long run.

I've written before about how many ads have recently blown up in advertisers' faces (Pepsi, Dodge, Nivea, Heineken, etc.) and thereupon required not simply remaking the ads themselves, but also cancelling national media buys and whole time-sensitive campaigns. (See https://www.inc.com/howard-tullman/catch-me-if-you-can.html .) I suppose the failure of New Coke will always be one of the classic examples of misplaced enthusiasm and horrible market research and the GAP trying to change the color of their logo will be one of the more seemingly trivial cases which nonetheless required immediate apologies and the abrupt abandonment of millions of dollars of new materials.

And, of course, my personal favorite - especially given just how high-flying Netflix is these days - was the *Qwikster* disaster which lasted all of two weeks (or maybe less) before the plug was pulled and Netflix retreated from the stillborn attempt to split up the DVD-by-mail and their streaming service into two separate businesses. Funny because today no one even remembers the little red envelopes any more than they recall the millions of AOL disks that they also got every day in the mail. Actually, my friend Mark Walsh swears that AOL only mailed a billion or so of the disks and that the rest were shoveled out of low-flying crop dusters which blanketed the entire Midwest.

And, talking again about the expanded impact of social media, if you get it wrong today, you not only have to deal with the actual unhappy customers and buyers, you also have to deal with the trolls and professional complainers who bitch just for the sake of seeing their own comments out there in the world and most likely never have used or will buy the products or services in question. (See https://www.inc.com/howard-tullman/there-are-no-good-trolls.html .)

So, who's done it right in the recent past and what can we learn from their example. Surprisingly, McDonalds did a great job with the whole McCafé transition and the world's pretty much none the wiser which means that they got it done literally right under the noses of their customers without anyone catching on and launch some crusade to turn back the clock.

Here's what happened. In the last few years, alternative coffee brands and other offerings have exploded, and these new choices were making a serious dent in the daily numbers at Mickey Dee's. In addition, coffee tastes in general were changing and, across the board, coffee has gotten both stronger and sweeter. In particular, younger coffee drinkers were looking for a lot more flavorful brew and various confections, but seniors (among the largest segments of McDonalds coffee customers) liked things just the way they were and didn't want expressos, lattes, syrups, or much of anything else except the good old regular brew. Starbucks dealt with the same issue years ago when they launched their Pike Place (which you and your friends all call Pikes Peak) line of drinks.

So, the company undertook a careful plan (probably close to two years in the overall implementation and completely under the radar) to slowly and consistently – month in and month out – increase the strength of their basic coffee without saying a word to anyone. Today, if you look at the menus, everything, including regular old coffee, is part of the McCafé family.

What's the lesson: it's easy by the inch, but hard by the yard. Sometimes slow is the way to go, with small and sure incremental steps, and you'll still get there - maybe a little later than you'd like - but with a whole lot less wear-and-tear and a lot happier and larger overall base of customers.

Having just returned from a short trip to Japan, I can tell you that, from a commercial perspective, the more some things change, the more others remain exactly the same. Doing business in Japan seems like it hasn't changed a bit in several centuries. I've been working and lecturing there for over a decade and most of the common business practices still seem stuck in time and firmly bound by custom and tradition. This isn't exactly a bad thing although it's probably one of the reasons that Japan's economy hasn't kept pace with the world's other leading economies. But for some willing and well-prepared foreign businesses, this situation can present real opportunities.

But as far as Japan goes, I'd say – until you really learn their rules of the road – you'd do better – for the sake of your own sanity – to skip the sake and save your money. If you really want to understand what the expression "slow as molasses" means, and also get a real appreciation for how business customs still vary radically from country to country, spend a little time exploring today's Silk Road.

The first thing that you need to understand is that – if you thought life in Key West was laid back – those Parrot Heads have got nothing on the Japanese. Osaka may be the place where "don't worry, no hurry" was invented because even the best businesses move at a glacial place and a sense of urgency is regarded as halfway between disrespectful and ungrateful. Everything takes more time than you can imagine – multiple introductory visits are mandatory – the first few meet-and-greets are typically more about food choices and family matters – nobody gets down to business on the first few dates - and don't forget the gift giving. It appears to me that – in the gift department – it's absolutely the case that it's the thought that counts most, the quality of the wrapping is probably in second place, and finally getting the timing right is also critical – not too soon or too late – just right on time.

If there's any good news about the whole process, it's that - after you pay your dues and build an authentic relationship – it's likely that you're in it for life. That's why they take their time and – as long as you're not an impatient American - it's not really a bad thing to be thinking about the lifetime value of each customer rather than going for quick hits and short turnaround times. Young entrepreneurs will learn an important lesson here about the need for patience and the criticality of investing in relationships.

The second thing that is radically different in Japan is that no one is willing to say "No". Every entrepreneur will tell you all day long that they much prefer a fast "No" to a long and painful series of "Maybes", but that's what you get in Tokyo. And you have to be very careful: (i) not to confuse very good manners with any kind of agreement; (ii) not to talk yourself into believing that you heard what no one said; and (iii) not to accept commitments made in so many words, but not from the heart. When you've come a very long way and you're looking to get something done so you can go home, it's too easy to start kidding yourself. I always try to remember the drunk who once told me "that hooker really liked me" whenever I need a reality check. No amount of wishful thinking ever actually gets things done.

Japan is a peaceful and pristine world of unfailing politeness, an absolute avoidance of conflict and confrontation, and a place where almost everything is about procedures and the process with only the most modest concern for progress. If you're in a hurry and have a plane to catch, you're in the wrong place.

But it may be that's there's a bit of a generational crack in the "friendly" façade. What we learned (without naming any names) is that – outside of the room and out of the presence of their superiors – the junior people you are dealing with will kick back a bit over a burger and tell you quietly that, while they admire the directness and honesty of American business men, the fact is that being frank and out front is such a foreign behavior in Japan that they fear things may never change.

And the last obstacle to overcome is a xenophobic pride in their own people and a staunch belief in their own internal ability to meet their needs. Doing business today in Japan almost inevitably means partnering with a local firm and - even then - such deals depend on the foreign party having complex skills and capabilities not otherwise available in country. As you might imagine, the general consensus is that, as regards the Olympics, there really are no skill sets so unique that they can't be provided by local companies.

My impression is that this overall attitude is so firmly rooted in the culture and politics of Japan that you can't even blame individual actors or attribute evil motives to them. It's in the air and it's everywhere. It starts with the aggressive refusal to even consider easing the restrictions on immigration at a time when the demographics of the shrinking population are headed in the wrong direction and there are growing health issues around providing in-home care for millions of elders who are aging in place. Surveys consistently report that the older citizens have a dramatic and overwhelming preference for their care to be delivered by robots rather than by immigrants. But no one would ever say anything like that directly to you.

Bottom line: Japan is the most welcoming closed society around. You are more than welcome to come – just don't plan on staying too long.

I blame Rupert and Fox. They brought yellow journalism back to the U.S. in spades and the "news" hasn't been the same ever since. The media game changed radically and rapidly and even those with the best of intentions had to adapt and adjust or go under. It's a painful race to the bottom of the barrel and a constant struggle to create more useless content to toss into the vacuous vortex. Everyone's obliged to feed the beast. Repurposing and spinning other people's content to keep up is what my friend calls "churnalism" and it's rampant. And, if you can't make it, then feel free to fake it. Just this week, a former Fox news analyst claimed that Fox News hosts regularly say things they know to be untrue just for the sake of ratings and notoriety.

Facebook can't figure out why they should bar the Holocaust deniers and the other made-up conspiracy scumbags from their site (and not just the newsfeed) when 99% of their users think the answer is obvious. But then, Zuck isn't about raising the bar – he's all about the bucks and he sucks. But the saddest part of the FB story is his constant claim that Facebook isn't a media business which makes its living selling small slices of your attention to advertisers, he says it's just a platform that happens to bring the "news" to billions of people every day. Give me a break, Zuck, and get real.

There was a time not too long ago when there was only one inviolate rule in journalism – the absolute separation between news and opinion. "Everyone is entitled to his own opinion, but not to his own facts" was the way Senator Daniel Patrick Moynihan famously put it, in 1989. If you, as a journalist, followed that simple rule, you could smoke like a chimney and drink like a fish, as long as you made deadline. If your writing style was breathless (as opposed to timeless) and halfway between cheesy and choppy, well that's what editors were for. And, in your haste to beat out your buddies, you could even occasionally get your facts a little messed up.

Of course, getting the facts straight was nowhere near as hard as it is today where the process is equal parts sloppy and intentionally skewed. Getting it right takes a daily and distant backseat to getting it out first and fastest. And, what's even worse, in a social media-centric version of Gresham's Law, fake news today tends to blot out and smother any semblance of legitimate, measured and meticulous reporting. Some 75% of the American public say they can't tell the difference between real news and the fake stuff and more than 50% no longer read or watch any mainstream media. In a democracy, without a common ground and some shared basic facts, it's impossible to have any kind of useful dialogue or discussion. And when the majority tunes out entirely, you're stuck with everyone settling for their own version of their "truth".

It's pretty sad that no one trusts the media any more, but the players don't have to lend its own helping hand to this sleazy slide into the cesspool. Reporters used to pride themselves above all on their independence, their neutrality and their objectivity. The television detective Joe Friday of *Dragnet* wasn't the only one focused on "just the facts, Ma'am." Writers weren't supposed to inject themselves and their theories, opinions and prejudices into their stories — that's what editorials were for. The suits sitting in the comfy suites upstairs would write their endless editorials intending to educate and edify us in so many important ways. But the guys and girls running around the city sourcing the stories just told their stories the best and most accurate way they knew how. Short, sweet and to the point. Today's digital media is quite short, but it's rarely sweet, and almost always pointless.

I'm not exactly sure when it started or what caused reporters to think that they were now mind readers and oracles, but practically every news story you read is full of reporters' snide asides, unwarranted observations and gratuitous jabs at somebody. The examples are legion, but it's not worth the time or space to list them. We read that this politician is "trying desperately to shed a certain label" or that another is only supporting certain legislative positions in order to "to position himself for higher office." Or the pieces are stuffed with fake facts, suspect statistics or phony factoids that fit the prejudices and predispositions of the writers.

The media's methods, motives and messages are all under constant attack for increasingly good reasons, but the really sad news is that it's the public's trust in just about anything that's been the most obvious and immediate victim of this wholesale rush to sensation, celebrity and notoriety. Most current surveys rank media just below politicians and used car salesmen and just a drop above pond scum.

We were also always told that there was an ironclad "Chinese wall" between the guys and girls running around the city sourcing the stories and the people selling ads and space. A sacrosanct separation between reportage and revenues – where craven cashflow considerations never seeped subtly into the deliberations or influenced the sometimes-delicate decisions about when and what the papers would be writing. It feels like the drama and hard calls made around the publication of the Pentagon Papers may have been the industry's high-water mark and that it's been all downhill since then. And, needless to say, back then, misleading and mendacious headlines weren't written with half an eye toward collecting clicks and aggregating eyeballs rather than highlighting critical content.

It's always important to highlight your material and it's still called the newspaper business because you've got to sell news, papers and advertising, and no one doubts that a great headline is still something to be valued and appreciated as it helps to launch the day's papers and websites into the hands of readers. But it never felt quite as slimy and sneaky (and cheap) as it does today— when it's all about SEOs trying to capture anyone and everyone's attention at any cost, hijacking someone's else's triumphs or tragedies, and driving people from site to site like rats in a maze. Our cellphones may be irradiating our earlobes, but the glut and pace of digital media is turning our brains to mush.

There's no happy ending in sight for these problems. And no easy answers either. It's clear that the media can't fix itself since it's totally hooked on hype, desperate for cash, and constantly competing for clicks. And sadly, none of us has the guts to go cold turkey and try to turn all this noise off because FOMO is almost as prevalent a disease these days as any other form of addiction. So, what can we do in our own businesses to help stem the tide?

Three suggestions. First, focus on what you can control and/or fix. Don't make things worse and don't contribute to the crap. Make it about providing good information for smart decision-making rather than slick selling. Second, when you reach out to customers and clients, say exactly what you mean to do and then do exactly what you said you would. Living well may be the best revenge but living up to your promises and delivering the goods is what makes for lifelong connections and a great business. And finally, make something every day that you can be proud of. Something you can stand by and for, that makes a difference, and that sometime soon, you can point out to your kids and say, "I made this".

Anyone who thinks that the misguided mopes who are writing clever copy, snarky headlines, and "news that no one needs" feel good about themselves or what they're doing is kidding themselves. They may be cynical, but even they aren't that stupid. They know they're just adding trash to the pile. But what they may not know is that when you do something every day that you don't believe in, it takes a little bit of your soul away and a sad soul can kill you quicker than any infection.

TULLMAN'S TRUISMS

ENGAGE ME, DON'T ENRAGE ME

274 – FACEBOOK IS FAILING AND TWITTER IS TOAST

Every once in a while, even the tech untouchables make mistakes which are so obvious and obnoxious that the world (and even the stock market) is forced to take notice. We're watching a few of these unrecoverable errors take hold right now and slowly leak into the consciousness of the general public and that can't be good news for these companies.

As Twitter continues to extinguish millions of fake accounts each week and discloses as a result that its recent apparent growth in users was gossamer, it's also becoming obvious that this is a race that they will never win because the machines can spawn new bots and fake accounts much more quickly, easily and cost-effectively than the troops at TWTR can swat these things away. And the situation at Facebook is no better and probably much worse because at least the guys at Twitter are trying to address the issues while the frauds at Facebook still largely have their heads in the sand.

I've been a big fan of FB forever (See https://www.inc.com/howard-tullman/facebooks-fabulous-future.html.), but I think the romance is finally over. As they lurch stupidly from one crisis to another and offer a continuing stream of lame excuses and amateurish apologies, they are increasingly showing the youth, insulation and inexperience of the management team led by the Zuck who looks more foolish and out of touch every time he opens his mouth. Anyone who thinks that there's nothing fake about denying the Holocaust is a moron and the Zuck is leading the pack straight into the swamp and taking a well-deserved beating at the same time.

Here's a flash. You don't ever want to be this season's pin cushion or poster boy for arrogance and ignorance when the world starts throwing shade and what we're seeing right now is Schadenfreude on steroids. It would ordinarily be somewhat entertaining to see the boys get their comeuppance, but unfortunately, when the big tech guys stumble, the little guys (like us) eventually take it in the shorts.

I expect that the longer-term (and surely negative) financial consequences are just beginning to be felt by the masses in the market and that can't be good news for anyone's IRAs or 401(k)s whether they're stuffed with tech stocks or just holding tracking funds which are subject to the same downturns. I think we could be looking at the beginning of the end of the party. The traders are already starting to make their moves and, typically in these cases of rapid and radical downturns, we civilians are always the ones left holding the bag because we can't get out of harm's way fast enough. FB, Netflix (which I think is gonna weather the storm and come back) and TWTR are just the first dominos to fall.

I say this notwithstanding my clear understanding that the vast majority of typical traders don't care about much of anything substantive except stock movement, velocity and volatility. I think that for them any directional action is apparently equally OK as long as things just keep moving up or down. As Jackson Browne once wrote in *My Opening Farewell*: "there's a train everyday leaving either way." And, I've also come to realize (no surprise here) that money doesn't really care who makes it and that morals and some basic decency don't really matter much to the market.

But I do think that when the world gets sufficiently angry and notwithstanding the fact that these "kids" have been given corporate protections and crazy governance provisions that essentially make them secure in their positions for life, there will come a time and a reckoning when even their clueless and greedy directors can't take the heat and have to make at least some cosmetic changes in the clubhouse and bring in some grown-ups.

This actually isn't good news for us or for these stocks because the grown-ups don't have any idea of how to keep growing these businesses (maybe no one does at this point) and they have even less ability to solve some of the nasty problems and clean up all the stuff that's been shoved into various closets. And worse yet, they're going to take their sweet time in doing anything because they don't want to make things worse if that was even possible.

All of which means that there's only one direction for the stock prices of these companies to move for the foreseeable future and that's further down. Hanging on to these stocks and hoping for the best is a lot like trying to nail Jell-O to a tree. Even the biggest hammer and the strongest nail won't keep the stuff from ending up in a puddle at your feet.

When our parents told us time and again to pay attention, we mostly thought it was a matter of courtesy and not of consequence. But, as it turns out today, attention has become a currency of its own that we are each free to spend and/ or to squander. If you want me to pay attention to your message, you've got to find me at the right time and place (See https://www.inc.com/howard-tullman/catch-me-if-you-can.html.) and give me a compelling reason to listen. Show me quickly how you're going to make my life better (save or spare me something – time, money, work, bad decisions, etc.) or I'll quickly show you the virtual door and be long gone.

Billions of dollars are being spent every day by millions of marketers trying desperately (and increasingly unsuccessfully) - amidst the growing noise and clutter - to attract, engage and direct our attention to their clients' wares and wonders. And, if it wasn't challenging enough in its organic form, the task is made ever so much more difficult in the digital world by the abundance of hucksters, scammers, bots, viral shysters (See https://www.inc.com/howard-tullman/the-trouble-with-social-media.html.) and every other manner of market manipulator selling phony video views, valueless virality, illegitimate likes, two-bit tweets and useless users.

Outbound and conquest marketing is just going to continue to get harder and harder and even less cost-effective which is why more and more effort is being directed to improving and deepening the connection and the experience of the viewers and customers which companies already have. (See https://www.inc.com/howard-tullman/why-knocking-on-old-doors-is-the-best-sales-strategy.html.) These folks are the lowest hanging fruit, the easiest to reach, and the most inclined to pay attention as long as you're meeting their progressively rising expectations and especially their increasingly shorter attention span. The game today isn't being played in weeks or days or even hours – it's a double-overtime, all-the-time, battle over seconds and – as far as I can see – right now, no one is giving this more thought than the sports guys. Watching the changes we're starting to see in the way professional sporting events are being broadcast and otherwise presented to and shared with the fans offers a number of important lessons for the rest of us.

With the digital observation and surveillance data now available and the mass of real-time metrics that mobile users supply, everyone has a far more accurate window on what works during every single second of these games than they ever had before. The smartest players are using all this information to better manage their users' experiences and – at the same time - to start to remake the games themselves to better suit both the core fans and viewers and to attract new populations to the pool.

The Big 3 sport leagues continue to have a unique edge (being live performances) over so much other media that can be readily and easily time-shifted (and consumed whenever and wherever), but this hasn't blinded them to the growing need to get ahead of the fidgety fans who are always on the lookout for alternatives. Their small steps and the experiments to date have been fairly modest because, while the club owners are good businessmen, they're also very conservative people (apart from my friend Mark Cuban) and baseball, basketball and football are highly entrenched and sacrosanct parts of the culture and traditions of this country.

Still, the concerns they're starting to address are very relevant to the ways that every business is going to need to assess and evaluate how they are interacting with consumers and prospects and how the overall experiences they are creating and delivering to their customers can be improved. All the dimensions are in play – how, when, where, what and to whom you are delivering your products and/or services.

Here are a few of the most important things to be looking out for:

(1) How Available Is It? (Access)
Everything is going global. Games will need to be played in the afternoon for European viewers and on weekend mornings for Asian audiences. Streaming games on Facebook (not contractually permitted in the U.S.) is already happening in India. How equipped is your business to sell to, service and support customers around the world? It's relatively easy to have your app downloaded in 100 countries. It's much harder to provide 24/7 customer support worldwide.

(2) How Long Is It? (Time)
Everything in business today is a function of time. No one wants to wait for anything. Games are being shortened thru mandating fewer standard-length time-outs and briefer halftimes, reducing coaches' trips to the mound, quicker pitching sequences, etc. because the average fan is only watching about half of the game. How quickly can you respond to your customers' inquiries, ship their goods, or dispatch service personnel to their sites when needed? The best businesses today respond to inbound customer calls in less than a minute.

(3) How Painless Is It? (Friction)
The customers all want to drive today, and they want a quick, easy and friction-free solution. In this era of mass customization, the individual wants to create and share his or her personal experience on the fly. The teams continue to work aggressively to add increased functionality to the in-home and mobile experiences including multiple selectable camera views, multi-lingual commentary choices, player, coach and referee microphones, fan cameras, etc. The goal is to supply everything you'd get in the stadium except the spilled beers and the screaming slob sitting next to you. In our own companies, the test is

similar. How easy is it to do business with your business? How long does it take to reach the right person or department? How many layers and gatekeepers do I need to deal with to get my problem resolved? How readily is help available if I get stuck on the website? These are all quantifiable and relatively simple questions to answer. But the process starts when you start paying attention because, if you don't care about these critical outcomes, no one else in your company will either.

(4) How Do I Find Out What's Going On? (Awareness and Discovery)
We're all connected, and nothing is more immediate or interruptive than a text. FOMO is rampant, and the teams are starting to use your phones and mobile messaging to let you know what's happening (or about to happen) and what you're gonna miss? Everyone wants to be in the room when it happens. This digital outreach has been especially effective in pulling in incidental and occasional fans and even newbies who don't want to miss the moment. How are you getting your messages out to the right audience at the right time and place so that they reach and resonant with both your current customers and new prospects as well?

(5) How Much of Me Do You Get? (Share of Attention/Stomach)
These days no one does anything important all by themselves. Given everyone's limited time and the difficulties of reaching the most desirable targets, new distribution and channel partnerships are being developed in sports and the teams are willing to "share" access to critical audiences and mindshare as well with their advertisers and sponsors in ways that would have been unthinkable just a few years ago. Split screens continue to display on-court or on-field action right alongside ads to avoid bathroom breaks and snack streaks where the audience disappears entirely. In the same fashion, most new and smaller businesses today are absolutely going to have to ride on other's platforms and rails or have no chance of reaching sufficient numbers of end users. (See https://www.inc.com/howard-tullman/whats-behind-door-number-two-it-better-be-you.html.)

None of this is simple except for the guy who doesn't have to make it all happen himself. But it's worth paying attention to, trying to get a little bit better all the time, and understanding that standing still is never an option. And, in the end, it all comes down to the Joe Maddon rule: "Try not to suck."

TULLMAN'S TRUISMS

ATTENTION IS THE NEW CURRENCY

If you just want to get what you've always gotten; keep doing what you've always done. If you want to change the old rules and get better, you've got to start aiming higher and thinking bigger. There's always a best seat in the house, the best row at a show, something desperately worth shooting for and we all know that you may not always get it. But shame on you if you don't at least go for it. If you don't ask, the answer is always "No". And today, I think there's no better example for companies and entrepreneurs of every size than SpaceX.

Notwithstanding Elon's current Tesla angst, the SpaceX engine which he built (almost as an afterthought) continues to fire on all cylinders, to make the impossible seem commonplace, and to raise the bar for big dreams being backed up by awesome deliverables. Dockless bikes, slick little scooters, and new offerings of gluten-free whatever all seem depressingly trivial compared to Elon's grand ambitions.

Things in the space biz may take a little longer than expected, and some of the beneficial by-products may even turn out to be better than what was initially sought or expected, but – in the end - the scale and the scope of what has already been achieved since SpaceX was founded in 2002 is unlike anything that has come before or after. Keep in mind that NASA was formed on 1958, more than 60 years ago, and these days it's getting help from Hawthorne and taking directions from Denver. Jeff Bezos (Blue Origin) has been in the "space" business since 2000 and he's got "bupkes" to show for it. Richard Branson is another big talker with Virgin Galactic which he founded in 2004, but it seems that he's perpetually "just six months away" from being in space. I wouldn't hold your breath.

And, as you might expect, seeing in this case just makes believing that much easier. You can't visit the SpaceX factory without coming away with one overwhelming impression. There's a palpable sense of possibility and the belief that virtually anything is achievable with enough time, effort, and perseverance. This isn't some cheap Silicon Valley talk or "pie in the sky" (no pun intended) prediction. It's an outgrowth and extension of an attitude that is as compelling as it is contagious. And it's backed in facts and in demonstrable results. These people are hard-core professionals - engineers and scientists – who spend their days head down and making things happen. Elon does the dreaming, but these are the hundreds of people who get the job done every day.

They might technically be manufacturing machines and missiles, but what they really make here are "believers." People who believe that the world is leaning in their direction and that success (albeit over time) is far more probable (not just possible) than any other outcome. I wish you could bottle this attitude because it's such a special combination of pride and practicality as well as concrete grounding and vast visioning that I think we should add it to the drinking water at every school and startup in the country.

So, what's the main message from SpaceX for the rest of us? We need to look further and wider if we're going to up the ante, make major changes, and leapfrog the competition. (See https://www.inc.com/howard-tullman/the-case-for-pursuing-massive-growth.html.) Using the best available data and basing our plans, programs and designs on real metrics and milestones (rather than make-believe) is an essential methodology, but, if it's the only view you have of the future, you'll find that your focus is far narrower than it should be and that your energies end up being directed mainly to short, sure wins instead of big jumps and new horizons.

This conservative approach leads to designs and choices that tend to be marginal improvements and incremental gains rather than game-changing moves. Successive approximation and consistent iteration are great tools ("getting a little better every day"), but the key word is "little" and what we need more and more of are bigger leaps and longer look-aheads.

It's not enough to simply try to keep getting closer and closer to a known goal because that approach and that perspective can often keep us from looking further down the road and really thinking about going for the gold.

277 – CLEANING HOUSE MAY BE HAZARDOUS TO YOUR HEALTH

I have been concerned for a while now - even as the stock market continues to explode upward and carry tech stocks to new heights - that things are getting tougher in the trenches. Securing follow-on financings is more challenging these days and the investors are both more realistic and more demanding as well as far less patient than they've been in the past. Not good news for newbies. (See https://www.inc.com/howard-tullman/your-days-are-numbered.html.)

I'm also seeing strategics take a step or two back and disappear at the last minute from deals that were "all done" except for the ceremonial dinner. Except that they weren't all done and the businesses waiting to cash those checks blew up instead and/or abruptly closed shop instead of celebrating. From the corporate's perspective, it's a lot better to have wasted a bunch of time looking at a deal than to lose a lot of money investing in a bad one. In the first case, it's likely to lead to a slap on the hand while the other's gonna be a kick in the pants for sure.

Maybe it's all an investor reaction to the upside and liquidity (ease of exits) that the market is currently offering as compared to the risks, brain damage, and multi-year struggles that even the best of startups represent. And when things are taking longer to blossom, and the far-off promise and remote horizon of actual profits continues to recede, the idea of making 50% to 100% returns on your money every 6 months with a few phone orders starts to look awfully attractive.

But the bigger issue for the entrepreneurs running businesses which are caught right now (hopefully momentarily) in that nasty space between nothing and nirvana is that their boards and investors start to get antsy as well and look for quick fixes, fire sale liquidations, or - perish the thought - changes in management. The typical tenure of a startup CEO isn't that long to begin with and when everyone is looking for "change" - without any real idea of what that means for a particular business - it's easy for the guy or girl running the business to feel like there's a target painted on his or her back.

It's not a happy prospect, and I think we are gonna see a lot more coming, but I'm actually OK with changing out the CEO when the ship has stalled and there's no real salvation in sight. But what I think is stupid are directors and investors who bring in a new leader and then watch while the whole rest of the management team is also shown the door as the new CEO "cleans house" so he or she can have their own team and too often ends up throwing out the whole baby with the dirty bath water.

If this kind of wholesale dumping of most of the existing C-level team is even arguably appropriate, it means that both the board and the prior CEO have been asleep at the switch for years. And I'm seeing this happen every week now in larger and smaller businesses where the mantra of change (almost for change's sake) without any real guidance, direction or plan is the flavor of the week and another way for investors and directors to buy time, ignore certain obvious realities about the business, and watch while the deck chairs are shuffled for the umpteenth time.

So, here are a few hints for both incoming CEOs and the boards that brought them in:

(1) The new CEO doesn't know where all the bodies are buried and what closets hold the most skeletons, but others on the team do know and, even if they aren't the best bet for the business in the long run, tossing them out prematurely is a sure formula for failure. And, I might add, that the board doesn't really know the new CEO that well either on Day One so giving the new leader unlimited license and adopting a laissez-faire approach makes very little sense. You don't have to look any further than the revolving doors at Hewlett Packard over the last ten years for clear evidence. And counting on your search firm to get the pick 100% right is equally foolish. Even the best of the headhunters suck at telling you the real story – they're just looking to close the sale.

(2) Adding a bunch of new people to any enterprise all at the same time (even if they've previously worked with each other at different places and under different circumstances) exponentially increases the risks of missing the boat and making major mistakes in the early going. Changes – especially in company culture – don't come easy and they actually rarely begin until the new management starts taking actual actions rather than just talking about what's going to happen. But, if a half dozen people are running around and making random decisions (especially about people) before there's even a clear alignment on direction and strategy, the message to the rest of the business couldn't be any worse or less productive. Measure twice, cut once.

(3) Your key employees (the ones you need to keep and re-recruit to the new mission) and your most important customers are also likely to be plenty nervous about the changes being made and looking for as much stability and continuity as possible. It turns out (in every case I've seen) that some of the senior people who are quickly shoved out not only knew a great deal about the business, they also knew and had long-standing personal relationships with a lot of the key customers.

Here again, some of those relationships and even customers may not have been helpful (or even profitable for the business), but you can't really determine that without spending some time looking under the covers and it helps to have a few knowledgeable people on board to assist and guide you in that process of discovering what's what.

Bottom line: wholesale house cleaning without taking the time to do it right can be very hazardous to the health of your business.

462

In the frenzied startup world where growth is the only real gospel, we're so taken with the idea of sheer size and the need to get "bigger quicker" that we sometimes lose sight of the fact that not everything that matters in life is about scale. The biggest crowd, the largest parade, the loudest voice, the most sales, etc. is only a small part of the story.

Sometimes, it's just as important to take the time to do something small and special just because it's the right thing to do and because it needs to be done. The truth is that no act of kindness or generosity – however small or modest it may be – is ever wasted. And it seems like we need a boatload of simple acts of kindness and charity these days just to try to help keep things in our country from running further aground.

These are harsh and difficult times. In fact, I'm pretty sure that - in my entire lifetime - I have never witnessed such disheartening and indiscriminate displays of political power and personal pettiness by our representatives on both sides of "the aisle" in Washington - although today it feels more like a sewer. And I'm afraid that the sorry show shows no sign of abating any time soon.

But it's in these very kinds of hard times - when you can take a few moments to give someone else a helping hand (with no expectation of reward or recognition) - that you somewhat restore your belief, hope and faith that things can get better. And you realize that you <u>always</u> get a lot more out of "giving" than you do from all the "getting" that occupies so much of the time and effort in our daily lives. Sometimes – in moments like these - it's the smallest things that can take up the most room in your heart – at least for a fleeting moment or two – and remind you of the good that exists in most people and in most parts of the country.

And for those of you who might say that you just don't have the time for organized (or even random acts of) charity or that you can't afford to take your eye off the ball even for a moment, I'd say that it's really important to whatever you're trying to build or accomplish that you find a little time to make a difference in someone's life other than your own. I like to remind young entrepreneurs that there's always more work, but you only have one family. But seeking the same equilibrium is just as essential in your business as well. If you don't get the balance correct between "making a living" and "making a life" right from the start, I can guarantee you that you won't like what you ultimately grow into and your business will suffer just as much as your personal life.

Getting the company culture correct has never been more essential or more critical to the success of new businesses than it is today. And the culture starts from the CEO down and is built through the day-to-day actions of the people in the business and from continued demonstrations of solid commitments to serious principles and not through spiffy slogans or endless conversations.

Show me, don't tell me. Or else I'll find a better place to be. The best and most talented employees today don't work for a company – they work for a reason and a purpose – and if your business can't demonstrate a purpose backed up by behaviors aligned with what they're looking for, they'll leave – typically in less than a year. And this isn't something that will keep until you eventually get around to it. Get started before they get going out the door.

Today, because our time is so scarce and the demands on it are so great, I think we all kid ourselves into believing that there will be all the time we need later in life to do those good deeds and to give back in meaningful ways. And then one day, in the not too distant future, we wake up to find that the time and many of the most important opportunities have passed us by. That's why there's no better time than the present to take up the task and get started.

It's not that hard to help and to make a difference. And just remember when you wonder if even the simplest gesture matters that it's not a matter of scale. It's a matter of sincerity, real interest and simply stepping up.

The difference that your efforts can make in even a single life are incalculable and the impact can be immediate and life-changing. Start now.

Perspective is one of the by-products smart entrepreneurs are expected to gain from being punched in the nose so many times by fate and misfortune. The theory is that the next time around, you'll be a little more perceptive, look a little longer before leaping, and take into account more of the variables and risks that you're facing. But honestly, there's no way to protect yourself in a fast-growing startup (especially in an uncertain area where you're a first mover) from making a multitude of mistakes regardless of how many times you've been around the track. The most you can hope for is that (a) you won't make the same mistakes over and over again and that (b) you will quickly recognize and remedy those unhappy cases where you're heading hurriedly down the wrong path. As they say down South, there's no education in the second kick of a mule.

We all know that it never feels good to be wrong, but it feels a lot worse when the pain and misery are self-inflicted. Getting important things wrong is somewhat easier to bear if you haven't shot yourself in the foot or put that foot in your own mouth. (See https://www.inc.com/howard-tullman/bring-back-the-peter-principle-please.html.) As Jim Croce used to say, there's no one to blame but yourself if you insist on spitting into the wind.

I get that sometimes circumstances conspire against us regardless of how hard we're trying or how good our intentions may be. Of course, the best entrepreneurs know that their job in those cases is to change the circumstances and make their own good fortune. When you're in the swamp, the steps are pretty clear: acknowledge the problem; admit the mistakes; put them behind you and get over the spilt milk (you can't water yesterday's crops); consider all the going-forward options – not in terms of saving face or salvaging something, but with a view toward the future and the best way forward; and then just get going and do it. You never get the time back that you spend in too much noodling and the rest of the world isn't waiting around for you to make your next move.

But avoiding the problems and trying to make the best choices and decisions possible in the first place is always the smartest route. Much better to avoid the potholes entirely than to get a great deal on the tow truck. And it's just as important to be sure that you have an approach and a consistent process in place that helps you make the right decisions under whatever circumstances you find yourself in.

Enhanced decision making is a set of skills and a discipline that can be learned and employed in just about any context to improve the ultimate outcomes. It starts with a simple proposition: you need to not only think bigger, you need to think broader. Expanding the consideration set is the single most overlooked way to improve the quality of your decision making.

Everyone tells new entrepreneurs to think big. I couldn't agree more. If I have a quibble, it's never with the vision - it's usually with the timing. (See https://www.inc.com/howard-tullman/why-its-okay-to-start-slow-and-snail.html.) Dream big, but start small; get it very right; and then scale up quickly. This approach still seems to be the smartest to me and the few, highly-visible, Unicorn-ish launches that are exceptions just help to prove the rule. Betting the farm, burning thru a boatload of bucks, and going big from the get-go is a bad plan 99% of the time. It may still sell in the Valley, but in the real world, slow and steady starts make the most sense. At the same time, what's also critical is to not let tunnel vision or ancient history (which means anything that happened more than a few days ago) cloud or obscure the full range of options and alternatives that are available to you.

One of the most powerful aspects of all the new technologies and data resources which we now have at our disposal is that we are no longer limited to evaluating binary, "either-or", choices and we can (and we need to) consider a much broader group of alternatives. You don't want to be stuck with Yogi Berra's useless advice that "when you come to a fork in the road, take it". There's no question that the more conscientious you are about considering a greater number of realistic alternatives, the more likely that your ultimate choice and decision will be correct.

So, it's not enough in the process to simply ask how these tools can help you do what you've always done better and more efficiently; the new and most critical question is what things can you do and accomplish today that you never even imagined were possible before. That's the next game and the key enabler of this approach is the ability to (and the necessity to) identify multiple new choices and alternatives rather than simply accepting the most immediate and obvious ones. (See https://www.inc.com/howard-tullman/five-reasons-your-market-is-bigger-than-you-think.html.)

We're all in a hurry and short on time but increasing your optionality and the range of choices is the best investment of a few extra hours of inquiry that you will ever make. It's important to think bigger in building your business; but it's just as important to think as broadly as possible in order to help make the best decisions.

Bottom line: the more choices, the merrier.

Last week Chicago lost a great mayor - as well as the most aggressive spokesman <u>ever</u> for the city's tech and entrepreneurial community - when Rahm Emanuel - the best big city mayor in the country - bar none - announced that he had decided not to run for a third term of office. Good news for him and his family and really hard news for the city. Family first. Period. (See https://www.inc.com/howard-tullman/your-work-is-not-your-life.html .)

His brief announcement as well as many comments he made in the aftermath (along with the few key interviews which he gave) had some important lessons for lots of us and especially for the pack of losers who had already lined up to run against him. If it wasn't so sad for the city, it would be comical watching these one-issue, nichy little midgets gripe, posture and position themselves as hopefuls and aspirants to a position many miles beyond their reach or grasp. It was a lot like seeing a group of 10th grade Pony league pitchers trying to throw shade at one of the MLB pros. If you want to beat Babe Ruth, don't play baseball.

It's so painfully easy to complain and criticize from the sidelines - I call these people solution-less soreheads - and considering that most of them are presently gainfully <u>unemployed</u> - I'm reminded of the old crew expression that the only one in the boat who usually has the time to complain is the one who isn't rowing and holding up his or her end of the deal. I'd feel sorry for most of them because of how sadly deluded they were, but their rank arrogance of thinking even for a moment that any one of them is up to the task makes it hard to sympathize with their stupidity.

And it didn't take the media mavens and the other scriveners long to start to realize (or maybe to grudgingly admit is a better way to put it) that there was a tremendous amount of important work that did get done in the last seven years for the good of the city and that most of it wouldn't have gotten done without the pushing, prodding, pleading and insistence of the Mayor. Substantial improvements in affordable housing, expanded access to public transportation, and the conversion of the Chicago river from a sewer to the spectacular Riverwalk were just a few of the initiatives that will serve the city well long after his departure.

Not surprisingly, the talking heads and commentators then turned their energies to whining about the fact that none of the current candidates was even remotely up to the job. Not much of a surprise to anyone who knew and understood what this overwhelming job really entails and requires, both personally and professionally, but apparently new "news" to the script readers and social media morons who never took the time to acknowledge exactly how tough and talented a mayor Rahm Emanuel has been for this city.

Sometimes a song says it all and no one ever summed up this sad situation better than Joni Mitchell in "Big Yellow Taxi" with the line: Don't it always seem to go that you don't know what you've got til it's gone". People who are even a little bit in the know know exactly how devastating a blow Rahm's departure is to the progress of any number of ongoing projects and business opportunities. This announcement may be the end of any number of new prospective investments in the city unless someone with real credentials and serious skills steps quickly into the breach and offers some serious prospect of stability and continuity. No one likes uncertainty and change less than long-term investors and institutions.

But, one of the succession difficulties is likely to be that the most qualified new possible entrants have - at best - a complex relationship and a mixed history with Emanuel. His own entry into office was aided immeasurably by a warm handoff from the incumbent and departing Mayor Daley. Of course, that hearty handshake was accompanied by a bucket full of hot messes which Rahm spent years trying to clean up and straighten out with substantial success. No other mayor ever tried – much less succeeded in large measure – in cleaning up Chicago's decades of mismanaged and underfunded pension plans for police, fire and teachers. No other mayor grew the tech sector in the city by tens of thousands of jobs year and year and made Chicago the nation's leader – 5 years running – for corporate headquarters relocations. And no other mayor expanded the public-school day and school year so that by graduation, Chicago public school students will have spent more than two additional years in class than when Emanuel arrived on the scene.

Of course, no one really expects a similar amount of support from the 5th floor of City Hall this time around for virtually any of the major undeclared candidates at this point. But, politics does make strange bed-fellows, so I guess we will just see what happens down the road. And, apart from the politics and the befuddled state of the city at the moment, there's a very important lesson for prospective entrepreneurs as well in Rahm's parting comments.

Being the boss means doing it ALL. Every day. All day. You don't get to pick and choose the fun parts. You don't get to delegate the hard conversations or the ultimate responsibility. And you don't have to shoulder the disappointments when people let you down or the hurt you feel when you suffer alongside the families and the kids who you wish you could have only helped a little bit more.

Only a few special people are up to jobs like this – be it mayor or CEO – and a lot of folks kid themselves into believing that this is what they want to do with their lives, but they have no idea of how all-consuming and enervating a task it is. And what it costs in terms of your personal life and health and the lives of your family.

My advice to every aspiring entrepreneur is to be very careful what you wish for and do your homework before you take the leap. (See https://www.inc.com/howard-tullman/seven-scar-of-an-entrepreneur.html.) Seven scars are just the beginning. The occasional highs are OK, but the inevitable and continual lows are brutal.

My advice to the clowns so far who are seeking to succeed Mayor Emanuel is to do yourself and our city a favor and keep whatever day job you may have

Christmas came early this year, but it's not very good news for the toy makers whose businesses and sales are still pretty much in the toilet across the board. And here's the thing – these guys can blame technology all they want and complain about all the kids with their noses glued to the screens, but they're pointing to the wrong part of the problem. It's not that the kids aren't excited about getting a pile of new presents; it's that their parents are much more concerned with buying the new and very expensive "tech toys" for themselves. Let the kids wait until December; the starting gun for their parents' shopping sprees is the annual Apple announcement of the latest and greatest new phones and watches. And this year's race is on.

And, once again, Apple is leading the charge toward the inevitable cliff's edge in a breathtaking game of "consumer chicken" that would scare even Evil Knievel if he were still around. It's becoming a question of just how high these prices can go for no good reason. And apparently, at least for the moment, there's no end in sight. This reminds me of the early days of the Intel Pentium chips when new chips kept rolling out even though the alleged incremental benefits in speed and processing power weren't apparent to any human beings that I knew. Of course, that didn't keep the geeks (and anyone not on a budget) from upgrading to the newest versions – need it and see it - or not. In fact, it was that dependable and consistent buyer response (a market-driven derivative of the Moore's law belief that things just keep getting better and more powerful) which set the behavior curve for the tech industry and its customers for years thereafter. Honestly, it's not that much different even today.

Mom and Dad don't want to corner the market for Bobby or Betty on this year's Beanie Babies so they all can brag to their neighbors and their carpool cronies. They just want the new giant iPhone XS MAX with a new Series 4 Apple Watch on the side. And Apple can try all they want to call this monster the "X-S", but what leaps immediately into anyone else's head is "EXCESS" and that says it all. Big dollars, big size, wretched excess at its finest. But knowing that it makes no economic sense and keeping yourself from falling once again into Cupertino's clutches are two radically different things.

In the old days, we used to complain about planned obsolescence in the auto industry (and we are also seeing it in the mobile phone world when our phones' performance suspiciously degrades right before new devices are rolled out), but Apple has also mastered the art of foolish functionality. The Watch is already approaching a level of complexity (like any other over-engineered product) where the lion's share of the embedded functions is unknown to most mortals and basically unusable by the vast majority of the users. In what I can only imagine was completely unintended irony, the additional 8 or 9 features that are displayed on the face of the new Watch are called "complications" and ain't it the truth. But the beat goes on. We're buying into the new stories against our better judgment and even when we know that the things are no great shakes and not really doing the jobs that we need done.

And, the really sad thing – particularly about the Watch with all its new bells and whistles – is that the battery life still basically sucks. How about fixing what's not working every once in a while instead of adding more battery-sucking functions that no one asked for. What good is a tracking device of any kind (especially one that's increasingly positioned as a medical management tool) if you can't count on it to last the whole business day and when you have to take the thing off every night and recharge it? Makes it a little bit challenging to measure your sleeping behavior if your Watch is sleeping beside you on the bed stand. I wrote about this angst a while ago (See https://www.inc.com/howard-tullman/fitbit-anxiety-is-part-of-a-larger-problem.html.) and things haven't changed a bit. If your tracker isn't tracking, what's the whole point?

Bottom line: No matter how much steak sauce you put on a hot dog, it's still a wiener.

Promises always come with the peril of non-performance. It's a bad plan in life (and in any business) to promise more than you can deliver. The fact is that, if you want people to believe your promises tomorrow, it helps a great deal if you kept them yesterday. And I'm sure that this sounds like old news to most of you since we've all been lectured from just after birth about the necessity (and the difficulty) of always trying to live up to your commitments.

I'm certainly guilty of a bit of this myself and I'm actually proud of it. (See https://www.inc.com/howard-tullman/to-succedd-be-the-one-everyone-can-count-on.html.) And I also clearly understand the basic concept and agree that it makes all the sense in the world, but the difference today is that maybe things have radically changed and the problem now isn't so much about arrogance or baseless bragging as it is how to deal effectively with the truth. Because the truth today is a lot stranger in some ways than fiction.

Given the powerful technologies which we now have at our disposal and the actual and concrete results that we can deliver, the somewhat novel sales problem that I'm seeing is that too many startups are so excited about the powerful possibilities and the real wonders which their solutions can work that, in their eagerness and enthusiasm, they're losing sight of who they're selling to and what kinds of solutions those buyers are looking for. In the old days we used to say that the main difference between a car salesman and a computer salesman was that the car guy knew he was lying to you. Today telling your prospects and customers too much about what your products and services can do is more likely to confuse them than to convince them.

Instead of offering simple initial implementations and step-by-step measured solutions - basically addressing and resolving the lowest and most obvious hanging fruit first - what I'm seeing and hearing too often in these kinds of conversations are broad claims and bold statements that "our software can do anything – just tell us what you need". And, even if that was true, which in some cases is almost certainly the case, it absolutely doesn't matter to the buyers. And – worse yet – it's totally off-putting because it shifts the onus of specifying the problems that need to be identified and dealt with to the buyers who – in all honesty – may know what they need, but have no real idea of what your products can do or how your solutions would be introduced and incorporated into their specific operations. So, their natural reaction is to take two steps back rather than buying into your pitch.

That's why it makes so much sense to start by sandbagging a bit instead of bragging. Under promise and then over deliver. Let me give you a real life and slightly sneaky example that you'll be every night on TV – if you ever watch TV. I say "sneaky" because I think this is a situation dictated by marketing, but it might also be to get around certain regulatory requirements about diet claims. If you watch the latest ads for several of the wonder drugs (no names please) - after they make all the over-the-top basic benefit claims for the drugs and after they list the 4 million side effects – you'll hear a little announcer aside which goes like this: "and you might just lose a little weight also". No promises. No guarantees. But, as good Samaritans, we thought you just might want to know. Right. That's under promising to "T".

And you need to be thinking the same way when you present your new products and services. Tone it down – don't go for the gold from the get-go. Prove your product a little bit at a time. (See https://www.inc.com/howard-tullman/why-its-okay-to-start-slow-and-snail.html.) New is a nasty word to millions of procurement officers, buyers and other decision makers. Novel and innovative are right up there as well.

In the real world, no one is looking for a miracle. They want risk-free, middle-of-the-road, mundane improvements which might save their companies some money, but will save their jobs for sure. They want immediate solutions, not ultimate salvation in part because they're not sure that they'll even be around for the big, long-awaited payoff. So, you need to plan, sell, and act accordingly.

Even if you can eventually move the moon, start with something that you can get done by next Monday.

I'm always amazed at how people you'd naturally assume were reasonably intelligent, somewhat experienced, and fairly mature can talk themselves into believing that hope is an effective strategy and that wishes regularly do come true. The staggering advances we've seen in technology over the last two decades could make a believer out of almost anyone, but take it from me, the "field of dreams" is still a fantasy which makes for a mighty good movie, but a lousy and costly) business plan.

You can build it, but there's no guarantee that anyone will come and, even if they do, that they'll be willing and able to pay for more than the privilege of your presence. No one likes to end up alone, but, at the very least, if you're an entrepreneur, you're with someone you dearly love. It's lonely at the top (even if it's a garbage heap), but at least it's not crowded. Maybe that's some small solace. The principal point is that patience these days is at a premium and investors are less and less willing to wait for miracles. (See https://www.inc.com/howard-tullman/no-dont-need-your-pointless-app.html.) Talking a good game isn't going to get it done in an era where real results and solid tech are basically the starting points.

But when those far-out dreams do occasionally come true (or at least start to offer a real glimmer of hope for a future), it's a thing of beauty to behold. Personally, I've been waiting for years for *Magic Leap*'s mixed reality technology to cross the chasm and get "real" (no pun intended) and in the latest demonstrations in my office where you can't fake a video or gin up a prototype that will never make it into production, I have to report that I'm impressed and think things may be finally getting there.

For me, any kind of broad adoption and implementation of augmented reality and mixed reality tools (as opposed to virtual reality products which I think may never get there) has always been about three primary considerations.

First, the system must have a very modest learning curve, simple controls, and minimal requirements and expectations for any material changes in the day-to-day behavior of the prospective users. The closer the new solutions remain to the ways in which business has traditionally been conducted; the more likely that there will be a rapid adoption and, most importantly, this permits an ongoing peer-to-peer education and instruction process which is essential to broad exposure and success. It's impossible to boil the ocean and train the whole world and so new systems need to promote, encourage and reward early adopters and influencers to spread the word. In a way, it's actually in their own interest as well because, not only do they get serious bragging rights, but also – as with all new technologies – the more users, the more powerful the network and the greater the benefits for all. This is *Metcalfe's Law* in practice. No one ever wanted to own the only telephone or fax machine in town. (See https://www.inc.com/howard-tullman/future-of-content-marketing-simplereach.html?cid=search.) The *Magic Leap* system and the handheld controller it employs took just a couple of minutes to learn and then even novice users were set to go. Far easier to use than the controls on the entertainment systems of any plane these days. Setting up the operating environment by "painting" the space took another minute or two and was roughly as challenging as moving your head around to teach your iPhone to use facial recognition.

Second, the new equipment has to be lightweight, non-invasive, and, above all, connected to markers and reference points in the real world. This last recognition may be the genius of mixed reality. In business uses, we don't have the slightest interest in being "taken away" or dropped in some new virtual world. Maybe it works for seated gamers, but for the rest of us looking for helpful tools; it's disruptive, foreign, hard to navigate and usually a little nauseating as well. Strapping on heavy duty googles and stumbling around the room like an idiot isn't fun or especially instructive and it's likely that this is the primary reason that *Facebook* quickly closed hundreds of *Oculus Rift* demo booths in *Best Buy* stores when it became clear that virtually no one was interested in the virtual experience. The *Magic Leap* headset (which will undoubtedly get even lighter and smaller as time progresses) are roughly the same as typical swim googles and just about as light and you can see the room you're in at all times so you're never "lost" or uncomfortable. Starting from a solid ground, you can quickly enter the environment and build your new world.

Third, the metaphors within the application itself have to be common, readily understood, and consistent with typical behaviors so that new users are not challenged, confused or threatened. Too many systems today adopt a layering strategy which requires either prior knowledge or extensive exploration in order to find essential components and tools. The charm of the basic *Magic Leap* application was that there was a simple resource bookcase with shelves that you can simply scroll up and down and, on each shelf, were located various objects that you could select and drag into your room and then employ in different ways.

Whether you were constructing structures, empowering or activating objects, or performing other simple operations like moving around the 3-dimensional space, two things were readily apparent – it was impossible to get lost in the process and there were no unrecoverable errors. Both of these attributes are invaluable for beginners and created an overall context in which trial, exploration and experimentation were encouraged without any penalties associated with mistakes or inadequate preparation or training.

Bottom line: a stimulating and exciting step forward for explorers and learners of any and every age. A dream come true.

They keep talking about ideas and changes designed to speed up the pace of baseball games which right now are a lot like watching paint dry - albeit even less colorful. I expect that it will be a few more years before anything major happens in the majors (no pun intended) although almost all of the leading sports teams (just like retailers) have finally realized that it's far smarter to encourage cellphone use and engagement in the ballparks and arenas than it is to try to shut it down by restricting or blocking Wi-Fi access.

Side-by-side real time commentary and even video replays on mobile only enhance and improve the fans' experience and engagement. As sports betting continues along the path toward complete legalization (right behind pot), the fans' phones will become an even more central part of the in-venue activities. And, of course, e-sports are exploding across the world with attractive demographics that couldn't be more appealing to the old white guys who continue to dominate the ownership of the country's sports teams. According to Nielsen, more than half of baseball fans are over 55 and the average fan age is around 53 as compared to the NFL average age of 47 and the NBA's 37. You can expect to see prunes at the concession stands pretty soon instead of pretzels.

Finally, a little-known fact, but a critical commercial consideration, is that in the course of the season, there are on average 4 times the number of butts in the good seats than the actual number of season ticket holders and the only consistently effective way to identify those folks (guests, season sharers, scalpers, etc.) is to grab their email addresses or cellphone numbers. Now especially, when the competition for attention is so fierce, "knowing all your customers" couldn't be more critical. It's unlikely that these folks are gonna download a bunch of different team apps – the incentives aren't great and the screen clutter on everyone's phone just keeps growing (See https://www.inc.com/howard-tullman/no-dont-need-your-pointless-app.html.) so, for one-to-one communications, direct phone texts are the best in-venue bet. But overall, don't look for the baseball experience to get much better anytime soon.

Meantime, in the rest of the world, we're already seeing a big change in the strike count. Today, for most businesses, it's two strikes and you're out. You get one chance to learn. Strike one. And you get one chance (after that lesson) to make some quick course corrections. If you don't react, respond, and rapidly change, that's strike two and you're out. No one has the luxury of plenty of time any longer and you can't wait for your people to eventually wake up and smell the coffee. They need to get started right now. Instilling a sense of urgency, showing them a path to success, and providing them with the tools and resources needed to get the necessary work done is your most important job.

But just talking about change without taking concrete actions is like wetting your pants in a dark suit. It gives you a temporary warm feeling, but no one else (hopefully) notices. Spoiler alert – forget the preceding passage if you haven't already seen the new version of *A Star is Born*. And talking about the same old stuff is also a formula for failure. The past prescriptions won't provide rapid or certain relief any longer and certainly not the promised and expected results of the past. Staying the course, sticking to your knitting, and doing things the way you always have are just as likely to be problematic strategies these days as productive ones.

You can't hide from the future, you can't afford to stand still, and you can't save your way to success. Gains secured by cost-cutting are short term salves at best and more likely to further set you back than to be a means of setting you up for the future. Growing your way out of your problems and fundamentally transforming your organization into a digital-first juggernaut are the only viable paths forward. Clinging to the past is a pyrrhic prescription for constant pain, growing confusion, and eventual extinction. It's OK to learn from the past, but you can't keep living there.

The very traditions which previously provided comfort, consistency, and assured (if modest) results are now at best excuses to resist inevitable change. Too many companies these days are working hard to catch up with their past (the "glory days") rather than focusing on what's ahead. But the fact is that no one becomes successful in the past – the trick today is to learn from the past, but not become a prisoner of it. And, more often than not, traditions and standard operating procedures create barriers and obstacles to taking the very actions most likely to preserve the good parts of the past and enable the progress necessary to secure the future.

Slow and steady just offers the false feeling of progress and stability when, in reality, you're slipping further and further behind. Experience in times like this can be your worst enemy and playing it safe won't keep the wolves at bay for very long. It turns out that you can't evolve your way into radical change. It's not a continuous or comfortable process. It's a series of abrupt actions, hard decisions, wrenching personnel changes, and painful compromises which may or may not eventually get you to where you hope you're headed.

You've got to make the critical changes happen because nothing very good ever happens by itself. And, at least if you're taking action and happening to the world (as Springsteen says) instead of letting the world hit you over the head, you're likely to still be in the boat (and in the race) when the distant shore finally appears.

It's not a short or obvious trip – there will be sacrifices galore and it's certainly not easy - but then again, there's not much of a choice or an option if you want your business to thrive – and not just barely survive.

Time has a very nasty way of turning your assets into liabilities. If you aren't moving forward or if you're spending too much time looking into the rearview mirror, you'll wake up one day soon and discover that you've been left behind. These days, either you make dust or you eat dust. No one is sitting around waiting for you to catch up – in fact, they're more likely to be trying to figure out how to run right over you on their own way to the prize. So, now's the time to giddy up.

It's all about making hard choices and taking action because it's only decisive action that ultimately overcomes and conquers your reluctance and fear. The slower your decision-making process is; the more likely you are to be losing ground and heading in the wrong direction. In fact, I think that every company (large or small) should have the same, very simple, motto to remind people day-in and day-out of the "need for speed". I'd suggest *"si non nunc quando"* which means "if not now, when?" because I think that says it all. Move it or lose it.

If you can't seem to make up your mind; if you're constantly revisiting settled matters and/or reopening old conversations; or if you're just kicking the can a little further down the road, you're in for a rude awakening and an unhappy and abrupt ending. Excessive waiting doesn't make for better decisions – it makes for lost time, demoralized people, and a devastating loss of direction and momentum.

Massive business plans and strategy documents, millions of meetings, extensive third-party consulting reports, and excessively detailed analyses are simply ways to hide from the truth and avoid making the tough decisions. Elaboration in these cases is often just a form of mental pollution.

Speed is everything today and startups understand that necessity much better than most big businesses because: (a) entrepreneurs all suffer congenitally from "hurry sickness"; (b) the race to self-sustainability for a startup is existential; if you don't get to some point of equilibrium where you can stop pedaling (and fundraising) for a moment or two in order to take stock of where you've been and where you're heading, you're gonna be toast soon enough (See https://www.inc.com/howard-tullman/slow-down-it-might-save-your-business.html); and (c) if you're not in a big hurry, you're probably already too late.

On the other hand, in too many large organizations, there's a striking lack of urgency, a reluctance to make hard choices, and a willingness to ignore the inevitable until it's too late. Hoping that the problems will resolve themselves and that the competition will go away isn't much of a strategy. As a result, mediocre projects are allowed to continue because no one has the courage to call a halt; make-work jobs and featherbedding flourish because there's no accountability and no one keeping score; and the business heads slowly and continually downhill into irrelevance and obscurity. No one ever said it better than T.S. Eliot: "This is the way the world ends, not with a bang but a whimper."

The "bad" behaviors, which bring about these results, are obvious, but, regardless of the size of your business, if you don't consistently root out and address the causes and concerns, you're never going to improve the current state of affairs or get yourself out of the deepening hole that you're slowly slipping into. We all see the symptoms, but we need to invest the necessary time looking into the reasons if we're going to come up with solutions.

This is clearly one of those cases where the big, old and tradition-bound businesses can learn a great deal from the examples which abound in the startup world. In fact, if I had to make a short catalogue of the issues that constantly recur whenever you see a business starting to go sideways, I'd start with the 5 basic fears:

(1) **Fear of Failure**

   This is the most common problem and frankly the one that's already been the most exhaustively discussed. It's still Number One on the hit parade, but I don't have a whole lot to add to the prior conversation. (See http://www.inc.com/howard-tullman/failure-happens-four-ways-to-do-it-well.html and https://www.inc.com/howard-tullman/forget-about-failing-fast-if-you-must-fail-forward-instead.html .) Suffice it to say, if you let your fears rather than your desires and goals drive your decisions, you're not going to get anywhere. Entrepreneurs don't have all the answers, but the one thing that they know for sure is that to pull off these new and special adventures, your faith (especially in yourself) needs to be stronger than your fears. They don't ask for permission; they wonder who's gonna stop them. And they run toward their fears rather than away from them.

(2) **Fear of Success**

   This is the least understood of the fears. Scaling is scary. You want to be sure that the path you're about to embark on isn't a gangplank that you're actually about to walk off. Rapid expansion along any dimension of your business isn't easy. Moreover, just as many businesses get in trouble because they couldn't handle the radically increasing demands of their customers as fail because the phones just stop ringing. (See https://www.inc.com/howard-tullman/its-not-about-failing-its-about-scaling.html .) In big businesses, everyone knows a story or two about an ex-employee who got too far out over his or her skis and is no longer there. There are very few prizes for being the one who's the budget buster even if the gamble looked unbeatable to everyone at the beginning. This is why I often say that – in the startup world – ignorance is a competitive advantage because you don't know what it is that you're not supposed to be able to do and so you just go out there and get it done.

(3) Fear of Choosing

I think of this problem as a version of pre-buyer's remorse. Someone has to be willing to step up to the plate and make a decision and then live with the consequences – right or wrong. And you need to strike a balance – too few alternatives and you make bad choices – too many choices and you never make a decision. Everything these days that we do or decide not to do is a choice – but sitting around and putting off the critical decisions is no longer an option. As all the great QBs like to say, when you cock your arm, you need to go ahead and throw it and not spend a lot of additional time thinking or talking about it. Entrepreneurs live by their wits and their intuition. In their world, so many decisions are made in real time and so quickly that analysis paralysis isn't really a problem although there's always a long line of investors happy to say "I told you so" when things go wrong. All that noise doesn't really matter much – any decision bets no decision all day long.

(4) Fear of Commitment

In an ideal world, everything would be reversible, and take-backs and do-overs would be as easy as pie. But in the world we live in, especially when you're dealing with a finite amount of resources, multiple options, and a very short window for action, you don't get a second chance and you're stuck with the choices you make. But that's no excuse for not choosing. It's a part of the leader's job and playing safe just won't do. You can't steal second base with one foot still firmly on first. You don't have to bet the farm every time – a luxury that startups don't have – but you can't be half pregnant either. And your team needs to commit just as fully – not in words – but in their hearts - and in their actions.

(5) Fear of Being Blamed

Playing the blame game is a waste of everyone's time and it's one of the most destructive parts of any company's culture. When things go wrong, there's no question that you need to find out why. But the goal isn't to beat someone up, it's to get better and avoid the problem the next time. In the best new businesses, there're are only two instances when we blame people: when they don't ask for the help they need and when they don't help their peers when they're asked.

Bottom line: there's really no mystery here. Take a look at your own business and your own team and see who's on the move – pushing the business ahead - and who's afraid to act and waiting in the wings to be told what to do.

As Bob Marley said: "You never know how strong you are, until being strong is your only choice."

TULLMAN'S TRUISMS

WAITING DOESN'T NECESSARILY GET YOU TO A BETTER ANSWER

I used to think that there was nothing more painfully staged or artificial than the mandatory "sharing" sessions where some world leader (or political candidate seeking the job) would be casually observed by a noisy posse of press and a gaggle of clicking cameras sitting in a classroom in front of a group of elementary school kids and allegedly reading meaningful passages to them from some picture book. These saccharine set-ups were regarded by most of us as just slightly more shameless (and almost as stupid a waste of time) as the mandatory state fair baby-kissings and/or the shots of someone chomping down on a steaming ear of fresh-grown country corn or a mustard-slathered corn dog.

Those of us of a certain age sadly recall a major media kerfuffle starting in 2002 when then President Bush was filmed and photographed in just such a session holding a book he was supposed to be reading to some students where the book's cover indicated that it was upside down. Turns out that the photo was a photoshopped fake, but the message about authenticity was still loud and clear and everyone else (except maybe the kids in the class) was pretty much in on the joke and gave the watching world a knowing wink. Complaining about the sloppy staging of a photo op is pretty much like sending your Big Mac back and complaining that you asked for it "medium rare" and not "well done" as if a Big Mac of any doneness is ever actually done well.

I sometimes think that when the press whines about how and why they lost all their credibility with a large part of the American public that one of the root causes may have been repeatedly subjecting us to scenes like this (ripe for selfies and social media) and insulting our intelligence (as well as serving as the worst kinds of willing flacks for the politicians). This seems to me to have been the beginning of the latest shift and sowed the newest seeds of the slippery slope into the cesspool. As we used to say, never interrupt your opponent when he is making a fool of himself. The media were more than willing accomplices to their own demise and, in their continued desperation for photo-ops and click bait, the decline just goes on and on.

I also often wondered if the politicians themselves would ever reach a point where they decided that it was just too embarrassing to continue to be a party to and a participant in such specious spectacles, but, at least to date, that doesn't appear to be the case. Even the ones who you would imagine have some semblance of dignity and seriousness can't resist the directions and dictates of their managers and the blandishments of the people that move their bodies (like hunks of meat) across the country and along the campaign trail according to the same time-old and time-tested conventions.

But more recently, I've come to realize that some of these sessions can and do serve an entirely different and beneficial purpose for the politicians <u>and</u> for those of us who understand the need to radically change our schools and our entire system of education. Today our schools – especially K-12 – continue to mortgage our kids' futures with processes and programs that haven't changed in a hundred years. The schools continue to put a premium on posture and punctuality rather than productivity and on memorization and imitation rather than imagination and innovation. Sadly, we're not born bored; it's something we learn to be at school. And it's gotta change.

We're not equipping our kids to succeed in a "new collar" jobs in a future where we know that the skills they will need are vastly different from the ones we learned so long ago. Today the only constant in their lives is constant change and the rate of the changes taking place continues to accelerate. And frankly, the only recourse that we as parents (and prospective employers) have is to convince the very same politicians doing these "dog and pony" shows in the schools that we need their help in recognizing, funding and effectuating some real changes in our schools and that we need those changes yesterday.

The somewhat encouraging news is that it turns out, as cynical, jaundiced, and beaten down as most of our representatives are these days, they still have something inside them that responds powerfully to seeing and interacting with young kids who are still curious and passionate about learning. Of course, they do have to be pretty young kids these days so that they don't talk back or say something snotty. But if you surround these guys with the right kids, the magic and their love of learning does come through.

Kids who still have a sense of ownership and agency in their futures and the imagination to think about how bright and wonderful those futures could be. Kids who haven't had their dreams snuffed and their naïve and native creativity crushed. And, at least in those moments, the optimism, the energy and their faith in the future is contagious and you have to hope that maybe just a little bit of it rubs off on their visitors.

It turns out – way back when – that it really didn't matter how President Bush was holding his copy of the book because the kid was reading to him, not the other way around.

I'm not much of a fan of manufactured mission statements and most pious platitudes and posters you see on the walls make me puke. I used to joke that these days you can buy a pro forma (and nicely laminated) mission statement for your business at Staples and probably a fill-in-the-blanks business plan as well. The truth is that you can't "ape" your way to success. Ya gotta make your own way and tell your own story.

And, in an age of lousy listeners and mixed meanings, it's even more critical to make sure that your message gets through to your team - clearly and consistently – and that you never make the mistake of thinking that once is enough. It pays to be obsessive about company communication because that's the only way to be sure that the story sticks and that everyone who's in the boat is on the program as well. Say it once and it's wasted – say it half a dozen times and they'll start listen – and, if say it all the time, they'll take you seriously. Repetition is the most convincing argument.

And it's also not enough to take a smile and a nod and think that you got the job done. Never confuse good manners with agreement and don't take anyone's word for things that aren't backed up by their actions. Especially when you're trying to change things, it's important to take these things very personally. Apologies without changes in behavior are really just insults.

This kind of crucial communication is especially essential when you're just starting out as the head of a new business. Everyone in the joint will be looking closely for signs and signals – keys and clues – trying to guess what's in your head and figure out where and how things are going. As if you knew. They're looking to you for leadership and guidance – to show them the vision, the path and how you'll all get there. You're on stage – all day – every day and your words and actions are contagious.

But, even in a small shop, communication is a challenge and a lot harder than you would think. And the stakes couldn't be higher especially right at the start when building the right culture is as important as building the rest of the business. As they used to say at NASA: "Off by an inch at launch; miss the moon by a mile". Cultures are fragile in the formative stages and can curdle and go south in a very short time if they're not curated, cared for, and mercilessly maintained/enforced. Businesses very quickly become the behaviors they tolerate and, once that slippery slide starts, it's almost impossible to reverse. It's not something that you can get right later – you get it right from the start – or you can forget about it.

But you can't do this all by yourself or try to get face-to-face with everyone and that's why you need a few shortcuts and step savers. The best leaders are great storytellers, but they are even better simplifiers. They're architects of aphorisms and crafters of clichés. And they've learned that the most powerful and memorable pronouncements are often the shortest. If you can't say it in a sentence or two at the most, it's either not worth saying or you don't understand the subject well enough to share it and sell it to your team, your clients, and your customers.

I've had thousands of employees in more than a dozen different businesses and I can guarantee you that – even 10 or 20 years later - most of them can still finish my sentences before I can when I'm spouting the old company lines. They aren't Yogi-isms quite yet, but they're on their way and they make a lot more sense. Every business needs their own (authentic) versions of these pithy phrases to act as ready reminders, great guardrails, and guides to the gospel.

I've got too many to share them all here, but I thought I'd give you a couple that have served me well for decades and are no less relevant or valuable today. Feel free to make them your own or adapt them to help you tell your own story.

(1) Your dog doesn't need email

Developers and especially engineers are shameless incrementalists. No feature or function is too excessive or unnecessary to add to the next release. They'll load it in whether we need it or want it or not. This is how we get products like Word or Excel where 99% of the users have no clue as to how to use 99% of the embedded and layered functions, but we all suffer from the inflated size of the installs and the painful delays every time we launch these monster programs. These guys are constantly inventing the cures for no known diseases. They don't understand that new users just wanna get started and not spend hours learning the ropes. Use this phrase as shorthand to head off feature creep and product bloat. It's also useful in swiftly stigmatizing utterly useless apps. (See https://www.inc.com/howard-tullman/no-dont-need-your-pointless-app.html .)

(2) There's never only one cockroach

Problems come in packs (three's not always a charm) and, even at the best-run businesses, it's too easy to fall into the trap of quick fixes which address only the most obvious symptoms rather than the root causes. Typically, because everyone's in a hurry, the next step is a rush to declare victory and a futile attempt to move on. The truth is that makeshift solutions distract you from the real underlying problems which rarely go away of their own volition. More often they fester and get worse.

In an age of growing interdependence, global connectivity, increasing complexity and the constant threat of unintended and unforeseen consequences, it just makes sense to slow down and take a deeper look at things. Einstein once said that he wasn't so smart, he just stayed with problems longer. It pays to keep looking. And it's also important to understand that "problems" are often just opportunities dressed up in overalls instead of Allbirds. (See https://www.inc.com/howard-tullman/so-youve-got-problems-thats-probably-great-news.html .)

(3) You never know who's gonna bring you your future

One of the reasons that many good entrepreneurs succeed is because they are narrowly and aggressively focused on the main opportunities which they see directly in front of them. They pride themselves on knowing when to say "No" which – in the startup world - is especially difficult because you're constantly confronted by hard choices, new and inviting distractions, and multiple tantalizing offers. But shutting yourself down like this is dangerous because, while lots of very bright people think that they're on top of what's going on in their fields and in the world in general, they're badly mistaken.

First, because things are just moving too fast for anyone to keep up with everything, and second, because the things that are likely to supercharge or strangle your startup aren't the things in front of you or being pursued by your closest competitors. They're the unexpected things – the outside entrants – the new market makers – the leap-frogging technologies - that are likely to be the most disruptive and/or devastating.

It's smart to always keep an ear to the ground and a watchful eye out as well, but as often as not, the real business breakthroughs will be surprisingly random – a kid who pitches you a new idea in an elevator – an article in a flight magazine that strikes a chord – advances in techniques so far from your field that you only see them on *60 Minutes* – and so on and so forth. (See https://www.inc.com/howard-tullman/five-reasons-your-market-is-bigger-than-you-think.html .)

And, believe me, if your head's 100% buried day to day in your business, these opportunities and inspirations will blow right by you. Look, listen and learn.

(4) It doesn't pay to put lipstick on a pig

When you're just starting out, short of cash, and trying to cover all the bases at the same time, there's a terrible tendency to spread yourself a mile wide and an inch deep. Too little time and too many demands and mouths to feed. So, you start thinking that doing something (anything) or even just doing a little bit is better than sitting still and doing nothing. If you can't do it right, at least do it quickly and don't look back. Because aren't startups all about speed?

This is a formula for failure and when you eventually do look back, you'll see a track record littered with losses, leftovers and losers because you and your team haven't learned the most basic rule of business: you should never try to do something cheaply that you shouldn't do at all. The best businesses do a few things really well and build from there. They don't do anything halfway or half-assed because these attempts never get you anywhere you want to go. Doing things to keep busy (or on the cheap) isn't the same as doing business and getting the right things done.

No matter how much steak sauce you put on a hot dog, it's still a wiener.

(5) Don't mistake a clear view for a short distance

Everything in Startup Land takes longer and costs more than expected. The only things that are consistently underestimated are, of course, sales, revenues and profits. It's all about the necessary passage of time which is that nasty little thing that keeps everything from happening all at once. You can only push a rope so far and honestly it doesn't matter how passionate you are, how hard you're willing to work, how well-funded you may be, or whether you've got the very best idea since the invention of sliced bread. It's still gonna take the boat a while to sail (and sell) and managing the realistic expectations of your team is just as important as delivering the straight scoop to your customers and prospects. It may, in fact, be even more important.

A little bit of early caution and some serious patience will pay serious dividends down the road. I realize that entrepreneurs rarely come with an on/off switch and that they're all true believers, but it's critical to realize that convincing yourself is easy. I call this the "that hooker really liked me" syndrome. But selling – especially something new and different - is time-consuming and hard. Even entrepreneurs so good that they could sell a muzzle to a mongrel or sell shoes to a snake learn eventually that nothing good happens overnight. You can't get to heaven in a heartbeat.

In the trenches of the real world, it's more a matter of diligent preparation, solid consistent execution, and pathological perseverance than one of hope and vision. No one likes sitting on the phone making 50 calls a day, but that's what it takes to build a business. A step at a time, one foot in front of the other, and always looking for the next hill to climb. Because nothing really matters until someone sells something to somebody.

Now's the time for you to get going on figuring out your year-end bonuses. As much as you'd like to, you can't really put it off any longer since December is right around the corner. Honestly, the whole deal would be so much easier and less stressful if we gave out bonuses in July or August instead of in the midst of the holidays. But, if you're a typical entrepreneur, your people are paid twice a month which means that you've got to distribute their bonuses with their first check in December, so they have a little time to spend it on holiday presents.

I was going to say, "time to decide what to do with it", but these days the idea of "saving" some of that extra cash doesn't even enter into the discussion. Half the time, I think these bonus payments are pre-spent which just makes the pressure greater on you to get the amounts right. This is no easy task in the age of social media sharing, profound entitlement, exaggerated expectations, and dysfunctional transparency. As hard as you try and as diligent as you can be, a bunch of your people are still going to be unhappy. Get used to it.

If you're a startup CEO who's even a little bit conscientious, and most of us are, you'll spend a lot more hours than you'd imagine stewing over these decisions, slicing up the fixed and often shrinking pie in a million different ways, and trying to do right by everyone which, of course, is unrealistic to begin with and impossibly subjective as well. You work really hard to try to do the best job you possibly can.

You can collect input and suggestions from your board, your accountants and other team members (who, as a rule, are always willing to spend more money than the company can afford to take care of their own folks) and you can look at "industry" guidelines which are usually just as useless. Because, especially at this time of the year, every business sits on its own bottom; has its own Rashomon history of the year just past; and a big bunch of explanations, rationalizations, and "woulda, coulda, shoulda" excuses.

So, there are no pat patterns, flawless formulae, or even good guidelines to really help you make these personal and highly emotional decisions. And, as you're sitting and sweating these decisions out in your study on the Sunday after Thanksgiving, you'll quickly realize that this is another one of those "the buck stops here" situations. I guess, if your business has had a lousy year, it's a little easier to be more modest in the bonus amounts but - nine times out of ten - those overall results weren't the fault or the responsibility of most of your hardworking employees, so it doesn't help to whine too much to them about the bottom line. It might work better on some of the managers who better understand the math, but I wouldn't count of any of them stepping up to take a bullet for the team either. I think it's fair to say that baseball is still the only place in the real world where a sacrifice is actually appreciated.

But even if every case is ultimately a little different, I think there are a few things to keep in mind and to learn from those who've suffered through the painful process over and over again. Here are a few basics to keep in mind.

(1) There's no silver bullet and it never gets easier.
At the end of the day, you're gonna be sitting opposite a bunch of people – one at a time - who think that you have measured their value and worth as human beings (not just as employees) and converted that opinion into dollars and cents. A lot of heat and emotion is bundled into that little bonus amount and you can count on some sparks to fly during those conversations.

(2) Percentages are a really poor proxy.
Comp committee members and other experts are notorious for telling you (with little or no basis in fact or even experience) that bonuses in "a new business like yours" should be around X% of most employees' salaries. In my experience, this advice always results in dollar bonuses amounts that you'd be afraid to give your doorman. My advice is to build your bonus structure up from the bottom starting with a dollar amount that you won't be embarrassed to present to your youngest and newest employees and go from there.

(3) Making mediocre people happy is a good way to lose your best performers.
Trying to buy peace so you won't get a bunch of dirty looks and evil eyes at the office party is a bad bet for the business overall. Some people are only alive because it's against the law to kill them and some people deserve exactly what they've earned (or not earned) and they shouldn't get one dollar more. It sends the worst possible message to everyone and really discourages the people who are hitting it out of the park. Get in the habit of sacrificing the few, if necessary, to save the many. Always be raising the average.

(4) Don't make promises you can't or won't be able to keep.
It's easy (in your haste to get out of the room and end the conversation) to fall into the "there's always next year" trap. But please don't. First, because it doesn't really help the situation – no one wants to be happy tomorrow. And second, because if you really think things are unlikely to improve, you're just putting off a harder and more critical decision. And, by the way, when you say to yourself that you don't know about a person, the truth is that you do. Try to always be able to say that your average employees now work somewhere else.

(5) **Buckets are much better than brackets or bands.**

Using systems of brackets or bands for comp or bonus determinations are OK, but they often miss a very central consideration which is that some of the most impactful and important people in your business could have relatively low salaries. So, the pure math can be misleading but, in your heart, and your head you know who these people are. And that's why I like the "buckets" approach. Start the whole process with 3 big buckets. Bucket 1 are the best people in the business – wherever they are and whatever they may be earning. These folks need to be <u>rewarded</u>. Bucket 2 are the vast majority of your employees and hopefully they're doing more than their fair share and contributing. These people need to be <u>recognized</u>. Bucket 3 are the people who are just doing their jobs and not much more. They're probably earning their salaries but not much more and, frankly, if they aren't getting better, they better be gone. These people need to be <u>reminded</u>. Use the bonuses to send the appropriate messages to each group.

And finally, just one more reminder. Don't take it personally when no one is grateful or thanks you. It's just another part of the job.

TULLMAN'S TRUISMS

ONLY THE WINNERS DECIDE WHAT THE WAR CRIMES WERE

Now is the time of year for some quiet reflection. But it's hard to make the time because entrepreneurs aren't particularly introspective or self-aware (as most of them are quick to admit) and they rarely like looking in the rear-view mirror or rehashing old news or past mistakes. If you need a current poster boy for this attitude, look no further than the Zuck who's all about future fixes and moving on and not interested in the least in talking about past failures and the damage done.

This "full speed ahead" attitude is actually a source of some considerable pride among the more arrogant executives in the Valley as they continue to lecture the rest of us on solutions to world problems and on how to improve our lives and society without opening their own kimonos to take a look at the messes they've made inside and out. We used to describe this approach as "often wrong, but never in doubt" and, in reality, it's clearly both a blessing and a curse for most business builders.

A blessing because the best entrepreneurs focus on possibilities more than problems - winning rather than worrying - and, above all, tomorrow and not yesterday. This astute and calculated ignorance is actually a competitive advantage for the newcomers who are building startups because when you don't know or focus obsessively on what you're not supposed to be able to do or what you're actually qualified for or even capable of; it often happens that you just go right ahead and simply get it done. You don't ever have to be bound by the limitations of others. That's the good news.

The curse is when you spend so much time seeing the "big" picture, setting the vision, and steering the ship, not around, but through the tough times; you can lose sight of yourself and how and whether things are still working for you. This isn't good news. Being the boss of any business is hard enough, but it's even tougher running a struggling startup (an oxymoron for sure because who isn't sweating every day in their business to get over or to get better) and it's almost impossible to do it well if your own head isn't fully in the game.

I wouldn't say that we should expect to be or need to be "happy" to take on these challenges, but we do have to believe in our hearts and heads that what we're doing is valuable, meaningful and likely to make a difference. Otherwise it's easy to become bitter. As always, Springsteen says it best in *Devils and Dust* when he sings: "what if what you do to survive kills the things you love.... it'll turn your heart black".

If you find yourself angry more often than amused - upset more often than uplifted - and pissed more than proud; it's time to take a break and take a close look at yourself. This is a hard topic to take up and it's never easy to have a heart-to-heart conversation with yourself, but it's essential and now's as good a time as any. I've written about this issue before in terms of when it's time to do something different, but here I'm talking more about a tune-up rather a termination. (See https://www.inc.com/howard-tullman/theres-never-a-great-time-plan-your-exit.html .)

If you want a quick and easy way to getting the process started, your own conversations may be the key. I call this "the I's have it" approach. It's a shorthand way to see if things are starting to slip and are going to require further examination and work. Listen carefully to how you're talking to your people and about the business. If too much of the talk is about "I" and not "we", it's a good bet that you're feeling angry or sorry for yourself or both and need to get yourself back on track.

Watch for these negatives:

(1) **"I don't really care…"** said NO entrepreneur ever. Of course, you care – it's your business and your baby. This is just a way of telling the team that you're unhappy without being honest enough to put it out there. So, you sulk and shut down. It's not just your unhappy employees who can suffer from "whatever" sickness. (See https://www.inc.com/howard-tullman/why-whatever-will-sink-your-business.html.) The good news about this is that sitting on the sidelines isn't in your DNA and you'll be back minding everyone else's business soon enough.

(2) **"I didn't know…"** about someone. As often as not, you did know or should have known, but this is just a handy way to deflect responsibility and blame someone else for something you should be doing or should have addressed. Great entrepreneurs sweat all the small details and there's very little that goes on or matters in their companies that they miss. And even if they missed it, there's always a parade of people waiting at their door to give them the unhappy news.

(3) **"I wasn't asked…"** about something. This is an especially sad cop-out because you built the whole business on people taking chances, risks and initiative and now you're whining that they didn't ask nicely for your permission. Or maybe you saw what was going on (and wrong or sideways) and you decided to be willfully ignorant and let the chips fall where they may. This isn't you either and it's pretty close to cutting off your nose to spite your face. Get over yourself and get busy fixing the problems.

(4) **"I didn't have…"** X or Y or Z. And I'd like to grow 10 inches and play center for the Chicago Bulls. Of course, you didn't have certain things. No one ever has it all – that's why you make do and do the best you can with the people and resources that you do have. It's just another part of the job – if it was easy and everything was handed to you on a silver platter - it wouldn't be much of a challenge. Entrepreneurs know that it's the journey – it's the work that you put into filling these gaps – inventing new work-arounds and solutions – and making these things happen - that's the real joy in building a business.

Bottom line: it's been a tough year in some ways for almost everyone. And it's easy for an entrepreneur to feel lonely and unappreciated. Sometimes the hardest work is thankless, but it's still important and it still needs to get done and done right. Take some time to take your own temperature and listen to yourself, suck it up, and then get yourself back in the game.

And remember that great entrepreneurs don't do this stuff because they want to; they do it because they have to, and they wouldn't be caught dead doing anything else.

TULLMAN'S TRUISMS

NO ONE CAN MAKE YOU FEEL INFERIOR WITHOUT YOUR CONSENT

For many years, I've maintained that – when a startup is trying to influence long-established consumer behaviors - it's always much smarter to design any new business processes and required actions so that they align with and move in the same directions as the prospective customers and existing users are already headed. It's simply not practical or cost-effective to try to alter or redirect people's ingrained actions and only then to discover that you're required to spend great gobs of time and money (which you typically don't have) in an upstream struggle where you're fighting to change millions of minds. It's much better to build on my behavior; help me do what I'm already doing faster or smarter; start with incremental adjustments which make me more productive; or provide the easy wins and successive rewards that save me time or money. But don't try to bully me into behaving or beat me over the head with your message.

Saying doesn't make it so – you've got to show me quickly and easily that it makes sense to "sign up" for your solution. It's all about speed, ease of access and convenience. Otherwise it's just gonna be a brutal uphill battle. And it's always faster and cheaper to ride on the rails that someone else has already built and funded. This can present itself as a variety of alternative opportunities: you can add value to equipment or facilities that someone else has already capitalized; you can add functionality to platforms that are currently up and operating; or you can create incremental and/or supplementary revenues from customers already being attracted to certain venues, services, etc.

But the thing we know for sure is that there's no upside in reinventing the wheel, creating the umpteenth version of the same solution, or trying to teach people a new way of doing something when they believe that their current plan already gets the job done reasonably well. We're not as choosy these days as we used to be, and we aren't really looking around for more of much of anything. We're basically lazy today and really stuck in our ruts. And the biggest rut and most pervasive tethers of all are our mobile phones.

But those very phones also represent a game-changing and fundamental shift in the way that brands, bars and businesses are going to have to reach out to their customers. Today, 95% of U.S. adults have a cell phone (75% of those are smart phones) and 80% of us automatically look at our phones within 15 minutes of waking up in the morning. I think the others are just too embarrassed to acknowledge that they do as well. We're all looking for that daily dose of dopamine along with our morning caffeine and things just accelerate rapidly from there. Typically, on a weekday, you'll look at your phone over 160 times which equates to about 3.5 hours a day. Weekends are even worse. And nothing's getting better.

In our lifetime, there's never been a more powerful and ubiquitous marketing platform than our phones. They possess 3 characteristics which are essentially super powers: they're intimate, immediate and interruptive. Simply stated, this means that, in our lives, they're omnipresent, they're always on, and they're impossible to ignore. They're much more of a buddy, an accomplice and a sidekick today than any of our BFFs. And, for marketers and merchants, they're the keys to the kingdom and the best way for anyone to break through the clutter in our lives. But it's easier said than done because the barriers to ready access continue to increase.

This is in part because, while the digital world continues to expand, our own personal worlds are shrinking given our limited ability to manage and focus our attention amidst the endless stream of fluff and flutter. We're more apt to try to shut down and shut off the outside world these days than to openly and excitedly embrace it. And, we're increasingly settling in our familiar ways; visiting the same few sites and platforms; using the same small number of apps; and largely loath to change or look elsewhere. (See https://www.inc.com/howard-tullman/whats-behind-door-number-two-it-better-be-you.html.)

As a result, effective engagement is hard enough to achieve these days – in a world of constant collisions, perpetual noise and distractions, and miniscule attention spans – even before a new entrant adds to the challenge by trying to change the order of things. In a word, if you want my attention; meet me where I'm at; go with the flow; and don't bust my bubble or mangle my mood. (See https://www.inc.com/howard-tullman/want-your-app-to-succeed-get-it-out-there.html.) Trying to launch a brand-new app today is like trying to teach a fish to ride a bicycle. Even if you could, why would you? (See https://www.inc.com/howard-tullman/no-dont-need-your-pointless-app.html.)

An equally significant barrier to new entry is the fact that the scarcest and most precious real estate anywhere these days are the apps pages of our phones. They're jammed with excess icons that we barely remember (and never use) because we're hoarders and lousy housekeepers. There's no more room for anything new and even less interest. And, just as we've learned about friends on *Facebook* and connections on *LinkedIn*; more itself isn't better – only better is better. It's almost impossible to pitch me on something new and improved if I'm not interested or paying attention. (See https://www.inc.com/howard-tillman/we-have-reached-peak-apps.html. And I'm never gonna hear about how much better your product or service is if I'm not looking or listening because I've got my nose stuck stubbornly in the space two inches from my phone. We're all clearly creatures of our habits and most of us are honestly reluctant to admit just how captive and dependent we have become on our digital devices.

Nothing in human history has ever rivaled the emotional and psychological attachment which we have to our phones and the degree of dependence is growing across all ages and across the world. In a very real sense, our phones have become an extension of our selves (avatars, animated personas and emoticons are just the start) and this connection and identification will only intensify as we increasingly come to depend on voice as our means of interaction. Killing the keyboard is the final frontier as we come to talk to our phones, not through them to another person.

So, if you can't pry my phone out of my hands and I'd rather die of hunger or thirst than download another app for my phone at some bar or restaurant, both you (and whatever venue I happen to be in) better figure out fast how to get my attention and get your messages in front of me. And, of course, the simplest solution is sitting right there in front of me. It's quick and easy. It's free. There's nothing to load or learn. And I can start in a second. It's called *Upshow* (https://www.upshow.tv/).

No, it's not some greasy and beat-up table tent. And the waitress is too busy table-hopping to tell me about tonight's special anythings – even if I could hear her. And frankly, even if you give me a terrific and shiny new tablet to order from, I don't really want to spend my time learning all about your system in order to order. But my phone's a whole 'nother thing.

I'm already an expert on *Twitter* and *Instagram*. I've already got those apps sitting open on my cell. And I've been taking selfies and other goofy shots of my buddies all night long while I'm trying to watch a dozen different games on the video screens which are stuck on every wall. But suddenly, I'm starting to see something else going on in the place as other tables start to point excitedly at the monitors because <u>their</u> selfies are starting to show up in real-time for everyone to see. And I think, what am I: "chopped liver"? So, I ask because I'm actually interested, and it turns out that I just add a hashtag with the bar or restaurant's name to my IG posts or my tweets and it's a done deal. All of a sudden, I'm "dualing".

There may be fancier names for this phenomenon – like screen convergence or shared media – but I like my word – <u>dualing</u> – because that's what's really happening. My content, my experience, and my attention are now in two places at once (and shared with the whole place) and I'm paying rapt attention to both because <u>I'm in charge</u> and I'm driving the show. I'm engaged, I'm open to offers, suggestions, contests, coupons, etc. because there's now a direct two-way channel to my phone. And I'm willing to listen as well.

This is a whole new game and the next big thing in digital in-venue engagement and entertainment. And it's basically "free" to everyone. 100% free to me. And whatever modest investment the venue might make in the *Upshow* backend system and software is peanuts compared to what they've already spent installing a zillion monitors everywhere. And did I mention that the vast majority of this "authentic" content is created for nothing by the users themselves and then sent (along with the venue's branding) to everyone on their social media networks.

The best promotion is word of mouth and a picture is worth a thousand words.

It's been a tough couple of weeks with a wrenching series of the unexpected deaths of friends – all entrepreneurs and/or educators in their own way - aged from their mid-50s to their mid-90s. Several died abruptly without the slightest indication of any serious illness – brutal bolts from the blue - and others left us at a time when we earnestly believed that they were in the midst of bouncing back and regaining their strength. So much the sadder given the immense struggle which preceded their demise.

And, say what you will, these are frightening episodes for all of us of a certain age because they are the most immediate and stark reminders of our own mortality. And whatever anyone else ever tells you, these painful passings are never easy or expected in terms of one being prepared for the event, ready for the surprising and palpable pain, or able to deal with the sinking sense of loss. Nor do we exactly understand the mixed feelings of relief which we experience in some morbid fashion on the putative behalf of the deceased. The truth is that, by definition, every death is unfairly premature and always comes too soon. It's never about getting over these kinds of things – it's just a matter of trying to successfully muddle through them – with some semblance of grace and respect. The pain may eventually lessen and the scars start to heal, but the wound remains forever.

But in those first and early moments of the searing knowledge – before the procedures and the protocols kick in – before life resumes and the rush of essential events takes over and moves things along with an irresistible (and grudgingly welcome) force of their own – you have a brief window of reflection where you realize that, while death may end a life, it doesn't extinguish the long history, the many mixed emotions, the complex connections, and the underlying relationships that were a part of your life together and which withstood the many trials and tribulations of time.

And, if you permit yourself, your exploration often extends beyond the immediate losses of certain individuals to recall and remember (and perhaps cerebrally celebrate) others who are also no longer a prominent presence in your life, but to whom you owe much. I've written in the past that entrepreneurs are lousy at saying thank you (See https://www.inc.com/howard-tullman/why-entrepreneurs-are-really-terrible-at-saying-thank-you.html.), but there seems to me to be an even deeper deficiency. It's not enough to thank our employees and our investors and random others if we don't also remember to reach out to thank the critical contributors who were steadfastly there at the start.

At our business schools, we regularly debate the "nature versus nurture" controversy - essentially discussing whether entrepreneurs are just born a certain way and destined to pursue new ventures or whether anyone with an interest (and hopefully some measure of passion) can be taught the critical skills for startup success. (See https://www.inc.com/howard-tullman/entrepreneurs-born-or-built-debate.html.) I'm firmly in the "it's in your genes" camp, except that I don't really think that heredity explains it all or that entrepreneurs themselves give enough credit to the critical importance of the roles played by their parents, professors, mentors and, to a much lesser extent, their peers.

And, by the way, I don't mean to suggest that the role and the impact of these other parties is necessarily or automatically a positive influence or a supportive one – just that it's often a very powerful one that is under-appreciated and only occasionally acknowledged. Everyone you encounter on the journey teaches you something – some are good examples and role models and others are just as important warnings about what not to be or do. Sometimes a blessing, sometimes no more than a passing breeze, and sometimes a boot.

But for so many entrepreneurs, the real start and the best part of the journey was when they were kids at home. Home where they have to take you in – home where the support and love is unconditional – and home where many of the essential habits, attitudes, and values are initially built, regularly reinforced and eventually absorbed. Who doesn't have half a dozen mottos, slogans or aphorisms burnt into their brain from Mom or Dad? These aren't just pithy phrases or cliques. It turns out that they're pretty important life lessons. And, although GEICO's ads make light of it, maybe turning into our parents in some ways isn't the worst thing that could happen. After all, they raised us and we turned out pretty well, so how bad could they have been?

So it's worth a moment from time to time – especially if you still have a chance to say it to their faces before they're gone – to think about and thank your parents for their patience and thick skins, their perseverance at times when you were clearly a lost cause, and their persistent part in your eventual and plentiful successes. No time like the present and never too soon or too often. Don't wait for a fire or a funeral and, for sure, don't wait until it's too late.

After all, they're the ones who taught us that it's not the tears and sadness, but the desire and the determination to move forward that ultimately makes the pain of loss bearable. So find an opportunity over the holidays and make it a moment of celebration and not sadness.

As the Boss says in *The Wish*: "Well tonight I'm takin' requests here in the kitchen. This one's for you, ma, let me come right out and say it. It's overdue, but baby, if you're looking for a sad song, well I ain't gonna play it."

As the year draws to a close, it's a good chance to catch your breath and spend a few hours just thinking--and not doing anything but thinking--about the year ahead and where you want to take your business. If you don't have a plan, or really care where you're headed, then any path will get you there. In that case, just make sure that you're walking down a path and not a plank. But the smart entrepreneur knows that even the most rapidly reactive organizations can't keep up with the rapid and accelerating rate of change today – where each change shortens the interval between changes – and the next abrupt shift is on top of you before you've even dealt with the last. So, you've got to get ahead of the curve, anticipate the action, and skate to where the puck is headed. Trying to catch the train after it's left the station is a loser's game.

I'm not talking about some foolish New Year's diet resolutions or your desire to definitely get in great shape this winter; to read a book a week and clean out the attic; or simply to be a much better person in 2019. I mean thinking strategically about how you can make the next 12 months a lot more valuable and productive for your company.

Not enough entrepreneurs do this simple exercise these days (we've all got plenty of explanations and excuses for why this is) and, as a result, too many lose sight of the critical things they should be doing and the most important questions they should be asking: Why did I get into this business in the first place? Am I doing any good and/or making any difference that matters in the long run? Does anyone outside of my friends, family, investors, and employees care about what we're doing? (See https://www.inc.com/howard-tullman/your-days-are-numbered.html?cid=search.)

Don't dwell on the past

While you are thinking ahead, I wouldn't waste much time reflecting on the past 12 months since: a) there's nothing you can really do about them; b) you ought to already know what you did right and wrong -- and hopefully have learned a lot from the experience; and c) fretting over mistakes and missed opportunities doesn't really move anything forward. You can't build your future on regrets and "shouldas, wouldas, and couldas."

Besides, looking in the rear mirror is distracting. It makes it easy to run off the road or smack into something big and ugly that could have been easily avoided if you had been looking ahead. That involves paying attention to the outside world and, even more important, to what your customers are doing and saying about their own pressing needs and their current desires. Customer expectations are progressive. If you're not on top of these needs, you'll soon be at the bottom of your customers' lists. (See https://www.inc.com/howard-tullman/keep-your-customers-by-thinking-ahead-of-them.html.)

And the most important reason that you don't want to get all wrapped up in analyzing the past is that doing so is almost always an invitation to spend your time navel gazing, making excuses, and bemoaning the bad breaks. And that's not where you need to be focusing your energy as you try to get your business set for the New Year.

Know what customers want

You need to get out there and find out what's going on now outside the four walls of your business, because that's where your future will be found. Remember, you will never get straighter or more useful answers to your questions than the ones you get directly from your customers. The truth -- with all its wonders and warts -- comes from the consumers and the users of your products and services. They don't have an agenda (apart from always wanting a lot more for a lot less), and they're the real reason you got into this business to begin with, so pleasing them and addressing their needs seems like the obvious thing to do. But it doesn't happen if you don't do it. When you take the time to look, think, and ask, you might just discover that there's a bigger and better opportunity right under your nose that you've been practically tripping over for months or years without ever noticing. (See https://www.inc.com/howard-tullman/five-reasons-your-market-is-bigger-than-you-think.html.)

Five questions to ask yourself

If you're ready to take the plunge, here are a few of the main questions to ask yourself. It's a pretty simple process, but, as you'll see, the results can be game-changing.

1. What's the problem you initially set out to solve?
2. Are you trying to solve the same problem today or doing something different?
3. Is the problem still important to your customers and worth their paying you to solve?
4. Are others offering cheaper, quicker, or easier solutions to the problem?
5. Are there new, more important, or different problems to be solved?

You'll notice that all of these questions address the customers' problem(s) and not your products or solutions. This isn't just a question of semantics. If you don't understand the pressing problems of your customers, you have no chance at all of building a successful product or service to solve them. You can keep building the greatest software never sold or discovering the cure for no known disease, but you won't be building a business that will be here at the end of next year.

TULLMAN'S TRUISMS

IT'S NOT WHO WILL LET US, IT'S WHO WILL STOP US

As the year draws to a close, it's a good opportunity to catch your breath and spend a few hours just thinking — and not doing anything but thinking — about the year ahead and where you want to take your business.

If you don't have a plan, or really care where you're headed, then any path will get you there. In that case, just make sure that you're walking down a path and not a plank.

But the smart entrepreneur knows that even the most rapidly reactive organizations can't keep up with the rapid and accelerating rate of change today, where each change shortens the interval between changes, and the next abrupt shift is on top of you before you've even dealt with the last. So, you've got to get ahead of the curve, anticipate the action and skate to where the puck is headed.

I'm not talking about some foolish New Year's resolutions or your desire to definitely get in great shape this winter, to read a book a week and clean out the attic, or simply to be a much better person in 2019. I mean thinking strategically about how you can make the next 12 months a lot more valuable and productive for your company.

Not enough entrepreneurs do this simple exercise. We've all got plenty of explanations and excuses for why this is and, as a result, too many lose sight of the critical things they should be doing and the most important questions they should be asking: Why did I get into this business in the first place? Am I doing any good and/or making any difference that matters in the long run? Does anyone outside of my friends, family, investors, and employees care about what we're doing?

Here are a few hints to get that conversation with yourself going:

Don't dwell on the past

While you are thinking ahead, I wouldn't waste much time reflecting on the past 12 months because there's nothing you can really do about them and you ought to already know what you did right and wrong and hopefully you have learned a lot from the experience.

Also, fretting over mistakes and missed opportunities doesn't really move anything forward. You can't build your future on regrets and "shouldas, wouldas and couldas."

Besides, looking in the rearview mirror is distracting. It makes it easy to run off the road or smack into something big and ugly that could have been easily avoided if you had been looking ahead. That involves paying attention to the outside world and, even more important, to what your customers are doing and saying about their own pressing needs and their current desires.

Customer expectations are progressive. If you're not on top of these needs, you'll soon be at the bottom of your customers' lists.

And the most important reason that you don't want to get all wrapped up in analyzing the past is that doing so is almost always an invitation to spend your time navel gazing, making excuses and bemoaning the bad breaks. And that's not where you need to be focusing your energy as you try to get your business set for the new year.

Find out what customers are going to want

You need to get out there and uncover what's going on outside the four walls of your business, because that's where your future will be found.

Remember, you will never get straighter or more useful answers to your questions than the ones you get directly from your customers. The truth, with all its wonders and warts, comes from the consumers and the users of your products and services.

They don't have an agenda (apart from always wanting a lot more for a lot less), and they're the real reason you got into this business to begin with. Pleasing them and addressing their needs seems like the obvious thing to do.

When you take the time to look, think and ask, you might just discover that there's a bigger and better opportunity right under your nose that you've been practically tripping over for months or years without ever noticing.

Ask yourself a few things

If you're ready to take the plunge, here are a few of the main questions to ask yourself.

(1) What's the problem you initially set out to solve?
(2) Are you trying to solve the same problem today or doing something different?
(3) Is the problem still important to your customers and worth their paying you to solve?
(4) Are others offering cheaper, quicker or easier solutions to the problem?
(5) Are there new, more important or different problems to be solved?

You'll notice that all of these questions address the customers' problem(s) and not your products or solutions. This isn't just a question of semantics. If you don't understand the pressing problems of your customers, you have no chance at all of building a successful product or service to solve them.

You can keep building the greatest software never sold or discovering the cure for no known disease, but you won't be building a business that will be here at the end of next year.

I'm sure one of your most fervent New Year's resolutions which you duly and promptly shared on social media was the annual "work less and spend more time with the family" promise - maybe with a kicker this year (thanks to Arianna Huffington's incessant whining) that you'll also get more sleep and thereby become a far more effective and infinitely better person overall. Every entrepreneur (and anyone else building a business) knows how these things go, especially today when we're all working longer and harder, spending less time with our families and loved ones, and feeling guilty about it. The fact that there are often good reasons for the extra time away or because the jobs we're doing are important, not just to ourselves, but to others as well, doesn't make that discussion any easier or less emotional. The truth is that there's always more work, but you've only got one family.

Very often in our familial conversations about work, we find ourselves explaining and trying to justify our efforts and our absences, especially to our kids. And, unfortunately, for lack of a better or more straightforward explanation, we often seize upon a particularly unfortunate turn of a phrase and a pretty lousy excuse. We say, in so many different ways and words, that:

- I work to make money to buy you (fill in the blank); or
- I work to make money to provide you with (insert here); or
- I work to make money so we can do or go (destination please).

Sound familiar? Maybe it's a spouse, but most often it's our kids. And just what are we telling them?

We're telling our kids that we work for money -- that money is what matters-- and that money is to buy things, places, people, etc. That "getting" is really the be-all and the end-all for our work. And that's too bad. Because it's a lame explanation, a dishonest excuse, and an awful message -- probably the worst message possible. This explanation is quick and easy, and we all fall into this trap from time to time. But we can do better and, frankly, we need to do better because our kids are already drowning in media messages that say -- a million times a day -- that life is all about the bucks.

So, I have a modest suggestion for the next time you find yourself in this particular fix. Change the context -- change the conversation -- and tell your loved ones the truth (or maybe what we hope the truth should be) whenever we're asked about why we work. I'd suggest spending a little time thinking about your own answer before the fat's in the fire.

What is the truth? What's an honest answer? It starts with being honest with yourself. When you're dragging, feeling a little sorry for yourself, can't take another day of work (and it's only Wednesday), and you find yourself mumbling and grumbling to yourself that "we need the money" or "I have no choice" or "I've got bills to pay", you're just kidding yourself just like we've all been kidding our kids for years.

If you don't know why you're working and what you're working for, or you can't think of a good reason to come to work, then do yourself and everyone else a favor and find something else to do. If you're not interested and at least a little bit excited about what you're doing -- most of the time -- leave it.

O.K. you say, but what is the right answer when the kids ask, as you're sneaking out the door on Saturday morning to spend the day at the office: "Hey Dad, how come you never come home?" Or maybe: "Why is work so important all the time, don't we come first?"

The truth and the best answer is that we work for two basic reasons: (A) to make ourselves proud and (B) to help other people. We don't really work for money. We work to be productive and creative. We work to make a difference in our lives and the lives of others. We work because we secure real satisfaction from what we achieve with our hands, our hearts and our minds.

There's no price tag on this stuff. Money isn't even a good way to keep score. Does anyone really think that a rock star's contribution is millions of times more valuable than a teacher's? That's just more media bullshit. We work to accomplish things that move our lives forward, that matter in meaningful ways, and that we can feel honestly and sincerely good about it. There's no shame or false pride in that. There's nothing to be embarrassed to tell your kids about. If you love what you do, let them know and pray that someday they'll have a similar experience and privilege.

Is it foolish, or do we sound selfish, if we admit that we work because it makes us feel good and fulfilled? I don't think so and I think it's a much more constructive, effective, and appropriate answer for everyone -- kids and grownups too. Don't tell your kids you work because you have to, or worse, that you work to buy them Christmas toys or other goodies. We work because work is important and that's what grown-ups do. Your career is something to be unashamedly proud of and to share with your kids and others. We're building things to make the world a better place.

And that's where Part B comes in. We're not isolated islands and in this thing all by ourselves. Everything we do or don't do impacts many others -- especially those of us who teach. So, it's just as important to understand, acknowledge and have our kids appreciate that, apart from the selfish motivation of making us feel good, we all work as well for a greater good and to help others by making their lives better and fuller as well as our own. Hard work and commitment is how life moves forward and how the world gets better. A lot of tiny steps by millions of people, a little bit at a time, and mountains move.

And that just leaves the matter of money. What should we say about money? I hope that the message I've shared with my kids is pretty simple. Money, beyond life's necessities, is for charity and for giving back. Money is not an end in itself or a game of running up the score. Money is not a worthwhile goal because there's no finish line and there's always someone with more. At best, it's an enabling and an ennobling tool to make valuable, important, and charitable things happen.

The bottom line: work hard and be proud of the work you do; love what you do or do something else; try to make a difference in this world every day in large and small ways; and use all of your talents, energy and resources to help others to better their lives. And lastly, hug your kids much too much, far too often, and until they squeal.

Have a Happy, Healthy, and Prosperous New Year.

TULLMAN'S TRUISMS

YOU GET WHAT YOU WORK FOR, NOT WHAT YOU WISH FOR

295 – HAPPY NEW YEAR. NOW STOP TRYING TO MAKE EVERYONE HAPPY.

This is the time for you to allocate more resources to your winners and kick the losers to the curb. Good leaders learn to use the word "No" and to stop propping up mediocre products-or people.

As you wrap up 2018, and start thinking about your business's budget for the next year, the toughest single task is always the allocation of inevitably scarce resources among competing ideas, opportunities and commitments. The hardest single word to say is "No" -- and also the most important. Because smart strategy in times like these is all about what you don't do.

Saying "Yes" is so much easier and a relatively painless way, at least in the short run, to keep poor projects alive or to try to do things cheaply. Things that you shouldn't do at all. And saying "Maybe" when you should just say "No" isn't doing anyone a service; it merely postpones the inevitable.

Get used to the idea that there's never enough to go around and you can never make everyone happy or please all of the people even some of the time. Don't even start down that path. Absolutely the most important thing not to do is to try to treat everyone "fairly" - by which I mean equally - because nothing about business is fair.

Business is all about frankness, not fairness. Telling your people the truth is the greatest favor you can do for them. Splitting the baby or trying to give everyone a little something dilutes the overall enterprise and diminishes everything you're trying to accomplish. It's a proven formula for stagnation, mediocrity and eventual demise.

This kind of equitable treatment, where every department gets a similar budget, or every department head gets the same raise and bonus, feels good in the moment. But it's a stupid plan to try to placate everyone instead of making the hard choices to assure the survival of your firm. And it's a lazy and cowardly way out. I understand that no one wants to be the bad guy in someone else's day and that these messages are always difficult to deliver, but not only is it a part of every leader's job, if you're not personally up to the task, then you shouldn't be in the position in the first place. The buck really does stop with you.

And believe me, survival isn't too strong a term these days; it's exactly the level of significance and severity that these choices and decisions deserve. I see businesses every day where the management is treading water, waiting to retire, and/or afraid to bite the bullet, shoulder their responsibilities, and take the necessary actions. As a result, time quickly passes, momentum and opportunities are lost, investors, donors and partners lose interest, funding disappears, and one day they turn around and there's nothing left to pursue.

The market for talent, as just one example, is fierce and unforgiving. If you aren't smart enough to understand that you've got to pay your best people better than the rest of the team and, if you still think that it makes sense to be equitable based simply on longevity or titles or job descriptions, you're living in the past. Those peak performers, who are the only ones that matter to your future, will soon be hired away. Not because they're ungrateful or disloyal; because they're not stupid.

It's the same with

(1) businesses you're in that are going sideways
(2) products you're producing that are getting tired and losing market share, or
(3) departments where there's no longer the same demand for or the value attributed to the services that they're providing

Spending money or other resources to prop these losers up, to keep failing operations afloat until they become someone else's problems, or because you're afraid to shrink them, sell them or shut them down means you're not doing your job, that you're kidding yourself and a lot of other people as well. Things only move all by themselves in one direction: downhill. Face the facts and fix the problems so that you have the funds to invest and bolster the businesses that are healthy and growing. Facts are stubborn things. They don't go away or change because you ignore them - they fester.

You've got to have a strict set of metrics (rank 'em or yank 'em), a clear view of where the future of the firm is likely to be (winners and losers), and some idea of the path(s) that will get you there. Every good venture investor will tell you the same thing: you starve your losers and feed or double down on your winners. This isn't rocket science. Most of the time, an outsider with even a fraction of the information you have can tell you which of your people are winners and what parts of the business are destined to grow dramatically and which ones are already the walking dead. Of course, if you were being honest with yourself, you'd admit that you also know who and what has to go. You just need to screw up your courage and get the job down.

And it's at budget time that things really come to a boil because the choices couldn't be clearer or more immediate. Are you really going to fund a flailing business for another year when every metric is headed in the wrong direction because things might get better? Are you really gonna lose a couple of your superstars just because you were afraid to pay them what the market made clear they're worth in order to keep the rest of the team happy? And, worst of all, are the people who once bet on you tiring of the same sad stories and mediocre results and getting ready to put their money and their attention to better and more productive uses elsewhere?

296 – EVEN IF YOUR MONEY'S IN YOUR MATTRESS, YOU'RE STILL IN THE MARKET

I have spent most of the last year (doing two live morning shows a week) on the web having a couple of actual experts and seasoned veterans, Tom Sosnoff and Tony Battista from tastytrade (https://www.tastytrade.com/tt/) trying to teach me how to trade options. We started my adventure with an account of $250,000 and ended the year (spoiler alert) with pretty much the exact same amount - give or take $500 - even after the December debacle.

If the mostly rotten month of December 2018 wouldn't have tossed the markets (and especially the tech stocks) off a cliff and screwed things up, I would have ended the year ahead by about $8000 to $10,000 which - considering that I never really had more than about $50,000 at risk at any given time - would have been a pretty impressive outcome for a complete novice. But it was not to be. Of course, if the Queen has a couple of different chromosomes; she'd be the King. So, who am I to complain?

And let me be clear, my results were just that - mine - because we wanted to see not just what the guys could "teach" me, but what I could actually learn. So, the choices I made, and the stock selections were all based on my preferences, prejudices, urges, guesses and gut feelings. And, notwithstanding their clear advice that, by and large over time, betting on the direction of the market or on the up-or-down movement of a specific stock was a losing proposition, I generally did exactly that - betting based on my ideas and beliefs regarding the merits of the specific underlying businesses and assuming that their stock prices would reflect what I thought was likely to be their actual operating performance. Think of this as the struggle of hope (mine) against history (theirs) and you'll have a pretty good idea of what went on. And, just to make things worse, I never let my complete lack of actual experience get in the way in the least or reduce the fervent intensity of my opinions. Sometimes wrong, but never in doubt.

But I have to say that overall it was a great experience. Experience - in case you don't know - is what you get when you don't get what you want. Or, as they used to say about Wall Street in general, they take your money and their experience and turn it into their money and your experience. So, I'm grateful to have broken even and to have learned a few things that I think are worth sharing.

And, even more importantly, thanks to Tony B, I realized, maybe for the first time, that even if your money's safely stuffed in your mattress at home, you're still in the market - whether you like it or not - whether you know it or not - and whether you want to be or not. Because no one really has a choice today including the mattress stuffers. If you're not playing, you're paying one way or the other. But I'll get back to that.

So, what did I learn?

(1) If you're going to play in this pool, you can't be an occasional participant or a part-timer. It's not a "set it and forget" deal like buying traditional stocks or mutual funds and putting them away for a decade or so in the belief that equities always increase in value over the long run. These markets move rapidly and radically every day and you've got to be there to watch and react to the movements pretty much in real time. Thinking that you'll set aside a couple of hours a week or a morning or two to play these markets like you were going to the race track is about the same as just rolling up your bankroll and setting it on fire.

(2) These markets are entirely driven by technology. If you don't have access to the proper tools and trading platforms, you're so dramatically disadvantaged that you might just as well give up. It's like bringing a knife to a gunfight. You can get the tools, you can learn the strategies and the technologies, and eventually you can participate in the process, but the very first investment you need to make isn't in a particular option or underlying stock, it's in spending the time to learn how to play the game. If you don't, the rule's exactly the same as in any poker session. If you don't know who the patsy is in the game, you're the patsy.

(3) If you decide (as I did) that you're going to generally be "directional" which means thinking that you know which way things are gonna move, and which the experts at tastytrade will tell you is a stupid strategy, then at least be prepared to be patient and stay the course. It takes quite a bit longer for systemic operational improvements or deficiencies to be reflected in the prices of these stocks and, in the meantime, between (a) short-term and often misleading media reports which can move prices the wrong way, and (b) your own worst instincts and adrenaline surges driving you to do something, you can overreact and change your positions for no good reason and to no good end. Doing things is not the same as getting things done.

(4) On the other hand, there will be times when you're proven quickly to be dead wrong and then you need to cut your losses and move on. Mistakes are always part of the process and it's OK to make them, it's just a really bad idea to stick with them once it's clear that the baby is ugly. Chasing your losers is a constant temptation, but one that the best and most disciplined traders almost never do.

(5) Size matters. Start small. New players need to stay in their own weight class for a long time because they're not generally prepared either financially or mentally for the kinds of big swings and serious hits that can happen in an instant if you get

too far ahead of yourself or to far out over your skis. Remember that there are pros, sharks and smart machines on the other side of every trade and they make their living every day in this business that you're just beginning to understand.

I had included another "lesson" when I made my first list which was all about the traditional advice that you give every gambler in any sport - don't bet or invest anything more than you can afford to lose. Be sure you keep some funds put away and on the sidelines for safety and security. You'll sleep much better at night and all your family members and relatives will also thank you.

Now I know that no one is ever plans to lose anything, just like no one wants to be happy later, but my initial thought was to suggest that this isn't a game to be playing with your retirement funds or money you need to live on or for emergencies. And then, I had a conversation with Tony B and he suggested something to me that really changed my mind. He said that we're all always in the market and that whatever choices you make about where to put your money (or if you decide to keep it all in your own little piggybank) are just shades and variations on market decisions in exactly the same way as any stock purchase or sale might be.

But the big difference today - especially for young entrepreneurs - who are already making big bets on their futures and their own businesses is that standing still - not having a strategy to grow your assets - is actually slipping backwards every day - especially in a period when the interest rates being paid on "secure" savings accounts and even CDs are embarrassingly modest and unlikely to remotely keep up with inflation. So, while you may think you're being cautious and playing it safe with some of your scarce dollars, you're actually mortgaging your future and digging yourself into a hole.

The trick is to make those precious few assets that you've managed to put aside work harder for you and that's all about using leverage which is precisely what options provide. A side note: even with my $250,000 account, I couldn't realistically do much of anything with Amazon or Google because the share prices were so high that to actually buy a bunch of the shares of either stock would have consumed big chunks of my funds in a very short time and given me way too much exposure to far too few underlying stocks. But I could simulate and model the interest that I had in these stocks by using options costing only a fraction of the cost of the actual shares. I could play with the big boys without betting the kind of bucks that made no sense and, if I did it right, as noted above I was looking at annual returns approaching 20% on my money rather than 2% from some savings account along with a free toaster.

None of this is easy or straightforward, but it's important to think about when you're looking at your own financial future. And no one becomes an expert in a year. But if you take the time, learn to trade for yourself, and start small before you scale, you'll be doing yourself and your family a big favor.

TULLMAN'S TRUISMS

YOU LEARN EARLY ON IN RACING THAT THEY DON'T WAIT FOR YOU

We keep hearing new statistics about the accelerating rate at which new information-; content of all kinds-; is being created both by humans and machines. The latter is accelerating at an exponentially greater pace, one that has been driven by machines exchanging data with other machines. There's no end in sight to this growth, and absolutely no slowdown is even imaginable at this point. One of the most interesting challenges for the next few years will be "throughput" - how will we keep the enormous flow of data from the machines, and zillions of sensors, from clogging or breaking the whole Internet?

And, if the non-stop output from the machines isn't bad enough, the explosive growth of big, slow and clunky videos on the web continues to increase congestion, impose constraints and raise complex questions about prejudicial pricing, inequitable throttling and other anti-competitive and anti-consumer conduct by the gatekeepers.

Companies like Xaptum (www.xaptum.com/), one of the first Internet of Things startups at 1871, the Chicago-based tech incubator I ran for many years, have been addressing the machine volume concern for some time. Xaptum is talking specifically about a separate edge pathway or an entirely new network devoted exclusively to M2M transactions. But today, no one has any good ideas about what to do with the equally problematic video situation. Because, in all fairness, no one expected that, virtually overnight, everyone in the world would become not only a consumer of video, but a creator as well.

The current statistics are interesting and demonstrate that, while we are clicking on more and more videos, we're watching fewer and fewer of them from start to finish. This has all kinds of implications for the ill-advised advertisers who are largely paying for the privilege of showing their stuff to no one who matters or cares. Our patience these days is non-existent, and our attention spans continue to shrink/www.inc.com/howard-tullman/catch-me-if-you-can.html>.

I haven't looked up the most recent estimates on this phenomenon, but the basic premise is that we've created more information (I'm reluctant refer to this unmanageable and overwhelming mass of media as "knowledge") in the last whatever than mankind has created since the beginning of time.

However these calculations are made, it's abundantly clear that this isn't especially good news for anyone and, in most instances, no one would even be tempted to describe this glut of infojunk as a source of pride or any cause for celebration. In fact, to call this flood of facts, factoids and fake news a mixed blessing is an understatement of a magnitude comparable to those old Vietnam-era military reports where we were assured that "to save the town, it became necessary to destroy it."

It's getting harder and harder every day to effectively connect to anyone as our attention becomes an even scarcer and a more precious commodity in our lives than our time, which is increasingly and wastefully consumed <www.inc.com/howard-tullman/mastering-social-media-is-a-pointless-time-suck.html> by slogging our way through all this stuff. If I'm not listening to what you're trying to say, you're just wasting your breath.

And keep in mind that this is a two-sided problem, where the pain is shared by both the companies and the customer/consumers. It's an enormous problem for each of us as individuals and an equally sizeable and critical problem for every business as well. If we can't figure out how to manage the overwhelming influx, to filter and focus the flow, and to create some tools to help infuse some meaning and value into the mess, the emergent digital communication channels will soon resemble all the crappy ad and coupon packages that we immediately discard on Sundays. Or all the 3rd class mail and catalogues that never even make it into the house.

And "meaning" in this context includes an appreciation of the context in which all this new material is being created. Today the context of most communications is more critical to successful reach, reaction and response than the content of the materials themselves. (See https://www.inc.com/howard-tullman/to-sell-more-your-marketing-must-embrace-smart-reach.html.)

In the same way, "metrics" don't mean anything when there's no one on the other end of the line/https/www.inc.com/howard-tullman/the-trouble-with-social-media.html>. We continue to hear more and more reports about problems with the actual impact of online ads. Retargeting ads are being shown to recent purchasers, which makes little or no sense. Targeting has become so narrow that the overall opportunity is in fact shrinking, not expanding. Ads are being counted and accumulated when it's obvious that they aren't being seen by human beings or visible at all.

If you can't find me or efficiently reach me with your message, all of the money you're spending on expensive online media is going down the drain and all the slick and detailed reporting you're receiving isn't worth the paper it's written on. Too little signal and too much noise.

I'm almost 100% cash and feeling pretty good about it. Whatever you happen to believe about equities appreciating over the long haul, the first half of 2019 is going to be a bumpy ride at best. The days of an explosive and expansive tech sector-- the FAANG stocks that have run the market to such incredible heights-- aren't likely to be seen again for some time. I'm seeing months of volatility ahead, which is going to be great for traders but won't do much for consumer confidence or any sense of stability, especially in a time of insane political instability.

Other than Microsoft, which I expect to continue to creep slowly and steadily upstream, I can't see a single one of the other FAANG-class companies (however you count them and whoever you choose to include) that isn't facing product, market, regulatory or serious competitive issues. These issues are far more likely to drive distractions and detours than any new initiatives or sustained and profitable growth. And, as the politicians gear up for the next election cycle, it's hard to imagine any lower-hanging fruit for the media-sick morons to pick on than the big guys in the tech sector. Unlike the NRA and the big pharma folks--they've long known how to buy off and hold off the pols-- the techies are political babes in the woods. Easy pickings.

So, I'm not looking for much in the way of good news any time soon and frankly, an Uber IPO or an Airbnb buyout isn't gonna really set the markets on fire either. Relative to their crazy and over-inflated private valuations, I'm betting that a public offering in this environment for almost any of these unicorns is going to look like a down round if you actually know the internal investment numbers and prior valuations. And that's before giving any effect to embedded repricing ratchets and other downward pricing protections that were undoubtedly built into these deals. In my general review of these deals, the entrepreneurs were almost entirely focused on keeping ridiculous levels of voting and board control. And, because everyone told them that the sky was the limit in terms of stock prices, they paid very little attention to the prospect and consequences of any decline in the price of their internal shares. They were smart, but not smart enough.

These bad vibes make me pessimistic about the funding future for startups and early-stage growth businesses-- especially those that are still chasing profitability. So my advice is very simple: get your business ready for the recession. It's coming and it's no longer really a question of "if" but rather "when" and "how bad." Now's the time to start trimming your sails and re-setting your course for at least a year. In a market and a time as crazy as today, there are far fewer penalties to waiting and hunkering down than you would typically incur. Doubling down on your commitments and speeding up expansion activities when everyone lacks visibility makes no sense. Don't be doing things (especially deals) just to keep busy. Busy-ness is a lot different than taking care of business. Random and reckless activity for activity's sake is a poor antidote for whatever actual anxiety you may be experiencing.

Here are a few suggestions about what needs to be done. But first, I want to modify a few of my own prior pronouncements. Not because they're wrong in the long run, but because they're not right for right now. So, think "yes, but" rather than "yes, and" for a while.

(1) Market share expansion occurs mainly in tough times.

Yes, it's definitely easier to grow your piece of the pie when the competition is down-and-out, and you're blessed with a recently-acquired war chest (at the moment) and some pricing flexibility, which lets you take advantage of the situation and make some very attractive offers to clients and customers. Or maybe, because the channels are less crowded and there's less demand, you're able to secure better deals or placements or exposure (or even long-term partnerships) that wouldn't be available to you in happier and healthier, but also more competitive times. These are definitely tantalizing prospects. But cutting your prices to grab customers will almost surely come back to bite you down the line; and there's no guarantee that, if things continue to slow down and get worse, that you may also be looking at some tough times and choices. So, you have my permission to be penny-wise for a while.

(2) Don't try to do something cheaply that you shouldn't do at all.

Yes, I've always been a very strong advocate of avoiding anything that amounts to "putting lipstick on a pig" or "steak sauce on a hot dog." It's usually smarter to just say "No" to these temptations to try to get by with less than your best but, here again, there are always going to be exceptions to the rule. Right now, my motto for your business--whether it's dollars for development, money for marketing, a new ad and branding campaign, or growing the team--is pretty simple. "Go for good for now, great can wait." Just because you've grown and even if you've got some bucks in the bank, take a breath and a moment to remember the old days when the only options were limited to guerilla, down-and-dirty, and get things done with smarts rather than simply more shekels. Try to get back to those days and those times.

(3) You can't save your way to success.

Yes, but saving a few bucks right now may be your path to staying in the game. In a startup, the only sin you can never rebound from is running out of cash. Because then they send you home. So, it's never worth the risk of cutting things too close or not making sure you've got enough for Plans B and C if it comes to that. Right now, I'd say that the exact things you want to be doing are pretty clear:

a. Conserve your cash
b. Shorten the length of your commitments
c. Stick with the team you have instead of making a bunch of additional bets on unproven players. Don't let your mouth or your ego write checks that you can't cash or cover.

In the end, it all comes down to money. Money doesn't really care who makes it. Money is always there; it's just the pockets that change. And money does talk. You just want to be sure that it doesn't say, "Goodbye."

TULLMAN'S TRUISMS

DON'T MISTAKE A CLEAR VIEW FOR A SHORT DISTANCE

I'd rather have 10% of a watermelon than 100% of a grape. A little slice of the price of every purchase in almost any area of commerce adds up to an impressive bundle of bucks in no time at all – especially once the underlying businesses begin to take off. Today, the truth is that you can't sell a stand-alone product; you also have to sell connection, support and service and deliver a first-class experience across all those dimensions. As a result, in the "right now" and "always on" economy, everything is, of necessity, transaction-based in one way or another. The only question is who are all the people getting a piece of the pie and how do you make sure that you get your share. It's getting harder and harder to get into the game because so much of the process is data-dependent and only a few of the biggest players have access to the answers.

We're starting to see the emergence of large and well-funded gatekeepers, toll takers, and all kinds of other middlemen in almost every industry and everywhere you look on the web. And they're here to stay because many of the markets and the disparate players which they serve couldn't continue to grow and expand without the concentration, centralization and organization which these entities provide. It's not exactly one-stop shopping yet, but, over and over again, technology channels tend toward two- or three-horse races or even "winner-take-all" configurations. You don't have to be the first; just eventually the best. (See https://www.inc.com/howard-tullman/dont-overlook-the-second-mover-advantage.html.) And, to stay in the race and maintain your position, you also need to have the technology and, most importantly, the data that it increasingly takes to compete at these levels of size and scale.

The new gatekeepers are becoming some of the most valuable businesses on the planet because, as we grow ever more connected and reliant on a few key channels to meet our basic and recurring needs; the people who own the pipes (the utilities) may be in decent financial shape, but the ones who are controlling the content and product flows and sitting astride the traffic in, out and through those pipes are much better positioned, further ahead of the game, and far more likely to be highly profitable. Controlling, delivering and charging for access to the content or products is a lot more appealing than having to handle all the hardware maintenance headaches. Poor AT&T and Comcast still have to pay attention to (and spend millions servicing and keeping up) all those POTS lines, cable boxes and telephone poles while digital content creators and e-commerce providers essentially ride their rails for free. Trump's not entirely wrong about how the e-commerce companies are taking complete advantage of the U.S. Postal Service which still has to get all those deliveries over the last mile and into our mailrooms and mailboxes.

It's a good start to know who and where the customers are, but the ultimate giants will be the ones who can track, influence and ultimately dictate our actions, choices and decisions. Companies which can provide invaluable evaluations and interpretations of the vast amounts of user data which are being constantly and exponentially generated will become new market leaders, but the best players won't share this data with the world – they will use it exclusively to improve and strengthen their own positions. This is where Amazon once again shines.

Amazon's dream state for its Prime customers is the complete elimination of thought in the purchase process. "One-click" is on its way to being "no clicks" at all. Think of this as "I see, I buy". I'm not even sure that needs or even desires will enter into this Pavlovian process of pre-conditioned responses for much longer. And, as for commodities and recurring purchases, it's going to be all about automated replenishment. The pantries of Prime subscribers will never be empty again.

But it's Amazon's newest foray into providing free samples to its Prime customers on behalf of brands that highlights the beginning of these new data-driven initiatives. No one has more detailed information on every aspect of our past, present and intended purchase intent and behaviors than Amazon and no one can do a better job for their brand "partners" than Amazon of putting these offerings directly and painlessly into the hands and the homes of the very best in-market prospects.

I t's always risky to ask an entrepreneur what he or she honestly thinks about venture capitalists. I used to say that entrepreneurs viewed VCs the way most dogs regard a fire hydrant. It's easy to find fault with these guys, but it's not always fair. Our opinions are colored by our own experiences – good or bad – and so, as an outsider looking in, you have to take every player's comments with a few grains of salt. Typically, things are never as good or bad as described and, if anything, prudence and reticence generally rule. As Thumper used to say, "if you can't say something nice, don't say nothin' at all."

The main reason to generally keep your mouth shut is pretty obvious. Since you never know when or where the next deal or critical financing may come from, no one wants to inadvertently burn any bridges or aggravate possible future investors. If you decide to blow someone off, just be sure to have a really good reason. You should earn your enemies, not make them carelessly or gratuitously because, while friends come and go, enemies accumulate. And the venture world is really a pretty small pond where everyone talks to each other all the time.

I realize that we take some things very personally and that take-backs and other disappointments sting a lot more than other "business as usual" busts might. It's not essential to forget and forgive these things, but you do need to get through them and get on to the new. Usually this isn't a huge problem because every good entrepreneur is already looking down the road at what's next and no one suffers more from selective memory than entrepreneurs. Of course, that can be every bit as much a blessing as a curse. You can't water yesterday's crops, but you also want to be sure that you're not being naïve, too trusting, or winding up making the same mistakes over and over again.

When a VC reneges and changes the long-agreed-upon terms of a deal, they do it knowingly and with a smile. When an entrepreneur says that something isn't the way he or she remembers it, as often as not, that's the absolute truth. It's not a case of chicanery; it's more often a matter of memory and attention (or really lack of attention to the details) than it is of accuracy or honesty.

You would be utterly astonished to learn how little the CEOs in some of the biggest financings around know about the actual nitty-gritty details of the deal itself. Isn't that what the lawyers and bankers are for? Even the smartest entrepreneurs tend to forget that these are usually one-off and infrequent deals for them, but the VCs do them every week and it's their bread and butter to make sure that every dotted "i" and crossed "t" leans in their direction. It's not their fault; it's their nature. Just like the scorpion told the turtle.

VC relationships are complicated at best and, for a variety of reasons, the emotions can run very high from Day One. And the conduct, tone and intensity of the due diligence and investment negotiating processes have a lot to do with where the parties end up mentally as well. Entrepreneurs are proud and prickly people and the truth is that in fundraising – especially for new businesses – you've got to kiss a lot of frogs before you find your prince. In the end, if there are remaining issues or hard feelings, it's usually more about the process than the money.

And, it's not like all the issues and instances of bad behavior are on the VC's side either. Entrepreneurs can be foolish and insistent pigs on valuation and try to drive too hard a bargain on other parts of the deal without appreciating that this is a bad long-term bet for their businesses. Early and growth stage investments are a lot more like marriages than financial transactions and how things begin has a whole lot to do with where they're likely to end up. In most cases, you're going to be living with these folks a lot longer than you ever imagined and you're also more than likely to need to go back to that very same well down the road.

A good CEO knows that he needs to get what the business requires in the deal, but not so much more that everyone ends up disappointed or disgusted. No one wants to be a 90-day wonder where a few months down the line, everyone is sitting around wondering how the deal ever got done.

The dream state is that each side gives up something near and dear to them in the end and everyone's just a little bit unhappy about what they left on the table. That's how things get done in the real world.

You take what you need and leave the rest.

Howard Tullman is the Executive Director of the Ed Kaplan Family Institute for Innovation and Tech Entrepreneurship as well as the first University Professor appointed at the Illinois Institute of Technology in Chicago. He was previously the CEO of 1871 (the home of 500 digital startups) which, under his guidance and leadership, tripled in size and was recently named the Number 1 university-affiliated incubator in the world. Prior to his role at 1871, Tullman was the Chairman and CEO of Tribeca Flashpoint College and the President of Kendall College. He is also the General Managing Partner of two early-stage venture capital funds, Chicago High-Tech Investment Partners, LLC and G2T3V, LLC which focus on identifying and funding disruptive innovators.

Tullman is a world-class serial entrepreneur and has successfully founded more than a dozen high-tech startups in his 50-year career and created more than $1 billion in investor value as well as over 6000 new jobs. He is a tireless supporter of entrepreneurs and a mentor to many startups, growing businesses of all sizes, political leaders and government agencies as well as a board member of several of Chicago's fastest-growing tech companies. He has written over 30 books and writes a regular weekly column on The Perspiration Principles for INC. Magazine. He lectures on technology trends, entrepreneurship and change management all across the world.

He can be reached:

By email at: h@g2t3v.com or h@kaplan.iit.edu

On twitter at: @tullman

On facebook at: facebook.com/tullman

At his blog: tullman.blogspot.com or website: www.tullman.com